Of Laws and Limitations

Of Laws and Limitations

An Intellectual Portrait
of Louis Dembitz Brandeis

Stephen W. Baskerville

Rutherford • Madison • Teaneck
Fairleigh Dickinson University Press
London and Toronto: Associated University Presses

KF
8745
B67
B37
1994

Associated University Presses
440 Forsgate Drive
Cranbury, NJ 08512

Associated University Presses
25 Sicilian Avenue
London WC1A 2QH, England

Associated University Presses
P.O. Box 338, Port Credit
Mississauga, Ontario
Canada L5G 4L8

The paper used in this publication meets the requirements
of the American National Standard for Permanence of Paper
for Printed Library Materials Z39.48-1984.

Library of Congress Cataloging-in-Publication Data
Baskerville, Stephen W.
    Of laws and limitations : an intellectual portrait of Louis
Dembitz Brandeis / Stephen W. Baskerville.
        p.   cm.
    Includes bibliographical references and index.
    ISBN 0-8386-3478-8 (alk. paper)
    1. Brandeis, Louis Dembitz, 1856–1941.   2. Judges—United States—
Biography.   I. Title.
KF8745.B67B37   1994
347.73'14'092—dc20
[347.30714092]   91-58957
                                                                   CIP

(continuation of copyright page)

Extracts from *Letters of Louis D. Brandeis*, edited by Melvin I. Urofsky and David W. Levy, are reprinted by permission of the State University of New York Press.

Extracts from Melvin I. Urofsky's critical edition of "The Brandeis-Frankfurter Conversations," published in *The Supreme Court Review*, are reprinted by permission of Chicago University Press.

Excerpts from Allon Gal's *Brandeis of Boston* are reprinted by permission of Harvard University Press.

Quotations from Edward F. McClennan's article, "Louis D. Brandeis as a Lawyer," published in the *Massachusetts Law Quarterly*, are reprinted by permission of the Massachusetts Bar Association.

Quotations from Dean Acheson's autobiography, *Morning and Noon*, are reprinted by permission of the Houghton Mifflin Company.

For Pielet
who alone knows how much it cost

New times demand new issues and new men,
*   The world advances and in time outgrows the laws*
That in our father's time were best;
*   And, doubtless, after us some purer scheme*
Will be shaped out by wiser men than we,—
*   Made wiser by the steady growth of truth.*

—Lowell, "A Glance Behind the Curtain"

Contents

Preface

When I first became interested in Louis Dembitz Brandeis more than twenty years ago, his ideas were decidedly unfashionable. In the United States context, to be a liberal meant being in favor of big government and supporting high levels of domestic expenditure by the federal authorities—this primarily with a view to alleviating the problems of poverty, racial discrimination, and urban decay that seemed everywhere to belie the nation's affluent and consensual self-image. With Lyndon Johnson's "Great Society" not yet cold in its grave, the very word "liberal" was already well on the way to becoming a term of abuse far beyond the conservative heartlands of Middle America. The concept of a "new federalism" that would see Washington sharing both revenue and responsibility with the several states was rightly considered a Nixonian idea, and thus anathema to all those on the center left of the political spectrum; worse still, the phrase "states rights" was generally regarded as the Old South's thinly veiled euphemism for white supremacy. Postwar reformers, it seemed, shared neither goals nor even a common discourse with the man who, at the time of his death in 1941, was widely regarded as one of the country's leading liberal figures.

In 1972, the political culture of the United States remained locked into a paradigm established by the reform agenda of the New Deal. Twenty years on, though, that situation has been transformed. Released from the intellectual stasis imposed by the cold war, Americans are once again free to ask themselves and their leaders searching questions about a range of issues that have long been taboo: about what the balance of power should be between the federal government and the states; about the individual's responsibilities to community, society, and self; about the behavior of giant corporations that pollute the environment even as they plunder the earth's resources; about the congruity (or lack of it) between the ideals on which the American nation was founded and the reality that its citizens now inhabit. When George Bush so thoroughly demolished the "liberal" candidacy of Michael Dukakis in 1988, few would have predicted that four years later the electorate would be found demanding the formulation of a new reform agenda—one capable of addressing the crises perceived to exist in education, health-care provision, drug-related crime, and even the functioning of government itself. In developing that agenda, those who contend for the right to do the public's business would do well to recall that the country has not one but two liberal traditions. For as well as the familiar Hamiltonian focus on centralized authority, social action, and the leadership of an informed elite, there is also the old Jeffersonian appeal to devolved power, individual responsibility, and participatory democracy.

No single individual since the Civil War has explored this alternative prospectus for national evolution with greater clarity or conviction than Mr. Justice Brandeis. Regrettably, however, the products of his intellect are widely dispersed, for in a long life devoted more readily to action than to contemplation, he never found time to sit down and write a book. Although the last twenty years have seen a veritable growth industry in Brandeis biographies, there has so far been no comprehensive attempt to reconstruct the complex processes of his intellectual development, nor to identify the principal sources from which he drew enlightenment. My objective in writing this book has been quite simply to supply this gap in the literature.

No one can complete an undertaking of this kind without incurring numerous debts of gratitude. The first obligation of any historian, especially one intent on treating a society other than her or his own, must be to the archivists and librarians without whom the tasks of research would be impossible. In the Library of Congress I have been aided over many years by people whose names I never knew, but whose unfailing courtesy and cheerfulness bolstered my spirits—even on those grey winter days when the volume of letters still to be read and references still to be checked seemed truly endless. The staff of the Roosevelt Presidential Library in Hyde Park provided a similar source of inspiration during the early stages of this project, quickly responding to my countless requests for manuscripts, books, and photocopies with a perennially smiling efficiency. At the Harvard Law School Library, Erika Chadbourn and Judy Mellins were both uncommonly generous with their time and assistance, thus ensuring that a necessary trip would also be remembered as an enjoyable one. Charles Cutter and his colleagues in the Judaica Department of Brandeis University Library went out of their way to make my all-too-brief visit as pleasant as it was rewarding. I am grateful also to Elizabeth Shenton at the Arthur and Elizabeth Schlesinger Library on the History of Women in America for helping me locate an English-language copy of Frederika Brandeis's *Reminiscences*. Last, but by no means least, I should like to record my thanks to all those at the University of Louisville who helped make my stay in the city of Brandeis's birth such a delightful one, and especially to Tom Owen, Janet Hodgson, and Sherrill McConnell for their expert knowledge, advice, and friendliness. In almost twenty years of visiting libraries and archives on both sides of the Atlantic, nowhere else have I found such a high standard of professional competence matched by such a full measure of personal warmth and hospitality.

Greatly appreciated as are all the facilities and kindnesses that the researcher encounters "on the road," her or his efforts there would be largely
in vain were the "home team" unwilling or unable to respond effectively to the
demands placed on it. In this context, I am greatly indebted to the staff of the
Brynmor Jones Library at Hull University, and particularly to those working
in the Inter-Library Loan Department, for their calm responsiveness and
persistent good temper in the face of burdensome requests for articles from
sundry obscure periodicals. Their searches were not always successful, but it
was not for want of trying.

It was never part of my plan to track down and interrogate all the surviving family members and secretaries who knew Brandeis in his later years—a
task already well performed by his biographers. Several of these first-hand
witnesses have, in any case, recorded their memories in print and, when applicable, my use of their writings will be found acknowledged in the notes
and bibliography. I did have certain questions, though, which only those
who had served in New Deal Washington or who had worked for the elderly
justice were capable of answering; several people were therefore invited to
share their recollections with me. Two of these deserve special mention.
David Riesman, Jr., wrote me two substantial letters in the spring and fall of
1981, and subsequently talked with me at some length about his former
boss. Paul A. Freund gave me permission to use the Brandeis "Court Papers"
preserved at the Harvard Law School, and likewise consented to a long
personal interview. It is thanks chiefly to the sometimes radically differing
perceptions of these two individuals that I was able to get what they and
others have written about "Isaiah" into some sort of critical perspective. I
am extremely grateful to them both. Other people willingly took the time to
respond in writing to my requests for information, among whom Thomas H.
Eliot and Leon H. Keyserling were particularly helpful; likewise interviews
with Ewan Clague, Thomas G. Corcoran, and Louis L. Jaffe all added useful insights from which this study has benefited in less tangible ways.

European students of the United States cannot long remain unaware of
the financial burdens imposed by the reality of having their primary–source
materials located across the Atlantic; without institutional assistance, few
would be able to bring their projects to a satisfactory conclusion. The initial
research for this book was made possible by my tenure of a Harkness Fel-
lowship of the Commonwealth Fund of New York, which not only enabled
me to spend two years in the History Department at the University of Maryland, but also facilitated regular and frequent access to the Library of Congress. Some years later, an award from the British Academy made possible
both a trip to Louisville and a return visit to Washington, D.C., and subven-
tions from the Department of American Studies at Hull helped fund my investigations at Brandeis University and the Harvard Law School. I am greatly beholden to all three bodies for the timely assistance that they provided.

My personal debts are more numerous but no less real. Historical research may seem a solitary occupation to those not involved in it, but without the advice and encouragement of friends and colleagues few of its fruits would ever see the light of day. On both sides of the ocean there are people to whom I owe special thanks. Let me start with the North American contingent. It was William E. Leuchtenburg who, during a year spent in Oxford as Harmsworth Professor, first sparked my interest in Brandeis and later helped arrange the logistics of my Harkness award; it was James T. Patterson who, by asking how the justice's Progressivism differed from that of Herbert Hoover, set me to thinking seriously about the former's intellectual development. Colleagues at College Park also contributed their mite: Keith Olson acted as a general guide and mentor; Jim Harris taught me how to find a parking spot on Capitol Hill, and proved to me that conversation is not a dying art; Myles Bradbury helped track down items in the United States that were untraceable in U.K. libraries; and Don Gordon helped more than he knows with a mischievous remark about the perfectibility of man. Elsewhere, George Abbott White made available the facilities of Eliot House's Matthiessen Room during my stay in Cambridge; Catherine and Gordon Bell twice provided a weekend's rest and recreation between long weeks spent in Hyde Park; and for more than fifteen years Toni Robinson has made sure that I have a home and a friend in Washington. Lastly, I should like to thank Andrea Hammer—my copyeditor—and all those at Associated University Presses who have helped in the tortuous business of turning my unwieldy manuscript into a book. Distance may indeed lend enchantment to a view; but when it is of transatlantic proportions it does little to speed up the more mundane processes of publication. I am therefore particularly grateful to my production editor, Regina M. Phair, for her patience and good humor.

In England too there has been no shortage of people ready to aid and abet my work. My greatest obligation is to Philip Taylor, without whom this book might never have been finished. By his questions and pertinent observations, his suggestions on and criticisms of two early drafts of the manuscript, my own thinking has been constantly challenged and refined; by his exhortation and example, my excuses for idleness and prevarication were finally worn away. I owe him much. Others helped me in different ways. My friend Hilary Hall afforded helpful comments on an earlier draft of the first chapter; Ed Abramson gave me valuable advice about the Jewish-American experience; John White pointed me toward the material on blacks in Louisville; and Dustin Mirick talked with me at length about Goethe and the Greeks. Louis Billington and Ralph Willett have acted as sounding boards for numerous ideas, and Herbert Nicholas, Tony Badger, Howell Harries and Copper LeMay have all contributed over the years to my understanding of Progressivism, the New Deal, and the role of law in American society. The errors in this book are, of course, mine alone; but many of the best insights belong to them.

Words cannot easily express the influence that my wife and son have had on the themes and perspectives offered in this book. Judy is not a historian, but she has helped me become a better one by altering the way I look at the world. John has grown up with "the Brandeis book," tolerated its intrusion into his adolescence, and filled with joy the long pauses in its twenty-year gestation. Some day, I might even persuade him to read it! To both of them I offer heartfelt thanks.

North Cave, England, 1992

Of Laws and Limitations

Prelude: The Good Grey Judge

Angels:
  Saved is our spirit-peer, in peace,
  Preserved from evil scheming:
  "For he whose strivings never cease
  Is ours for his redeeming."

—Goethe, *Faust*

When he died in the fall of 1941, a few weeks before his eighty-fifth birthday, Louis Dembitz Brandeis had been regarded as an American institution for more than a quarter of a century. As is the case with most public figures, his place in the perception of ordinary people was defined by a series of formal images or impressions, sharp in outline, simple in form, that served to conjure up a readily identifiable persona in the minds of millions who would never know the man. For most practical purposes it did not matter that these often jarring images were made to compose a timeless, unchanging amalgam; that they were drawn from a public career spanning some six decades and made to coexist in a vague continuous present; that they were at once unrelated to personal ambition, unresponsive to the pressures of the historical context, and wholly lacking the dynamism and vitality of an intellectual development continually tempered and channeled by wide experience.

Even those personally close to the elderly justice were inclined to accept uncritically the holism and internal consistency of his outlook, whether directed toward the ephemera of national and international affairs or to the eternal axioms of the human condition. They mostly took for granted the happy congruity that appeared to exist between the public profession of his ideals and the frugal, ascetic demeanor of his private life. A law clerk's subsequent observation that his was truly "a mind of one piece" merely encapsulated the almost universal feeling of Brandeis's contemporaries, that he was a man of singularly harmonious intellect. Yet in the years since his death, even his admirers have been reluctant to go beyond this to the assertion that he possessed and acted on a rationally articulated system of belief amounting to a coherent philosophy of civilized man as a morally responsible social being. They remember instead his pragmatism and his liking for inductive processes of reasoning; they stress the eclecticism and essential simplicity of his prescriptions for the good life; and they underscore his personal integrity and independence of mind. In short, they attempt to draw

19

the fire of his critics' charge that he was at heart a classic nineteenth-century liberal, adrift in a modern world whose life-style he shunned and whose problems he failed to comprehend. Few, though, are willing to go onto the offensive, to assert with Harold Laski that Brandeis was the greatest of John Marshall's successors on the Supreme Court bench precisely because "his decisions were the consummate expression of a legal philosophy which he tried to fit, with a coherent amplitude, into the needs of his time."[1]

Any attempt to claim for Brandeis the title of "philosopher" is at first sight confounded by the sparsity and ad hoc nature of his published writing. The plain fact is that he never wrote a book. Even his best-known work, *Other People's Money—And How the Bankers Use It* (1914), is a compilation of articles that had originally appeared in *Harper's Weekly*, and is in any case couched in the didactic language of the muckraker rather than the considered prose of the dispassionate and disinterested scholar. Moreover, even if one considers the later collections of essays, addresses, briefs and official testimony, all edited by others and the largest not published until the last decade of his life, the overwhelming bulk of his most widely quoted work was actually written during the relatively brief period separating his fiftieth birthday in 1906 from his appointment to the United States Supreme Court just ten years later.[2]

As for his correspondence with other public figures, as well as the numerous letters he penned to family, friends, and professional associates, this material is a good deal more varied in its range and extends over a much longer period; however, it is widely scattered, and only became readily accessible to scholars during the 1970s thanks to the editorial efforts of Melvin Urofsky and David Levy. It could certainly do nothing in Brandeis's own lifetime to amend or augment the printed record of his views on public issues, and may in any event constitute a misleading guide to the depth and nature of his intellect. "I am not one of those who believe any letter of a great man is worth publicity," wrote his friend and longtime associate Felix Frankfurter in 1956, claiming this observation to be "particularly true of a man [i.e., Brandeis] whose normal mode of conveying his greatness was not put in correspondence." The "great mass" of his letters were "matter of fact, very businesslike," he went on, "because of the demand of his work on his time and energy."[3]

Of course, there is one further, if long underused, portion of the printed record that is both substantial and written entirely after 1916: namely, the 528 opinions that Mr. Justice Brandeis wrote while on the bench. Yet until recently, few people outside the legal profession had read more than a tiny fraction of this immense corpus of material, let alone attempted to integrate its substantive elements into a comprehensive exploration of his thinking. Early biographies, most notably that by Alpheus T. Mason, considered only a handful of the most celebrated opinions, mainly dissents; and diligent though such authors undoubtedly were in other areas, they scarcely began to explore the latent potential of Brandeis's judicial writings for making possible a fuller and more finely delineated portrait of the mind that created them. To some extent the specialized studies of his judicial ideology and methods published by Samuel Konefsky and Alexander Bickel in the mid-1950s made up for this deficiency, but not until the recent biographies by Philippa Strum and Lewis Paper did the process of integration begin to achieve convincing results.[4]

For most Brandeis scholars, however, the paucity and intractability of their subject's literary output has been more than offset by the vivid recollections of those who encountered him during his later years, be they friend or opponent, law clerk or supplicant, disciple or critic. To those who knew him only as an old man, already turned seventy when the Great Depression struck, the justice was an imposing figure. The strength and energy of his personality, and perhaps more especially the clarity of his vision in a period of profound uncertainty, inspired respect among the New Deal politicians and government officials who called at his California Street apartment for tea and counsel; in the minds of the impressionable young men, fresh out of Harvard Law School, whom Frankfurter sent to work in his office, these qualities frequently generated something closer to awe.

One such "impressionable young man" was Paul Freund, who served as Brandeis's legal secretary during the 1932–33 session of the Court. His postgraduate year in Washington witnessed both the bleakest winter of the depression and the heady excitement of Franklin Delano Roosevelt's first hundred days in office. Interviewed some fifty years later, Freund could still recall several characteristic views but no connecting principle in the elderly justice's thought:

> He was not a philosopher in any systematic or formal way. He had some grounding in German liberalism; he liked to quote Goethe, but in my experience he didn't rely on the classical libertarian philosophers. . . . As he himself said, he had no systematic, formal philosophy, but he was accustomed to dealing with discrete, individual problems, on the basis largely of his own experience and observation, and the things he read [which] he appreciated tended to be the things that confirmed the views that he had already formed. I don't think reading or study of the philosophers was formative with him, except possibly the German experience when he was in Dresden as a young student. It was in the air, I suppose. He got it in the air . . . and from family background and tradition, rather than from formal philosophical study.[5]

If not a philosopher, then, what was Brandeis? In Freund's view, which he propounded before members of the American Historical Association in 1956, the answer was twofold: he was a moralist and a lawyer. "The inner daemon which drove him from one harsh encounter to another, struggling against wilfulness and inertia all about him, was a passion for the moral life, the life that is free to develop character through the exercise of responsibility." As a lawyer he sought to achieve some amelioration of the social order, whereby the freedoms enjoyed by ordinary men and women might be developed and extended; but in the search for desirable ends he never ceased to weigh the morality of the means to be employed. Searching through the pantheon of American democrats, Freund chose to compare Brandeis with Lincoln, as a lover of freedom "who insisted that freedom could be secured only within principles of order, of structure and process, of which the Federal system is a design to be cherished."[6]

In old age, Brandeis's outstanding intellectual quality seemed to be his empiricism: that immensely practical cast of mind which continually subordinated theory to utility, and believed the solution to any problem would be found through patient study and imaginative experimentation. The near collapse of corporate capitalism following the stock-market crash of 1929 came as no surprise to him, but merely served to justify his long-held conviction that "bigness" was inherently self-destructive. As a human tragedy the Great Depression evidently disturbed him greatly, "but not in a maudlin or sentimental way," as Freund recalled in 1983:

> He did not stress individual cases of hardship. He was looking for structural faults and cures. He felt that to concentrate on the individual cases of hardship was enervating. He didn't like hard-luck stories, but he did like discussion of what to do and what was wrong, and to what extent "bigness" was responsible, and why we couldn't have regularity of employment. . . . I don't mean that he was callous, but I think that he felt that energies that were concentrated on the hardship cases could better be employed in working for structural change.[7]

Freund had expressed himself more fully on this theme in his 1956 address. Brandeis was there represented as a "tough-minded, unsentimental, . . . morally deep-cutting" man, very different from "the bleeding heart or the good grey judge of popular legend;" several anecdotes were adduced to illustrate the point. For instance, to the woman who asked him anxiously at the depth of the depression whether he thought the worst was over, he replied cheerfully: "Oh, yes. The worst took place in the years of prosperity before 1929." To Harold Laski, while conceding that he found the widespread suffering, the economic helplessness and the general dejection quite appalling, he wrote in 1932: "But the process of debunking continues; and if the depression is long continued—which seems likely—America will gain much from her experience." And to a visitor bemoaning the plight of the millions of young people unable to find a job, he reportedly remarked: "There is one thing that any able-bodied young man can do to earn a living—he can join the army." Though Freund himself seems to have found this last comment rather shocking, he does offer some explanation for it:

Had the comment come from someone else, it would be put down to callous inhumanity; coming from Brandeis, who drove himself unsparingly in the cause of his fellow man, the remark showed rather his annoyance at the doughy sogginess of mere lamenting, which had neither the tang of moral indignation nor the nourishment of a constructive idea. To think of Brandeis as a shining white knight riding off to every call of distress is to confuse the prophet Jeremiah with the all-American boy.[8]

Reliance on such recollections, though, unless supported or qualified by other sources of information, must inevitably distort our understanding of how Brandeis's mind worked when in its prime, and perhaps more seriously tends to conceal the processes by which the fundamental principles of his creed had developed and evolved over the years. For while it is true that he was deeply troubled by the events of the 1930s, as much by the rise of Hitler as by the collapse of the old economic order, it remains equally true that he saw these manifestations as proving the validity of postulates he had already made and conclusions he had already reached rather than as suggesting the need for fundamental rethinking on his part. In other words, he viewed the crisis of capitalism as calling for action not contemplation, and ideally for action aimed at implementing his own political prescriptions. If we are fully to understand the philosophical foundations on which these calls for action were based, it is to earlier years that our attention must first turn—years all too cursorily glossed over by most of his biographers.[9]

What then were the hallmarks of this fundamental philosophy? On the face of it, Brandeis was a Wilsonian Progressive, committed to realizing the Jeffersonian ideals of Democracy, Individual Liberty, and Social Justice. In the mouths of many politicians, then and since, the ritual capitalization and solemn utterance of such words has had the paradoxical effect of devaluing them to the level of base platitudes—to the point indeed where for some they have become a hollow catechism, intoned on public occasions as the rhetorical emblem of a glib and facile Americanism. For Brandeis, though, they were much more than empty labels: They were essential goals to be pursued and achieved by concrete means.

Viewing his intellectual progress with the considerable benefits of hindsight, several distinct facets of the human condition appear to have engaged his attention, following in rough sequence one upon another. Each achieved a temporary prominence in his mind for a given period of his life before being absorbed into and reconciled with the wider ramifications of his thinking; yet each also left an indelible impression on the peculiar configuration of his mind. Three personal discoveries, first made in the 1870s, 1890s, and 1910s respectively, and comprehended more fully in later years, led him to erect a new intellectual edifice on foundations originally supplied by the culture of German liberalism that was his familial inheritance. First, at Harvard and afterward in private legal practice he discovered law, both as a passive framework for the maintenance of social cohesion and as an active agency for the promotion (or prevention) of social change. Second, while furthering his professional career in Boston, and observing from that vantage point the world and its ways, he encountered for the first time the realities of class conflict, and came increasingly to discern in the corporate forms of organized capital a growing threat to the already distended fabric of America's industrial society. And third, in the midst of an apparent reevaluation of personal identity, he discovered his own Jewishness, and by embracing Zionism came to perceive more clearly the importance of community and belonging as the indispensable context within which to develop the values of self-sacrifice and individual responsibility. In each of these phases of his intellectual development, however, the positive awareness of individual potentiality was tempered and in part counterbalanced by a negative perception of the barriers to progress imposed by the limited capacity of all human beings for complex thought and sustained action. "The worldly wise are not wise, claiming more than mortals know" was among the aphorisms he quoted most frequently.[10]

The ideas associated with each new enthusiasm might revise and temporarily obscure, but they never came close to eradicating the lessons taught by earlier contemplation and experience; the result was a growing complexity and sophistication of thought that by the 1920s was indeed worthy of being called a philosophy. It was in many respects a radical philosophy, affording its adherents a coherent system of socioeconomic, political, and legal ideas; but it was also one that appeared increasingly at variance with the dominant trends of twentieth-century life. Nonetheless, its author, never much concerned to find himself swimming against a prevailing tide, remained firmly convinced that his basic precepts were sound and that time and circumstance would eventually persuade intelligent men of their relevance. Had he left behind him a great treatise setting forward in elegant prose his provocative analysis of industrial America, and his belief that citizenship was bound up with participation in local democratic processes, Louis Brandeis might well have stood alongside C. Wright Mills, Paul Goodman, and Herbert Marcuse as one of the chief intellectual mentors of the sixties generation. In the event, interest in his ideas waned rapidly after his death, as first war and then affluence diverted American minds into more congenial and less austere modes of thought and discourse. Watchmen sounding the tocsin, prophets proclaiming the imminence of disaster if truths were ignored, held little appeal for those to whom the power of corporate wealth and the salience of corporate ideology were a natural and welcome part of the American way of life. For good reason was Brandeis known in his later years as Isaiah—the Old Testament prophet who inveighed against the men of Judah for their transgressions and self-pride, yet also foretold the building of a New Jerusalem on the ruins of the old.

Not only did Brandeis fail to write a great treatise; he also declined to interpret his own actions in the light of his beliefs. When asked after his retirement from the Court in 1939 whether he was going to write his memoirs, he responded in characteristically Delphic fashion: "I think you will find that my memoirs have already been written." The task of conveying the essence of his life to remote posterity thus fell to others, not least among whom were co-workers like Frankfurter, anxious to claim his jurisprudential mantle for their own special inheritance. Indeed, so transcendent and pervasive did his explicitly legal thinking seem to these friends and disciples, that after his death those closest to him were at pains to insist that the only proper measure of his life would be a "judicial biography": a full-scale intellectual study that firmly rooted the actions and programs of the social reformer in the fertile and creative mind of the jurist.[11]

Frankfurter had been contemplating such a book for many years, making detailed notes of conversations he had had with his mentor on visits to the latter's summer home at Chatham during the 1920s, and soliciting memoranda from the favored students whom he sent to clerk for the justice over the course of two decades. "I want you to do something very concrete and as soon as may be," he wrote imperatively to David Riesman in 1936.

> This is strictly between ourselves. One of these days I shall have to do a full dress analysis of your Justice, I hope not for many years. I ought to have for that a detailed account of his intellectual procedure in a case that is of importance from every angle of significance, the acuteness of technical questions, the popular implications of the controversy, the sharp conflict within the Court, etc. etc. And so I wish you would pound out on your typewriter a detailed and comprehensive analysis of everything that bears on the jurisdictional opinion and the other opinions in the T.V.A. case. And do this as soon as may be.

The numerous surviving letters from other law clerks providing similar reports to that sought from Riesman would strongly suggest that Frankfurter issued such peremptory requests as a matter of course.[12]

The "judicial biography" was *his* project, however, not Brandeis's—a fact underlined by his stated intention to delay composition until after the death of its subject, and his concern that the matter should remain strictly *entre nous*. In fact, the justice had plans of his own that would eventually result in Alpheus Mason's semiofficial biography, *Brandeis: A Free Man's Life*, published in 1946. Mason would subsequently insist that Brandeis had cooperated fully in the writing of this book. "His decision to permit me to undertake a task, vast in scope and heavy with responsibility, was not a snap judgment," he told Frankfurter angrily in 1960, after more than two decades of the latter's spiteful obstruction. "It came after he had known me and my work for a full decade. . . . He authorized me to prepare his biography." For this purpose, Mason claimed, he had been given "unrestricted access to the Justice's papers"—to all, that is, except the so-called "Court files," which had been handed over to Frankfurter for safe keeping in 1939, and to which he was repeatedly denied access.

> Apparently the inference you would have me, and others, draw, is that I did not enjoy Brandeis' confidence, or even his good will. . . . Massive evidence, much of it of record, refutes you—the ten days I spent with [him] at Chatham in the summer of 1940, when he recalled intimate details, pouring out, in a way most unusual for him, his heart and soul on various aspects of his life and work; the letters he wrote his friends bespeaking his confidence, and requesting their cooperation; above all, the proof stamped on pages of the biography itself.[13]

Thus while Professor Mason, and others committed to producing broadly gauged estimates of the late justice, had to content themselves with the printed record, and with working through such epistular remains of his public career as came to be housed in the Law Library at the University of Louisville, Frankfurter retained a jealous and restrictive control over Brandeis's Court papers, eventually depositing them in Cambridge. At first it continued to look as though Frankfurter intended undertaking the "judicial biography" himself; however, his own work in Washington soon persuaded him of the need to find a surrogate. In fact, two were chosen: Paul Freund, by then a faculty member at the Harvard Law School and Alexander Bickel of Yale. For more than twenty years these men were to enjoy exclusive access to the working papers assembled by the justice and his clerks in the course of more than two decades spent on the Supreme Court bench. As Frankfurter himself advised Bickel in 1958:

> Wisdom, I believe, "precludes," to use a favorite Brandeisian word, lawyers or even writers from grubbing among the Brandeis materials as a basis for interpreting, either by qualifying or confirming, the official texts of opinions. It is one thing for Paul and you to use such materials in whatever writings you will be doing, with the kind of regard you will inevitably exercise. It is quite another thing to have [others]. . . . make use of them as dictated by their special interests.

Only the members of a narrow priesthood, it seemed, were pure enough to handle such sacred documents without defiling them![14]

From the materials thus placed at their disposal, these two able lawyers were supposed to distill the judicial essence of his social philosophy and political outlook. The major undertaking, Frankfurter reminded Freund in 1951, was to extract from them "the study of a mind and the nature of the judicial process." The endeavor was to prove chimerical. Bickel found, and in 1956 published along with a perceptive commentary, a series of hitherto unpublished Brandeis opinions that had been suppressed, or at any rate remained undelivered, either as a consequence of judicial horse trading or because the case in question had become moot. Freund wrote several insightful and illuminating articles about his old chief, rounded out by personal recollection and anecdote, and on occasion by quotations from discarded early sketches of the more celebrated opinions, but nothing more substantial. Toward the close of 1958, Frankfurter was still claiming that his protégés were designated as the official eventual biographers of the justice, but the "big book" of his imagination was never written.[15]

The question arises: Why not? In part the answer lies in the nature and limited usefulness of the very Court Files in which both Frankfurter and Mason in their different ways placed such great faith. For fascinating though it may be to trace the growth and elaboration of a Supreme Court ruling from rudimentary first draft to mature delivered opinion, or to observe the tutorial relationship between judge and law clerk, these processes do not, and cannot by themselves, reveal the totality of the judicial mind at work. But more significant by far is the nature of the quest itself, and in particular the questionable validity of Frankfurter's perception that Brandeis was at bottom a juristic thinker. This is at best an unproven hypothesis; arguably, as we shall see in later chapters, it is both misleading and untenable. It was an indispensable starting point, however, for those wishing to claim the late justice as a disinterested champion of the canons of judicial self-restraint and thereby the most adept precursor of their own embattled school of jurisprudence. Thus, in 1947, Frankfurter could write enthusiastically to Louis Jaffe after reading the former law clerk's review of the Mason biography:

> Your disassociation of Brandeis from the "activists" is as true as it is good. Is it preoccupation with my own job [as a Justice of the Supreme Court] which makes me wonder why those of the legal professoriat who know better are doing so little of this sort of elucidation, and are leaving the field largely to those who really think that law is only the "manipulation of symbols" for immediate predetermined ends.[16]

Lawyers, though, were not the only participants in the posthumous struggle to appropriate Brandeis's reputation. Zionist leaders too had an obvious interest in claiming his memory for themselves—a prospect that at least one of his long-standing associates in that movement found difficult to stomach. Learning that Solomon Goldman was "jumping into print" within a few months of his old friend's death, Stephen S. Wise, himself one of the most respected figures in American Jewry, was frankly appalled. In his judgment, the principal danger was that Goldman would "make it appear that L.D.B. was a sort of Chasidic rabbi, who in his work and speech sought to parallel some of the Midrashic wisdom of earlier sages in Israel." Nothing, he believed, could be less appropriate or further from the truth. "I need hardly tell you, who knew him best," Wise confided to Frankfurter, "that Brandeis was first and last an American; that he was an American jurist, that he was an American judge; and that only in the last twenty-five years of his life did he give much of his great mind to Zionism. To write a book on Brandeis, the Zionist, at this time will give a distorted picture of the man." Having corresponded with Brandeis for more than twenty-five years, he had himself amassed a considerable body of material on the subject—sufficient "to make a large and important book bearing on Zionism"—but this, he felt, was not the overriding priority. For as he told his correspondent:

> the first book on L.D.B., which you are supremely qualified to write—but which, of course, in view of your judicial obligations you may not be able to do—ought to be a book about Brandeis, the American Statesman, Jurist, Judge, etc. . . . It will be unjust to [his] memory . . . for Jews to claim him as though he were solely our own. "Er war unser," but, first and last, he was American Statesman, Prophet, Jurist.[17]

With the emphasis it gave to statesmanship as well as law, Wise's vision was in some ways better rounded than that of the man to whom his remarks were addressed; both nevertheless tended to perceive their hero in the context of their own experiences. To Frankfurter, who first heard Brandeis speak about "The Opportunity in the Law" at a meeting of the Harvard Ethical Society in 1906, he would always be seen as the ideal legal practitioner. "Our present task is to fortify ourselves by his example," he wrote in 1941, "by his passionate dedication of great gifts to great purposes, by the use of the versatile resources of the law for the liberation and enrichment of the potentialities of man." For Rabbi Wise, though, Brandeis's greatness entailed something rather more elusive: "One felt as one sat with him in his modest little study, unadorned save by the radiance of his personality, that one had drawn a little nearer to the sources of truth and justice." As he went on to explain in a magazine editorial written shortly after the justice's death, he had known Brandeis as "a man whose spirit has given me fresh insight into the possibility of the Jew at his highest." What was the particular characteristic that Wise found so inspiring? True enough, like Frankfurter, he had perceived in the object of this eulogy the great legal mind; but he had seen something more beside: the "American Prophet."[18]

The present volume is not intended as just another biography, even though cast within a comprehensive framework of necessary biographical information. Rather it is an attempt to explore the content of the prophetic vision which, as reformer and judge, Louis Brandeis offered to his contemporaries during a public career spanning four decades—a vision which, in the last years of the twentieth century, begins to assume renewed relevance for a society increasingly ill at ease with moral relativism, corporatist values, and the souring fruits of "bigness" in all its forms. It is also an attempt to discover the intellectual roots of that vision, and to rescue the story of its complex evolution from the deracinating strategies adopted by most previous commentators, keen to press ahead toward what they consider its final, mature, perfected formulation. By so doing, it becomes possible to debunk not merely the myth of "the good grey judge," but likewise the postmortem fabrication of the juristic monk, whose legal idealism remained wholly detached from, and unsullied by, the desire to achieve worthwhile social ends.

The resultant picture is of a more human and ultimately more attractive figure, whose enduring legacy is a dual and paradoxical perception: of the dynamic potential of law to overcome the limits imposed by human frailty; yet also of the inherent limitations of legalism as an operational philosophy capable of ordering the actions and relationships of man in society. If the final touches to this portrait will depict details added in old age, the first broad brushstrokes must lay down an outline of ideas already present in youth.

1

The Wishes of Youth

I can hardly revive the spirit of those days, and indeed you would not be able to understand them. The tendency of the times is different, even in Germany, and even the spirit of youth. It has different ideals, different feelings, even if in the main everything remains fundamentally the same since the world began.
—Frederika Dembitz Brandeis, *Reminiscences*

Nobody comes into the world with ideas and values predetermined by their genes; rather their thought patterns and ideologies are the evolving product of social context and human contact, of education and environment. Throughout childhood and adolescence, available role models are emulated or rejected as an individual's personality and character take shape and develop slowly toward their distinctive adult formations. Thereafter, though experience of the world will inevitably modify and overlay much of the limited philosophy acquired in youth, its essential configurations are rarely jettisoned completely, but continue to delimit as long as life endures the permissible pathways of thought and motivation. The sources from which youthful ideas are drawn will of course vary markedly, depending on period and location as well as on education and upbringing; in most cases, however, the thought and value systems offered by family and friends, teachers and favorite authors, can be expected to exert a powerful influence on the unformed mind, particularly when they are held in common by members of a close-knit family and located within a stable and self-confident culture-community.

Louis Dembitz Brandeis was raised in just such a setting during the third quarter of the nineteenth century; for this reason it is worth exploring in some detail the family background from which he came, and the values and life experiences of those most responsible for his upbringing and education, in order to discover what assumptions he grew up with, and what perceptions he subsequently took from home into the wider world. For if, as the German proverb relates, "the wishes of youth are garnered in age," then some recognizable features of the elderly Supreme Court justice should be foreshadowed in the aspirations of the fresh-faced boy, growing to adulthood in what was then the richest and most go-ahead region of the American Midwest.[1]

31

His parents, Adolph and Frederika, were among the younger members of an extended family of Bohemian Jews who, after quitting their homeland in the late 1840s, eventually came to rest like many other German-speaking émigrés amid the agrarian prosperity and commercial hurly-burly of the middle Ohio Valley. In the strictest use of the term, they were not "Forty-Eighters"—at least, not in the sense of being politically active radicals forced to leave Europe after the collapse of the 1848 revolutions.[2] Their motivation was as much economic as political, and the decision to leave their home in Prague was being considered well before the revolution broke out. At the core of the group was part of the senior generation of the Wehle family: Gottlieb, his bothers Moritz and Siegmund, and their sister Amalia. With Gottlieb came his wife Eleanore and their twelve children; Moritz brought with him his wife, daughter, and cousin; and Amalia was accompanied by her brother-in-law Dr. Siegmund Dembitz and his children, Frederika and Lewis, over whom she and Moritz had exercised a quasi-parental responsibility since the death of their sister Fannie in 1840. This tight little band of migrants was completed by the two Brandeis brothers, Adolph and Samuel ("Semmi"), both long-standing friends of the family, fiancés respectively of Frederika Dembitz and Lotti Wehle, and brothers-in-law of Moritz Wehle, who was married to their sister Emma.

The Wehles were a respectable and industrious clan, whose ancestors had lived ln Prague for generations. As Gottlieb later wrote in a memorial for his children, they were men of good standing in the city's Jewish community, "well-known for their learning, their great charity, their upright and irreproachable lives, their wealth and peaceable dispositions." His father, Aaron Behr Wehle, ten of whose seventeen children survived into adulthood, had owned a substantial silk company with extensive business connections in the Italian peninsular. What became of this firm is far from clear, but most probably it passed into the hands of his eldest children. In any event, the family fortunes of Gottlieb Wehle were dependent not on silk but on Bohemia's cotton-print textile industry, for which he imported dyestuffs from Hamburg. By the 1840s this business was in decline. The Napoleonic wars had disrupted trade, and postwar economic policies had led to a long-term depreciation of the currency; moreover, the belated onset of the industrial revolution in Austria was rapidly undermining the viability of the traditional hand-block printing companies (like those run by Moritz Wehle and his father-in-law Simon Brandeis) for whom Gottlieb's firm acted as middlemen. The newer, better-capitalized textile manufacturers now appearing at the forefront of technological change were setting up their own machine-printing operations, and taking advantage of improved transportation and communication systems to deal directly for their dyestuffs with shippers and suppliers in Hamburg and the other ports from which such materials could be had. In the meantime, like other Jews, the Wehles and Brandeises remained subject to special discriminatory taxes as the price of continued toleration. Given such conditions, not only their business, but with it their livelihood and social status, could only look forward to an increasingly bleak future—unless they too joined the drive for mechanization, which they were apparently unable or unwilling to do. Perhaps their resources were already too far depleted; for as Frederika's Aunt Amalia would recall years later in Indiana, these were times when prosperous families like theirs "went to bed worth one hundred thousand gulden and woke up worth only twenty thousand."[3]

It was their appreciation of this dismal socioeconomic reality that first led the family elders to consider selling up in Prague and moving to the New World; but it may have been the political events of 1848 which finally determined the matter. The Wehles and their kin were men and women of pronounced liberal sympathies who favored greater political freedom and the right of self-determination for the ethnically diverse provinces of the sprawling Hapsburg Empire. Moritz Wehle, for instance, had long been a frequent traveler to Italy, perhaps in connection with his late father's silk business, and during the 1820s and early 1830s had apparently been an active participant in the clandestine Carbonaro revolutionary movement. Similarly, his brother-in-law Dr. Siegmund Dembitz sympathized greatly with the abortive Polish rebellion of 1830–31, and went so far as to place his medical skills at the service of the Polish revolutionaries in 1848. This being said, there is no evidence to suggest that either man was ever identified as a dangerous dissident by the Austrian authorities, or that either's decision to emigrate was forced on him by political necessity.[4]

What may have proved a more decisive factor than any personal fears of repression was the rapid growth of Slav nationalism among the Bohemian Czechs, the smouldering embers of which were suddenly fanned into flames during 1848 by the March revolution in Vienna and by the calls to German unity voiced in the Frankfurt Parliament in May. German speakers were a minority in Bohemia, and German Jews a minority within a minority. Thus, however much they may have approved the revolutionary changes in principle, the growth of anti-Semitism among the urban proletariat, and the hostile and ethnically intolerant noises coming from the Pan-Slav Assembly when it met in Prague that June, must have left even the liberal Wehles feeling decidedly uneasy about their situation. How well would middle-class Jews fare in a newly democratic and decentralized Austria, where political and economic power could be expected to pass inexorably into the hands of the ethnic group dominant within each province?

As early as 1844, rioting cotton-print workers had vented their anger on the Jewish entrepreneurs who dominated the city's textile industry, blaming them for the twin evils of falling wage rates and rising unemployment, both brought on by the introduction of new machinery. Ironically, as we have already seen, the Wehles and Brandeises were economic casualties of precisely the same industrialization processes; but an angry mob was hardly likely to take note of such niceties. Anti-Semitic rhetoric, inter-spersed with occasional attacks on Jews and their property, became an increasingly common feature of the mid-1840s, and with the economic reces-sion of 1847 was to take on a fresh intensity. Though bakers and grain mer-chants suspected of profiteering were the initial targets, during the first weeks of the revolution in March and April 1848 the growing power of the urban proletariat was accompanied by widening harassment of Jewish mer-chants and other unpopular individuals. This rising tide of working-class re-sentment and bitterness, propelled by a spate of racist pamphlets, slogans, and cartoons, finally spilled over during two days of ferocious anti-Jewish riots at the beginning of May, producing what one informed commentator has called "the worst anti-Jewish outbursts of the revolutionary era."[5]

As if this were not enough to contend with, the dilemma facing liberal-minded Jews was made even more acute in mid-June, when a violent con-frontation developed between radical insurgents and the Austrian forces sent to quell them. With the Jewish quarter barricaded against any further hostile attacks from whatever side they might come, its inhabitants, like most Germans in the city, remained neutral as they watched events unfold. On 17 June, however, after the accidental shooting of his wife at the start of a week of clashes between students, workers, and regular troops, General Alfred Windischgrätz, the imperial commander-in-chief, bombarded the city, suppressed the popular uprising, and routed the Assembly. Neutrals now found themselves caught between manifestations of imperial tyranny on the one hand and the excesses Czech nationalism on the other. It was at *this* point, rather than with the suppression of the Vienna Reichstag some four-and-a-half months later, that the elders of the Wehle family determined at long last to seek a new life for themselves in the United States, and to send the young and resourceful Adolph Brandeis on ahead to spy out the lie of the land. The members of the Wehle-Brandeis migration were not so much keen fomenters of revolution in 1848 as concerned onlookers, fearful lest they should become its victims.[6]

Perceiving as early as 1842 that his father's impoverished cotton-print business could provide him with neither financial security nor personal inde-pendence, and failing to meet the preliminary educational requirements needed to study chemistry at university, Adolph had taken a course in agri-culture and management at the Technical School of Prague; and after three more years of working for his father and Moritz Wehle, in 1846 he had gone to Hamburg in search of more rewarding opportunities. He soon became disillusioned, and not long after arriving in the city could write his brother Samuel:

> After my long journey I seem to have gone backward rather than forward, and to stand again at the beginning of a career. The caprice of fortune has set me back in the very first class after I had passed many a hard examination in life's school, and I see that in spite of my 24 years, I must play the schoolboy again, perhaps again

for nothing. The first problem is to find a good position, which seems to be very difficult. The pay of the best clerks is worse than in Prague, and as for any hope of independence, no one can tell about that.

The possibility of a move across the Atlantic was apparently already under consideration, for he continued: "If everything fails, I cast my eyes on the near ocean and what lies beyond. Perhaps sometime we can be happy there together. I was never happier in the thought than now, that is, if it is shared by those dear to me." In the event, his prospects took an early turn for the better, and for the next eighteen months he found himself gainfully employed in the grocery business, initially in Hamburg and then for a while in England, where he went (or perhaps was sent by his employers) to investigate the workings of the British colonial trade in such items as tea, coffee, sugar, and spices. This enabled him not only to acquire useful knowledge and experience of the wider commercial world, but also afforded an ideal opportunity to become reasonably fluent in the English language—both of which accomplishments would later be put to good use in North America. Learning of the revolutionary spirit breaking out at home in the spring of 1848, he sought to return to Bohemia via the Netherlands; but his return being delayed by a bout of typhoid contracted on the journey, he was prevented from playing any active part in the Prague uprising and scarcely had time to take stock of the political situation there before being packed off back to Hamburg en route for America. Nevertheless, his extant correspondence is sufficient to indicate his concern for the outcome of these upheavals; and once in the United States, his letters home make pointed reference to that "wonderful year" in which "the spirit of the Lord informed the peoples of Europe and His mighty voice overthrew the tyrants."[7]

Thus it was that Adolph Brandeis, a bright and ambitious young man already promised in marriage to Moritz Wehle's niece and ward Frederika Dembitz, set sail for New York in the summer of 1848. As the person deemed best qualified by experience, training, and youthful energy to assess the Wehles' prospects, he was charged with responsibility for choosing a suitable spot in which to establish the farm colony by which the family elders hoped to restore their ailing fortunes. On his arrival, the young Bohemian set to work at once to fulfill the commission with which he had been sent over. Traveling south through Pennsylvania into Maryland and Virginia, he then struck west to explore Ohio and Indiana. There he visited farms and country estates, talked with everyone from whom he could elicit relevant information about agricultural conditions in the region, and even went so far as to hire himself out as a farm laborer to gain first-hand experience. By the beginning of 1849 he was working for a wholesale and retail grocery business in Cincinnati, and becoming ever more dubious about the choice of frontier farming as a suitable occupation for middle-class city dwellers, several of whom were already well advanced into middle age. Despite an initial reluctance to abandon the romantic idyll of a farm in the wilderness, the older

Wehles were eventually brought around by the force of Adolph's arguments and continuing uncertainties at home, and in April 1849 a family party of twenty-six members took ship in Hamburg for the New World, weighted down by several massive chests containing not only clothes, feather beds, and copper kitchen utensils, but also books, paintings, and two grand pianos. From New York they made their way by canal and train to Cincinnati; and after spending a month there to get the measure of their situation and formulate new plans for their future, all but two of the group decided to settle in the small but rapidly expanding business community of Madison.[8]

During his exploratory tours of the previous summer, Adolph Brandeis had been struck by the boom and bustle of Louisville and Cincinnati, and by the commercial opportunities that seemed to exist all along the middle reaches of the Ohio River. Situated between these two larger neighbors, Madison was an Indiana town of some 10,000 people, that with the recent completion of a railroad link to Indianapolis seemed destined to develop rapidly as the principal economic gateway of that state. Once it had become evident to him that farming was out of the question, Adolph had begun to ponder the possibility of manufacturing some basic commodity like sugar, soap, or starch that could be supplied in bulk along the trade routes radiating outward from these river ports, and took the wise precaution of recommending his correspondents to find out about the Bohemian process for making cornstarch (then in short supply in America) before leaving Prague. Reviewing their options in Cincinnati a few months later, the group decided on a twofold strategy for securing their future prosperity: They would build a factory in Madison for the manufacture of cornstarch. To bolster their income, however, and to make the most of Adolph's recently acquired expertise, they would also establish a grocery and produce business in the town. The factory quickly foundered, because none of the group had any real understanding of how to set up and manage such an enterprise; but the grocery concern flourished, providing the Wehles with a modest livelihood, and providing Adolph Brandeis with the contacts and experience on which he would subsequently build a thriving wholesale business of his own.[9]

Adolph and his fiancée were married in September 1849. Because of the stresses of her childhood, Frederika Dembitz was in many respects a stronger and more resilient person than her husband; yet at the same time, because of her greater aesthetic awareness and cultured upbringing, she perhaps gave up more than he when the Wehle family decided to turn its back on the Old World. Her father, Dr. Siegmund Dembitz, though born in Hungary to once-wealthy Jewish parents of Dutch and Portuguese descent, had received his medical training in Prussia; and because his qualifications did not enable him to practice in Austria, he spent much of his early professional life in the towns of Prussian Poland, eking out a meager existence, and associating whenever possible with German officials and the lesser Polish nobility. Although Frederika always maintained a great affection for him, she resented at heart the way in which his restless spirit had condemned her mother to years of wandering across Europe, separating herself from family and friends, and destroying her health in the process. Remembering him as "full of eloquence and enthusiasm" and "more brilliant than most men," she also recalled that he was "very impractical and inconsiderate," possessed of a character that was "irritable, passionate and eccentric."[10]

Nevertheless, despite her father's incessant roaming and her mother's early death, Frederika managed in the circumstances to maintain a surprising degree of equanimity about her situation, and, thanks in large part to the devotion and good sense of her Wehle aunts and uncles, emerged into adult life as a capable, liberally educated and socially cultivated young woman. At the age of sixteen she was, by her own estimate, "a thoroughly healthy, lively, hearty girl" who, though she "had already experienced much of life's tragedy, and knew that starlight and roses alone cannot make us happy," could still be "happy in [her] dreams, and indeed was gay and of good cheer." Thus the amenities of Madison, and even Louisville, must have appeared rather provincial and unrefined at first to one with so cosmopolitan an upbringing and lately accustomed to reveling in the culture and bourgeois gaiety of Prague. On the other hand, she was no stranger to loneliness and privation either, and married life in America seems to have afforded her the emotional comfort and domestic stability that had been almost totally absent while she was growing up. Born in either Chzarnievew or Strzelno (she knew not which) in 1828, during the next seventeen years she was to live successively in Zirke (Sieraków) in the province of Posen (Poznan), Drossen (Osno) in Brandenburg, Müncheberg and Frankfurt an der Oder, both close to Berlin, and Sagan (Zagan) in Silesia. Whenever her father went off to look for another new town in which to try his luck, she would go to stay with her relations in Prague, at first with her mother but later alone, and frequently for months on end. From 1845 onward she lived there permanently until, with her fiancé and other members of the Wehle tribe, she set out for the United States.

Zirke she remembered as "the paradise of [her] childhood," where she had visited the grand houses of the Polish nobles whom her father served as physician and played in the gardens with their children. Following the abortive Polish revolution of 1830–31, Dr. Dembitz's fortunes declined steadily, his improvident and querulous nature rapidly alienating friends and potential clients in every community where his family subsequently settled. Even Frederika's Aunt Amalia, an unhappy widow who gave up her own business to keep house for him when his wife died, found him impossible to live with, and together with her brother Moritz Wehle waged a remorseless and ultimately successful battle within the family for control of her sister's children. During the last years spent in Dr. Dembitz's itinerant household. Frederika recalled that they lived in "very poor and depressing circumstances": and it was probably her father's financial dependence on the the charity of his brothers-in-law that enabled Moritz and Amalia to call the tune with regard to the children's later upbringing.[11]

The recollections of her life in Europe. which she wrote down for her son Louis in a series of letters penned during the 1880s. reveal clearly the range of her interests and accomplishments. Though she spent less than two years in regular schools. she did receive formal lessons during the greater part of her girlhood. at first from her father and private teachers. and then for a time in Müncheberg from Superintendent Waizmann. a Lutheran clergyman who introduced her to "history, in particular ancient history and literature." During the winter of 1835–36. which she spent in Prague with her mother. she was sent to a knitting school to keep her occupied. and there learned French grammar and conversation from Madame Sanuci. the old woman who ran the establishment. She also took dancing lessons with children from the neighboring Mauthner and Brandeis families. occasions which not only became the basis for lasting attachments in later years but which long remained "among the pleasantest recollections" of her childhood.[12]

It was Dr. Dembitz. though. who layed the most enduring foundations for her later education by first opening to her (and later to her brother Lewis) the elements of writing, arithmetic, and French. "He was an excellent teacher," she remembered half a century later, "and knew how to make the lessons very interesting, exciting our curiosity and introducing into every subject something beautiful and instructive." At the age of eight he was teaching her Greek mythology, and telling her the stories of Croesus and Solon. Soon afterward he was reading her Schiller's *Burgschaft*. Not surprisingly, perhaps, the games that she and her brother played reflected the content of their lessons. Thus in the garden of the parsonage at Müncheberg. they acted out the Trojan wars with the Waizmann children. using an old hobby horse for the Wooden Horse and a few ivy-covered rocks for the city walls. Here too, on another occasion, they tried making glass "according to a Phoenician recipe." After the death of his wife, Dr. Dembitz became an increasingly sorry figure—his eccentricities more pronounced and his temper frayed—but his mind continued to exercise "a powerful influence" over the intellectual development of his children. "His enlightened point of view seems to me more admirable the older I grow," Frederika would write in later life. "If he had only been more practical, with his genius and charming personality he would have occupied a prominent position in the world of scholars."[13]

Even before her mother's final illness, however, responsibility for Frederika's education was beginning to pass into the hands of her Wehle relations. From June 1839 until the following summer she lived with her Uncle Moritz and Aunt Emma in Prague, and with no children of her own age in the house soon buried herself in her studies. A precocious child who had been fascinated by libraries from a very early age, she now "read with enthusiasm every book that I saw or that I had not been forbidden to read: children's books, novels, the classics, everything that I could spell out,—even Moses Mendelsohn's Plato, which was lying around." She also had formal lessons, at first with a student and then with her "first Jewish private teacher," one Herr Edeles, "an old gentleman reminiscent, in behavior and dress, of the scholars of the 'Ancien Regime'—delicate cuffs and rings with seals, refined speech and compliments; also stories about his circle of aristocratic pupils, and in between a little history and literature."

In part, Moritz Wehle's solicitude stemmed from his desire to see his niece raised as a lady, not as a ragamuffin. To this end a certain training in decorum was required which Frederika found frankly irksome. It was not that she lacked companions; the Mauthner children lived close by, and she loved the time she spent in their company. But she could no longer run freely from house to house as she had done in Müncheberg; in polite society, visits had to be arranged beforehand. Then there were the proprieties of walking out in public. Frederika remembered her experiences with anguish "Oh, how going out walking bored me, again and again over the Graben or on the Bastei! If it meant going alone with Emma, it was bearable; but when Onkel Moritz went along and I had to walk two steps in advance according to rule, then despair overcame me." Her only compensation was to sit beneath the trees at Schubert's coffee house, and there to talk or play with the children of family acquaintants. In the evening, they would sometimes go to the *Färberinsel* (Dyers' Island), and, as she later recalled, "although we only walked up and down very stiffly or sat down even more stiffly," nevertheless she was delighted by "the music, the brilliantly lighted garden which seemed like fairyland to me, and the sight of so many elegant people."[14]

During her next sojourn in Prague, which began in the summer of 1842, she and her brother found themselves living with their Uncle Lassar, another of the Wehle brothers, and his wife Therese. Now almost fourteen years old, and mature for her age, Frederika was treated by her elders "with great consideration and often as if [she] were grown up"; however, on occasion they would also criticize her, and when this happened she was left feeling lonely and dejected. In retrospect she supposed the family thought her specially gifted but were wary lest she became conceited. In truth, it was not so much conceit as intellectual self-assurance that caused her the greatest difficulty; for despite having been brought up by her mother and Aunt Amalia to have nothing but "the greatest respect and admiration" for her elders, she quickly came to perceive that her Uncle Lassar was a man possessing "no culture of any kind," and that he was therefore ill qualified to be her mentor. "This I realized because he wanted to teach me," she wrote later.

Once he even slapped me because I insisted on some point, and in spite of his getting angry, I was, of course, right. I had grown up in too good a school. My father always knew the facts, just as my brother did, and if he did not, he searched until he found them. So I was accustomed to accept his decision as absolutely correct and I was surprised that this uncle knew so little.

She got on rather better with her Aunt Therese, who shared many of her enthusiasms and treated her as a friend and confidante despite the difference in their ages. They read Goethe and Schiller together, and Therese let her young charge assume the lead in their relationship. Among her other relatives in Prague, Adolf and Jenni Wehle always treated her with tenderness and indulgence; but it was her mother's youngest brother, Uncle Siegmund, who became her favorite. "He often delighted me by giving me presents which were not merely useful and therefore much more enjoyed," she later reminisced. He also took her to concerts, including one on the *Färberinsel* given by a celebrated harpist, and on the way bought her a pair of kid gloves and treated her to an ice—small kindnesses that would remain clear in her memory after more than forty years. More important perhaps, certainly in relation to her education, he gave her the run of his extensive library without censoring her choice. With hindsight, she considered this "perhaps . . . not entirely wise," but was convinced that she had come to no harm by it. In this way, she encountered not only Klopstock's *Messiade* but also the rather more dubious *Contes Moraux* of Marmontel. Uncle Siegmund, though, was always very proud of her learning and read French with her whenever the opportunity offered.[15]

Music was already an important part of her life. While staying with Moritz and Emma Wehle in 1839 she had taken piano lessons from a "half crazy" tutor, Herr Austerlitz, who for twenty years had been reckoned the most distinguished music teacher in Prague and had the reputation of being something of a martinet. In the event, she practiced conscientiously, and he behaved graciously toward her, but afterward she thought it a wonder that "he did not destroy forever all my love of music." Three years later she was taking lessons from Wilhelm Kuhe, a talented young man related to her aunt, and benefiting too from frequent contact with the Mauthners' new governess, Auguste Auerbach, who had received her own musical instruction from Felix Mendelssohn in Leipzig.

Amateur theatricals were another of Frederika's childhood enthusiasms. With Betti, Yetti, and Peppi Mauthner in Prague she would extemporize elaborate productions, just as she had done in Müncheberg with her brother and the neighbors' children. "The parts were distributed, the subjects only outlined, the end usually tragic, and the development of the plot was left to each actor." Thus with "all the declamations, all the faintings and unhappy love affairs" which these playlets contained, they enjoyed themselves immensely. With the arrival of Fräulein Auerbach the repertoire widened to include the performance of operas, the composing of poems, and the writing of novellas. "When I think of the entertainments we arranged for ourselves at that time," she recalled in middle age, "I must confess that they really were brilliant, and anyone who watched us might have expected us to do far more than we accomplished later."

In fact, as she herself came to realize, these theatrical games represented merely one small part of the fantasy world into which she fled more and more to escape the loneliness and uncertainties she was experiencing in the real world. Of politics she knew nothing at all. Indeed, her recollections contain little to indicate that she apprehended anything of the economic and social tensions developing ln Prague during the 1830s and 1840s; nor that she was aware of the concerns, aspirations, or even the existence, of a large Slavic population, either there or in provinces of Prussian Poland where she had grown up. In this respect, however, her ignorance of the forces that were shortly to produce the revolutionary outbursts of 1848 was scarcely remarkable, being equal to that of most foreign visitors of both sexes who almost uniformly insisted on regarding Bohemia as a German land.

During her first lengthy stay in Prague she was alone much of the time, which, as she later reflected, "encouraged me to continue my earlier indulgence in daydreams and to color whatever happened to my liking. All the people whom I met, everything that attracted me I fitted into a picture or a story, perhaps compared them with events and people out of books. I really lived a kind of double life." As we have seen, on subsequent visits to the Bohemian capital her relations took greater pains to ensure that her life there was both edifying and enjoyable; however, as she grew older this only made her more acutely aware of the stark contrast between the richness and color of her life in Prague and the impoverished, humdrum existence she endured as her father's housekeeper in Frankfurt an der Oder and later in Sagan. There she might attend dances, but much to her regret was forbidden to take part in theatricals. Wrenched back to the provinces after spending a brief six weeks with Moritz and Emma in 1845, she remembered for decades the agony of mind that her father's sudden arrival had occasioned: "My heart almost stood still with pain. I felt as if a beautiful part of my life had ended."

Finding on her return to Sagan that her best friend had gone away, she threw herself into emulating the writers of the Romantic school, reading, penning letters and composing poems in the approved Romantic style. But, she subsequently recalled, "as I had to keep house very economically, and had much to do, and also played the piano a good deal, my romanticism could not get the upper hand, and I think I retained my common sense in relation to practical life." Indeed, this "innocent romanticism" evidently provided some consolation for her loneliness, and probably prevented her from becoming embittered by her misfortunes. In fact, she remained generally of "a happy nature," and remembered herself as "always lively," dancing rather than walking through the rooms of their house.[16]

As well as providing us with a detailed picture of her own emotional and intellectual development, Frederika's *Reminiscences* also cast important light on her family's religious beliefs, and on the extent and nature of their identity as Jews. In the 1840s, the Jewish community in Prague consisted of some ten thousand individuals, or one in ten of the city's inhabitants, which made it the largest single enclave of Jews in the Austrian Empire. Most were poor craftsman and their families, living out their lives in the cramped tenements and winding alleys of the *Judenstadt*. At one level, cultivated middle-class Jews like the Wehles were themselves a part of this community, but unlike their humbler brethren they were also able to move freely in the wider world beyond the ghetto. It is perhaps of significance that, in the years during which Frederika visited and sometimes lived in the old, rambling *Durchhaus* belonging to her grandparents, the little gate that had formerly led into the Jewish quarter was kept locked, and the house's main entrance opened into the Christian section of the city.[17]

Nevertheless, a generation earlier her grandfather, Aaron Behr Wehle, had evidently been highly regarded in the Jewish community, as much for his learning and religious zeal as for his commercial success. Despite all the burdens of bringing up a large family, it was his wife Esther who ran the family silk business, since, in common with other prosperous Jewish patriarchs, Aaron preferred to spend his time studying the Bible and the Talmud. However, he and many of his relations and friends were members of the mystical Shabbatean sect founded by Jacob Frank in the mid-eighteenth century, whose principal article of faith was a belief in the imminent coming of the Messiah. Indeed, his brother Jonas is described as the "spiritual leader" of the sect in Prague. More generally, the Frankists rejected the dry, casuistic reasoning of orthodox Judaism, and abandoned dietary laws and elements of ritual in favor of a "mystic idealism that opened an almost boundless prospect of intellectual and moral expansion." As Gottlieb Wehle wrote ln 1866, toward the end of his life:

> even the most fanatical of their opponents had to accord to these heretics the possession of the highest intelligence, blameless mode of life, the most rigid sense of morals, justice and charity—in fact all most desirable virtues.
>
> It was their conviction that man, the image of God and his masterpiece, would again reach the condition of perfection with which he was endowed when he came from the Creator's hand; that he would again be as innocent as he was before his fall, that he would be free from vice and sin.
>
> This was in general their belief, the aim of their studies, and their striving for deeper insight into the nature of God.[18]

The Wehles therefore saw themselves as men who had broken with tradition; who valued liberty of conscience above the good opinion of their neighbors, and who were ready to sacrifice wealth and social standing for their beliefs. Frederika took a less charitable view, referring variously to the "crazy beliefs" of the Shabbateans, and to the "religious ecstasies and illusions" entertained by her elders. Why otherwise level-headed and intelligent men should have devoted so large a proportion of their energies and substance to the furtherance of such notions, she could never understand, unless it was that they were so "unhappy and depressed by the state of the Jews" that they were ready to adopt any faith that promised to ameliorate their condition. She clearly blamed some of her father's improvidence on his own adherence to this sect, and was convinced that he had been "drawn into all kinds of adventures through his romantic nature and his sense of exaltation." Likewise, her Aunt Amalia had suffered loneliness and despair for the same cause, sacrificing "the happiness of her youth" to the belief that it was "a pious act not to marry, but to await the Messiah unfettered by earthly desires." When at last she came to "recognize her illusions," she entered into a sad and loveless marriage with another sect member for no better reason than that she felt herself indebted to him. Precisely when "these infatuated people came to their senses" she did not know, but reckoned that they were probably reluctant "to admit that they had been deceived." By contrast, she considered it a mark of her mother's clear-headedness that she had held herself aloof to some extent from "the general religious exaltation of her family." Her grandmother too had endeavored to resist the sect's appeal. "A simple, good, pious woman," she recalled, Esther Wehle "suffered much in seeing her children abandon the old religious practices and give up the old dogmas"; in later years, out of consideration for her feelings, they continued to observe "all the proper ceremonials" whenever she was present. Frederika remembered particularly the Sabbath feasts when "all her children and in-laws came to her for dinner Friday evenings, and it was a fine sight to see the handsome men and their wives, bright and talkative, seated around the gayly laden table."[19]

Another of the reasons why Moritz and Emma Wehle took their eleven-year-old niece to live with them in Prague in 1839 was their concern about her religious upbringing. Most of the people visiting the Dembitz household in Müncheberg were Christians, and Frederika's playmates were the children of a Protestant minister. They were either afraid that she would "turn too much towards Christianity," or else they wanted to introduce her to the tenets of Reformed Judaism, which they in common with several other former Shabbateans had lately come to espouse. Such fears would not have been wholly groundless. "I saw that my parents were good Jews," she would observe many years later, "and yet did not associate with Jews and were different from them"; thus there developed in her, as a consequence, "more affection for our race as a whole than for individuals." Forty-five years on, she did not know precisely what her parents believed, nor "what Jewish doctrines they discarded" through their association with Frankism; "but I do know," she wrote, "that they believed in goodness for its own sake and they had a lofty conception of morality with which they imbued us and which I developed further for myself." Her mother's close friendship with Frau Waizmann and her own intimacy with the pastor's children had, it is true, fostered in her "a great admiration for Protestantism"; however, with the passage of time, this "toned down into tolerance," and not necessarily as a direct result of her aunt's and uncle's intervention. "I had been brought up in too enlightened and rational an atmosphere," she noted, "not to be more antagonized than attracted by sentimental mysticism and anything unnatural or miraculous." In short, she found the Christian Messiah no more appealing than the Jewish one so eagerly awaited by her relatives. "I had serious inner struggles just as most thoughtful young people do who have not been brought up with any formal religion, and that these doubts did not make me unhappy is due to the moral atmosphere in which I grew up."[20]

In Prague she was not only taught by her first Jewish private tutor, but also became interested in the religious services at the Reformed Temple, where the celebrated Dr. Michael Sachs was then making his reputation as an orator. To Frederika he seemed "a noble man with a beautiful and Christ-like countenance," and he impressed her every bit as much as he did the adults who flocked to hear him preach. A Christian visitor to Prague in 1841 observed that Sachs had lately become so popular that his listeners at the synagogue frequently included Protestants and Catholics in their number. After attending a service there himself, he described the scene thus:

> The women, like the men, were sitting in the lower space of the temple, with this difference only, that the men occupied the centre, and the women the side aisles. The choir was composed of a number of young men and boys, in a black costume, with small black velvet caps. As they sung [sic], they were accompanied by a small organ, and the psalms had been rendered into a pure and well-written German version.

The accessibility of this form of worship, not to mention its similarity to Christian practices, clearly made an impression on Frederika's mind, but it was insufficient to offset either the rationalism of her education or the deep-seated antipathy she felt toward fervent zeal of any kind; so it was with something approaching dismay that she viewed her brother's conversion to an ardent Jewish orthodoxy at the tender age of thirteen.

In brief, she absorbed the inner moral purposes of religion while explicitly rejecting the outward forms of conformist piety. "I do not believe that sins can be expiated by going to divine service and observing this or that formula," she wrote uncompromisingly in 1884.

> I believe that only goodness and truth and conduct that is humane and self-sacrificing towards those who need us can bring God nearer to us, and that our errors can only be atoned for by our acting in a more kindly spirit. Love, virtue and truth are the foundation upon which the education of the child must be based. They endure forever. . . . God is the consummation of all virtue, truth and nobility. To strive for these should be our aim wherever life leads us.

This, in essence, was the moral creed by which Frederika lived, and the one whose principles she sought to instill into her own children. On its face, it represented a private rather than a public code, but in practice Jewish thinking found little use for such distinctions. As our Christian visitor to Prague in 1841 noted: "Religion among the Jews forms naturally a subject of constant and familiar conversation, as having been the element in which their political and moral relations have at all times been developed." For Louis Brandeis, religion as such would never occupy an important place in his life; as we shall see, however, the secular faith of Zionism would come to provide him with a very similar context for the development of both thought and action during the latter part of his life.[21]

Adolph and Frederika spent only two years in Madison before detaching themselves from their Wehle relations and moving the fifty-odd miles downstream to Louisville, Kentucky, where their fourth child, Louis, was born in the late fall of 1856. Here Adolph quickly established a wholesale grain and produce business, and when the wheat crop failed in New York's Genesee valley in 1855, he made the first shipments of grain from Kentucky to the eastern states; later that same year he went into partnership with Charles W. Crawford with a view to exploiting further the rich potential of this and other urban markets. During the years that followed, their fledgling firm expanded rapidly until by the early 1870s it was responsible for running a flour mill, a tobacco factory, an eleven-hundred-acre farm and a river freighter, the *Fanny Brandeis*, in addition to its staple commerce.[22]

As well as possessing the intelligence, imagination, and good fortune needed to succeed in business, Adolph also seems to have set great store by developing and maintaining close personal contacts with his suppliers. From the earliest days in Madison, he traveled the backcountry on horseback or in his buggy, up to twenty or thirty miles inland on both sides of the Ohio River, getting to know the farms and communities from which his produce came. Undertaken partly to promote his business interests and partly to provide himself with congenial company, Adolph's journeys through Indiana, Ohio, and Kentucky brought him "into contact with all sorts and conditions of persons," and allowed him to see for himself the parochial roots of American democracy at a time when political differences and public affairs of great moment were the common talk of livery stables and corner groceries across the nation. Because German speakers constituted the largest immigrant group in the region, he could continue to preserve some tenuous links with the cultural milieu in which he had grown up through the relationships he fostered among the farmers, merchants, and mechanics of the interior. Josephine Goldmark, herself a member of the Wehle-Brandeis clan, later showed a perceptive understanding of the part these regular business trips played in Adolph's life:

> He would ride or drive inland in the early mornings; he would buy a standing field of ripe produce and then remain in the vicinity several days in order to attend to its packing and shipping. He would fraternize with the farmers, playing dominoes, talking German, and drinking beer, interested always in human relations and in the observation of the human species.[23]

The 1850s were a decade of political ferment in the United States, and for no group more so than the German immigrants of the Ohio Valley. Not only were they harassed by a disturbing wave of nativism, symbolized by the rise of Know-Nothingism, but there was friction too within the German community itself, between Catholics and Protestants over social and doctrinal issues, and more damagingly between conservative "Greys" and radical "Greens" about the extent to which the reform programs of the Old World were relevant also in the New. The Germans of Louisville, who had followed European events closely during the fateful year of 1848, continued for some time afterward to hope for a renewed effort against the forces of reaction in their homelands. In 1850, there was a group in the city predicting that a new uprising would take place the following spring, and calling for "a regiment of mounted artillery" to be raised and ready to sail when hostilities began. Two years later, they were still said to be "sponsoring picnics and sharpshooting tournaments to provide the sinews of war for another attack upon the kings and princes of Germany"; and when the hero of the Hungarian revolution, Louis Kossuth, spoke in Louisville during his American fund-raising tour of 1852, the city's German community contributed fifteen hundred dollars toward his cause.[24]

1854 saw the arrival in Louisville of the extreme republican, Karl Peter Heinzen, for what was to prove a short but tempestuous career as a newssheet editor in the city. Calling on fellow radicals to help organize a "new reform party" in America, he took a leading role in formulating the declaration of principles that subsequently became known as the "Louisville Platform." Among its other positions and demands, the platform opposed all privileges based on class or race, and came out forcefully against the toleration and extension of slavery; it called for an end to mindless partisanship and to what was seen as sinister clerical influence in politics; and it advocated not only free land for actual settlers, but (more controversially) equal social and political rights for blacks and women as well. Heinzen and his associates also wanted naturalization procedures to be made easier and quicker, a comprehensive program of social legislation and infrastructural development (termed "internal improvements" in the jargon of the period), and an end to American isolationism. Most tendentious of all were their proposals for sweeping constitutional reforms aimed at promoting direct popular government, which would have involved the abolition of both presidency and Senate, an end to the separation of powers, and the effective dismantling of federalism.

The Louisville Platform quickly became the subject of fierce and protracted debate among German Americans, and divided some communities for several decades; yet it was far from being the most extreme example of radicalism to arrive from Europe with the refugees of 1848. Socialists and communists were probably few in number, but their violent rhetoric could make them highly visible. The Louisville-based *Beobachter am Ohio*, for instance, launched outspoken attacks against all forms of private property, and called for capitalists and clerics to be hanged together, according to the "philosophy of the guillotine and the gallows." Not surprisingly, such ideas soon attracted the unwelcome attention of nativist Americans, who now added German "radicals and infidels" to their list of the immigrant bogeymen to be extirpated from their communities. This led directly to the ugly Know-Nothing riots that occurred in Louisville during a local election in August 1855. Carl Wittke's graphic description clearly indicates the seriousness of these incidents:

> Houses, taverns, and groceries of German and Irish citizens were raided, looted, and in some cases destroyed, and there were numerous casualties. Many immigrants left the city with their belongings, even though the state legislature took steps to indemnify the sufferers, and papers like the *New Yorker Staatszeitung* and the *Buffalo Demokrat* appealed for funds for the relief of Irish and German victims of the outrage.

Another object of nativist hostility during the 1850s was the growing Turner (*Turnverein*) movement, whose members combined a devotion to physical fitness with a commitment to radical political positions including most notably support for abolition. In Louisville, the Turner Hall was burned down in circumstances that strongly hinted at arson. In considering this and the other disturbances of 1855, however, it is important not to ignore the economic dimensions of ethnic hostility. Know-Nothings were particularly strong in the waterfront wards of the city, a fact not wholly unconnected with widespread unemployment and severe wage cuts that were the combined result of a general economic recession and the halting of all commercial traffic on the Ohio River the previous summer, the latter being caused in turn by a fierce drought experienced throughout the midwestern region. Recent immigrants from Europe thus represented a convenient scapegoat for the economic misfortunes of those who earned their livelihoods from the river. After the excesses of 1855, long remembered in Louisville as "the Know-Nothing year," the intensity of intercommunal antagonism lessened appreciably, but anti-German feeling in the city continued to smolder beneath the surface right down to the Civil War, with open violence breaking out again at a German picnic as late as 1859.[25]

Although most Forty-Eighters plainly rejected revolutionary socialism, and regarded the radical proposals of Heinzen and his coadjutors as both dangerous and impracticable, that is not to say they were apolitical. On the contrary, most were quick to obtain their citizenship so that they could exercise the democratic rights and responsibilities denied to them in Europe. For the older generation of Germans and for some of the newcomers, it was the Democrats who still in the 1850s best represented the interests and aspirations of the immigrant, and some of those who identified with the "Grey" faction would indeed remain loyal to the party of Jackson well into the next decade; however, the inexorable rise of the slavery issue, and especially the passage of the Kansas-Nebraska Act in 1854, proved increasingly corrosive of traditional party allegiances, and the meteoric rise and fall of Know-Nothingism between 1854 and 1856 effectively signaled the end of the Second Party System. Consequently, in the political realignment that followed, many Germans, including most of those identified as "Greens," found that the new Republican Party afforded them a congenial political home, and this despite the nativist tinge given to the emerging coalition by the inclusion of substantial numbers of former Know-Nothings. For most Protestants, and perhaps for some Jews, this can best be explained by an inveterate hatred of Roman Catholicism; but for others the cause might just as plausibly have been a determination to prove their Americanism as opponents of slavery and defenders of the Union. In either event, it was a political decision of the greatest moment.[26]

In common with most German Jews arriving in America during the middle decades of the nineteenth century, Adolph Brandeis appears to have experienced little difficulty becoming fully integrated into the wider German-speaking community, though whether he joined the Louisville *Turnverein*, or thought of himself as a "Green" or a "Gray," no evidence survives. Similarly, we know little about his party political orientation during the 1850s beyond the fact that he began the decade as a fervent admirer of the Whig Henry Clay and ended it as a supporter of the Republican Abraham Lincoln. We do know that most of the family's other members evidently shared his views. For instance, his brother-in-law, Lewis Dembitz, who had started up a law practice in Louisville after completing his studies in Cincinnati, also became an enthusiastic Republican: a champion of John Charles Frémont in 1856, and one of Kentucky's delegates to the Chicago convention that nominated Lincoln for the presidency in 1860. Only Moritz Wehle, it would seem, identified with the Democrats. Writing to his cousin Julia Wehle during the 1856 campaign, and noting with approval that both she and her father Gottlieb were good Republicans, Dembitz was at a loss to understand how their uncle "as an old Carbonaro and revolutionary can have wandered into the Dough-face or Douglas party, in company, as Greeley puts it, with ballot-box-stuffers, baggage-smashers, shoulder-strikers, pothouse-brawlers, etc." Even in Louisville, well known for its Democratic sympathies, "The most intelligent, most honest and most cultivated people are all more or less openly on the side of Frémont."[27]

If there appears to be a significant measure of class consciousness lurking just beneath the surface of this casual restatement of a familiar partisan stereotype, we should perhaps not be too surprised. For it is important to remember that Louis's father and uncle, like all the other members of the Wehle-Brandeis clan, were "bourgeois liberals" rather than working-class radicals: people who, since the mid-1840s, had found themselves repeatedly on the receiving end of class antagonism, and violence meted out by poorly paid artisans and unemployed workingmen. Emotionally wedded as they were to the forms and nostrums of democracy—universal manhood suffrage, trial by jury, freedom of the press, speech, assembly and religion, and an improved educational system to civilize the masses—they were nevertheless fearful, probably with good reason, of anything that smacked of Jacobin revolution in Europe or unbridled mobocracy in America. They readily identified their interests with those of farmers and tradesmen, and could easily share the latter's justifiable resentment of those who claimed special privileges on the basis of their wealth and power; however, they had little in common with the emerging proletariat of the cities. Adolph Brandeis and Lewis Dembitz were not men to sympathize with the objectives of the Louisville Platform; and as we shall see, their social conservatism was to have a profound influence on the social outlook of Louis Brandeis during his early years at the bar and in public life.[28]

Despite Adolph's fluency in English and his bubbling enthusiasm for almost all things American, at home the Brandeises retained their identity as German-speaking Jews; but while their religious faith seems to have been worn lightly, their linguistic and cultural inheritance appears to have pervaded their whole life-style. It was a Germanic rather than a Jewish cultural tradition in which the young Louis was raised and with which he would identify subconsciously until his death. In the field of literature, it was Goethe and Schiller who represented the "great authors," and through whom he perhaps first developed his contact with the world of classical antiquity; it was toward the string quartets of Mozart and Beethoven and the *lieder* of Schubert and Schumann that his musical sensibilities were directed. When at the age of seventeen he was deemed ready for an education in the wider world beyond Kentucky, it was on a trip to the cultural capitals of Europe and thence to school in Dresden that he went rather than to a Yankee college in the East. It is hardly surprising, therefore, that the basic matrix of his thinking should have been formed and nurtured within the rational and optimistic paradigm of German liberalism. What is more remarkable is that so few of his numerous biographers have made any serious effort to explore the intellectual ramifications of such a humanistic upbringing, or sought to explain the fundamental principles of his mature philosophy by reference to this youthful orientation.[29]

Admittedly, there survives little direct evidence to demonstrate the manner in which the habits, attitudes, and personal example of Adolph and Frederika combined to influence the early emotional and cognitive development of their children. Only one extant letter, a travel diary, and a few fragmentary recollections are available to illuminate the thinking and behavior of their son Louis before the middle of his first year at Harvard Law School. Likewise, the extent to which he and his siblings were conscious of, and affected by, their European heritage can only be a matter for informed speculation. We do know, however, that he loved to hear his mother talk about her life in Europe, about her parents, friends, and numerous relations, and that mother and son shared a love of literature and classical history. Arguably too, it was her personal creed that provided the moral bedrock on which his later social philosophy would be built. "It is such happiness to be your mother," she wrote when he was in his late twenties; "to feel . . . that all my dreams of high ideals and purity are united in you."[30]

The domestic environment in which Louis Brandeis grew up was one of emotional warmth, middle-class comfort, and steadily growing material prosperity, accelerated during the early 1860s by lucrative federal contracts to supply the Union Army with grain. As children, he and his older brother Alfred were particularly close, despite a three-year difference in their ages; indeed, they were to remain on the most intimate terms of friendship with one another until Alfred's death in 1928. "There never were two brothers who complemented one another so perfectly and were so completely one," Frederika would recall, as she looked back on their early years together. Moreover, still scarred perhaps by the tragedy and loneliness of her own youth, and the enforced maturity thrust upon her shoulders by the premature death of her mother, she seems to have been determined that her own progeny would go through life with fond memories of a leisurely and carefree childhood. Louis was therefore allowed to grow up as a lively, not to say boisterous, child who, when he was not teasing the little girls of the neighborhood, ringing doorbells after dark, or playing tricks on the family servants, could often be found whiling away his time by the Louisville waterfront, watching the riverboats as their cargoes were loaded and unloaded, and running barefoot in the summer heat. While celebrating the Fourth of July in 1864, he and Alfred were "nearly blown into eternity" when a powder flask exploded while they were setting "fuses" with damp powder. Among the gang of Huckleberry Finns with whom they played, he was also reckoned to be quite handy with his fists, and although the youngest member of their group, was regularly put up to fight "the Little Lord Fauntleroys" of the city. During his penultimate year in high school, he even fought one of his brawnier classmates for the affections of a local belle named Emma; as a newspaper reporter found many years later, this "physical contest . . . appears to have eclipsed in interest the memory of his excellence in scholarship in the minds of at least a few of his early associates."[31]

It is his outstanding academic record, however, which merits our closer attention. In Louisville as elsewhere the arrival of the Forty-Eighters inspired a revitalization of both private and public education. In 1852 a German-American school was organized in the city, which within two years had more than two hundred children on roll. It offered a wholly secular curriculum, and despite financial difficulties remained open until 1863, thereafter bequeathing a strong tradition of academic excellence to its successor institutions. After a period at Miss Wood's private school, Louis proceeded first to the German and English Academy of Louisville and then to the city's Male High School. At the former, the course of study comprised French, German, Latin, composition, chemistry, algebra, and trigonometry, with the main emphasis being placed on mathematics and languages. He generally achieved the top grade 6 (denoting perfection) in all these subjects, and on his report card for the fall semester of 1868 the school principal gave him a "special commendation for conduct and industry." Similarly in high school, where Greek among other subjects was added to the curriculum, his work either was, or else fell just short of being, "without fault"; and at his graduation in 1872 he was awarded a gold medal "for pre-eminence in all his studies," thus becoming the youngest pupil ever to gain his diploma from the school.[32]

It seems likely, however, that a considerable proportion of his education took place at home, outside the confines of formal lessons. With all talk of business affairs banned from the dinner table by Frederika's explicit prohibition, mealtime conversations naturally turned instead to discussions of history and current affairs, of literature and the arts. The 1850s had witnessed a remarkable renaissance of interest among German Americans in the classical works of their own culture, and in the years of Louis's childhood German-language books and newspapers were readily available in Louisville and other major centers of Teutonic settlement. As early as 1854, a recent arrival from Europe could claim that more German classics were being sold in the United States than in Germany itself. "Schiller, Goethe and the other classicists [sic]," he insisted, "are to be found in thousands of copies in the huts of workers, on the counters of merchants, in the blockhouses of the western farmers." Even allowing for some degree of exaggeration, it still seems more than likely that such works were present also in the Brandeis household.

That Louis read widely from an early age is beyond dispute; doubtless he was encouraged and directed by Frederika, just as she herself had been guided and spurred on by Dr. Dembitz and Siegmund Wehle. No exhaustive listing of books and authors first sampled in these childhood years can be compiled; however, from isolated fragments and later scattered references a generalized picture may be inferred. Louis was undoubtedly familiar from an early age with the works of Goethe, whom he remained fond of quoting throughout his life. He probably had some acquaintance too with the writings of Schiller and Heine, since both were among his mother's favorites. His initial perceptions of the antique world, however, are more problematic; for it is far from clear whether he acquired his knowledge of its history and philosophy from secondary sources, or by reading the works of ancient authors. Frederika and her brother had certainly read Homer as children, and Louis may well have been prodded into following their example. Since Latin formed part of his studies at school, it is at least conceivable that some Roman authors were attempted in the original, whereas, having no Greek before going to high school, he would probably have been obliged to tackle Hellenic writings via the medium of English or German translations. In later life, the dramatic poetry of Euripides would frequently serve him as a source of entertainment and inspiration, and it is not unreasonable to assume that his initial introduction to Greek tragedy was effected early under his mother's tutelage. English and American authors, such as Shakespeare, Byron, and Emerson, were not neglected either (though he would become even more familiar with the latter during his years in Cambridge); so it might reasonably be claimed that, by the time he was ready to sally forth into the world, Louis Brandeis had already been the recipient of a liberal, and in some senses a classical, education.[33]

Another of her own enthusiasms that Frederika fostered in her children was music. Spartan as life in Louisville may have been compared with Prague, it was far from being a cultural wasteland, and the arrival of Louis H. Hast around 1850 had done much to enhance the musical amenities of the city. As Louis would tell his niece Fannie many years later:

> It is to this romantic German piano-teacher that Louisville owes the beginnings of its appreciation of the great chamber and orchestral music. In lofty enthusiasm he formed the quartette and quintette clubs. With untiring devotion he guided them. Courageously he organized an amateur orchestra. Thus he afforded the opportunity of gaining knowledge and understanding through doing. And the joy of the doing was experienced.

Another Fannie, Frederika's first-born child, was the family's "musical impresario" during the childhood years; at her instigation Louis became a reasonably proficient violinist, and played himself in one of Hast's orchestras during the summer of 1875, before leaving Louisville for Harvard Law School. A few years later, Frederika would share with him her delight at spending three days at the Cincinnati Music Festival, and her admiration for Theodore Thomas, "a musical genius and a great conductor." Decades later still, long after he had abandoned the violin himself, Louis and his wife Alice would enjoy the consolation of gramophone records played on their "wee Victrola"; even in death, his coffin surrounded by grieving relatives and friends, the rites of passage consisted not of Jewish ritual, but at his own request of a selection from Beethoven's string quartets. Music, in short, constituted an important, if often private, part of his spiritual being.[34]

If young Louis owed his idealism and the greater part of his cultural education to his mother's influence, his knowledge of the world and his ambition to succeed in it were nurtured and developed first and foremost by his father and his Uncle Lewis. It was the former who encouraged him to read modern history and biography, and the latter who first aroused his interest in the law. Both, drawing on their different fields of expertise, stressed the importance of facts and valued practical experience above abstract theorizing; together they imbued the future Supreme Court justice with a reflexive impulse toward the rational and the pragmatic that would eventually become the hallmark of his professional methodology. It would be a gross oversimplification, though, to imply that hard paternal realism somehow came into conflict with soft maternal ideals in the course of Louis's adolescence. For one thing, as we have seen, Frederika too had been brought up with a profound respect for facts, and had seen enough of life's tragedy to make her as hard-headed as her husband or brother. For another, her son never considered pragmatism and idealism to be mutually exclusive. "In my opinion the only thing of real value in life is the ideal," he would tell a Zionist colleague in 1915, "and in this I am certain that Professor James, from a 'pragmatic point of view,' would have wholly concurred." Similarly, both parents must share some responsibility for the boundless self-confidence that their son rapidly exhibited in the exercise of his mental powers, sometimes to the point where it must have resembled sheer arrogance. One can but wonder what the treasurer of Louisville's Websterian Debating Society must have thought when told by an unsmiling ten-year-old boy that his accounts contained a forty-cent discrepancy![35]

Family background, however, is far from being the only molder of a young person's character; the wider environment, the world beyond hearth and home, must also be considered when examining the earliest sources of outlook and perception. In the decades before the Civil War, Louisville was a vibrant and fast-growing city, ideally situated on a bend of the Ohio River to dominate the commercial activity of its rich agrarian hinterland. Its population increased by 58 percent during the 1850s and by 48 percent during the 1860s to stand at 100,753 in the census of 1870, making it the fourteenth largest urban center in the nation. In 1870, almost 15,000 (15 percent) of its citizens were black, and more than 25,600 (26 percent) were foreign born, including 14,380 Germans and 7,626 Irishmen; Bohemians, counted separately, numbered just sixteen.[36]

The Louisvillians had always enjoyed a lucrative trade with their southern neighbors in the lower Ohio and Mississippi valleys; and with the coming of the Louisville and Nashville Railroad in the 1850s there began to develop a remunerative business with the North and West as well. Thus for this thriving community of merchants, traders, and manufacturers, as for the inhabitants of most border cities, commercial self-interest combined with the ties of kinship to make the choices of 1861 particularly awkward. Kentucky eventually entered the war on the side of the Union, but perhaps as many as a quarter of the 100,000 Kentuckians who took up arms during the struggle were enlisted in the Confederate army. As one commentator later put it: "Kentucky's head was with the Union and her heart was with the South."[37]

In the antebellum period Kentucky was a slave state, though in the 1850s its legislature reckoned that non-slaveholders outnumbered slaveholders seven to one.[38] The incidence of the "peculiar institution" was, however, very uneven, with the great majority of slaves confined to the southwestern section of the state, to the Bluegrass district around Lexington, and to Louisville itself. Although blacks, both slave and free, constituted only 10 percent of the Louisville population in 1860, with the onset of war they were viewed with extreme hostility and suspicion by many of the city's whites, and throughout the conflict suffered severe hardship and repression. The Brandeis family were forthright abolitionists and Republicans in a city dominated by Democrats and, on occasion, sympathetic to the Confederate cause. Tokens of the dissension around him were among Louis's earliest memories, including "the licking" he got in school the morning after Bull Run. "I remember helping my mother carry out food and coffee to the men from the North," he recalled in later years. "The streets seemed full of them always. But there were times when the rebels came so near that we could hear the firing. At one such time my father moved us across the river."[39]

He may well have been aware too of the many blacks now moving in his environment. On the eve of the war, there were some 6,820 black residents in the city, 28 percent of whom were freemen. In March 1864, despite strong opposition, the recruitment of blacks into the Union army began in Kentucky, and after their enlistment the black troops were stationed in Louisville. By the spring of 1865, as fugitive slaves converged on the city from all over the state, its black population was growing at the rate of about two hundred people a week; on the Fourth of July, General John M. Palmer, commander of the Union forces in the state, addressed a crowd of between twenty thousand and fifty thousand blacks who had assembled there to hear him proclaim their symbolic emancipation.

These developments were viewed by most whites in the city with dismay, and in the months and years ahead would lead to a growing resentment of black efforts to secure political and educational rights for themselves. When peace returned, the dominance of ex-Confederates within the city's political and professional elites ensured that what George A. Wright has termed "polite racism" prevailed in Louisville for the remainder of the century. This is especially ironic because, although the economic fortunes of Kentucky as a whole were undoubtedly damaged by the war, those of its largest city remained comparatively buoyant, bolstered by its role as a supply center for the

Northern armies. Moreover, even when the black population was swelled after the war by the influx of freed slaves from the surrounding country-side, this prosperity continued, and jobs remained relatively easy to find.

After the Civil War, the Brandeises and their close relatives became part of a small but influential coterie of liberal whites who challenged the pattern of race relations then emerging in Louisville, and sought to respond more humanely to the social needs and aspirations of their city's expanded black community. At the head of this group were two influential Republicans, John Marshall Harlan and Benjamin H. Bristow, both of whom settled in Louisville after the war, and who during a few brief years provided the political drive and intellectual leadership behind which those opposed to the spread of discrimination and segregation could muster their limited strength.[40] If not exactly color-blind, at least these people were compara-tively free of the ingrained racial prejudices so evident in the rhetoric of Democratic spokesmen like the nationally known editor of the *Louisville Courier-Journal*, "Marse Henry" Watterson, or the entrepreneur and liter-ary critic, Basil Duke.[41]

At a domestic level, though, racial attitudes are more difficult to pin down. For example, when the household of Adolph and Frederika Brandeis moved from First Street to exclusive Broadway after the war, they staffed it with black servants and employed "their first Negro coachman," like all the rest of their middle-class neighbors;[42] however, it would be unwarranted to draw any inferences from this fact concerning their personal relationships with individual blacks or their sentiments toward the black community as a whole. Indeed, while there is little direct evidence on such matters, it might be observed that Lewis Dembitz is known to have been a close associ-ate of Harlan and Bristow.[43] More pertinently, perhaps, Wright notes that in Louisville "several leaders of the Jewish community were consistent sup-porters of black civil rights"; that several black institutions in the city were only kept open by means of the donations made to them by the Jews serving on their boards; and that members of the Brandeis family "worked in volun-teer organizations that made improvements in black neighborhoods." Inter-viewed many years later, their black cook Lizzie gave an example of what she considered Frederika's outstanding generosity:

> I 'member once when I was on a committee to raise funds for an orphan asylum for colored children—it was mah duty to raise $25—and where the money was comin' from I sho' didn' know. For money come awful hard in those days.
>
> But I asked Mis' Brandeis if she would give a little something towards it, and she said, right off: "I certainly will. Doan' you worry about that, Lizzie." And what do you suppose she did? She sat right down and wrote Lizzie a check for $25. That's what she did! And do you think Lizzie ever forgot that? No, sir!

At this distance, it is impossible to discover just how paternalistic the spirit was in which such gestures were made; but in the circumstances it would seem unreasonable to discern here either a family or a wider Jewish community characterized by latent racial prejudice.[44]

Important as the political and racial climate of his hometown must have been in the development of his later outlook, there were also other environmental influences at work on his psyche from an early date. For in just the same way that his mental horizons were expanded from infancy by stories and reading, so too the physical landscape he inhabited was not long confined to the Louisville city limits. In 1862, Frederika and the children went to visit the Wehles in New York. Moritz and his family had left Madison in 1852, followed by Gottlieb, Eleanore, and their children four years later; now Moritz and Emma were on the point of moving back to Prague. In 1864, the Brandeises traveled East again, this time to spend the summer in Newport, Rhode Island; and the following year Louis and his brother accompanied their parents on a circular tour that took them to Niagara Falls, across the border into Canada, and again to Newport. Seventy-five years later, in a conversation with Alpheus T. Mason, the retired Supreme Court justice could still recall the schoolboy's excitement at seeing the falls, the ocean, and "real Indians." At Newport much time was taken up with swimming, boating, and fishing; the boys also rode donkeys, read books in the local library, and got to know the children of other vacationers. For Adolph the trip provided a rare opportunity to reminisce at length with Dr. William Taussig, an old friend from the Prague days, who was also there with his family. Frederika wrote her daughters back home in Kentucky how "our good Papa sits with him recalling old stories of his youth and laughing till the tears run down." It is probable that Louis and Alfred listened to some of the stories as well. Thereafter, shorter trips between Louisville and the Taussig's home in St. Louis became a frequent occurrence for all members of the family. In the following decade, Alfred would spend a year at that city's Washington University; Fannie would marry one of his classmates, Charles Nagel, and make a home there; and Louis himself would spend several months in the city after graduating from law school, working for the firm of William's brother, James Taussig.[45]

One might also surmise that, as they grew older, the boys would sometimes have accompanied their father on his business trips to the farms and villages of the Ohio Valley backcountry. Here Louis would have seen for himself the "island communities" that throughout a long lifetime represented his ideal image of "the good life." If they were not always as orderly and harmonious as the idylls of romantic myth might suggest, they were nevertheless demotic, industrious, largely self-sustaining places, where personal relationships, both good and bad, took shape on a face-to-face basis, and where a man's worth rested on the estimate of his neighbors. They afforded a setting in which people still figured prominently in the landscape, where life still retained a human scale. What he saw there would never make Louis want to become a farm boy, or even a wholesale produce merchant like his father and brother; doubtless it gave him a sight of bigotry and exploitation as well as of hopeful striving and communal endeavor. But it did imbue him with a deep and enduring respect for the little, independent folk of this world: the farmers and artisans, the shipping agents and storekeepers, the clerks and country lawyers, for whom the small town was no temporary staging post on the road to quick riches and sprawling power, but the best American life to which they could aspire. In later years, his reification of the ideal context for humane living would inevitably change and become plural; the simple model would diversify until it could accommodate both factory village and desert kibbutz; but it was in all probability his youthful observations of the Ohio Valley towns that provided the core cerebral images around which his vision of community was originally conceived.[46]

If travel across the northeastern United States and into Canada was a significant feature of Louis's childhood and early adolescence, the journey to Europe that the Brandeises undertook in 1872 represented a vital element of his preparation for adult life. During the 1860s the family had come to take financial prosperity very much for granted; but with the scaling down of federal contracts and a mounting failure rate among their southern clients after the war, a new decade had opened with the firm of Brandeis & Crawford beginning to incur heavy commercial losses. Rather than lose everything he had worked so hard to build up, Adolph decided to wind up his business affairs in Kentucky and to use some of his remaining capital to take Frederika and the children on a fifteen-month tour of Europe.[47]

This journey would also serve to bring the younger members of the family closer to their German cultural roots. The differences of faith and faction that had caused such bitter division among German Americans during the 1850s had begun to diminish in intensity when put into perspective by the larger, bloodier battles of the Civil War; it was only with the defeat of Napoleon III and the unification of the German states under the king of Prussia, however, that the last remaining signs of former disunity were swept away. By the close of 1871, even most of the severe critics and erstwhile victims of continental absolutism found themselves spellbound by Bismarck's military and diplomatic achievements in Northern Europe. Louisville Germans, their houses festooned with American and German flags, greeted the Prussian victories of 1870 with cannonades and mass meetings, and marked the triumph at Sedan with a "Fraternal Festival" and parade. Despite their Austrian connections, members of the Brandeis household seem to have been carried along by the tidal wave of popular fervor. In his first extant letter, dated September 1870, Louis mentions his sister Fannie's intention to attend "the Prussian meeting" being held the following day, details Uncle Lewis's proposed punishment for the French Emperor, and tells of a neighbor's plans to raffle off a picture of Heidelburg to raise funds for the wounded. Quite apart from their healing effect on the German community within the

United States, the seismic changes of 1870–71 led many old Forty-Eighters to reassess their feelings toward the European countries they had left behind; though Adolph and Frederika set sail from New York in August 1872 with every intention of returning to the United States in due course, the possibility that Louis might remain in Europe to become a doctor like his Uncle Samuel was at least discussed during the trip.[48]

Having landed at Liverpool on 18 August, the party passed quickly via London, Dover, and Ostend into German-speaking territory, and during the next few weeks traveled by way of Cologne, Frankfurt am Main, and Stuttgart till in late October, after a lengthy stopover in the Tyrolean summer resort of Ischl, they at last arrived in Vienna. There they spent the winter, visiting the sights, going to concerts and the theater, and in Louis's case taking private lessons and auditing classes at the university as well. Toward the end of March 1873 they moved on into Italy where they spent the next two months indulging their tastes for architecture, sculpture, and painting in one ancient city after another. By July they had journeyed from Milan, via Como and the Italian Lakes, into the Swiss Alps, where Adolph and his sons spent many blissful days scrambling along rocky mountain tracks and tracing rivers to their source. This was the emotional high point of a trip that Louis would remember in graphic detail for the rest of his life. Letters exchanged between himself and Alfred throughout the next half century would allude repeatedly to places and incidents encountered during that enchanted year—the last the family would spend together before physical infirmity, financial ruin, marriages, and careers separated them for good.

In the fall of 1873, Alfred took ship for America, intending to start up in business for himself in Louisville. Adolph, Frederika, and the two girls, however, were prevented from making the journey home by the serious illness that now beset Fannie, and being dissuaded even from crossing the Alps to visit Prague, returned to Vienna to fall back on the aid and comfort of relatives. Louis, meanwhile, had determined to further his formal education in Europe and, finding that he lacked the preparation needed to pass the examination for entry into the University of Vienna, was persuaded by the promise of a personal introduction to try his luck at the *Annen-Realschule* in Dresden. In the event he went to Germany alone, and having charmed his way past the principal's bureaucratic disdain for his American qualifications, spent almost a year and a half as an honor student at the school, taking twelve courses at a time, and steadily improving his performance to the point where nine of his final term's marks were at the grade 1 or *sehr gut* level. By the exacting standards of his German teachers, his knowledge of languages was comparatively weak, but even here he managed a respectable grade 2 (*gut*), and in such subjects as literature, mineralogy, geography, physics, chemistry, and mathematics, he excelled. Before leaving Dresden in March 1875, he was awarded a prize by the faculty out of the Heymann Endowment for his "industry and good behavior," and in keeping with his already strong attraction to the world of classical antiquity chose to receive a book on Greek art, A. W. Becker's *Charakterbilder aus der Kunstgeschichte*. Seven weeks later, with Fannie well enough to travel, he and his family were once again on board an ocean liner, this time bound for New York and home; a few days later, while Adolph and Frederika were in Massachusetts renewing their acquaintance with friends in Brookline, their son made the short journey to Cambridge to arrange matriculation into the Law School of Harvard University.[49]

Louis Brandeis returned to the United States confirmed and confidant in his Americanism. The orderly precision of Bismarck's militaristic state held no charms for him whatever, whereas the freedoms he enjoyed in the New World were now appreciated with a fresh intensity. "I was a terrible little individualist in those days," he told Ernest Poole many years later, "and the German paternalism got on my nerves." He vividly remembered returning home late one night and discovering that he had forgotten his key.

> I whistled up to awaken my roommate; and for this I was reprimanded by the police. This made me homesick. In Kentucky you could whistle. . . . I wanted to go back to America and I wanted to study law. My uncle, the abolitionist, was a lawyer; and to me nothing else seemed really worth while.

Much as he had enjoyed the cultural life of Austria and Italy, and the companionship of mountain walks in Switzerland, the social atmosphere of Europe seemed stale and claustrophobic, and its political systems little changed from those that had existed in 1848. If the trip helped him to comprehend better the nature and context of his European heritage, it also enabled him to realize how much of his personal makeup was now firmly rooted in the new, abrasive, democratic cultures of his own native soil.[50]

2
The Spirit of the Law

When . . . a young man's youth falls in a pregnant age, when production outweighs destruction, so that he is early stirred to a presentiment of what such an epoch demands and promises: then, forced by outward inducements to active interest, he will lay hold on this side and on that, spurred by a desire for manifold activity.

—Goethe, *Poetry and Truth*

Brandeis's initial perceptions of the law were empirical rather than theoretical, based in part on observation of his uncle's legal practice in Louisville, but also perhaps on a semiconscious awareness of the vital role that legal forms and procedures played in maintaining the channels of commerce from which his family had drawn their prosperity. If private property and a market economy were the primary institutions of mid-nineteenth-century America, then courts of law were among its most hallowed temples, and lawyers and judges occupied positions of high status and prestige within its hierarchy of priests. As early as 1830, Tocqueville was ready to regard members of the bar as the youthful republic's closest approximation to an aristocracy, and there can be no doubting the important contribution made by lawyers to the nation's public life. As James Willard Hurst, one of Brandeis's brightest protégés, later put it: "By training and means of livelihood [the nineteenth-century lawyer] became one of the few who did the community's serious reading, spoke its thought, and struggled to bring together its diverse interests." To make a good career at the bar, therefore, was self-evidently a sensible and worthy ambition for the son of educated immigrants, for whom involvement in public issues was an integral, not to say a natural, concomitant of life in a civilized society.[1]

The legal culture that attracted Brandeis's attention in the 1870s was a complex, dynamic, and, at root, a profoundly ambivalent one. Though devoted to sustaining the institution of private property, its principal sympathies rested not so much with those seeking protection for what they already possessed but with "those who wanted the law's help positively to bring things about." It is this developmental orientation which goes a long way toward explaining the courts' preoccupation with contract law, especially during the first three-quarters of the nineteenth century; for the constructive innovation witnessed in this area clearly reflected the needs of a rapidly expanding commerce, whose relationships were increasingly national or international in scope. Moreover, as the century wore on, the principles distilled from the emphasis on the nature and enforcibility of contractual obligations in trade and manufacturing were gradually extended into such diverse spheres as employment, agency, banking, and insurance, where a similar faith in the benevolence and efficacy of free markets held sway. It is important to note, however, that the major buttresses to this developing framework of law were set in place not so much by legislators as by judges. Thus, by and large, the functional edifice that emerged was the fruit not of statute (state or federal) but of the common law.[2]

It would be wrong, though, to perpetuate the myth that American governments were committed to a policy of legal as well as economic laissez-faire during the nineteenth century. In reality, they showed little reticence about resorting to positive legal action whenever the need for it became manifest, but the contemporary definition of "need" has to be clearly understood. As Hurst has observed: "Not the jealous limitation of the power of the state, but the release of individual creative energy was the dominant value. Where legal regulation or compulsion might promote the greater release of individual or group energies, we had no hesitancy in making affirmative use of law." In practice, however, most Americans remained naïvely optimistic, at least as far as the mid-1870s, about the simplicity of the mechanisms by which this goal might be achieved. Again to quote Hurst:

> Our prime inheritance was of middle-class ways of thinking. We continually experienced the tangible accomplishments of individuals, small groups, and local effort, with a heady sense of living in a fluid society in which all about him all the time one saw men moving to new positions of accomplishment and influence. Our background and experience in this country taught faith in the capacities of the productive talent residing in people. The obvious precept was to see that this energy was released for its maximum creative expression.

The result was an "instrumentalist" view of the law, which saw courts, and lawyers, and legal formulas as tools to be employed whenever they seemed useful. Consequently, although it developed rapidly in the course of the century, the fabric of law remained largely passive in terms of its interaction with the changes occurring more widely in American society—industrialization, mass immigration, the rapid growth of cities: reactive rather than *dirigiste* in its style, "acted upon by other social forces, more often than acting upon them." Larger issues, such as the proper method of organizing and/or limiting the exercise of power in a democratic society, were left to future generations for their resolution.[3]

This was the face of American law that Brandeis first encountered. As a law student he would be trained to work within its institutions; as a practicing lawyer he would remain for almost two decades steeped in the compel-

ling inner logic of its fundamental assumptions; only in the 1890s, when presented with a patent disparity between legal metaphysics and social reality,
would he begin seriously to question the operational validity of a narrowly
"instrumentalist" jurisprudence. Yet, notwithstanding the bourgeois-liberal
aversion to mobocracy that he inherited, the hold that the common law and
its principles exerted on his mind ought not to be considered as proof of a
simplistic, standpat conservatism, but should be taken rather as evidence of
commitment to the shared values of his generation and class: a belief in
limitless possibilities for self-improvement and in personal responsibility for
success or failure; an assumption of socioeconomic homogeneity and of
equal opportunities guaranteed to all by constitutional fiat; an abiding faith
in the moral worth of individual endeavor and in the transcendant value
of material development. Far from representing a static conservatism,
this complex amalgam of secularized religion, rationalized self-interest, and
genuine social aspiration constituted a powerful, if blinkered, teleology of
dynamism.

During the summer months of 1875, following his return from Europe,
Brandeis set about preparing himself to become a law student. This he did
by wading through the four weighty volumes of James Kent's *Commentaries
on American Law*, a standard introductory text that had gone through no
fewer than twelve editions since its original publication between 1826 and
1830. In the estimate of one eminent legal scholar, Lawrence M. Friedman,
though not exactly exciting to read, Kent's style was "at all points clear, the
exposition transparent," and he even managed to turn the odd memorable
phrase. More important from the neophyte's perspective, he possessed "a
sure and impressive grasp of the whole fabric of American law. His jurisprudential thought was not original or profound; but his attitude toward the
living law was pragmatic, hard-boiled, and often shrewd." Admittedly he was
no romantic liberal, but neither was he the narrow, unreconstructed Tory
that he has sometimes been made out to be. In fact, Friedman's description
of Kent resembles closely Hurst's broader assessment of the legal culture in
which he was embedded:

> He had no use for the obsolete, no aversion to productive change. . . . He had a
> deep respect for property rights, but a tremendous concern for enterprise as well.
> He loved law as an instrument both of security and of mobility. He had no sen-
> timental attachment to tradition, if it interfered with the "stability and energy" of
> property. He wanted law to serve the cause of economic growth; to protect institu-
> tions that worked.

Thus Louis Brandeis's first formal introduction to American law was not
only congenial in the main to his own developing modes of thought but was

at the same time fully representative of the dominant legal ideology of the age.[4]

The years he spent at Harvard Law School were to furnish him with the first truly formative experiences of his adult life, establishing the habits of mind and contributing some of the ideas that would characterize his philosophical outlook to the end of his days. Arriving in Cambridge in the fall of 1875, not yet nineteen years old and lacking a college degree, he became one of the earliest beneficiaries of the revolutionary methods of legal training introduced at Harvard in the 1870s by the Law School's innovative dean, Christopher Columbus Langdell. By substituting the study of actual cases for the memorization of textbook verities, Langdell hoped to encourage a more disciplined and critical attitude of mind in his students, and demonstrate to them that the doctrines and principles of which the law was composed were themselves the product of an aggregating process, evolving and growing by slow degrees in response to the changing needs of society. The inductive reasoning explicit in Langdell's approach struck a responsive chord in the mind of the young Louisville scholar, freshly returned from a Germany where scientific rationalism pervaded the intellectual atmosphere. As one of his later acquaintances shrewdly remarked: "He would have been irked greatly by the older fashioned methods of studying law."[5]

The team that Langdell had gathered around him at Harvard came ultimately to share not only a new method of legal instruction but also a new conception of the law itself. As Brandeis summarized it in 1889, gone was the operational theory that the law possessed "neither beginning nor end . . . , neither fundamental principle nor natural development"; in its place came the proposition "that the law was a science, and should be studied as such." Proceeding from this conviction, and recognizing that adjudicated cases constituted the well-springs of his jurisprudence, Langdell argued that, in common with other modes of scientific enquiry, study of the law necessarily involved recourse to the original sources of the discipline. After all, that was where the writers of textbooks had acquired their own understanding. "No instructor can provide the royal road to knowledge by giving to the student the conclusions deduced from these sources," Brandeis would later assert in an approving gloss of Langdell's position. The tutor should aim instead to show his students how "to think in a legal manner in accordance with the principles of the particular branch of the law" being studied. "He should seek to inculcate and develop in legal reasoning the habit of intellectual self-reliance." From the recipient's viewpoint, the critical study of actual cases, and the subsequent induction of legal principles from them, was likely to prove both intellectually stimulating and pedagogically effective. As Brandeis could recall from his own experience, "The points thus incidentally learned are impressed upon the mind as they never could be by mere reading or by lectures; for instead of being presented as desiccated facts, they occur as an integral part of the drama of life." While the principles of the law were admittedly numerous, indeed almost innumerable, the truly fundamental ones were comparatively few. It was these alone that the law student needed to acquire; for once acquired, they would be "found springing up" again and again. "They are immediately recognized and located; they are the guide-posts that point the lawyer unerringly to his destination, however numerous the cross-roads or alluring the by-ways."[6]

It would, however, be a great mistake to overstate the completeness of the Langdell revolution at Harvard during the 1870s. As Brandeis himself noted, "several of the professors declined for many years to adopt the system" advocated by their dean. In the 1875–76 session, for example, the teaching faculty comprised just five members. The venerable Emory Washburn, a former governor of Massachusetts, taught courses on real property, criminal law, and criminal procedure; Langdell himself offered equity and civil procedure; James Bradley Thayer taught evidence, trusts, and those parts of equity not covered by the dean; and the newly appointed John Chipman Gray held classes on sales, partnership, and other elements of mercantile law. The most junior member of the team was the controversial James Barr Ames, who had been appointed assistant professor in 1873 barely a year after graduating from the school himself. He was responsible for teaching contracts, torts, and bills and notes. In terms of pedagogical style, only Langdell and his protégé Ames employed the new case method; their three colleagues continued to lecture in the time-honored manner. Indeed, as at least one perceptive observer has pointed out, without the unfailing support of the university's dynamic young president, Charles W. Eliot, Langdell's innovatory techniques would almost certainly have been stillborn, such was the initial resistance to them from students, professors, and the wider legal community alike.[7]

The sharpness of the contrast between the new methods and the old is well illustrated by the recollections of Franklin G. Fessenden, who was a member of the first cohort of students to pass through the Law School after Langdell's arrival. The traditional mode of instruction was by means of formal lectures, in the course of which the professor would read from prepared notes or a textbook (not infrequently his own), breaking off only occasionally to elaborate a point or to answer a question. Informal discussion between a lecturer and his students was rare. Langdell, on the other hand, would circulate sheets containing reprints of reports on a selection of cases (or in later years assign sections of the appropriate casebook) for critical scrutiny before the class. In either event, the headnotes were deliberately omitted. In the class itself, Langdell offered no formal exposition of the rules of law that were applicable in a particular case, but instead engaged the students one by one in a process of dialectical interrogation. Preliminary inquiries about the facts of the case, the arguments of counsel, and the opinions of the bench were followed by further questions designed to draw out of the student his own views about the issues thus raised. To many the process was bewildering; for as Fessenden recalled a half-century later, "nearly all, if not all, failed to see at the beginning that the method was to analyze the case closely and to extract the essential elements, and in this way to grasp the real legal principles involved."

Doubtless the puzzlement quickly evaporated, but continuing criticism and the generally sparse attendance at Langdell's classes during the early years suggests that it was not quickly replaced by universal approbation. In fact, the consequence was rather to produce rival camps within the student body, with a small cadre of enthusiastic Langdell supporters being readily distinguishable from a much larger body of traditionalists who regarded communication of legal rules and formulas as the only legitimate function that a law school could perform. Fessenden summarized the differences of outlook involved as follows:

> The results of the method of Langdell was active search and inquiry; that of the other professors was passive absorption. One produced work and constant discussion outside the lecture room among the students; the other, acquiescence in what was read by the lecturer. One excited earnest inquiry; the other produced a feeling of satisfaction in hearing the rule announced. On the one hand, accuracy of thought and expression were encouraged, tending to clear perception of sound distinctions and to the discovery by the student of the principles involved. On the other hand, acceptance of the conclusions of some one who announced the law was the expected and acceptable result. The second was by far the more popular method among members of the School; and it practically had the general approval of professors, graduates, and those engaged in the practice of law.[8]

To some extent these polarities may be overdrawn. Certainly by the time Brandeis entered the school there was more discussion in the "lecture" classes, and the prior preparation of relevant cases was more widely encouraged. Similarly, it should be understood that Langdell, and later Ames, had no a priori objection to the use of textbooks by their students, provided these were employed to complement the scrutinizing of specific cases. As one modern commentator has observed, "many judicial opinions are [themselves] textual essays on some area of the law, and the study of cases can be a sort of textbook study." Moreover, when it came to editing their own casebooks, both men adopted the practice of appending indexes and/or textual summaries, which amounted to statements of doctrine. Thus, even if there was no actual convergence of teaching methods during the 1870s, at least some measure of common ground does appear to have emerged between the new dean and his more eminent colleagues.[9]

Pedagogical style, however, was only one element of the Langdell revolution. Equally innovative, and to some critics infinitely more shocking, were collateral changes in tuition fees, course structures, student access, and the examination system, which for a while appeared to threaten the economic viability of the school. In 1871, for example, the course was lengthened from eighteen months to two years, and in 1876 to three years, with progress from one session to the next being made conditional on satisfactory performance in formal written examinations. Likewise, from 1875 onward the course's admission requirements were tightened so that only those with a college degree or capable of passing a stiff entrance examination were admitted to candidacy for the bachelor of laws degree. Despite a short-run decline in enrollment, in the longer term these reforms had the desired effect of increasing the number as well as the intellectual caliber of Harvard-trained lawyers, and of successfully beating off competition from both the newer law schools and the older tradition of law-office apprenticeships.[10]

Langdell's most courageous challenge to the ruling conventions of legal education, though, came with the appointment of Ames to the faculty in 1873. Up till then, it had been customary for students of law to be instructed by "active judges and practicing lawyers who gave part of their time to teaching." Ames, by contrast, had spent the year since his own graduation teaching history courses in Harvard College, and had no firsthand experience of legal practice whatever. To make matters worse, he made no secret of his disdain for what others regarded respectfully as the wisdom of the judiciary. As Brandeis told his cousin and future brother-in-law, Otto Wehle, in 1876, "it seemed to be Ames's great aim and object to convince us that nine-tenths of the judges who have sat on the English Bench and about ninety-nine hundredths of the American Judges 'did not know what they were talking about'—that the great majority of the Judges were illogical, inconsistent and unreasonable." Even as late as 1882, one of President Eliot's closest colleagues, Ephraim W. Gurney, could express fears that by "breeding within itself its Corps of instructors" the Law School was running the danger of becoming cut off "from the great current of legal life which flows through the courts and the bar." He objected to Langdell's conception of the law as "an exact science," and excoriated both the dean and his still-young subordinate for exhibiting the attitude of mind that must inevitably result "from a too academic treatment of a great practical profession." As evidence for his charge, Gurney cited

> the contemptuous way which both Langdell and Ames have of speaking of Courts and Judges - not simply those of the day, but the men of the past whom the profession looks up to as its great ornaments. The trouble in their mind with those judges is that they did not treat this or that question as a philosophical professor, building up a coherent system would have done, but as the judges before whom the young men are going to practice will do. I pardon this in Langdell, who has a right to knock bigwigs about; but it seems to me to sit with an ill grace on Ames as yet, and I can easily understand some prejudices against the School, if an old lawyer hears some youngster in his office fresh from the School take this tone.

Yet if Brandeis's own reaction was anything to go by, such fears were perhaps misplaced. For as he noted, although Ames's attitude toward the bench was indeed extreme, his newly appointed colleague, Charles Smith Bradley, was just as passionately committed to an opposite prejudice, going even so far in his deference to judges "as to avoid offering any criticism of what has become settled by decisions, however unsupported by reason." Indeed, it was this very clash of styles and perspectives that Brandeis found so appealing. As he observed to Wehle, "it is very interesting to hear the different professors successively express their views on the same things or persons. Frequently they are diametrically opposed to one another." Moreover, though he was as we shall see clearly influenced by his teachers, he was never in awe of them, and was not about to swallow any single set of opinions whole, merely because of the conviction with which it was voiced. If Langdell's methods achieved nothing else, they did succeed in cultivating in his students the critical faculties of judgment and discrimination.[11]

In fact, though, Gurney's nightmare vision of a Law School faculty wholly divorced from the professional world of legal practice and judicial administration was not what Langdell was aiming for; rather he sought to establish a disciplinary balance between forensic expertise and academic insight from which an atmosphere of creative tension might be expected to emerge. In pursuance of this goal, Harvard Corporation would long continue to appoint both judges and scholars as the proper means of ensuring the best possible development of young legal minds.[12]

For better or for worse, this was the brave new world of intellectual ferment and professional controversy that Brandeis entered in the fall of 1875. His obvious zeal and capacity for hard work quickly enabled him to come to terms with the rigorous demands of the Langdell regime, and it was not long before the young Kentucky scholar began making a deep and lasting impression on his fellow students. As one of them recalled in 1916: "Mr. Brandeis had barely taken his seat in our class room before his remarkable talents were discovered and his claim to immediate distinction allowed." After an interval of nearly forty years he could still bring to mind

> the pleasant voice of that youthful student, his exact and choice language, his keen intellectual face, his lithe figure, his dark yet handsome aspect, and finally the unaffected suavity of his manner, that had in it something of the polish of the Old World. Intellect, refinement, an alert and receptive spirit, were written all over his attractive personality.

Moreover, Brandeis clearly relished the opportunities afforded by Langdell's new-model curriculum. "Law schools are splendid institutions," he informed his cousin after only six months at Harvard.

> Aside from the instruction there received, being able continually to associate with young-men who have the same interest and ambition, who are determined to make as great progress as possible in their studies and devote all their time to the same—must alone be of inestimable advantages. Add to this the instruction of consummate lawyers, who devote their whole time to *you*, and a complete law library of over fifteen thousand volumes and then compare the opportunities for learning which a student of the law has at Harvard Law School and in a law-office. After one has grasped the principles which underlie the structure of the Common

Law, I doubt not, that one can learn very much in an office—That first year at law is, however, surely ill-spent in an office.[13]

Throughout his own "first year at law" Louis worked hard at his studies, preparing cases, participating avidly in class discussions. He also began familiarizing himself with the subtle intricacies of courtroom practice in the private but challenging forum provided by the Pow-Wow Club, one of Harvard's early and exclusive precursors of today's moot courts. "The members of this club were attendants on Langdell's lectures," Franklin Fessenden would later recall.

The deepest interest was taken. Able arguments were made, some of them equal to the best made in [the] highest courts; and apparently as much was felt to be at stake as if the case were real. This practice, coupled with the mental discipline gained in Langdell's lectures, brought out the best there was in the men. . . . This developed a thoughtful and studious set of men, and formed in them habits of industry which followed them in their later years of active work in practice at the bar and on the bench.

Brandeis's own appraisal was equally enthusiastic. Law clubs were, he believed, "grand institutions, a great incentive to labor and the work for them is a pleasant change." He was evidently pleased to muster with the pro-Langdell faction as one of "Kit's Freshmen," and quickly imbibed the principal tenets of the new order. "A lecture alone is little better than the reading of textbooks," he told his cousin authoritatively, "but such lectures as we have here in connection with our other work are quite different things. Idem non est idem." As for textbooks themselves, some of the professors were "trying to inculcate in us a great distrust [of them] . . . , and to prove to us the truth of the maxim—'Melius est petere fontes quam sectari rivulas.'" Some texts, he conceded, were fairly awful, being "loosely . . . written" and full of "startling propositions. . . unsupported by the authorities cited to sustain them"; but others received "almost unqualified praise," especially a number of recent English ones. Evidently by 1875–76 Brandeis and his fellow students were being encouraged to benefit from the best features of the older pedogogy alongside the more exciting methods of the new.[14]

During his second year at the Law School, Brandeis was particularly impressed by a recent recruit to Langdell's team, Charles S. Bradley, a former chief justice of Rhode Island whose views on the judiciary we have already noted. The new professor was evidently an important early stimulus to Louis's thoughts on the significance of equity pleading within the fabric of the common law; he attended three lectures a week on the subject, the largest single element in his 1876–77 course schedule. As he told Wehle,

Bradley is the greatest advocate of the Roman Law and of the Equity system in our jurisprudence, rejoices over the gradual growth of Equity doctrines in our law and the ultimate rule of real justice and right. Whatever is "against conscience" is to him the subject of abhorrence. He desires that there should be no distinction between what is "legally right" and what is "morally right." Considering the end and aim of all law, to keep the world whole, [he] shys [*sic*] at any conclusion which leads to palpable hardship.

As will become evident in later chapters, however, Brandeis's initial confidence in the value of equity procedures would later diminish considerably as he came to appreciate that a latitude capable of *facilitating* justice might just as readily be used to *frustrate* it.[15]

In purely academic terms, his performance at the Law School was truly exceptional, his two-year average score of 97 marks out of 100 representing a level of achievement unsurpassed during his lifetime by any other student. Yet since he was still not twenty-one years old when his course ended in 1877, he was only permitted to graduate by special permission of the trustees. The class that he headed comprised more than two hundred of the brightest graduates that the colleges of New England could provide, but as the classmate already quoted later observed: "I think it would be admitted by every surviving member of that class, however distinguished, that . . . [he] had the keenest and most subtle mind of all." For his own part, when interviewed by Ernest Poole in 1911, Brandeis remembered his student days as among the happiest of his life. "I worked!" he told Poole. "For me the world's center was Cambridge."[16]

Happy Louis's days at Harvard may have been, perhaps even exhilarating, but they were not without their hardships and anxieties. Money was tight. His father's finances, already weakened by the effects of the postwar depression on his old firm's clients in the South, had been further depleted by the "panic" of 1873 and the family's longer than intended sojourn in Europe. Worse still, the cotton business that Adolph set up in Louisville on his return never prospered, and two years later failed completely, leaving him demoralized and with the collection of bad debts as his sole source of income. One inevitable consequence of these straitened circumstances was that Louis had to pay his way through the Law School without any prospect of financial support from his parents. Indeed, had it not been for the few hundred dollars loaned him by his brother, he might never have gotten to Cambridge at all.

Once he did arrive, there was a first-year tuition fee of $150 to find, with the result that, during the 1875–96 session at any rate, he had little choice but to restrict his wants and live frugally. At the year's end he applied for and was granted a scholarship, but was persuaded by Bradley to try his hand at tutoring instead. Beginning with the professor's own son, he soon found himself with enough young pupils to cover his living expenses in Cambridge, pay his fees, and even provide him with a small financial surplus. These tutorial activities continued during his graduate year as well, though perhaps on a reduced scale; for by then his resources were being further augmented by a proctorship in Harvard College, which paid fees for invigilating at university examinations. By the end of 1878 Louis had been able to pay back Alfred's loans, and to accrue a capital of between twelve and fifteen hundred dollars, which he invested in U.S. Treasury certificates and an Atchison Railroad bond.

Though not troubled thereafter by immediate financial worries, Brandeis would retain the habits of thrift he had acquired in Cambridge throughout his life so as never again to feel the pressures generated by want of money. As Alfred Lief has observed, by contriving to live so far within his means, he succeeded in establishing for himself "a measure of financial independence, relieving him of having to do objectionable things for money needed to sustain a more expensive scale of living. This apparent strain of austerity owed less to the Puritan atmosphere than to close reasoning. Sacrifice and self-denial were not involved; it was choice." Expenditures were prioritized, and those things that were considered of least value, like cigarettes and later alcohol, he ultimately chose to live without. Time was rationed too: He stopped playing the violin because, being a far from gifted performer, he felt the hours taken up could be better employed doing other things at which he was more proficient. In short, the self-discipline first developed in Cambridge would grow rather than diminish in later life. Moreover, it would by no means be confined to the working environment of study and office, library and courtroom, but would extend naturally into the domestic sphere as well, influencing everything from diet and furnishing to leisure activities and personal relationships. The Harvard experience was, in a literal sense, quite fundamental.[17]

Another difficulty from Brandeis's student days that would have profound long-term consequences was the poor state of his health, and in particular the deteriorating condition of his eyesight. It has been claimed that he was physically frail even before his arrival at the Law School, and that the director of the newly opened Hemenway Gymnasium, where paradoxically he went to "keep fit," found his muscles on examination to be weaker than those of any other student he had yet seen. This is difficult to square with the image of a schoolboy who skated on frozen ponds, ran barefoot along the Louisville waterfront, and was good with his fists; or with the summer spent hiking in the Alps with his father and brother. It becomes readily understandable, though, if we picture instead an indigent law student, working too hard and eating too little, to the point where his constitution begins to suffer. But whatever the cause of his frailty, the regime of limited but regular exercise prescribed for him seems to have provided the cure; and in coming to terms with the fact that a healthy mind does indeed require a healthy body to sustain it, Brandeis learned a lesson from which he would profit throughout his life.[18]

Problems with his vision, however, represented something more serious: a potential barrier between him and a career in the law. He suffered eye strain from the long hours of reading by gaslight in his rooms and in the cramped library of Dane Hall; and during the summer of 1876, while working with his cousin in Louisville to gain experience of how a law office functioned, he found it increasingly difficult to focus his eyes properly. The Cincinnati oculist whom he consulted that August warned him against further reading and "prescribed total abstinence from the law" until his eyes recovered; however, a few weeks later he was back in Cambridge, though evidently far from cured. In Boston he saw another specialist, Dr. Haskett Derby, who, when his eyes failed to respond to the exercise treatment that had been recommended, advised him to abandon the law altogether. Adolph, now every bit as alarmed as his son, urged Louis to go and see Dr. Knapp, a highly regarded oculist in New York, who, on finding nothing organically wrong with his eyes, advised him "to read less and think more." For a law student coming up to his final examinations, this was easier said than done; however, with the help of fellow students who read to him, and the conscious improvement of an already remarkable memory, he not only succeeded in completing his second year, thereby gaining his LL.B, but did so, of course, in the truly exemplary manner already referred to.[19]

Nevertheless, his eyes evidently continued to disable him, and early in 1878 he wrote explaining his situation to a former classmate, Walter B. Douglas:

> My eyes have been troublesome ever since last spring. The oculists agree that they are perfectly healthy, that their present useless condition is merely a freak of the nearsighted eye which will pass over. I am able to use them hardly three or four hours with most careful use but my oculists promise me a brilliant future. Hence am not doing very much nor very satisfactory work this year.

He was, in fact, attending a wide range of lectures and relying heavily on what he called "the absorbing process"; but he also continued to depend on a number of "kind friends" who acted as readers for him. On Monday and Wednesday nights he studied "Sales" with William R. Richards; on Friday nights and Saturday afternoons it was "Equity" with Richards and William A. Keener; on Thursdays it was "Trusts" with Samuel D. Warren, Jr.; and on Tuesdays the "Real P[roperty] Club" met. By June he was reporting further progress to his brother: "Today I reached one hour in my reading & shall hence forth be allowed to write one half hour each day instead of so much reading. The last week has made me more confident than ever of the efficacy of the cure and I hope by September to have my eyes strong again." On Dr. Derby's advice, though, he had decided not to visit Louisville that summer lest "the heat may debilitate me & thus injuriously affect the eyes."

As he told Alfred portentously: "It is probable that I shall remain in New England. . . . Cambridge is beautiful now & I am becoming more & more attached to the place."[20]

During his years at Harvard, the law unequivocally dominated his life; but while legal study clearly absorbed the greater part of his time and energy, it did not prevent him from indulging in a variety of leisure activities. Although he felt able to spend comparatively little time reading for pleasure, even after his eyes began to trouble him he did so as often as he could. "I have managed to spend a little time every evening with English & German authors," he wrote his cousin in November 1876, "and have at least the consolation that in course of time: 'Many a little will make a pickle.'" He was also coming to admire increasingly the work of Ralph Waldo Emerson. "I have read a few sentences of his which are alone enough to make a man immortal." Even when he could no longer read for himself, as we have seen others were persuaded to read to him, and this, as he explained to Walter Douglas at the beginning of 1878, extended to works of European literature as well as to law books: "The whole of every Sunday morning is spent with my friend [Philippe] Marcou in reading (listening to—on my part) the German Classics—Goethe, Schiller, Lessing, Grillparzer."[21]

Thanks to the survival of the *Index Rerum*, which he bought in 1872 and kept up diligently during his years at Harvard, we know that Brandeis actually read a good deal more widely than this. "Reading, equivalent to drinking," he observed, "maketh a full man." Almost nothing was entered in the book until he returned from Europe in 1875, but thereafter quips, jokes, and a few biblical quotations were jotted down alongside evidence of more intensive study. The topics represented at greatest length in the *Index* were "Law" and "Boston," and one suspects that this accurately reflected the twin enthusiasms of its compiler's life. Nevertheless, in a separate volume, he also commented on, and copied out quotations from, the works of literature that he was sampling. These included fragments from English authors like Shakespeare, Swift, Horace Walpole, De Quincey, Milton, Swinburne, Tennyson, Stevenson, and Matthew Arnold but also from the Americans Lowell, Longfellow, and Emerson. He seems to have written down everything that struck him as particularly edifying or perceptive, thereby perhaps justifying to some extent Professor Mason's characterization of his reading habits as "utilitarian." Emerson, more than any other writer, encapsulated for him several key concepts that would one day be thought of as touchstones of the Brandeis philosophy. On self-reliance, for example, he noted: "It is easy in the world to live after the world's opinion; it is easy in solitude to live after our own; but the great man is he who in the midst of a crowd keeps with perfect sweetness the independence of solitude"; and on being willing to change one's mind: "A foolish consistency is the hobgoblin of little minds." To the philosophy implied by these and other quotations stored up in this little notebook we shall be be returning at intervals throughout the present study.[22]

Conviviality also had its attractions; and in the late summer of New England's intellectual renaissance, good company was as much the stuff of enlightenment as were good books. Though hardly a practiced socialite, Brandeis moved with increasing ease in the cultured circles of Boston's Brahmins, on one occasion finding himself at Denman Ross's discussing Ruskin's views on the decline and fall of Gothic architecture, and on another being invited to Professor Thayer's house to hear a lecture on education by Emerson himself. In June 1878, he could write to his brother about one reception to which he had lately been invited in Boston: "[There] I saw (literally) Longfellow & Holmes & just missed Curtis and Whittier. Celebrities are so numerous here one cannot take the trouble to look at all of them." He was also welcome in several private homes as a dinner guest, where he was happy to while away an evening devoted to nothing more mentally taxing than good food, pleasant conversation, amateur music, and frivolous parlor games. Yet such occasions were perhaps all the more appreciated because of their rarity. "[S]eeing only comparitively [sic] little of 'Society' I generally enjoy myself in it," he confided to his sister Amy; but then added with more than a hint of sarcasm: "Very much of society would surely bore me. I could discuss the merits of Mr. Porter's portraits or Mr. Hunt's landscapes fourteen times with considerable interest—but not oftener." At times, therefore, he was content to relax into a reflective plebeian anonymity. On the Fourth of July 1878, for example, after a day spent with friends in Cambridge, he decided to go alone into Boston for the evening. "There was an immense crowd on the Common to listen to music & gaze on the fire-works," he reported to Alfred, "& their enthusiasm for the display & pleasure in the show was truly Italian. The crowd was unusually orderly & the naturalness with which the[y] stretched themselves on the grass regardless of dirt & the kicks of passers & stumblers reminded me also of the descendants of the Romans."[23]

During these years as a student, Brandeis did his best to maintain close links with his home and family in Kentucky. Apart from a regular correspondence with relatives and friends, he also managed to spend his first two summer vacations in Louisville. In 1877 his annual visit chanced to coincide with the wave of labor unrest then sweeping through the nation, and as the mood of the city's striking railroad workers soured, Louis and his brother had no qualms about joining with other "respectable" citizens to defend both property and the status quo. When the windows of the family's house on Walnut and First Streets were put out by the mob, the Brandeis boys responded by attending public meetings and mustering with a group of armed vigilantes formed to patrol the streets and defend the engine sheds. Recalling this incident in an interview he gave a short while before his death, the retired liberal justice was concerned to play down the ideological significance of his actions, claiming sheepishly that he had probably been at greater risk from the gun he carried than any potential rioter or arsonist. But the fact remains that, in the early skirmishes of an embryonic class war, he had ostentatiously taken the side of capital and public order against the ragtag forces of labor and the perceived threat of social unrest. Far from representing a foolish youthful aberration, this clear-cut identification with a system of conservative middle-class values was patently in line with actions and attitudes manifested by older family members since being forced to quit Prague in the 1840s. Moreover, as we shall see, it would remain symptomatic of Louis's own inner reaction to the struggles of working people up to, and perhaps beyond, the violent industrial conflicts of the early 1890s. He would in the event be almost forty years old before beginning to reflect seriously on the axiomatic principles of social order with which he had been raised.[24]

Much as he undoubtedly appreciated the intellectual atmosphere and incomparable opportunities for learning that the Law School had afforded, according to Edward F. McClennen, one of his later law partners, Brandeis evidently regarded his formal training in Cambridge as merely the first steps in legal scholarship, and so remained "a constant and diligent student of law" into the mid-1890s when the increased burden of public causes at last forced some temporary curtailment of his search for further erudition. McClennen recalled, for instance, his habit of annotating the margins of his early law books, whenever later decisions afforded fresh lines of interpretation. The product of such labors was a comprehensive grasp of the law in all its facets: "In some branches of law and in knowledge of law as a whole he was unsurpassed." Though always an avid collector of facts, he developed early the knack of reaching through the mystifying fogs of detail to seize the essential core of issues that lay beyond. McClennen perceived that his inclination was "to see the principle on which a decision rested, and not merely the decision itself," and correctly reasoned that it was this habit of mind which "enabled him to carry over from one branch of the law, into another, the essence of a decision, which some might regard as insulated from such an escape." He cited the fiduciary obligations of a trustee or agent by way of example: To Brandeis such responsibilities were not merely a technical feature of the law of trusts or of agency, but rather a requirement to be imposed by law on all those in whom confidence was reposed, regardless of whether the terms "trustee" or "agent" were applied or not. "The reason for the rule," McClennen observed, "arrested his attention more than the rule itself."[25]

In the summer of 1878, however, scholarship had to yield precedence to the need to begin earning a living. After a brief but frustrating attempt to set himself up in St. Louis, Harvard's star graduate in law returned to Boston, and thus to the influence that professors and former classmates could wield on his behalf. Here, in the close-knit world of Brahmin society, word of his brilliant academic attainments, added to the personal links he had formed in Cambridge, served to smooth his path into private legal practice. Such advantages, McClennen suggested, "greatly diminished the need for connections of wealth, of commercial prominence and of social position, even in as definitely classified a city as the Boston of 1879." But that was only because these essential preconditions for success could be provided by somebody else.[26]

During the summer of that year, Brandeis went into partnership with his friend, fellow law student, and erstwhile reading partner, Sam Warren, who had graduated second in the class of '77, and whose family ran a successful paper-mill business in Massachusetts. "I wish to become known as a practicing lawyer," he told Warren; in discussing the terms of their proposed association before reaching a final decision, however, he made no secret of the part he expected his friend to play. As well as wanting him to examine "the prospects of a young law firm," he was more especially concerned with Warren's "own prospects of securing business" by means of his "social and financial position." The latter's father was not only a successful local manufacturer but also a greatly respected member of Boston's business community, whose recommendation, if it could be secured, was tantamount to a guarantee of the proposed partnership's survival. "Brandeis never tired," wrote McLennen, "of telling how [the elder Warren's] success had come so largely from a far-seeing, broad-minded commercial sagacity that sought to advance trade not by overreaching acuteness, but by liberal regard for the interests of his customers and in a reliance in times of stress on their proven honesty more than on their accumulated assets." Not only was he Brandeis's ideal of the "professional" businessman; he was also an indispensable source of future commercial patronage.[27]

His arrangement with Warren did not prevent Brandeis from actively exploring other avenues of professional advancement. Although an early idea for procuring the editorship of a legal periodical failed to materialize, within weeks of returning to Boston he had managed to secure a position as law clerk to Horace Gray, chief justice of the Supreme Judicial Court of Massachusetts, who in 1881 was to become an associate justice of the United States Supreme Court. As with the opportunities afforded to his own clerks after 1916, the association with Gray provided Brandeis with invaluable experience in the researching and writing of judicial opinions; it also offered an effortless entrée into the innermost social circles of the Boston bar. Back in Missouri, his brother-in-law, Charles Nagel, was quick to see the potential benefits:

> The situation with the Chief Justice seems to be the most desirable of all the chances offered you in Boston. It must be in every way instructive and fortifying. . . . No one can help seeing that such a connection means a chance at every desirable position offered in Boston and even at Cambridge. I presume you still prefer to enter upon active practice and with that in view, the above position is particularly important. You will probably be able to get on the right side of the Justice; although I can imagine that a man of his description might make a pleasant relation impossible for you.

In response, though still a trace unsure about the wisdom of his decision to quit the practice he had joined in St. Louis, Brandeis revealed an almost limitless confidence in his own abilities. "I find much comfort & consolation," he wrote Nagel, "in the feeling that whatever I have achieved, or may achieve here is my own—pure and simple—unassisted by the fortuitous circumstance of family influence or social position." Although this assertion was technically correct, in that it was indeed his own intellectual endeavors which had brought him to the favorable attention of men of power and influence, its implication of the possibilities for further independent advancement would have been profoundly misleading to a less sophisticated correspondent.

The arrogance and impatience for which Gray was apparently renowned on the bench were mercifully absent from his more intimate dealings, and Brandeis found himself in a situation whose pleasantness exceeded his "fondest hopes." The chief justice was, he told Nagel, "the most affable of men, patiently listening to suggestions and objections & even contradiction." The relationship he proceeded to describe bore many similarities to that reported in later years by Paul Freund and others among his own clerks; so much so that it is difficult to escape the conclusion that Brandeis consciously modeled his judicial demeanor, in this context at least, on Gray's.

> Our mode of working is this. He takes out the record & briefs in any case, we read them over, talk about the points raised, examine the authorities' arguments—then he makes up his mind if he can, marks out the line of argument for his opinion, writes it, & then dictates it to me.
>
> But I am treated in every respect as a person of co-ordinate position. He asks me what I think of his line of argument and I answer candidly. If I think other reasons better, I give them; if I think his language is obscure I tell him so; if I have any doubts I express them and he is very fair in acknowledging a correct suggestion or disabusing one of an erroneous idea.
>
> In these discussions & investigations I shall learn very much. Many beautiful points are raised and must be decided.

Brandeis was particularly appreciative of his chief's remarkable knowledge of the statutes and legal precedents of the commonwealth itself, and anticipated "much advantage in this respect"; soon he would be beholden to Gray for the even more material advantages that accrued when the latter took steps to facilitate his early admission to the Massachusetts bar.[28]

Whether or not his mentors at Harvard were instrumental in fixing up the position with Gray is uncertain, but they certainly approved wholeheartedly. Brandeis identified Bradley, Langdell, and Thayer, in particular, as regarding the job as a "very valuable . . . stepping stone" toward further advancement. His ties with members of the Law School faculty were close and would remain so for the next twenty years; moreover, it is clear that, in the beginning, both he and they had the possibility of an academic career for him at Harvard very much in mind. As early as March 1878, while Brandeis was still a graduate student undertaking a third year of course work, a young friend took notice how "the Profs. listen to his opinions with the greatest deference." Sixteen months later, Nagel observed how his brother-in-law appeared inclined to the idea that his "real talent" lay in teaching. "It may well be so," he conceded; "and if you turn to it, you seem to have the President [i.e., Eliot] and half the corporation for you now. . . . On the whole, your chances seem brilliant." Brandeis readily acknowledged his interest, and accepted that a choice between the academy and the courtroom would have to be made eventually:

> I have not made up my mind yet, because it is not necessary but, as far as I can analyze my feelings, I think it was the prospect of teaching that kept me here [sic]. I recognize that my being here would make it easier to get the place should I want it—& that it would be much easier, too, to test my capability & love for such a position—without risking all.

If a suitable opportunity were to offer itself, and if his eyes then appeared equal to the task, he thought himself on the whole predisposed to accept it.

> The law as a logical science has very great attractions for me. I see it now again by the almost ridiculous pleasure which the discovery or invention of a legal theory gives me; and I know that such a study of the law cannot be pursued by a successful practitioner nor by a Judge (I speak now from experience). Teaching would mean for me writing as well. However, this is all talk. I may feel differently in three months and the wrangling of the Bar may have the greatest attraction for me. It surely is not distasteful to me now. It is merely a question of selecting between two good things—They are both good enough for me. I question only which I am good for.[29]

Brandeis's dilemma was to remain unresolved for several years more. In 1882, however, he was invited by President Eliot to give the course on "Evidence—that neglected product of time and accident" normally taught by Thayer; and the following year he received the offer of an assistant professorship in Harvard's Faculty of Law. His family were delighted; but although they made no secret of their preference for a teaching career, they also left Louis in no doubt that the final choice must be his alone. After much soul-searching he decided to turn the offer down. He did not lose his fascination with legal scholarship, nor was this to be his last stint as a lecturer; but never again after 1883 would he seriously entertain an ambition to make his reputation as a professional academic.[30]

His ties with Harvard, though, were far from being severed by this decision. Even after more than a decade spent in private legal practice, the enthusiasm for law schools he had first evinced as a freshman had scarcely abated. "All lawyers concede that a short apprenticeship in the office of a practitioner is valuable," he wrote in 1889, "but a thorough knowledge of legal principles is essential to higher professional success, and this knowledge, which under all circumstances is difficult of acquisition, can rarely be attained except as the result of uninterrupted, systematic study, under competent guidance." Although pupilage in a law office might indeed have provided an adequate substitute at the turn of the century, "when the scope of the common law was narrow and the reported cases comparatively few," it now had to be recognized that the utility of such a training had been rendered increasingly ineffective by the growth of commercial enterprise in England and America, with its concomitant proliferation of legal principles and its explosion in the volume of litigation. Moreover, in the United States, the diversity of legal decisions reached by independent state judiciaries only served to further complicate the situation that the would-be lawyer faced. Specialization in both training and study were thus made essential.

Brandeis's interest in and support for legal education would continue undiminished throughout his life. Already deeply involved in fund-raising activities, and largely responsible for securing the donation that brought Oliver Wendell Holmes, Jr., temporarily to the Law School faculty in 1882, Brandeis continued to labor indefatigably on its behalf until his appointment to the Supreme Court in 1916. He was particularly influential in setting up the Harvard Law School Association, becoming its first secretary in 1886; a year later he could be found playing an equally prominent role in the establishment of the *Harvard Law Review*, which he went on to serve as both trustee and treasurer; and in 1890 he accepted an invitation from the Board of Overseers to join the committee of visitors responsible for monitoring the affairs of the school. In each instance his motive for participation was the same: He wanted to see the Harvard Law School expand both its range and reputation till it might at last take its place as the nation's leading center for legal education. With this object in view, he was never reticent about suggesting improvements in the curriculum, nor about criticizing the performance of the staff, if by doing so he thought that the quality of the students could be bettered. In particular, his determined focus on the need for a thorough grounding in state practice, though at odds with Langdell's own views on the subject, should be seen as a harbinger of future concerns, being but the first element in an evolving philosophy of localism that would eventually become the keystone of a wider social perspective.[31]

Nevertheless, for all its pedagogical novelty, the sort of legal education that Brandeis had himself received at Harvard in the 1870s, and in which he displayed such a keen interest thereafter, was predicated on the increasingly dubious assumption that common-law principles and procedures not only constituted, but would continue to constitute, the operational bedrock of America's legal culture. Such a view was in fact becoming more and more anachronistic in the professional world that Langdell's pupils entered after graduation. The tides of state legislation and administrative regulation, which had begun their almost imperceptible rise in the years immediately following the Civil War, were running strongly by the 1880s; and although social reformers and special interest groups of all kinds plainly welcomed the phenomenon of public responsibility being shouldered by statutory agencies, those trained in the mystique of the common law did not.[32]

It was this mounting disquiet about legislative encroachments on the proper preserves of the common law, combined perhaps with a genuine interest in the *Harvard Law Review* and a determination to make known his views on matters of public policy thought relevant to the firm's clients, that persuaded Brandeis to collaborate with Sam Warren in the writing of three articles that were published in the new journal between 1888 and 1890: the first two concerned with the use of water resources in Massachusetts, and the third dealing with the individual's right to privacy.

In "The Watuppa Pond Cases," as the authors explained, the central issue was a number of civil suits, decided or pending mainly in the courts of the commonwealth, concerning the riparian rights of property owners in manufacturing districts to an unrestricted flow of water in rivers and streams fed at some point along their course by large ponds. Most of the principal watercourses of New England fell into this category, and many of the smaller streams depended almost wholly on such ponds for their water supply. Although it had long been a settled principle of law that state legislatures could not authorize the taking of water from such a pond without at least compensating owners of water power on the outlet stream for damage resulting from the diminution of its flow, the position in Massachusetts and Maine was complicated by the status of "great pond" accorded to all sheets of water greater than ten acres in extent by the "Colony Ordinance and Ancient Charter of 1641–7." These great ponds were not to pass into private ownership, but were to be retained by the state and devoted to the use of the public at large.[33]

Already by the mid-nineteenth century, the courts had perceived that a growing conflict of interest existed between those who wished to use the pure water and favorable location of these ponds to supply the needs of nearby cities and towns, and those dependent on the ponds or their outflow streams for the very survival of their businesses. Chief Justice Shaw adumbrated the nature of the problem as early as 1852:

> What the rights are of adjacent or riparian owners of and bordering on such ponds, has, we believe, never been the subject of adjudication or discussion. Some rights, we suppose, have always been exercised by such proprietors, such as a reasonable use of the water, for domestic purposes, and for watering cattle. But in the advanced state of agriculture, manufactures, and commerce, and with the increased value of land and all its incidents, there will probably be hereafter increased importance to the question, whether and to what extent such riparian proprietors have a right to the use of the waters, for irrigating land, for steam-

engines, for manufactories which require a large consumption of water, and for
the supply of their own ice-houses, for delivery to neighbors, and for more distant
traffic.[34]

When, in 1871, the Massachusetts legislature allowed the city of Fall River
to draw on North Watuppa Pond to help meet its growing need for fresh
water, and when as a consequence the flow of water in the Quequechan River was substantially reduced, the Supreme Judicial Court awarded heavy
damages to the mill owners along the river bank. In 1886, the city authorities sought to increase the volume of water to be drawn from the pond and
hit on the idea of writing into the bill a provision to exempt them from
paying compensation to the mill owners. The bill passed into law over the
governor's veto and two years later came before the Supreme Judicial Court
for review. There, though the judges were all agreed that common-law rules
in general prevented the legislature from depriving injured parties of a right
to compensation, nevertheless the majority found that North Watuppa's designation as a great pond permitted the state of Massachusetts to grant to a
city the right of taking water from it, without compensating riparian owners
on the outlet stream, because such a grant constituted "a public use."[35]

Brandeis and Warren sided with the dissenting opinion of the minority,
who argued that the Colony Ordinance gave to the commonwealth the same
rights over great ponds that individual proprietors enjoyed over lesser
bodies of water, and nothing more: In short, the right to use them, and to
keep them available for public use, *as ponds*, that is, for gaming, sporting
and other recreational purposes.

> No authority could be found for the proposition that the proprietary interest of a
> State in a piece of land in which it owns the fee is not held subject to the same
> limitations as that of a private owner. . . . It would hardly be supposed that the
> State, any more than a private individual, could dig on its land to the injury of
> adjacent land, or maintain a nuisance thereon.

Therefore, any different or more extensive right held by the state over the
waters of a "great pond" would have to be grounded on its existing sovereign
powers; yet a search of the Colony Ordinance itself, and an examination of
the manner in which its provisions had been understood and applied hitherto, in terms of either legislative or judicial practice, revealed no evidence
of any such sovereign rights. After a detailed exploration of earlier decisions
by the courts of Massachusetts and Maine, the writers asserted their conviction that the Watuppa Pond cases had been decided in error; that all available precedents pointed to the conclusion "that the right of the public in
'great ponds' was to their use *quâ* ponds," and that consequently the legislature had a right to regulate their use but not a right to destroy them to the
detriment of others.

To lay down, under such circumstances, a doctrine which overturns what had previously been regarded as an established rule of property, thus affecting most seriously many valuable water privileges, seems like a near approach to *judicial legislation*, and that, too, of doubtful expediency. It is a wide departure from the spirit which has in the past led the Commonwealth of Massachusetts to foster its manufacturing industries by every means in its power, and the decision is to be regretted especially, because it comes at a time when all the restraints imposed by the Constitution and the courts are *needed to protect private property from the encroachments of the Legislature.*[36]

The partnership's second foray into the field of legal scholarship was really a sequel to its first, being devoted in large measure to the demolition of an article on "Great Ponds" that had appeared in the intervening issue of the same journal. The writer's principal contention, according to Warren and Brandeis, had been to show that "the right of riparian proprietors to the undiminished flow of a stream of water depends upon the law of water-courses, or of running water; that a watercourse must have a perceptible current; that when the water is still, or has no perceptible current" a separate body of law applies. More materially, he had gone on to assert that there existed no legal rule against the diversion of such "still water," even where it was integral to a waterway otherwise subject to such limitation. By a skillful and technically informed evaluation of the cases adduced, the authors proceeded to eviscerate every contention of their adversary until nothing remained of his supposed distinctions. It also gave them an opportunity to rehearse the underlying arguments of their earlier article. In particular, it enabled them to refine still further their objection to what they considered a clear abuse of judicial interpretation:

It may be that legislation enacted before our Constitution, even though originally an encroachment on private property, if long acquiesced in, because in accord with the spirit of our institutions, should now be upheld by the court as a rule of property . . . ; but it is quite another thing to extend by forced interpretation an ancient ordinance to a new application subversive of a well established and long undisputed rule of property, in order by indirection to avoid the plain prohibition of our present constitution, which forbids the taking of private property for public use without compensation to the owner.[37]

As we can now see, the principal purpose of these literary excursions was to stress the importance of preserving established rights, particularly when these were threatened by statutory encroachments on the part of the legislature. To Edward McClennen, when he looked back on this episode, Brandeis's subtlety of thought in these articles (and he appears to give Warren almost no credit for them whatsoever) seemed to reveal "the fine common law mind which, in declaring the law out of the void, has done it with regard to what was best for the community or the state to be ruled by. His

approach was free from that deference to forms and shells which have restricted vitality." However, it could be argued with equal plausibility that
Brandeis's exposition of the law of ponds amounted to little more than a
conservative exhortation to *stare in vias antiquas*, elevating the private property rights of factory owners above the paramount need of a wider public to
secure to its use a healthy and ample supply of fresh drinking water. In point
of fact, neither proposition is wholly valid. His primary concern in the
Watuppa Pond cases was not to restrict the state's right of eminent domain,
and even less to forestall its efforts to protect and promote the welfare of its
citizens, but rather to prevent it discharging its responsibilities toward one
set of individuals at the expense of another set, without due compensation.
In this respect, his argument anticipates precisely the opinion he was to de-
liver in the *Radford* case, almost half a century later, where at issue was the
federal government's right to ameliorate the effects of the bankruptcy laws
by abridging the rights of mortgage holders: "however great the Nation's
need, private property shall not be thus taken even for a wholly public use
without just compensation. If the public interest requires, and permits [ac-
tion] . . . , resort must be had to proceedings by eminent domain; so that,
through taxation, the burden of the relief afforded in the public interest may
be borne by the public."[38]

The allegation that the judges' behavior in the Watuppa Pond cases constituted "a near approach to judicial legislation" may at first sight appear
confusing, because the primacy of "judge-made" law over statute could be
read as the essential subtext of their entire argument. In fact, what they
clearly found so objectionable was not the determination of the Massachusetts courts to establish a coherent framework for future action but
rather their willingness to do so on political rather than judicial grounds.
That judges might respond to the same commercial and interest-group pressures as legislators was a new and worrying idea that Brandeis was not yet
ready to grapple with; but it was certainly one whose potential implications could not easily be squared with the conservative sociolegal philosophy that he currently espoused.

The third and last article to issue in the joint names of Warren and Brandeis was to be of more enduring significance; for it constituted both a substantive contribution to a hitherto neglected area of civil liberties and an
important source of evidence by which to identify and interpret Brandeis's
early attitudes toward the scope and potentialities of the common law.
Yet although it is somewhat better known to his biographers than the
Watuppa Pond pieces, "The Right to Privacy" has received scarcely more
attention from them as an intellectual product worthy of critical analysis.[39]

The article posits the existence of a common-law right to privacy, analogous to those recognized in the law of defamation or in the rules protecting literary and artistic property, but distinct therefrom. The authors were especially concerned by the activities of journalists and press photographers who, with new technologies at their disposal and a readership ever eager for tittle-tattle, were now regularly seen to be "overstepping in every direction the obvious bounds of propriety and of decency." Scandalmongering had become a busy trade, pursued with boldness and industry by its practitioners. "To satisfy a prurient taste the details of sexual relations are spread broadcast in the columns of the daily papers. To occupy the indolent, column upon column is filled with idle gossip, which can only be procured by intrusion upon the domestic circle." Moreover, such unwarranted violations were increasing at the very moment when a quickening in the tempo of social interaction made the ability to opt for personal seclusion ever more valuable. "The intensity and complexity of life, attendant upon advancing civilization, have rendered necessary some retreat from the world, and man, under the refining influence of culture, has become more sensitive to publicity, so that solitude and privacy have become more essential to the individual." Not only were the the victims and their families subjected to unjustifiable mental anguish by the exposure of their private lives to common gaze, but the sensibilities of the public at large would soon become dulled and inured to the sufferings that their voyeurism caused. The result could only be a lowering in the standards of public morality.

Even gossip apparently harmless, when widely and persistently circulated, is potent for evil. It both belittles and perverts. It belittles by inverting the relative importance of things, thus dwarfing the thoughts and aspirations of a people. When personal gossip attains the dignity of print, and crowds the space available for matters of real interest to the community, what wonder that the ignorant and thoughtless mistake its relative importance. Easy of comprehension, appealing to that weak side of human nature which is never wholly cast down by the misfortunes and frailties of our neighbors, no one can be surprised that it usurps the place of interest in brains capable of other things. Triviality destroys at once robustness of thought and delicacy of feeling. No enthusiasm can flourish, no generous impulse can survive under its blighting influence.[40]

The problem was to discover whether an appropriate legal remedy for this social malaise already existed. Thus in large part the article was devoted to an exploration of those cases, mostly from the English courts, from which a theoretical basis might be derived for the right that Brandeis and his partner were seeking to affirm: what Judge Cooley had called, in everyday language, "the right to be let alone." They were confident that the common law, as it had been developed in England and America, retained the flexibility required for their purpose. "Political, social, and economic changes entail the recognition of new rights," they maintained, "and the common law in its vitality, in its eternal youth, grows to meet the demands of society." In this way, legal rules originally designed to protect life and property from forcible interference were at a later date extended, so that the right to life became the right to enjoy life, and the term "property" was deemed to include the abstract as well as the concrete. Judicial shields against physical harm, adequate enough in a rougher age, were thus refined to effect also some "recognition of man's spiritual nature, of his feelings and his intellect." A whole series of more specific rights were identified and made enforceable at law: the right to protect oneself against nuisances of all kinds; the right to defend one's reputation against defamation by libel or slander; the right to defend as property the products and processes of one's mind.

> This development of the law was inevitable. The intense intellectual and emotional life, and the heightening of sensations which came with the advance of civilization, made it clear to men that only a part of the pain, pleasure and profit of life lay in physical things. Thoughts, emotions, and sensations demanded legal recognition, and the beautiful capacity for growth which characterizes the common law enabled the judges to afford the requisite protection, *without the interposition of the legislature.*

The recognition of a correlative right to privacy ought to be viewed, therefore, as merely the latest extension of a long-established civilizing process, begun centuries earlier and theoretically limitless in its potential for modification.[41]

In seeking to identify a principle that might be invoked to supply the protection they envisaged, the authors canvassed a range of possibilities. While bearing a superficial resemblance to invasions of privacy, the wrongs dealt with by the law of defamation were found to injure the individual in his relations with others, with no account being taken of damage to peace of mind or self-esteem. The consequences were in effect "material rather than spiritual," or, as we might say, psychological. "That branch of the law simply extends the protection surrounding physical property to certain of the conditions necessary or helpful to worldly prosperity," they explained. It made no general provision for compensating plaintiffs merely for injury to their feelings, though there were several exceptions to this rule. Indeed, the distinction between those cases in which injured feelings did constitute a cause of action (or were taken into account for the assessment of damages), and those where they did not, owed more to practicality than to logic. As the authors averred, "The decisions on this subject illustrate well the subjection in our law of logic to common-sense."[42]

A more fruitful analogy was the common-law right that secured "to each individual the right of determining, ordinarily, to what extent his thoughts, sentiments, and emotions shall be communicated to others," more commonly termed the "right to intellectual and artistic property." Although frequently held to arise directly from the right to protect more tangible forms of property, a careful examination of the relevant cases suggested to Brandeis and his co-author that its foundation in fact rested on a somewhat less definite principle, vaguer yet capable of a more general application. It was to begin with entirely separate from the statutes defining copyright, the purpose of which was to secure to the author, artist, or composer the full profits resulting from publication or performance of his work; the common-law right was to determine whether and under what conditions publication or performance should occur at all. It also gave a man the right to prevent another publishing, summarizing, cataloging, or even describing not only products of literary or artistic merit, but indeed any note, thought, daub, or ditty he chose to set down for his own private amusement or edification. Warren and Brandeis were struck by the fact that the judges' reasoning in the relevant cases often betrayed a concept of privacy wider than the notion of property on which the more straightforward decisions quite easily rested. Publishing the fact that a man had "written to particular persons or on particular subjects," for instance, was deemed by the English Court of Chancery a potententially injurious act, involving "a disclosure as to private matters" that might legitimately be made the subject of an injunction. Seizing on this and similar examples, the authors were quick to point out the implication of their discovery; for once privacy was "recognized as a right entitled to legal protection," the ability of the courts to act would no longer be dependent on the nature of the injuries sustained as a consequence of its violation. This in turn led to a broader conclusion: "that the protection afforded to thoughts, sentiments, and emotions, expressed through the medium of writing or of the arts, so far as it consists in preventing publication," was an instance not of the enforcement of a right of property but rather an invocation of "the more general right of the individual to be let alone," which derived its force instead from the principle of "inviolate personality." Such a right, if it existed, was clearly not restricted to literary or artistic works alone. If their inference was correct, and if there were indeed precedents for assuming "a general right to privacy for thoughts, emotions, and sensations," then it followed that these should be as inviolable when expressed "in conduct, in conversation, in attitudes, or in facial expression" as when they occurred in writing, painting, or music. At last they had reached a principle that might protect the citizen from surreptitious photography or exposure in the gossip columns, as readily as it already protected his private correspondence from publication.[43]

Well aware that they might come under fire for promoting a significant extension of judge-made law, Brandeis and his partner were initially at pains to underscore the immanence of their doctrine in previous decisions of the courts. The law would have "no new principle to formulate," they insisted, if it were to extend the existing protection of personal writings and the like to cover such things as "personal appearance, sayings, acts, and . . . personal relation, domestic or otherwise." The right to privacy that they were affirming applied with equal validity to both classes of things. "The application of an existing principle to a new state of facts is not judicial legislation," they explained in a footnote.

To call it such is to assert that the existing body of law consists practically of the statutes and decided cases, and to deny that the principles (of which these cases are ordinarily said to be evidence) exist at all. It is not the application of an existing principle to new cases, but the introduction of a new principle, which is properly termed judicial legislation. . . .

The cases referred to above show that the common law has for a century and a half protected privacy in certain cases, and to grant the further protection now suggested would be merely another application of an existing rule.

Thus far their argument was an orthodox restatement of what Langdell and his Harvard colleagues had taught them at the Law School, and anticipated the line that Brandeis would faithfully pursue three years later in his lectures at the Massachusetts Institute of Technology (M.I.T.). What came next, however, represented an extraordinary departure from this customary approach; for the footnote continued:

But even the fact that a certain decision would involve judicial legislation should not be taken as conclusive against the propriety of making it. This power has been constantly exercised by our judges, when applying to a new subject principles of private justice, moral fitness, and public convenience. Indeed, the elasticity of our law, its adaptability to new conditions, the capacity for growth, which has enabled it to meet the wants of an ever changing society and to apply immediate relief for every recognized wrong, have been its greatest boast.

And so their point should not be misunderstood, there followed a pointed quotation from a well-known treatise on jurisprudence:

"I cannot understand how any person who has considered the subject can suppose that society could possibly have gone on if judges had not legislated, or that there is any danger whatever in allowing them that power which they have in fact exercised, to make up for the negligence or the incapacity of the avowed legislator. That part of the law of every country which was made by judges has been far better made than that part which consists of statutes enacted by the legislature."

Evidently Brandeis was still some way from formulating his mature opinion that the cardinal virtue for any judge was self-restraint![44]

The origin and significance of this article have been widely commented on. It is generally asserted that the ideas for it were developed in the context of disclosures about Warren's social life in the pages of Boston's *Saturday Evening Gazette*. In fact, there is virtually no evidence to support this contention. Recalling the circumstances of the project's inception some fifteen years later, Brandeis agreed that the initial suggestion had come from Warren, whose "deepseated abhorrence of the invasions of social privacy" had led them to take up the inquiry; however, this was not the same thing as saying that Warren's own privacy had been violated. Whatever the truth of such assertions, most biographers have clearly paid a good deal more attention to disentangling the background to the article than they have to analyzing the novel legal arguments that it deployed. Such unwarranted emphasis on trivial points of personal detail has tended to obscure the wider intellectual relevance of the issue, and in any event to mistake the occasion for the cause of the enterprise, thereby incidentally providing support for the authors' belief that a fascination with gossip inverts "the relative importance of things."

Brandeis and his partner were in reality motivated by a concern less mean than mere revenge and less parochial than personal interest. They were aware of, if not indeed influenced by, E. L. Godkin's essay, "The Rights of the Citizen: To His Own Reputation," which had explored a similar topic in *Scribner's Magazine* some months before. Moreover, their own article cited details of a recent case before the New York Supreme Court, in which a Broadway actress had brought suit to prevent unauthorized use of photographs showing her in tights, taken without her knowledge or permission. It was these incidents, rather than the supposed harassment of Warren, which defined the scope and texture of their investigations. The latter's personal experiences, or those of friends or family, might conceivably have raised their consciousness on this issue, but it did not limit or seriously impinge on the substance of their reasoning about it.[45]

Regarding the article's importance as a contribution to legal philosophy, a piece by Elbridge B. Adams in the *American Law Review* for 1905 described it as a paper "which in originality of conception, in facility of reasoning, and in the results to which it has led, is one of the most brilliant excursions in the field of theoretical jurisprudence which the recent literature of the law discloses." Seven years later, a note in the *Columbia Law Review* accorded it "the unique distinction of having initiated and theoretically outlined a new field of jurisprudence," and suggested that using the analogy of literary property rather than that of defamation was a particularly ingenious strategy. By 1916, Roscoe Pound, then dean of Harvard Law School, could declare that it had done "nothing less than add a new chapter" to the law. Although the courts were at first reluctant to acknowledge the validity of its central claim, the doctrine of a right to privacy had "steadily made its way," until at last it enjoyed, according to Pound, a "growing preponderance in its favor."

As the years passed, the authors too watched the progress of their brainchild with interest. Brandeis, who on reading the proofs of the article in 1890 had expressed disappointment at not finding it as good as he remembered it to be, was nevertheless pleased on reading Adams's piece in 1905 to discover that it remained "a vital force"; a week later he was even more delighted when, after finding for the plaintiff in a suit alleging invasion of privacy, the presiding justice of the Georgia Supreme Court wrote informing him of the decision and expressing his opinion that recognition of a legal right to privacy "would before long become the established doctrine of our law." What emerged, however, was a severely qualified right, the limitations of which were still occupying Brandeis in 1928, when he wrote his celebrated dissent in the *Olmstead* case opposing the legality of wiretaps. Evidently, the appeal of the subject remained enduring; and when *The Curse of Bigness* was being compiled in 1934, a reprint of "The Right to Privacy" was included at Brandeis's own suggestion, as being "of more interest to the general public and the profession" than almost any other item among his early writings.[46]

By the time of their collaboratlon on these three articles, the legal partnership between their authors was effectively at an end; Warren had ceased to play an active part in it after the death of his father in 1888, a circumstance that caused him to devote all his future efforts to the family business. The firm of Warren & Brandeis, however, continued to prosper as it had done through the 1880s, and Brandeis's own reputation as a lawyer grew steadily during the 1890s, not only among the businessmen and intellectuals of Boston, but likewise in other cities and states, especially among those who had known him at Harvard or who kept in close touch with the affairs of the Law School. As yet, however, he remained primarily concerned with the task of establishing his fledgling business as a paying concern, displaying little inclination to champion social causes of any kind, unless lecturing on the duties of citizenship can be deemed promotion of a "social cause." Even here, his views were conventional: Taxation was a necessary evil, but prudent control over the public purse was essential as a countervailing virtue; suffrage was a privilege that imposed civic duties inappropriate to the female sex. As McClennen subsequently recalled, "The interest in public affairs and in the general betterment of the community about him, which became so intense in later years, had nothing in it abnormal in the eighties. He was in the common sense of it just a practicing lawyer of the first water and an unusually attractive and cultured gentleman."[47]

That is not to say he remained unconcerned by political affairs, however. The bitter partisan divisions of his native city, and his family's courageous support there for the Republican cause, ensured that even after he settled in Boston his first allegiance would be to the G.O.P. "Am feeling considerable interest in politics and hope Garfield will be elected," he wrote his brother during the election campaign of 1880. "Can't quite reconcile myself with the idea of a Democratic rule yet." But four years later, when the Republicans chose to nominate the much despised James G. Blaine as their presidential candidate, Brandeis swallowed his remaining scruples and joined with other Boston "Mugwumps" including President Eliot and the Warrens, to vote for Grover Cleveland.

In the same year he gained election to the executive committee of the Civil Service Reform Association in the Fifth Congressional District, and in

1887 became a member also of the Boston American Citizenship Committee. Yet these were the respectable group affiliations of a "genteel" reformer rather than the radical driving-engines of a firebrand, and the connections they afforded would prove more of a help than a hindrance to his legal practice. When in 1890 he received "a very urgent invitation" from the Democratic State Central Committee to accept nomination as a candidate for the state legislature, he declined the offer. "It could be very interesting," he told his fiancée, Alice Goldmark, "but of course I cannot do it. It is one of the many things one must postpone or leave wholly undone." As always when political offers presented themselves, he was determined to put his career in the law first.[48]

The demanding professional schedule that enforced his distance from politics during the 1880s left little room either for family life. Following his return to New England in 1878, his visits to Louisville were both few and fleeting, though he kept in close touch with affairs "at home" by means of regular letters to and from his brother. His mother's letters record the brief visits that Louis made to Kentucky in 1881, 1883, and 1884, but the longest time they spent together in the five years during which she was writing her *Reminiscences* was six weeks in Newport, Rhode Island, during the summer of 1886. Separated thus from the son she adored, Frederika was consequently more sensitive to small changes in his personality whenever they did meet. Returning from a four-week vacation in Mattapoisett in the summer of 1882, during which Louis had traveled down from Boston at weekends to be with his family, she reflected on the earnest frame of mind in which she had found him. "Perhaps you were in a more serious mood than I realized," she wrote. "I had always been sorry that the seriousness of life had been impressed on you at too early an age, and that your tender childlike disposition had been too deeply affected. But I hoped that your youth and your successes would obliterate or at least allow these impressions to fade." Two years later she again commented on his quiet and serious temper, but observed also, she thought, a greater contentment: "Your eyes sparkle, your expressive face reveals the nobility of your soul, a child-like smile often plays around your lips."[49]

An equally interesting perspective on these occasional get-togethers (and incidentally a further sidelight on Brandeis's own attitude toward race) is provided by the recollections of the family's black servant Lizzie. She too was at Mattapoisett in 1882, accompanying Fanny Brandeis Nagel and her baby who were there for the summer. It was her first experience of the seashore, and though given a bathing costume by Fanny she was afraid to venture into the ocean. This went on for three weeks until Louis came down to spend Sunday with them, and the whole family went in bathing. "I walked down on the beach," she recalled,

and there was Mr. Louis lying flat on his back on the sand. I said, "Why ain't you in bathing, Honey?" An' he said, "I'm waiting for you, Lizzie." "Go on," I said. "I ain't goin' in. I'm afraid o' the salt water." "That's all right," he said. "I won't let it hurt you. An' I ain't goin' in one step until you come along."

So, rather than have him lose the nice swim he enjoyed so much, I jes' had to go and put on that bathing suit, and he led me in just like I was a fine lady.

After that, she could not get into the water often enough, so enjoyable did she find the experience. More than anything else, it was this simple human gesture that stood out in her mind when she looked back. Even after Brandeis went onto the Court in 1916, she would continue to think of him as "the sweetes' and thoughtfules' boy in this world."[50]

Much as he apparently enjoyed summer vacations by the sea, he was still young enough to relish the prospect of backpacking expeditions in wilder terrain, which served perhaps to remind him of the Alpine jaunts of 1873. The summer of 1885, for instance, was spent trekking through the Canadian wilderness with a few like like-minded friends, "fleeing from overcivilized Boston for the forest primeval," as his mother put it, but equipped with "sufficient comforts to make the experiment not too trying." Yet whether on the beach or in the mountains, whether canoeing, sailing, hiking, or horseback riding, these leisure breaks constituted a carefully planned and increasingly self-disciplined program for physical and spiritual renewal. Work had to be measured by intensity as well as duration, and only a fresh mind, he believed, was capable of rising to meet the unforeseen challenge. There had to be time for "that unconscious thinking which comes to the busy man in his play." Thus he never suffered the slightest pangs of guilt about taking time out when he felt it was needed. Indeed, far from hindering completion of the multiple tasks he set himself, the timely resort to recreation alone rendered it practicable. "I soon learned that I could do twelve months' work in eleven months," he recalled in old age, "but not in twelve."[51]

The nature of his practice was from the beginning geared more to consultancy than to trial work, and Brandeis's appearances in court were usually to litigate on behalf of long-term clients. Any wider regard he enjoyed as an advocate at this date resulted not from the novelty of his courtroom methods, so much as from the esteem naturally accorded to painstaking groundwork and reliable performance. Fellow lawyers who saw him in court "recognized quickly the masterly way in which he conducted a trial and his thorough understanding of his case, gained as only it could be by a combination of careful, and often laborious, preparation and a very unusual capacity to acquire and to remember information and to regulate its use to the best advantage." Yet although his forensic skills were remarkable for their superb workmanship rather than for their spectacle, ample evidence survives to show that Brandeis positively relished the adversarial challenges of the courtroom. Any initial reservations about whether he would enjoy "the wrangling of the Bar" were quickly dispelled, and during the 1880s the letters written to Alfred Brandeis in particular contain several excited references to the legal battles in which he was currently engaged. In March 1887, with no serious trial work in the offing, he readily admitted his hankering for a really drawn-out tussle:

> Except a few cases before the Supreme [Judicial] Court [of Massachusetts] this month I have tried few causes within the last weeks, and I really long for the excitement of the contest—that is a good prolonged one covering days or weeks. There is a certain joy in the draining exhaustion and backache of a long trial, which shorter skirmishes cannot afford.[52]

Such expressions of satisfaction notwithstanding, his personal appearances in court grew steadily more infrequent during the decade that followed, as consultancy work increased in volume and more and more time was spent in the service of public causes. Often his presence in court, when it did occur, was designed to calm the nerves of an anxious client who believed that the success or failure of his suit might depend on it. More typically by the early 1890s, he displayed a willingness to place a greater reliance on the other members of his firm, in the promotion of whose careers he took a keen and active interest. Brandeis had by now become, moreover, a confirmed believer in the advantages of professional specialization and was loth to dabble personally in areas where other members of his team were better versed. "As to that class of things which the individual makes his own, he must in the office in time become the principal," he told William H. Dunbar in 1896; "for those dealing with the office learn that he is considered the authority there on those things and shortly follow suit." Aside from the areas in which he was regarded as the expert, there would always necessarily remain much for each individual, Brandeis himself included, "as to which he is the associate, the Junior or Senior of the others in the organization and every man must stand ready to give every other man full aid. Every man also must hold himself to a stricter performance of his task—on account of his relations to the others." The success of the great New York law firms, he felt, proved his point "that such organizations are the most effective means of doing the law work of this country—so far as clients are concerned." The financial rewards of an increasingly lucrative practice were always scrupulously shared with those who did the work, and Brandeis did his best not to steal the professional credit and public recognition properly due to his younger associates. Yet even so, the more experienced among them must have found his often paternalistic advice grating on their self-esteem; and none could help noticing that within the business community of Boston, from whom the greater part of their clients were drawn, they long continued to be known simply as Brandeis's firm.[53]

The clientele, always a diverse assemblage, as Edward McClennen observed, tended to broaden rather than narrow as the years went by: "He acted for manufacturers, for merchants, for investors, for brokers, for associations of these different ones, for labor unions, for the injured, for the successful, for the unsuccessful, and for benevolent institutions." Only the fields of patent, admiralty, and criminal law were largely unrepresented, and even here his talents would occasionally be exercised. His own particular areas of expertise, though, were well known to clients and partners alike, and ranged from the laws governing commercial relations and fiduciary obligation, through the intricacies of public-utility rate making, to the reciprocal legal rights and responsibilities of employers and employees. With Sam Warren he all but invented the law of the right of privacy, and in every area of his practical knowledge he was always acutely aware of questions of appropriate jurisdiction and the significance of constitutional limitations to action.[54]

During the early years, it was not surprisingly those aspects of the legal process most likely to affect his business clients that occupied the greatest share of his attention. Though not in the usual sense of the term a "corporation lawyer," he did undertake his share of work for large corporate clients. "I even worked for a trust or two," he told Ernest Poole in 1911. "Perhaps that is one reason why I am not a corporation lawyer now." In the sphere of commercial law, with its emphases on property rights and contractual obligations, common-law questions were the regular stuff of legal controversy. Brandeis was also aware that local customs and the prior determinations of state courts would frequently decide the outcome of litigation. Thus during the late eighties and early nineties, he was particularly concerned in his dealings with Harvard Law School to promote the study of Massachusetts law as part of the curriculum there, with the stated intention of developing in its graduates a familiarity with state practice and procedure equivalent to that already evident in students graduating from the Law School of Boston University. "The course should not be confined to the peculiarities of Massachusetts law of pleading, practice and evidence," he told Dean Langdell, "but should extend generally to the main branches of substantive law." It should include "those variations from the general law which have been made by statute, and those which have been the result of peculiar local practice or decision"; in short it should constitute "a Massachusetts supplement to the general instruction at the School." The need for such a supplement had been brought home to him, both as an examiner for admission to the Suffolk County bar, and in the course of his own legal career in the state. "So far as my experience goes," he insisted to Langdell, "I find that throughout my ten years' practice I have been confronted with unfamiliarity with Massachusetts law generally, and I find my own experience painfully confirmed by my observation of others."[55]

McClennen was in no doubt about the nature of Brandeis's appeal to his clients. "They sought his advice as a lawyer," he observed, "but as a lawyer with an unusual grasp of common affairs." This characteristic had doubtless matured considerably by the 1890s, but the seeds of it were there from the beginning. He had been brought up to take a broad view of the human condition, forever testing and confirming by observation the truth of the humanistic values for which his parents stood. It was this expansive attitude of mind, combined with a passion for truth and a deeply ingrained sense of duty, which, even more than the raw power of his intellect, marked him out from his contemporaries at the bar. Furthermore, there were added to these general characteristics his particular abilities as a legal practitioner:

> a composite of a righteous disposition, great perceptive and reflective qualities, necessity to work, susceptibility to good influences, a broadening schooling in fundamental law, an acquisitive and retentive mind, a charming personality, and a rare capacity to select and to use forcefully the men available and the instruments at his command.

For McClennen, though, the unifying factor was what he termed Brandeis's "creative imagination," a depth of insight "which mapped out the way for his great industry and his intelligent grasp to follow," and which placed him "in the front rank of greatest lawyers."[56]

Perhaps the clearest insight into Brandeis's notion of the legal process during his early years as a lawyer is to be found in the text of the lectures he wrote for a course on business law at the Massachusetts Institute of Technology. The precise dating of this text is as important as it is difficult. The typescript preserved among Brandeis's papers at the University of Louisville was compiled in 1907 by his secretary, Alice H. Grady, and is headed "M.I.T. Course on Business Law, 1892–4." However, the contents show little evidence of the seismic changes in outlook and perception that Brandeis would later ascribe to the violent events at Homestead in 1892, and which are plainly displayed in the course outline and case notes privately printed for his students in the 1895–96 session. Therefore, the suspicion must remain either that the Louisville text represents the lectures as they were written before 1892 but never delivered, or that the lessons of Homestead took longer to suffuse his thinking than he later recalled. For reasons that will be become clear in the following chapter, there can be little doubt that the latter explanation is indeed the correct one.[57]

In this series of lectures, Brandeis endeavored to set out his views on a multiplicity of issues in more or less systematic form, and devoted considerable attention to examples drawn from the Massachusetts courts. The subjects covered range from the legal status of partnerships, corporations, and trusts to the permissible limits of economic regulation by government; from the rights and responsibilities of organized labor engaged in strikes or boycotts to the economic imperative of suppressing monopoly and upholding competition. He gave thoughtful consideration to more technical matters as well, such as the rights of defendants in judicial proceedings and the enforceability of contracts; permitted himself a modicum of theoretical discussion on the nature and origins of the common law, the breadth and importance of written law, and the historical development of equity pleading; and he even committed to paper a few fragmentary thoughts on the constitutional basis of judicial review and the undesirability of government by referendum. As will be seen later, these lectures illustrate with unrivaled clarity not only the scope but also the socially conservative character of Brandeis's early thoughts about the law; at the same time, however, they also demonstrate his elemental perception of it as a positive framework for legitimized social action.[58]

In his view, the justification for including legal studies in the general education of the institute was twofold: first that "an understanding of the general principles of law, and of its administration [was] an essential part of a liberal education"; and second that "such knowledge [would be] of great practical value to men engaged in active life," because it would enable them to solve, or better still avoid altogether, difficulties likely to arise in the conduct of their business affairs. Its importance ln the general educational context, however, was even more fundamental. As he told his students, "the conduct of life is to so large an extent determined by the existing legal institutions, that an understanding of the legal system must give you a clearer view of human affairs in their manifold relations, and must aid you in comprehending the conditions, and institutions by which you are surrounded." It was not his intention in these lectures to deal per se with the theoretical principles that underlay the legal system, much less to provide his business-oriented students with a thorough working knowledge of the law, for such considerations were properly the province of jurists and lawyers, respectively. Rather he sought to offer them a conceptual understanding of how the common law worked in practice and how it might affect their commercial dealings; to show them that, though legal systems developed from the English tradition were particular in their application to a given place and time, they were also organic in nature, representing the accumulated wisdom of countless generations of judges and legislators, each responding to the problems of their own day within a framework of past rulings and decrees. He wanted to demonstrate moreover how this gradual process of accretion still continued down to the present; how, in order to remain alive and relevant, the law must always develop and grow in relation to the complex substantive issues of an ever-changing world. Despite differences between the legal systems of different countries and states, there existed among those in the common-law tradition a "general basis" underlying the surface features, and this fact justified the illustration of general contentions by reference to the experience and practice of a single state (i.e., Massachusetts), because "a comprehension of the legal system of any one of these states would doubtless answer fully" the general purposes for which the course was undertaken.[59]

With these considerations in mind, Brandeis sought to reach a definition of the common law that might adequately indicate something of its richness and scope. Only a small part of the law, as he was at pains to point out, took the form of explicit prohibitions or commands, in the sense of legislative acts or constitutional provisions. The great bulk of legal precepts could more accurately be described as "rules of human action, rules of human justice sanctioned by authority." They had been developed by courts and judges over the centuries and provided a system of elementary justice as basic to the American as it had long been to the English way of life. These rules of conduct could be likened to the so-called "laws" of the physical sciences, or with greater accuracy to the "laws" of political economy, ethics or good health. They differed from such rules or laws only in one main particular, Brandeis explained, namely that:

> An authoritative method of determining them has been devised, and a definite penalty has been affixed for a breach of them; if as to the laws of political economy there is a doubt, if the statesmen or professors disagree, there is no appropriate tribunal to decide the matter; if the laws of political economy are transgressed what the penalty would be is undetermined. If the rules of law are in doubt, a means exists for authoritatively deciding these questions in the courts, and the coercive power of the state is applied to secure obedience to this law.[60]

But where had these rules come from, and how had they been arrived at? In marked contrast to the views expressed by himself and Warren in their recent articles, and indeed to the opinions he would subsequently profess during his years on the Supreme Court, the answers offered to his students in 1892 were uncontroversial, even glib. For Brandeis now stuck resolutely to the premise "that the law was there to be found, not that the judges made the law," which was something he now insisted they had no power to do. Each case decided, each precedent, was "but evidence of the rule of law"; it was not the law itself. Such precedents were like dots or points on a plane: "A line is drawn connecting them all and when drawn becomes the principle. These dots become so numerous that every conceivable case may be covered by precedents, and even if the dots are not numerous, the curve may be understood, the principle may be asserted with positiveness." At first there was no record of the judges' decisions, and even when records did start to be kept they generally consisted of little more than a statement of the facts proved and the judgments entered. The appearance of the first proper law reporters led not only to the publication and wider availability of legal decisions, but in time also to the incorporation within their reports of the arguments presented to the court, and the process of reasoning by which the judge had reached his decision. Eventually, with the development of appellate proceedings, "these questions of law were discussed more fully, and generally it was only the decisions of cases in the appellate courts that were so recorded and published, and became authority." Thus there developed a vast body of recorded decisions "covering the innumerable complications which arise in human affairs," the dots on the plane, from which the law might be known. Again, though, Brandeis stressed the precise status of the precedents:

> No decision was itself the law; it was the evidence of what the law was. But the principles in the course of time became settled. Every possible variation of questions arising in a particular connection would become exhausted, and the rule would become generally adopted, covering all such cases; it would become, as it is called, a settled principle of law. And thus the law, so far as evidenced by these decisions, is of constant growth. *New principles are being developed as controversies arise upon new facts.* The collection of principles evidenced by these numerous decisions contained in the reports of the different courts is called the Unwritten or the Common Law, and it is this which gave rise to Tennyson's description of "the lawless science of our law, that codeless meriad [*sic*] of precedent, that wilderness of single instances."

Just how these "new principles" were being developed, and by whom, he left infuriatingly vague; but no perceptive student could have failed to realize that, with the application of this formula, the alleged dividing line between "judge-made" and "judge-found" law was in grave danger of becoming an extremely fine, if not indeed a wholly spurious one.[61]

Brandeis also gave his class a brief summary of how the principles of equity had come to be developed. The common-law courts had not always been renowned for their flexibility, he explained; judges in medieval England often applied their principles narrowly, deference to custom and precedent inducing them to deny relief in new cases where there were no precedents on which to rely. By such manifestations of rigid legalism, the dictates of morality and natural justice were not infrequently frustrated. "While the common law as thus administered did grow to a certain extent with the growth of the community," aided in particular cases by the enactment of appropriate statutes, in general "it failed to meet all the exigencies of the times." Increasingly, cases arose where the law was itself defective, and the resulting injustices became so flagrant that eventually appeals were made to the Crown for redress. As a consequence, there grew up a separate system of so-called equity courts, presided over by the Lord Chancellor and his officials in Chancery, and in time these too came to rely on a corpus of precedents for their determinations. The system was, of course, different in several respects; otherwise it would have served no useful purpose. In the first place, it applied only to cases in which the common-law courts were unable or unwilling to grant relief; in the second place, it drew its inspiration from an alternative philosophy of justice. For whereas the common law had its origin in custom, the equity system "had its roots in conscience and morality, in the desire to grant relief." Its development did not put an end to injustice, because there remained many individual instances where the rules as administered worked hardship on the litigants; yet in their mature form, the equity courts offered alternative kinds of relief to anybody who felt they had a legal grievance; henceforth, their choice between the different courses of action available to them would depend on the nature of the remedies offered, the ills suffered, and the cures sought. Although in the United States the two systems had quickly become merged to provide a unitary system of courts, administering between them the whole body of the law without regard to the origin of any particular principle being invoked, nevertheless, in Brandeis's opinion, the philosophy of justice underpinning the equity courts had bequeathed to the common law in America a vital legacy of procedural flexibility and high moral purpose.[62]

Within this conception of customary justice, the role and prestige of the judge was obviously of crucial importance; for if the common law was not judge made, it was at least, as Brandeis insisted, judge found. In seeking to explain the judicial function to his students in the 1890s, he chose to quote at length from James R. Carter's analogy between the methods of the law and those of the physical sciences. Judges, so Carter maintained, set about determining the law in precisely the same way that naturalists set about the classification of plants and animals:

The naturalist arranges the plants and animals in classes, according to some common feature which they exhibit, the higher and more general including the lower. When a new specimen is found, the questions which science asks are, to what order, genus and species does it belong, or is it a new discovery for which some new species must be framed? To answer these questions the naturalist observes the features of the specimen, and compares them with those which have been before examined and classified. Judges do the same; they observe the transactions of men and arrange them in orders, families, genera or species, according to their proper description, and the particular custom and feature which they exhibit. When a novel transaction makes its appearance, the function of the judge is to closely scrutinize its features, and to determine to what class, that is, to what custom, each should properly be assigned.[63]

On the face of it, we should be hard pressed to find the functions of the judiciary being imbued with more inertness than they are in this exposition; yet there is nothing in the context of the citation to suggest that Brandeis had any quarrel with it. On the contrary, he evidently regarded it as a masterly summation of the way in which judges were supposed to behave. They were not required to transform or embellish the law, merely to adduce and administer it. Certainly in practice this might involve a declaration of the principles by which a particular decision was reached, but it was not their province to usurp the prerogatives of the legislature by creating substantive law. Transfer this philosophy into the sphere of public law, add to it a measure of socioeconomic awareness among members of the judiciary, and one seems to have the rudiments of the latter-day principle of judicial self-restraint.

The much-altered condition of mid-twentieth-century law, however, was not the context in which Brandeis was writing in 1892, and surface appearances can be deceptive. For in the predominantly common-law environment then prevailing, his role as taxonomist left the judge with a surprisingly wide latitude for creative jurisprudence. Moreover, even under so highly restrictive and largely mechanistic a definition of the judiciary's responsibility, there remained one vital question to be answered. If judicial rulings were merely "evidence of what the law was," to what extent should they be considered binding in future cases? Brandeis's attitude was characteristically subtle, almost to the point of sophistry. Because judges, particularly on the nation's highest courts, frequently did seek to explain the reasoning that lay behind their rulings, and thus expounded by the way certain propositions of law, it was his belief that a "great distinction" needed to be made "between the weight of the decision itself and of the reasoning or statement of the rule." He proceeded to elucidate the grounds for such a distinction and the reasoning that followed from it. Regarding an *obiter dictum*, or a statement of law "not necessarily involved" in deciding the case before a court, judges were generally not loath to overrule it in deciding subsequent cases. Conversely, in considering an earlier case where the decision did "necessarily involve a proposition of law," they were strongly inclined to accept such prior determination as a binding precedent. Any point definitely decided by a court would ordinarily be followed by that same court "for all time subsequently," even though judges, finding themselves obliged to pass on a similar question thereafter, might "on the whole think [that] a different decision would have been better." Such in essence was the common-law doctrine of *stare decisis*.

Brandeis, however, already perceived limits to its application. Thus, even as he quoted Sir William Jones's observation that "the courts were bound by authority as firmly as pagan deities were supposed to have been bound by the decrees of fate," Brandeis was anxious to qualify its significance:

> While the regard for precedent is unquestionably great, so that it will always be followed on points which might reasonably be decided either way, yet where a decision is manifestly erroneous, and would lead to injustice in its application in the future, courts will, instead of merely limiting the scope of the decision, if necessary, actually overrule it. The decision whether an erroneous adjudication shall be overruled or not, resolves itself into a mere question of expediency depending upon the importance of consideration, of the importance of certainty, in the rule, and the extent of property to be affected by it, the courts being always more reluctant to change a rule which is a rule of property, than to change a rule which is merely one of action.

As we shall see in later chapters, both as an advocate and as a judge, he would have cause to ponder the widom of these limitations many times in the years ahead.[64]

Brandeis's downright hostility to the very idea of widespread legislative intervention in the fields of social policy and economic regulation was at bottom an issue of constitutional principle, as we shall see more clearly in the next chapter; but it was also in part a matter of professional self-interest. For the proliferation of statute law and administrative regulation, if allowed to develop unchecked, clearly threatened to alter the legal landscape in fundamental ways, thereby undermining and devaluing the most essential skill possessed by members of the bar: namely, their thorough working-knowledge of the principles, formulas, and procedures of the common law. This was the core of their professional expertise, and quite naturally they both feared and opposed its obsolescence. If invested with sufficient legislative backing, investigative agencies and administrative tribunals might prove resistant to judicial review. Even more assuredly, statutory interference would soon come to pollute the limpid waters of the common law, and by the generation of endless ripples distort the sharply focused images of society reflected off its surface. Brandeis was as susceptible to such fears as any of his professional colleagues.

This having been said, it is evident from his discussion of the limited deference due to precedent, and from his pronounced sympathy for the spread of equity principles within the common law, that his thinking in 1892 contained a large measure of ideological confusion about the appropriateness of judges acting as law givers. Was the tendency toward judicial activism implied by the overturning of bad decisions, and the tempering of fixed rules by reference to principles of morality and natural justice, to be welcomed or decried? He was unable to give a clear answer. Related to this area of doubt was another equally profound: By becoming locked into a constitutional system with the separation of powers as its governing precept, had the American judiciary been effectively divested of its quasi-legislative function; or did it retain the right to mold and refine the common law as new facts presented themselves, to extend and reformulate its principles as new and unforeseen situations arose? For a lawyer with scholarly pretensions and an acute mind, these were philosophical problems of the greatest moment that demanded an early resolution.

Despite specious indications to the contrary, the underlying logic of the M.I.T. lectures remained the same as that of the articles on water rights and privacy, namely, that judges working within a carefully articulated framework of principles and precedents were less likely to infringe the liberties of the citizen than were legislators who, ever mindful of the next election, found themselves ground remorselessly between the upper millstone of self-seeking special interest and the nether millstone of an easily manipulated public opinion. This was a gut belief, and one he would only be brought to disavow with the greatest reluctance. Though his faith in the disinterested independence of the judiciary would often be sorely tested in the years ahead, even in the new century his confidence in the advantages to be gained from judicial flexibility would remain an important motive force behind his adumbration of a new, sociologically based jurisprudence. The important difference between the legal ideas he espoused in the early 1890s and those to which he would hold some twenty years later lay not so much in any radical change of heart about the wisdom inherent in judges, but rather a newly awakened perception of the federal Constitution as the instrumental frame of reference within which the judicial function in America was performed. So it is from the business of common-law adjudication to that of constitutional interpretation that we must now turn our attention.

3

Constitutional Limitations

*The capacity of indignation makes an essential part of the outfit
of every honest man, but I am inclined to doubt whether he is a
wise one who allows himself to act upon its first hints.*
—Lowell, *My Study Windows*

Constitutional law did not occupy a prominent position on the American
legal landscape during the middle decades of the nineteenth century. The
creative genius of Chief Justice John Marshall may indeed have secured extensive powers of judicial review for the nation's judges, but his successors
on the bench used their right of veto sparingly. It was no small thing to declare the considered actions of a legislature unconstitutional, and the judiciary was wary of appearing to use its prerogatives recklessly. In fact, tempta-
tion was not often put in its way. Common-law adjudication and statutory
construction remained the principal elements of a judge's professional task
until the 1890s; and as late as 1875, fewer than one in ten of the cases coming before the Supreme Court in Washington turned on issues of
constitutionality.[1]

This emphasis on the common law and its formulas was reflected in contemporary law-school curricula, of which courses on property, contracts,
torts, criminal law, and criminal procedure represented the major part. At
Harvard in the 1870s constitutional law was reduced to the status of an elective, squeezed in alongside sales, bailments, agency, negotiable instruments,
partnership, shipping, insurance, equitable jurisdiction and procedure, principal and surety, domestic relations, marriage and divorce, wills and administration, corporations, conflict of laws, and debtor-creditor relations.
Although Brandeis is known to have taken several courses on equity, there
is no record of his ever having attended a single lecture on constitutional
law. It is not even clear who was deputed to give such lectures during his
years at the Law School. Langdell and Ames seem unlikely candidates for
the job; Washburn and, after him, Bradley were certainly not specialists on
the subject; and Thayer, who would later become an expert on the Constitution and write eloquently about its origins and scope, probably had his hands
full teaching evidence, trusts, and parts of equity. Neither in the mid-1870s
was it likely to have been the new Story Professor, John Chipman Gray,
though he certainly was "the great teacher of property law" referred to by

Felix Frankfurter, who, being "called upon late in life to teach constitutional law . . . , after a brief trial, gave it up in despair on the ground that constitutional law 'was not law at all, but politics.' "[2]

Gray's remark was not merely despairing but also shrewd. Despite the restrictive potential inherent in the commerce and contract clauses of the federal Constitution, and the doctrine of "vested rights" developed to afford a measure of protection to private property, the decades before the Civil War had witnessed the emergence of a politically stable consensus regarding the right of state legislatures to initiate and regulate activities deemed to be in the public interest. In forward-looking men like Lemuel Shaw of Massachusetts were found jurists willing and eager to interpret broadly the "police powers" of the states, provided entrepreneurial zeal and the free flow of commerce were not stifled in the process. Far from being channeled by the judiciary into a restrictive policy of laissez-faire, state legislatures were permitted, even encouraged, to assume an activist role in the development of a vibrant and viable commercial culture. "It was natural," observes Willard Hurst, "that legislators rather than judges should be the prime exponents of the policy of shaping environment to enlarge men's range of choice. This called for more general and novel policy-making than common-law tradition envisaged as within the scope of judicial power." Thus at precisely the same time that courts were becoming preoccupied with the release of private resources and energies through developments in the field of contract law, state legislatures were similarly employed in improving communications, creating new financial institutions and mechanisms, and generally promoting an increased scale of economic activity.[3]

In many states, this harmonious identity of interests between bench and legislature continued unabated into the 1870s and beyond; but elsewhere, most notably in New York, Pennsylvania, and Illinois, rapid industrial expansion and the mass of regulatory legislation that followed in its wake led to mounting friction between the political and judicial branches of government, as the parties most affected by these changes sought relief from different quarters. Just as state legislatures were pressed to expand the scope of investigative and regulatory activities recognized as coming within the remit of their police powers, so state courts were asked to recognize and enforce new constitutional limitations on the rights of such legislatures to impair liberty of contract or fetter the use of private property. Moreover, given the centrality of the constitutional issues raised in these disputes, particularly those stemming from the "due process" and "equal protection" clauses of the Fourteenth Amendment, and involving definition of the terms "person," "liberty," and "property," it was inevitable that the most contentious cases would come before the justices of the United States Supreme Court for their ultimate resolution.[4]

Against a background of mounting social tension, and not a little paranoia among some of the more reactionary elements of the legal establishment, the decade culminating in the War of 1898 saw a series of significant conservative victories in the nation's highest tribunal against the forces of reform. As late as 1888, in *Powell v. Pennsylvania*, the Supreme Court appeared ready to countenance further extensions of the police power on the ground that the validity of a state law prohibiting the manufacture of butter substitutes involved "questions of fact and public policy which belong to the legislative department to determine." But two years later, in *Chicago, Milwaukee & St. Paul Railway. Co. v. Minnesota*, the Court's decision to overturn a state law establishing a railroad and warehouse commission and empowering it to set reasonable rate schedules marked a singular new departure. In particular, the assertion that "the reasonableness of a rate of charge for transportation . . . is eminently a question for judicial investigation" appeared to reverse a rule of action to which the Court had held firm despite more than a decade of requests to reconsider its position: since 1877, in fact, when Chief Justice Waite, in disposing of *Munn v. Illinois*, had declared unequivocally that "For protection against abuses by legislatures the people must resort to the polls, not to the courts." Admittedly the *Chicago, Milwaukee* case was complicated by an explicit denial in the enabling statute of any judicial appeal from the decisions of the new commission, and in two subsequent cases involving no such provision, determined in 1892 and 1894, respectively, the regulatory power of the states was upheld. But in *Reagan v. Farmers Loan and Trust Co.* also decided in 1894, the Court found rate schedules drawn up by a Texas railroad commission to be "unreasonable," and in quashing them effectively sounded the death knell of Waite's principle. Moreover, following such a blatant demonstration of the Court's newfound willingness to take seriously criteria of reasonableness rooted in the "implied limitations" of natural law, the contention that constitutional guarantees of "due process" might admit of a "substantive" as well as of a "procedural" interpretation could no longer be shrugged off as the wishful thinking of a few judicial extremists.[5]

From a progressive standpoint, worse was yet to come. Early in 1895, the Court all but emasculated the Sherman Act by its ruling in *United States v. E. C. Knight Co.* that manufacture was not a part of commerce, and that consequently Congress had no power to break up an acknowledged monopoly operated by the American Sugar Refining Company. Four months later, in the notorious *Pollock* decision, the Justices went on to invalidate by a 5–4 majority the income tax provisions instituted by Congress during the previous year, and one week later still they voted unanimously to uphold the labor injunctions granted by a lower court in connection with the 1894 Pullman strike. Returning thereafter to the issue of economic regulation, the Court also decided cases in both 1896 and 1897 which narrowed considerably the authority of the Interstate Commerce Commission; established a rule in *Smyth v. Ames* (1897) that transportation rates set by any public authority should yield a fair return on "the present value" of the property thus regulated; and in *Holden v. Hardy* (1898), while agreeing to sustain a Utah statute limiting the hours worked by miners, gave notice that, in the interest of "freedom of contract," states would be required henceforth to show special justification for interposing themselves between employers and employees to determine hours, wages, or conditions of work. Taken together with scores of other decisions reached in state and federal court-rooms across the country, these rulings have been identified as evidence of a "new judicialism" emerging during the 1890s: an evolving corpus of legal doctrine that not only claimed for judges a greatly expanded role in the de-termination of what was constitutionally proper, but also furnished them with the judicial tools and precedents they needed to intervene decisively in the "irrepressible conflict" between the forces of labor and capital, which many thought to be imminent.[6]

Members of the bar and bench were deeply divided ln their reactions to such novel assertions of judicial power, and the intensity of their debates is amply evidenced in the reports of state bar associations and the pages of contemporary law journals. Legal progressives were at one in condemning judicial interventionism and supporting the further extension of socioeco-nomic regulation by state authorities, whereas conservative opinion was divided between "radicals" who advocated the rigorous implementation of a laissez-faire regime and "traditionalists" whose determination to resist the leveling tendency of popular majorities was tempered by a deep-seated re-gard for the sanctity of legal precedent and an almost reverential respect for an older conception of constitutional propriety. However, a pronounced hardening of attitudes occurred as the crisis of the 1890s unfolded: the sud-den eruption of the People's party onto the national political stage, and the strident demands contained in its 1892 Omaha Platform; the violent scenes associated with industrial unrest at Homestead, Pullman, and Coeur d'Alene; the consequent heightening of awareness among middle-class Americans of the socioeconomic dilemmas generated by two decades of rapid industrialization, sprawling urban development, and mass immigra-tion. All these factors combined to polarize "respectable" opinion, even among those previously inclined to favor traditional ways of doing things; and if some moderates did eventually rally to the Progressive cause, by far the greater number were drawn into the orbit of an increasingly fearful and beleaguered conservatism.[7]

The 1890s were in retrospect as crucial a decade for the development of Louis Brandeis's social outlook as they were for that of so many other Americans of his age and class. As they opened, a dozen years after his gra-duation from Harvard Law School, his knee-jerk response to the political issues of the day remained remarkably similar to that of other high-minded

men with whom he had become acquainted during his years as a student—
Eliot, Langdell, and Warren among them—who were now sufficiently repelled by the mounting level of corruption in public life to consider bolting
the party of Lincoln and joining with northern Democrats in a modest program of "liberal" reform. Yet though linked to it by a shared commitment to
protect and extend individual freedoms, the liberalism espoused by such
"Mugwumps" was far removed from the brand of progressive reformism,
already developing elsewhere in American society, which after 1900 would
increasingly succeed in getting the term "liberalism" equated with its own
belief in the duty of government to legislate, regulate, and spend on behalf
of individual citizens—ordinary people otherwise powerless to defend their
freedoms in a society dominated by the private might of corporate organizations and other large-scale institutions. The doctrines to which Brandeis and
his associates subscribed were closer to those of classical liberalism, with its
commitment to sound money, free-market economics and cheap, limited
government—a simple, homespun philosophy, whose key motive values
were honest efficiency and disinterested public service.

Yet however well intentioned they may have been, such exhortations to
civic virtue were beginning to look increasingly threadbare in a new era
typified by the clash of warring interests and discordant ideologies. The
quickening pace of economic change had brought in its wake not only rich
opportunities for individual advancement, but also a welter of seemingly intractable social problems that included bad housing, inadequate public facilities, widespread crime, and dangers to public health; and although these
might all be made worse by graft and inefficiency in the conduct of federal,
state, and municipal administration, civil service examinations and independent auditors could only effect improvements at the margin. Indeed, perhaps
the most worrying ruptures in the social fabric did not involve the activities
of government at all; for as the rapid growth of corporate business from the
1870s onward had been paralleled, though scarcely matched, by the organization of the first effective industrial and craft unions, the resultant impact
on labor relations had come by the turn of the century to resemble a battlefield on which the early skirmishing might soon be followed by unrestricted class warfare. To those conscious of the stresses and tensions to
which social cohesion was being subjected, and ready to place the good of
the commonweal before merely private interests, the need for a more comprehensive program of reform was rapidly becoming self-evident. In the
event, though, Mugwump enthusiasm for cheap and honest government did
not translate automatically into a broad humanitarian concern for the plight
of the poor, the underprivileged, and the oppressed; almost as many civil
service reformers joined the ranks of conservative reaction after 1900 as enlisted beneath the campaign banners of Progressivism.[8]

Nevertheless, genuine moral outrage at the behavior of unscrupulous
businessmen and shady politicians often did provide the springboard needed

to launch some "genteel" reformers into more robust careers of public crusading. In Brandeis's case, moral indignation surfaced early. At the beginning of 1891, he began to have thoughts about writing another journal article. "You know I have talked to you about the wickedness of shielding wrongdoers & passing them off (or at least allowing them to pass themselves off) as honest men," he wrote Alice Goldmark, the young woman who would soon become his wife. "If the broad light of day could be let in upon men's actions, it would purify them as the sun disinfects." His theme was to be "The Duty of Publicity," a sort of counterpart to "The Right to Privacy," and one, as he now confided, "that would really interest me more." The article never materialized, but the concern with upright conduct in public life represented a powerful impetus to action, eventually combining with others to involve him ever more deeply in the service of public causes.[9]

In the closing days of 1890, he had been urged by George F. Williams, a prominent member of the Massachusetts legislature, to throw at least his name behind the "liberal" measures then being pushed by the state's reform-minded governor, William E. Russell. "Knowing . . . how heartily you sympathize with such work," wrote his correspondent, "I venture to ask, if you cannot get time to study some particular measure and identify yourself with it: this much for the State." Williams's own interests were avowedly partisan, but he lived in hopes that Brandeis might be persuaded to support the Democrats' reforming initiative: "Some of us have given ourselves up to this work, and I believe our participation in politics has done much to steer the people toward Democracy. You belong with us and your influence would help amazingly, if only exercised incidentally." Brandeis did offer some limited assistance to the reformers, meeting with a group of legislators, for example, to consider a bill to require publication of election expenses; but his primary response to these exhortations must have seemed decidely quixotic.[10]

Early in 1891, he decided to take up the cause of the Massachusetts Protective Liquor Dealers Association, who were endeavoring to *prevent* passage of legislation promoted by the state's temperance lobby, which was threatening to put them out of business. He agreed to act as counsel for the association's members on condition that they call an immediate halt to the campaign of wholesale bribery that had hitherto characterized their activities and pay close attention to his advice. "All the morning I was before a legislative Com[mit]tee," he told Alice one day in early February, "fighting the errors & hypocracies [*sic*] of so-called temperance people & carrying out my pet reform of the liquor trade by making the dealers respectable. . . . At times I think I can accomplish much with them."[11]

His basic contention was that existing liquor laws in the commonwealth were harsh and unenforceable. In theory, alcoholic drinks could only be sold as part of a meal; in practice, though, this prohibition was widely evaded, serving only to make criminals out of otherwise legitimate traders and to invite corruption into the political process. "You can make politicians of shoemakers or farmers," Brandeis told the committee; "you can make politicians of any class of people, or of those in any occupation if you harass them, if you make it impossible for them to live unless they control, unless they have secured power to determine when, and how, and where they may live." Liquor dealers could be removed from politics by the simple expedient of making the liquor laws more, not less, reasonable. Since it was *excessive* drinking that constituted the real social evil, the legislature's chief concern should be to ensure that sales of liquor were properly regulated. To achieve this it was essential that the licenced traders should be turned into honest citizens; "self-respect and prosperity," he insisted, rather than outlawry and graft were "the most effective guardians of [public] morals." Impressed by his arguments, the politicians decided to follow his advice.[12]

As this episode illustrates, Brandeis's moral indignation did not at first incline him to favor the efforts of social and economic reformers. On the contrary, his whole conception of constitutional government made him deeply critical of those demanding statutory remedies for all of society's ills and inequities. State legislatures, he believed, succumbed too easily to the pressure exerted by lobbyists seeking special privileges for corporate clients or organized interest groups, and were frequently induced to pass laws that benefited one section of the community at the expense of another. This was not only bad policy; it was more important a denial of the "due process" guarantees of equal opportunity and fair treatment enshrined in virtually all state constitutions. If the political model underpinning these views can be traced back to the basic principles of Jacksonian democracy, the proximate source from which Brandeis derived and absorbed their legal implications was almost certainly Thomas Cooley's *Treatise on the Constitutional Limitations which Rest upon the Legislative Power of the States of the American Union*.

First published In 1868 and widely read for the next two decades, this monumental work exerted an enormous influence on the development of American legal thought during the last quarter of the nineteenth century, and not least on Supreme Court Justice Stephen Field and the other leading proponents of "negative judicial activism." However, those who would dismiss Cooley as one of the principal ideologues of laissez-faire capitalism and a mere apologist for large corporate interests do scant justice either to the ambivalence of his public career or to the subtlety of his ideas about the law. A Jacksonian Democrat turned Liberal Republican by the Civil War, for more than twenty years Cooley managed to combine a zest for careful scholarship with an active career on the bench. As well as serving as an associate justice of the Michigan Supreme Court from 1864 to 1885, he was an energetic faculty member at the University of Michigan Law School, and indeed the text of *Constitutional Limitations* grew out of a series of lectures that he wrote for his students there. Later, after resigning from the bench, he was installed as chairman of the newly created Interstate Commerce Commission, and there played a vigorous role until his retirement on health grounds in 1891.[13]

As to the salient themes of his jurisprudence, in his scholarly works as in the opinions he wrote while on the bench, Cooley was staunchly opposed to the granting of special privileges to corporations and offered only qualified support for the judiciary's claimed power to nullify legislative acts. One legal historian has characterized his stance as a judge in these terms:

> In some respects Cooley's judicial decisions were closer to those of Taney than to those of Field. He construed the obligation of contracts clause strictly and was suspicious of its use to protect corporate privilege. He asserted the supremacy of legislative power against private claims: a municipality, he maintained could not delegate its powers to some private individuals to seek redress against others. He articulated a narrow theory of judicial review of legislative, executive, or administrative activity; and in a celebrated case involving the Michigan Tax Commission in 1882, he not only upheld the autonomy of the Commission's operations, he also inveighed against judges who "assaulted" statutes because they "did not like the legislation."

Yet he also implied that equality of opportunity could be secured by the simple expedient of preventing governments from interfering in the economic affairs and relationships of their citizens: a congenial idea that others, closer than he to the outlook of America's new economic elites, were quick to develop and exploit for their own advantage. Even so, he

> stopped short . . . of fashioning the limitations of the due process clause into dogmas such as the doctrine of liberty of contract, through which [other] judges, by maintaining the fiction of equal bargaining power in industrial workers and their employers, invalidated much of the welfare legislation passed by states in the late nineteenth and early twentieth centuries. For Cooley constitutional limitations were two-edged: they functioned not only to protect private enterprise from undue legislative supervision but also to prevent it from securing special benefits.

Thus, if he was indeed a leading progenitor of the conservative concept of "substantive due process," he was a largely unwitting one.

In fact, at the root of Cooley's constitutionalism lay an even more fundamental article of faith which many of those who seized gratefully on the notion of "limitation" failed to grasp: namely, that it was both feasible and desirable that judges should interpret the law so as to render its operations predictable. "That state of things when decisions conflict, so that a citizen is always at a loss in regard to his rights and his duties, is a very serious evil," he observed in an early chapter of *Constitutional Limitations*, "and the alternative of regarding adjudged cases as precedents in future controversies resting upon analogous facts, and brought within the same reasons, is obviously preferable." Moreover, whereas certain common-law rules of action might be modified over time, as society changed and the facts of daily living to which they were applied came to assume wholly novel configurations, written instruments, and especially constitutions, Cooley reasoned, ought always to receive "an unvarying interpretation" and to be construed uniformly.

> A constitution is not to be made to mean one thing at one time, and another at some subsequent time when the circumstances may have so changed as perhaps to make a different rule in the case seem desirable. A principal share of the benefit expected from written constitutions would be lost if the rules they established were so flexible as to bend to circumstances or be modified by public opinion. It is with special reference to the varying moods of public opinion, and with a view to putting the fundamentals of government beyond their control, that these instruments are framed: and there can be no such steady and imperceptible change in their rules as inheres in the principles of the common law.

In short, whereas the common law afforded judges a measure of flexibility within which they might respond effectively to promote or hinder change, written constitutions provided fixed boundaries beyond which legislatures, and even judges, could not legitimately trespass.[14] As we shall see, all of these ideas left a deep imprint on Brandeis's receptive mind, and many were to find their echo in the lectures that he delivered at M.I.T. in the early 1890s. As the decade progressed, however, a corrosive mix of personal reflection and wider experience began to challenge the smug certainties of his outlook, and to reveal the logical inadequacies of this potentially rigid legal philosophy. Between 1891 and 1897, his ideas would undergo a major reappraisal, and on several important issues his own position would emerge completely reversed. Nevertheless, the key question must be addressed: What manner of experience could have proved traumatic enough to have brought about such seismic changes in the intellectual makeup of a man rapidly approaching the peak of his professional career?

According to Brandeis's own recollection of events, there was one incident in particular which, more than any other single influence, helped turn a rather complacent corporate lawyer into a committed reformer. "I think it was the affair at Homestead which first set me to thinking seriously about the labor problem. It took the shock of that battle, where organized capital hired a private army to shoot at organized labor for resisting an arbitrary cut in wages, to turn my mind definitely toward a searching study of the relations of labor to industry." His course on business law at M.I.T. had been scheduled to start in the school year 1891–92; but, although a set of lectures was already in preparation, ill health forced him to postpone its delivery until the following session. His original theme, he remembered, was to have been "the evolution of the common law in its relation to industry and commerce," but the events at Homestead caused him to alter both his plans and his ideas in dramatic fashion:

> One morning the newspaper carried the story of the pitched battle between the Pinkertons on the barge and barricaded steel workers on the bank. I saw at once that the common law, built up under simpler conditions of living, gave an inadequate basis for the adjustment of the complex relations of the modern factory system. I threw away my notes and approached my theme from new angles. Those talks at Tech marked an epoch in my own career.[15]

Unfortunately, this neat explanation cannot be squared with the surviving evidence. The typescript of his proposed M.I.T. lectures preserved at Louisville conforms closely to the original thematic program just outlined. As we saw in the last chapter, and will see again shortly, in many respects it constitutes a decidedly unprogressive treatise, and one might be forgiven for assuming that it was written prior to the supposedly formative summer of 1892. A note at the foot of the contents page, however, explains that the compilation was "prepared *in the fall*" of that year, for a series of "*contemplated* lectures" at the Institute. Although "finalized" might have been a more appropriate word than "prepared," bearing in mind that the text extended to some 361 pages and was based on materials collected over a three-year period, the fact nevertheless remains that these must be the lectures actually delivered during the academic session 1892–93. If further proof were needed that this is the text as "revised," then the inclusion of explicit references to Homestead in the sections dealing with organized labor must be regarded as conclusive.[16]

It is patently impossible to reconcile these circumstances with Brandeis's own subsequent claims to have discarded his notes and begun again from scratch immediately after reading about the clashes; more pertinently perhaps, the substance and tone of the passages dealing directly with events at Homestead give no support whatever to the idea of any sudden "conversion" experience. Given that the critical confrontations occurred a mere two months before the start of the new school year, we should not expect to find Brandeis undertaking to rewrite his lectures completely; but shortage of time can hardly be adduced as a explanation for the unmistakably hostile character of the interpolations that were made. Two conclusions therefore seem inescapable: first, that the lecturer's more liberal ideas about labor relations developed at a somewhat later date than he himself recalled; second, that factors other than his learning about Homestead in the newspapers must be called on to explain his change of heart. For what is certain is that Brandeis's mature perspective on the legitimate rights and expectations of working people represented a marked departure from his earlier thinking on such matters.

What philosophical beliefs did he hold before his intellectual realignment, then; and in particular, what did he have to say about relations between employers and employees? As already indicated, even the 1892 "revision" of his "talks at Tech" reveals a much less sympathetic attitude toward combinations of workers than has generally been recognized hitherto.[17] After surveying the history of organized labor in America since the seventeenth century, he went on to discuss those cases decided in the courts of Massachusetts that best illustrated the principles used in determining the legality of strikes. From this analysis, he was able to conclude that although the law would always permit a strike, regardless of how much embarrassment or hardship it might wreak on the employer, and would allow the strikers to use whatever influence or persuasion they possessed to prevent others from taking their jobs, it would not countenance violence on their part; nor would it accept any interference by threats or force with the business or property of the employer. "If the strikers attempt to take possession of the factory of their employer," he observed, "they cannot complain if they are repelled by such force as the employer is able to command and [is] required to use."[18]

With reference to the situation at Homestead, he found no grounds for distinguishing the legal rights of the parties concerned from those already outlined. Although the strike itself was legal, the subsequent seizure of the mills, and the strikers' declaration that they should not be operated by non-union labor, "far exceeded the bounds of the law." As for the contention that the Carnegie Company did likewise by employing Pinkerton Detectives "to recover possession of their property" he was less certain. "Ordinarily a man in possession of his property has a right to protect it from the legal interference of others," he told his students, "and may use such means as are reasonably necessary for this purpose." Where the issue was one of repossession rather than sitting tight, however, similar though arguably more circumscribed rights probably prevailed. "In practice," he continued generally, albeit in terms clearly relevant to the circumstances at Homestead,

> the employers found at times that they could not summon among their own loyal men, a force sufficient to repel the strikers. They found at times also, they could not rely for assistance upon the sheriffs or the police. They undertook, therefore, to hire men, who as their agents, should aid them in holding possession of their property, and protect it against strikers. These men were frequently, often necessarily, armed. They were supplied first and principally by the Pinkerton Detective Agency. Such employment, and the injury resulting to individual strikers would not constitute any legal ground of complaint on their part, but the public, through the Criminal Law, could probably punish the act of the Company, as tending to a breach of the peace, as they could also that of the employees.

Although it could be argued that this explanation represents nothing more than an accurate and objective statement of the law as it stood in 1892, and implies no necessary endorsement on Brandeis's part of the morality or wisdom of the judgments involved, such a construction is difficult to reconcile with either the surrounding discussion or his practice in dealing with other topics. Critical observations on statutes and rules of law with which he disagreed occur throughout the text. The inescapable conclusion is that he found nothing objectionable in the legal situation he was describing.[19]

Strikes were not the only aspect of the industrial relations scene to which Brandeis's lectures directed their attention. One of the main themes running through the course echoed a line that he and Sam Warren had adumbrated in their Watuppa pond articles and in "The Right to Privacy": namely that, in the broad field of socioeconomic relationships, determinations of the common law by judicial process were generally preferable to statutory intervention on the part of state legislatures. Whereas judges were to be regarded as disinterested experts, politicians too readily appeared as the tools of special-interest groups. He was particularly disturbed by the activities of professional lobbyists, hired to promote or hinder the passage of legislation by people interested in the outcome obtained. Although it was perfectly legitimate for individuals or companies to procure the assistance of lawyers, either to present their case before a legislative committee or to draft appropriate clauses for insertion into the bill proposed, members of the lobby all too frequently went beyond simple advocacy of a measure to exercise a more underhand influence over legislators. In other words, graft, or at least the potential for it, had become an everyday feature of the State House and required extirpation.[20]

Though one of his original purposes in agreeing to lecture at the Massachusetts Institute of Technology had been to counteract the influence of the "monied interests," he was equally unhappy about the pretensions of organized labor. The courts, he believed, had adopted a generally permissive attitude toward combinations of workers but had been rather less liberal with regard to employers seeking to make similar arrangements for protection against their employees; the law had even undertaken to punish employers who tried to prevent the organization of their work forces. However, "the laborers and their sympathetic friends" regarded the ample legal remedies already granted for their self-protection as wholly inadequate, and had sought to invoke "the power of the legislature" to bring about the workers' further "elevation." The political influence of the labor unions had combined with "the humanitarianism of the present day" to produce "a mass of legislation more or less crude" aimed at improving the workingman's lot. Statutes had been passed, as Brandeis observed, "to reduce competition, to limit the hours of work, to improve the conditions under which it is performed, and to regulate the time, the manner and the medium of payment therefor." Several states, including Massachusetts, had even enacted measures to prevent companies employing Pinkertons as guards. Indeed, the commonwealth had "probably been foremost in the movement. A hundred octavo pages, ten times the space filled by the federal Constitution, would not suffice to contain all the laws passed on this subject within [the last] fifteen years."[21]

Among the various kinds of meddlesome legislation previously itemized, he was especially concerned by attempts to regulate hours of labor, which he clearly regarded as unconstitutional. "It is indeed difficult to see how the infringement of the rights of the individual liberty [*sic*] can be carried farther than by limiting the number of hours a day that a man may be employed to work," he wrote. Although such laws generally took the form of a prohibition against the employer, it was obvious that their effect lay equally on the employee, "because it must shut to him all avenues of longer employment in the particular line to which he chooses to devote himself." Interestingly enough, he was prepared to make an exception in the case of regulations dealing with child labor; he explicitly approved of attempts to limit the hours worked by children, to prohibit their working at night or during the school term, and to secure regular mealtimes for them. Given their recent achievement of full legal status, he was less certain about the position regarding women, though he seemed willing to consider specific cases on their merits. Otherwise, though, he was quite contemptuous of arguments that the state had a responsibility to protect the health of its citizens by limiting the number of hours each might work. Such a thesis, he declared, if pursued to its logical conclusion, would "justify the legislature in interfering with" almost every aspect of an individual's life.

> Working long hours in the day would probably be no more injurious to the health than not taking exercise, or than the eating of mince pies by people with weak digestions, and the legislature might as well on principle undertake to control these matters of private concern as to prevent adult people from overworking, simply on the ground that it is injurious to their health.

A state government's duty was limited to the protection of the *public* health; private health was not its concern. Thus it could properly intervene to prevent people living in conditions likely to cause an epidemic but only because the wider interests of the community were at stake. He firmly rejected the contention that legislators had a constitutional interest in the well-being of every citizen and were entitled "to control the living of the individual" as a consequence. "If that be true" he averred, "there is no such thing as a guaranty to individual liberty." Interference on the part of the state could only be regarded as legitimate when the problem singled out for action could be shown to have direct, immediate, and harmful effects on the community as a whole. His one consolation was a belief that the courts would ultimately declare the broadest interventionist statutes void.[22]

This reasoned condemnation of most prolabor legislation was no mere paraphrase of judicial opinions but an uneqivocal expression of Brandeis's own views. He was equally forthright in saying what he thought about the rise of corporate business, and once again his views differed in significant respects from those associated with his name in later years. His principal reaction was highly positive: Without the growth and widespead use of "corporate combinations" it was difficult to see how the great commercial and industrial expansion of America during the nineteenth century could have taken place. "The wealth, or at least the courage of single individuals," he asserted,

> would not have been equal to the task of constructing our railroads, of extending the systems of telegraph over the continent, of erecting the gas and water works, of establishing banks and insurance companies and the huge factories. In many of these enterprises great aggregations of capital were indispensable; in many they were desirable as a means of lessening the cost of the service rendered.

Nowhere had the value of such "aggregations of capital" been more evident than in manufacturing industry, where significant economies of scale had resulted from the scale of operations achieved by large business corporations. In there proper sphere, therefore, these developments had proved wholly beneficial to the community.

Increasingly, however, "combinations in business" were being used to suppress competition rather than as an aid to raising capital or cutting unit costs. It was now considered more desirable to monopolize the market altogether, by fair means or foul, than to gain a competitive edge in sales by improving one's service or product. At least where commerce and manufacturing were concerned, Brandeis was already vehemently opposed to such developments. "The maxim that competition is the life of trade and is demanded by public policy," he averred, had long since become established among the English-speaking peoples. It was firmly entrenched as a principle of the common law; and he was able to cite precedents going back to the fifteenth century, which served to illustrate the receptive hearing the courts had always been willing to give to those protesting against monopolistic combinations.[23]

Competition could be taken to extremes, however. When rival firms sought to annihilate one another by cutting their prices below cost, and by taking losses on a scale that only large accumulations of capital could sustain, not only were otherwise sound businesses driven to the wall, but a strong incentive to further combination was created; for only those with the greatest reserves of capital could hope to survive in such a cutthroat environment. Yet, it was easier to disapprove of such methods than it was to find a legal principle by which they could be eradicated. The plain fact was that all competition was permissible in law unless self-evidently fraudulent, oppressive, or unfair; moreover, in practice, the terms "oppressive" and "unfair" were defined within exceedingly narrow limits. As Brandeis tried to explain:

> If the Standard Oil Co[mpany] seeing a competitor spring up determine to undersell him at any cost to themselves, and thus crush out the new competitor, their ac-

tion may, in a popular sense, be oppressive and unfair, for the stronger to get an advantage over the weak; but it is not illegal. The Standard Oil Company can give away their product if they please, or sell it for half its cost, and no one has a legal right to complain of their action, even if thereby he is driven out of business.

Competition only ceased to be fair in the eyes of the law when fraud or deception could be proved, or where property rights had been infringed. "The mere doing of those acts which are necessary to increase one's own business," he continued, "does not become unfair because it diminishes the business of the other men." Conflicts of attrition, though, could be highly damaging to the winners as well as the losers; thus in the recent past it had become much more common for corporate predators to seek to eliminate their opponents by merging with them rather than by forcing them out of business.[24]

It was this tendency that had led to the formation of what were popularly called "trusts." These were trade combinations designed to achieve "a union more or less complete of all competing concerns" in a particular industry. Some were nationwide in scope, others operated over a more limited area; but the purpose in either case was to exercise monopolistic control of the marketplace. There were also, as he pointed out, many commercial concordats of a less formal nature: Bilateral or multilateral agreements could be concluded between independent companies to maintain prices, divide territories, and fix production quotas; or else central bodies could be set up to control patterns of marketing and distribution. Compacts of the first kind were difficult to enforce, however, in view of the courts' longstanding disapproval of contracts placing *unreasonable* restraints on trade, whereas the latter type had also been declared invalid because the group-marketing features were deemed part of a broader plan to create a series of territorial monopolies. Trusts properly so called, where boards of trustees exercised control over production and distribution, might be invalidated by their constituent companies' charters of incorporation, which in many states required stockholders to exercise their responsibilities personally. Even the outright merging of assets into a unitary concern could be declared void if it could be shown that the purpose had been to create a monopoly.[25]

Whether achieved by cutthroat competition or granted by a government patent, monopolies had always been "regarded as contrary to the spirit and policy of the common law." Their malign effects on the wider community, as summarized in Brandeis's account, had altered little since the days of Lord Coke: The prices of items engrossed by a single supplier generally rose to whatever levels the market would bear, while the quality of such commodities tended to decline; also monopolies frequently closed the pathways of opportunity previously open to small businessmen, craftsmen, and traders by removing the basis of their independence, and menacing the livelihood of themselves and their families. Indeed, as the depression of the early 1890s deepened, this last incident of monopolization took on an immediate and particular significance whose implications Brandeis was not slow to grasp:

> A society in which a few men are the employers and the great body are merely employees or servants, is not the most desirable in a republic; and it should be as much the policy of the laws to multiply the numbers engaged in independent pursuits or in the profits of production as to cheapen the price to the consumer. Such policy would tend to an equality of fortunes among its citizens, . . . and lessen the amount of pauperism and crime.

All monopolies, however they were created, threatened both the price level and the preservation of "industrial liberty" to the same degree. "By the invariable laws of human nature," he asserted, "competition will be excluded and prices controlled in the interest of those connected with the combination or trust."[26]

Nevertheless, in spite of all the problems and potential ill consequences attendant on their operations, the granting of monopolistic privileges to private interests was sometimes unavoidable. Modern civilization required elaborate systems of communication; highways and railroads, mail, telegraph and telephone services were all "indispensable." Similarly gas, electric, and water supplies were an essential adjunct of urban living. A "special exercise of power" was needed before any of these facilities could be made widely available. "It is difficult to conceive of the building of a highway or railroad without passing over the lands of many people," Brandeis observed, "and likewise the distribution of water or artificial light, or the sending of messages by telegraph or telephone involves the use of the public's property or that of other individuals." In many other countries, and to some extent in the United States, the responsibility for supplying these services had been assumed directly by either governmental or municipal authorities, generally to the exclusion of would-be competitors. In practice, though, states whose constitutions did not prohibit the patenting of private monopolies, were just as likely to delegate such functions to licensed contractors over whom they would thereafter exercise a measure of regulatory control. All such public franchises came with legal strings attached; and it was clearly right that they should, since, without a specific grant of authority from the sovereign power, no citizen or company could engage in a business that required the use of property belonging either to private individuals or to the people as a whole. Furthermore, when special privileges were required, a state was entitled to use its discretion in deciding how, and on whom, they should be bestowed; nobody could complain that a right had been granted to another but denied to him. In other words, the granting of monopoly privileges in such circumstances was perfectly legal, so long as without it the individual would have no right to carry on the business. It was important to notice, though, that except where cities were explicitly mandated to make their own arrangements, this power to grant patents of monopoly was generally reserved to state legislatures; where municipal administrations had attempted to usurp it, their efforts had frequently been declared void.[27]

Quite apart from the attitude of the common law, and the limitations and prohibitions found in many state constitutions, the due process and equal protection clauses of the Fourteenth Amendment were likewise generally held to outlaw the granting of exclusive franchises to private interests, unless these were clearly intended for the performance of public functions. Yet a practical exception to this consensus of disapprobation could arise in certain circumstances from the exercise by the states of their so-called "police powers". These permitted state governments to regulate such "unwholesome trades" as the slaughtering of animals, or such potentially dangerous activities as storing gunpowder, building with combustible materials, or burying the dead within the city limits; the plain intention was to protect thereby the health, safety, and general welfare of the public and its property. As Brandeis explained, by exercising these powers, states were simply fulfilling their obligation to ensure "that every person ought to use his property as not to injure his neighbors, and that private interests must be made subservient to the general interests of the community." The practical effect of such wide-ranging authority, though, might easily lead to the granting of licenses to a limited number of people, and could on occasion be held to justify outright monopoly.

With special privileges come special burdens, however. For it was a well-settled principle of law that a legislature could impose such conditions as it saw fit on anyone acquiring such privileges for their business. "If the parties are not satisfied with the conditions," Brandeis observed, "they need not accept the grant, and if these grants were made subject to be revoked or amended at any time, the condition need not have been invoked at the outset, but it may be imposed subsequently." Given the public nature of businesses like railroading, gas supply, and so forth, a legislature might undertake, probably by setting up a regulatory commission, "to control the affairs, investment, compensation, etc." of the companies involved, as well as "in some measure the conduct of such persons who engage in the business." Thus, without exactly denying employees the right to strike, it might "compel them to give a reasonable notice before quitting work." A stipulation to this effect in their contracts of employment would probably prove ineffective, however, because the workers could not usefully be sued for breach. Thus enforcement would require the creation of a new criminal liability, and Brandeis was clear in his own mind that such a development of the law could readily be justified "by the interest of the public in securing uninterrupted means of transportation and communication." In fairness, though, he was equally keen to see a "corresponding obligation" laid on employers "to give notice of the intention to dismiss the men."[28]

Up to this point, at least, he had no quarrel with either the logic or methods by which such regimes of regulation operated in respect of quasi-public corporations; the legal and economic doctrines underpinning such activities were, he believed, wholly sound. But "in their zeal to appease public clamor," state legislatures had gone further:

> Not content with regulating price in those businesses which were dependent for their existence upon grants from the state, they undertook to determine also what the maximum charge should be in businesses which individuals had established and were carrying on under the ordinary right of a free man to engage in his chosen occupation.

He went on to relate the situation of the Chicago grain elevators, through which by the early 1870s the grain of seven or eight midwestern states was passing annually. Despite the fact that these elevators "had been built without special grants of privilege on land bought in the normal way" (i.e., without claiming the right of eminent domain), the Illinois legislature had bowed to the pressure of the Grangers and moved to regulate their operations by means of a statutory commission. The elevator owners had naturally appealed to the courts. They objected to the state's interference on the grounds that the setting of maximum rates deprived them of their property without due process of law, and that, in any case, the "reasonableness" of their rates was a matter for judicial rather than legislative determination. In the landmark decision of *Munn v. Illinois* (1877), a majority of the United States Supreme Court rejected these contentions, holding that any business "affected" or "clothed with a public interest" was liable to regulation by virtue of the police powers reserved to the states. The fact that state power was open to abuse was not of itself an argument against its existence or validity, declared Chief Justice Waite, who went on to assert the principle already discussed, that those who felt aggrieved at the actions of their elected representatives should seek redress via the ballot box rather than through the courts.[29]

To all such assertions of democratic hegemony, Brandeis in 1892 was unequivocally opposed. He regarded Justice Field's dissent in the *Munn* case as a "masterly opinion," and appeared fully to endorse its insistence that a state could only intervene to fix compensation where a business depended for its existence on a governmental grant of privilege. The reasoning of the majority, subsequently reaffirmed in a case involving the grain elevators in Buffalo, turned on the fact "that a monopoly had actually been created which the public interest demanded should be regulated." It was a line of argument that he found every bit as unsound as its consequences were dangerous. Nonetheless, he viewed with optimism the fact that three justices had dissented in the more recent case, and looked forward to the day when this "growing minority" would ultimately control the court.[30]

We have already seen that, at the time these lectures were written, Brandeis was squarely opposed to regulatory statutes being used to achieve social goals; liberty of contract and the freedom to employ private property for any lawful purpose were rights guaranteed by the Constitution and protected at common law, and ought not to be infringed by state legislatures responding to pressure from special-interest groups. Such views have widely been regarded as typical of laissez-faire conservatism at this date, and it is frequently suggested that constitutional scruples of the type commonly claimed by Justices Field and Brewer were, in reality, little more than a fig leaf of respectability for the principle of private greed and the ethics of mass exploitation. Today's liberal cynicism has little time for the notion that such opinions should be considered at face value; that in large measure the constitutionalists were sincere in their beliefs; and that the "public interest" doctrine, beginning to gain ground rapidly by the early 1890s, did indeed pose a genuine threat to the liberties of individuals, small as well as great. Brandeis, like Field, held fast to the Jeffersonian belief that governmental power was something to invoke rarely, and then only when the need was clear and pressing; the Constitution had identified the proper occasions for its exercise, and there was no reason to expand its sphere of competence. During the latter half of his life Brandeis would come to modify these views, but he could never abandon them completely; for an intuitive sense of the fragility of freedom, and the allegorical example of Faust's fateful striving after worldly power, lay too deep within him to be dismissed with equanimity.[31]

Some forms of regulation were plainly sanctioned by both custom and common sense; measures to protect the public health and to prevent fraud or physical nuisance fell easily into this category. But what about moral nuisances like alcohol abuse or gambling? How far should the state go in controlling these? Evidence from the lectures in this area throws valuable light on Brandeis's decision the previous year to defend the interests of the Massachusetts liquor dealers. In the first place, he was clear in his own mind that the liquor business was one "properly the subject of regulations." Whatever might be said in favor of drinking as a pastime, the production and sale of alcoholic beverages could obviously lead to serious social evils if not properly conducted. Not only minors but the community as a whole needed protection, and the state was fully entitled to prescribe appropriate safeguards. For instance, it could limit the number of licenses issued; exercise discretion in the selection of licensees; prevent liquor being sold on Sundays, close to schoolhouses, or at times of the day when it was likely to encourage breaches of the peace. Gambling was even more damaging to society, and its prohibition by law eminently reasonable, though in Brandeis's own opinion, the extension of the term "gambling" to include speculation in commodity futures was a decidedly dubious proposition. There was nothing "inherently immoral" in such transactions, and it could be argued that "the possibility of making such contracts is essential to the conduct of business as now carried on."

It was not the prevention of damage so much as the guardianship of morals that Brandeis found objectionable. "Gambling in all its forms and prize fighting are generally deemed contrary to good morals," he wrote.

> But the question of the validity of the laws regulating business supposed to be contrary to good morals becomes more doubtful. Where the doing of the act or the use of the article is not in itself a crime, but a wrong only in its abuse, as the drinking of liquor, the question is often asked, can the business relating to such [an] act be prohibited?

In the case of liquor, it had been forcefully argued that, although its sale could be regulated, prohibition was only valid with reference to "minors, lunatics, confirmed drunkards, or persons intoxicated." To prohibit manufacture and sale altogether would be to infringe the individual's "constitutional rights to liberty 'and the pursuit of happiness.'" The courts had again found otherwise, however, upholding the states' right to eradicate a trade many considered injurious to the public. Brandeis's own opinion was that "the proper scope of legislation in a free country is not to suppress vices, but crimes; that the legislation should be limited to the doing of that which may be injurious to others and not extended to that which in the opinion of the legislature may be injurious to the particular individual." Such a principle was arguably as much a plea for the recognition of civil liberties, as it was a conscious defense of libertarian economics.[32]

The central question when public health, safety, and welfare issues were involved was precisely the same as when the regulation of monopoly was mooted: How far should the police powers of the states be held to extend? It clearly did not follow that every law ostensibly passed for the promotion of worthy ends was to be accepted as a legitimate exercise of the police power, and there was a respectable body of legal opinion that stressed the judiciary's responsibility for ensuring that genuine purposes were distinguished from specious ones. Speaking for the Court in *Mugler v. Kansas* (1887), Justice Harlan had stated the matter succinctly, and Brandeis quoted at some length from his judgment:

> There are, of necessity, limits beyond which legislation cannot rightfully go. . . . The courts are not bound by mere forms, nor are they to be misled by mere pretences. They are at liberty—indeed, are under a solemn duty—to look at the substance of things whenever they enter upon the inquiry whether the legislature has transcended the limits of its authority. If, therefore, a statute purporting to have been enacted to protect the public health, the public morals or the public safety, has no real or substantial relation to those objects, or is a palpable invasion of rights secured by the fundamental law, it is the duty of the courts to so adjudge, and thereby give effect to the Constitution.

However, by deciding to uphold Kansas's sweeping prohibition of the liquor trade, despite these reservations, it appeared that Harlan and his brethren were unwilling to acknowledge the logic of their own principle. If, to achieve its stated purpose of guarding the community against the evils of excessive consumption, the state legislature believed it necessary to ban production of all alcoholic drinks, even those intended for the maker's own use, then it was "not for the courts, under their views as to what is best for the community, to disregard the legislative determination of that question." Yet if Brandeis had reservations about the validity of moves against the liquor business, he was even unhappier about recent attempts in Massachusetts to restrict the manufacture and sale of cigarettes. "The theory," he supposed, "was that some boys smoked too many, and that as a law prohibiting sales to minors might not be easily enforceable, it is better to prohibit them altogether." He doubted that such legislation, even if passed, could withstand scrutiny in the courts. If cigarettes could be suppressed on such grounds, why not other forms of tobacco, or mince pies, or bicycling, or "notably foot-ball"? "It is obvious," he concluded, "that the horse of protecting the health and morals of the community may be ridden too hard; you may deprive the individual of all opportunity or at least of all obligation to take care of himself, and the 'inalienable' right of life and liberty may be reduced to a nullity."[33]

There remained one final category of business regulation to which Brandeis believed some attention was due, and that involved firms whose operations were dependent, wholly or in part, on property or rights belonging to the general public. The fish in lakes and rivers, for example, together with all kinds of game, were public property; everyone enjoyed equal rights to them, and the state was duty bound to regulate the taking of such fish or game with a view to upholding those rights. A few years earlier, in their articles concerning water rights in Massachusetts, he and Sam Warren had noted a similar purpose in the Colony Ordinance's designation of "great ponds," and had strongly supported the commonwealth's right to control, though not to alienate or destroy, property held in common for its citizens. Moreover, he was now ready to link the preservation of such property with the granting of rights and privileges. "It is upon the same theory," he declared, "that laws regulating legal monopolies or businesses involving grants of public franchises may rest."[34]

As Brandeis saw matters in the fall of 1892, the individual liberties protected by settled principles of law and guaranteed by the United States Constitution lay under serious threat of abrogation. Special-interest groups, in particular labor organizations and their "humanitarian" supporters, were pressing state legislatures to interfere ever more comprehensively in a whole range of socioeconomic situations, contrary to wise constitutional restraints provided by the Founding Fathers; worse, a growing body of legal opinion that included both lawyers and judges seemed ready to countenance these unwarranted claims. One effect of the resultant expansion of statute law, hitherto largely ignored, had been a concomitant shift of emphasis away from civil suits toward criminal prosecutions. "The civil relations of man to man mainly occupy the attention so far as law is concerned," he expatiated.

> But the multitudinous legislation of a socialistic nature, based upon the idea of advancing the general welfare of the community, has added very extensively to the extent and scope of the law of crime within the last twenty years. The power of the state through its criminal procedure is, at least on paper, being invoked to compel people to live and do business according to notions which vary much from their existing habits and customs.

Not only were the statutes obtained by reformers a derogation of personal liberty and frequently coercive in nature; they were also intended to provide one section of the community with rights achieved at the expense of another.

The problem was that, even with a full separation of powers, the legislative branch of government could be induced to enact new statutes at such a rate as to swamp the traditional wisdom of the common law. Only the fundamental law of the Constitution could provide a bulwark against these encroachments, and even here a number of recent Supreme Court decisions gave Brandeis cause for concern about the apparent mutability of its interpretation. In fact, though, the underlying conflict between case law and statute had been long developing:

> While the common law was vigilant in preserving freedom of trade, and encouraging all fair competition, the Legislature during much of our country's life has been active in checking it [sic]. . . . Wherever individuals or classes have been strong enough to secure the act of the Legislature to protect them from competition and to disregard the maxim of the Common Law [that "competition is the life of trade"], the aid of the Legislature has been invoked.

Examples of such intervention were legion. Trade unions had successfully lobbied for the banning of alien contract labor, just as business groups had secured tariff legislation; state laws had been enacted against dressed meats, ostensibly as public health measures but actually at the instigation of fresh meat interests; workers had pressed for legislation to restrict access to certain occupations and competition from convict labor. Perhaps the most effective campaign of all had been mounted by the nation's dairy industry, which, not content with obtaining state action against oleomargarine, had carried its case for discriminatory taxation all the way to Washington, D.C. There, as Brandeis explained with evident disgust, the dairymen had

> invoked the power of the United States to protect them from the competition . . . , and after inducing a number of state legislators and state courts to pervert in their favor the police power, they induced Congress to pervert the powers of the Government to raise a revenue by imposing a tax on the business of manu-

facturing and selling oleomargarine, at a time when the principal activity of congressmen should have been devoted to devising means of reducing the revenue of the government.[35]

By means of these and similar strategies, narrow pressure groups were busily reordering the economic, social, and legal fabric of the nation, making over an established pattern of reciprocal rights and duties that had served Americans well since the foundation of the Republic. Their purpose was as selfish as it was potentially destructive: in brief, the single-minded pursuit of their own private advantage, regardless of cost or detriment to the public weal. The resulting social conflict was as though two rival armies, each brandishing its own philosophy of law, stood facing one another across a constitutional battlefield. For his own part, Brandeis seemed to have no doubts whatever about the rightness of mustering among the forces of tradition and precedent.

Notwithstanding the apparent firmness and overall coherence of these convictions, during the next two or three years they would be subjected to wide-ranging reassessment, and within a decade by far the greater part would be repudiated, or at least drastically amended. The question thus presents itself once more: If his immediate reactions to the violence and bloodshed of Homestead cannot be seen as the cause of these changes, what other events, experiences, or personal contacts can? One key element of the answer is suggested by Allon Gal, who points appropriately to the extent of Brandeis's involvement with trade-union activist Mary Kenney and her reporter husband John F. O'Sullivan, then president of the Boston Central Labor Union. Kenney had been to Homestead before the strike in 1892 and had seen for herself the company's preparations for a siege: high walls built around the mill compound with "apertures for guns." Two years later, having married and settled in Boston, she and Brandeis shared a public platform to debate issues raised by the Haverhill shoe-workers strike. Her brief apparently was to talk about conditions faced by the workers; his was to speak about the legal rights of their employers. It was from that point in 1894, according to Gal, that Brandeis "began to reformulate his approach and to realize that trade unions were important to both labor and management." Not long after this disputation, he and the O'Sullivans met again socially, brought together by their mutual friend Elizabeth Glendower Evans. Mary recalled the circumstances in her autobiography: "It was all joy for me when he and Jack O'Sullivan discussed one after the other the problems of industrial betterment. Mr. Brandeis had to be shown and it wasn't easy. He had been thinking on the other side so long. However, his mind was at all times open to conviction. If ever a man talked facts, it was Jack

O'Sullivan." With her own firsthand experiences of labor disputes to relate, she too found Brandeis an "attentive listener"; and as his sister-in-law later noted, "The workers's side on those struggles lost nothing in her telling." In the next few years he spent many evenings in the O'Sullivans' home, and through them came to know a widening circle of Boston's Irish labor leaders. Perhaps this then, rather than his own gut reaction to the Homestead strike, was the source of his education in both trade unionism and the aspirations of America's working classes.[36]

Another important factor leading to Brandeis's intellectual reorientation was the publication of Henry Demarest Lloyd's *Wealth against Commonwealth* (1894), whose highly detailed exposé of the Standard Oil Company's operations greatly impressed him. Perhaps because of perspectives afforded by those who knew him only late in life, there has been a widespread tendency among Brandeis biographers to discount the influence books had on the development of his thinking. Yet because his eyesight enabled him to read relatively few volumes each year, those he did read often had a disproportionately large impact on his outlook. Thus in November 1895, we find him pressing hard for a popular version of Lloyd's rather weighty tome. "The excellent work that he has done should be put in form, so that it will reach the people," he told a magazine editor who had given the book a favorable review. The big problem with trying to take action against the trusts was that such efforts lacked public support.

> The American must be educated. The man who has consciously suffered from the trust is the individual competitor, and, in some instances, the producer. The public as a whole have perhaps suffered in many instances, but not suffered consciously. Our people still admire the Captains of the trusts. The facts collected by Lloyd would, if presented to the people, tend to remove this admiration and make Americans conscious of the dangers under which they are living.

No progress could be achieved against "the trust phalanx" otherwise.[37]

It will be evident from these remarks that Brandeis's attitude toward corporations generally had hardened considerably from those he had been expressing barely three years before. On the limited evidence available, however, it is difficult to say whether this hardening amounted to much more than a readiness to see the trusts now as the prime constitutional malefactors: a role he had previously ascribed to labor organizations and sundry, nameless "humanitarians." There is little reason to think that he had yet jettisoned, or even significantly modified, his belief in the primacy of common law over statute, nor to assume that his strictures about the evils of prolabor legislation had yet been withdrawn or moderated. It is equally doubtful whether the change of focus perceived by Philippa Strum in the published outlines of his M.I.T. lectures for 1894–95 and 1895–96 really deserves the construction she places on it; for on closer inspection the constituent elements of the new section headed "The Legal Relation of Labor and Capital" can be shown to have had their precise counterparts in the earlier transcription. Furthermore, the inference she draws from his abandonment of the more abstract discussion of legal philosophy appears contradicted by a letter he wrote to a Stanford law professor early in 1894. For then, in terms reminiscent of the introduction to his 1892 text, he could still observe:

> Studying law should be conceived as part of a general education, in which the mind is enriched and disciplined. Good teaching relies on adapting the subject to the needs of the student, which vary greatly. Law, like history, economics and philosophy—perhaps even more—can be seen as part of the general growth of the mind, and courses to that end could be developed.

In fact, the continuities of outlook in such expressions are a good deal more obvious than the novelties, and it is probably just as unwise to search for a single moment of conversion in 1894, or 1896, as it surely is to do so in 1892. The likelihood is that Brandeis rethought his theoretical underpinnings piecemeal, whenever personal encounters or new professional experiences could no longer be integrated successfully within the logical patterns of his earlier thinking. Consequently, echoes of this older philosophy would continue to reverberate beneath the surface of his letters and public pronouncements for years to come.[38]

There are, however, two further stimuli to this process of rethinking that seem worthy of more serious consideration than they have hitherto received. The first is the rise of "negative judicial activism" discussed earlier in this chapter. Because of the paucity of his extant correspondence from the 1890s, we have little direct evidence concerning his reaction to the behavior of the judiciary during this critical period, and nothing at all on what he thought about the Supreme Court decisions of 1895; however, it would be dangerous to assume that the ideas which, barely three years earlier, had informed his retrospective approval of Field's dissent in the *Munn* case continued to have his unqualified endorsement. His own courtroom experiences may have begun to give him cause for disquiet. As he told his sister Amy in February that year: "I have spent much time of late before juries and am becoming quite enamored of the Common Sense of the people—and somewhat doubtful of the uncommon Sense of the judges." Yet, in spite of this observation, he evinced little sympathy for Populism, and during the presidential election campaign of 1896 came out strongly against the "fusion" ticket of William Jennings Bryan. "I wish you would see Mr. O'Sullivan," he wrote Bess Evans in August, "and make sure that he does not commit himself to silver." Brandeis was anxious to "take up this question with the workingmen, through him" and warn them off endorsing what he considered the dangerous panacea of monetary inflation. "They are the people most interested—they will lose the ground gained in so many years struggle—if Bryan wins." A newfound enthusiasm for the potential of organized labor was clearly in evidence here: "l look to the workingman's seriousness for our general political salvation," he continued. "I want to talk only to them." From this one might well deduce that his later hostility to the use of the labor injunction originated, in part at least, from the treatment meted out to Debs and his colleagues, and it is just as likely that his subsequent positions on the commerce clause and "substantive due process" were influenced by the *Knight* and *Holden* rulings; however, such speculations lack proof. All that can be said with certainty is that a lawyer of Brandeis's perspicacity and intellectual range could scarcely have ignored the professional and constitutional implications inherent in these and like decisions; and if he long remained suspicious of the potential for tyranny represented by legislative majorities, he was by no means oblivious to the similar threat posed by self-opinionated judicial minorities.[39]

The other spur to self-appraisal and reanalysis was a private one: his marriage at the age of thirty-four to his second cousin, Alice Goldmark. Despite occasional pangs of loneliness, during the 1880s Louis had found little difficulty in putting off thoughts of matrimony until his business was established and his personal finances were secure. Indeed, writing to Charles Nagel in 1879 about his plans for finding a suitable partner when the time came, he revealed an attitude toward women that was as shallow as it was patronizing: "I should become very nervous already, seeing desirable girls marrying & engaging themselves so fast were I not convinced that there are more fish in the sea than were ever caught." Women, he observed to his brother two years later, were "very strange people"; and although he had long enjoyed the company of bright, sophisticated ladies whom he could engage in serious conversation at dinner parties, from stray comments in letters to family and friends it is difficult to resist the conclusion that he regarded most of the younger females with whom he came into contact as frivolous, empty-headed creatures.[40]

Louis first became fully aware of Alice in the spring of 1890. He had been called back to Louisville by the tragic death of his sister Fannie, and on a visit to his Uncle Samuel's discovered that two of his Goldmark cousins were staying there as houseguests. Since their last meeting, Alice had matured into an intelligent, cultured, and vivacious young woman, with whom the successful Boston lawyer found he had much in common. Summer saw the Goldmarks and Brandeises vacationing together in the Adirondacks; and as the days passed, their intellectual and physical attraction blossomed into love. Engaged by September, they were married in a civil ceremony at Alice's apartment the following March. Since childhood, Louis had been used to keeping his emotions in check; to rationalizing his academic and professional successes as the result of "a deep sense of obligation" rather than of private ambition. But now the discovery of a previously unfulfilled passion located deep within his psyche seems to have rocked him on his emotional bearings. "I long for the time when you will be with me always," he wrote his fiancée a few months before their wedding day.

You have become so large a part of my life that I rattle about sorely when you are absent. Is it not strange? For seventeen years I have stood alone—rarely asking— still less frequently caring, for the advice of others. I have walked my way all these years but little influenced by any other individual. And now, Alice, all is changed. I find myself mentally turning to you for advice and approval—indeed, also for support, and I feel my incompleteness more each day. I feel myself each day grow- ing more into your soul, and I am very happy.[41]

Quite apart from its immediate impact on his style of living and sense of personal identity, this newly awakened perception of his own "incomplete- ness" would come to have a lasting effect on Brandeis's wider philosophical outlook as well. Although his faith in the efficacy of logical thought and rational action was too deeply ingrained in him to be set aside, after his mar- riage to Alice the external objectives toward which thought and action were directed would never again be determined without reference to a set of ethical criteria that were themselves, at bottom, emotionally determined. Rigid social attitudes, derived as much from old legal formulas as from out- worn political verities, gradually gave way before a more flexible, if some- times still conservative, pragmatism that was yet balanced and rendered dynamic by a countervailing idealism bordering at times on the Messianic.

Perhaps the first solid evidence of a more enlightened and flexible approach to social problems gaining the upper hand came toward the end of 1894, when he was persuaded to turn his attention toward the problem of pauperism, and in particular toward maladministration of the state-run poorhouse located on Long Island in Boston Harbor. After protracted in- vestigations by a special committee of the Board of Aldermen had revealed widespread abuses in the care and management of this facility, on the re- commendation of his friend Bess Evans, Brandeis agreed to let himself be hired by wealthy philanthropist Alice Lincoln to press for the dismissal of the superintendent and his officials. On looking into the matter with his cus- tomary thoroughness, he concluded that the main fault was incompetence rather than corruption and went on to urge the adoption of new approaches to the care of paupers. Though remaining averse to the indiscriminate outlay of public funds, he became convinced that economy and humanity repre- sented far from incompatible goals, and that the misdirection of effort was as wasteful as the squandering of resources.

In Brandeis's view, the aim of institutional care should rightly be to cure, or better still to prevent, the problems of personal inadequacy and destitu- tion that gave rise to dependency. He strongly supported a case-study approach, by means of which the handicaps of individual inmates could be classified and adequate remedies could be instituted, such as better health care for the sick and a requirement of work from the able-bodied. "There

should be a law passed to provide and compel work," he told the committee, "not merely because it will save the city expense, nor only because it
will decrease the number of inmates, but because it will improve the character of those who work, making them self-supporting and giving them self-
respect." This modern-sounding justification of "workfare," however, was
accompanied by a somewhat less than typical concern for the broader welfare, and indeed the essential personality, of the inmates themselves. Such
people were not machines but human beings, Brandeis insisted, with "emotions, feelings and interests" just like everyone else. The provision of work,
therefore, was only a part of what was needed to effect their rehabilitation.
"They should have entertainments, they may be literary, they may be musical, they may perhaps be of a class hardly worthy to be called either. . . . But
each one of them, and all of them, can be raised and raised only by holding
up before them that which is higher and that which is better than they."
Since men became "degraded" through circumstance rather than choice,
society had a duty to help them where it could and to provide some hope at
least of a better life. "Unless you bring the outer life, the outer sunshine,
into the darkness of the lives of these unfortunates," he told the city fathers,
"you can never expect to get that moral growth to which this institution
should ever strive to bring its inmates. These are the main considerations.
All else is subsidiary."[42]

"Moral growth" had never been a merely rhetorical concept for Brandeis
but constituted the proper goal of all human endeavor. Although ambivalent
about the ultimate perfectibility of man, he believed strongly in the capacity
of each individual for self-improvement. Everything he had experienced,
everything he had read since his youth, only served to reinforce the validity
of this creed. However, the conditions he saw on Long Island, the writings
of contemporary social critics like Henry George and Edward Bellamy,
the violent clashes at Homestead, began during the 1890s to undermine his
naïve conviction that untrammeled opportunity was the birthright of all. As
the decade progressed, he came gradually to appreciate how economic
power, buttressed by the power of the state, could and frequently did distort
the lives of those unlucky enough to fall across its path. For many Progressives in the years ahead the most appropriate response to this situation
appeared to lie in efforts to realign the instrumentalities of state power behind the common people; but for Brandeis the attractions of this solution
would always remain decidedly limited. If individuals had difficulty coping
with corporate bureaucracies, how much better would they fare with government officials? In any case, how ready were politicians to abandon their support of those already rich and powerful? In 1897 he got his first chance to
find out.

In January, he traveled to Washington to testify before the House Ways
and Means Committee on the Dingley tariff bill. He went as counsel for the
New England Free Trade League, an association of small manufacturers

formed to lobby for the lifting of all duties and trade restrictions affecting their industries; his opening remarks, however, made it clear that he regarded himself as holding a wider brief as well. He was appearing "on behalf of the consumer and a large number of workingmen in New England," the committee heard; not to call for free trade but "to object to a change of conditions which are very far removed from free trade." Many of the duties it was now proposed to augment at the behest of special interest groups, already stood at 40 percent or more. The people he represented were not seeking further protection but wanted merely to be left undisturbed so that their businesses might have time to recover from the ravages of the recent depression. He believed he was speaking up for a broader spectrum of interests than those that had held sway hitherto: "for those who want to be left alone, those who do not come to Congress and seek the aid of the sovereign powers of the government to bring them prosperity." He concluded with a sharp indictment of those who relied on state interference for the advantages it afforded them:

> This asking for help from the government for everything should be deprecated. It destroys the old and worthy sturdy principle of American life which existed in the beginning when men succeeded by their own efforts. That is what has led to the evil of protective tariff and other laws to that end, by which men seek to protect themselves from competition.

Such observations did not go down well, even with Democratic members of the committee. What they resented was not so much his advocacy of laissez-faire values, which after all many of them shared, as it was his insistence that these constituted the only means by which the rights and well-being of ordinary citizens could be preserved and promoted. It was a lonely and exposed position to adopt. As one veteran reformer observed in a letter to the *Boston Herald*, with the exception of Brandeis, "not one word of public spirit, not one sentiment implying a thought of equal rights and privileges, has relieved the monotonous record of corporate and private greed which casts its shame upon popular government."[43]

It is clear, therefore, that the insights gained during the 1890s, particularly in the course of defending the inmates of public institutions and opposing high protective tariffs, did not cut Brandeis off completely from the patterns of thinking that had served him well for forty years; much less from his intellectual roots. What they did was to develop still further the concern for ordinary working people, being nurtured in him throughout the decade by a wider range of social experiences and the new set of personal contacts that came along with them. While it may be true, as Edward McClennen alleges, that his participation in public campaigns did not come about because of any "peculiar affection for the underdog," but on the contrary grew out of "the refined lawyer's desire to bring about justice," it is equally the case that Brandeis had emerged from them by the turn of the century with a pattern of attitudes and opinions markedly different from those he had been expressing only a few short years before.[44]

Whatever the precise catalytic ingredient that produced this apparent *volte-face*, there can be no doubt that it constituted only the final element in a complex process of intellectual reevaluation. Although Brandeis's discovery of the Zionist cause after 1912 would ultimately provide him with a novel guiding theme around which to reformulate his ideas about democracy, and in the development of Palestine after 1917 would even afford him a human laboratory in which to see them applied, the ideas themselves were clearly derived from different perceptions, evolved at a much earlier date. His conception of the democratic principle as something more extensive and responsible than mere exercise of the voting franchise stemmed initially from his increasing involvement in public affairs during the last decade of the nineteenth century, and would become increasingly sophisticated thereafter as his activities as a municipal reformer served steadily to deepen his understanding. More specifically, it was his determination to regard working people as possessed of a legitimate claim to take part in decisions affecting their terms and conditions of employment that most directly led to his formulating a broad definition of the democratic process, and to his espousal of a radical program of industrial as well as of political democracy.

On these initial foundations he would eventually construct a superstructure of ideas, not only concerned with the mediation of labor disputes, but also involving such diverse themes as the function and structure of labor unions, the socioeconomic potential of producer and consumer cooperatives, the optimum scale of corporate business, the regulatory responsibilities of government, and much else besides. But the unifying element in each of these considerations would be the same: how best to provide for the personal growth of the individual within a context of personal responsibility and self-respect. Now, in applying his mind to the problems raised by these issues, and perceiving more clearly than before what he believed to be the inescapable limitations inherent in the human condition, he became convinced that institutional structures that failed to take account of such limitations were worse than useless. In this congeries of insights and prescriptions lies the very core of Brandeis's mature philosophy.

However, in view of the considerable reputation as a jurist that he was to achieve in later years, some further interpretation of his remarks about the inadequacies he came to perceive in the common law after 1892 is needed here as well. In the first place, it seems clear that he was not ready to belittle the value of the common-law tradition in general terms but objected principally to its mechanical application, particularly with reference to industrial relations issues. What he learned from the bitter confrontation at Homestead was that the precepts of this tradition were, by themselves, an insufficient guide to the conduct of public policy, particularly where legal formulas and socioeconomic realities appeared to require the adoption of divergent and irreconcilable courses of action. In the second place, he evidently believed that the common-law tradition could and should be supplemented by less prescriptive legal instruments. This in turn led him to try reestablishing the concept of social justice on broader legal foundations, at first by dint of the judicious application of the rules of equity, themselves rooted in the moral principles of natural law; then, when the flaws inherent in equity proceedings became apparent, by calling for a more flexible interpretation of the federal Constitution.

The latent potential of the Constitution as a vehicle for permitting if not exactly promoting social change was probably first inculcated upon his mind by the arguments of James Bradley Thayer, whom he regarded as his "best friend among the instructors at the Law School" and with whom he remained on terms of intimacy thereafter. By the 1890s, Thayer was regarded as a distinguished constitutional theorist, and is remembered as a forthright exponent of the view that this ambiguous document possessed "ample resources within itself to meet the changing needs of successive generations"— a conviction that Brandeis's rich experience at the bar before and after the Homestead strike led him to share. First as an advocate and later as a judge, Brandeis came to regard the Constitution, as Felix Frankfurter later put it, not as "a literary composition but a way of ordering society, adequate for imaginative statesmanship, if judges have imagination for statesmanship."[45]

Whatever previous discussions they may have had on constitutional topics, it was probably not until the fall of 1893 that Brandeis fully internalized the significance of Thayer's thinking on such questions. In that year, the October issue of the *Harvard Law Review* carried the latter's celebrated essay on "The Origins and Scope of the American Doctrine of Constitutional Law"—regarded by Frankfurter as the most important single contribution ever made to discussion of the subject; and although there is no *direct* evidence that Brandeis ever read the article, the parallels between its central emphasis on the need for judges to exercise restraint and his own subsequent position on the limited nature of the judicial function seem too close for mere coincidence.[46]

The core of Thayer's essay was a historical inquiry into the stages and processes by which the American practice of judicial review had evolved to the point where, by the 1890s, judges seemed able to nullify legislative acts at will. The universal acceptance of such a power to be exercised by the judiciary had been slow and far from automatic, and in Thayer's opinion had probably been "helped into existence" by a theory widely canvassed around the time of the Revolution that "courts might disregard such acts if they were contrary to the fundamental maxims of morality, or, as it was phrased, to the laws of nature." However, "where it was the single and necessary ground of the decision," this doctrine had never been implemented by the courts. "Nor can it be," the writer added with an eye to arguments then emerging about the natural-law basis of substantive due process, "unless as a revolutionary measure." Although he claimed to be restating "more exactly and truly" an accepted doctrine, rather than advocating a new one, Thayer was acutely aware that contemporary developments were threatening to undermine it; and toward this he expressed his opposition in uncompromising terms:

> The checking and cutting down of legislative power, by numerous detailed prohibitions in the constitution, cannot be accomplished without making the government petty and incompetent. This process has already been carried much too far in some of our States. Under no system can the power of courts go far to save a people from ruin; our chief protection lies elsewhere.[47]

For Thayer, the proper scope of judicial review was limited to determining whether, for the narrow purpose of deciding a question duly brought before the courts, a disputed exercise of the legislative power was *explicitly* prohibited by the Constitution. Not only did such questions

> call for a peculiarly large method in the treatment of them, but especially they require an allowance to be made by the judges for the vast and not definable range of legislative power and choice, for that wide margin of considerations which address themselves only to the practical judgment of a legislative body. Within that margin, as among all these legislative considerations, the constitutional lawmakers must be allowed a free foot. In so far as legislative choice, ranging here unfettered, may select one form of action or another, the judges must not interfere, since *their* question is a naked judicial one.

Legislators were entitled, indeed required, to reach their own decision as to what was and was not permissible within the state and federal constitutions under which they operated; and only when litigation arose could this prior determination be questioned. Even then their judgments were deserving of respect; for statutes might "accomplish results throughout the country of the profoundest importance" before meeting with any judicial challenge to their constitutionality. This was no accidental occurrence, unforeseen by the constitution makers, he insisted, but a prerogative deliberately entrusted by them to the legislative branch of government—a power

> not merely of enacting laws, but of putting an interpretation on the constitution which shall deeply affect the whole country, enter into, vitally change, even revolutionize the most serious affairs, except as some individual may find it for his private interest to carry the matter into court. . . . The judiciary may well reflect that if they had been regarded by the people as the chief protection against legislative violation of the constitution, they would not have been allowed merely this incidental and postponed control. They would have been let in, as it was sometimes endeavored in the conventions to let them in, to a revision of the laws before they began to operate.[48]

To the specious argument that these observations mistook the nature of the judicial function, and that judges exercised "the mere and simple office" of comparing two written documents and giving force to the superior obligation of constitution over statute whenever the two were found to be in conflict, Thayer entered a scathing rejoinder:

> This way of putting it easily results in the wrong kind of disregard of legislative considerations; not merely in refusing to let them directly operate as grounds of judgment, but in refusing to consider them at all. Instead of taking them into account and allowing for them as furnishing possible grounds of legislative action, there takes place a pedantic and academic treatment of the texts of the constitution and the laws. And so we miss that combination of a lawyer's rigor with a statesman's breadth of view which should be found in dealing with this class of questions in constitutional law. Of this petty method we have many specimens; they are found only too easily to-day in the volumes of our current reports.[49]

What was missing from much contemporary discussion of judicial review, Thayer believed, was any admission that the doctrine enunciated by Marshall in *Marbury v. Madison* (1803) had for many decades thereafter been "supplemented by a very significant rule of administration" succinctly expressed in the words of a Pennsylvania chief justice: "that an Act of the legislature is not to be declared void unless the violation of the constitution is so manifest as to leave no room for reasonable doubt." A member of the Georgia bench was rather more expansive: "No nice doubts, no critical exposition of words, no abstract rules of interpretation, suitable in a contest between individuals, ought to be resorted to in deciding on the constitutional operation of a statute," he maintained incisively. "This violation of a constitutional right ought to be as obvious to the comprehension of every one as an axiomatic truth, as that the parts are equal to the whole." What these and like qualifications amounted to was a plain rule that statutes should be accorded a presumptive constitutionality, unless their subversion of accepted rights was self-evident. "This well-known rule," observed Thayer in a footnote, "is laid down by Cooley, . . . and supported by emphatic judicial declarations and by a long list of citations from all parts of the country."[50]

One further aspect of recent judicial decisions exercised the writer's mind: whether or not it was appropriate for the courts to determine if a legislative act was reasonable. Clearly there was a sphere within which such powers of review might be fully justified.

> If a legislature undertakes to exert the taxing power, that of eminent domain, or any part of that vast, unclassified residue of legislative authority which is called, not always intelligently, the police power, this action must not degenerate into an irrational excess, so as to become, in reality, something different and forbidden,— e.g., the depriving people of their property without due process of law; and whether it does so or not, must be determined by the judges. But in such cases it is always to be remembered that the judicial question is a secondary one. The legislature in determining what shall be done, what it is reasonable to do, does not divide

its duty with the judges, nor must it conform to their conception of what is prudent or reasonable legislation. The judicial function is merely that of fixing the outside border of reasonable legislative action, the boundary beyond which the taxing power, the power of eminent domain, police power, and legislative power in general, cannot go without violating the prohibitions of the constitution or crossing the line of its grants.[51]

Clearly, though, there was a growing body of opinion that wanted to see the courts adopt a more intrusive approach to questions of reasonableness, and to this point of view Thayer remained implacably opposed. In the end, he like John Chipman Gray recognized that constitutional questions had more to do with politics and the stability of society than with law as it was normally defined; the quintessential attributes required by judges were thus statesmanship and the capacity for self-restraint. "What really took place in adopting our theory of constitutional law was this," he explained:

we introduced for the first time into the conduct of government through its great departments a judicial sanction, as among these departments,—not full and complete, but partial. The judges were allowed, indirectly and in a degree, the power to revise the action of other departments and to pronounce it null. In simple truth, while this is a mere judicial function, it involves, owing to the subject-matter with which it deals, taking a part, a secondary part, in the political conduct of government. If that be so, then the judges must apply methods and principles that befit their task. In such a work there can be no permanent or fitting *modus vivendi* between the different departments unless each is sure of the full co-operation of the others, so long as its own action conforms to any reasonable and fairly permissible view of its constitutional power. The ultimate arbiter of what is rational and permissible is indeed always the courts, so far as litigated cases bring the question before them. This leaves to our courts a great and stately jurisdiction. It will only imperil the whole of it if it is sought to give them more.[52]

Whether he read them, or heard them from the writer's own lips, Brandeis appears to have found these arguments extremely persuasive; so much so that they would rapidly come to supersede opinions that he had held and confidently espoused from the time of first embarking on a legal career. Moreover, as he pondered Thayer's exposition, he may well have been especially struck by the professor's suggestion that judges should give full and proper consideration to the grounds on which legislators decided to take action. For this to be done effectively, it would become incumbent on counsel to collect and present in court all the evidence relating to the disputed enactment—not merely evidence as to comparable statutes and judicial precedents, but evidence capable of illuminating the social, economic, and moral considerations that had led to its framing and passage. Herein lay the intellectual seed that would one day germinate and reach full flower as the "Brandeis Brief."[53]

It was thus to insights gained from economics and sociology that Brandeis would be attracted increasingly as the nineteenth century drew to a close; indeed, to a large extent, the "new angles" that he remembered developing with growing conviction after 1892 were provided by his openness to a range of perspectives provided by these new social sciences. Given the professional development of the subject since the 1930s, it is perhaps difficult to take seriously the fact that Louis Brandeis regarded himself, and was regarded by others, as a student of economics. As we have already had occasion to observe, he began his public life with the economic outlook of any Cleveland Democrat. Even in the late 1890s, as his remarks at the tariff hearings amply demonstrated, his conception of political economy remained bounded by the standard liberal virtues of free trade, honest government, and sound money. Harvard's Frank Taussig seems to have been an important early influence in the formation of his economic thinking, just as its president, Charles Eliot, was a potent force propelling him toward the advocacy of Mugwump political principles. But gradually, as Allon Gal has observed, Brandeis became "aware that social and economic justice were not necessarily served by these principles alone." It was this realization that turned him in the direction of Progressivism and toward his growing obsession with the evils of what he liked to call "Bigness."[54]

As we have also seen, however, the awakening of Brandeis's social conscience was in reality neither as sudden nor as monocausal as he later remembered it. Yet another key factor in its development was undoubtedly, as Gal suggests, the firsthand experience he gained in the carrying on of his legal practice. Frankfurter made a similar point in 1936, when he observed that Brandeis's views were "not the products of speculation, but the deposit of an extraordinarily wide and deep experience with the various industries of which . . . [he] for many years was counsel." It will be recalled that the clientele of his law firms (Warren and Brandeis, 1879–97 and Brandeis, Dunbar and Nutter, 1897–1916) were mainly merchants and independent manufacturers, especially in the paper, shoe, and leather industries. Significantly, neither practice had clients in the textile business, nor among Massachusetts's financial and transportation interests. Small and medium-sized companies predominated. Not only did they impress Brandeis with their sense of vigor and enterprise, but their owners tended to share and reinforce his own views on money and the tariff. If many of these people failed to follow him into the Progressive fold, they did at least provide him with some of the formative experiences and associations on which his later intellectual development was based.[55]

It was in the law, though, rather than in economic and social science per se, that this early professional experience led him to seek solutions to the burning social issues of the 1890s. In his perception, the burgeoning urban and industrial problems then belatedly capturing his attention stemmed not from the ineluctable logic of social Darwinism but from uncontrolled industrial development, promoted in the interests of private economic gain. Poverty, crime, labor unrest might become better understood as a consequence of painstaking scholarship in the social sciences, but their amelioration and ultimate eradication required greater legal, not economic, realism. The skepticism he would later develop toward the abstractions of classical economic theory was the effect rather than the cause of the changes in his legal philosophy; for his experiences as a commercial lawyer eventually convinced him that, far from being the inevitable victims of impersonal economic forces, American workers and small businessmen were being sacrificed for reasons that were wholly *avoidable*. Economic relationships existed within a mutable framework of positive law, some of it enshrined in statute, but most of it fabricated by judicial interpretation of the Constitution and the common law. This process of judicial interpretation was not mechanically determined, but developed organically in response both to political pressures and to the arguments of counsel, acting increasingly in the late nineteenth century on behalf of powerful corporate clients.

Likewise, social problems arose in a specific context determined as much by political power as by inanimate market forces; economic resources might indeed be finite, and their supply dependent on factors largely beyond human control, but their distribution was a matter of deliberate choice. Huge differences of wealth and power had developed in America since the Civil War as the direct consequence of decisions taken personally by self-serving politicians, industrialists, financiers, and judges. Recognition of the central role played by legal decisions gradually became a matter of vital, if not paramount, importance for Brandeis. Within his evolving conception of social dynamics, law would continue to be viewed as the keystone of America's class structure; and the reform of judicial policy and practice would thus continue to be viewed as the essential prerequisite of meaningful social change.

4

Toward a New Freedom

The growth of the nation . . . and all our activities are in the hands of a few men who, even if their action be honest and intended for the public interest, are necessarily concentrated on the great undertakings in which their own money is involved and who necessarily, by very reason of their own limitations, chill and check and destroy genuine economic freedom. This is the greatest question of all, and to this statesmen must address themselves with an earnest determination to serve the long future and the true liberties of men.

—Wilson, *The New Freedom*

Few movements in American history are as complex, as seemingly all pervading, yet as elusive as Progressivism; consequently, as might be expected, no informed consensus exists regarding the best way of interpreting it. What may appear as an act of concerned altruism to one scholar, for instance, may frequently be taken as proof of a self-interested conspiracy by another, and such a major difference over motivation may just as easily be replicated with reference to other key issues like the relative importance of ideas, the social profile of participants, or the critical evaluation of socioeconomic outcomes. It cannot be the function of this study to provide a lasting resolution of these and similar disagreements, but Brandeis's involvement in several of the most controversial reform campaigns of the period does appear to make a schematic depiction of the Progressive landscape desirable, if not indeed essential.[1]

Whatever else it may have become, the wave of reforming zeal that swept across America during the first two decades of the twentieth century was in origin and essence a response to the manifold problems thrown up by industrialization. The "crisis of the 1890s" was primarily a crisis of perception, leading to a widespread fear among the nation's elites that the established order might soon collapse into chaos; but if in retrospect these anxieties seem to have been exaggerated, the evidence of social dysfunction on which they fed was real enough. Great commercial cities and raw industrial towns positively heaved with the weight of humanity pouring into their factories, sweatshops, and tenement houses, and were patently ill equipped to cope with the problems of sanitation, transportation, education, and public order that resulted. Whether the newcomers were peasants from Calábria or farm boys from Kansas, their influx meant a steadily mounting physical burden for the already teeming urban environment to bear, and presented municipal governments with a welter of conflicting demands which they generally lacked the resources to meet. If the economic depression of the mid-1890s naturally fastened the public's attention on agrarian discontent and industrial violence, the returning prosperity that ushered in the new century left room for the expression of more general doubts. Fears of epidemic disease, cultural inundation, and moral enfeeblement took their places alongside the already well-established specter of proletarian insurgency in the minds of a growing number of middle-class Americans, and were soon given an even sharper focus thanks to the graphic literary skills of novelists like Upton Sinclair and journalistic "muckrakers" such as Lincoln Steffens.[2]

If this were not enough to contend with, the older issues of corruption in government and combination in industry remained high on the agenda of "liberal" reformers; indeed, the growing awareness of urban degeneration and squalor actually lent them a new urgency and relevance. Orderliness and efficiency in local administration could now be proffered as the only reasonable and cost-effective means of responding adequately to the multiple demands for action pressing in on City Hall. At the same time, the wave of mergers that occurred between 1897 and 1904 revived worries that had lain largely dormant since the passage of the Sherman Act in 1890, and led to renewed calls for state and federal action to halt the rapidly increasing trend toward economic concentration and monopoly. As a result of this felicitous conjuncture of issues, after 1900 the optimism and vitality found particularly among the new social-welfare reformers was engrafted on the more deeply rooted stock of an older "genteel" liberalism, producing thereby not one but a series of Progressive types: some focusing on "good government" issues, others on the trust question; some campaigning narrowly against child labor and alcohol abuse, others throwing their weight behind the broader struggle for social justice. Tariff reduction, women's suffrage, conservation, labor legislation, the elimination of prostitution, and the provision of better public education—these and many other issues were thrown into the hopper of Progressive reform.[3]

These differences of focus and emphasis were not, however, the only lines of cleavage apparent within the rapidly developing coalition for change. For one thing, reform campaigners came from a variety of different occupational backgrounds, and brought with them widely differing sets of values and social aspirations. As well as lawyers and doctors, social workers and academics, there could also be found a substantial leaven of career politicians, battle-hardened journalists, and Protestant ministers inspired by the Social Gospel. Most significant of all, perhaps, especially among the antitrust and "good government" sections of the movement, were those members of the business community who, rather than standing four-square behind the status quo, opted instead to work with and shape the thrust of reform in ways that were congenial to their own outlook and interests. In marked contrast, though energetic in pursuit of measures to improve their own conditions, labor activists and black leaders were conspicuously absent from the broader sweep of reform agitation; reciprocally, industrial relations and racial discrimination were evidently of little interest to most "social justice" reformers. Nevertheless, although the "typical" Progressive was likely to be a young professional man or woman from a well-to-do Yankee family, such a profile was by no means universal; already in his midforties as the new century opened, a Southerner, and of course a Jew, Brandeis himself was by these tokens far removed from the textbook template of what a Progressive reformer ought to be.[4]

Diverse backgrounds tended to make for diverse goals. If social workers and evangelical ministers were generally energized by motives of altruism and compassion for the disadvantaged, albeit within an austere judgmental framework of bourgeois values and moral certainties, the forces driving other Progressives are often more difficult to identify. The "status anxiety" thesis first advanced by Richard Hofstadter, and the allied notion developed by Samuel P. Hays and Robert H. Wiebe of middle-class groups seeking to establish for themselves a niche within the ruling elite by virtue of their professional expertise, doubtless go some way toward explaining the participation of many reformers. Likewise, the concern of some business leaders to stabilize markets by involving government in the processes of regulation has been amply demonstrated by Gabriel Kolko and James Weinstein, even if their "corporate liberalism" theory is conceptually inadequate to account for the widespread involvement of businessmen in municipal reform campaigns. At this most parochial level, the delicate task of warding off violent social upheaval at the same time as keeping taxes low and morals high was arguably at the root of much reform activity, and especially of the drives for order and efficiency in which local chambers of commerce frequently played so prominent a role. In practice, though, several of these spurs to action might easily overlap one another, with personal frustrations and setbacks combining in the same individual with principled indignation, fears of disease and disorder, or the promptings of a Christian conscience. In short, Progressivism was rarely the result of a single motive impulse.[5]

As the years went by, however, more serious rifts began to develop within the reformist camp—rifts that reflected fundamental differences of ideology between the different groups. For many Progressives, reform was a moral crusade in which clear ethical principles not only required their involvement and informed their analysis, but also determined the agenda to which they worked. This group placed a high value on helping the individual achieve both economic and moral autonomy, and required that ordinary people be permitted and prepared to accept responsibility for decisions affecting their own lives. The archetypical arena for its activities was small-scale and local;

certainly most of its members saw the family and community, city and state as more relevant contributors to meaningful socioeconomic change than the nation and its political counterpart, the federal government. At the opposite pole of Progressivism were those more deeply influenced by the philosophy of pragmatism, for whom moral relativism seemed a concept more fully attuned to the realities of twentieth-century existence. For those thus inclined, broad collectivist planning, worked out and applied by an interventionist federal bureaucracy, was infinitely preferable to the application of localized, piecemeal solutions. Social and economic problems that were national in scope demanded national solutions by way of response. Allowing for the inevitable compromises and confusions that attend any attempt to embody ideas in institutional form, this was the ideological gulf that divided reformers during the presidential election of 1912; for the latter group bulked large among the supporters of Theodore Roosevelt's "New Nationalism," whereas the former saw their ideas encapsulated in the "New Freedom" program propounded by Woodrow Wilson. And if in the next few years the practicalities of office and war went some way toward blunting the ideological sharpness of such distinctions in the minds of President Wilson and his administration colleagues, they often remained somewhat clearer among supporters and advisers who lacked any direct responsibility for turning ideas into policies, and policies into workable laws. Among these, Louis Brandeis must be considered one of the most prominent.[6]

Although it followed a familiar pattern of development from local to state and from state to national level activity, Brandeis's Progressivism is not at all easy to classify, and many previous attempts to formulate valid generalizations have either wrecked on the shoals of overwhelming detail or strayed off course in pursuit of some particular strand of argument or activity. Moreover, few observers have paid sufficient attention to the evidence for his continuing intellectual growth and progression in the two decades after 1900, and even fewer have given the stabilizing counterweight of his earlier conservatism its proper due in their evaluation of his later Progressivism. One who has is Richard M. Abrams, and his assessment is worth quoting at some length. Brandeis, he notes,

> shared with "the classes" of his adopted city [i.e., Boston] the traditional tenets of the American faith: that there are certain eternal moral truths which inhere in the human soul, that men of all classes can agree on and have an interest in upholding these truths, and that America has a mission to cultivate the principles of goodness in all men. Fundamentally, Brandeis represented an advanced variety of the "Mugwump type." Once the Mugwumps had thought character was enough; social conflict emanated, they believed, from dishonesty, irresponsibility, and ignorance. Many of them never became emancipated from this view. Others, like Brandeis, shifted their role from defenders of established moral values to critics of the social order, even while they continued to assume the validity of those values.

What makes Abrams's estimate of particular value is less its generalized insight into the mind-set of genteel-reformers-turned-Progressives than the specific explanatory framework within which this elucidation is embedded.[7]

The essential burden of his argument is that as the new century dawned Massachusetts already made contributions to the general welfare of its citizens more far-reaching, and enforced standards of behavior in business and politics more stringent, than those campaigned for by Progressive reformers elsewhere in the country; and that, since these standards tended to place the commonwealth at a disadvantage alongside the laxer regimes of its competitors, any change in public policy was likely to be in the direction of their erosion. Thus the major campaigns waged in Massachusetts by Brandeis and his associates in the Public Franchise League can easily be viewed as both Progressive and conservative at one and the same time. "Significantly," Abrams observes, "they did not contend for *reforms*; they made their fight for the preservation of the traditional view of the Commonwealth's relationship to business and public service corporations." Briefly stated, this "traditional view" was that

> the state bore the principal responsibility for enforcing the honest management and true valuation of corporate properties; it regarded capital stock as a measure of the owners' interests in a corporate enterprise as well as a guarantee fund for the corporation's creditors; it included in its definition of fraud the issuing of stock dividends, borrowing beyond existing capital stock, and operating a corporation before all the capital had been paid in.

By the close of the nineteenth century practically no other state in the Union continued to interpret its responsibilities in this paternalistic light. "Modern" opinion preferred to give corporate managers a much freer rein, and the exercise of such autonomous power was fundamentally incompatible with an intrusive regulatory regime designed to protect as its first priority the interests of investors and the wider community. In Brandeis's own case, as we have seen, respect for the more traditional way of doing things was in part a facet of his own familial inheritance; more important, however, it was a product of his legal training and of two decade's practice as a commercial attorney acting for small and medium-sized firms—firms with justifiable fears about the effects that deregulation of already huge corporate businesses might have on their own commercial prospects. In a period that had witnessed the development of several large center firms seeking to overcome the financial, social, and legal obstacles standing in the way of their further expansion and consolidation, the novel arguments adduced in court by smart corporate lawyers hired to promote their clients' interests by whatever means came first to hand may have contributed something to the widespread image of the legal profession as one characterized by unprincipled iconoclasts; but as one distinguished constitutional historian commented shrewdly in 1917, "the normal function of the law is conservative, and not even the reformer would have it otherwise, once he has obtained his objective."[8]

For all its perception and utility, however, the picture that Abrams paints of Brandeis's Progressivism remains static and incomplete. Positions taken or views articulated in 1902 are assumed to refer equally in the altered circumstances prevailing a decade later—a point well illustrated by the erroneous inference that he continued to support the use of labor injunctions and remained opposed to women's suffrage. Furthermore, while it illuminates a field of operations in which the "people's attorney" was largely *reactive* against developments occurring elsewhere and actuated by others, as with his crusade against the New Haven Railroad, Abrams's interpretation neglects and leaves obscure those areas in which Brandeis was *proactive*, such as the forms of legal advocacy, the harmonization of industrial relations, and (especially after 1912) the regulation of business by federal agencies. It is also true that, although his activities may appear somewhat atypical when measured beside those of such "insurgent" Progressives as Wisconsin's Robert M. LaFollette or California's Hiram Johnson, Brandeis's enthusiasm for the empirical study of social phenomena, whether as the groundwork for a legal argument or as a means of comprehending the ramifications of economic change, places him squarely in the mainstream of Progressive social thought. Similarly, his wholehearted endorsement of Frederick W. Taylor's theories of "scientific management," and his own insistence that organized labor might actually benefit from their adoption by American industry, associates him closely with that passion for efficiency and order which many commentators have identified as such a key component of the Progressive matrix. Thus if Brandeis was not exactly a liberal pragmatist in the mold of Theodore Roosevelt or Herbert Croly, neither by 1912 could he be thought of as a standpat conservative in the image of Henry Cabot Lodge.[9]

To a considerable extent, the characteristic features of Brandeis's Progressivism were determined in relation to the continuing evolution of his jurisprudence. Increasingly central to his conception of the law in the years after Homestead was his understanding that the logic of legal reasoning could not by itself suffice to settle contentious questions of public policy. What lawyers and judges required to make their arguments and opinions relevant and decisive in the real world—the world of subconscious motives and conflicting interests—was an up-to-date knowledge of the social, economic, and political circumstances surrounding the case at hand. "Know thoroughly each fact," he counseled himself in an an early memorandum on what practice of the law ought to include.

> Don't believe client witness. Examine documents. Reason; use imagination. Know bookkeeping—the universal language of business: know persons. Far more likely to impress clients by knowledge of facts than by knowledge of law. Know not only

specific case, but whole subject. Can't otherwise know the facts. Know not only those facts which bear on direct controversy, but know all the facts and law that surround.

Needless to say, perhaps, few opponents would ever catch Brandeis out on a question of fact.[10]

Characteristically, practices and habits of mind that he found to be of utility in his own career were then frequently pressed onto other people as though the reasoning behind them were axiomatic. "You are prone in legal investigation to be controlled by logic and to underestimate the logic of facts," he had admonished a junior colleague early in 1893. "Knowledge of the decided cases and of the rules of logic alone cannot make a great lawyer." In Brandeis's view, an intimate "knowledge of human necessities" was indispensable, and for this broad experience and a wide circle of acquaintance were essential prerequisites.

No hermit can be a great lawyer, least of all a commercial lawyer. When from a knowledge of the law, you pass to its application the need of a full knowledge of men and of their affairs becomes even more apparent. The duty of a lawyer today is not that of a solver of legal conundrums; he is indeed a counselor at law. Knowledge of the law is of course essential to his efficiency, but the law bears to his profession a relation very similar to that which medicine does to that of the physicians. . . . The great physicians are those who in addition to that knowledge of therapeutics which is opened to all, know not merely the human body but the human mind and emotions, so as to make themselves the proper diagnosis—to know the truth which their patients fail to disclose and who add to this an influence over the patients which is apt to spring from a real understanding of him [sic].[11]

Twenty year's later, his advice to a frustrated young man, then working in a business office by day and studying law at night, ran along similar lines. His time spent in "a commercial house" was by no means wasted, Brandeis informed him, because proficiency in the law demanded familiarity with affairs, men, and human nature, as well as technical know-how. "The time that you spend in business," he prophesied, "may ultimately prove to be the most profitable preparation for an honorable and useful pursuit of your profession." He should therefore use wisely the opportunities it afforded for observation and self-education. "Learn, above all things, to understand thoroughly business, business habits of mind, business practices, and business men; and treat every activity in life with which you come in contact as simply educating you to a better performance [in your chosen profession]."[12]

This emphasis on the facts of business life was not simply a consequence of his being engaged in the practice of commercial law, but followed naturally from his growing awareness that the changes occurring in American industry and finance constituted the most important single feature on the contemporary political landscape. He realized too that, since the fundamental parameters of American politics were themselves determined by the exis-

tence of a written constitution, lawyers and judges were inevitable participants in the political process, whether they entered into their roles reluctantly or with relish. As he told a meeting of the Harvard Ethical Society in
1905, a lawyer's training made him well suited "to grapple with the questions which are presented in a democracy"; and particularly so in America,
where political issues so frequently presented themselves in legal form.
Those charged with a young lawyer's legal education aimed at the development of his judgment as well as the increase of his knowledge.

> His early training—his work with books in the study of legal rules—teaches him
> patient research and develops both the memory and the reasoning faculties. He
> becomes practiced in logic; and yet the use of the reasoning faculties in the study
> of law is very different from their use, say, in metaphysics. The lawyer's processes
> of reasoning, his logical conclusions, are being constantly tested by experience. He
> is running up against facts at every point. Indeed it is a maxim of the law: Out of
> the facts grows the law; that is, propositions are not considered abstractly, but
> always with reference to facts.

Yet a lawyer's investigation and use of facts differed markedly from the
methodology of scientists and scholars, who properly refrained from
reaching conclusions till all the available evidence had been collected and
weighed. Lawyers had perforce to reason from the limited range of facts
within their grasp. "If the lawyer's practice is a general one, his field of
observation extends, in course of time, into almost every sphere of business
and of life. The facts so gathered ripen his judgment. His memory is trained
to retentiveness. His mind becomes practiced in discrimination as well as in
generalization. He is an observer of men even more than of things."[13]

This is not to suggest that Brandeis was entirely sanguine about the legal
profession, or about the education of those being prepared to embark on
it—far from it. When in 1909 a magazine editor sought his views on the usefulness of a series of articles that challenged lawyers to "raise the standard
of their professional ethics," he expressed warm approval. "They need to be
educated," he asserted. "Many of the best men of the profession recognize
no ethical standard above that of loyalty to clients and prudent honesty with
the court. They fail to realize their responsibility to the community and to
others than their clients for the proper use of the tools which their professional training and ability have forged for them." A year later, during the
celebrated Ballinger-Pinchot controversy, he referred bitterly to lawyers
who had "prostituted the law to their purposes," and who had "made legal
decisions the excuses for reversing policies which did not suit them"; and in
1912 he could write of improving the education of lawyers as a necessary
step toward "overcoming the inefficiency of the law." As he told a prominent magazine editor: "This involves primarily the specialization of legal
education, and that in turn requires that lawyers should not merely learn
rules of law, but their purpose and effect when applied to the affairs of man.

In other words,—a study of the facts, human, industrial, social, to which they are to be applied."[14]

As a practical corollary to these views, Brandeis became convinced of the need to make the judiciary take cognizance of socioeconomic circumstances before reaching decisions that might entail dire social and economic consequences for working people and their families. Such was the intellectual rationale behind the sociologically oriented "Brandeis brief" put before the U.S. Supreme Court in *Muller v. Oregon* (1908), which involved legislation intended to limit the maximum hours worked by women in that state to ten a day. Prior to the revolutionary argument presented in the Oregon case, wrote Felix Frankfurter in 1916, "social legislation was argued before our courts practically *in vacuo*, as an abstract question unrelated to a world of factories and child labor and trade unions and steel trusts." Now, for the first time, counsel was attempting to marshal before the highest court in the land "the facts of modern industry which reasonably called for legislation limiting hours of labor."[15]

However, such novelties of presentation should not obscure the fundamental fact that in *Muller*, as in all other public causes that he agreed to take up, Brandeis believed himself to be acting in a quintessentially "lawyer-like" way, to be upholding the best traditions of American legal practice. This is a point made forcefully by Edward F. McClennen, a member of Brandeis's firm in 1908, who later insisted that the proper significance of the case had been largely overlooked by supporters and critics alike. Frequently cited for the light it shed on his character, or "as a specimen of his work for the oppressed," McClennen believed that the real importance of the Oregon brief lay in its exemplification of his work *as a lawyer*. As he explained many years later:

> It is true that he was importuned to go into it by those interested in the welfare of overworked women. This was a course which had a strong appeal to him. It was enough to make him look into the questions involved. This done, the impelling cause of his taking the case up was that in the state of the decisions [*sic*] he saw grave danger that a judicial error might be made if the case were presented in the routine manner, and that therefore he ought to do what he could to secure the right decision.

Having reformulated the problem in this way, he was able to set about rethinking the means needed to solve it. "It did not require the inclinations of a sociologist or the attributes of benevolence," McClennen maintained. "It required the perception of a skillful lawyer."[16]

Roscoe Pound made a similar point, a few days after President Wilson nominated Brandeis to a seat on the Supreme Court in 1916. "His friends . . . make a great mistake in urging as his chief qualification his views upon social questions and the eminent services he has performed in the public interest," he wrote the chairman of the Senate subcommittee charged with investigating the nominee. "Important as these matters are, their importance does not lie immediately in the direction of qualification for the bench. What is not generally known is that Mr. Brandeis is in very truth a very great lawyer." He then went on to identify the revolutionary nature of the brief filed in *Muller*, whose real point, he believed, was not so much its advocacy of social legislation, as it was "the breadth of perception and remarkable legal insight which enabled him to perceive the proper mode of presenting such a question."[17]

The majority decision three years earlier in *Lochner v. New York* (1905), where a law fixing maximum hours of work in bakeries had been held unconstitutional, seemed on the face of things to have established a precedent for invalidating the Oregon statute as well. Certainly there was little reason to believe that a law applying to women only would fare any better on that ground alone. The State of Oregon had enacted its law in 1903, before the *Lochner* decision was handed down, taking its cue from the ruling in *Holden v. Hardy* (1898), which had upheld a law restricting the working day of miners to an eight-hour maximum because of the hazards associated with the industry. Ignoring the orthodox approach, which would have required him to search out such favorable precedents and to make as much as he could of the distinctions in the unfavorable ones, Brandeis based his case instead on the Court's own ruling: namely, that a state legislature might legitimately interfere with liberty of contract, provided it could be shown that such interference was needed to protect the health of workers; and moreover that the legislature was entitled to determine for itself, subject to judicial review, whether such a restriction of liberty was required, and, if so, the appropriateness of the means adopted for the purpose. The measure to be employed was the *reasonableness* of the legislation thus enacted. What he did in his brief and oral argument was, as McClennen put it, "to present not refinements or extensions of principles of law, but facts disclosed by scientific investigation"; to assert that the "matters of general knowledge," which the justices might be expected to take into consideration, could not be equated solely with what professional lawyers knew. In Brandeis's view, the majority decision in *Lochner* represented not so much a departure from the relevant principles of law as a misapplication of those principles, brought about by an ignorance of the facts of common experience. The chances of obtaining a reversal of opinion in the *Muller* case, he believed, turned on his ability to provide the justices with "a convincing sense of these facts."[18]

To achieve this goal, he presented the Court with a brief containing two pages of legal argument and more than a hundred pages of "sociological" evidence compiled by his sister-in-law, Josephine Goldmark, and her team of researchers. The citations were taken not from law reports and legal treatises, but from the statements of physicians, factory inspectors, social workers, and industrial commissioners: expert testimony from a dozen countries and some of it going back more than half a century. One legal historian has summed up its principal findings thus:

Brandeis's brief showed that every reliable nonjuridical authority in Western Europe and North America knew that excessively long hours of work are harder on women than on men, and further, that because women bear children the physical well-being of humanity requires that their working hours be limited. One citation after another proved that long hours of work led to breakdowns in women's health and morals—to illness, to alcoholism, and to prostitution.

The Oregon law was reasonable, Brandeis maintained, because the health of working women and the welfare of the community as a whole required that excessive hours of toil for women should be outlawed. The justices listened to the argument with respectful attention, and after almost six weeks taken to consider the evidence decided unanimously to uphold the statute.[19]

After 1908, though he might often be dismayed and depressed by the decisions of individual courts or exasperated by the reactionary reasoning of individual judges, Brandeis never seriously questioned the practical utility of fashioning the American legal system into an instrument for social advancement. The relationship that ought to exist between the judicial and the legislative branches of government, and more particularly between the judiciary and the executive, would come to demand more and more of his attention in the years ahead; yet he remained from choice a jurist rather than a politician, and such difficulties as the separation of powers presented (and in practice he found them to be few) did little to alter his underlying conviction that the fabric of the law should both determine and reflect the fundamental order of a civilized society.

Brandeis's victory in *Muller v. Oregon* not only constitutes a landmark in the development of "sociological jurisprudence," but in the private sphere also marks the culmination of a lengthy process of intellectual reevaluation that had started more than a decade before. We saw in the last chapter how external events and personal experiences combined during the 1890s to fracture the intellectual certitude and complacency that had carried him through law school and the early years of legal practice. Not only did the experiences of marriage and parenthood predispose him toward the adoption of a more humane and sympathetic social philosophy, but rather more significantly the facts and observations that accumulated as a by-product of his professional method progressively undermined the theoretical underpinnings of his world view. Faced with the growing disparity between a perception of social reality informed by hard evidence and a body of sociolegal doctrine absorbed more or less uncritically during more than three decades of self-education, it was characteristic of the man that he should *begin* the highly unsettling task of questioning the relevance of his ideas rather than take the easier course of quietly ignoring or explaining away facts which he found ideologically inconvenient. But that did not mean that all his earlier thinking was automatically jettisoned, or that some alternative philosophy was adopted wholesale. Some notions were indeed modified or abandoned altogether, but the majority were carefully reworked until the resulting framework of thought was capable of explaining the external world as he had come to perceive it. What barely changed at all was his underlying system of values, inculcated in youth and perfected in early manhood, which not only gave meaning to his perceptions, but also served to direct his actions both public and private. Self-reliance, civic virtue, and responsibility for one's own moral development would remain the watchwords of his personal creed throughout life, and not infrequently provided the yardsticks by which he measured the merits and achievements of others.

Yet the most important word in the foregoing paragraph is "begin"; for what is clear is that the process of reassessment which got underway after Homestead was far from being completed when the Progressive Era opened, or for that matter when he took up his seat on the United States Supreme Court. Rather, the critical reappraisal and reformulation of old ideas became for Brandeis an almost continual mental process from the mid-1890s onward, giving some substance to the charges of inconsistency that were leveled against him at his confirmation hearings. It was as though, having been forced to give up one fixed system of thought, he became reluctant to commit himself to any other, lest it too should become untenable.

The result was an outward persona that soon became associated in the public consciousness with action rather than with ideas; and behind it the brooding intellect of an unexpectedly private man whose surviving correspondence, though voluminous, provides historians with few insights into the workings of his mind. As Thomas K. McCraw has recently observed with reference to the collected edition of these seemingly opaque documents:

> None of the letters conveyed the impression of a deep conceptual intelligence. In them there was little evidence of reflection, none of rumination. There was no . . . agonizing over one's proper role in life or relationship with God, no self-doubt on any score. Instead the letters depicted a quick, confident, and often rigid mind preoccupied with some immediate practical task—a controlled, carefully managed life with no wasted motion, little humor, and no frivolity.

However, while these remarks may constitute a more or less valid description of the letters considered in isolation, there is other evidence contemporary with them to suggest that the inferences drawn constitute rather too hasty and trite an assessment of the letter writer himself. For in his defense it may be argued that philosophical premises, even inarticulate ones, can frequently be identified as the wellsprings of action, and that a focus on the particular does not necessarily preclude the processes of inductive reasoning by which more general principles may in time be reached. What is needed before a more penetrating assessment of Brandeis's mature outlook can be reconstructed is a longer perspective and a more analytical approach.[20]

Before his participation and victory in the *Muller* case, almost all of Brandeis's public activities took place within Massachusetts, and many of these within the city of Boston and its immediate environs. Though not much taken up with party politics at any time in his life, throughout the 1890s he identified nominally as a Democrat, having become a member of the Young Men's Democratic Club early in the decade. Happy enough with the local reformism of William E. Russell, in 1896 a poll of the club's members revealed that more than three-quarters of them were ready to distance themselves from their party's Chicago platform and from Bryan's presidential candidacy. At the end of July these "Gold Democrats" issued a manifesto reaffirming their commitment to sound money, limited government, and individual liberty, in which they decried the leadership's capitulation to the extreme demands of Populist agitators. Brandeis was among the signatories, and for the remainder of the campaign volunteered his rhetorical skills to the anti-Bryan cause.

One explanation for this conservative reaction is that Bryan's patent animus against the eastern business community alienated many of those who, like Brandeis, saw businessmen as a potential agency for promoting social change within the urban environment. Another, equally plausible reason, given our knowledge of Brandeis's earlier views, is that he still identified more closely with the attitudes of Boston's Brahmin elite than he did with the aspirations of its critics and detractors. This second interpretation is perhaps given further weight by the fact that, as "the people's lawyer" of later years, he came to view the Populist rank and file, if not their eponymous champion with a measure of retrospective sympathy. "I forgive the great West its Bryanism—and all the vagaries economic and social which that broad term comprises," he wrote Alice from Nebraska in the fall of 1899. The rigors of the agricultural depression "might well have robbed the sanest of reason—and of hope, within the realm of ratiocination." He evidently continued to regard the monetary nostrums offered by Bryan himself as misguided; his letter referred to "the cruel torture" of deflating Populist hopes "slowly through a long series of years" and asserted his belief that it would "have been a mercy [to] shatter at a blow" the chimerical dreams of their leaders. Yet the finality of this judgement was tempered by a new sense of compassion. "Prosperity here would be only tolerable," he concluded. "Adversity must have been indeed dreadful. Let those who believe in gratitude give deepest thanks tomorrow that they live in Massachusetts."[21]

Whatever the motives behind it, Brandeis's stance in 1896 did nothing to endear him to Democratic party regulars, some of whom even went so far as to challenge his presence at a ward caucus held shortly after the election; and though he survived this attempt to oust him altogether from the party fold, and continued to regard himself as a Democrat, the public crusades he undertook in subsequent years could only succeed in mustering intermittent and lukewarm backing from members of his own party. Indeed, according to

Geoffrey Blodgett, the perceptive historian of genteel reform in Massachusetts, it was this lack of reliable partisan support that more than any other factor helped determine the nature and scope of his early Progressivism. Noting like Professor Abrams that Brandeis's campaigns were generally negative in purpose, intended primarily "to prevent things from happening," Blodgett takes the argument a stage further. Hindered by "the bankrupt condition" of the commonwealth's Democrats after 1896, he observes,

> he was rarely in a position to initiate positive or corrective reforms without substantial Republican support. It was not until Brandeis escaped from the political matrix of Massachusetts and could identify himself with the regenerated national Democratic party after 1910 that his Progressivism bloomed in full creative fashion.[22]

In fact, his association with urban campaigning had actually begun a few years before Bryan's divisive nomination, when in 1893 he joined with other protesters to oppose the West End Railway's plans to extend its tracks across Boston Common. His intervention at the public hearings was evidently impressive. "Never before this morning," a delighted correspondent informed him afterward, "has it been my good fortune to hear so logical, clear and convincing an argument on the very important question of street franchises as that made by you at the state house. I wish that your remarks could be printed and sent to every taxpayer in the city." But though he would later refer to the West End fight as his "first important public work," he was not yet by any means the accomplished master of obstruction that he would soon become; neither did his involvement in this particular local issue necessarily betoken any broader urban commitments, at least in the short term. "I ought to be reading on Municipal Reform in which I am credited with being interested," he wrote his sister early in 1895. "But my ignorance is quite dense. On the whole I warn you not to believe anything Alice reports me as doing."[23]

During the next two decades, however, the problems associated with local and regional transportation systems were to become one of his principal interests; and it was his activities in this field, more than any other, that were to lead to the crystallization of his thinking about the twin phenomena of monopolistic enterprise and corporate scale. But this was not the only area of concern to engage his attention: One after another, such diverse issues as the rates charged by power utilities, allegations of dishonesty leveled against public officials, and the job of setting up a viable negotiating machinery for the New York garment industry were subjected to the incisive scrutiny of his powerful intellect. A sustained involvement with these and similar subjects also led inevitably to the gradual widening of his Progressive horizons from their initial focus on Boston and its hinterland, through an intermediate concentration on the larger economic landscape of the New England region, to the ultimate emergence of a genuinely national perspective. This evolution-

ary process would culminate at length with his participation in the ideological conflicts of the 1912 campaign and the struggle to establish an audacious
legislative agenda for Wilson's first term as president.

It is not the intention here to imitate the excellent detailed accounts of
Brandeis's Progressive involvements already made available by his numerous biographers; more important for our purposes will be the delicate task
of plucking from the morass of information about his activities the vital flin-
ders of evidence capable of identifying and illuminating his thoughts. Nevertheless, some brief discussion of his principal campaigns is needed to provide a context for subsequent analysis.

Between 1897 and 1902 he was deeply involved in legislative wrangling
over the terms of the franchise sought by the Boston Elevated Railway
Company to consolidate and develop the city's new electric railway system.
Those opposed to the company's plans for taking over the assets of the West
End Railway, consisting mainly of elements of the Reform Club, the Municipal League, and the Associated Board of Trade, proceeded to orchestrate
a brilliant public awareness campaign in the local press, and to organize a
series of public assemblies protesting the creation of an effective monopoly
on terms disadvantageous to the community. In 1901, after four years of in-
conclusive skirmishing, the Elevated at last appeared to be gaining the upper hand when a bill giving effect to its demands for a long-term franchise
with guaranteed immunity from enforced rate reductions passed through
both chambers of the Massachusetts legislature with decisive majorities.
Even the accession of the Boston Chamber of Commerce, the Boston Central Labor Union, and the newly formed Public Franchise League to the
opposing coalition was insufficient to resist a measure that enjoyed biparti-
san support among the city's political leaders. Only the governor's veto
prevented the company achieving its goal. Yet this was to prove sufficient,
for the following year its directors capitulated by accepting the lease of crucial subway connections on the more restrictive terms demanded by the
protesters.[24]

Brandeis played a leading role in these efforts to thwart the company's
plans. First as a private citizen, then as counsel to the Board of Trade, and
latterly as founder and principal motive force behind the Public Franchise
League, he worked tirelessly to ensure that the time-honored relationship
between the commonwealth and a chartered corporation created by it
should be upheld. The principles underlying this relationship were essentially those espoused in his lectures at the Massachusetts Institute of Technology ten years before, and grew out of his conception of what the common
law and Constitution required of politicians and business leaders alike. In
rhetorical terms, though, he and others were inclined to represent the issues

raised as a fight between "the People and the Trusts," thereby linking public conceptions of a specific commercial question to a general and highly contentious interpretation of socioeconomic developments occurring within the nation at large. For the moment this analysis was one they were rather more keen to assert than to prove. More accurately, as Richard Abrams has suggested, the contest was one "between a dynamic, speculative element in the business community which aspired to exploit modern financial techniques, and a conservative element which cherished traditional business methods and the traditional state-corporation relationship." Moreover, it was clear that the Elevated's scheme enjoyed a considerable measure of popular support, both from those who saw it as a source of employment and those who welcomed the provision of a much-needed public improvement that did not require the city to dip into its own coffers.

Even accepting that there was an element of speculation involved in this project, and that the company's backers were seeking to make the best deal they could, it remains a fact that the relatively high returns offered by industrial securities from the late 1890s onward made new capital difficult to obtain for investment in public-service corporations forced to operate within the regulatory straitjacket favored by Brandeis and his associates. Neither, at the time, was there anything to suggest that the latter understood or even recognized the nature of such financial constraints. Yet when the dispute flared up again in 1911, Brandeis was ready to adopt a rather different tack. Taking up the cudgels once again to oppose to the company's contention that generous concessions were needed to attract the necessary investment, he succeeded in securing an arrangement whereby the city agreed to fund and build the new subways required to meet user demands, and the Elevated agreed to operate these new municipal facilities on leases subject to termination after twenty-five years. "Boston has thus established the policy of retaining control of its transportation system," he commented in contemplation of final victory. "The city will own all the subways, and through this ownership and the right to revoke surface locations, will control the entire traction system, with power to compel corporations to pay what may seem from time to time adequate compensation for the use of the streets."[25]

In his dealings with Boston's gas combine, Brandeis took a rather more flexible line from the beginning. In 1903 an application was made to the Massachusetts legislature for permission to rationalize the several small companies then supplying gas to the city's consumers into a single business entity. The following year, an attempt was made by the Boston Consolidated Gas Company to have its assets valued at more than $20 million, this pursuant to a stipulation in the enabling act that capital issued by the new corporation should not exceed the "fair value of the plants and property" previously owned by its constituent companies. Again using the Public Franchise League as a front, Brandeis challenged the figures, arguing that more than $5 million of the amount claimed was not represented by either stock or funded debt but consisted of "accumulations from excessive payments exacted from gas consumers" and should thus not be capitalized. After a year of sometimes bitter confrontation, the company's president, James L. Richards, eventually backed down and, as well as accepting Brandeis's valuation, agreed to allow a special commission nominated by the governor to recommend an appropriate mechanism for reconciling the interests of investors and consumers.[26]

The result of their deliberations was the Boston Sliding Scale Act, which became law in 1906 despite, as Brandeis later recalled, "the strenuous opposition of both conservatives and radicals." Its principal feature, borrowed from schemes operated in a number of British and Canadian cities, was an arrangement by which the rate of dividend paid to stockholders rose as the price of gas charged to customers fell. Within two years the cost of gas in Boston had fallen by 20 cents per thousand cubic feet and the return to investors had increased proportionately. When the scheme's opponents argued that successive price reductions would soon enable the company to pay very large dividends, Brandeis's considered response was unexpectedly cool and pragmatic. "The Public Franchise League," he wrote in 1907,

recognized fully that after a few years' operation under the act much larger dividends would probably be paid than capital as capital is entitled to when employed in a business which is not only safe because it enjoys a substantial monopoly, but which also receives from the community without the payment of any compensation the license to lay and maintain its pipes in the public streets. The League insisted, however, that the proper aim of the public must be not to limit dividends, but to secure gas of good quality at low prices; that a limitation of dividends was desirable only when it conduced to that end; and that under proper conditions a reasonable assurance of the undisturbed enjoyment of large dividends might be the best method of attaining cheap gas.

Investors and the consuming public would benefit pro rata from any improvements in operational efficiency; and in any event the act provided for an automatic review after ten years of the price-dividend relationship to take account of changed circumstances. In Brandeis's view the Boston system was a compromise between private enterprise and public ownership, "an experiment" aimed at discovering "the best practical solution of the public-utilities problem." It created "substantially a partnership between the public and the stockholders of the gas company—a partnership in which the public will secure an ever-increasing share of the profits of the business."[27]

In his successful efforts to resolve the gas question in Boston, Brandeis appears to have been motivated in part by a desire to ward off radical demands for widespread municipal ownership of public service corporations, even though a few years later he was ready to advocate limited public ownership himself. However, in the case of the New Haven Railroad Company's ambition to rationalize and integrate the transportation systems of Southern

New England public ownership was not the issue; the specter of monopoly was. In August 1903, just as the gas fight was getting under way, financier J. P. Morgan decided to appoint the widely respected Charles S. Mellen as president of the New York, New Haven & Hartford Railroad. In the course of just six years Mellen succeeded in consolidating the region's interurban street railways and intercoastal steamship lines, and between 1907 and 1909 capped these achievement by effecting a merger with the Boston & Maine Railroad.[28]

The issues raised by the New Haven's expansionary activities were first brought to Brandeis's notice in the summer of 1905, when he attended hearings held before a special joint committee of the Massachusetts legislature to investigate the purchase of street railways by steam railroad companies. He had not intended to speak himself, but in the event was persuaded to make a few extempore remarks. As he explained to the committee's members, the question of whether established railroad interests should be allowed to fend off competition by acquiring the assets of the newer, high-speed trolley lines was probably the most important matter to come before the legislature in the period of which he had knowledge. In essence the issue was a simple one: "whether or not there shall be accorded at this time an absolute monopoly of the transportation interests of this Commonwealth." The manner in which it was finally settled would have serious and wide-ranging implications for the future commercial prosperity of the state, and not least for the numerous smaller communities located at a distance from the most profitable trunk routes. He regarded as misplaced the committee's concerns about possible stock watering and its preoccupation with the need to secure an equality of privilege as between "foreign" corporations and those chartered in Massachusetts, because the legislature already possessed the necessary regulatory powers and institutions to deal with such matters. It ought instead to be "determining what is in the interests of the Commonwealth" as a whole, and whether the monopoly being proposed was desirable. Yet significantly he refrained from committing either himself or the Public Franchise League to any general indictment of monopolistic enterprise despite being pressed repeatedly to express his views on the subject. He preferred, he said, to reserve his position until the committee had assembled sufficient evidence and was ready to place its own recommendations before the legislature. "I don't think we ought to assume anything in regard to the matter until it has been fully discussed, until we can weigh the reasons pro and con."[29]

Not prepared to wait for the politicians and other interested parties to work out a transportation policy that would best serve "the interests of the Commonwealth," Mellen began the first of a series of devious maneuvers aimed at acquiring control of street railway companies without the approval of either the legislature or the Massachusetts Railroad Commission. Brandeis and the Public Franchise League continued to dither on the question of whether such acquisitions should be supported or opposed as contrary to the public interest, and only came down off the fence in 1907 when news broke of the New Haven's proposed merger with the Boston & Maine Railroad. The dispute that followed was bitterly fought. Though much of the subsequent debate centered on the questionable ethics of the New Haven's directors, and drew from Brandeis several prophetic warnings about the company's financial condition, there were also a number of serious economic issues at stake in the merger battle. Chief among these was the very real fear that a railroad empire with major terminals at other Atlantic ports might use its control of the Boston & Maine system to divert New England freight traffic away from Boston altogether, or at very least do away with the very favorable pricing regime that allowed the region's manufacturers to compete effectively in Western markets. Brandeis presented a bill in the General Court that would have forbidden the New Haven from acquiring either direct or indirect control of the Boston & Maine system and have required dispersal of the stock already acquired by the following April, on pain of criminal penalties.

However, the state's Republican leadership, though anxious not to appear as a champion of the merger scheme, was equally concerned not to antagonize such powerful supporters as the railroad magnates; consequently a compromise proposal was steered through the legislature that deprived the New Haven of the right to vote its Boston & Maine stock for twelve months, but also gave implicit recognition to the company's ownership of that stock. Brandeis's bill was quietly sidelined. When in May 1908 the New Haven's acquisition of its street-railway properties by the use of holding companies and "voluntary associations" was declared illegal by the courts—a ruling which cast a long shadow over the railroad merger as well—Mellen calmly transferred the company's Boston & Maine shares to one accommodating stockholder and its trolley-line assets to a dummy corporation. Moreover, in 1909 his victory was confirmed with the passage into law of the Boston Railroad Holding Company Act, which, while purporting to reaffirm the prohibition of railroad mergers brought about without legislative consent, and forbidding the New Haven to regain possession of the Boston & Maine stock it had formerly owned, in fact nullified these gains by locating the stock in a new holding company over which the New Haven was permitted to exercise a controlling interest. A rival suggestion that the commonwealth itself should purchase the Boston & Maine shares, put forward by the state federation of labor and endorsed by a number of leading Democrats, apparently received equally short shrift from both the Republicans and the antimerger forces whom Brandeis represented. Thus with no alternative buyer in sight, resistance to the New Haven machinations effectively petered out. The opposition were to have the last laugh, though. By 1910 Mellen's sprawling transportation empire was beginning to run into financial difficulties; in 1913 an investigation by the Interstate Commerce Commission revealed that the company's books had been doctored to cover up evidence of its weak financial position. To this extent at least, Brandeis's hostility to the merger had been vindicated.[30]

If the New Haven episode served to broaden his campaigning horizons beyond the confines of Boston, three other involvements must share the responsibility for drawing his attention toward public-interest issues whose principal focus lay outside the New England region altogether. Each can be dealt with briefly. His association with maximum-hours legislation for women has already been referred to in connection with the novel brief he entered in the *Muller* case; it should be noted, however, that this was merely the first of a series of court appearances in which he successfully upheld the right of state legislatures to protect the welfare of their citizens through the "reasonable" exercise of their police powers. His dealings with Boston's labor leaders, as we saw in the previous chapter, had begun to develop during the mid-1890s and his defense of maximum-hours and minimum-wage legislation in the years after 1908 went some way toward enhancing his credibility with workers' organizations elsewhere in the country, as did his advocacy of a scheme for savings-bank life insurance. It was as a direct consequence of his perceived respect for workingmen, that between 1910 and 1916 he was called on to serve as unpaid chairman of the Arbitration Board for New York's garment workers, during which time he drew up and implemented a protocol to regulate employer-employee relations in the industry during a tense and turbulent period in its history.[31]

However, it would be wrong to regard him as an uncritical "friend of labor" in the these years. It was simply that his evolving conception of an efficient and harmonious capitalism required that workers should benefit from the system as equal partners, and thereby come to identify with and share its social values. "This fellow Brandeis is the most dangerous man in the United States," the Wobblies' leader "Big Bill" Haywood is said to have remarked after studying the garment industry protocol.

> Brandeis knows something about capital and labor. He isn't one of these highbrow reformers who is sure to make a fool of himself. That's why I say he is in our way. The workers trust him even when he goes against them. Think of it. He tells them they're wrong here and wrong there, he defends the manufacturers more than half the time, and still they believe him. They even say he was right sometimes when he decided against them. They're a pretty sentimental lot in the working class, and I think they'd follow Brandeis to Kingdom Come because they say nobody can buy him, that he's not in this for himself, and that he's the whitest man who ever mixed up in the class struggle. That's what makes him so damned dangerous. If he were a fool, if he didn't know all about everything, if he were in it for Brandeis, if there were only something the matter with him, he wouldn't be messing things up for the I.W.W. wherever he goes.[32]

One episode more than any other, however, was responsible for establishing Brandeis on the national political stage. This was his involvement in the Ballinger-Pinchot affair, according to one recent commentator "the most sensational controversy of the Progressive Era." The case began simply enough with a young civil servant, Louis Glavis, bringing allegations about fraudulent mining claims to the attention of his boss, Interior Secretary Richard A. Ballinger, who dismissed them for lack of evidence. Matters began to escalate when Glavis decided to appeal for support to Chief Forester Gifford Pinchot, who in turn brought the story to the attention of President Taft. Having explained his own actions to Taft's satisfaction, Ballinger proceeded to fire the incautious plaintiff for insubordination. The dispute might well have ended there had Glavis and Pinchot not decided to go public by leaking their account of the affair to the muckraking editor of *Collier's Weekly*, Norman Hapgood, and had he not published a cover article impugning Ballinger's integrity. In the public furor that ensued, during which the chief forester was also dismissed from office, Brandeis was initially hired to defend the magazine against the anticipated writ for libel and ended up as Glavis's attorney demolishing Ballinger's reputation before a congressional committee charged with investigating national conservation policy.[33]

Subsequent developments in the controversy have been amply covered both in specialist studies and by Brandeis's biographers. Discovering that there was little or no documentary evidence to back up Glavis's original claims of wrongdoing, the Boston lawyer determined to deflect attention instead onto the administration's handling of the subsequent inquiry. In a series of withering forensic displays he succeeded in turning the case into a simple confrontation between truth and falsehood, between virtue and corruption, between good and evil. Though there were, in fact, real issues at stake concerning the accountability of public officials and the best way of conserving national resources, these were subjects for which he evinced little overt enthusiasm. As his public statements and private correspondence both testify, he became absolutely convinced that the interior secretary was a blackguard who had to be brought to book at all costs; indeed there was something almost sadistic about the way in which the inquisitor and those close to him set about their task. After Ballinger's own cross-examination, Brandeis's longtime secretary, Alice Grady, would note with obvious relish "the masterful way" in which her boss had "stacked and shuffled the facts and presented them sweetly one by one to the consternation of his wriggling victim."[34]

Yet for all the discussion about the merits of the case against Ballinger, and the rather unsavory aspect of Brandeis's character revealed by his handling of the "prosecution," the fact remains that this dispute tells us a good deal more about the latter's personality than it does about either his thought processes or his attitude to the policy issues raised. For a man who had always found the wilderness a refreshing antidote to the pressures of urban living, and who was easily persuaded of the depredations to be expected from big business, it seems strange to find him neglecting in this incident an obvious opportunity to influence federal conservation policy and perhaps to fix a large mining corporation in his sights. Perhaps he was toying with the idea of running for public office himself and endeavoring to use the Ballinger-Pinchot dispute as a launch platform for his own ambitions; however, it is more likely that he was seeking to raise his profile among the reform-minded politicos opposed to Taft, with a view to influencing the national political agenda of Progressivism. Certainly the "New Freedom" philosophy that Woodrow Wilson expounded during the 1912 presidential campaign coincided with Brandeis's own views in many particulars, and parts of the legislative program enacted during Wilson's first term in office bore the clear imprint of his advice. Far removed as his coldly calculating performance in the Ballinger case may now appear from the world of ideas, it was probably instrumental in gaining for him a position from which to turn some of his own into realities—a sad irony indeed for one who would continue to deny throughout his life that worthy ends could ever justify the use of despicable means.[35]

Be that as it may, by 1912 if not before, Brandeis had succeeded in distilling from the thoughts and observations of half a century a complex socioeconomic philosophy whose internal coherence depended on the relationship between a series of distinct if related thematic focuses. During the preceding decade, consideration of the problems surrounding monopoly and the associated phenomenon of corporate gigantism had come to exert an increasingly dominant influence over his thinking, and now provided him with fresh insights into the proper definition of the term "efficiency" when employed in an industrial context; likewise, the implications of scientific progress and the uses to be made of new technology had provided him with plenty of food for thought. Reviewing his experiences and beliefs in the light of one another, he now sought to formulate a model of industrial society capable of reconciling his long-held belief in the ideal of personal responsibility, exercised within a supportive framework of law, with the present reality of individual weakness in the face of vast, and seemingly lawless, corporate power. The result was a new, and ultimately radical vision of how democracy should operate in an advanced industrial society—a vision that required both flexibility and self-restraint from the forces of labor, capital and government alike.

Self-restraint, however, was not a prominent characteristic of America's corporate capitalism in the first decade of the twentieth century, especially not when it came to the efforts made by large-scale businesses to dominate the marketplace in which they functioned. The rhetoric of the Progressive Era is heavily encrusted with references to "trusts" and "combinations," and to this spoil-tip of words Brandeis contributed as freely and articulately as any of his contemporaries, which has led many commentators to equate his often quoted denunciations of "bigness" with a straightforward opposition to monopoly. Certainly his awareness of the trust problem was an essential factor leading him beyond the laissez-faire liberalism of his early career. The antimonopoly writings of Henry George and Henry Demarest Lloyd evidently impressed him; and together with a sympathetic identification with the interests of his Boston clients, they may well have been instrumental in converting the quiet advocate of free trade into the rather more forthright and outspoken champion of regulated competition better known to later generations.[36]

Nevertheless, the conversion of Brandeis into an opponent of monopoly per se was a slow, tortuous, and ultimately incomplete one. As noted earlier, when pressed by a Massachusetts legislative committee in 1905 to place on record his views about monopolistic enterprise, he responded evasively. Although such unaccustomed reticence might be interpreted as a tactical device intended to make the promoters of street railway consolidation reveal their own hands first, there are grounds for believing that he was as yet genuinely ambivalent about what his attitude toward monopoly should be. His confusion of thought was evident in what he did say to the committee:

> It may be that we have reached that point in the development of this subject and our street railway system, that we are ready for monopoly. We have concluded in regard to steam railroad systems that a regulated monopoly is the best form of steam railroad legislation [sic], but it doesn't follow as of course that in the development of the street railway system we have reached that point. It may be that we shall reach that point or it may be that we shall never do so. It may be that there are such differences in the street railway and railroad systems that they should be kept apart. Those limits [sic] may preclude the possibility—in the interests of the whole people—of allowing amalgamation.

In certain circumstances at least, he was now apparently ready to accept "regulated monopoly" as the form of organization most appropriate to particular kinds of quasi-public undertaking. Because this in turn meant recognizing the need for competent guardians to monitor and on occasion to discipline the corporate entities involved, he held a commensurately high opinion of the Massachusetts Railroad Commissioners. Next to the commonwealth's judicial system, "and ranking with it," he regarded the commission as "one of the proudest and most efficient examples of the work of public officials that can be presented in the whole country."[37]

This unexpected flexibility of mind on an issue that would prove an insuperable bar to his supporting Roosevelt's third-party candidacy in 1912 receives additional confirmation from the personal recollection that Brandeis set down in that year. For as he told Senator Moses E. Clapp, as late as the spring of 1906 he had been "of the opinion that under some conditions monopoly in industry could operate beneficially to the public, or, in other words, that there were 'good trusts' as well as 'bad trusts.'" The corporation

in question here, however, was not a public utility but a manufacturing concern, the United Shoe Machinery Company, which Brandeis served both as
counsel and as a director before resigning at the end of 1906 over the firm's
use of "tying clauses" in its leases. The shoemakers who came to United for
certain patented machines crucial in the manufacturing process found themselves obliged by these clauses to obtain all their other equipment there as
well. At first United's customers did not complain, because in other respects
the company treated them well, denying quantity discounts to the larger
operators and making it possible for smaller businesses with limited capital
to compete on equal terms. Indeed, this last factor was the principal reason
behind his support for the company: that while it monopolized producer
goods in the shoe industry, it actively promoted competition among manufacturers of consumer goods. But as resentment against its restrictive leases
grew, and bills to outlaw such agreements were presented in the Massachusetts legislature, he began to reconsider his opinion. After all, several
of the region's leading shoe manufacturers were clients of his law firm, and
when together with a group of these headed by W. H. McElwain he failed to
persuade United to drop its tying clauses, he determined to sever all remaining connections with the company. As he told the senator,

> The facts then developed and the further consideration given the subject con-
> vinced me fully that, while the policy and methods of the company had, on the
> whole, operated beneficially up to that time, they must, if pursued, eventually
> prove injurious both to the community and the company's interest; and I urged
> most strenuously upon [the United directors] that these methods be changed, that
> the policy of monopoly be abandoned, and particularly that the tying clauses be
> eliminated from the leases.

By 1912, however, the propriety of Brandeis's subsequent actions against
the company was being publicly called into question, and these last remarks
to Clapp must be read primarily as an exercise in self-justification. In reality,
what had altered was not the degree of virtue inherent in United's business
methods, but Brandeis's own reaction to them.[38]

Evidently, by the summer of 1907, his uncertainty about the desirability of
combinations in business had begun to resolve itself. "I am now, and always
have been, directly opposed to distinct monopoly," the *Boston American*
quoted him as telling the legislative committee charged with investigating
the Boston & Maine merger in June—a claim which, if indeed he had made
it, would have been highly disingenuous. In fact, though, the official transcript shows him being rather more circumspect in his choice of words. "I
believe within limits in consolidation," he informed the committee.

> If I might state the general principle which I may go on, it would be this: there is
> for the community a certain limit of greatest efficiency, commercial efficiency, and
> if there are no other considerations that general limit of commercial efficiency, in-

dustrial efficiency is the limit one may go to. But I believe, on the other hand, that it is extremely important that the community should not be subject to a complete monopoly in any branch of business, and that, applying it to this particular case, we have here a proposed combination of railroads, but which through its scope practically covers all transportation, or is in danger of doing so.[39]

Even in these more measured terms, his position was still not altogether consistent with that he had taken little more than a year before with regard to the shoe-machinery trust. This having been said, though, the outlook revealed in this 1907 testimony did at least possess the virtue of greater clarity than he had managed to adduce on the street railway issue in 1905. On this occasion, be came before the committee as the legal representative of two Boston & Maine stockholders, Samuel and William B. Lawrence, to speak in support of his bill to prevent the merger taking place; yet in response to a question about his own views in the matter he made no attempt to conceal the force of his opposition to the proposed consolidation. "I feel as strongly individually as I do as counsel in the matter," he told the committee.

I believe that it is of the utmost good to the Commonwealth to maintain what there is left of a separate ownership in our transportation system. I think that the three systems that are left are at least as little as we ought to have. And that has become the more important, it seems to me, in view of the fact that the New Haven road has acquired a large ownership in trolley interests and is now practically sharing with the Morse interest a control of all coastwise transportation.

There was no longer any suggestion that the time might come when a monopoly of street railways might actually serve the public interest. Indeed, the prospect that the New Haven might further tighten its grip on the passenger and freight networks of Southern New England plainly filled him with foreboding.

That is a situation which it seems to me the community cannot regard except with the gravest alarm, that we are practically turning over to one corporation in the first instance, but in the next instance to . . . a foreign corporation, all of our transportation system. I think that would be a very great danger; in fact, I know of none so great that our industrial community has been exposed to in the time that I have given to our more general public interests.

Traditional mechanisms seemed inadequate to control such an all-embracing enterprise as the New Haven empire; and the Massachusetts Railroad Commission now looked a rather fickle bulwark against the potential abuses of monopoly power. Brandeis had little confidence in the governor's talk of additional safeguards. "I don't believe that you can create a board of control which would be great enough to safeguard [the state's] interests," he told the committee; neither did he believe that the Boston & Maine stockholders could be relied on to do so. "It seems to me that the only way to safeguard them is to create the possibilities of some free action on the part of some other corporation." Genuine competition seemed the only answer.[40]

On the second day of the hearings, once the promerger forces had had their say, Brandeis was invited to make a second statement. This time, after briefly summarizing his earlier testimony, he tried appealing to local pride in past achievements. "Every change is not progress," he asserted defiantly, and the revolution being pushed through by Mellen and his cohorts was an undesirable one, intended to bring into being "an absolute monopoly in the hand and under the control of aliens to Massachusetts." With this simple utterance, the invidious distinction between domestic and foreign corporations that he had sensibly rejected during the 1905 inquiry into street-railway takeovers was shamelessly appropriated into his expanding rhetorical armory.

> If the time comes, which I hope it never may, when Massachusetts in its laws, in its morals, in its principles and its traditions, shall not rise higher than the average of the United States, we may well be content to be governed in important matters by the whole country or by men of other states; but it has been the pride of Massachusetts and the striving of Massachusetts in the past to lead, and not to be subject to others. Why should we not lead? Why should not a Commonwealth as rich as ours, rich in brains as well as rich in money, control itself?

But his argument went deeper than mere provincial vainglory; for he also perceived that ownership of the transportation network was a matter of vital importance to the economy of the state. To a suggestion from Lucius Tuttle, the Boston & Maine's president, that the proprietorship of a railroad was a matter of little consequence, provided the state retained the power to legislate and to enforce the laws that it made, Brandeis entered an emphatic disclaimer. To him it mattered a great deal whether the managers of such a vital enterprise were men whose "whole existence and welfare" were bound up in the interests of the community their business served, or not.

> Isn't it of the utmost importance in life that we have one allegiance, and not a divided allegiance? When you have a railroad system controlled by Massachusetts men, whose prosperity is distinctly dependent upon Massachusetts prosperity, and Boston prosperity if you will put it, doesn't it make a difference in the safety with which the thing may be done whether it is that, or whether you are but one of a large number?

The New Haven would not intentionally injure the city, he believed, but harm could nonetheless be expected to occur "in the ordinary course of events." Only those with sole and unequivocal commitments to the welfare of Boston and its parent commonwealth could be entrusted with what Tuttle himself had called "the fundamental condition of our prosperity and well being."[41]

To Brandeis, then, the sprawling New Haven empire represented the most unacceptable face that industrial capitalism could present: absentee ownership and banker-management combined with monopolistic control of assets vital to the economic health of an entire region. Yet it should be noted that his continuing insistence that some monopolies could be more acceptable than others was no mere figure of speech. The point recurs again and again. In 1910, for example, he was approached by a group of Louisville businessmen associated with a "committee of one hundred" that included his brother Alfred, and asked to comment on the desirability of a proposal to consolidate the city's gas and electricity companies. His correspondent, one Henry M. Johnson, left him in no doubt that the committee's members were opposed to the particulars of the scheme, despite being aware of "a pretty well defined sentiment" that the merger should take place. Characteristically, Louis was reluctant to commit himself before he had all the relevant facts to hand, and wrote back to request from Johnson "a full and detailed statement of the present lighting situation in Louisville," including information about the existing franchises, the capitalization and investments of the operating companies, a full schedule of the present and past charges for gas and electricity, and a candid assessment of the current profitability and future prospects of these businesses.[42]

In almost every respect, this was a duplication of the research he himself had undertaken in connection with the Boston gas combine six years earlier. The main difference here was that two distinct species of public service corporation were due to be merged—a move that threatened to stifle in his hometown the keen and seemingly healthy competition that continued to exist between the rival power utilities of Boston. In October, Brandeis summarized his thinking on this issue in a letter to Louis B. Wehle. "Don't . . . let the Louisville people be misled in favor of a merger by the argument that monopoly in public service corporations is a good thing," he warned his nephew. "A gas company with a monopoly may be a good thing; an electric company with a monopoly may be a good thing, but gas and electricity are different methods of supplying one's wants, and you cannot get the best results unless you maintain a competition between these two methods of lighting." He was ready to concede, however, that this maxim might not be universally applicable. "In the smaller cities," he continued, "it is often desirable to consolidate the two methods of lighting partly because there are parts of the city to which the gas mains cannot be extended without undue expense, but in a large city the merger of gas and electric light companies is certainly an evil." Therefore he was implacably hostile to the suggestion that the consolidated power company should be granted a twenty-year franchise: "I should infinitely rather have for Louisville municipal ownership, with all its dangers," he declared ominously, "than either a merger or a long term agreement." The following spring, due in part no doubt to the detailed advice supplied to the protesters at Brandeis's instigation, the merger proposal was roundly defeated.[43]

Between 1907 and 1910, then, the need to define ever more precisely the circumstances in which monopoly might or might not be acceptable to the community at large had led him inexorably toward a thoroughgoing reappraisal of the social and economic benefits to be derived from its reciprocal condition: competition. In this context it was important to strike a reasonable balance between the rival demands of efficiency, fairness, and practicality, which, more often than is generally recognized, is exactly what he attempted to do.

In an article on competition written in 1913, he developed at some length the allegation that monopolistic combinations were frequently the result of unfair practices:

> no monopoly in private industry in America has yet been attained by efficiency alone. No business has been superior to its competitors in the processes of manufacture or of distribution as to enable it to control the market solely by reason of its superiority. There is nothing in our industrial history to indicate that there is any need whatever to limit the natural growth of a business in order to preserve competition.

At first sight, it would seem from this candid expression of his views that, by 1913, Brandeis had come to regard monopoly as a universally undesirable and artificial condition of the marketplace, while by implication he considered competition both desirable and natural.

But was this in fact his contention? To make sense of this passage, we must first endeavor to understand what he meant by the terms "monopoly" and "competition." Consideration of what has been said already in this chapter, combined with even a summary analysis of his essays and later opinions on the subject, will reveal that only rarely did he use the word "monopoly" with technical precision, to imply total domination of a market by a single company. For Brandeis, as for many other Progressives, monopoly was defined rather as the condition resulting whenever competitive market forces became seriously impaired in their operation, either by economic circumstances, or as a consequence of deliberate collusion between rival firms. The number of business concerns involved was of only marginal importance; to most intents and purposes, he used the word "monopoly" where a professional economist might prefer the more precise if less elegant term "oligopoly." Thus, in his view, trusts, pools, and trade associations might be every bit as "monopolistic" as the sole supplier of a good or service.

Yet as he had been ready to admit on numerous occasions since 1900, this did not necessarily mean that they were a bad thing. He was well aware that ruthless competition had all too often in the recent past been a prelude to takeovers and mergers, and that its effects could be both debilitating and socially harmful. If he had little sense that businessmen might have a legitimate objective in wanting to stabilize the markets in which they operated, at least he appreciated that limited cooperation between them might prevent the unnecessary waste of effort and resources.[44]

Conversely, as we have seen, he also recognized that there might be situations in which monopolies could prove not only advantageous to the community but for all practical purposes unavoidable as well. His most unequivocal statement about the possible legitimacy of monopoly came many years later in his dissenting opinion in the Oklahoma Ice case, written at the depth of the depression in 1932, where he managed to find perfectly acceptable justifications for upholding a local monopoly in the ice business:

> Particularly in those businesses in which interest and depreciation on plant constitute a large element in the cost of production, experience has taught that the financial burdens incident to unnecessary duplication of facilities are likely to bring high rates and poor service. There, cost is usually dependent, among other things, upon volume; and division of possible patronage among competing concerns may raise the unit cost of operation as to make it impossible to provide adequate service at reasonable rates.

Thus, provided it could be suitably controlled and regulated by the local community it was intended to serve, a market monopoly might not only be allowable but even socially desirable.[45]

On the face of it, the view that Brandeis expressed in this celebrated opinion would seem to be at odds with the enthusiasm he evinced for competition in the years immediately preceding his appointment to the Court. In this period, he more frequently identified incentive and development as the welcome incidents of a competitive economy, and argued that the accompanying wastes were relatively insignificant. Those that did occur he regarded as the unavoidable price society paid for "a system which urges men on to action, enterprise and initiative." He rejected the assertion that monopoly was preferable because it prevented waste and led to efficiency. The economies of monopoly were superficial and delusory; its efficiency was temporary at best. "Undoubtedly competition involves waste," he wrote in 1912. "What human activity does not? The wastes of democracy are among the greatest obvious wastes, but we have compensations in democracy which far outweigh that waste and make it more efficient than absolutism." As with democracy, so too with competition. Yet he was at pains to stress that there was no need to equate competition with cottage industry: "A large part of the American people realize today that competition is in no sense inconsistent with large-scale production and distribution." It was all a matter of degree.[46]

From an early date, though, he was willing to introduced an important qualification into this line of argument—one that would eventually find its echo in the Ice case opinion. What could not be tolerated, he maintained, were those "wastes of competition which do not develop, but kill." These the law could and should eliminate whenever possible by regulating competition rather than monopoly. "Competition consists in trying to do things better than someone else," he explained in 1913; "that is making or selling a better article, or the same article at a better cost, or otherwise giving a better service." It was not legitimate competition to "resort to methods of the prize ring, and simply 'knock the other man out.' That is killing a competi-tor." Therefore prices should not be rigged; the health and safety of workers should not be jeopardized; wages should not be withheld arbitrarily. If com-petition in any particular industry or public service was thought conducive to the wider interests of the community, then the benefits involved ought not to be bought at the expense of either workers or consumers; neither should cutthroat methods be permitted to effect a monopoly in situations where a healthy competitive market could be preserved by timely government intervention.[47]

The most significant stage in the development of Brandeis's thinking on the subject of competition was probably reached during the summer of 1911, when he played a leading role in drafting the antitrust bill that Robert M. LaFollette laid before the United States Senate at the end of August. The new measure, intended to supplement the Sherman Act of 1890, was made necessary by the Supreme Court's decision in May 1911 that only "unreason-able" restraints of interstate commerce were outlawed by the existing law. This was nothing short of judicial legislation, in effect extending to the Sher-man Act the "rule of reason" already invoked to restrain the scope of reg-ulation permitted to the states in the exercise of their police powers. Hastily denying a press report that he regarded the Court's ruling as "very fortunate for the consumer and the country generally" and "valuable" as a stimulus to competition, Brandeis arrived in Washington only three days after it was handed down, and there participated actively in the decision of leading Progressives to press for a change in the law that would deny the courts dis-cretion to protect the interests of big business.[48]

A central feature of the draft bill that Brandeis produced for Senator LaFollette was its insistence that the preservation of competition necessarily entailed its regulation as well. "The Sherman Law as interpreted by the Supreme Court leaves in vast uncertainty the question as to what, in any case, will be deemed a reasonable restraint," he told the veteran editor of the *Boston Post* in September.

> The LaFollette bill utilizing the experience of twenty years specifies a series of acts which in practice have been proven to be unreasonable as destroying competition. Such acts as these are declared unreasonable, thereby giving certainty and effec-tiveness to the law. Examples of such practices are that of refusing to supply a cus-tomer, if he purchases also from the Trust's competitor, or cutting prices in a par-ticular district to kill a competitor, as was so often practiced by the Standard Oil [Company].

It was now more difficult than ever to secure compliance with the Sherman Act, since, as well as proving the existence of a combination to restrain trade, the prosecution had also to demonstrate that such restraint was unreasonable. The senator's bill stood this requirement on its head by stipulating that, once the existence of a particular combination had been proved, the defendants in the case should have the burden of showing that it was reasonable.[49]

In fact, one of the specifications included in the version of the bill submitted to Congress was rather more restrictive than Brandeis had intended or thought wise. This was a clause that defined as an unreasonable restraint of trade any business that controlled more than 40 percent of the market for a given product, whether that market was national, regional, or local in scope. True enough, the final element reflected his concern that, if the nation were regarded as a single market, "It would be perfectly possible for concerns to establish practical control of particular districts and still be far under the forbidden percentage of the business of the whole country." As he told LaFollette at the end of May: "Some of the most dangerous combinations have been those that limited their operations to particular cities or states." But the 40 percent figure disturbed him nonetheless.

> I am confirmed in the opinion that though it is very tempting and would be useful in many instances to make the control of a certain percentage of the business conclusive of unreasonableness, it would be very dangerous to do so. We should undoubtedly find numbers of instances in different branches of trade where almost any provision making a fixed percentage conclusive would create hardship, and be against the public interest.
>
> Furthermore, if we fixed a percentage that was conclusive, it would have to be reasonably high, and it would be taken as practically legislative sanction that control of anything under that percentage would be reasonable.

In other words, whereas LaFollette and his congressional supporters appeared to be looking for a rigid mechanism to root out something clearly labeled "monopoly," Brandeis thought it essential to retain flexibility in the regulatory process, even if this meant the end of unrestricted competition.[50]

This involvement with the national antitrust movement was the Boston attorney's first association with Progressive *reform* as such, but even here the regulatory regime he sought to establish was as much intended to preserve something old as to engender something new. He certainly did not see the proposed legislation as an end in itself, but rather as a means of halting and then reversing a process that had already succeeded in distorting an older status quo that he still considered preferable to the new order. If giant conglomerates could only be defeated by the imposition of criminal penalties and the threat of imprisonment, then so be it; but he was not irrevocably committed to this particular course of action if a better and more effective method of coercion could be found.[51]

In fact, the first glimmer of an alternative was to present itself sooner than he could possibly have expected. At the beginning of 1912, an independent tobacco retailer from New York City, Alfred Samuel, wrote to Brandeis after reading an article he had written about the Supreme Court's holding in the Tobacco Trust case. His letter offered a novel solution to the problems of monopoly: If sound antitrust laws were going to be made inoperative by decisions of a partial judiciary, why not make combinations of capital futile by means of taxation? "If a mon[o]poly is taxed to the extent of rendering the enterprise unprofitable to its promoters," he wrote, "there will be no need of any Anti Trust legislation and there cannot be any objection to such taxation, if the chance is given to the promoters of such Trust, to avoid such taxation by dissolving such Trust into the different original firms, under which they previously existed." Despite its inelegant phrasing, the force and attractiveness of this argument was readily apparent, and in his acknowledgment the "people's attorney" promised to give "careful attention" to Samuel's "valuable suggestions." Although the idea of invoking the tax weapon against large concentrations of corporate power was not immediately incorporated into Brandeis's thinking on the subject of trust regulation, by the 1930s it had become the centerpiece of his strategy to halt the spread of "bigness" in America.[52]

Unhappy as Brandeis undoubtedly was with certain technical aspects of the LaFollette's approach to antitrust matters, the two men shared an essentially common faith in the importance of preserving a competitive business environment. However, several academics at the University of Wisconsin, notably Charles Van Hise and Edward A. Ross, were beginning to develop a radically different analysis of the nation's socioeconomic ills. To members of this group it seemed that increased efficiency might with good reason be substituted for trust busting as the main aim of social reformers. Economies of scale made industrial concentration appear positively desirable as the best method of achieving both social justice and greater material abundance, and the regulation, even the promotion, of such combinations could therefore be defended as the legitimate function of a Progressive government committed to acting in the public interest. Outright monopoly might be avoided in most cases by means of affirmative action taken to preserve independent producers and keep the doors of entrepreneurial opportunity open for newcomers; but where the competitive pressures thus produced were insufficient to prevent monopolies from forming, an Interstate Trade Commission, modeled on the existing Interstate Commerce Commission, should be called in to regulate prices. The Sherman Act ought to be "retained as a club by which to induce combinations to place themselves under federal control," but could be amended so that only those corporations that indulged in a few specific types of discrimination, price cutting and patent manipulation would henceforth be regarded as combinations in restraint of trade.[53]

Brandeis first became aware of these views in November 1911 when Charles R. Crane, a Progressive acquaintance from Chicago, showed him a letter he had received from Ross outlining the main points of the Madison group's thesis. A few days later he received from Van Hise an advance copy of the lecture entitled "Concentration in Industry," which the latter was scheduled to give at Harvard on the 14th of that month; and sometime later still he met with Van Hise in Washington to discuss their respective positions. At about the same time, Brandeis secured from Frank Taussig an up-to-date reading list of books and pamphlets dealing with the twin subjects of monopoly and competition, together with a brief description of the stance adopted by each author. R. T. Ely's *Monopolies and Trusts* and J. B. Clark's *The Control of Trusts*, for example, were identified as "books which approach the combination problem from your point of view," both writers being said to argue that, provided "bullying" tactics were outlawed, competition was capable of maintaining itself in all sections of the economy. The only exceptions they recognized were the public utilities and those "industries where natural resources [were] strictly limited."[54]

However, in a letter dictated prior to reading Van Hise's paper and at least a week before he heard from Taussig, Brandeis had already set out the basis of his extensive disagreements with the Wisconsin group's position. "I think the progressives would make a most serious mistake if they should commit themselves to a programme as outlined in Ross' letter," he told Crane. Although he accepted that the Sherman Law as presently enforced was inadequate to deal with the trusts, he rejected this as an argument for legitimizing their existence.

> What the law should undertake to do is not to restore "unrestricted competition" but to preserve and make possible competition stripped of those abuses which have led in large part to combination and monopoly. The talk about "economies of combination" is apt to create in the mind a great exaggeration of what actually has been gained in economy through combination and a failure to recognize the immense gain in economy which has come through competition.

The fixing of prices by a federal commission he considered "unwise" because, among other things, it failed to make due allowance for "the vast difference between the relatively simple and uniform problems of transportation and the ever varying and complex problems of industry." In any case, price controls would "meet only the least of the evils of monopoly." There were other, more pressing things for the authorities to do. "The proper function of government is to encourage not combination, but co-operation." This, he told Crane, was "the large field for constructive legislation."

He was concerned too by the amorality of the group's argument; they seemed not to have considered "the effect of legalizing wealth and power obtained illegally and in open defiance, in many instances, of law." If the flouting of legal norms were to be condoned in this way, it could have unfortunate consequences for the future stability of the social fabric. In his view "such legalization would bear fruit in the long run infinitely more serious to society than any temporary disturbance of business through enforcement of law." Ross's statement failed to indicate any consideration either "of the immense development of capitalistic power which would attend the carrying out of a programme along the lines indicated in the conclusion." Above all, however, it failed to recognize "the social value of small as distinguished from large units, and of the importance of developing individuality in business." Here at last was the critical shift of emphasis from the problems of monopoly to those of corporate size—a new emphasis that would characterize Brandeis's socioeconomic outlook for the remainder of his life.[55]

By 1912, there can have been few Progressives who seriously doubted that a combination of capital seen to be operating against the public interest *could be* dismantled given a plausible economic justification, the political will, and a modicum of judicial flexibility. The great divide lay apparently between those who considered such atomization socially and economically desirable, and those who did not. Yet the question might reasonably be asked: Might not the sheer scale of a corporate undertaking place damaging constraints upon its viability—*even where no market monopoly existed*? Brandeis evidently thought so. If the New England Puritans, whom he greatly admired, were troubled by the limitations imposed on mankind by sinful human nature, he was far more concerned with those defined by physical and mental capacity. Man's ability to exercise weighty judgments was, he believed, severely restricted, and nowhere was this incapacity of greater consequence than in the sphere of financial and industrial management. Thus in several of the essays collected in 1914 under the title *Other People's Money* he roundly condemned the practice of financiers directing the affairs of enterprises about whose business they themselves had little or no personal knowledge. "Banker management," he wrote, "contravenes the fundamental laws of human limitations: First, that no man can serve two masters; second, that a man cannot at the same time do many things well." Apart from distortions of judgment, resulting from self-interest or merely from general concerns about the "market," banker-managers simply did not have the time to acquire sufficient information about the workings of the companies they undertook to guide. The following year, in testimony before the United States Commission on Industrial Relations, he expanded further on the awareness of industrial and social conditions possessed by financial directors in large corporations:

> neither these same men nor anybody else can properly deal with these problems without a far more intimate knowledge of the facts than it is possible for men to get who undertake to have a voice in so many different businesses. They are prevented from obtaining an understanding not so much because of their point of view or motive, but because of human limitations. These men have endeavored to

cover far more ground than it is possible for men to cover properly, and without an intimate knowledge of the facts they cannot properly deal with the problems involved.[56]

Furthermore, in Brandeis's opinion the size of an individual concern could tax the capabilities of a manager just as much as a large number of separate concerns, and as we shall see later this was one of the principal arguments leading him toward his concept of the "unit of greatest efficiency," first referred to during the Boston & Maine merger hearings in 1907. He recognized, of course, that the delegation of responsibility within the framework of an organizational structure could substantially reduce the burdens weighing on the man or men at the top, and greatly increase the efficiency of the enterprise, but he remained skeptical of claims that this alone could solve the problems he perceived. "No matter what the organization," he wrote in 1913, "the capacity of an individual man usually determines the success or failure of a particular enterprise, not only financially to the owners, but in service to the community. Organization . . . can never supply the combined judgment, initiative, enterprise, and authority which must come from the chief executive officers." Nature, he believed, set limits on what human beings might accomplish; and by way of illustration he quoted a German aphorism found in Goethe's autobiography: "Care is taken that the trees do not scrape the skies."[57]

If not the ultimate source of his philosophical outlook, a preoccupation with the consequences of industrial scale was indeed to become the major socioeconomic concern of Brandeis's later years. As far as we can see, the opinions he held on *this* subject, as distinct from those he had developed concerning monopoly, owed little to any formal economic theory, be it classical or heterodox; their formulation was almost wholly empirical. In the years between 1897 and 1911, his legal battles against the Boston Elevated, the gas combine, the shoe-machinery trust, and especially the New Haven empire had given him personal experience of large-scale enterprises. As we have seen, these encounters led him to have grave doubts about the effectiveness of the existing antitrust legislation, so that from the summer of 1911 onward he was ready to work closely with LaFollette and his congressional colleagues who were determined to see the Sherman Act strengthened. However, it was the question of size not monopoly that came increasingly to dominate his thinking, and his involvement with the Armstrong, Clapp, Stanley, and Pujo committees that did most to sharpen his focus on that issue. From the evidence gathered during their hearings, added to his own personal observations, he drew two important conclusions: first, that finance capital posed a special threat to business competition; and second, that large size could itself prove to be a source of commercial inefficiency, as well as a major obstacle to the development industrial democracy.[58]

There can be no doubt whatever that Brandeis saw the problems of bigness and monopoly as intimately related. The principal thesis propounded in *Other People's Money* is that the trusts were a creation of the investment bankers. He rejected the bankers' contention that concentration of capital was a direct result of the financial needs of an expanding industrial base; that larger banks and closer cooperation between them were essential to the efficient performance of the nation's business. The huge securities issues of recent years had not been floated by the banking syndicates to finance new industrial undertakings, or major improvements in existing plant and equipment, but for the sole purpose of effecting combinations, and that frequently in contravention of existing statute law and contrary to the "laws" of business efficiency. The concentration of finance capital and the development of trusts in the public utility, transportation, and manufacturing fields had arisen in the service of one another; they enjoyed, Brandeis believed, a wholly symbiotic relationship. Size achieved through "natural growth" might well be beneficial to the community, and thus desirable in the public interest, but size achieved through combination he regarded as an unmitigated evil. Its purpose was not so much the promotion of efficient production, extraction, or service, as it was the extension and peremptory exercise of corporate power. "Size we are told, is not a crime. But size may, at least, become noxious by reason of the means through which it was attained or the uses to which it is put," he insisted. Neither was he much impressed by the argument that these problems might be alleviated by widespread stock ownership in the hands of small investors. Anticipating the findings of Adolph Berle and Gardiner Means a generation later, he told the Industrial Relations Commission in 1915:

> These corporations are not controlled through a majority of the stock; they are controlled very largely by tradition. And it is an almost inevitable result of the wide distribution of stock . . . [which,] instead of being a blessing, constitutes, to my mind, one of the gravest dangers to the community. It is absentee landlordism of the worst kind.[59]

Yet if Brandeis regarded bigness and monopoly as connected phenomena, he did not regard them as identical or synonymous. In the last year of his life he would still be emphatic that the one gave rise to the other: "there could be no monopoly without 'bigness,'" he would write with purposeful exaggeration. It was one of his few enduring criticisms of the Wilson administration that the president and his political advisers had directed the thrust of the New Freedom against monopoly rather than against size; "because," as he recalled years later, "Americans hated monopoly and loved bigness." The provisions of the 1914 Clayton Act had consequently failed to live up to initial expectations; several clauses drafted by himself had been omitted from the version finally passed by Congress, and the phraseology of others had been amended so as to weaken their effect. A 1930 précis of his dissent ten years earlier in *Federal Trade Commission v. Gratz* explains his opinion of Wilson's antitrust legislation quite succinctly: "The view which finally prevailed with respect to concentration [i.e., monopoly] in industry and commerce was that concentration was a source of evil; that existing combinations could be disintegrated by perfecting the judicial machinery and that further concentration could be averted by providing additional remedies and regulating competition." This emphasis was wrong, he told a correspondent in 1931: "In my opinion the real curse was bigness rather than monopoly."[60]

This having been said, however, it would be wrong to equate Brandeis's growing preoccupation with the malign effects of vast institutional size with an automatic rejection of technological change, or with a neo-Jeffersonian hostility to industrialism and urban life. Of all the cities in which he had lived since early adolescence—Louisville, Dresden, St. Louis, Boston—none had a population of less than 100,000 people, and most were a good deal larger. Although he was concerned to improve the spiritual condition of America's toiling masses, he also recognized the preeminent need to promote their physical well-being; and like anyone else aware of economic processes, he saw that the key to material prosperity lay in higher levels of productivity. As he testified in 1914, such progress as had been made toward improving the standard of life for working people, especially during the preceding fifty years, had been made possible by the application of mechanical invention. It was the introduction and development of machinery that had so greatly increased the productivity of the individual worker. The only trouble was that as corporate capitalism had elaborated and extended its institutional structures, so labor had increasingly found itself squeezed out of the economic picture, with the result that workers failed to receive their fair share of the rewards made available by technology.[61]

Far from being an opponent of industrial technology—during the Progressive period anyway—Brandeis frequently blamed the so-called trusts for seeking to hamper further technical progress, and actually advocated a role for government operating on behalf of smaller-scale producers in the research and development field. Positive advances in processes and methods of production were to be welcomed, provided that they resulted in a better or cheaper product and were not socially harmful. Value judgments about machinery were pointless if made in the abstract; it was the social context in which it had to be received, the uses to which it might be put, the effects it might have on human behavior and relationships, that best determined whether technological change was for good or ill. He looked forward to the time when men would "think as hard, as intensively, about their social problems as they . . . [did] about automobiles, aeroplanes, and wireless telegraphy." If they would only do so, then nothing would be impossible.

Yet when all was said and done, he believed that men were more important than machines. "When we come to think about it hard and really try," he told an interviewer in 1913, "how much more rapidly we shall be able to produce results with people than from any other raw material. All the raw material from which man produces his mechanical miracles is inert. But the people, as raw material can help. They have will." It did not seem to occur to him that "the people" might well harbor ambitions different to his own. In fact, his fundamental optimism regarding the nature of men in society, and his apparent inability to comprehend the irrational element in human behavior, led him to discount totally the logical alternative: the possibility that those who had the will to help might, if it suited their purposes, choose to hinder instead. Here, in short, was one human limitation that he could neither perceive nor understand.[62]

The yardstick that Brandeis intended to use for measuring the value of technological advances was their efficiency. "Efficiency," he wrote, "is the hope of democracy. Efficiency means greater production with less effort and at less cost, through the elimination of unnecessary waste, human and material." How else, he asked, could Americans hope to see their social ideals realized? He had become a firm believer in the potential benefits to be derived from the application of scientific management techniques, but only if these could be introduced with the approval and cooperation of the work force. "It is most important that it [i.e., Taylorism] shall be applied democratically," he insisted. "It cannot be successfully applied otherwise." Expertise would always have to give way in the end to the exercise of personal judgment, and experts would have to respect consensual feelings that did not accord with their prescriptions. Self-restraint was not an injunction, its seems, which Brandeis reserved solely for the judiciary.[63]

Nevertheless, it was to legal devices and institutions that he still turned most readily when contemplating the best means of resolving society's most deep-seated problems. For a responsive system of law to evolve, however, it was essential that legislators as well as lawyers should begin to reassess the values their society held most dear; this in turn required both the wider dissemination of progressive social thinking, and a higher degree of public participation at all levels of the political process. Brandeis's growing conviction that ordinary working people should take responsibility for decisions affecting their own lives led him also to reconsider the high value he had previously placed on professional knowledge and skill. "I trusted only expert opinion," he recalled in 1913; but "experience of life" had made him look again at democracy, and at the patent nostrums of "the worldly wise." "I began to see that many things sanctioned by expert opinion were wrong." This realization constituted a significant departure from the views held by most Progressives, whose own professional expertise regularly served as their principal warrant for political activism. But it also represented a major paradox; for this was also the man whose victory in *Muller v. Oregon*, barely five years before, had been wholly dependent on the marshaling and skillful deployment of expert testimony.[64]

Perhaps the conflict between these two positions is more apparent than real, though. Brandeis objected to claims of specialist knowledge because they were too often used to support arbitrary action, and this he abhorred regardless of whether the prescriptive authority in question was judicial, administrative, or corporate. The value of experts, he believed, ought to lie in their intrinsic neutrality, in their capacity to serve as disinterested witnesses of fact. Their proper role was to enlighten judges, to advise politicians and businessmen, to inform public debate; it was not to take and implement decisions on their own authority. Although most Progressives were inclined to subordinate public opinion to professional expertise, when it came to the crunch, Brandeis wanted to make those in positions of power more fully answerable to the public they were supposed to be serving. He preferred increasingly to rely on the commonsense wisdom of a culturally differentiated and democratic populace, made capable of developing its potential for self-government to the full by education and opportunity.

One section of that populace for whom the opportunity to participate in any kind of government remained strictly limited was made up of American women. Speaking in opposition to women's suffrage had been one of Brandeis's earliest political activities, and there is no evidence to suggest that his attitudes softened appreciably before the turn of the century. By 1905 he was ready to acknowledge his belated approval of women voting for members of the Boston school committee—something they had actually been doing since 1879!—but he still thought it inadvisable for the present "to change the caucus law so as to permit them participating in the selection of candidates." Six years later, however, he could be considered an outright friend of votes for women. In June 1911, he agreed to preside at a meeting of the National Congress of Charities and Correction held in Boston's Jacob Sleeper Hall, where, among others, Jane Addams and Sophonisba Breckenridge were scheduled to speak on the suffrage question.

In the event, he was reluctantly persuaded to address the conference himself and to explain why he had shifted his position from one of hostility to one of advocacy. "That change in opinion is the result of my own experience in the various movements with which I have been connected," he told an expectant audience.

> As years have passed I have been more and more impressed with the difficulty and complexity of [the social, economic, and political problems that have presented themselves] and also with the power of society to solve them; but I am convinced that for their solution we must look to the many, not to the few. We need all the people, women as much as men. In the democracy which is to solve them, we must have not a part of society but the whole.

His contacts with labor activist Mary Kenney, and even more the long and intimate friendship he and Alice enjoyed with Elizabeth Glendower Evans, may have done much to blunt his early prejudice; however, it was probably the research done by Josephine Goldmark and Florence Kelley for the revolutionary *Muller* brief that did most to revise his opinion of the work women were capable of performing in public life. Indeed, he may well have had this very case in mind as he continued:

> The insight that women have shown into problems which men did not and perhaps could not understand, has convinced me not only that women should have the ballot, but that we need them to have it. This is specially the case because these problems will have to be solved largely through collective action in which legislation is necessary.[65]

From this point onward, Brandeis became an increasingly vocal proponent of women's suffrage; it fitted comfortably into an evolving philosophical perspective that stressed development of the individual through active involvement in the wider community. In February 1913 he testified during hearings on the proposed constitutional amendment for equal suffrage in Massachusetts, and thereafter worked hard for the campaign to secure the ratification of this and similar measures being put forward in other states. "Women's suffrage must be generally adopted," he wired a staff editor of *Strauss Magazine* in March 1913, "because the participation of women in political affairs will promote social efficiency. Much that is required to be done to improve social and industrial conditions can be done only with women's aid. We cannot relieve them from the duty of taking part in public affairs." Two years later, in a special edition of the *Boston American* devoted entirely to the franchise debate, he took the opportunity to expand on his views in some detail.[66]

He began by taking issue with the old cliché that a woman's place was in the home. A century of industrial evolution had ensured that the occupations which had once kept her there—spinning, weaving, making clothes, preparing food for the family—no longer took up the amount of time and effort they once had, the domestic needs in question now being met in large part "by our immense factory and commercial systems." During the same period, the quality and availability of education for women had developed rapidly, to the point where an equal share in the suffrage was not only fair but, in due course, inevitable. "No power on earth," he declared confidently, "can maintain equal educational standards for all classes, side by side with political inequalities." Hand in hand with these changes had come "tremendous possibilities for the individual development of men and women": not only for making money but also for "living harmoniously." Modern life differed "very materially from collective life a few generations back," and now presented Americans with a series of "urgent and evergrowing social and political problems" that threatened the well-being of the whole community. "Government no longer consists merely of preserving order," he observed emphatically;

we passed that period of national existence long ago, but of a necessity it also includes the doing of those things that make life livable.

That our present-day women are pre-eminently fitted to carry work forward by education as well as by temperament absolutely is beyond question.

To suggest that "public service of the highest possible character" was not conducive to the development of "admirable feminine traits" was nothing short of an insult. Yet despite being "highly educated and by nature especially fitted to help carry forward the work of modern government," women were still being held back, denied "the real force of citizenship." True, women the world over were already contributing "to the welfare of humanity in numerous capacities," but they found themselves frustrated and handicapped in their endeavors through lack of any "positive power to secure remedial legislation." The need for universal suffrage was indeed great. "It is utterly beyond belief," he declared rhetorically, "that the perplexing problems confronting all democracies can be solved without utilizing every particle of assistance available in the entire community." All women, regardless or their age or marital status, "must be given an opportunity to work for the great human family."

The article concluded by linking the issue of women's suffrage to the preservation and future development of democracy itself, and as a concise statement of Brandeis's political creed is worth quoting at length:

> Universal suffrage does not imply that every citizen with a vote will use that vote wisely, but it does mean that we would have universal responsibility and a universal power to advance the best interests of the community in which we live.
>
> While it is true that man may have a special mission in life, it is also obviously and undeniably true that woman's viewpoint on social and moral questions is so different that all factors entering into those problems cannot be weighed in the balances of public opinion without equal suffrage. . . .
>
> Democracy has proved of far greater value to the world than the super-man, and the rule of reason a safer reliance than anything offered by brute force and nation-wide despotism.
>
> Yet complete democracy is no longer possible in any government that refuses woman a legitimate right to contribute of her zeal and intelligence for the good of all, herself included.
>
> I shall vote YES on the suffrage amendment at the next State election, aside from any question of women's rights, because it is my manifest duty to do so in the interests of true democracy.[67]

The informed and responsible exercise of political liberty, however, was only one of the fundamental rights he thought appropriate for citizens in a truly democratic society. For what practical use was the right to vote for those wielding political power in the state, if those controlling the economic resources of industry and commerce continued to behave in a totally arbitrary fashion, displaying contempt and disdain for the interests and wishes of the men and women whose working lives they had come to dominate? In his

pre-Court days as the "people's attorney" Brandeis became closely identified with that body of reform-minded Progressives who sought to improve
the physical welfare of working people, directly through the passage and
judicial acceptance of social-welfare legislation, and indirectly through the
organization of labor unions.

Here as elsewhere, the range and complexity of his ideas has given rise to
much confusion and misunderstanding; however, some elements of his
thinking stand out clearly enough. For instance, when he came to testify before the Industrial Relations Commission in 1915, he would be quite forthright in his opinion that the improvement of material conditions and physical
well-being were not, by themselves, a sufficient objective for which to aim:

> It is the development of manhood to which any industrial and social system should
> be directed. We Americans are committed not only to social justice in the sense of
> avoiding things which bring suffering and harm, like unjust distribution of wealth;
> but we are committed primarily to democracy. The social justice for which we are
> striving is an incident of our democracy, not the main end. It is rather the result
> of democracy—perhaps its finest expression—but it rests upon democracy, which
> implies the rule of the people, and that involves industrial democracy as well as
> political democracy.

Individual development could not occur unless men and women were properly housed and fed, and unless they had proper facilities for education and
leisure. Yet one might achieve all these things and still have "a nation of
slaves." It was not uncommon for a corporation to offer wages and conditions significantly more attractive than those sought by organized labor, as a
means of undermining union influence and buying-off pressures for democratization of the company's decision-making machinery. To give way before
such blandishments was a grave error, he believed: "Men must have industrial liberty as well as good wages"; and although improved conditions might
"contribute a very material amount" to both the quantity and quality of life,
care should be taken that such provision did not constitute "a bribe to forgo
that which is more important."[68]

The task of reconciling the modern industrial system with the ideals of the
nation's political democracy was, Brandeis had declared as early as 1905,
"the greatest problem . . . before the American people in this generation."
In an interview for *La Follette's Weekly Magazine* eight years later, he
sought to measure the progress already made by workers along the road to
industrial democracy.

> In my judgment, we are going through the following stages: We already have had
> industrial despotism. With the recognition of unions, this is changing into a consti-
> tutional monarchy, with well-defined limitations placed about the employer's
> formerly autocratic power. Next comes profit sharing. This, however, is to be only
> a transitional, half-way stage. Following upon it will come the sharing of respon-
> sibility, as well as of profits. The eventual outcome promises to be full-grown in-
> dustrial democracy.

And he concluded rather cryptically: "As to this last step the Socialists have furnished us with an ideal full of suggestion."[69]

It was the experience of taking responsibility for one's own life which he regarded as the creative, evolutionary force in human development. "No remedy can be hopeful," he would write in 1922, "which does not devolve upon the workers participation in, responsibility for the conduct of business; and their aim should be the eventual assumption of full responsibility—as in cooperative enterprises." Thus if his earliest response to labor relations had been, as Allon Gal suggests, to take up a position "somewhere between the interests of the employer and those of the working man," the logic of his maturing philosophy was to adopt a much more radical stance. The views he articulated in these later years were in fact quite unequivocal. Not only was the worker's participation in and ultimate control of industry a prerequisite for his personal development; it was also an essential step toward the attainment of a proper social justice by wider distribution of the fruits of industry.[70]

"Bigness," though, got in the way of such developments. By the time he gave testimony before the Industrial Relations Commission in 1915, he had evidently devoted considerable thought to the phenomenon and was ready to elaborate on its ramifications. His main objection to the very large corporation was that it made possible, perhaps inevitable, what he called "the exercise of industrial absolutism." Organized labor battled with massive corporations on a wholly unequal basis, lacking both their power and their economic resources. Such contests, thought Brandeis, "though undertaken with the best motives and with strong conviction on the part of the corporate managers that they are seeking what is for the best interests not only of the company but of the community, lead to absolutism." It was this absolutism, whether malevolent or benign, which made the great corporations so dangerous. "There develops within the state," he warned, "a state so powerful that the ordinary social and industrial forces existing are insufficient to cope with it." The impersonality of these institutions militated against any semblance of industrial democracy. Remote directors, "absentee" stockholders, and complex executive hierarchies prevented employees from participating in management decisions or even from influencing them. Plant managers, situated near the bottom of the executive structure, became little more than stewards, overseeing the successful operation of their factories and having almost no say in the planning of corporate strategy. Yet paradoxically it was they alone who came into regular personal contact with the labor force. "Thus we lose," claimed Brandeis, "that necessary cooperation which naturally flows from contact between employers and employees— and which the American aspirations for democracy demand."[71]

Such a working environment was hardly conducive to that development of human potential which he had long regarded as vital. Some years later, Dean Acheson, his law clerk in the early 1920s, put his finger precisely on the thing that made Brandeis so angry about this state of affairs:

He thinks that the great end in life lies with the individual mind, in its building up its own worlds, in its explorations and darings and triumphs over weaknesses and fears and laziness, and, perhaps, something more . . . that I don't even guess at. But he sees that for most the road to this is quite shut off and for the rest it is getting more and more impassable as great stupid institutions, growing larger and larger, fall across the way and crowd into the little space which the individual has.

From Brandeis's perspective this could only lead to futility and frustration, and these in turn might be expected to lead to outbursts of antisocial violence. In 1912, for instance, referring to the use of explosives by saboteurs in Los Angeles, he sought to place the responsibility for such outrages where he felt they properly belonged. Why had they occurred? What drove the perpetrators?

Was it not because they, and men like them, believed that the wage earner, acting singly, or collectively, is not strong enough to secure substantial justice? Is there not a causal connection between the development of these huge indomitable trusts and the horrible crimes now under investigation? Are not these irresistible trusts important contributing causes of these crimes—these unintelligent expressions of despairing social unrest? Is it not irony to speak of the equality of opportunity, in a country cursed with their bigness?[72]

Much as he might sympathize with workers driven to such acts of violence (and it is perhaps significant that he discounted the possibility that they might have been ideologically motivated), sabotage and armed struggle were not activities of which he approved. Instead he favored an assault on what he saw as the root causes of social alienation, and so sought to improve communication and understanding between workers and their employers, as a first step on the road to industrial democracy. Any implication that, as a Progressive, Brandeis was antilabor, or that he struck a half-hearted balance between the divergent interests of labor and capital, is profoundly misleading; for his experience of industrial relations from the 1890s onward was sufficient to convince him that, potentially at least, the two sides of industry enjoyed a real community of interests. What was needed was a forum in which they might be brought together. "Problems existing in a trade are those of the employer and employee both," he asserted in 1915. Profit sharing alone could not provide solutions to such problems:

There must be a division not only of profits, but a division also of responsibilities. The employees must have the opportunity of participating in decisions as to what shall be their condition and how the business shall be run. They must learn also in sharing that responsibility that they, too, must bear the suffering rising from grave mistakes, just as the employer must. But the right to assist in making decisions, the right of making their own mistakes, if mistakes there must be, is a privilege which should not be denied to labor.

Industrial democracy was thus defined as not only a voice but a vote as well; "not merely a right to be heard, but a position through which labor may participate in management." When asked whether the scheme he envisaged ought to come about by voluntary agreement or whether some kind of compulsion might not be desirable, he professed himself a believer in voluntary agreements, "certainly for the present." In the short run the most important work was to educate the parties involved, to make them aware of their interdependence. Success required not only goodwill but also a large measure of continuing effort; workers would have to learn some of the skills of management. Industrial democracy was only possible, he had written in 1905, among people who could think:

among people who are [of] above average intelligence. And that thinking is not a heaven-born thing, that intelligence is not a gift that merely comes. It is a gift men make and women make for themselves. It is earned, and it is earned by effort. There is not effort, to my mind, that is comparable in its qualities, that is so taxing to the individual, as to think, to analyze fundamentally. The brain is like the hand. It grows with using.[73]

In his testimony before the U.S. Commission on Industrial Relations he cited the New York garment industry as an example of what could be achieved, referring particularly to the provisions of the protocol drawn up at his own instigation in September 1910. Having himself served as chairman of the industry's Board of Arbitration, he was well qualified to explain its virtues. Under the protocol certain grievances had been removed, but whereas similar results had been accomplished by many agreements between employers and employees in other industries, in the garment trades the process had been taken a stage further. According to Brandeis, the protocol had "created a system of government" for owners and workers alike:

In many agreements between employers and unions, you find a provision for a grievance committee, but such committees are only for occasional use. The protocol establishes a government with administrative officers, courts, and a legislature always ready to take up questions arising in the trade. . . . It is absolutely as continuous as our political government.

So long as capital and labor, employers and employees, retained distinct functions and identities in industrial society, then only by creating something akin to a government for each trade, a forum within which problems might come up for consideration and solution as they arose from day to day, could any approach to genuine democratization be made.[74]

Yet while *preferring* voluntary moves toward the implementation of industrial democracy, Brandeis confessed himself pessimistic about the possibilities. Once again, the problem he perceived was the autocratic attitude of the larger corporations. As long as such concentrations of power existed, he believed, no effort to secure democratization on the part of working people could possibly be effective. Much of the country's protective legislation consisted of prohibition of things that had been found dangerous according to common experience. For example, it had been found necessary to set limits on the maximum size of trucks permitted to use the public highways. "Concentration of power," he told the commissioners, "has been shown to be dangerous in a democracy, even though that power may be used beneficially." It was the mere existence of such power and not the manner of its use that constituted the real problem.[75]

When it came to an industrial concern as large and powerful as United States Steel, applying the concept of democratization was an objective fraught with enormous difficulties. The company was so large that Brandeis thought it unimaginable that the men in control could be made to realize the necessity of yielding a part of their power to their employees. "It is almost inconceivable to my mind," he declared, "that a corporation with powers so concentrated as the Steel Corporation could get to a point where it would be willing to treat with the employees on equal terms. And unless they treat on equal terms there is no such thing as democratization." This required more than merely making a contract with the work force; it required a continuing relationship, the elaboration of a system of industrial government. Yet it was scarcely reasonable to expect large corporations to reform themselves. In his view, the evidence regrettably was all to the contrary:

> I think all of our human experience shows that no one with absolute power can be trusted to give it up even in part. That has been the experience with political absolutism. Industrial democracy will not come by gift. It has got to be won by those who desire it. And if the situation is such that a voluntary organization like a labor union is powerless to bring about the democratization of a business, I think we have in this fact some proof that the employing organization is larger than is consistent with the public interest. I mean by larger, is more powerful, has a financial influence too great to be useful to the State; and the State must in some way come to the aid of the workingmen if democratization is to be secured.[76]

Regulation, or so Brandeis maintained, was as essential to the preservation and development of healthy competition as it was to the preservation and development of liberty; for excesses of competition would lead to monopoly in the economic sphere just as surely as in the political sphere excesses of liberty would lead to absolutism. "The right to competition," he wrote exactly twenty years before the Oklahoma Ice case dissent, "must be limited in order to preserve it." The proposition that regulation of some kind was required in the economy was something on which Progressives were generally united. As we have seen, the only real contention among them was whether it was competition or monopoly that needed to be regulated. According to Brandeis, those like himself who advocated the regulation of the former insisted

> that competition can be and should be maintained in every branch of private industry; and that [it] can be and should be restored in those branches of industry in which it has been suppressed by the trusts. They believe that no methods of regulation ever have been or can be devised to remove the menace inherent in private monopoly and overweaning financial power; and that if, at any future time, monopoly should appear to be desirable in any branch of industry, the monopoly should be a public one—monopoly owned by the people and not by the capitalists.

Though not directly spelled out here, the assumption clearly implicit in this manifesto was that the newly competitive environment Brandeis wished to see could only be brought about if oversized businesses were broken up into smaller, more effective units, and could only be maintained thereafter if government stepped in to prevent the great lords of capital from recombining their assets for reasons of private advantage. If disaggregation were to prove genuinely impracticable, then public ownership should be considered preferable in the last resort to continued corporate control of large-scale monopoly.[77]

By the time when these words first appeared in *Harper's Weekly* in November 1913, their writer was becoming concerned lest Woodrow Wilson might fail to follow through with the enactment of new antitrust legislation adumbrated during his 1912 presidential election campaign. Brandeis's faith in federal regulation was at its height, and the finality of his judgments quoted above needs to be interpreted in that light. It will be recalled that as late as November 1911 he had explicitly rejected the notion of a federal commission being established to regulate monopoly; yet within a year he was ready to accept without quibble that the effective control of either monopoly or competition would require not merely a clear legislative framework but a regulatory agency to boot.

The first evidence of his "conversion" to the idea of federal regulation came in the draft of a letter on antitrust policy that he penned for Governor Wilson's use in September 1912. Hitherto, he believed, the Sherman Act had been "little more than a declaration of our economic policy"; and though experience gained under the act had served to establish the soundness of that policy, it had also pointed up defects in the legislation that stood in the way of its effective implementation.

> To make that Sherman law a controlling force—to preserve competition where it now exists, and to restore competition where it has been suppressed—additional and comprehensive legislation is necessary. The prohibitions on combination contained in the act must be made more definite; the provisions for enforcing its provisions by the Courts must be improved; and they must be supplemented by other adequate machinery to be administered by a Federal Board or Commission.

With regard to the third of these proposals, he was able to justify it with
some force:

> The functions of government should not be limited to the enactment of wise rules
> of action, and the providing of efficient judicial machinery. . . . The Government,
> at least where the general public is concerned, is charged with securing also com-
> pliance with the law. We need the inspector and the policeman, even more than
> we need the prosecuting attorney; and we need for the enforcement of the Sher-
> man law and regulation of competition an administrative board with broad powers.

Precisely what the scope of those powers ought to be was a matter that
could safely be left to Congress, but the board should clearly be entitled to
gather information about corporate abuses, to cooperate fully with the Department of Justice, and to aid directly in securing compliance with the law.
Moreover, he thought it probable that "whatever powers are conferred upon
the Board at the outset will be increased from time to time" as experience
showed what additional authority it might usefully and safely be invested
with. This, then, was the essence of what Brandeis recommended to the governor prior to his election as president in November 1912; indeed, it was to
become the very essence of the New Freedom program itself.[78]

Yet, if many specific features of the New Freedom's antitrust program
plainly owed much to Brandeis's outlook and industry, in at least one
essential—their attitude toward the nature and scope of governmental
intervention—he and Wilson differed markedly. Deep down, despite his
public endorsement of the regulatory regime established in 1914, the latter
continued to affirm the traditional creed of his party that the best kind of
government was that which governed least. He was a late convert to "trust-
busting" and a reluctant proponent of the view that new institutional
mechanisms might be needed to achieve it. His speeches in 1912 are full of
righteous indignation against the evils of monopoly, but apart from moral
suasion and vigorous imposition of the criminal penalties prescribed by the
Sherman Act they had little new to offer. Brandeis, though, took a more
positive stance. As Melvin I. Urofsky has observed:

> If Wilson approached the trust problem in the role of political moralist, his most
> trusted advisor came in the garb of social and economic engineer. Louis Brandeis
> did not share Wilson's belief in the basic goodness of men but leaned toward
> Adam Smith's view of the basically greedy nature of economic man. Before Con-
> gressional hearings on trust legislation he maintained that any real effectiveness of
> anti-trust measures would never be brought out through criminal proceedings. To
> another committee he said he saw no hope that searing the monopolists "alleged
> consciences" would produce any results at all. The proper method would be to de-
> cide on the desired goals and then frame just laws which reasonable men would
> follow.

But Urofsky also argues that what Wilson found so appealing about the
Brandeisian program against bigness was its apparent compatibility with his

own commitment to limited government. Provided it were possible to re-store and maintain a competitive economic environment, then the basic inefficiencies of bigness would bring about its demise. If this was indeed Wilson's reasoning, it is evident that he had failed to understand the fundamental lineaments of Brandeis's proposals. The latter's "unit of greatest efficiency" was not envisaged as the institutional fulcrum of a free-market economy, through which some kind of leverage might be applied against the trusts, nor yet the automatic product of market forces seeking to establish some classical notion of economic balance; it was a social goal to be worked for, intelligently and pragmatically. It mattered not that, as Richard Hofstadter claimed, "no one, not even Brandeis, knew how to define or measure superior efficiency, or to draw a line in the progress towards bigness, beyond which it would lose, rather than gain, in efficiency." There was never any intention on his part to fix such lines of demarcation once and for all in legislative form; rather they were to be determined on a case-by-case basis within a framework of rules laid down by Congress.

If the vision thus held out to Wilson did not involve the creation of a vast federal bureaucracy to bring it to fruition, this was only because the machinery Brandeis considered essential for enforcing compliance was not to be administrative so much as judicial in nature. For all its practical deficiencies, the Interstate Commerce Commission provided him with his model of a regulatory tribunal, nominally part of the executive, but exercising quasi-judicial functions derived from the time-honored procedures of the common law and courts of equity.[79]

It will be recalled that, in his draft memorandum of September 1912, Brandeis had urged Wilson to pursue three separate but related lines of attack against the trusts: clarification of the Sherman Act by means of supplementary legislation; the taking of steps to ensure that the courts enforced the law as amended; and the creation of an investigative board or commission to help secure compliance with its provisions. Generally speaking, an undue concentration on the first and last of these proposals has been accompanied by an unwarranted neglect of the second. In Brandeis's view, the main obstacle to the proper imposition of existing antitrust policies—lately exemplified in the "lamentable failure of the proceedings against the Standard Oil and the Tobacco Trust"—was not the courts' inability "to prevent or to disintegrate illegal combinations," but rather involved "defects in judicial machinery or methods." The division of trust-owned properties into identifiable segments did not by itself make the resulting components "separate and distinct," if it permitted them to be owned and controlled by the same stockholders. In this respect the Supreme Court's decrees were clearly deficient. Furthermore, by failing "to afford redress for wrongs done in the past" to a large number of independent business concerns, they had connived at "a failure of justice destined to bring into disrepute not only the Sherman Law, but all law." The remedy for such ills, and the means of ensuring that they were not repeated in future cases, lay at hand, however, if the government were willing to make the courts operate effectively. "Efficient judicial machinery," he observed,

> will give relief to the people by effecting a real disintegration of those trusts which have heretofore suppressed competition and will also enable individuals who have suffered from illegal acts to secure adequate compensation. Efficient judicial machinery will be even more potent as a deterrent than as a cure; for inefficient judicial processes is [sic] the greatest encouragement to law-breaking.

It obviously would not require a wild leap of the imagination to substitute for the mild term "inefficiency" a rather more caustic phrase such as "judicial bias in favor of concentrated capital"; yet, in fact, Brandeis was at pains not to personalize his indictment. "This failure is not inherent in judicial processes," his memorandum asserted.

> It is due wholly to a surprising lack of effective legal method and machinery. The judicial determination of the illegality of the combination and its practices should result, under any proper system of law, as a matter of course, in compensation to the injured, and reparation to the public in some form for the profits wrongfully obtained. The Sherman Law contemplated in part such a result, for it provided that anyone injured by an illegal combination might recover three times the damages actually suffered. But that provision has been practically a dead letter; because under the general rules of law the decisions in proceedings instituted by the government do not enure in any respect to the individual benefit of those who have been injured.

It was necessary for the aggrieved parties to institute independent proceedings, in the course of which as private litigants they could expect to "derive no legal aid from the decree in favor of the government." This, Brandeis thought, was a bizarre state of affairs that had granted the trusts effective immunity from private suits for damages. Yet the evil consequences of it might easily be avoided by the adoption of a simple device suggested in bills currently pending in Congress. This would

> provide in substance, that whenever in a proceeding instituted by the Government a final judgment is rendered declaring that the defendant has entered into a combination in unreasonable restraint of trade, that finding shall be conclusive as against the defendant in any other proceeding brought against the defendant by anyone, so that the injured person would thereafter merely have to establish the amount of the loss suffered; and the danger of losing the right to compensation (while awaiting the results of the Government suit) is averted by the further simple device of providing that the Statute of Limitations shall not run while the government suit is pending.

The significance of these observations resides less in the merit or otherwise of the specific remedies being proposed, than in the confirmation they afford to Edward McClennen's remark that, even in his reform activities,

Brandeis was used to operating within a mental framework defined by legal ideals and procedures. Although he might have considered accepting the post of attorney general in Wilson's cabinet had it been offered, there seems little doubt that he had long since decided against pursuing a career in politics, just as decades earlier he had eschewed a career in the classroom. At what point he first set his sights on becoming a judge it is impossible to say, but the nature of the advice and assistance he gave to Wilson, both as candidate and as president, seems wholly consistent with the developing self-image of a legal elder statesman. To the man who within four years would nominate him for a seat on the nation's highest court he wrote: "These are a few of the many improvements in judicial machinery which, if adopted, would go far toward making the Sherman law a controlling force." And then, generalizing the point, he went on: "It is largely by similar improvements in our judicial machinery, and not by the recall of judges, that the inefficiency of our courts will be overcome and a just administration of law be attained." This was true enough, but it was doubtless true as well that the appointment to judgeships of men who combined in their hearts a healthy respect for the power of law with a steadfast determination not to abuse it might be even more conducive to the end sought. If such a proposition occurred to him, he of course left it unstated.[80]

In a perceptive examination of the extent to which Wilson relied on Brandeis for economic advice during the 1912 campaign and the first year of his administration, Melvin Urofsky has rightly pointed to the Boston lawyer's decisive support for a federal reserve system under governmental control as the key factor impelling the president to repudiate more conservative proposals being put forward in the summer of 1913.[81] Yet as we have already seen, for Brandeis banking reform represented only one small step along the road to genuine economic liberty, and before the end of the year he had begun privately urging key figures in the administration to press ahead with more direct means of combating large concentrations of capital. "The President's policy of New Freedom involves necessarily the hostility of the great banking and financial interests," he told the new interior secretary, Franklin K. Lane, in December; "for they want industrial and financial absolutism, while we want industrial democracy. The conflict between us is irreconcilable." Publicly, in a muckraking article in *Harper's Weekly*, he repeated the advice he had earlier given in confidence to Wilson:

> The Money Trust cannot be broken, if we allow its power to be constantly augmented. To break the Money Trust, we must stop that power at it source. The industrial trusts are among its most effective feeders. Those which are illegal should be dissolved. The creation of new ones should be prevented. To this end the Sherman Law should be supplemented both by providing more efficient judicial machinery, and by creating a commission with administrative functions to aid in enforcing the law. When that is done, another step will have been taken toward securing the New Freedom.[82]

However, despite this public shift of ground in the direction of an activist program against the trusts, in private he remained far from sanguine; from other published sources we know that he was gloomily aware of the practical difficulties likely to attend any new efforts at implementing a policy of federal regulation. The desirability of trade agreements between competing firms in the same industry would need to be determined, probably case by case; further steps would need to be taken to outlaw incestuous relationships between railroads and their customers, thus bringing about a complete divorce of transportation from industry. Even more problematic was the question of rate and dividend regulation. The establishment of any rule fixing maximum returns on capital might threaten efficiency and lead to a reduction of corporate effort; the difficulties of distinguishing larger net earnings due to managerial efficiency or workers' productivity from those rightly designated excess profits seemed virtually insuperable. Likewise, attempts to secure low prices by means of government price fixing were liable to prove as unworkable as statutory efforts to control railroad rates by limiting the dividends payable by railroad corporations.[83]

Perhaps the most serious obstacle of all, though, was the sheer scope and magnitude of the technical difficulties involved: the lack of uniformity between industrial activities and between different plants in a single industry; the quantity of data to be collected and analyzed; the need to act flexibly and effectively within a reasonable time scale; the impracticability of assessing "reasonableness of rates" where costs of production or provision were fiercely debated, or where pools and other forms of monopoly made meaningful comparisons impossible. Even if these problems were capable of solution—and his awareness of human limitations led him to believe otherwise—there would remain the matter of effective enforcement. One of his principal concerns, as he told Wilson at the outset of their relationship, was to ensure that any regulatory commission established should be empowered to aid in securing compliance with antitrust legislation, not only in the interests of the public as a whole, but at the request and for the benefit of those particular individuals or businesses who had been injured, or who feared injury, as the result of unfair competition. In view of the obvious inequality of resources between the giant corporations and their smaller competitors, he believed that equality before the law could no longer be secured merely by the provision of adequate enforcement machinery. It was essential that the government should intervene positively to prevent injustice.[84]

A strong Federal Trade Commission bill, to which the People's Attorney had contributed liberally during later stages of the drafting process, did in fact become law in the summer of 1914, as did the much-amended Clayton Anti-Trust bill referred to earlier. Almost immediately, however, the outbreak of hostilities in Europe began to restrict the attention those in Washington felt able to devote to purely domestic affairs, so that by 1915 Brandeis had become even more skeptical about the possibilities for further action against bigness—at least where the national government was concerned. He may also have become disillusioned by Wilson's failure to comprehend fully the implications of the distinction he drew between bigness and monopoly. Asked whether existing state and federal legislation was adequate to prevent industrial abuses, he now confessed to having "grave doubt as to how much can be accomplished by legislation, unless it be to set a limit upon the size of corporate units," and went on to argue that, when the results of great size became a danger to the welfare of its citizens, the *community* might have to impose limits. Here, Brandeis appeared to be addressing himself once more to the desirability of state rather than federal regulation; a reversion which, when developed to its logical conclusion, would lead him inexorably toward the "community control" position that he would adopt years later in his Ice case opinion.[85]

The standard interpretation of the New Freedom as a "basically conservative" ideology is well established and has done much to color received opinion concerning Brandeis's mature social philosophy. According to the representative summary afforded by Urofsky, it

> looked not to reform and to redo society in a new mode but to return to an idyllic (and mythical) past in which the various economic groups of the country existed in near-perfect harmony. To the extent that it favored popular democracy against a *status quo* favoring a wealthy elite, it was progressive, but its liberalism was of the nineteenth-century *laissez-faire* type, which called for an impotent government with a minimum of regulation.

There may indeed be some truth in this analysis, especially as it relates to the gut instincts of Wilson himself, but as a synoptic view (at least by association) of the future justice's thinking it is a patent travesty.[86]

It is certainly the case that Brandeis, like the president, "feared letting government go too far," and was therefore implacably hostile to the New Nationalists' concept of an intrusive bureaucratic state, which, in the name of efficiency, would subordinate individual liberties to the abstraction of a higher public interest. But if for Wilson the defense of individualism was an ideal with largely negative connotations, for Brandeis it had come to imply the need for a series of positive institutional developments. Partly as a result of his professional experiences as a corporate lawyer in Massachusetts, and partly as the product of his growing involvement in public causes at both the local and national levels, he had become ever more convinced that the limited capacities of human beings required the interposition of a coherent and accessible framework of law between each citizen and the wider community of which he or she was a part. Living under a constitutional system of government, he believed, individuals should be able to depend on the law as the best means of ordering relationships between one another, and of protecting them from any accretion of power—be it personal, corporate, or governmental—which appeared to threaten their autonomy, deny them opportunities for personal development, or diminish their moral responsibility for decisions affecting their own lives and the lives of others.

If he now expressed greater respect for legislators than he had been wont to do thirty years earlier, and appreciated the need for judges to exercise self-restraint in their interpretation both of constitutions and of statute law, he continued nevertheless to regard the judicial function as a vital adjunct to the necessary processes of legislative reform. The only trouble was that, to be successful, this philosophy required that judges as well as politicians should behave responsibly and in accordance with the dictates of reason; for this he was able to provide no guarantees beyond those afforded by education, exhortation, and example on the part of those who engaged in public life. At first sight, this might appear to lead back toward specious parallels with Woodrow Wilson, whose moral preachments became the hallmark of his presidential career at home and abroad; in fact, however, Brandeis's social vision was much broader than this.

Though his projections of the good life are easily viewed as the reflex of a bourgeois-liberal outlook, his willingness to contemplate such radical innovations as producer-cooperatives, industrial councils, and even the public ownership of natural monopolies serve to establish his credentials as a man ready to face the future with imagination and creativity rather than as one bent on retreating to the idyll of a mythical golden age. Admittedly, his radicalism was to some extent backward looking: at least as far as the Massachusetts of his early adult life, and quite possibly to the Ohio Valley of his boyhood. Yet these had been functioning polities, not vaporous utopias; he had seen these pasts at firsthand and knew that they worked. By allowing bigness to strangle both individualism and free enterprise, Americans had set out along a false path, and wisdom now required that they should retrace their steps. If breaking the trusts meant creating new regulatory agencies, disciplining the courts, and laying the foundations for a thoroughgoing industrial democracy, then so be it.

As we have seen, the paths that led Brandeis to this individualistic conception of Progressivism were many and varied; but while his pragmatic responses to external events and experiences were doubtless of considerable importance, especially in relation to his views on bigness, it would be a mistake to ignore the primacy of the social philosophy that had been evolving and maturing in his mind since childhood. For him, the enactment of legislative programs and the establishment of judicial restraints were primarily viewed as the means to an end. Such activities represented goals of secondary importance when compared with the more ambitious objective of controlling and channeling the forces of industrial growth, and of doing so in ways that would enhance rather than restrict the opportunities for personal development available to ordinary Americans. For against his idealistic awareness of the potential for social and economic progress was set a realistic assessment of the frailties and imperfections of individual human beings, even the most dextrous and intelligent—of all perhaps except himself!

5

A Gift of Prophecy

And he shall set up an ensign for the nations, and shall as-
semble the outcasts of Israel, and gather together the dispersed
of Judah from the four corners of the earth. . . .
For the Lord will have mercy on Jacob, and will yet choose
Israel, and set them in their own land: and the strangers shall be
joined with them, and shall cleave to the house of Jacob.
—The Book of the Prophet Isaiah

Interested though Brandeis was in influencing the content and sustaining the momentum of liberal reform measures, it was legal rather than political activities that played the dominant role in his life during the first eighteen months of the new administration—particularly his work as special counsel for the Interstate Commerce Commission—that culminated in the "freight-rate" decision handed down by the commission in July 1914. Yet behind the familiar picture of the "people's attorney" as a legal magician and sometime legislative draftsman, as a Progressive campaigner with access to the inner recesses of presidential power for as long as Woodrow Wilson remained in the White House, it is possible to discern the steady emergence after 1912 of another, less tangible image: that of elder statesman and confidant to men in high places; of oracle and prophet.[1]

It sprang not simply from a difference of years, for although Brandeis was somewhat older than many of the Progressive activists who sought his advice, he and the president were almost of an age. In part his new role grew out of a widely held perception that he was one of the most talented and ingenious public figures of his generation. It was no idle whim, for example, that persuaded Wilson to offer him the chairmanship of the proposed Commission on Industrial Relations in the spring of 1913, and with no intention to flatter that he wrote: "There is no one in the United States who could preside over and direct such an inquiry so well as you could." Moreover, according to Navy Secretary Josephus Daniels, this high regard was not confined merely to the early years of the New Freedom. "Wilson often wished the concept of his counsel in matters on which he was an authority," Daniels noted in his memoirs. "Not once, but a number of times discussing humanitarian or progressive policies, he would say to me: 'I wish you would go to see our friend Brandeis, acquaint him with the problem and get his reaction.' "[2]

More than knowledge, expertise, or intelligence, however, the indefatigable Boston lawyer seemed to possess the faculty of wisdom: an ability to help others see clearly the best means of resolving their own problems. "A talk with Brandeis always sweeps the cobwebs out of your mind," observed the president in 1915; and the following year, in a letter supporting his controversial nomination of Brandeis for a seat on the Supreme Court, he went even further:

> I have known him. I have tested him by seeking his advice upon some of the most difficult and perplexing public questions about which it was necessary for me to form a judgment. I have dealt with him in matters where nice questions of honor and fair play, as well as large questions of justice and the public benefit, were involved. In every matter in which I have made test of his judgment and point of view, I have received from him counsel singularly enlightening, singularly clear-sighted and judicial, and, above all, full of moral stimulation.

Nor did Brandeis's appointment to the Court put an end to his role as counselor and sage, rather the opposite; for though his public pronouncement were henceforth confined to judicial and, as we shall see, to Zionist matters, his private views continued to be sought and offered on an ever-widening range of subjects.[3]

To cite just one particularly noteworthy example: when, toward the end of 1917, after America's entry into the war, Wilson was persuaded to take over the nation's congested railroad network, he at first questioned the expediency of asking his son-in-law, William Gibbs McAdoo, to head up the agency charged with administering it, especially since the latter insisted on retaining his cabinet post as Secretary of the Treasury as well. On Friday, 7 December, Joseph P. Tumulty, Wilson's private secretary, and Robert W. Woolley of the Interstate Commerce Commission went to see Brandeis at his Washington home in the hope that he might use his influence with the president to secure McAdoo's appointment. The justice was sympathetic to their arguments, but considered that basic human limitations must prevent any man from doing two such onerous jobs; furthermore, he was unwilling to go to the White House on McAdoo's behalf unless Wilson explicitly asked him to do so. Steps were set in train, therefore, to arrange the appropriate summons for Sunday the 9th, but morning wore into late afternoon without the expected telephone call coming through. Then, at precisely five o'clock, the president appeared in person at Brandeis's Stoneleigh Court apartment, flanked by two secret service agents. "I could not request you to come to me," Wilson explained, "and I have therefore come to you to ask your advice." For three-quarters of an hour the two men discussed the issues involved, closeted in the justice's tiny, book-lined study;

before leaving the president announced his intention of appointing McAdoo without requiring him to relinquish the Treasury first. Recalling this extraordinary visit for her sister several months later, Alice Brandeis was struck by the symbolism of the scene rather than by the decision it produced. "The room was fairly dark," she wrote,

> with only one strong desk light. He had been working at some opinion, consulting authorities, and law books were lying everywhere about—on his desk, on chairs, even on the floor. . . . Here surely was the scholar, the student at his work. And yet it is as a practical man of affairs, a statesman, that Louis's advice is so much sought.[4]

Certainly his public stature had been enhanced by the donning of a judge's robes in 1916, but this was not the only transformation that had occurred since the New Freedom campaign of 1912 in which he had played such a prominent part. Even more significant was his growing involvement with Jewish and especially Zionist affairs, which after the outbreak of war in Europe saw him propelled onto the world stage as a leader of and spokesman for the international Zionist movement, and as a tireless worker for the establishment of a Jewish homeland in Palestine.[5]

The precise factors that led Brandeis to identify himself as a Jew remain unclear. For the first fifty years of his life and more, he wore the mantle of Jewishness lightly, preferring to regard himself, and to be regarded by others, as the son of German immigrants driven from Europe by the Revolutions of 1848. Neither of his parents was actively religious; indeed, they appear to have avoided the formal rituals of worship as a matter of principle. "I do not believe that sins can be expiated by going to divine service and observing this or that formula," his mother had written in the 1880s; "I believe that only goodness and truth and conduct that is humane and selfsacrificing towards those who need us can bring God nearer to us, and that our errors can only be atoned for by acting in a more kindly spirit." She justified bringing her children up without any definite religious beliefs on the grounds that she had "wanted to give them something that neither could be argued away nor would have to be given up as untenable, namely, a pure spirit and the highest ideas as to morals and love." This was intended as the language of agnostic rationalism rather than of atheism, and it helped to establish the pattern of moral self-sufficiency that was to characterize her son for the rest of his life. But it also cut the young Louis off from the ethical values and rich cultural resources of Judaism, the loss of which he only began to appreciate fully in middle life.[6]

Yet at their deaths, in 1901 and 1906, respectively, even his mother and father were prepared to yield a little to the claims of ethnicity and religion by being interred after Jewish burial services in the Adath Israel cemetery belonging to Louisville's Reform congregation; for tenuous as their links to Judaism may have been, neither Adolph nor Frederika had ever been minded to convert to Christianity. Moreover, there were other adult role models available within the family circle in which Brandeis was raised, several of whom were more conscientious in matters of religious observance than his parents. For example, Dr. Samuel Brandeis, Adolph's brother, was a leading figure among the city's Reform Jews, though to what extent he adhered to Judaic customs at home is not recorded. On the other hand, Lewis Naphtali Dembitz, Frederika's brother, was a devout Orthodox Jew, whose book *Jewish Services in the Synagogue and Home* (1898) would long serve as a primer for those of his faith in America wishing to preserve the more conservative religious traditions of their European homelands. Dembitz was Brandeis's favorite uncle, the man for whom he had been named. Even in old age, the justice could still remember the early perceptions of Judaism he had formed in childhood; for although the Jewish Sabbath was not celebrated in his parents' home, he remembered well

the joy and awe with which my uncle . . . welcomed the arrival of the day and the piety with which he observed it. I remember the extra delicacies, lighting of the candles, prayers over a cup of wine, quaint chants, and Uncle Lewis poring over books most of the day. I remember more particularly an elusive something about him which was spoken of as the "Sabbath peace" and which years later brought to my mind a passage from Addison in which he speaks of stealing a day out of life to live. That elusive something prevailed in many a home in Boston on a Sunday and was not wanting at Harvard on the same day. Uncle Lewis used to say that he was enjoying a foretaste of heaven. I used to think, and do so now, that we need on earth the Jewish-Puritan Sabbath without its oppressive restrictions.[7]

Despite the obvious attractions of such a warm and humane religiosity, not to mention the enveloping web of culture to which it was attached, for Brandeis, at least, it was not enough. The rationalistic outlook instilled by his parents' example left little room for belief in an after-life, or even perhaps in a personal God; and without faith in a covenant promising ultimate salvation, all rituals and formulas of worship, be they Jewish or Christian, must have seemed empty and pointless indeed. The attractiveness of Lewis Dembitz lay in attributes other than his piety. "To those of my generation," Brandeis told his Dembitz cousins in 1926,

he was a living university. With him life was unending intellectual ferment. He grappled eagerly with the most difficult problems in mathematics and the sciences, in economics, government and politics. In the diversity of his intellectual interests, in his longing to discover truths, in his pleasure in argumentation and in the process of thinking, he reminded us of the Athenians. He loved books as a vehicle of knowledge and an inciter to thought; and he made his love contagious.

It was not therefore as a Jew, but rather as a scholar and intellectual that Brandeis sought to emulate his uncle's example.[8]

This having been said, though, there is little evidence that Louis ever consciously repudiated the nonreligious aspects of his Jewishness: the Hebrews' passion for intellectual excellence, their moral sensibility and respect for law, all reinforced by their self-perception as a "People of the Book," represented a vital cultural tradition which his uncle personified; and in general terms at any rate, Brandeis was always ready to claim these strands of the Jewish heritage as his own. In this he may have drawn a measure of inspiration after his marriage to Alice from the example of his brother-in-law, Felix Adler, founder of the Society for Ethical Culture, who, being by Allon Gal's description "critical of the Jewish religion and of traditional religions in general," propounded instead a philosophy of moral action unrestricted by narrow sectarianism. Certainly, Adler's insistence that continual striving after social justice represented a historical commitment of the Jewish people would later find a clear echo in Brandeis's own writings. Such beliefs did not at first require their holder to lead in any sense a distinctively Jewish life; on the contrary, well into the sixth decade of his life Brandeis was as fully assimilated to "the American Way" as any son of European immigrants could be. Yet when it did come, his "conversion" to Zionism was quite definitely an intellectual as distinct from a mystical phenomenon. Even once he had become the leading Zionist in America, this fastidious man, raised to be suspicious of all forms of dogmatic or formulaic belief, continued to be selective in his Jewishness. If he took a greater interest in the customs and rituals of Judaism than he had during the greater part of his life, he still shunned regular public worship, and at his death rejected all formal rites of passage out of the world.[9]

It was another secular Jew, the English socialist Harold Laski, who perhaps came closest to defining the spiritual dynamism exemplified in the mind of his longtime friend. For Laski, true religious insight took the form of a transcendental humanism quite independent of churches, liturgies, creeds, and priests. What he termed "its power to elevate" was derived from a "profound sense of an infinite universe so complex, so mysterious, so certain, as each of its immense problems are explained, to present us with new problems still more immense." Its essential quality was that "inner and passionate impulse which drives those who possess it beyond and above themselves" to the point where they are able to rise above short-term wants and whims to "search for a fraternal relation with all who suffer and all who are broken by the tragedy of a pain they cannot face." Religion thus defined "can never compromise with the world; it must be willing to break it or be broken by it rather than to yield the imperative passion in which it finds its supreme expression. It is not a spirit which makes for personal contentment." Something of that spirit was innate and individual, inseparable from the character of its possessor; but some other part of it resulted from a productive interaction between that characteristic self and its experience of the world. Such a religion gleamed as a light "in the controlled, yet impressive emotions" which, in Laski's opinion, the careful reader could discern in many of Brandeis's own writings. Its essence was nowhere better put, he believed, than in the Book of Proverbs: "Where there is no vision, the people perish."[10]

Brandeis first spoke publicly about Judaism in 1905 in a brief address before the New Century Club to celebrate the arrival of the first Jews in America 250 years before. Much of what he had to say anticipated his later pronouncements: Americans should not harbor dual loyalties, but must pursue in their individual lives the same democratic ideals that were embodied in the nation's institutions, and participate to the fullest extent of their capacity in the business of government. For those Jews who had chosen to make their home in America, he went on, there was no inherent conflict between their own traditional values and those of their adopted country; both emphasized the need to maintain the highest ethical standards and the importance of taking individual responsibility for one's own actions. In fine, Jewishness and Americanism were not merely compatible terms; to all intents and purposes they were synonymous. Moreover, unlike many others of his generation and national origin, Brandeis viewed the recent arrival of Jews from Eastern Europe with some optimism. "I am inclined to think there is more to hope for in the Russian Jews than from the Bavarian & other German," he wrote his father the day after this talk. "The Russians have idealism & reverence." Viewed in context, though, and with a skeptical eye, these 1905 remarks may be thought to have had rather more to do with attempts to broaden the base of the Democratic party in Boston than with any sudden reawakening of ethnic consciousness.[11]

Up to this point, in fact, Brandeis's contacts with Jews of any stamp remained decidedly limited. The major wave of Jewish immigrants from the cities and shtetls of Russia and Poland had not broken on America's shores until the 1880s, and then Boston was not a major destination when compared with New York or Chicago. It did have its own ghetto, though, as the anti-Semitic Frederick Jackson Turner found to his disquiet while walking around the city in 1887. "I was in Jewry," he wrote, "the street consecrated to 'old clothers,' pawnbrokers, and similar followers of Abraham." The area was "filled with big, Jew men—long bearded and carrying a staff as you see in a picture,—and with Jew youths and maidens—some of the latter pretty—as you sometimes see a lilly in the green muddy slime." It was only "after much elbowing" that the ruffled historian managed to free himself from "this mass of oriental noise and squalor."[12]

It is unlikely, though, that Brandeis was ever himself a frequent visitor to the thronging alleyways of Boston's Jewish quarter. Indeed, as we have seen, it is rather easier to document his associations with Boston's Irish laborers than it is with the workingmen of his own race. His relations with members of the German-Jewish business community were rather better developed, as the Hechts, Eisemanns, Filenes and others constituted an important element of his legal practice. Yet with few exceptions these relationships appear to have been purely professional in nature. Brandeis did not habitually socialize with his Jewish clients any more than with his Gentile ones. Philippa Strum is almost certainly correct, therefore, when she asserts that, prior to this date, Brandeis "used his German-Jewish connections in Boston as a source of business." Indeed, he even employed a Jewish law clerk for the specific function of handling the affairs of his firm's Jewish clients. Although he did pay membership dues to the United Hebrew Benevolent Association and the Federation of Jewish Charities, and later supported the Hebrew Industrial School, his donations to such organizations were small, and his further involvement in their activities did not extend beyond helping them from time to time in his professional capacity. In all his contributions to Jewish Charities down to 1912 totaled less than $1,500. He was attached to no church group; the *Jewish Encyclopedia* did not even mention his name. In short, within the city's Jewish community he possessed almost no ethnic profile at all.[13]

Between 1910 and 1912, however, his own cultural origins began to take on new meaning for him: a profound personal transformation that appears to have had two main causes. The first of these stemmed from his growing involvement with New York's predominantly Jewish garment workers. Among the journeymen of the Lower East Side he found a keen intelligence and an almost biblical sense of justice: attributes that intimate acquaintance convinced him were related to their Jewishness. This, as he later recalled, was his first real experience of "Jews en masse, with employees and employers and with many who were but recent immigrants." Here, in the midst of a heated strike, men confronted each other with quotations from the prophets, and measured one another by a timeless standard of racial pride. "*Ihr darft sich shemen! Passt dost far a Idn?*" he heard one Yiddish speaker challenge his neighbor: "Shame! Is this worthy of a Jew?" Yet despite all the "bitterness and rancor" usually associated with such quarrels, he found that "each side was willing to admit the reality of the other fellows' predicament. They really understood each other, and admitted the understanding. They argued, but they were willing to listen to argument. That set these people apart in my experience in labor disputes." Reflecting on these observations a few years later, he remembered being "deeply impressed, that these Jews with whom I dealt showed in a striking degree the qualities which, to my mind, make for the best American citizenship, that within them there was a true democratic feeling and a deep appreciation of the elements of social justice." As in his 1905 address, he could discern no incompatibility between their Jewishness and his Americanism; on the contrary, there seemed to be a definite similarity between the values which each tradition held dearest. "Observation and study revealed to me that was not an accident," he continued, "that it was due to the fact that twentieth century ideals of America had been the age-old ideals of the Jews."[14]

The second factor impelling Brandeis toward a reappraisal of his cultural identity was a developing acquaintance with Jacob De Haas, editor of the *Boston Jewish Advocate* and a former secretary to the father of modern Zionism, Theodor Herzl. The two men met at the beginning of 1909 to discuss Brandeis's savings-bank insurance scheme, which the *Advocate* subsequently endorsed as a means of promoting social justice while avoiding socialistic legislation. In the following year, the Jewish weekly also provided its New England readers with sympathetic coverage of Brandeis's activities among the garment workers of New York, published another article on his insurance proposals, and generally sought to provide him with a platform from which to influence the thinking of Jewish voters during the two-year run-up to the 1912 election campaign. De Haas also gave Brandeis an opportunity to express in print his thoughts about Judaism and the nature of the Jewish heritage. Interviewed by a reporter from the *Advocate*, and asked whether he accepted the proposition that the Jews were a chosen people with a historic mission to preserve and promulgate their religion, he agreed that they were. "I believe further," he went on, "that the Jews can be just as much of a priest people to-day as they ever were in the prophetic days. Their mission is one that will endure forever. The Jewish prophet may struggle for truth and righteousness to-day just as the ancient prophets did." He took pride in the success of individual Jews, and believed that America afforded great opportunities for Jews (as for other immigrant groups) to make their mark in the world, and to define their own role within the framework of an evolving pluralistic culture. Asked too about his attitude toward those trying to secure an independent Jewish homeland, he replied that he had considerable sympathy for the Zionists: "The movement is an extremely deserving one. These so-called dreamers are entitled to the respect and appreciation of the entire Jewish people."[15]

Sympathy, though, did not automatically equate with knowledge or commitment. Such fellow feeling as Brandeis was able to evince for the Zionist Movement, rested "primarily upon the noble idealism which underlies it," as he told the editor of the *Maccabaean* a few weeks after this interview; it also reflected his "conviction that a great people, stirred by enthusiasm for such an ideal, must bear an important part in the betterment of the world." There was nothing here to indicate any awareness of the suggestion that a national homeland once established might serve as a refuge for the persecuted Jews of the Russian Empire, or that Herzl himself had been prepared to consider Uganda as a more practical destination than Palestine. Right through the early months of 1913, small "contributions to the cause" and further vague expressions of good will continued to represent Brandeis's only tangible associations with Zionism; though persistently courted by leading figures in the national Federation of American Zionists (F.A.Z.) by virtue of his growing importance in Progressive political circles, he continued to decline all requests to play a more active role in Zionist affairs.[16]

In August 1912, however, De Haas went to see Brandeis at his summer home in South Yarmouth on Cape Cod, ostensibly to discuss ways of promoting Wilson's candidature among the Jewish voters of Southern New England. But as well as representing the interests of the Democratic National Committee, the *Advocate*'s editor also took the opportunity to raise with Brandeis the subject of his Uncle Lewis's Zionism; and having elicited from his host an encouraging response, he proceeded to launch into a four-hour seminar about Herzl's vision of a reconstituted Jewish state, and about his own firsthand experiences in the movement. De Haas evidently told a good story, and during the winter of 1912–13 the two men came together on several more occasions to continue Brandeis's education in the history of Zionism. According to the latter's own testimony, it was not until this fateful South Yarmouth meeting that his interest in the subject was fully aroused, and for the remainder of his life Brandeis would continue to acknowledge De Haas as his "teacher" in Zionism: the man chiefly responsible for bringing him actively into the cause.[17]

Yet just as the "people's lawyer" exaggerated the significance of the Homestead Strike as the catalyst for transforming his social outlook during the 1890s, so likewise the Jewish Supreme Court justice placed rather too great an emphasis on the part played by De Haas in awakening his Zionism. It was not in 1912 that Brandeis first heard about Herzl and the colonization movement in Palestine, but more than a dozen years earlier when he read an article in the *North American Review*. An earlier date is also implied by what he told Lord Balfour in 1919. "As an American," he confided to the British minister, "he was confronted with the disposition of the vast numbers of Jews, particularly Russian Jews, that were pouring into the United States year by year. It was then that by chance a pamphlet on Zionism came his way and led him to the study of the Jewish problem and to the conviction that Zionism was the answer." This suggests that Brandeis, in common with many other Americans of German-Jewish origin, was becoming profoundly concerned by the late 1890s that the influx of Yiddish-speaking Jews from the East had begun to stoke the flames of anti-Semitism in the United States, and that this development now threatened even the social acceptability of fully assimilated Jews like themselves. He seems to have feared too the radical "disposition" of these newcomers and was perhaps inclined to view Zionism, at least in part, as a means of funneling their potentially disruptive energies into courses of action that were rather more in tune with bourgeois American values. For as he told Balfour regarding those Jews left behind in Europe: "The very same men, with the same qualities that are now enlisted in revolutionary movements would find, and in the United States do find, constructive channels for expression and make positive contributions to civilization." Thus in 1912, he may not have been quite so ignorant of Zionist aspirations as he later claimed. Be that as it may, as an after-dinner speaker at the New Century Club in March 1913 he was at pains to make clear that it was "his deep solicitude for the spiritual and moral welfare of the Jews" that had given rise to his interest in Zionism rather than the political objective of a sovereign Jewish state. This would seem to place his views rather closer to those of "social" and "cultural" Zionists than to those of De Haas and of other politically oriented followers of Herzl.[18]

Similarly, the newfound willingness to participate in Zionist activities conventionally ascribed to 1913, was neither as momentous nor as marked at as some commentators have alleged. Although it is true that Brandeis agreed to join the F.A.Z.'s Associate Executive Committee in July of that year, the committee's functions were largely advisory and the responsibilities of membership nominal; anyway he attended few of its meetings before the fall of 1914. Moreover, less than a week after accepting this first invitation, he declined a second, more exacting one to serve as an F.A.Z. delegate to the forthcoming World Zionist Congress in Vienna, plausibly citing other engagements as his excuse. This leaves as the only substantial evidence of a closer association the mere fact that he was even nominated, which, as Urofsky and Levy have pointed out, "does not indicate the extent of [his] involvement at this time so much as it shows the small number of available leaders upon whom the Zionists could draw." The truth is that, as late as the summer of 1914, his readiness to work openly with those in the mainstream of American Zionism was still far from being whole-hearted.[19]

Whatever may be said about this continuing lack of public commitment, it remains clear nevertheless that his knowledge and understanding of the "Jewish problem" in Europe were beginning to develop apace, and that this in turn was leading him to a greater appreciation of the importance of Palestine as the proper focus of Zionist aspirations. His rapidly increasing level of awareness can best be seen in the remarks he addressed to Nahum Sokolow at the beginning of August 1913. An energetic figure in European Zionism, and a close associate of Chaim Weizmann, Sokolow was in the United States to drum up American support for the movement generally and for the World Zionist Congress in particular. After recording expressions of regret about his own inability to go to Vienna, Brandeis's letter goes on to outline for the first time his own thinking about the development of Palestine, and to indicate those matters which he felt the Congress ought to discuss.

Typically, he began by stressing the need for Zionist efforts to be concentrated "upon a few undertakings"—perhaps inevitably so, given his known feelings about the limited capacities of human beings, and his recognition of the meager financial and personnel resources then available. His other suggestions, though, showed a much more sophisticated grasp of local detail than had been apparent only a few months before. His main emphasis was no longer on developing "the spiritual and moral welfare of the Jews" but rather, in view of the rapidly mounting pressures being put on those in Eastern Europe, on "opening up Palestine to the masses." In his opinion, this required not only "the possession of large tracts of land" but, of equal importance, obtaining "such concessions from the Turkish government as will give to our people freedom of movement, control of our operations, and security for the investments necessary to the development of the land we may own." In this connection, he was confident that "the offer of our movement to introduce into Turkish possessions an intelligent and industrious population" was bound to influence the political calculations of that country, and thought that a recent Turkish offer to sell the Jews further real estate in Palestine represented "a much sought opportunity to achieve a position of permanent value to our people." Land, however, was not the most pressing issue. "We need at the same time," he told Sokolow, "a large immigration of our people into Palestine. Numbers are necessary to rendering our position secure." This meant ensuring "such conditions of settlement as will leave our people free from such entanglements as have arisen in the past, and which necessarily arise in the future if the Jews are not afforded an opportunity to act in their own behalf with the mutual consent of the Turkish government." Provided these fundamental needs were recognized, he concluded, any reasonable plan put forward by the Congress would assuredly "meet with the hearty approval and financial support" of American Jews.[20]

The Vienna Congress spent much of its time debating problems of economic and cultural development in Palestine, and the progress being made by the Jewish settlements there. To the disquiet of uncompromising "political" Zionists, primary emphasis was put on the need for "practical" measures to ensure that colonization proceeded on a secure financial footing, and this in turn was perceived to rely heavily on the involvement of long-term, ideologically committed investors rather than commercial opportunists with an eye only for short-term profits. Brandeis's letter to Sokolow, which was read out to the delegates, evidently chimed in well with the prevailing mood. As Arthur Ruppin, head of the Zionist Organization's Palestine Office in Jaffa put it bluntly: "For a long time to come our progress in Palestine will depend entirely on the progress of our movement in the diaspora." With its studied use of "we" and "our," and the tone of authority with which its writer claimed to speak for American Jewry, the Brandeis note could be read in retrospect as a bid for leadership of the Zionist movement—at least in the United States and perhaps beyond.[21]

It is, of course, possible that this heightened degree of "practical" awareness, and the new level of identification with Zionist goals that accompanied it, were the result of more frequent contacts with De Haas, who since their South Yarmouth meeting had begun to act not merely as Brandeis's teacher but also informally as his secretary in relation to Jewish affairs. It seems likely, however, that De Haas's influence was not the only factor at work here. Of equal, if not greater, significance was his first meeting with Aaron Aaronsohn, the celebrated Jewish agronomist generally acknowledged as the discoverer of "wild wheat." Brandeis first heard of Aaronsohn's work as head of the Jewish Agricultural Experiment Station in Palestine at the beginning of 1912, and was thrilled by the possibilities it seemed to offer for "scientific agriculture and utilization of arid or supposedly exhausted land"; however, it was not until the following May that the two men actually met face to face in the lawyer's home. Despite his guest's rather halting grasp of the English language, Brandeis later described him to Norman Hapgood as "one of the most interesting men I have met" and according to one account was subsequently heard to credit the Palestinian farmer with responsibility for his final conversion to Zionism.[22]

More certainly, we know that he was particularly impressed by Aaronsohn's descriptions of Jewish life in the new Israel. Two weeks after their first meeting, in an address to the Young Men's Hebrew Association of Chelsea, Massachusetts, Brandeis recounted part of what he had been told: "That in Palestine, [in] the little communities which have grown up in the last thirty-two years and now number 150,000 Jewish souls, not a single crime was known to have been committed by one of our people during all that time." Then, in his own words, he continued: "There has developed there, and there can develop still more in that old land to a higher degree, that spirit of which Mr. Aaronsohn speaks . . . this manhood." The image of Palestine which Aaronsohn conjured up in Brandeis's mind was not merely that of a land without crime, but seemed to correspond in many respects to his vision of the ideal society: its communities and institutions small in scale; its people vigorous, autonomous, and morally responsible for their own actions; its social and economic goals clearly defined and held in common. "Every member of those communities is brought up to realize his obligations to his people," the agronomist had insisted. "He is told of the great difficulties it passed through, and of the long years of Martyrdom it experienced. All that is best in Jewish history is made to live in him, and by this means he is imbued with a high sense of honor and responsibility for the whole people." As an experiment in human development, being carried on by people of his own race, this was patently something that Brandeis considered deserving of his enthusiastic support.[23]

The outbreak of war in Europe in 1914 threw the World Zionist Organization into chaos and thrust the erstwhile Progressive campaigner into the forefront of American efforts to support the Jewish colonies in Palestine. On 30 August, only a few brief years after his first tentative expressions of interest in things Jewish, Louis Dembitz Brandeis became chairman of the Provisional Executive Committee for General Zionist Affairs and as such a principal spokesman for American Jewry. The irony of this situation was not lost on him, and at first he seems to have felt inadequately prepared and poorly qualified for the weighty responsibility he had assumed. "Throughout long years which represent my life," he confessed on accepting this office, "I have been to a great extent separated from Jews. I am very ignorant in things Jewish." Moreover, in the months that followed, he continued to express similar sentiments in addresses to fund-raising rallies across the country. "During most of my life my contact with Jews and Judaism was slight," he told his audiences. "I gave little thought to their problems, save in asking myself, from time to time, whether we were showing by our lives due appreciation of the opportunities which this hospitable country affords."[24]

From what has been said earlier, there can be little doubt that, according to his own lights, Brandeis's espousal of the Zionist cause was a sincere one; yet even amid the desperately serious business of saving Jewish settlers in Palestine from starvation, he was anxious to stress that his interest in the Jewish people, and in their aspirations for a national homeland in Palestine, was at root a special case of his more general concern to promote the achievement of true democratic freedoms and a larger measure of social justice *wherever* they were capable of being secured, and particularly in the United States. "My approach to Zionism was through Americanism," he now declared in a telling phrase that was reminiscent of his 1905 speech to the members of the New Century Club. "In time, practical experience and observation convinced me that Jews were by reason of their traditions and their character peculiarly fitted for the attainment of American ideals."[25]

This identification of American aspirations with traditional Jewish values would long continue to form a major element of Brandeis's individual conception of Zionism—a conception that he never found any difficulty harmonizing with the other characteristic features of his mature social philosophy. In a lengthy address to a conference of the Eastern Council of Reform Rabbis in June 1915, he returned once more to what was by then becoming a well-worn theme. There was, he asserted, no inconsistency whatever between being a loyal Jew and a loyal American: "The Jewish spirit, the product of our religion and experiences, is essentially modern and essentially American." This much he had said before, but now he was ready to develop the idea more fully. Not since the destruction of the Temple had Jews been so fully in harmony, both in spirit and ideals, with the fundamental objectives of the country in which they resided.

> America's fundamental law seeks to make real the brotherhood of man. That brotherhood became the Jewish fundamental law more than twenty-five hundred years ago. America's insistent demand in the twentieth century is for social justice. That also has been the Jews' striving for ages. Their affliction as well as their religion has prepared the Jews for effective democracy. Persecution broadened their sympathies. It trained them in patient endurance, in self-control, and in sacrifice. It made them think as well as suffer. It deepened the passion for righteousness.

Indeed, he argued, loyalty to America demanded that every American Jew become a Zionist; for only through the ennobling effects of their own striving to secure a Jewish homeland in Palestine (for others if not for themselves) could Jews develop the best that was in them, and give to their adopted country the full benefits of their great inheritance.[26]

This perceived analogy between Jewish and American traditions of democracy and social justice enabled Brandeis to read the lessons of American history into a Jewish context with total freedom, and from 1915 onward he rarely failed to make use of this facility whenever a suitable opportunity arose. For example, he frequently drew parallels between the characteristics he thought necessary to the success of the Jewish settlements in Palestine and those of the early Puritan colonists in America. Duty, he believed, must be regarded as "the dominant conception in life," just as it had been in the pioneer days of New England, "when American democracy had reached there its fullest expression." Old Testament virtues were as central to Calvinist as to Jewish theology, and the Puritans had been "trained in implicit obedience to stern duty by constant study of the Prophets." Both shared a profound respect for high levels of intellectual achievement. "Democratic ideals," he asserted, "cannot be attained by the mentally undeveloped. In a government where everyone is part sovereign, everyone should be competent, if not to govern, at least to understand the problems of government"; to this end public education was essential. Thus the common school system had been established by the Puritan colonists immediately upon their arrival in the New World, and Harvard College had been founded a mere six years after the first settlement of Boston. Had he been of a less secular disposition, Brandeis might also have noted one further characteristic that the early New Englanders shared with the children of Israel: an unshakable belief that they were a people chosen of God.[27]

Brandeis was by no means the first person, however, to note the parallelism existing between the American and Hebrew political traditions. Thirty years before in his book on *The Origins of the Republican Form of Government in the United States* (1885), Oscar S. Straus had pointed to a striving after liberty and equality as the common civic heritage of both cultures. Indeed, he went further by asserting that the Founding Fathers, like the Puritans before them, had consciously based their political institutions on Jewish models. "Thus we see," Straus wrote in a chapter headed "The Hebrew Commonwealth, The First Federal Republic,"

> at this early period of mankind—1,500 years and more before the Christian era, before Rome had obtained a foothold in history, 500 years before Homer sang, and 1,000 years before Plato had dreamed of his ideal republic, when all Western Europe was an untrodden wilderness—the children of Israel on the banks of the Jordan, who had just emerged from centuries of bondage, not only recognized the guiding principles of civil and religious liberty that "all men are created equal," that God and the law are the only kings, but also established a free commonwealth, a pure democratic republic under a written constitution, "a government of the people, by the people, and for the people."

Straus subsequently enjoyed a highly successful political career, becoming the first Jew to achieve cabinet rank as Theodore Roosevelt's commerce and labor secretary; he stood as a Progressive candidate in 1912 for the governorship of New York and went on to serve as United States Ambassador to Turkey. Yet nothing in these experiences led Straus to search for the fulfilment of his Jewish identity in Palestine, as he made abundantly clear in an address delivered before a meeting of the American Hebrew Congregations in 1911. "While Zionism is a pious hope and vision out of despair in countries where victims of oppression are still counted by millions," he told his audience, "the republicanism of the United States is the nearest approach to the ideals of the prophets of Israel that ever has been incorporated in the form of a State. . . . Ours is peculiarly a promised land wherein the spirit of the teachings of the ancient prophets inspired the work of the fathers of our country."[28]

Whether Brandeis was familiar with Straus's views is not clear, though it is not improbable. The two men certainly displayed a common approach to the uses of historical analogy; for like Straus, who never became a fervent Zionist, Brandeis too endeavored to read back into the annals of early Jewish history the political struggles of a later age. Thus in December 1915, in a Hanukkah message directed to all American Zionists, we find him seeking to portray the revolt of the Maccabees against the Seleucid rulers of Palestine in 167 b.c. as an event of more than purely Jewish significance. It was not, he insisted, merely a victory over external enemies, the Greeks, but also over more dangerous internal enemies, the Sadducees. It was the victory of "democracy over aristocracy"; "of the many over the ease-loving, safety-playing, privileged, powerful few, who in their pliancy would have betrayed the best interests of the people." These were images clearly paralleled in the contemporary world with which his readers were familiar, and he went on to make explicit the universal truth revealed by the particular example:

> As a part of the eternal world-wide struggle for democracy, the struggle of the Maccabees is of eternal world-wide interest. It is a struggle of the Jews today, as well as of those of 2,000 years ago. It is a struggle of America as well as of Palestine. It is a struggle in which all Americans, non-Jews as well as Jews, should be vitally interested because they are vitally affected.[29]

Straus was a democrat as well, but a more conservative one than Brandeis. As Sam B. Girgus puts it: "he felt so secure in his marriage of Judaism and Americanism that he failed to fully understand that the strength of both traditions rested in part on their ability to change and grow." Like many other Americans of German-Jewish descent, he saw no reason to go beyond the tested formulas of classical liberalism that had provided his family with a homeland free from persecution and an open economic system in which they had prospered. For such men, the "American Way" offered its adherents a package of self-evident truths that was both timeless and changeless. Yet despite coming from a similar background, and being only six years his junior, Brandeis had managed to transcend the ideological limitations binding the other man to this static vision. "Like Straus," Girgus continues, "Louis D. Brandeis believed in the importance to human history of the union between Judaism and Americanism. In contrast to Straus, however, [he] saw that such marriages should produce new ideas and institutions in order to enable future generations to assume control over their own destiny."[30]

Brandeis's use and exposition of the Maccabean revolt is itself illuminating with regard to what it tells us of his own intellectual orientation during these years. His interpretation of this episode shows no trace of the *Kulturkampf* exegesis that had been prevalent, especially in German intellectual circles, since the 1870s. Neither does it reflect the preconceptions of earlier post-Enlightenment scholars, who generally portrayed the persecutions that sparked off the revolt as the crude imposition of a uniform state religion. Rather he depicts the revolt as a sociopolitical event with an important internal as well as the obvious external dimension. In this respect, although his simplistic polarity between democracy and aristocracy is clearly anachronistic, and his reference to the Sadducees equally dubious, he unconsciously prefigures the central thesis of Elias Bickerman's scholarly reassessment, not published till 1937, that "the Maccabean movement was, above all, a civil war, a religious struggle between reformers and orthodox"; that the Maccabees had taken up arms not against "some form of culture or state" but to preserve their lives and the ordinances of their religion. "It was not a national fight," Bickerman asserts,

> but a struggle within the nation itself, i.e., a religious war between two groups of Jews: between the polytheists who sacrificed God in order to save their people through assimilation to the surrounding world, and the monotheists, who were ready to give up their lives and that of the people in order to preserve the law of Moses. The first party relied upon the secular power of the Seleucids; on the side of the Maccabees, however, fought God.

Of course, Brandeis was completely unfamiliar with the specific historical features of Bickerman's analysis. The irony is that, culturally at least, he like many other American Zionists had a good deal more in common with the reformers in this scenario than with their Maccabean adversaries.[31]

By the end of 1915, however, he patently knew a good deal more about Jewish history and culture than he had three years earlier at the time of his South Yarmouth meeting with De Haas; and it is taking nothing away from the latter's role as guide and mentor to assume that much of his new knowledge came out of books. We know that he devoted much of the summer of 1914 to reading about Judaism and its history, and more especially about the rebirth of an ancient dream: that the Jews of the Diaspora might one day return to Zion. "Exactly what Brandeis read that summer is not known," Strum observes in her biography.

His letters and speeches in the following months show a familiarity with Herzl, the Hebrew philosopher Achad Ha'am (Asher Ginzberg), Edward A. Ross's *The Old World in the New*, Arthur Ruppin's *The Jews of Today*, Israel Cohen's *The Zionist Movement*, Abraham Geiger's *Judaism and Its History*, Ignatz Zollschan's *Jewish Question*, and Leopold Zunz's *The Sufferings of the Jews During the Middle Ages*.

In her view, though, more important to Brandeis than any of these was Alfred Zimmern's *The Greek Commonwealth* (1912): a book that "he quoted throughout his life and made certain that all the members of his extended family read." As Strum has amply documented, Zimmern's description of political life in fifth-century Athens bore a close resemblance to Brandeis's own conception of the ideal community: small in scale, decentralized, and efficient; its citizens dedicated to the proposition that justice and political freedom could only be maintained in a polity whose members played an active role in the work of government. Moreover, he like Brandeis believed in the contemporary relevance of historical models. "Greek ideas and Greek inspiration can help us today," he wrote in the preface to the book's second edition, "not only in facing the duties of the moment, but in the work of deepening and extending the range and meaning of Democracy and Citizenship, Liberty and Law, which would seem to be the chief political task before Mankind."

Nevertheless, it is difficult to go along with Strum's suggestion that Zimmern's writings "may have been the catalyst for the ideas already circulating in Brandeis's mind, or [that] he may have offered Brandeis a new way of looking at Zionism." What Brandeis found most appealing about *The Greek Commonwealth* was not that its ideas complemented or in some way augmented his own, but that its lucid exposition helped demonstrate and confirm the viability of opinions which he already held. Zimmern could teach Brandeis little that was new about Greek civilization, for the Boston lawyer had been reading about and internalizing its system of values since his childhood in Kentucky; but the persuasive prose of this half-Jewish scholar from Oxford University might yet be used to acquaint others with the timeless relevance of social and political ideals that he, Brandeis, and the ancient Greeks all held in equally high esteem. As for the book's impact on Brandeis's progress toward Zionism, it would be difficult to prove that it had any at all; though it is certainly conceivable that Zimmern's frequent comparisons between Greece and Palestine may have helped germinate in his mind a concrete image of the kind of society that might one day become possible in the new Zion. It is just as likely, however, that Brandeis derived his vision of the future from stories told him by Aaronsohn: not of Jewish life as it had been in the remote past, but of life as it was now in contemporary Palestine.[32]

Even assuming that Brandeis did indeed draw some useful insights from Zimmern's historical analogies, there is little evidence to show that he ever gave much serious thought to the similarities and connections existing between the ancient civilizations of Greece and Israel. In view of Strum's claim that Zimmern's book "was one of the few that Brandeis considered central to his life," it is worth noting that his 1915 Hanukkah message displayed neither knowledge of nor sympathy for what might be termed the pro-Hellenic interpretation of the complexities surrounding the Maccabean revolt, even though such a perspective had been popular in German accounts through the 1870s, and should have been readily obvious to any man whose enthusiasm for the civic virtues of Periclean Athens had recently been reinvigorated. By their own lights, the Hellenicized Jews of Seleucid Jerusalem were seeking to apply the teachings of the Greek enlightenment to their own people; for to the Greek mind, Jewish hostility to and withdrawal from the Gentile world was nothing less than an expression of defiant barbarism. As a contemporary Stoic fragment put it: "He who created us, created us for the common life with all men." Thus in seeking to end the particularism of Mosaic laws and customs, the Hellenic party in Judea saw itself as engaged in a struggle to expunge the barbaric features of their traditional culture.

What is truly remarkable is that a man like Brandeis, who throughout his life shared Goethe's love of classical Greek civilization and idealized the participatory democracy of the Greek *polis*, should fail to perceive the tension existing between his own deeply rooted ideals and such an emotive identification with *the* signal victory of Jewish separatism. Like so much else about his newly acquired Zionism, his knowledge of its historical antecedents remained to a considerable extent both selective and superficial.[33]

Although he had already begun to refer to the Jews as "my people" by 1910, as previously indicated it was the outbreak of hostilities in Europe four years later that finally compelled Brandeis to become active in the Zionist cause. The World Zionist Organization was torn apart by the conflict; and it soon became clear that if the Jewish settlements in Palestine were to be preserved, and the interests of East European Jews were to be represented properly at any subsequent peace conference, much of the burden would now have to be taken up by Jews living in neutral countries, especially those in the United States. At the beginning of the war, however, American Zionism was in a sorry state, both numerically and financially; the Federation of American Zionists, for example, at its 1914 convention could claim barely 12,000 members. Faced with this reality, during the next few years Brandeis devoted much of his energy to improving the structure and efficiency of the organization, and most important to increasing its membership. With numbers, he knew, would come both money and influence. Stripped of their rhetoric, therefore, his numerous addresses to Jewish groups during these years generally boiled down to a simple formula: "Men! Money! Discipline!" In November 1915, he wrote explaining the situation to the readers of *The Wahrheit*:

The outstanding problem which confronts the Jews in America is one of organization. Unless we are efficiently organized, reaching down into the ranks of indiffer-
ence and apathy, and drawing strength from every element, class or party in Israel,
we cannot hope successfully to cope with the great and pressing difficulties of the
Jewish problem.

Organization not for its own sake, but for the purpose of creating a bulwark of
strength behind propositions tending to solve the Jewish problem, is essential.

By 1919 the newly formed Zionist Organization of America (Z.O.A.)
could boast 176,000 members, with many thousands more belonging to
the Zionist-labor and Orthodox religious groups that remained outside its
ranks.[34]

Yet as his letter to *The Wahrheit* illustrates, Brandeis remained fully conscious of the broader issues behind which the resources of American Jewry
were being mobilized. As he explained to Gustave Hartman in June 1915,
the "Jewish problem" had two separate aspects: "the one involving the Jew
as an individual, and the other involving Jews collectively." Hartman, who
was in the process of setting up a Jewish civil rights organization to be called
the American Jewish Emancipation Committee, was plainly focusing his
attentions on the former, and Brandeis agreed wholeheartedly with his
objective; however, he urged his correspondent not to ignore the wider
matter of collective rights. "[Do] not be silent on the large phase of the
problem," he wrote, "for individual liberty depends for its exercise in large
part upon the development of the group of which the individual is a part."
Since in his view it was this "large phase of the problem" that Zionism
was intended to tackle, he proceeded to explain his own conception of the
movement:

Zionism seeks to establish in Palestine, for such Jews as choose to go and remain
there and for their descendants, a legally secured home, where they may live
together and lead a Jewish life. And in spite of the fact that this movement has
seemed to many a dream, it is now on the way to realization. What is needed for
the acceleration of this movement is the determination of the Jews themselves to
further the aims of Zionism, and that the world at large, the great humanitarian
and progressive world, should express itself as sympathetic to these aims, and also
help to further them whenever their voices may be heard.[35]

The plain fact is that Brandeis realized from the very beginning that,
although it was thrown into sharper relief by the war, the suffering of Jews
outside America was really the consequence of the more fundamental and
deep-seated problems of intolerance and prejudice, which required the
adoption of a determined and far-reaching strategy for their effective solution. In particular he was aware of the oppression and discrimination practiced against the great masses of Russian Jews before and during the war;
and in looking forward to the peace process that would eventually end hostilities, he was convinced that treaties and disarmament alone could not se-

cure a lasting peace—at least not one from which the Jewish peoples of Central and Eastern Europe might expect to benefit. "Peace can exist only in a world where justice and good will reign," he told a mass meeting of American Jews assembled in Carnegie Hall at the beginning of 1916. "Justice and good will involve not merely toleration of differences, but the grant of full rights, despite differences. There must be justice and good will not only between individuals, but between different peoples. All peoples must have equal rights."

In general terms, of course, as his letter to Hartman showed, he supported the proposition that only by the establishment of a Jewish homeland in Palestine could the "Jewish problem" be removed definitively from the international agenda. Nevertheless, he remained acutely conscious of the stark reality that, even granted the existence of a reborn Israel, a majority of Jews, whether from choice or circumstance, would probably continue to live and work in other lands. In his Carnegie Hall speech, therefore, he focused exclusively on the need to secure international recognition of civil rights for Jews as part and parcel of any peace settlement. Such rights, he maintained, could only be gained by "traveling the same road which other peoples travel, the road of democracy," which required ordinary Jewish people to assert "their own authority in their own interest." Participation was the keynote of his address:

> The demand for democracy in the consideration of the Jewish problem is not a matter of form. It is of the essence. It is a fundamental Jewish conception, as it is the basic American method. It rests upon the essential trust in the moral instincts of the people; potent to create their own well-being; to perfect it; and to maintain it, if an opportunity is given.

Here, in a Zionist context, to strengthen and sustain his plea to "trust the people," Brandeis did not hesitate to call on the moral authority of Herzl, just as in a non-Jewish context he might have felt impelled to call on the example of Jefferson or Lincoln. The principle, though, in either case was essentially the same: only by taking personal responsibility for their own lives could men, be they Jews or Gentiles, Russians or Americans, be truly free.[36]

The Balfour Declaration of 2 November 1917, with its promise to help facilitate "the establishment in Palestine of a national home for the Jewish people," transformed the situation, appearing to bring the prospect of an autonomous Jewish territory considerably closer than any Zionist could have dreamed only three years earlier. For Brandeis, who had not hesitated to use his personal credit and friendship to secure President Wilson's approval of the British commitment, a golden opportunity now presented itself to influence, perhaps decisively, the kind of society that would be developed in the new Israel. The only obstacle in his path seemed to be Chaim Weizmann, who had emerged during the war as the chief spokesman for a fragmented European Zionism and was now de facto leader of the world movement. As a first concrete step toward implementation of his aims, Foreign Secretary Balfour authorized the Zionist Organization to send a commission of inquiry to Palestine under Weizmann's chairmanship. Its remit was a wide one; for as well as collecting information about the existing Jewish settlements and advising on the possibilities for their further development, it was also charged with placating the Arabs, aiding the hard-pressed Jewish colonists, and liaising between them and the British authorities. The Wilson administration was at first reluctant to countenance American involvement with the enterprise, and Brandeis was himself disinclined to give it his blessing before being satisfied that the European Zionists shared his own vision of Palestine's future.[37]

Accordingly, on 13 January 1918, he wrote apprising Weizmann of his concerns. One matter in particular he considered to be of fundamental importance: "The utmost vigilance should be exercised to prevent the acquisition by private persons of land, water rights or other national resources or any concessions for public utilities. These must all be secured for the whole Jewish people." The experience he had gained during the Ballinger-Pinchot controversy and in numerous franchise fights now led him to approach the subject of Palestinian development with extreme caution. "In other ways, as well as this, the possibility of capitalistic exploitation must be guarded against," he warned, and went on to suggest a greatly expanded role for the Anglo-Palestine Company as "one of the most effective means of protection." Equally necessary, though, was "the encouragement of all kinds of cooperative enterprise," especially of schemes connected with the land. Self-reliance and active participation in economic decision making had long been goals that he hoped to see achieved one day in the United States; however, in Palestine, there appeared to be few, if any, vested interests present capable of blocking their immediate attainment. A Jeffersonian image of sturdy yeoman-farmers resisting the blandishments of an urban-industrial way of life might no longer be capable of realization in sophisticated America; but based on what Aaronsohn had told him, Brandeis considered it still eminently appropriate to the potentially fertile wilderness that was to be Israel. "Our pursuit must be primarily of agriculture in all its branches," he told Weizmann. "The industries and commerce must be incidental merely— and such as may be required to insure independence and natural development." Clearly, if Brandeis could prevent it, there would be no serpents to tempt men and women in the new Eden.[38]

At its founding convention the following June, the Zionist Organization of America adopted a statement of principles drafted by Brandeis (subsequently known as the Pittsburgh Platform), which, alongside other planks dealing with equal rights, public education, and the Hebrew language, included all the points previously raised in the letter to Weizmann. Despite being accepted unanimously by the delegates, it was soon revealed as a divisive document whose social-justice philosophy held little appeal for the Yiddish-speaking masses. Melvin Urofsky makes the point succinctly: "it totally lacked any of the mystic nationalism that they saw as part of redemption from exile." For Brandeis, though, it represented the quintessence of his belief that progressive American values and Zionist goals were ultimately identical—an article of faith that even the traumatic wrangling that took place at the Z.O.A.'s Cleveland Convention three years later would do little to diminish.[39]

In 1919, once the Supreme Court had risen for the summer, Justice Brandeis crossed the Atlantic to take part in a string of meetings with Zionist leaders in London and Paris, including his first face-to-face encounter with Weizmann. He then journeyed on by way of Egypt to Palestine in the company of De Haas and Zimmern. The justice and his companions were fêted wherever they went; reception committees, singing children, and honor guards turned out to greet them as they traveled from settlement to settlement and from town to town. Yet it was not so much the people as the place itself that captivated him. "It is a wonderful country, a wonderful city," he wrote Alice from Jerusalem. "Aaronsohn was right . . . The ages-long longing, the love is all explicable now . . . The marvelous contrasts of nature are in close juxtaposition . . . It was a joy from the moment we reached it at Rafia . . . even in the hot plains the quality of the air was bracing . . . It is indeed a Holy Land." At Zichron Yaacov, where Aaronsohn lived and where the villagers had built a special gate in his honor, Brandeis abandoned his customary reticence toward religious observance and went twice to synagogue. Everything he saw during his sixteen days in Palestine provided him with a context of experience for years of reading and countless hours of private conversations; it gave him faith in a Jewish identity that had previously received only intellectual affirmation. "I had read much about it, heard much about it . . . and reasoned much about it," he told an audience in 1923.

> But it was only by going there that I could convince myself in fullness how much was open to us and why we should endeavor to work out the problem, not as a dream but as a beautiful reality . . . If . . . persistence, devotion and ingenuity, readiness of self-sacrifice and self-control . . . is manifested by those who have an interest in it, there is nothing worthy which cannot be realized there.

At the age of sixty-two his identification with Zion was at last complete.[40]

During the summer of 1920, Brandeis again took ship for Europe, this time to attend the World Zionist Conference in London. The meeting was not a happy one. Relations with Weizmann, hitherto businesslike and at time verging on the cordial, broke down in mutual recriminations; the

American Zionist leader returned home feeling betrayed. While on the high seas, he wrote a detailed paper outlining the policy objectives he thought the Zionist Organization should pursue. Although his disagreements with the Weizmann faction were ostensibly about appropriate mechanisms for raising the funds needed for Palestinian development, this "Zeeland Memorandum" (so-called because it was drafted on board the SS *Zeeland*) reveals a continuing commitment to the aims which Brandeis had proposed and the Z.O.A. had accepted back in Pittsburgh.

Large-scale work, and especially the provision of adequate public utilities, he insisted, could not be left to private enterprise "because the capitalist would not, with other investment opportunities at hand, incur the risk without the prospect of corresponding profit, and this . . . does not exist at all or if it exists, could be effected only through exploitation contrary to the Pittsburgh Program." The only alternative was for the colonists to live frugally and to make themselves economically self-sufficient as quickly as they could. "We cannot attain our objective of a manly, self-supporting population," he wrote, "unless the settlers are made to realize that they must, and unless they actually do incur, in some form, hardships equivalent to those incurred by hardy pioneers in other lands." He did not doubt that such pioneers could be found: "The present misery of the Jews elsewhere, together with their traditional longing for Palestine, makes possible the necessary immigration." He was equally confident that "within a comparatively short time" they would "develop into a homogeneous people with the high Jewish ideals; [would] develop and apply there the Jewish spiritual and intellectual ideals; and [would] ultimately become a self-governing commonwealth."[41]

As he had told the British foreign secretary in Paris the previous summer, a Jewish Palestine needed "economic elbow room" in which to grow strong and "self-sufficiency for a healthy social life" to develop. That in turn meant securing "adequate boundaries, not merely a small garden within Palestine." It did not mean immediate nationhood, however. For Brandeis the first step along the road to Zionism's ultimate goal was to consist of an externally funded program of economic development; for only within a solid economic framework, he believed, could a society dedicated to the promotion of self-discipline and democracy be expected to evolve. In his view, nationalistic fervor, religious zealotry, and demands for sovereign independence represented merely a congeries of blind alleys.[42]

More than four years before his visit to Palestine, Brandeis had already set out in an article for the *Menorah Journal* what he believed the Jewish conception of democracy involved. "Among the Jews," he wrote, "democracy was not an ideal merely. It was a practice . . . made possible by the existence among them of certain conditions essential to successful democracy." These he proceeded to enumerate: (1) an all-pervading sense of duty in each and every citizen; (2) relatively high intellectual attainments in the population at large; (3) voluntary submission to leadership as distinguished from authority; and (4) a developed sense of community. The second of these requirements has already been alluded to, but the others require some elaboration, because they are crucial to any proper understanding of Brandeis's liberalism. As we have seen, duty was a value that he had come to prize highly, not for abstract reasons alone, but because he perceived that, without the assumption of personal responsibility on the part of ordinary men and women, power must inevitably pass into the hands of those present in any society ever eager to exercise authority on behalf of and over their fellow citizens. Democratic ideals could not be achieved merely by emphasizing the Rights of Man, important though these undoubtedly were. Even recognition "that every right has a correlative duty" would not meet the needs of a healthy democracy. In any conflict of interests, the duties must come *before* the rights, since only by acceptance of the duties could the rights be preserved.

However, Brandeis was careful to distinguish between authority, which he unfailingly regarded as suspect, and true leadership, whose qualities he always rated highly. "Democratic ideals," he wrote, "can be attained only where those who govern exercise their power not by alleged divine right or inheritance, but by force of character and intelligence." But if the dangers of elitism were to be avoided, certain positive qualities were also requisite among ordinary members of the body politic. This implied "the attainment by citizens generally of relatively high moral and intellectual standards"; furthermore, he added, "such a condition actually existed among the Jews. These men who were habitually denied rights, and whose province it has been for centuries 'to suffer and to think' (which is the essence of a democracy and social justice), but also to accept voluntarily the leadership of those highly endowed, morally and intellectually."[43]

As we have seen in earlier chapters, none of these first three "conditions for democracy" was new to Brandeis's philosophy; and none for that matter would have struck the majority of his Progressive contemporaries as particularly original. Certainly there was nothing uniquely Jewish about his formulation, even if one accepts his contention that, at some unspecified period in their history, the Jews had displayed these characteristics in some exemplary fashion. His fourth condition, though, was a different matter altogether. By identifying the "sense of community" as a prerequisite for democratic participation, Brandeis not only went beyond his own previously declared positions, but in so doing succeeded in defining and qualifying the context in which his other conditions would operate. This in turn gave his conception of the basic political process highly distinctive features that inevitably distanced him from the Progressive mainstream, and implied the need for some radical new departures in the way that Americans conceived and structured their political institutions.

It may indeed be the case, as Brandeis observed toward the end of his life, that his mother had passed on to him in his youth her own "sense of duty to the community, not so much by preaching as by practice"; however, for the greater part of his adult life he appears to have given little thought to precisely what the term "community" actually meant. Moreover, although most commentators have pointed out the pronounced communitarian strand in Brandeis's social philosophy, usually describing it as characteristically Jeffersonian, it is surely significant that this element was almost completely absent from his pre-1915 writings; in fact, it was almost certainly developed first in connection with his Zionist declarations.[44]

It was the community feeling present among Jews during the long centuries of oppression that, in Brandeis's view, rendered the imperatives of duty particularly effective. Whereas Western Christendom had fostered belief in the immortality of the individual soul, thereby enabling the downtrodden to bear the sufferings of this world in the hope of meriting the reward of a better life in the next, Judaism had stressed the importance of harmonizing men's social relations and of obtaining a full measure of social justice for all in the mortal world of everyday existence. "To describe the Jew as an individualist is to state a most misleading half-truth," Brandeis insisted. "He has to a rare degree merged his individuality and his interests in the community of which he forms a part." And to illustrate this contention he went on to quote a highly significant passage from the pen of Ahad Ha-Am:

> Judaism did not turn heavenwards and create in Heaven an eternal habitation of souls. It found "eternal life" on earth, by strengthening the social feeling in the individual; by making him regard himself not as an isolated being with an existence bounded by birth and death, but as part of a larger whole, as a limb of the social body. This conception shifts the center of gravity not from the flesh to the spirit, but from the individual to the community; and concurrently with this shifting, the problem of life becomes a problem not of individual, but of social life. I live for the sake of the perpetuation and happiness of the community of which I am a member; I die to make room for new individuals, who will mould the community afresh and not allow it to stagnate and remain forever in one position. When the individual thus values the community as his own life, and strives after its happiness as though it were his individual well-being, he finds satisfaction, and no longer feels so keenly the bitterness of his individual existence, because he sees the end for which he lives and suffers.

Was not this "beautiful" passage, asked Brandeis rhetorically, "the very essence of the truly triumphant twentieth-century democracy"?[45]

Ahad Ha-Am (literally "one of the people") was the pseudonym of writer and philosopher Asher Ginzberg, a Ukrainian-born Jew less than three months older than Brandeis, and widely recognized as the leading proponent of "cultural" Zionism. Brandeis's discovery of Ahad Ha-Am came at a crucial moment in his intellectual and emotional development; for not only was he looking to reestablish in middle age his own Jewish identity, but was also looking for a secure moral foundation on which to fasten his ideas about democracy and social justice. At such a juncture, he was profoundly influenced by the ideas of a writer who sought to teach emancipated Jews "how to live Jewishly"; a man whose "idealism [was] guided but not subdued by a sternly objective apprehension of realities." If any single writer should be credited with having helped Brandeis to harmonize the goals of his social philosophy with the objectives he now perceived for himself as a Zionist and a Jew, that writer is surely not Alfred Zimmern but Ahad Ha-Am.[46]

As we have already seen, with the sole exception of a new and particular emphasis on the importance of community feeling, all the essential lineaments of Brandeis's thinking about democracy, which after 1915 can be found woven into his statements and addresses on Zionism, had been developed initially in a non-Jewish context before that date. Nevertheless, Ahad Ha-Am's evocation of the relationship that ought to exist between the individual and his community evidently made a forceful impression on Brandeis's mind. It may even help us to comprehend the personal asceticism that was to become the hallmark of his private life in later years; for in his talk of shifting life's emphasis away from the satisfaction of individual wants toward the achievement of communal goals, Ahad Ha-Am was adumbrating a theme that would henceforth become the dominant feature of Brandeis's personal behavior as well as of his social thought.[47]

Looking back from the perspective of 1921, and the vitriolic schism which then occurred in the ranks of world Zionism, most commentators have perhaps exaggerated the extent of Brandeis's commitment to a purely politico-economic approach toward advancing the Zionist cause. The rhetoric of "Washington against Pinsk," the claims of the East Europeans that Brandeis stood for a policy of "Zionism without Zion" and lacked a "Jewish heart," have tended to obscure the degree to which he had internalized the "spiritual" elements of Ahad Ha-Amism. The volume of Ahad Ha-Am's articles that Brandeis read during the winter of 1914–15 had been produced some two years earlier in Philadelphia. As its editor explained in 1922, "the selection was confined, by the express desire of the publishing Society, to essays dealing with the broader aspects of Judaism and Jewish thought; essays of a more polemical character, in which the author has defined his attitude to the modern Jewish national movement, were designedly omitted." Thus the only writings of Ahad Ha-Am we can be certain Brandeis ever read did not give any direct intimation of the writer's hostility toward political Zionism in general and Herzl's conception of the Jewish State in particular. They did, however, expatiate on several themes which struck deep into Brandeis's consciousness.[48]

The words "spirit" and "spiritual" occur frequently in Ahad Ha-Am's essays, but they are not intended to denote religious as opposed to secular values; the distinction lies rather between underlying ideas and their outward expression. His "cultural Zionism" was essentially a secular phenomenon. The spirit is that of which thought and action are the external embodiment; it is the inner or "real" life, the inwardness of existence. For Ahad Ha-Am the spirit of the Jewish nation was to be sought not in statehood, nor even in Judaism, but in the Jewish cultural tradition. If this included the Law of Moses it also encompassed Hebrew language and literature, Hebraic conceptions of justice and mercy, of the individual and the commonwealth, and much else besides. His principal indictment against the political Zionists was that they had narrowed the basic definition of Zionism to exclude all these cultural dimensions. "Zionism—unqualified by any epithet—existed before," he wrote, "but it knew nothing of any problem of culture. It knew only its own plain and simple aim: that of placing the Hebrew nationality in new conditions, which should give it the possibility of developing all the various sides of its individuality." Yet claims to the effect that the social and economic problems of all Jews could be solved by the creation of the Jewish State alone had increasingly diverted attention toward the purely political aspects of Zionism, to the point where the original conception had "lost half its meaning." While this did not threaten the work being done to revive Jewish culture, it held potentially devastating consequences for the future of Zionism itself. "Every true lover of Zionism," Ahad Ha-Am believed,

> must realize the danger which it incurs through the diffusion of the idea that it has no concern with anything except diplomacy and financial transactions, and that all internal national work is a thing apart, which has no lot or portion in Zionism itself. If this idea gains general acceptance, it will end by bringing Zionism very low indeed.[49]

Brandeis's absorption of these ideas about the Jewish spirit was characteristically selective. He had little interest in Yiddish or Hebrew culture in the narrow sense, but was captivated by the notion of a broader cultural tradition in which the Jews were seen to have originated and preserved many of the values and attitudes that he believed most vital to social development and human happiness. Moreover, when Ahad Ha-Am insisted that those who believed or felt that the Jews were still a people had "the right to believe equally, without looking for any special proof, that the Jewish creative genius still lives, and is capable of expressing itself anew," Brandeis had little difficulty accepting the proposition. For the remainder of his life he would delight in pointing up examples of Jewish inventiveness and enterprise, and labor naïvely to refute or discountenance any imputation of Jewish shame or wrongdoing. Although he always placed a higher value on Palestinian settlement than Ahad Ha-Am was willing to do, he also shared some of the latter's concern for educational development, being willing to see the embryonic Israeli State not merely as a physical magnet for Jewish settlers but equally as a spiritual beacon for all Jews throughout the Diaspora.[50]

Somewhat more specific and a good deal closer to home were Ahad Ha-Am's strictures about emancipated Jews like Brandeis himself, living outside Eastern Europe, and partly or wholly assimilated into the mainstream of Western culture. The essayist regarded their abandonment of Jewishness as a disturbing phenomenon, and one in large part responsible for the perceived sterility of Hebrew cultural activity. He noticed with regret "the tendency to sink the national individuality, and merge it in that of other nations," and identified two major consequences of such a trend:

> on the one hand, the conscious and deliberate neglect of our original spiritual qualities and the striving to be like other people in every possible way; on the other hand, the loss to ourselves of the most gifted men whom we have produced in the last few generations, and their abandonment of Jewish national work for a life devoted to the service of other nations.

Yet paradoxically these men were themselves living proof of the creative potential of the Jewish people, if only it could be harnessed and put to work for Zionist ends. Though critical elsewhere of such reasoning, his discussion of Jewish characteristics in these essays seemingly entailed an implicit conception of culture as something almost innate, genetically transmitted, and ultimately inalienable despite the passing of generations. Inherited traits would out in even the most assimilated Jews.

> For try as they will to conceal their Jewish characteristics, and to embody in their work the national spirit of the people whose livery they have adopted, the light of literary and artistic criticism reveals quite clearly their almost universal failure. Despite themselves, the spirit of Judaism comes to the surface in all that they attempt, and gives their work a special and distinctive character, which is not found in the work of non-Jewish laborers in the same field.

Though these particular remarks were addressed specifically to the work of artists and intellectuals, no emancipated Jew could have been left in any doubt that their message was intended to be of general application.[51]

If Brandeis could see his own situation described obliquely in these words, there were other passages close by that must have challenged him even more directly. It was the Jews of the East, Ahad Ha-Am asserted, "the poor who believe," who possessed the means to reawaken the Jewish spirit lying dormant in their Western brethren.

> We will fill your spiritual emptiness with Jewish feeling; we will bring you Judaism, not the fair-sounding, meaningless lip-phrase which is your confession of faith, but a living Judaism of the heart; inspired with the will and the power to develop and to renew its strength. And then you will change your tune about slavery and emancipation.

If you have eyes to see what is going on around you, use them! Here are these paupers coming from the East, and beginning already to exercise an influence on your communities, while you disdain to take notice of them. Even so the lordly Romans in their day looked down with contempt on the "paupers from the East," until these paupers came and overturned their world.[52]

The bitter clashes of 1921 would show that Brandeis and his supporters were unwilling to cede control of American Zionism to the "paupers from the East," at least not without a struggle; however, we should not assume that he remained unmoved by the charge of having abandoned his cultural heritage. His irrational defense of the Maccabees against the claims of Hellenicized Jews to be promoting a higher level of civilization would suggest otherwise. When Ahad Ha-Am contrasted the "harmony and wholeness" found in the lives of Jews settled and working among their own people with the sundered personality of those living "among an alien people," he undoubtedly touched a raw nerve. For as he delved deeper into Zionism and his own Jewishness, Brandeis became increasingly aware of the alienness of American life, if not to his own perceptions then at least to many a Jew from the East:

[working] in a world that is not his own, and in which he cannot become at home unless he artificially change his nature and the current of his mind, thereby inevitably tearing himself into two disparate halves, and foredooming all his work to reveal, in its character and its products, this want of harmony and wholeness.

Yet if Ahad Ha-Am's solution to this psychic tension was to be the cultural revitalization of Jewish communities in the Diaspora, nurtured and directed from a new "spiritual center" in Palestine, Brandeis's solution would be to press on Jewish immigrants the underlying identity of interest and character between Judaism and Americanism, thereby implicitly denying the relevance of the assimilation argument to conditions in the United States. Yet this did not prevent him working wholeheartedly for what Ahad Ha-Am termed "the internal national life" of the Jews. On the contrary, as we have seen, it was part of his creed that Zionism and Americanism were not only mutually compatible but mutually obligatory aspirations for Jews in the United States. Moreover, he probably accepted the essayist's assertion that the founding of material settlements and the creation of a spiritual center in Palestine were interdependent objectives. Education was something he valued, and had it not been for the alteration in circumstances brought about by the Balfour Declaration, he might well have agreed that the founding of an independent center of Jewish learning in Palestine was both a high priority and one capable of more rapid realization than the further expansion of material settlements. He certainly entertained no illusions that the establishment of a Jewish state there would provide a physical refuge for all the world's Jews, but the "spiritual" relationship of even assimilated Jews to their ancestral home was a concept with which he could readily identify. It is doubtful, though, whether he could ever have gone along with the notion that the winning of cultural souls was more important work for Zionists than supporting the settlements already in place; nor could he have accepted the implications of Ahad Ha-Am's dictum that "One Jewish soul saved from the snare of assimilation is worth never so many [subscriptions and] shares."[53]

However, these complex issues were not the only, nor indeed the primary, concerns that Brandeis found illuminated by his reading of these essays. Ahad Ha-Am's conception of the relationship between justice and mercy, for instance, was clearly a matter close to Brandeis's professional and philosophic heart. The essayist believed that justice was the the bedrock of Jewishness, the heartblood of Hebraic culture. Mercy, or love, was a secondary virtue by comparison, of value only when combined with equity. "Mercy stands high on the ladder of moral development," he observed, "but Justice is the moral foundation upon which the ladder stands." Employed by itself to adjust the many conflicts of human life, mercy was potentially destructive of all natural and social rights, a doctrine that if universally applied "might well reduce the world to a condition of moral chaos." Justice, on the other hand, required probity on the part of those who sat in judgment, a self-disciplined application of the moral law within a coherent code of ethical behavior. The two combined offered a desirable and necessary mean; justice tempered by mercy was not merely a platitude, but a value essential to the well-being of all human societies. "There are in every generation," he wrote, "a few righteous men who arrive at this middle position; who by dint of habit come to make Justice a need of the individual Ego. These are the men who bear the banner of moral progress, the end of which is to make peace between the individual needs and the social, and to impose on both one law—the law of Righteousness." Such had been the prime function of the Old Testament prophets; and, as Brandeis might well have thought, it was not a bad ideal against which to measure the performance and moral stature of contemporary judges either.[54]

Of equal importance to him was Ahad Ha-Am's formulation of the proper relationship between the individual and the community, which we have already seen Brandeis quoting as the Jewish ideal in his "Call to the Educated Jew" of January 1915. Twelve years later, following a discussion about communism with his friend Felix Frankfurter, he recalled the passage as indicating "that the remarkable quality of living for the future salvation of the class—as distinguished from the individual—is a Jewish trait." Leaving aside the fact that Ahad Ha-Am had not generalized his discussion to the level of social classes, it is true that he regarded some conception of the future direction of social development as crucial. In sections both before and after that cited by Brandeis, he placed considerable emphasis on the need for a coherent purpose in the corporate life of nations. Suffering could be endured only so long as "the life of the community has an end of such importance as to outweigh, in the judgment of the individual, all possible hardships." Shifting the focus of social responsibility from the individual to the group did not obviate the need for a purpose to life; for why then did the community live? "The problem of the cause is a logical one," he wrote, "and the demand for its solution is therefore absolute and common to all human beings; whereas the problem of the end is a moral one, and the demand for its solution is accordingly relative, varying with the degree of moral development in the individual." Judaism had been forced to extend this quest from the personal to the national level, "to find an answer to the problem of the communal life." It needed to identify "some aim of sufficient grandeur and importance to uplift the individual, and to give him satisfaction at a time when his own particular life was unpleasant." It was for this reason, Ahad Ha-Am believed, "that Israel as a community became 'a kingdom of priests and a holy nation,' a nation consecrated from its birth to the service of setting the whole of mankind an example by its Law." Yet as he noted elsewhere, even Mosaic Law, for all its "logical principles," would ultimately be swept into oblivion, unless the Jewish people cherished a hope for the future. Let a nation "but make the future an integral part of itself, though it be only in the form of a fanciful hope," and it will have found a source of spiritual health and vigor sufficient to "preserve and sustain it for many a long year, despite all its ailments and diseases."[55]

In the Old Testament, the task of connecting the past of the Jewish nation to its hoped-for future belonged to the prophets, and it was to the role of prophecy in Hebrew culture that Ahad Ha-Am devoted some of his most pregnant reflections. As his editor and translator, Leon Simon, glossed his views in 1912, materialism had never been a vital part of the Jewish outlook. Indeed the Hebrew mind had not even been directed "towards the spiritualized materialism that finds its expression in in beauty of form and language"; rather its primary focus had always been upon "the discovery of fundamental truths about the universe, and the embodiment in actual life, of fundamental principles based on those truths." Its spirit, therefore, was "essentially religious and moral"; its prime objective "the attempt to found a social order based on God's will." The prophets were thus the quintessential products of that spirit: "men whose special gift it is to see into the heart of things, and to enunciate moral laws based on the spiritual truths which are revealed to their superior insight." Their ideal was a society based on perfect justice, or by another name righteousness:

a society, that is, in which each individual does that which is right from the point of view of the whole, without regard to his personal interest or convenience. And that which is right from the point of view of the whole society is that which is right from the point of view of the whole universe: for such a society embodies in human life the principle of right on which the universe is based. It is, in religious phraseology, a society which works out the will of God on earth.[56]

At first glance it might be thought that so secular a person as Brandeis would find little appeal in this sort of religious imagery. But that was just the point: Ahad Ha-Am's essays afforded a series of symbolic *images*, a complex metaphor, through which the writer's immediate concerns for the Jewish nation could be extended to encompass the concerns of all humanity. The fact is that Zionism could never have taken such a hold on Brandeis but for the *universal character* of the ideas he believed it enshrined, and their essential resonance with those he already entertained, whether based on his experience of American life or his reading of Goethe and the Greeks. In this particular context, moreover, Ahad Ha-Am's depiction of the prophetic character and of the seer's relations with those around him seemed to be describing not only Brandeis's own sense of social mission but likewise the frustrations and hostilities that it had encountered. The prophet, he averred, was "essentially a one-sided man," for ever at odds with the world and its prevailing wisdom.

A certain moral idea fills his whole being, masters his every feeling and sensation, engrosses his whole attention. He can only see the world through the mirror of his idea; he desires nothing, strives for nothing, except to make every phase of the life around him an embodiment of that idea in its perfect form. His whole life is spent in fighting for this ideal with all his strength; for its sake he lays waste his powers, unsparing of himself, regardless of the conditions of life and the demands of the general harmony. His gaze is fixed always on what *ought* to be in accordance with his own convictions; never on what *can* be consistently with the general condition of things outside himself. The Prophet is thus a primal force. His action affects the character of the general harmony, while he himself does not become a part of that harmony, but remains always a man apart, a narrow-minded extremist, zealous for his own ideal, and intolerant of every other. And since he cannot have all that he would, he is in a perpetual state of anger and grief; he remains all his life "a man of strife and a man of contention to the whole earth."[57]

The "gospel of justice and charity" preached by the Hebrew prophets did not require the "revelation of some new theoretical truth" and its subsequent proclamation around the world; rather was their mission "to influence practical life in the direction of absolute Righteousness—an ideal for which there never can be a complete victory." It was both a national and a universal mission, but the role of the Jews in maintaining and promulgating it was always seen to be special, their duty as a "chosen" people. The prophets saw the work involved as needing the participation and commitment of "a whole community," not as something to be undertaken by "scattered individuals, approaching it sporadically, each man for himself, at different times and in different places." But as Ahad Ha-Am observed, this prophetic ideal, once abroad in the world, came into conflict with "other forces, which hindered its progress, and did not allow it free development." Compromise became the new watchword; and with the decay of prophecy, "the universal dominion of absolute justice" became an idea without a standard- bearer.[58]

It does not really matter whether the foregoing argument represents an admissible, or even a credible, interpretation of Jewish history. Its significance for our purposes lies in the impact it had, or may have had, on Brandeis's mind. The prophet as described by Ahad Ha-Am was a man of moral courage and intellectual integrity, possessed of a boundless belief in the rectitude of his own ideas, and as such was a figure with whom, either consciously or subconsciously, Brandeis could not help but identify. If he were going to think of himself as a Jew, then why not as the highest type which the Jewish people had produced? In the America of the 1910s, Progressivism permitted temporary and qualified acceptance of such a man in public life, as muckraker, political critic, or social reformer; however, his legitimacy remained precarious, his dissidence always suspect. The dominant Anglo-Saxon tradition shied away from zealotry of all kinds, assigning no long-term role to social ideologues, whose uncompromising idealism it found profoundly unsettling. But what the American liberal tradition lacked, Ahad Ha-Am's brand of Hebraism provided abundantly: justification for holding and expounding a morally grounded vision of the just society, regardless of whether the ideal proposed was supportive or corrosive to contemporary values and goals.[59]

As we saw earlier in this chapter, Brandeis spoke explicitly about the contemporary relevance of the prophetic ideal in the course of the interview he gave to the *Boston Jewish Advocate* in 1910, maintaining that "The Jewish prophet may struggle for truth and righteousness to-day just as the ancient prophets did." This in turn led the *Advocate*'s representative to compare his sense of mission with that displayed in the Old Testament. The original "prototype" for Brandeis, he believed, was Daniel: "And how much like the great Daniel, prophet of old, who struggled against historic wrong and injustice, is this mighty modern Jewish prophet." For Allon Gal, convinced that Brandeis became the object of increasingly vicious anti-Semitism after his tussle with the New Haven Railroad, the comparison plainly seems an appropriate one:

Daniel's situation, indeed, of that of all the ancient prophets, best characterized Brandeis's position in 1910. The Daniel stories took place not in the Jewish homeland but in Babylon. The Jews there were respected and their God honored. Daniel and his friends underwent many trials but finally triumphed. Moreover, no one was wiser than Daniel; only he was able to read the menacing writing on the wall at Belshazzar's feast, indicating the imminent death of the king. The image of Daniel whose famous trials in the lions' den were a universal symbol, may have been more immediately appealing to Brandeis than that of other prophetic figures like Isaiah who, although exhibiting far greater social concern, lived in Palestine and prophesied the ingathering of the exiles. Like Daniel's, Brandeis's battlefield was outside of Palestine; Brandeis, too, was a man with a mission to pursue in the framework of a non-Jewish society.[60]

This is an interesting speculation, though one that perhaps loses some of its credibility if we decline to accept Gal's central thesis, which depicts Brandeis as a marginal man, conscious of his social rejection by Boston's Brahmin elite. An alternative "prototype" is suggested by Sam Girgus, who stresses the formal similarity between the writings of those comprising his "New Covenant" tradition and the jeremiads of New England's Puritan past:

In the manner of Jeremiah, who describes the making of "a new covenant with the house of Israel and the house of Judah" (31:31–32), these Jewish thinkers in America often write with the vision and sensibility of prophets and judges who stand between the American Way and the people. In this sense the Jews, who had been a model for the Puritans, become the "New Puritans," and Jewish writers and thinkers function in the role of "New Jeremiahs" preaching to the people to understand the meaning of America.

At first blush this synoptic profile might seem nearer to Brandeis's own prophetic ideal, especially in its implied evocation of America as the New Zion; but on closer inspection the correspondence here too begins to break down. Although it is indeed true that in his public utterances Brandeis dwelt frequently on the essential compatibility between Jewish and American values, and denied that Zionism necessarily entailed a divided loyalty for those American Jews who espoused it, it remains a fact that his work to establish a national homeland on the banks of the Jordan cannot readily be made to fit inside the "New Covenant" paradigm. With all due respect to Gal and Girgus, such activities bespeak the language of Isaiah more than they do that of Daniel or Jeremiah.[61]

It may indeed be the case, as his critics charged, that Brandeis tended to see the Jewish settlement of Palestine in largely American terms, as illustrated by his reference to the colonists there as "Jewish Pilgrim Fathers"; however, as previously stated he harbored no illusions that the new Israel being built by these modern pioneers could or should be expected to provide an ultimate destination for all the Jews of the Diaspora. For much as he felt moved by his visit to Palestine, he never seriously contemplated living there himself, nor did he encourage other Jewish-Americans to do so. Although, like Isaiah, he foretold the coming together of the scattered tribes of Israel and Judah, for Brandeis the gathering point was as much a spiritual as it was a geographical one. The need was for a context in which Jews could live freely and productively *as Jews*, living up to the values and ideals handed down to them across the ages. For many this would only be possible in

Palestine on the soil that God gave to Moses; but for many others, including himself, it could be achieved just as well in non-Jewish societies, provided these same values and ideals constituted an essential part of their cultural tradition.

Convinced as Brandeis was that cultural pluralism offered the only viable road along which the United States could progress, his Zionist activities were at bottom an exercise in ethnic altruism: a spiritual gift from one whose family had already found their own Zion in the New World to the poor and oppressed masses they had left behind in Europe. The psychological space that Brandeis inhabited during the last twenty-five years of his life was not unlike the Wehles' old *Durchhaus* in the Prague of the 1840s. Viewed from the outside, it appeared to cut through the walls dividing the Jewish and Gentile worlds from one another; but inside the door opening onto the culture of the ghetto was kept firmly locked. The bourgeois residents of the house were identified as Jews, were even widely respected in the Jewish community; but they had no need, either practical or mystical, for the security that the *Judenstadt* afforded to others of their race. From choice they walked abroad in a wider world.[62]

Within two years of reading Ahad Ha-Am's essays, Brandeis came to wield the power of a judge on America's highest judicial tribunal: the culmination of an outstanding legal career that had begun almost forty years earlier. Yet as well as an unsurpassed professionalism, long honed and tempered in his years at the bar, he would also increasingly display the obsessiveness and gnomic style of speech regarded as characteristic by those who observed him only in old age: young men in the main to whom he did indeed become known—simply, and without apparent irony—by the name of Isaiah.

6

Freedom and Justice for All

But when the laws are written, then the weak
And wealthy have alike but equal right.
Yea, even the weaker may fling back the scoff
Against the prosperous if he be reviled;
And, armed with right, the less o'ercomes the great.
— Euripides, *The Supplicants*

Brandeis's involvement in Zionist affairs during the first two years of the war severely restricted the time and energy he was able to devote to other concerns; nevertheless, he did what he could. "Have been supplementing Jewish activities by woman suffrage, gubernatorial, garment workers arbitration and public franchise excursions," he observed in October 1915. The note addressed to his brother was hastily written in New York; later the same day he would be in Philadelphia explaining to labor leaders why they ought to be in favor of scientific management techniques and how workers could benefit from the increased industrial efficiency these engendered. "Thus," he complained half-seriously to Alfred, "is the honest practice of a profession interfered with." It was an almost wistful remark; for although much of the business coming into the law firm of Brandeis, Dunbar, and Nutter had been handled for some years past by his trusted senior partners, Brandeis's own ability to put on the big forensic display was ironically at its peak. When an Oregon minimum-wage provision came before the United States Supreme Court for review in December 1914, his oral argument in defense of the measure struck a District of Columbia judge who happened to be present in the courtroom as "one of the greatest" he had ever listened to. "He not only *reached* the Court, but he *dwarfed the Court*," this observer wrote afterward, "because it was clear that here stood a man who knew infinitely more, and who cared infinitely more, for the vital daily rights of the people than the men who sat there sworn to protect them." In the event, it was to be his last major performance at the bar; before the justices could arrive at a decision in the case, the "people's lawyer" had himself been appointed to fill a vacancy in their ranks.[1]

It has been argued throughout this study that it was the law and its principles that provided Brandeis with his most enduring frame of reference within which to analyze and interpret the fabric of American life. As attorney, and subsequently as judge, he used its precepts and logical modes of reasoning as a surgeon might use a scalpel: to cleave truth from obscurity; to cut with delicacy and precision between several fine shades of meaning, and with as much acuity between their divergent though attendant consequences. It was not a faculty that everyone found appealing. Writing at the time of the controversial Senate confirmation hearings in 1916, former Secretary of State Elihu Root evidently found it both distasteful and perplexing. He readily acknowledged that President Wilson's nominee had some good qualities and was very able, but he was deeply concerned by the way in which Brandeis's "extraordinarily acute mind seems to draw distinctions and enable him to justify himself in conduct which I do not think to be in accordance with the standards [to be expected from a Justice of the Supreme Court]."[2]

During Brandeis's years on the bench, however, the subtlety and keenness of mind that so scandalized Root and other critics of his nomination were generally to prove a source of delight for his supporters. They gave a semblance of rigor to his judicial arguments on socioeconomic issues that most Progressives and liberals, and not a few conservatives, found both authoritative and compelling. Moreover, as the passage of time distanced him increasingly from the reformist campaigns of the prewar years, the rhetorical strategies he deployed appeared to be less and less bound up with matters of *political* contention, and more and more to be about reshaping the foundations of American jurisprudence. Yet unlike, say, Benjamin N. Cardozo, his liberal contemporary on the Court, Brandeis wrote no serious legal treatise that might serve as a guide to the core of his mature thinking about the law and its functions; and the literary fragments we do possess are too diverse and widely scattered in time to make juristic continuity or progression easy characteristics to identify and assess. Most of the published work was written before 1916, and the greater part of that, including the handful of articles published in legal journals between 1881 and 1890, as well as the numerous legal briefs written during his thirty years at the bar, is too specific and narrow in its focus to offer much of a clue to the wider orientation of his legal thought. In any case, as we have seen in previous chapters, the animating principles revealed in his 1892 lecture at the Massachusetts Institute of Technology differ considerably from those that directed his actions from the mid-1890s onward, which makes the earlier material of at best dubious relevance for an estimate of the intellectual stance he subsequently adopted as a judge.[3]

Fortunately, we also have the two addresses on legal and judicial practice that Brandeis gave in 1905 and 1916, respectively—the latter especially affording a fair summary of his professional outlook on the eve of his appointment as a member of the judiciary. In "The Living Law," delivered to the Chicago Bar Association at the beginning of January 1916, he spoke at length about a widespread dissatisfaction with the way legal institutions functioned in the contemporary world. At the root of the public's disquiet, he maintained, was the failure of most lawyers and judges to bring their thinking into line with the many profound changes that had taken place in the fabric of American society during the preceding three decades. The loss of independence and status suffered by many skilled artisans and small businessmen; the rise of mass production and the accompanying specialization of both managerial and labor tasks; the fundamental transformation of economic relationships epitomized in the substitution of corporate for individual enterprise—all had combined to make the welfare of the community increasingly dependent on the behavior of a few big employers, and had saddled the state with ultimate responsibility for ensuring that these titans of industry and finance used their power in ways regarded as compatible with the public interest. The people wanted not merely "legal justice" but "social justice" as well; they required government to "keep order not only physically but socially," and the law to "protect a man from the things that rob him of his freedom, whether the oppressing force be physical or of a subtler kind."[4]

Yet faced with such demands, the law had failed to adapt. The limited capacity of human beings to resist or control such powerful forces unaided was ignored. Judges had been more inclined to heed the claim of corporate lawyers that new protective legislation violated the natural rights of their clients in plain contravention of recognized constitutional limitations. The "natural vent of legislation" had thus been stifled. "Where statutes giving expression to the new social spirit were clearly constitutional," Brandeis argued, "judges, imbued with the relentless spirit of individualism, often construed them away." Whereas the fledgling social sciences were fully alive to the dimensions and consequences of these revolutionary economic developments, "legal science—the unwritten or judge-made law as distinguished from legislation—was largely deaf and blind." Its key practitioners, both on the bench and at the bar, had been trained as common lawyers and knew little of the methods or findings of recent socioeconomic research. "One can hardly escape the conclusion," he pontificated, "that a lawyer who has not studied economics and sociology is very apt to become a public enemy."

The answer proffered to his audience was a variation on the model adumbrated eight years earlier in *Muller v. Oregon*: the courts would have to be made aware of the facts of modern life and in future must give as much weight to the imperatives of public welfare and social harmony as they did now to the precedents of case law involving statutory construction and constitutional interpretation. "What we need is not to displace the courts, but to make them efficient instruments of justice; not to displace the lawyer, but to fit him for his official or judicial task." The "distorting effects" of professional specialization had to be corrected by means of "broader education—by study undertaken preparatory to practice—and continued by lawyer and judge throughout life: study of economics and sociology and politics which embody the fact and present problems of today."

The Constitution "was not obsolete," Brandeis insisted, but it had become encrusted with unnecessary layers of interpretation that reflected the economic prejudices of the modern judiciary more than the motivating precepts of the Founding Fathers. As far as the nation's appellate tribunals were concerned, the invocation of laissez-faire principles to interdict the actions of both Congress and state legislatures was in fact a relatively new phenomenon, and in his view one to be profoundly regretted. It had been "the traditional policy of the Supreme Court," for instance, to presume that legislation enacted under the police powers of the states was valid "until its violation of the Constitution [was] proved beyond all reasonable doubt." In recent years, however, this procedural axiom had been stood completely on its head, so that now the states were required to meet the highly restrictive conditions imposed on them by the nebulous concept of "substantive due process" and to demonstrate that their enactments were constitutional according to the test of "reasonableness." If the law was to remain a vital and respected force in American life, developments such as this had to be resisted and, wherever possible, reversed.

Not only has this address usually been read with hindsight as a manifesto outlining Brandeis's own subsequent behavior as a judge; perhaps even more significantly, it has been held to illustrate succinctly the extent to which his early, naïve faith in the common law and its interpreters had been forced to give way before a more sophisticated and doubtless more realistic evaluation of the legal function—an evaluation predicated on personal experience and the overwhelming weight of accumulated evidence. Gone apparently was his former preference for judge-made law over statute; gone too were his open hostility to social legislation and scarcely veiled belief in the judiciary as an autonomous, quasi-political force ideally suited to mediating the myriad conflicts of society. Law, it seems, had now to be conscious of social phenomena beyond the direct experience of judges and lawyers; restrained in its application of rigid formulas; mindful of other forces at work within the national polity. Such, if we take his remarks at face value, was the altered conceptual frame of his jurisprudence as he prepared to embark on the final phase of an already outstanding career in the law.

In stark contrast to the paucity of suitable material from which to infer the basic configurations of his legal thinking before 1916, the opinions, and particularly the dissents, that he wrote during his time on the Supreme Court are both plentiful and illuminating. For while the occasions for opinion writing are always by definition singular and limitative, Brandeis, in common with most other judges, often took full advantage of the customary latitude for philosophizing from the bench. Consequently, his *obiter dicta* on numerous subjects provide a rich, if sometimes problematic, source of ideas and pronouncements for anyone with the time and patience to sift through them. Yet Judges do not merely contemplate the law; in a very real sense they are frequently called upon to make it as well—even those operating under a voluntary injunction of self-restraint. Thus the mother lode, so to speak, too often overlooked by those in search of surface glitter or intellectual cohesion, is to be found less in the gloss of juristic speculation than in the more prosaic body of constitutional interpretation and statutory construction itself. Thankfully, the digest of Brandeis's opinions compiled by Harry Shulman in 1930 helps the researcher to open up a whole new world of legal thinking otherwise locked away in the largely unread texts of forgotten determinations; for subject to certain qualifications, it can safely be treated as highlighting those matters and cases that the justice himself considered significant.[5]

Taken together, then, the disparate materials identified in the foregoing paragraphs, although far from constituting an ideal range of sources, do permit us to evaluate with some degree of precision the principal features of Brandeis's judicial philosophy; and of course they can often be supplemented by the recollections and commentaries of those who worked with him, or who have attempted to analyze and weigh the importance of his personal contribution to the evolving fabric of American constitutional law. The nature of that contribution, however, was not always what it might appear at first sight; the testimony of "The Living Law," written after all when he was still a practicing attorney and an active reformer, may not always be an accurate forecast of his subsequent behavior as a Supreme Court justice.[6]

Considering the essential elements of the much-publicized "Brandeis brief"—particularly its appeal to judicial pragmatism, its stress on the open-minded consideration of socioeconomic evidence, and its demand that judges free themselves from the death grip of legal precedent—one is immediately struck by the relative rigidity of Brandeis's own attitude as a judge to the technicalities of judicial procedure. Though this lack of flexibility did not generally extend to matters of constitutional interpretation, nonetheless, even here his willingness to innovate would often be tempered by a considered respect for the determinations of his predecessors.

This is to be explained in part by an apparent unwillingness to abandon completely his early enthusiasm for the common law as inherited by the American colonists from their English forebears. Prior to the late 1890s when, as we have seen, he began to busy himself more and more with public issues involving constitutional rights and responsibilities, his main interests in the law, both intellectual and professional, lay in the allied fields of commerce and property. These were areas of legal activity in which constitutional questions tended to occupy a much less prominent position than common-law precedents and matters of statutory interpretation. Even as a first-year student at the Harvard Law School, the young Louis Brandeis had regarded a grasp of "the principles which underlie the structure of the Common Law" as *the* essential prerequisite of a successful practice, and this primary orientation continued to direct and shape his legal thinking, even on constitutional issues, for the remainder of his life.[7]

Nor was this an unreasonable viewpoint for a lawyer of his generation to adopt. For if, by the time he became an associate justice, the work of the Supreme Court characteristically concerned the interplay between government regulation and economic enterprise, forty years earlier, as Felix Frankfurter pointed out in 1930, it had been a very different story: "[In 1875] the Court wrote 193 opinions. But these still predominantly dealt with common law topics or technical legal questions of not wide public concern, while only 17 cases, less than 10 percent, involved questions of constitutionality, taxation, and like issues of public import." During Brandeis's time on the Court it virtually ceased to function as a common-law tribunal, focusing almost exclusively on matters of public law rather than on "the ordinary legal questions involved in the multitudinous law suits of *Doe* v. *Roe* of other courts." But even as construction of important federal and state legislation and interpretation of the the Constitution came to be the staple business of the Supreme Court, the fact is that, despite the obvious implication of his Chicago address, Brandeis continued to apply many of the principles and methods of the common law in his manner of dealing with constitutional cases.[8]

Slavish adherence to judicial precedents did not, it should be admitted, feature high on his list of such principles. The common-law doctrine of *stare decisis*, for which he had managed to evince such fervent and barely qualified approval in the 1892 draft of his M.I.T. lectures, became increasingly suspect during the four decades or so that followed, and anything but the straightforward principle of law that the explanation intended for his students had implied. What had begun in England as a maxim of the common-law courts had been readily assimilated into the practice of the United States Supreme Court from its earliest days, even on the rare occasions that it was called on to settle issues of constitutional significance. However, it was the rapid development of public law in the last quarter of the nineteenth century, and the equally alarming growth of litigation which followed in its wake, that brought matters of constitutional interpretation to the forefront of the Court's docket. In this context, given the political sensitivity of the issues involved and the socioeconomic outlook of most of the Court's members, the mechanical invocation of *stare decisis* was a practice that would cause Brandeis considerable disquiet during his years on the bench.

How then ought we to characterize his approach to the judicial function? Among those best qualified to discern the values and legal principles guiding his actions as a judge was Harlan Fiske Stone, appointed to the Supreme Court by President Coolidge in 1925 and made its chief justice by Franklin Roosevelt in 1941. Despite his earlier connections with Wall Street, Stone soon identified himself with the Court's liberal minority, and during the 1930s his name was frequently joined in dissenting opinions with those of Brandeis and Cardozo. In December 1942, at a special meeting of the Court held to honor Brandeis's memory, Stone used the opportunity afforded him to analyze the lineaments of his former colleague's jurisprudence. At its core he discovered a firm conviction that the American legal system—based squarely on the traditions of the common law, kept relevant by statute, and articulated by means of the federal Constitution—encompassed both the flexibility and the resourcefulness needed to make real the principles of liberty and equality to which the nation was in theory dedicated. "Only as we are aware of his passion for *freedom and justice for all men*," Stone asserted, "and of the means by which he translated it into action through a profound understanding of both the function of law in a changing world and the techniques by which law may be adapted to the needs of a free society, do we gain insight into the true sources of his power and influence as a judge."[9]

Progress in the law was rarely easy or swift, and such advances as were made depended heavily on the efforts of a few individuals: men whose vision saw the necessity of protecting or controlling the diverse elements of their society, and whose craftsmanship made possible the adjustment of old formulas to novel situations. In this respect, he likened the contribution made by Brandeis to that of Lord Chancellor Mansfield, who in eighteenth-century England had perceived the necessity and created the means for adapting the elements of a feudal common law to the circumstances of an expanding commercial society. In the twentieth century, the socioeconomic problems generated by an increasingly industrial and urban nation had called for similar innovation and creativity to be shown by America's judges. Everywhere the strength and bargaining power of different groups and classes within the community seemed unequal: Organized labor demanded legal protections for workingmen; reformers demanded tough action to suppress monopolies and to regulate public utilities; government demanded the recognition of new administrative agencies. "These were problems to tax the technical skill and training of lawyers and judges," the chief justice observed, "but their solution demanded also sympathetic understanding of their nature and of the part which the legal traditions of yesterday can appropriately play in securing the ordered society of today. In the long history of the law few judges have been so richly endowed for such an undertaking as was Justice Brandeis."

His earlier career at the bar had revealed not only his readiness to pursue justice in contentious issues of public concern, but also his pertinacity in finding ways to use the existing machinery of law for their resolution, thereby preserving the essential character of American institutions. Stone considered the key traits of Brandeis's character and personality ideally suited to these tasks: "social conscience and vision, infinite patience, an extraordinary capacity for sustained intellectual effort, and serene confidence that truth revealed will ultimately prevail." Yet uncommon as this combination of talents was, they would still have proved inadequate but for "his insight into the true significance of a system of law which [was] the product of some 700 years of Anglo-American legal history." While numerous others have commented on Brandeis's zest for facts, Stone is almost unique in relating this observation to an imaginative understanding of how it should be integrated into the broader pattern of his legal thinking. "Justice Brandeis knew," he remarked shrewdly,

> that throughout the development of the common law the judge's decision of today, which is also the precedent for tomorrow, has drawn its inspiration—and the law itself has derived its vitality and capacity for growth—from the very facts which, in every case, frame the issue for decision. And so, as the first step to decision, he sought complete acquaintance with the facts as *the generative source of the law.*

Thus he would insist on painstaking research into the socioeconomic context of each case before him, whether it concerned the wages and hours of labor, rate making for public utilities, the consequences of a monopoly, or whatever. It was a stage in the preparation of each opinion with which every one of his law clerks was familiar, because it was they who were generally called upon to do the leg work. This he regarded as the essential prerequisite for adapting rules of law developed in simpler days to the complex realities of modern industrial civilization.

> For what availed it that judges and lawyers knew all the laws in the ancient books, if they were unaware of the significance of the new experience to which those laws were now to be applied. In the facts, quite as much as in the legal principles set down in the lawbooks, he found the materials for the synthesis of judicial decision. In that synthesis *the law itself was but the means to a social end*—the protection and control of those interests in society which are the special concern government and hence of law.

The factors most crucial for achieving such a working synthesis were balance, selectivity, and self-discipline. Because Brandeis rejected the automatic supremacy of precedent, it did not mean that he failed to respect the wisdom of earlier jurists. His prime objective of accommodating the law to fit society's changing needs was always to be attained "within the limits set by the command of Constitution and statutes, and the restraints of precedent and of doctrines by common consent regarded as binding"; the desideratum of legal continuity was constantly "to be weighed against the pressing demands of new facts, and in the light of the teachings of experience." To a greater or lesser degree, such approaches to the decision-making process were common to all good judges. However, according to Stone, what made Brandeis judicial career distinctive "was his clear recognition that these are boundaries within which the judge has scope for freedom of choice of the rule of law which he is to apply, and that his choice within those limits may rightly depend upon social and economic considerations whose weight may turn the scales of judgment in favor of one rule rather than another." This was not a unique method of proceeding; it had been followed by great judges in the past, many of whom had "practiced the creative art by which familiar legal doctrines [were] moulded to the needs of a later day." But it was unfamiliar, and particularly at the time of his appointment and during his early years on the Court had caused his actions and motives to be widely misunderstood. Only with the passage of time, and a growing acceptance of his reasoning, did a general recognition develop "of his integrity of mind and purpose and of his judicial wisdom."

As already noted, Brandeis believed that by its very nature constitutional interpretation involved principles related to, but ultimately distinct from, those required for the construction of statutes or the application of common-law rulings. Intended by its framers as a timeless statement of fundamental law, necessary in all its provisions for the survival and prosperity of a free people, the Constitution could not be read "with the narrow literalism of a municipal code or a penal statute"; its essential meaning had to be approached and comprehended with subtlety and intelligence, "so that its high purposes should illumine every sentence and phrase of the document and be given effect as a part of a harmonious framework of government." The common-law doctrine of *stare decisis* should not be invoked to stifle the progressive evolution of that framework, even if the only alternative was a periodic reconsideration of basic values in the light of new experience, and on occasion the overruling of time-hallowed interpretations. In short, Brandeis reckoned that judicial relativism was preferable to judicial sclerosis.

In any case, he had long ago abandoned the notion that the Constitution set out to establish and protect one particular set of socioeconomic views to the exclusion of all others; on the contrary, it was clearly intended to preserve the rights of majorities and minorities alike. He thus became known as a stalwart defender of civil liberties, determined to uphold the rights of any fair-minded individual, however much he might disagree with the values or opinions for which that person stood. Yet whatever flexibility he might have urged in construing, say, the *general* restraints imposed by the due process clause, he was prepared to entertain no such latitude regarding "the *specific* constitutional guaranties of individual liberty and of freedom of speech and religion," or to the need for a strict "adherence by all who wield the power of government to the principles of the Constitution," seeing in these fixed precepts of law "the great safeguards of a free and progressive society."

Equally close to Brandeis, though in a totally different context, was his erstwhile law clerk, David Riesman, Jr. In the fall of 1935, like many before him, the future sociologist was sent to Washington on Felix Frankfurter's recommendation. The year was not a happy one for Riesman, who had wanted to clerk for Justice Cardozo; and once established, he found himself increasingly out of sympathy with Brandeis's judicial methods. Moreover, he soon came to feel that he was toiling ineffectively in the shadow of his talented predecessor Paul Freund; for by general consent, Freund had been not only an outstanding student at the Harvard Law School but had also proved himself an equally outstanding law clerk during his year with Brandeis, capable of contributing in material ways to the substance of the justice's opinions. Looking back on his own experience in a 1983 interview, Riesman was conscious of Brandeis's difficult position. He thought that it should be remembered in fairness that the justice was already an old man when they first met and was nearing the end of his service on the Court; "whatever resilience he may have had earlier was gone." As demonstrated by his opinions written during that session, particularly his dissent in the *Ashwander* case, it was evident that Brandeis saw himself as "fighting a strategic action, a holding action, against the conservatives on the Court." Yet despite his awareness of these circumstances, in retrospect the former secretary remained highly critical both of his boss's general outlook and more particularly of his ethics as a judge.[10]

Riesman's reservations about Brandeis's broader philosophy will be considered more fully in the next chapter. What troubled him a great deal more, both in the 1930s and subsequently, was a growing perception that the great champion of sociological jurisprudence might have feet of clay. His disillusionment began with a minor case that involved the legitimacy of an Oregon law requiring the boxes used for shipping berries grown in the state to be of a certain size and shape. It was, in fact, the very first case he ever researched for the justice, and he found the investigations at the Departments of Agriculture and Transportation a good deal more rewarding than mere "digging in the lawbooks." He quickly amassed boxes of documents and pamphlets, all of which seemed to point to one conclusion:

> Far from being an improvement, the Oregon berry boxes were a handicap. The only purpose of the law was to protect Oregon berry box manufacturers against those who could not make that kind of box from the redwood trees of Northern California—clearly the law was a violation of interstate commerce and was intended as a protective tariff. I explained all this to Brandeis, who was not in the least interested. What he wanted to do in his strategic way of thinking was to sustain state laws against federal attack, both to elevate the states and to pull down
> . . . the federal judges from their height. He really believed in judicial restraint, not because of a great admiration for the plebs, but because he did not think the judges any marked improvement. He also did have the hope that states would learn from their mistakes. Thus the Oregon berry box law was unanimously approved by the Court, and Brandeis suppressed the inconvenient evidence.[11]

This experience convinced Riesman that the justice's celebrated inductive approach to legal questions, the basis of the so-called Brandeis brief, was a fraud; that beneath the cloak of disinterested empiricism, Brandeis was as committed as any of the Court's conservatives to furthering the political and social objectives in which he believed, and to treating the law as a tool that could be twisted and manipulated to serve extrinsic ends. Already to some degree ambivalent about his new chief, Riesman was genuinely surprised to find that Brandeis's judicial method, in this case at least, was anything but a "search for factuality." The discovery bred in him a creeping cynicism, sufficient for example to send him back to the transcript of Brandeis's confirmation hearings. "It was generally thought by liberals," he recalled in 1981, "that he was opposed because of his progressive political views and out of anti-Semitism, but the hearings showed that there was a good case to be made against him on ethical grounds." He bore comparison with Ralph Nader, whose single-minded zeal Riesman considered "also unscrupulous and out to 'get the bastards,' no matter what." As for Brandeis: "The worst thing he had done was to have been counsel for the United Shoe Machinery Company and then used that information [sic] in getting the government to file an anti-trust suit against the company." For Riesman, the Oregon Berry Box case confirmed the darkest suspicions voiced in 1916: if not actually "dishonest," then Brandeis was at least "a legal trickster."[12]

Writing to Frankfurter in the late spring of 1936, however, Riesman's estimate of the justice had been much less critical, and while perhaps going further in identifying the nonjudicial sources of his thought, had been similar to Stone's 1942 appraisal in many respects. Skepticism of power and of human abilities, he then believed, lay at the bottom of Brandeis's constitutional philosophy during the 1930s. His seemingly paradoxical faith in men's potential for growth and development was itself predicated on a firmly held belief that the individual freedoms of the many could only be preserved by dint of delicate constitutional mechanisms, designed and perfected to frustrate the accretion of power in the hands of the few. "Among my friends," he told Frankfurter, "the views of Justice Brandeis are treated with disdain. Even his former secretaries whom I know adopt the shallow philosophy of the 'Nation.'" For his own part, he was inclined to think that "a thorough understanding of his philosophy should precede acceptance of one of the more dogmatic creeds which are fashionable today." He considered the justice's views "a challenge, an abrasive against which to rub panaceas," and his personal asceticism a moral example that would "grapple with me throughout life."[13]

As an arbiter of the Constitution, he rated Brandeis as greatly superior to Mr. Justice Holmes, whose opinions he had come to regard as "superficial and often grievously in error"; their constitutional import was negative only, and they disclosed no coherent scheme. Holmes, he believed, would eventually be remembered as a teacher and writer rather than as a judge.

On the other hand, Brandeis has reached his flowering on the bench. He did not take it easy as I suspect Holmes did on reaching that pinnacle. Opposing bad decisions with as much vigor as Holmes, he has tried also to lay the ground work of a pattern of constitutional interpretation. Holmes and T. R. Powell are in the main of the same constitutional school,—if the legislature wants it, that is enough. Justice Brandeis went further. He realized that constitutional government was not merely a somewhat delayed and palliated form of majority rule but an actual separation of powers which could prevent the majority having its way—and that however persuasive its action, if it ignored certain standards of conduct or acted oppressively or impaired certain freedom almost absolute.

In treating the matter of Brandeis's judicial ethics, however, this contemporary estimate breaks ground left untilled in Stone's eulogy, though it contrasts even more sharply with the later expression of Riesman's own views. The imputation of deceitfulness is there, but it is pressed obliquely and a reasonable defense is made:

> Many of my friends think Justice Brandeis intellectually dishonest. They believe that he is not sufficiently dispassionate to be as good a judge as say—Holmes or Cardozo. They suspect that his decisions are guided by his predilections rather than by "the law" or "the facts." To my mind, this question is like most one of more or less and that [sic] Justice Brandeis comes closer to the judicial ideal than is generally realized. I think the first lesson in achieving dispassionateness is to be aware of the problem,—for this, a certain amount of sophistication is essential. One must always watch one's self.

In flat contradiction of his recollected findings on the Oregon Berry Box case, Riesman was unequivocal about the rigor of Brandeis's judicial method, claiming that he always insisted "upon an absolutely accurate statement of the facts"; these, though his personal interests might determine the precise emphasis given to one element or another, he would never subsequently "warp or distort." The justice also placed great faith in the oral argument of counsel, preferring "a bad argument to none" at all; moreover, he constantly sought to apply "all the resources of learning to illumine the facts" before him, so that he not only comprehended everything directly pertinent to the case, but "the peripheral problems" as well. In stating the facts in an opinion, he was "careful to answer all the contentions of losing counsel even where he [considered] them fanciful"; for in so doing he was obliged to give due consideration to all their claims and offer a reasoned response to them. "He is indeed less deferential to the law than to the facts," Riesman continued,

> but it is his belief that the law should spring from the facts and he feels more secure in the ground work of actuality than in [the] superstructure of precedent. The only count on which an indictment of intellectual dishonesty could be sustained would state that in the work of the Court, he acted strategically and with concern of consequences. This is a matter on which I have no light.

David Riesman thus presents us with two distinct and at times conflicting interpretations of Brandeis in his role as Supreme Court justice, and similar differences of opinion can readily be found in the writings of historians and legal theorists. To some extent, of course, the discrepancies can be reconciled without too much difficulty; however, we perhaps ought not to be too hasty in our attempts to smooth over such differences of perspective. Beneath this deeply ambivalent attitude toward Brandeis, running as it does the complete spectrum between profound respect and intellectual disgust, there exists an important and disquieting truth. For in a career as long and complicated as Brandeis's, there must necessarily occur a great many situations, ideas, deeds, remarks that are difficult if not impossible to reconcile within a single, unitary framework of rational interpretation. A man can act both ethically and unethically in the same lifetime, or even in the same day; he can be reasonable and unreasonable, sensitive and insensitive, sophisticated and naïve in his response to different issues, or even to the same issues at different times. To search for consistency of thought and action on every occasion is surely to search for a comforting but transparent delusion. Brandeis, like most figures worthy of historical attention, displayed a multifaceted personality, the unity and harmony of whose mind was more apparent than real. As the divergent impressions made upon his colleague and law clerk demonstrate, deep-seated conflicts and contradictions lay but thinly concealed beneath his Olympian facade of intellectual and emotional severity.[14]

This being once said, however, some effort to comprehend the cardinal features of Brandeis's judicial method must be made; for the differing perspectives offered by Stone and Riesman raise a number of pertinent questions that need to be answered. In what circumstances, for instance, was Brandeis willing to see the previous rulings of his Court set aside; and did he indeed behave "strategically" in considering his votes? What was his thinking in respect of civil liberties; and to what extent was his judicial reasoning predetermined by a priori assumptions about the rights of states or the wisdom of judges? Most important of all, perhaps, what was the "pattern of constitutional interpretation" that he sought to develop during his years on the bench. On all of these issues his carefully worded opinions are capable of shedding an appreciable amount of light and when augmented from other sources can generally provide us with a reasonable picture of the way his mind was working.

From his earliest years as a member of the federal judiciary, Brandeis earned a reputation for operating within a coherent and firmly held set of ideas about the way in which cases coming before the courts ought to be decided. In theory, at least, the principles of action he considered important when constitutional limitations were invoked were the same regardless of whether the case in point involved the regulation of public utilities or the alleged infringement of personal freedoms. First, he was held to be a staunch believer in the desirability of reaching a decision on the narrowest ground possible, and of only passing upon constitutional questions when the application of common-law rules or the explication of statutory provisions failed to provide a satisfactory solution. Second, he began by insisting on a presumption of constitutionality, leaving the burden of proof to those who would have the actions of state or federal authorities declared invalid. Third, he asserted that not only the reasonableness of a statute but also its constitutionality must be determined by a full consideration of the facts pertaining in the particular case before the Court rather than by the application of abstract, a priori assumptions. With what consistency he applied these three principles himself is a matter to which we shall return later; but even the most cursory scanning of his opinions will reveal the frequency with which these general concepts were invoked. Taken together, they constituted the warp threads around which the subtle and variegated fabric of his jurisprudence could be woven.[15]

Of the characteristic elements of that fabric, as identified by Stone and Riesman, let us first consider once more his attitude toward the common-law precept of *stare decisis*. Although Brandeis's basic inclination was to yield a good deal to the claims of precedent, in a series of clearly worded dissents written between 1924 and 1932 he was at some pains to emphasize the extent to which the doctrine required qualification in constitutional cases. This being once said, in many respects there remains a remarkable continuity of language between these judicial utterances and the lectures on business law he had written some thirty-odd years before. In *Washington v. Dawson* (1924), for example, he picked up on his earlier distinction between rules of property and rules of action. Modification, he insisted, was the lifeblood of the law, and the doctrine of *stare decisis* should not deter the Supreme Court from overturning prior determinations when, on reconsideration, they were found to have been either erroneous or unfortunate. This was particularly true if the earlier decision had not created rules of property and vested interests that could be unsettled by a change of ruling. In *Jaybird Mining Company v. Weir* (1926), he pointed out to his colleagues that, when called upon to adjust the respective powers of the states and the nation, they had not allowed a rule to end with its enunciation, but had limited and qualified such rules when it became necessary to consider new and unforeseen facts that had arisen or come to light since the earlier decision was handed down. This, he believed, should be the pattern followed also when dealing with matters of public law. Brandeis continued to recognize that it was usually more important that a rule of law should be settled than that it should be settled right and even conceded that this logic applied equally to most constitutional principles; yet in *Di Santo v. Pennsylvania* (1927) he argued vigorously for flexibility of mind. The Supreme Court, he maintained, should not feel itself powerless to correct the errors of previous decisions in the field of constitutional law, especially where the point at issue involved the adjustment of conflicting claims made on behalf of federal and state governments.[16]

After 1929, the onset of the Great Depression only served to underscore his belief in the desirability of leaving legislators free within broad limits to experiment with new regulatory mechanisms in the socioeconomic sphere. He was more convinced than ever that judges ought not to recast the law (or the Constitution for that matter) in their own ideological image; however, he was also determined that legislators, especially at the state level, should have the right to act boldly, subject only to the explicit limitations of the Constitution and the tolerance of their constituents. Such was clearly the burden of his splendid peroration in *New State Ice Company v. Liebman* (1932); and in *Burnet v. Coronado Oil and Gas Company* (1932) he urged his fellow justices not to go searching for such limitations. Interpretations of the federal Constitution had to be undertaken with particular caution because, unlike erroneous rules of law, failings of constitutional exegesis were practically impossible to correct through legislative action. He believed the Supreme Court ought to recognize that the process of trial and error, so fruitful in the physical sciences, was appropriate also to the judicial function, and with this in mind should bow to the lessons of experience, as in several other recent decisions, by overruling its earlier holding. Indeed, the justification for doing so was even clearer when, as in the Burnet case, the constitutional question involved had been decided essentially on a determination of fact. In Brandeis's estimation, such a decision was not entitled to the same sanction, in later controversies between different parties, as would ordinarily obtain where the earlier decision had involved a pure proposition of law.[17]

Nowhere, though, did Brandeis express himself more clearly on this subject than in his dissent in *Stratton v. St. Louis Southwestern Railway Company*, written in 1930 but never delivered. Paradoxically, his purpose in this opinion was to defend an earlier ruling from which a majority of his brethren now wished to depart; however, to achieve his goal he needed to explain the proper scope of *stare decisis* as he conceived it. "I do not question the propriety of the Court's overruling, in cases of this character [i.e., tax cases], any decision which experience and reconsideration prove to have been mistaken," he asserted, and cited his own earlier dissents in *Washington v. Dawson and Company* and *Di Santo v. Pennsylvania* in support of this contention. He invoked the authority of Chief Justice Taney's declaration in the *Passenger Cases* (1849): "that it be regarded hereafter as the law of this court, that its opinion upon the construction of the Constitution is always open to discussion when it is supposed to have been founded in error, and that its judicial authority should hereafter depend altogether on the force of the reasoning by which it is supported." A principle derived from the common law could not be applied *unthinkingly* to the determination of constitutional questions; for the position of the Supreme Court in cases involving the application of the Constitution was "wholly unlike that of the highest court of England, where the doctrine of *stare decisis* was formulated." In *McCulloch v. Maryland* (1819), Chief Justice Marshall had reminded his fellow justices that it was indeed a constitution that they were required to construe, a framework of fundamental principles by which other laws could be measured. Brandeis proceeded to impress the same point upon his own colleagues:

> We must never forget that the Federal Constitution, unlike an Act of Congress or the Constitution of a State, cannot be easily amended. We must never forget that what is called interpreting the Constitution is a function differing materially from that of passing upon the questions ordinarily arising at common law or in equity and that the function is rarely comparable to mere interpretation of a statute.

Sometimes, to be sure, constitutional questions could be decided by the correct reading of some specific provision; but in his view, the cases that had most engaged the Court's attention since the passage of the Fourteenth Amendment and the tremendous expansion of interstate commerce presented "no dispute as to the meaning of words or clauses." They dealt rather with "the application of admitted constitutional limitations to the varying and illusive [*sic*] facts of life." Again he became philosophical:

> Life implies growth. Only change is abiding. In order to reach sound conclusions in such cases, we must strive ceaselessly to bring our opinions into agreement with facts ascertained. We must never forget that the judgment of men is fallible, being influenced inevitably by their views as to economic, social and political policy. Our effort to reach sound conclusions will be futile if we substitute formulas for reasoning. Formulas block the paths to truth and wisdom. *Stare decisis* is always a desideratum, even in these constitutional cases. But in them, it is never a command. For we may not close the mind to the lessons of experience and abdicate the sway of reason.

In the case then before the Court, however, he believed that experience merely served to reinforce the processes of reason underpinning a well-established constitutional doctrine: namely, that states were permitted to tax corporations for the privilege of doing intrastate business. He could therefore see "nothing in reason or experience to warrant . . . overruling a well-founded practice of three-quarters of a century."[18]

The *Stratton* case was eventually dismissed for want of jurisdiction, but evidence survives to show that in a few cases dissents already prepared by Brandeis were subsequently discarded, and that in several others dissentient views were voluntarily suppressed without him ever writing at all. The reasons for such behavior are too many and varied to justify any simplistic, monocausal interpretation, least of all the suggestion that Brandeis regularly bargained away his opposition to certain decisions in return for support in others about which he felt more strongly. In *Sonneborn Brothers v. Cureton*

(1923), for instance, the dissent he had originally written in response to an inadequate majority opinion from Justice McReynolds was dropped when Chief Justice Taft assumed responsibility for the case and wrote a fresh opinion substantially in line with Brandeis's views. On other occasions, such as in *American Railway Express Company v. Kentucky* (1927), he appears to have drafted "memoranda" (as his early drafts were generally styled) with the specific intention of influencing his fellow justices before the case was considered in conference, or of reversing a tentative decision already reached. And in *St. Louis, Iron Mountain & Southern Railway v. Starbird* (1917) his willingness to go along with a unanimous Court's finding for the plaintiff, after previously writing in favor of dismissal for lack of jurisdiction, was largely the consequence of a natural concern that the first dissent of his judicial career should be on a matter of greater substantive importance. In this instance, however, he may also have been anxious to avoid drawing undue attention to the Court's recklessness in disregarding major jurisdictional problems merely to reach a decision on the merits of the case at bar. Since the nature of the transgression lay buried in the record, it probably seemed advisable to leave it there; for, as Felix Frankfurter later observed in a somewhat different context, "The scope of a Supreme Court decision is not infrequently revealed by the candor of dissent."[19]

It was in a series of conversations he had with Frankfurter during the 1920s that Brandeis expressed his views on dissenting most clearly. There were all sorts of good reasons for withholding a dissent, he explained, and silence in any particular case did not necessarily imply concurrence in the decision and reasoning of the majority. One highly pertinent consideration was the number of times any single justice could afford to register his disagreement; "there is a limit," he observed, "to the frequency with which you can do it without exasperating men." Another determining factor could be the amount of time available. Holmes, for one, liked to "shoot them down so quickly" and got irritated when anyone held him up. He recalled how in *United Zinc & Chemical Co. v. Britt* (1922) the elderly justice had seen "a chance to decide one of his pet theories." Brandeis voted against granting *certiorari* and then against the majority opinion, but was unable to go along with Clarke's dissent. He thus found himself in a difficult position. "I was rushed with other work & so would have had to hold up Holmes if I was going to write a dissent & to hold him up from firing off is like sending an executioner after him. I had dissented recently in a number of cases, [and] Holmes cared a good deal about this opinion, he had gone with me in my dissents so I let it go, without dissenting." Another key factor was the relative importance of a case, and whether it involved constitutional issues or merely construction of a statute. Thus, from time to time, Brandeis was prepared to endorse or "acquiesce" in an opinion with which he did not agree. In *Railway Commission of California v. Southern Pacific Railway* (1924), for example, a case involving the right of states to regulate railroad facilities following passage of the federal Transportation Act in 1920, he was again faced with a dismal opinion from the pen of Mr. Justice McReynolds. Though he had no love himself for the proposed union station in Los Angeles whose enforced construction was at issue in the case, Brandeis found in McReynolds's opinion "too many glaring errors" that might return to haunt the Court in future years. He therefore wrote what he considered "a really stinging dissent," and only agreed to suppress it when Taft, not wanting the Court "shown up that way," took over the writing of the opinion. The decision still did not come out the way Brandeis would have liked; but as he told Frankfurter, it was "after all . . . merely a question of statutory construction & the worst things were removed by the Chief."

A strategic element was not wholly absent, then, from Brandeis's choice of when and how to dissociate himself from the decisions of the majority, but he was far from being a trend-setter in this respect. "The whole policy is to suppress dissents," Brandeis commented in the summer of 1924. Holmes was "always in doubt whether to express his dissent, once he's 'had his say' on a given subject & he's had his say on almost everything." Willis Van Devanter was especially active, working tirelessly during the 1920s to persuade his brethren to suppress dissents for the good of the Court; time and again an initial 5 to 4 split in conference appeared as 7 to 2, or even as unanimity, when the opinion was eventually handed down. This "private working with individuals," what Holmes called "lobbying," was the antithesis of everything that Brandeis valued in the judicial function. It meant that results were achieved "not by legal reasoning, but by finesse & subtlety." As he told Frankfurter:

> in the middle ages, Van Devanter would have been the best of Cardinals. He is indefatigable, on good terms with everybody, ready to help everybody, knows exactly what he wants & clouds over difficulties by fine phrases & deft language. He never fools himself, and his credit side is on the whole larger than his debit. But he is on the job all the time. One can achieve his results by working for them, but I made up my mind I wouldn't resort to finesse & subtlety and "lobbying."

Before Taft became chief justice in 1921, Brandeis recalled, his colleagues had shown themselves ill disposed

> to follow my views. . . . I could have had my views prevail in cases of public importance if I had been willing to play politics. But I made up my mind I wouldn't—I would have had to sin against my light, and I would have hated myself. And I decided that the price was too large for the doubtful gain to the country's welfare. . . . I could have had much influence with [Chief Justice] White—I did in the beginning, but I made up my mind I couldn't pay the price it would have cost in want of directness & frankness.

His own view was that the Court generally paid insufficient heed to dissenting opinions, and he was particularly sensitive to what he saw as their special function where constitutional issues were involved. There might indeed be a good deal to be said for not having dissents in "ordinary cases," where "certainty & definiteness" were the chief requirement, and where it did not "matter terribly" how things were decided so long as they were settled. Constitutional cases, though, were a different proposition, for every decision involved the element of statesmanship. Here, he mused "nothing is ever settled—unless statesmanship is settled & at an end."[20]

The scope and scale of the present study do not afford room for a comprehensive analysis of all the opinions that Brandeis wrote during more than twenty-two years as an associate justice of the United States Supreme Court; nor even for a rounded assessment of the many thematic concerns that both informed, and flowed from, his judicial reasoning. Instead, the principal features of his behavior and, more important, of his intellectual orientation as a judge will be exemplified by paying particular attention to just two broad issues—civil liberties and economic regulation—on which he was required to focus repeatedly during his lengthy tenure of office.[21]

The challenge to civil liberties during and after the Great War raised a whole string of constitutional questions about which Brandeis felt passionately, and in this sphere at least the pressure to suppress dissenting opinions was forcibly resisted. Yet although he is best remembered for a series of landmark opinions broadening the concept of individual privacy and upholding freedom to speak and assemble, one should not forget either his enthusiastic and comprehensive enforcement of the Prohibition laws. The logic of his thinking in each of these areas will be considered shortly; but first of all it is important to appreciate the way in which he approached such issues, because it seems unlikely that Brandeis ever regarded the freedoms of the citizen as a distinct category of law requiring the application of separate principles. Such freedoms were either guaranteed by the Constitution or recognized at common law, and his main concern was to ensure that both courts and legislatures showed consistency in according to the rights of persons the same degree of protection they already accorded to the rights of property. As a consequence of this orientation, his manner of dealing with civil liberties issues was in no way unique, but stemmed directly from the general ideas about constitutional interpretation identified earlier.

Brandeis perceived the federal Constitution as a framework of law designed to harmonize relationships between conflicting interests within the nation, to order the dealings of its citizens with one another and to guarantee norms of conduct on the part of those placed in positions of authority. Separation of the powers of government was not meant to make each of its branches autonomous but to create between them a vital measure of interdependence. It was no part of the framers' purpose to foster thereby the efficiency of government, but rather, by means of an inevitable friction, to preclude the exercise of arbitrary power and preserve the people from autocracy. The liberties of the citizen had been further strengthened by the provisions of the Bill of Rights, which, though frequently imprecise in terms of language, had clearly been intended to bestow upon him specific privileges and immunities thought essential for the well-being of a free people. Within this frame of order the federal judiciary had a crucial function to perform, by defining more precisely the personal liberties that individuals could expect to enjoy, and securing them against every attempted encroachment, erosion, or abrogation. Laws that threatened the rights of the individual were as offensive to the Constitution as those that menaced property, and in Brandeis's view the Court possessed both the responsibility and the power needed to strike them down. Personal freedoms were too important to be frittered away by the invocation of specious technicalities.[22]

At the foundation of all civil liberties lay the vital principle that all government officials should be subject to the same rules of conduct as other citizens and were to be denied any exceptional position before the law. The claims of "executive privilege" so familiar to modern ears would thus have received short shrift at the hands of Mr. Justice Brandeis.[23]

What was to be done, though, when public officials did violate the law ostensibly to protect the interests of the community? Dissenting at length in the case of *Olmstead v. United States* (1928), Brandeis set out the issues he believed to be at stake. The case put forward by the defendants turned primarily on the claim that their rights under the Fourth and Fifth Amendments had been violated by government agents, who had procured the evidence needed to convict them of conspiracy to smuggle illicit booze from Canada by using an illegal wiretap. Speaking for the majority of the Court, Chief Justice Taft chose to ignore the flagrant breach of a Washington State law prohibiting such taps, and dismissed Olmstead's assertion that the actions of federal officers amounted either to unreasonable search or to involuntary self-incrimination as proscribed by the Bill of Rights.

Building on some of the themes that he and Sam Warren had first developed in "The Right to Privacy," Brandeis disagreed with his chief on both counts. "The makers of our Constitution," he wrote,

> undertook to secure conditions favorable to the pursuit of happiness. They recognized the significance of man's spiritual nature, of his feelings and of his intellect. They knew that only a part of the pain, pleasure and satisfactions of life are to be found in material things. They sought to protect Americans in their beliefs, their thoughts, their emotions and their sensations. They conferred, as against the government, the right to be let alone—the most comprehensive of rights and the right most valued by civilized men.

It was the Court's responsibility to keep abreast of technological innovations, and to construe the protections afforded by the Constitution in the light of the latest scientific knowledge available. Government already possessed far subtler means of invading the privacy of its citizens than those envisaged by the Founding Fathers, and it was naïve to assume that even more insidious methods would not become available in the future.[24]

Moreover, it was no justification for official law-breaking that the object in view was wholly worthy. "Men born to freedom are naturally alert to repel invasion of their liberty by evil-minded rulers," he warned, but they might have a good deal more to fear from "men of zeal, well-meaning, but without understanding." To condone the actions that had brought Olmstead and his coconspirators to trial was not merely a degradation of the Constitution but a fortiori an incitement to further wrongdoing:

> Our government is the potent, the omnipresent teacher. For good or for ill, it teaches the whole people by its example. Crime is contagious. If the government becomes a law-breaker, it breeds contempt for law; it invites every man to become a law unto himself; it invites anarchy. To declare that in the administration of the criminal law the end justifies the means—to declare that the government may commit crimes in order to secure the conviction of a private criminal—would bring terrible retribution. Against that pernicious doctrine this court should resolutely set its face.[25]

Despite the force of the constitutional argument in the final version of this dissent, Brandeis's original inclination, even once the views of his brethren became known, had been to dispose of the case on the nonconstitutional ground that the federal courts should not permit the continuance of a prosecution where the evidence needed to secure a conviction had been obtained in violation of state laws and by the improper conduct of federal officials. These illegal actions were themselves the product of a conspiracy; and although the government as such had not authorized the unlawful behavior in advance, and was therefore presently guilty of no crime, it was Brandeis's firm opinion that the subsequent prosecution threatened to implicate not only the government but the Court itself. In one of the earliest printed drafts of his dissent he observed:

> if the Government, knowing of its officers' crimes, undertakes to avail itself of the fruits thereof to accomplish its own end of punishing these defendants, it assumes, in morals, the responsibility for the officers' acts; and if this Court should say that the Government may achieve its end by these criminal means, it would, in my opinion, amount in law also to a ratification.

Was the Court willing, he asked rhetorically, "to sanction such conduct on the part of the Executive?" The preferable course would surely be to adopt the principle long and widely applied to civil cases in both equity and law: "that courts of justice will not redress a wrong done when he who seeks the redress comes into court with unclean hands."

Thus, though eventually persuaded by his law clerk, Henry Friendly, that the constitutional question also needed to be addressed, Brandeis's initial focus on the narrower issue affords a good illustration of how his general axioms of judicial decision making were applied in practice. It is somewhat ironic, therefore, that when the Warren Court voted to overturn the *Olmstead* ruling in *Katz v. the United States* (1967), and cited this dissent extensively in support of their decision, it was his appeals for a broad construction of the Fourth Amendment, rather than his use of the "unclean hands" doctrine, which most attracted them. But perhaps Brandeis too was at length persuaded that the constitutional issue was the more important. Writing to Frankfurter a few days after the 5 to 4 decision upholding Olmstead's conviction was handed down, he commented ruefully: "I suppose some reviewer of the wire tapping decision will discern that in favor of property the Constitution is liberally construed—in favor of liberty, strictly."[26]

Derogation of personal freedom resulting from the overzealous behavior of government officials was only one aspect of a wider problem that concerned Brandeis from his earliest days on the Court. The war in Western Europe and the Bolshevik Revolution in Russia combined after 1917 to sour the optimistic, reforming atmosphere that had prevailed in the United States since the turn of the century, and in the following decade the tides of repressive intolerance ran strongly throughout the country. The Espionage Act, passed by Congress after America's entry into the war, and the complementary laws enacted thereafter by several state legislatures together provided a mechanism for the suppression of dissent. Pacifists, socialists, labor "agitators"—indeed all those radically opposed to the values or institutions of the conservative mainstream—found their views stigmatized as disloyal and un-American, and themselves marked down as potential subversives against whom society needed protection. Not since the Civil War had freedom of speech and assembly been in greater need of judicial defense. Speaking for a unanimous Court in *Schenck v. United States* (1919), Mr. Justice Holmes was willing to uphold the Espionage Act as a permissible expedient in wartime, but was also at some pains to establish the criteria used to determine when the suppression of free speech was legitimate. "The question in every case," he declared, "is whether the words used are used in such circumstances and are of such a nature as to create a *clear and present danger* that they will bring about the substantive evils that Congress has a right to prevent."[27]

In *Schenck*, the defendant had been charged with inciting military personnel to insubordination and obstructing recruitment, both in time of war. Here, where Holmes's "clear and present danger" test pointed clearly to the validity of a conviction, his brethren found little difficulty in supporting it, but in a series of more doubtful cases coming before the Court subsequently for review their willingness to accept its inner logic was found sorely wanting. In 1920, for example, they sustained the conviction of Peter Schaefer for reprinting articles from German newspapers, holding that the minor factual errors reproduced in his pamphlets constituted "false reports" under the terms of the Espionage Act. There was something unseemly, they believed, about the spectacle of men who had sought to subvert and destroy the institutions of constitutional government clamoring for the right to share in its protections. Applying the Holmes formula to the facts of the case, however, Brandeis found no justifiable basis for the majority's decision. "In my opinion," he averred in dissent, "no jury acting in calmness could reasonably say that any of the publications set forth in the indictment were of such a character or were made under such circumstances as to create a clear and present danger, either that they would obstruct recruiting, or that they would promote the success of enemies of the United States." Freedom of expression, like the liberty of contract to which his fellow judges were so partial, should be taken as the social and legal norm, and limitations should only be placed on it where the evil anticipated was both great and imminent; the holding and dissemination of unpopular opinions was not of itself a valid ground for repression. "Men may differ widely as to what loyalty to our country demands," he continued; "and an intolerant majority, swayed by passion or by fear, may be prone in future, as it has often been in the past, to stamp as disloyal opinions with which it disagrees."

A week later, in *Pierce v. United States*, he dissented again with Holmes in support, this time against the suppression of a Socialist party leaflet that claimed America had only entered the war to protect the economic interests of the capitalist class. This was hardly an original observation, as Brandeis pointed out; similar arguments had been voiced on the floor of the Congress when the war resolution was debated. In any case, the clear purpose of the present publication was to further the cause of socialism, not to obstruct the prosecution of the war, and as such it was entitled to the protection of the First Amendment.

> The fundamental right of free men to strive for better conditions through new legislation and new institutions will not be preserved, if efforts to secure it by argument to fellow citizens may be construed as criminal incitement to disobey the existing law—merely because the argument presented seems to those exercising judicial power to be unfair in its portrayal of existing evils, mistaken in its assumptions, unsound in its reasoning, or intemperate in its language.[28]

Although both of these cases concerned the limits to free speech considered applicable during a war, the wording of Brandeis's dissenting opinions indicates plainly that he was somewhat more concerned about how these precedents would be viewed in peacetime. They were written, or so he was later to claim, "to put on permanent record what we were not allowed to say." He soon came to regret his concurrence in the *Debs* and *Schenck* cases, wishing he had chosen to rest the convictions "on the war power" instead of on Holmes's formula, so that "the scope of espionage legislation would be confined to war," while in peace "the protection against restrictions of freedom of speech would be unabated." As he later explained to Frankfurter: "I had not then thought the issues of freedom of speech out—I thought at the subject, not through it. Not until I came to write the *Pierce* [&] *Schaefer* cases did I understand it. . . . You might as well recognize that during a war . . . all bets are off. But we would have a clear line to go on. I didn't know enough in the early cases to put it on that ground."[29]

Whatever abuses of civil liberty may have occurred in implementing the federal espionage law Brandeis was shortly to discover that several states had enacted statutes possessing an even greater potential for mischief. In April 1917, for instance, the state of Minnesota had passed a law that made it a crime to discourage enlistment into the armed forces, and in effect prohibited the teaching and advocacy of pacifist doctrines for all time to come, regardless of whether the country was at war or not. Thus when Joseph Gilbert of the Nonpartisan League subsequently addressed a public meeting on the subject, he was indicted and found guilty under its provisions. When the case came before the Supreme Court in 1920, Justice McKenna on behalf of the majority ruled that the act was a reasonable exercise of the police power, and pointed once again to the absurdity of claiming constitutional protection for the activities of anarchists and enemies of the United States. Although this too was a wartime conviction, it clearly stood in a different category from the *Pierce* and *Schaefer* cases, not only because the use of a state law raised the possibility of due process issues under the Fourteenth Amendment, but more especially because it was intended as a permanent and not merely as an emergency restriction. This time Brandeis dissented alone. The Minnesota statute, he declared, was not only a usurpation of functions reserved exclusively to the government of the United States, but was clearly "inconsistent with the conceptions of liberty hitherto prevailing"; it invaded "the privacy and freedom of the home," and denied the right of parents to pass on to their children whatever system of values and ideas they chose. The free communication and discussion of one's beliefs was not just a right, he asserted, but a duty, essential for the development of an informed and self-reliant citizenry. Harmony in national life resulted from the creative friction between different ideological forces, with the best guarantee of governmental wisdom lying in the frank expression of conflicting opinions. Their suppression, by contrast, was ordinarily attended with the greatest peril for the whole community.[30]

A substantial part of Brandeis's opinion was devoted to considering the claim of Gilbert's counsel that the subject matter covered by the Minnesota law was a purely federal concern. Not only was waging war the exclusive business of the national government, but by enacting the Espionage Act Congress had already defined the limitations on individual liberty it considered necessary for the country's defense, and had thereby foreclosed the possibility of state actions in the same area. Despite the fact that Chief Justice Taft also supported this contention, the arguments deployed in its favor were less than totally convincing. Control of its militia, for example, was one area in which a state government was plainly competent to act. More ingenious, and potentially more fruitful for Brandeis's purpose, was the ground on which the defendant had rested his claim to liberty of expression: viz. that as a citizen he possessed an "inherent right of free speech respecting the concerns, activities and interests of the United States of America and its government." McKenna had, in fact, conceded that the freedom asserted was both "natural and inherent," but cited *Schenck* to support the correlative contention that it was not "absolute." Although tacitly accepting that Congress might indeed be empowered to restrict the exercise of that freedom in certain circumstances, Brandeis made every effort to show that a state legislature was not.

The right to speak freely about functions of the federal government was, he maintained, "a privilege or immunity of every citizen of the United States, which, even before the adoption of the 14th Amendment, a state was powerless to curtail." It was well established that a citizen possessed the right to go wherever he wished "in pursuit of public or private business"; that he was entitled to play a full part in the conduct of the government and in the making of federal laws; and that this necessarily included "the right to speak or write about them" and "to endeavor to make his own opinion concerning laws existing or contemplated prevail." He could, in short, expound the truth as he saw it on any subject. "Were this not so," Brandeis insisted, "'the right of the people to assemble for the purpose of petitioning Congress for a redress of grievance or for anything else connected with the powers or duties of the national government' would be a right totally without substance." If the matters dealt with by the Minnesota law had been of state concern only, then the First Amendment would not have been applicable; but such was not the case. "The state law affects directly the functions of the federal government," he continued. "It affects rights, privileges, and immunities of one who is a citizen of the United States; and it deprives him of an important part of his liberty. These are rights which are guaranteed protection by the Federal Constitution; and they are invaded by the statute in question."

Despite the earlier, specious reference to rights implied by the First Amendment, precisely which constitutional guarantees he was alluding to in this last sentence Brandeis left deliberately vague. The Minnesota law was invalid, he concluded, "because it interferes with federal functions and with the right of a citizen of the United States to discuss them"; however, by what Article of or Amendment to the Constitution could such a right be sustained? The First Amendment was explicitly worded to prevent Congress alone from "abridging the freedom of speech," and the Court had subsequently ruled in *Barron v. Baltimore* (1833) that neither this nor any other protection afforded by the Bill of Rights could be invoked against the actions of the several states. Two possibilities did, however, suggest themselves under the terms of the Fourteenth Amendment. The first of these grew out of the notion that free speech might be a "liberty" protected by the due process clause; but this could not be made the driving engine of the opinion, if only because defense counsel had made so little of it in the initial trial. Nevertheless, Brandeis was unable to resist a sideswipe at his more conservative colleagues. Surely, he insisted with a scarcely veiled tone of sarcasm, if the due process clause could be used to invalidate state laws that threatened the freedom of contract or the freedom to hold property, it could be invoked just as legitimately to strike down those which menaced the freedom of expression. "I cannot believe," he concluded, "that the liberty guaranteed by the 14th Amendment includes only liberty to acquire and to enjoy property."

The second possible approach involved the privileges and immunities clause. Here, what he needed was some basis for arguing that the "privileges or immunities" explicitly protected against state interference by the Fourteenth Amendment were synonymous with the civil liberties enumerated and defended against federal violation by the Bill of Rights. But in the *Slaughter House Cases* (1873) and again in *Twining v. New Jersey* (1908), the Court had definitively rejected this proposition, and nothing in Brandeis's reasoning suggested that he was optimistic about securing a reversal. It is, therefore, difficult to see on what legal basis his sonorous prose could be supported.

By the time the case of *Gitlow v. New York* came before the Supreme Court on a writ of error in 1925, the clouding factor of the wartime emergency had largely evaporated, and even the more conservative judges seemed willing to recognize the need to bring their handling of civil liberties questions into line with the treatment of property. "For the present purposes," declared Justice Sanford, explaining the Court's decision to uphold New York's Criminal Anarchy Act, "we may and do assume that freedom of speech and of the press—which are protected by the First Amendment from abridgment by Congress—are among the fundamental personal rights and 'liberties' protected by the due process clause of the Fourteenth Amendment from impairment by the states." They were rights, however, subject to restriction under the police power, and state laws designed to establish appropriate limits should be accorded the presumption of constitutionality, unless their provisions could be shown to be either arbitrary or unreasonable. Brandeis did not write in the case himself, but supported instead the dissenting opinion of Justice Holmes who argued that the "clear and present danger" test, accepted by the Court in *Schenck* as applicable to federal statutes, should be adopted also for the evaluation of state legislation.[31]

Nevertheless, during the following session of the Court, it soon became evident that Brandeis was determined to express his own considered opinion on these matters, and to try in the process to make his colleagues realize that acceptance of Holmes's reasoning was the minimum requirement for achieving justice in such cases. An ideal opportunity for so applying the "clear and present danger" formula was presented by the circumstances pertaining in *Ruthenberg v. Michigan*. The plaintiff in error, Charles E. Ruthenberg had been convicted of "voluntarily assembling" with the Communist party of America at a secret convention, held in the isolated settlement of Bridgman, close to the shores of Lake Michigan, in 1922. Because the Communist party was held to be an organization "formed to teach or advocate the doctrines of criminal syndicalism," according to the laws of that state the mere act of attending such a gathering constituted a felony, despite the remoteness of the spot, and the fact that every one of those present was already well versed in the principles and policies of revolutionary socialism. As Brandeis's then law clerk, James Landis, observed, the case for a reversal was even stronger than in *Gitlow*; for provided the scope of the right of peaceful assembly and that of free speech were admitted to be the same, the absence of a "clear and present danger" here was even more apparent.[32]

This was the point that Brandeis endeavored to emphasize from the very first paragraph of his dissent. "The accused is to be punished," he wrote, "not for violence or threat of violence, not for attempt, incitement or conspiracy, but for a step in preparation which, if it threatens the public order at all, does so only remotely." Could a statute that assigned guilt with so little regard to the particular facts of the situation, and that sought to punish acts so far removed from any apprehended evil to the community, be regarded as compatible with existing definitions of due process? What tests should be applied in order to find out? Brandeis proceeded to set out his own answers to these important questions.

> The right to liberty obviously does not prevent a State from taking action reasonably required to protect itself from destruction, or from serious political, economic or moral injury. To this end, it may, in the exercise of its police power, ordinarily adopt any measure which the governing majority deems necessary and appropriate. But, despite arguments to the contrary which had seemed to me persuasive, it has been settled that the State's power, so far as its exercise involves fundamental rights of the citizen, is restricted by the due process clause in matters of substantive law as well as procedural law. Whether a particular measure is reasonable and appropriate, may therefore present a justiciable federal question.

The right of peaceful assembly was self-evidently one of those "fundamental rights," akin by its nature to right of free speech, a free press, and the freedom to teach, with which it was "closely associated." The limitations that could reasonably be placed on it were likewise capable of objective definition. "The protection extended by the Constitution to the right of assembly," he believed, "must . . . be as broad as that enjoyed by these other fundamental rights. Like them, it may be restricted only if, and to the extent that, its exercise involves clear and present danger."

While fully accepting that the validity of the Michigan statute would have to be decided eventually by an examination of the specific facts of the case, Brandeis chose first to grapple with the hitherto neglected task of determining more generally what the phrase "clear and present danger" might actually mean. In order to reach a sound conclusion here, the prime need was to understand why a state was "ordinarily denied the power to prohibit dissemination of social, economic and political doctrines which a vast majority of its citizens believes to be false and fraught with evil consequences"; why, in other words, "free speech and assembly were made constitutional rights." He began by elaborating a theme he had adumbrated in *Gilbert v. Minnesota*:

> In a democracy public discussion is a political duty. This principle lies at the foundation of the American system of government. Freedom to think as you will and to speak as you think are means indispensable to the discovery and spread of political truth. Without free speech and assembly discussion would be futile. With them, discussion affords ordinarily adequate protection against the dissemination of noxious doctrine. Those who won our independence by revolution valued liberty both as an end and as a means. They believed liberty to be the secret of happiness and courage to be the secret of liberty. They did not fear political change. They did not exalt order at the cost of liberty. They recognized that the greatest menace to freedom is an inert people; that the greatest menace to stable government is repression; and that the fitting remedy for evil counsels is good ones. Believing in the power of reason as applied through public discussion, they eschewed silence as coerced by law—the argument of force in its worst form. Recognizing the occasional tyrannies of government majorities, they amended the Constitution so as to guarantee free speech and assembly.

Drawing support from this classic statement of the philosophical foundations of civil liberty, he proceeded to outline a practical rule of thumb for the identification of preventable abuses. "To self-reliant men, with confidence in the power of reason applied through the processes of popular government," he asserted, "no danger flowing from speech can be deemed clear and present, unless the incidence of the evil apprehended is so imminent that it may befall before there is opportunity for full discussion." Repression could only be justified in cases of acute emergency; even then the danger anticipated had to be of a serious nature to justify tampering with "functions essential to effective democracy." The probability of "a relatively trivial harm" being done to society would consequently be insufficient ground on which to prohibit freedom of speech or assembly. After a lengthy rehearsal of the case at bar, during which the nature and immediacy of the threat posed by communism to American democracy were fully explored, Brandeis was able to conclude that according to these criteria the Michigan statute represented an unreasonable assertion of the police power, and that Ruthenberg's conviction should be quashed.[33]

Between August and November 1926, this proposed dissent went through a series of drafts; but then Ruthenberg died, and in March 1927 the case was dismissed as moot. Still anxious for an opportunity to express himself on the issues raised, Brandeis quickly shifted the focus of his attention to another case that had been proceeding toward a decision in parallel to Ruthenberg's. In 1919, Anita Whitney had fallen foul of California's Criminal Syndicalism Act by virtue of her membership in the Communist Labor party of California, by assisting in its organization and by attending its meetings. The cases were similar in many respects. Here, as in *Ruthenberg*, the right denied was the right of free assembly; the statutes involved were comparable in scope and purpose, and the views held by the two plaintiffs were for all practical purposes identical. Nevertheless, there were several important differences of fact that made *Whitney v. California* (1927) a much less satisfactory vehicle for Brandeis's statement of principles than *Ruthenberg v. Michigan* had been. First, Whitney was closely involved with the executive structure of her party and had been an active participant in the framing of its constitution; second, the intention to propagate the ideas of revolutionary socialism with immediate effect, and to advocate its doctrines to people previously unfamiliar with them, was evident from the record; and, third, though it had been claimed during earlier proceedings in the state courts that the California statute violated her rights under the Fourteenth Amendment, neither there nor in argument before the Supreme Court was any attempt made to extract a ruling on the "clear and present danger" formula. Moreover, even if this test had been applied, it was far from obvious that no such danger had existed. Brandeis thus found himself with no valid grounds on which to dissent. Instead, lifting passages wholesale from the *Ruthenberg* dissent, he wrote a concurrent opinion, agreeing to uphold Whitney's conviction but setting out an argument which, if it had been raised by her counsel, might just possibly have secured her acquittal. Despite the majesty of its prose, the clear and logical flow of his original opinion was lost, and the whole tendency of the exposition sat awkwardly alongside the result. In short, Brandeis would have been better advised to bide his time and wait for a more tractable case to come before the Court; for if his opinion in *Whitney* represented a "marker" that both counsel and his colleagues could follow in future cases, it also provided further evidence of the "advocacy" that even his friends found inappropriate for a judicial forum.[34]

What clearly lay behind Brandeis's thinking in this whole sequence of cases was an inarticulate belief that the protections afforded by the Bill of Rights *ought to apply* to the states as well as to the federal government. What he lacked was any coherent theory of law by which such a desirable goal could be turned into reality. The fundamental weakness of his position in *Gilbert*, and to some extent in *Whitney*, stemmed from the simple fact that for more than a decade he had consistently argued *against* the Supreme Court's right to adjudge the reasonableness of state laws. The Court's majority, on the other hand, was perfectly willing to engraft onto the Constitution those "natural rights" cherished by employers and property owners, and had frequently done so by making recognition of them a requirement of due process; but they had proved to be a good deal more chary about according the same privilege to "natural rights" of personal liberty.

Brandeis thus found himself in a logical bind. At root he was personally convinced that the Fourteenth Amendment's due process clause should apply only to matters of procedure, and that matters of substantive law should not be touched by it. For decades the concept of "substantive due process" had been used to strike down state laws otherwise constituting a valid exercise of the police power. Yet although a purely procedural interpretation of due process would doubtless enable the states to experiment freely in the field of social legislation, it would also render repressive statutes like those objected to in the *Gilbert*, *Ruthenberg*, and *Whitney* cases even more unassailable. More recently, the equal protection clause had also shown itself liable to distortion. "[It] looms up even more menacingly than due process," Brandeis observed in 1924, referring to the way in which a New York statute prohibiting night work for women had almost fallen because it discriminated between different categories of labor; he regarded the use made of it by Taft in *Truax v. Corrigan* (1921) as nothing short of "dreadful."

Only by scrapping the concept of "substantive due process," severely limiting the scope of "equal protection" and applying the Bill of Rights directly to the states could the appropriate distinctions be drawn; and each of these courses of action seemed forever precluded by the class alignments of the judiciary and by settled principles of constitutional interpretation. The alternative of repealing the Fourteenth Amendment outright enjoyed a certain vogue in liberal circles during the 1920s, but failed to tackle the issues of how procedural due process and equal protection for racial and religious minorities might be guaranteed without it. In the circumstances, therefore, Brandeis's only remaining option was to conduct a psychological war of attrition; and even then, despite his best efforts to shame the brethren into according civil liberties at least the same degree of protection as was regularly allowed to liberty of contract, any lessening of the prevailing inequities of application was restricted narrowly to the margin.[35]

The enduring paradox attaching to his position on privacy and free speech questions was that, in general, he favored enlarging, not restricting, the sphere within which state governments were permitted to act. What his colleagues failed to understand, he told Frankfurter, "is that recognition of Federal powers does not mean denial of State powers." What he objected to was not so much the increase of the former as the curtailment of the latter. This can be seen clearly in his attitude to the Prohibition cases coming before the Court during the 1920s, where he consistently upheld the right of federal and state authorities to punish violations of their respective liquor laws.

In *Ruppert v. Caffey* (1920), for example, he ruled that the federal Congress was entitled to prohibit the sale of intoxicating drinks under its war power without affording dealers an opportunity to dispose of their existing stocks; and in *Albrecht v. United States* (1927) held that Congress was entitled to punish separately, without infringing the double jeopardy clause of the Fifth Amendment, both possession and sale of the same illegal bottle. He had found much earlier in *Barbour v. Georgia* (1919) that a state which passed its own prohibitory legislation could forbid the acquisition of fresh liquor stocks between the statute's enactment and its coming into effect. In a 1926 opinion upholding the section of the Volstead Act that restricted a physician's right to prescribe alcohol therapeutically, he could discern no right to practice medicine that was not subordinate to either the police power of the states, or the power of Congress to pass any law thought necessary for the enforcement of the Eighteenth Amendment. In short, whereas privacy, free speech, and free assembly were "fundamental rights"—rights that could not be overridden by the police powers of the states, or by an illegitimate extension of the Congress's war power—the manufacture, sale, and consumption of alcohol were not. Consequently, within reasonable boundaries, legislative majorities were free to restrict such activities as they saw fit.[36]

These decisions can scarcely be considered arbitrary; nor can they readily be circumvented as though they constituted some kind of ideological aberration. True, there is plenty of evidence to show that Brandeis's attitude to the consumption of alcohol had hardened appreciably since the days in 1891 when he had defended the interests of the Massachusetts distillers against a hostile legislature; indeed, it is clear that he was personally in favor of Prohibition by the 1920s. Yet even if he had been fiercely opposed to it, the entire matrix of his constitutional philosophy would have militated against his declaring the Prohibition laws invalid. The Eighteenth Amendment, as enacted and duly ratified, explicitly granted concurrent power to Congress and the several states to enforce compliance by means of legislation. Consequently, when the laws thus sanctioned were challenged in court, Brandeis's predilection for deciding cases whenever possible on the narrow ground of statutory construction and his overarching presumption of constitutionality left little room for argument. There was no disagreement as to fact, and to have recognized substantive due process constraints as having the power to forestall implementation of the Eighteenth Amendment would not merely have flown in the face of his whole judicial style and purpose; by subordinating the objective substance of one Amendment to the due process clause of another, it would have erected a dangerous new constitutional principle whose possible ramifications none could foresee.

In addition to distorting constitutional means, it would also have had the effect of frustrating desirable social ends. Any line of reasoning sufficiently cogent to strike down either the Volstead Act or its state counterparts would have killed stone-dead the still much-debated prospect of obtaining a Child Labor Amendment. Simultaneously, and more importantly, it would have destroyed any remaining chance that other types of social-welfare legislation might be sustained when they came before the Court in future. Therefore, when Alpheus T. Mason suggested that on "moral" issues "Brandeis took a stand strangely out of key with his customary liberalism," he misunderstood not only the legal basis for the stand, but the structural foundations of the liberalism as well.[37]

When it came to the crunch, however, Brandeis needed little encouragement to sustain such morally uplifting legislation, what he termed "an experiment noble in motive," and was particularly anxious that the states should play their full part in the enforcement process. The intention of the Eighteenth Amendment, he reminded Woodrow Wilson in 1923,

> was that each government [federal and state] should perform that part of the task for which it is peculiarly fitted. . . . To relieve the states from the duty of performing [their tasks] violates our traditions; and threatens the best interests of our country. The strength of the nation and its capacity for achievement is, in large measure, due to the federal system with its distribution of powers and duties. . . .

Only by trusting the states, he believed, and relying on them to legislate and administer their own laws fairly, could the federal system be made to realize its full creative potential and flexibility. Without the Fourteenth Amendment, he told Frankfurter at about the same time, the states would have been forced to shoulder their constitutional responsibilities more. As it was they both passed the buck and failed to give adequate consideration to problems properly within their remit.

Subsequently during "the Depression decade," even when at his most gloomy about the operations of the national government, Brandeis would continue to retain an optimistic faith in the potential for differentiated development inherent in the states. As he told Alfred Lief as the First New Deal reached its high-water mark in 1934: "The United States is too big to be a force for good; whatever we do is bound to be harmful." The country "should go back to the Federation idea, letting each State evolve a policy and develop itself. There are enough good men in Alabama to make Alabama a good State."[38]

A faith in the value of federalism was, next to a devout belief in democratic participation, the most potent element of the justice's political creed. His conviction that the states represented the most appropriate arena for social experimentation was coupled with a pervasive sense that ordinary people needed to identify with a context both local and particular before they could perceive and exercise fully their democratic responsibilities. Like the city republics of Ancient Greece or the pocket states of the Holy Roman Empire, the scale of a Kentucky or a Massachusetts (or a Palestine) was something men and women could get their minds around, a forum within which the arts of citizenship and statesmanship might develop and flourish. It should come as no surprise, therefore, to discover among the principles guiding his behavior as a member of the judiciary a firm commitment to upholding the sovereignty of the states, especially in instances where their reserved powers clearly entitled them to promote and protect the social and economic welfare of their citizens. Only when state authorities sought to abridge the basic civil rights granted to their inhabitants *as citizens of the United States* did he believe it incumbent on federal judges to intervene. If the distinction invoked here was a subtle one—indeed some might even have considered it arbitrary, entailing just the kind of logic chopping that had led Elihu Root to oppose his confirmation in 1916—it was nevertheless one to which Brandeis seems to have attached the greatest importance.

From a holistic standpoint, he believed, the Constitution of the United States was to be regarded quintessentially as a framework for federalism, a structure of rules whose prime function was to preserve, and if possible to enhance, the "dual sovereignty" inherent in the concept of "a more perfect Union." Just as he saw in the Eighteenth Amendment a valuable instrument for encouraging the extension of federal-state cooperation, in efforts to eliminate child labor by means of punitive federal taxation he discerned a worrying arrogation by the Congress of responsibilities properly falling on the State House. Consequently, in 1922, he readily endorsed the Court's decision to invalidate the tax, and was explicit in his reasoning. "Perhaps it will be recognized some day as the beginning of an epoch, the epoch of State Duties," he told Norman Hapgood, applauding Taft's opinion in the case. "State Rights succumbed to the Rights of Nations. State Duties were ignored and State Duties atrophied. The extremes of concentration are proving its failure to the common man. . . . The new Progressivism requires local development—quality not quantity."[39]

In the field of socioeconomic regulation, Brandeis faced little of the technical and moral ambivalence that served to complicate his reasoning on the subject of civil liberties. As we have seen in previous chapters, his early hostility to social-welfare and regulatory legislation, enacted by states as an exercise of their police powers, did not survive the 1890s. Ironically, the rapid liberalization of his own outlook during the course of that decade coincided with the steady growth of conservatism in the legal profession as a whole—a development that was fully reflected in the behavior of the federal judiciary in general, and the United States Supreme Court in particular. Throughout his years on the bench, therefore, Brandeis found himself fundamentally at odds with the majority of his brethren on several vital issues of public policy and constitutional interpretation; among these, none was more intractable than the question of whether, and in what circumstances, state legislatures should be permitted to promote, regulate, or prohibit the social and economic activities of their citizens.

Reversing completely the opinion he had held in 1892, Mr. Justice Brandeis maintained quite simply that in most cases it was inappropriate for the courts to review and overturn regulatory laws enacted by popularly elected state legislatures. The only exceptions he was ready to admit were where a statute, or the administrative orders issued under it, clearly denied the citizen's entitlement to *procedural* due process; where a state had usurped functions explicitly delegated by the Constitution to the federal government; or where (just as with laws infringing civil liberties) the legislation being challenged sought to abrogate fundamental rights considered inseparable from citizenship in a free republic. Where he parted company with the Court's majority was over the question of precisely which rights were "fundamental"; over their willful nonobservance of jurisdictional limitations; and on the dubious practice of measuring the acceptability of state laws by reference to a set of arbitrary propositions—substantive requirements derived not from the letter of the Constitution but from the supposed dictates of natural law. It was in the process of distancing himself from this interventionist jurisprudence that Brandeis developed the general principles previously identified as the hallmark of his judicial method: that judges should not pass on constitutional questions unless it was absolutely necessary for them to do so; that they should approach all laws with a presumption of their constitutionality; and that they should decide matters only after full consideration of all the available facts. Taken together this added up to a dissident jurisprudence, characterized by the twin virtues of self-restraint and social awareness.

The area of dispute was wide and still widening. The regulation of business generally, and of public utilities in particular; restrictions on the use and abuse of private property, and on the permissible activities of trade unions; the setting of rates and prices, and the fixing of maximum hours and minimum wages for labor; the proper scope and purpose of taxation—all afforded grounds for disagreement and dissent. For one thing, Brandeis's methodological maxims did not encapsulate the common practice of the Court. His fellow justices frequently assumed jurisdiction over cases appealed from state courts in which no obvious federal questions presented themselves, usually with the express intention of settling a constitutional issue. "Few of them realize," he complained to Felix Frankfurter in 1923, "that questions of jurisdiction are really questions of power between States and Nations." Holmes and Taft, he believed, knew little about the subject and cared less, albeit for rather different reasons: "Taft because he likes to decide questions as a matter of expediency, where controversies arise"; Holmes, though caring little for "expediency," because he "likes to decide cases where interesting questions are raised." Van Devanter, on the other hand, "knows as much about jurisdiction as anyone—more than anyone. But when he wants to decide, all his jurisdictional scruples go." Brandeis himself recognized a very different order of priorities. "The most important thing we do," the asserted, "is *not* doing."[40]

As for a presumption of constitutionality, the Court's majority was rather more inclined to an opposite point of view, especially where the untrammeled use of property or the liberty of contract were threatened. Since they had repeatedly held that the due process clause of the Fourteenth Amendment permitted consideration of substantive issues, Brandeis was obliged to fall back on the third of his principles whenever his brethren chose to disregard the imperative force of the second. For if the Court was determined to assess the reasonableness of legislation, he would counter by insisting that only by a comprehensive study of the particular circumstances of the case at bar could such "reasonableness" be fairly ascertained. Usually, as for example in *Jay Burns Baking Company v. Bryan* (1924), a detailed rehearsal of the relevant context would form the bulk of his opinion, frequently a dissent from the majority's decision to strike down a measure as repugnant to the Constitution. The *Bryan* case arose in connection with a Nebraska law fixing standard weights for bread loaves. In Brandeis's view, the Court could not properly decide whether the statute before them was an "unreasonable, arbitrary, or capricious" measure, unless they knew the facts upon which legislators had acted. "Knowledge is essential to understanding," he declared; "and understanding should precede judging." But it was not sufficient merely to consider the facts appearing in the record; indeed, much of the evidence that he considered most important, and to which he referred in his dissent, was to be found in "the history of the experience gained under similar legislation" in other states, and from "the results of scientific experiments made, since the entry of the judgment below." It was essential that the Court take judicial notice of such matters, but it was not their job to weigh the evidence thus adduced. "Put at its highest," he contended,

> our function is to determine, in the light of all facts which may enrich our knowledge and enlarge our understanding, whether the measure, enacted in the exercise of an unquestioned police power, and of a character inherently unobjectionable, transcends the bounds of reason. That is, whether the provision, as applied, is so clearly arbitrary or capricious that legislators, acting reasonably, could not have believed it to be necessary or appropriate for the public welfare.

To find the Nebraska statute invalid by these criteria was, in his opinion, "an exercise of the powers of a super-legislature,—not the performance of the constitutional function of judicial review."[41]

It should not be thought, however, that Brandeis's colleagues were single-minded in their own attitude to substantive due process. If in 1924 a majority of the justices were unhappy with a state law requiring bread baked for sale to be of certain specified weights, eight years earlier, in *Hutchison Ice Cream Company v. Iowa* (1916), they had apparently seen no objection to another regulating the percentage of butter fat in ice cream. Moreover, in this his first opinion, Brandeis had already nailed his colors firmly to the mast, observing of the details presented in the record that "the legislature may well have found in these facts persuasive evidence that the public welfare required the prohibition enacted." Such inconsistencies in the reasoning of the Court were in fact common. When Frankfurter remarked years later that what bothered him most about the opinions of the Court was their incoherence, that "they don't hang together from week to week," he found that Brandeis was of like mind. "They don't," he agreed; "the trouble is [the other justices] don't know enough to keep them coherent!"[42]

For our purposes, perhaps the more important question is: Did Brandeis know enough to be coherent either? David Riesman, we know, thought otherwise, and he was not alone among the justice's later law clerks in taking such a view. For Nathan L. Nathanson it was his work on *Nashville, Chattanooga & St. Louis Railway v. Walters* (1935) that led him to question the openness of Brandeis's judicial methods. "It may be shocking to mention them in the same breath," he confided to Frankfurter, "but I sometimes wonder whether the Justice or McReynolds votes more in accordance with his prejudices, albeit they be of a different order. On occasion, at least, it is difficult to distinguish policy from prejudice." He was unhappy too with the form of Brandeis's opinions "which assume their conclusion, and then mow down the opposition."

These remarks were written on the very day that the *Walters* decision was handed down. The case concerned an order of the Tennessee Highway Commission requiring the railroad to bear half the cost of constructing an underpass where the line of a new section of the developing national road system intersected its tracks. The company then sought judicial review of the relevant statute, claiming that the order deprived it of property without due process of law by the requirement that it in effect subsidize a form of crossing designed for the convenience of its road-using competitors. Nathanson was set to work collecting all the available data, including everything he could find about federally aided highways. When his research at length uncovered a breakdown of state expenditures, with a diagram to illustrate the proportion spent in each area, the justice was shocked to see that a relatively large segment of the state budget was devoted to highway construction, whereas a much smaller amount was being spent on education. Yet in spite of the fact that Tennessee's spending priorities were almost completely the reverse of Brandeis's own, his oft-repeated assertions about the presumption of constitutionality, not to mention his long-standing antipathy to the concept of substantive due process, appeared to leave him no option but to defer to the judgment of the state's legislators.

Nathanson was dismayed, therefore, when the justice not only voted to quash the order but insisted on delivering the opinion of the Court himself. When the clerk protested, Brandeis reminded him of the test applied by Justice Holmes when deciding whether to invoke the notion of substantive due process: "Does it make you puke?" Nathanson saw the point—"but to think that autos and Federal-aid should have that effect!" According to Brandeis, there were three settled principles involved in the case at bar: first, that a statute valid with respect to one set of facts might be invalid with respect to another; second, that even though valid at the time it was enacted, a statute might become invalid as a result of changing circumstances; and, third, that the police powers of the states did not extend to actions that were arbitrary or unreasonable. The development of motor transportation facilities with federal assistance, he argued, had altered the economic conditions in which the elimination of "grade crossings" took place. It was now the automobile, rather than the railroad, that reaped the benefit; moreover it paid inadequately for the privilege and was itself the primary cause of dangerous accidents. In light of this altered situation, the purposes intended by the Tennessee statute now constituted an unreasonable exercise of the state's authority. Logical as its reasoning might appear in the abstract, it was all but impossible to square the finding of this opinion with the principles of law that Brandeis had been expounding ever since his arrival in Washington. Little wonder that Nathanson thought he discerned its source amid the miasma of social prejudice rather than in the wellspring of judicial policy.[43]

To Felix Frankfurter, his old mentor's holding in *Walters* was important for the "retrospective light" it appeared to shed on his support some fifteen months earlier for the judgment handed down in *Southern Railway Company v. Virginia* (1933). The legislation assailed in that case had sought to make railroad companies responsible at their own expense for the substitution of overhead for grade crossings at points where their tracks cut across the line of a state road. Federal aid had not been involved; but the statute gave rise to a case justiciable in the federal courts by virtue of a provision that empowered the state highway commissioner to designate without notice or hearing the crossings where such work was to be carried out, if in his opinion it was "necessary for public safety and convenience." Moreover, the act established no procedure for a judicial review of his decisions, except where it could be shown that he had exercised his granted powers in an "arbitrary" fashion. In the appellant's view, this constituted a deprivation of property without due process of law contrary to the *procedural* guarantees of the Fourteenth Amendment, even if Virginia's *substantive* right to order the elimination of grade crossings were recognized as a legitimate exercise of its police powers.

Delivering the opinion of the Court, to which Brandeis did not demur, Mr. Justice McReynolds reiterated "the firmly established rule that every State power is limited by the inhibitions of the Fourteenth Amendment." There was an important distinction to be drawn, he maintained, between the power inherent in legislators and that granted officials to act with their authority. If it were assumed

> that a state legislature may determine what public welfare demands and by direct command require a railway to act accordingly, it by no means follows that an

administrative officer may be empowered, without notice or hearing, to act with finality upon his own opinion and ordain the taking of private property. There is an obvious difference between legislative determination and the finding of an administrative official not supported by evidence. In theory, at least, the legislature acts upon adequate knowledge after full consideration and through members who represent the entire public.

The statute was consequently found to be invalid, although Stone, Cardozo, and the chief justice dissented on the ground that it had indeed constituted "a lawful delegation" of the state's "power to declare the need for the abatement of a nuisance through the elimination of grade crossings dangerous to life and limb"; and that "adequate opportunity [had been] afforded for review in the event that the power [were] perverted or abused."[44]

Discussing this case ten years later with Louis L. Jaffe, who had been Brandeis's law clerk when it came before the Court and was now professor of law in Buffalo, Frankfurter was ready to admit to doubts about the justice's motives for concurrence in the decision. Had the case, he wondered, been "completely unembarrassed by Brandeis' strong convictions regarding the influence of the automobile on our national life"? Would he have reached the same result if the case before him had "involved state revocation, let us say, of a liquor license, or an order by a state agency touching some financial control"? He accepted Jaffe's assertion that Brandeis acted generally on the principle of resisting all unwarranted, even if well intentioned, exercises of governmental power.

It is that principle, as you well know, which underlay his strong feeling in the *Morgan* case, and it is that principle which many of your friends and mine seem to think old-fashioned, if not reactionary, when they are at the controls. With their short-sightedness thay seem not to appreciate that two can play at the game of self-willed power. And, what is more important, that those who have humane and civilized ends are not likely to be allowed to pursue for long those ends without check except their own will. Or, if you will, self-willed authority does not for long pursue merely humane and civilized ends.

What bothered Frankfurter, by then himself a justice of the Supreme Court, was the application of this principle to the *Southern Railway Company* case.

For his part, while acknowledging some relationship between *Walters* and the *Railway* decision, Jaffe remained skeptical about the imputation that Brandeis might have been influenced by narrow considerations in both cases; and he dismissed his correspondent's "liquor license" and "financial control" analogies as red herrings. "I think that to some extent one must distinguish between the occasion for formulating a doctrine and the scope of it," he observed. His own assessment of the justice's motivation was characteristically more wide ranging.

It may be that the automobile problem led Brandeis to highlight the issue in the

Southern Railway case, though, in my opinion, it was more the recent coming of the Nazis to which he, at the time, made explicit reference. But I do not think that from this it can be argued that the doctrine of the case had significance for him only in matters involving railroads v. automobiles.

Frankfurter agreed. He had been "concerned with the contemporaneous considerations that led Brandeis to his view," he explained, backtracking somewhat. "I am sorry to have implied that for him it became thereafter merely a railroad v. automobile doctrine." He accepted too Jaffe's point about the need to distinguish between the situation giving rise to a legal doctrine and the subsequent scope of its application, but thought nevertheless that a vital connection existed between them; for in his view, "not the least interesting physiological aspect" of jurisprudence was "the extent to which a doctrine, propelled by particular circumstances, acquires a life of its own."[45]

Willard Hurst was troubled by something else. Writing to Frankfurter in May 1938, he confessed to harboring some concern about his boss's "departure from canons of judicial restraint" in the recently decided *Tompkins* case, where Brandeis had not only changed "a matter of important statutory construction after nearly a century lapse" but had sought to reach a constitutional issue that none of the parties in the case had thought to raise. The justice's purpose had been simple: to reverse the decision in *Swift v. Tyson* (1842) that had effectively subordinated the unwritten law of the states to the application of "general law" as interpreted by federal judges. This, he maintained, had been a grievous error; for as a draft of his opinion flatly declared, there was no such thing as a "federal general common law." Far from being uneasy about so prominent a display of judicial activism, with a majority of his brethren sharing in his view of the case he quickly came to see it as a source of considerable "satisfaction." As he told Hurst: "It has already relieved our Court (see the several cases disposed of on Certiorari); should relieve the lower federal courts; and, which is most important, tend to develop the morale of the State courts & the quality of their work."[46]

Neither had his behavior in *Tompkins* been an isolated occurrence. In *Thompson v. Consolidated Gas Utilities Corporation*, decided the previous year, Brandeis had again chosen to dispose of the case on due process grounds where a narrower, nonconstitutional construction of the statute involved might well have served his purpose. "On some occasions last year I was somewhat taken aback and puzzled," Hurst told Frankfurter, "by the Justice's drive to decide a substantive constitutional point without the tender regard for limiting doctrines which, *a priori*, I would have expected of him." Though Hurst himself had later formed the opinion re *Thompson* that "the only reasonable construction of the statute was that under which it was unconstitutional," Brandeis, he believed, had never "come to that degree of conviction." Instead, he had reasoned that, so long as the construction was open to a measure of doubt, the Court was entitled to settle the constitutional point. "I don't think it would do justice to the complexity of the problem of appraisal and analysis involved," Hurst concluded, "if one were to interpret very dogmatically his whole attitude towards judicial self-limitation. A notion of the day-to-day pragmatic aspect of the judicial process was a very sharp impression which I took away from last year's experience."[47]

In no single instance was this pragmatism better exemplified than in *Ashwander v. Tennessee Valley Authority* (1936), one of the most important cases to come before the Court during the period of David Riesman's clerkship. Although a wide range of parties and interests were vitally concerned in its outcome, the central issues raised in this suit were narrow, technical ones. It was perhaps for this reason that none of the justices except McReynolds appeared anxious to see *Ashwander* become a test case for the constitutionality of the Tennessee Valley Authority Act—this despite the fact that only six weeks before, in *United States v. Butler et al.*, they had been more than ready to invalidate the greater part of the New Deal's agriculture program by a majority of 6 to 3. In January 1934, the Alabama Power Company had entered into a contract with the Tennessee Valley Authority (TVA) to sell it "certain transmission lines, sub-stations, and auxiliary properties," and to purchase from the agency the "surplus power" generated by its hydroelectric plant at Muscle Shoals. The contracting parties had also agreed "mutual restrictions as to the areas to be served in the sale of power" produced by their respective operations. The plaintiffs in the case at bar were holders of preferred stock in the power company, who, having failed to persuade its directors to annul the contract as "injurious to the corporate interests [sic] and also invalid, because beyond the constitutional power of the Federal Government," had brought suit in the U.S. District Court to enjoin performance of the agreement and determine its constitutionality. The annulment and injunction granted in the lower court were subsequently set aside on appeal, and the case at last came before the Supreme Court in December 1935 on writs of certiorari.[48]

Delivering the opinion of the Court, Chief Justice Hughes followed the Circuit Court of Appeals by confining his judgment narrowly to the validity of the contract complained of which he affirmed, and pointedly refrained from passing on any of the wider issues dwelt on at length by counsel for the plaintiffs. These included such potentially explosive questions as the government's "right to acquire or operate local or urban distribution systems"; "the status of any other dam or power development in the Tennessee Valley"; "the claims made in the pronouncements and program" of TVA; and, most important of all, the validity of the act under which the authority functioned. He did, however, accept the right of preferred stockholders to bring such suits, and, after reviewing a substantial number of similar cases, went on to sound an ominous warning:

A close examination of these cases leads inevitably to the conclusion that they should either be followed or frankly overruled. We think that they should be followed, and that the opportunity to resort to equity, in the absence of an adequate legal remedy, in order to prevent illegal transactions by those in control of corporate properties, should not be curtailed because of reluctance to decide constitutional questions.

He rejected the government's contention that the plaintiffs, suing-in the right of the corporation, were estopped from questioning the constitutionality of the TVA by a series of technical errors. "Estoppel in equity," he declared unequivocally, "must rest on substantial grounds of prejudice or change of position, not on technicalities."

In fact, the only thing preventing the Court from reaching an immediate determination of the wider constitutional questions raised was the remoteness of the plaintiffs' standing to have these addressed in resolution of the suit then before the Court. As the chief justice explained,

the pronouncements, policies and program of the Tennessee Valley Authority and its directors, their motives and desires, did not give rise to a justiciable controversy save as they had fruition in action of a definite and concrete character constituting an actual or threatened interference with the rights of the persons complaining. The judicial power does not extend to the determination of abstract questions.

The issues disputed in the present case, though, were a good deal more precise: Had the federal government been entitled to construct the Wilson Dam between 1917 and 1926, and did it now have the constitutional authority to dispose of the electrical power being generated by the dam? The answer, so the Court believed, was plainly "yes" to both questions.[49]

Despite the legitimacy it afforded the TVA's operations at Muscle Shoals, this judgment seemed to offer the Roosevelt administration only temporary relief while further litigation was prepared for initiation in the lower courts; for with three of the Court's four conservative judges—Butler, Sutherland, and Van Devanter—ready to concur in its reasoning, Hughes's holding was plainly intended to leave the door open for a more carefully framed challenge to the authority's constitutional validity. It was probably this circumstance that caused Brandeis to write his own opinion, which, though not disavowing the outcome, took up the task of showing that no constitutional determination should have been reached at all—at least not on the basis of a stockholders suit.[50]

Beginning with his very first dissenting opinion in *Adams v. Tanner* (1917), the new justice had adopted the practice of supporting his juristic assaults on what he considered the narrow legalism of the Court's conservatives with copious references to law reviews, academic texts, and other nonjudicial sources. In fact, the technique used in these "Brandeis opinions" was similar to that developed in the celebrated "Brandeis briefs" that he had filed in *Muller v. Oregon* and a number of subsequent social-welfare cases. "Spendidly done!" wrote Mr. Justice Clarke after reading a draft of his dissent in the *Adams* case. "Your selections are admirable & the restraint of comment discreet having regard to your purpose. The authority attaching to such a statement from a member of this court will make of it a great public service. I am glad you are circulating it in advance. The experiment is worth trying." When Brandeis wrote on behalf of the Court, though, his style was somewhat different, as John W. Johnson has observed:

> when Brandeis authored majority opinions upholding the constitutionality of regulatory economic statutes, he seldom resorted to massive barrages of statistics and testimony. In such cases, he apparently believed the constitutional presumption for economic regulations was a sufficient rationale in and of itself to allow appellate courts to uphold such laws.

Perhaps surprisingly, then, his partial dissent in the *Ashwander* case (sometimes referred to as a "special concurrence") eschewed any reference whatsoever to information about the hydroelectric-power industry or to the socioeconomic condition of the Tennessee Valley, but provided instead a tightly argued exposition of the precedents for self-restraint on the part of judges. In Johnson's view, the resulting opinion constituted "one of the classic apologies in American legal history for judicial circumspection." More important, though, it read, and indeed was meant to read, like the ruling of the Court.[51]

Brandeis had no hesitation in accepting the government's contention that the plaintiffs had "no standing to challenge the validity of the legislation" that authorized TVA's activities; and he was adamant that such an objection could not be sidestepped by the invocation of proceedings in equity. "The obstacle is not procedural," he observed. "It inheres in the substantive law, in well settled rules of equity, and in the practice in cases involving the constitutionality of legislation." First, as regards the law, it was generally understood that the courts would not interfere with the management decisions of a public corporation unless evidence of manifest illegality were produced, and the complaining stockholders could prove that their property rights were seriously threatened. In the present case "there was no showing of fraud, oppression, or gross negligence. There was no showing of legal duress. There was no showing that the management believed that to sell to the Tennessee Valley Authority was in excess of the company's corporate powers, or that it was illegal because entered into for a forbidden purpose." Second, as pertaining to equity practice, any party seeking an injunction was required to demonstrate that a danger existed "of irreparable injury" to their interests if equitable relief were not granted. The preferred stockholders in the case at bar had failed to show that the contract complained of in any way imperiled their property rights.[52]

The third obstacle he identified, the established practice of the courts in constitutional cases, provided the core of Brandeis's opinion. The undoubted convenience of a prompt decision regarding the validity of the TVA Act, both to the parties involved in the case and to the general public, was not a sufficient reason, he believed, to depart from the "settled rules of corporate law and established principles of equity practice" just outlined. Indeed, the very fact "that such is the nature of the enquiry proposed should deepen the reluctance of the courts to entertain the stockholder's suit." Moreover, in support of this assertion he was able to cite a passage from Cooley's *Constitutional Limitations*: "It must be evident to any one that the power to declare a legislative enactment void is one which the judge, conscious of the fallibility of human judgment, will shrink from exercising in any case where he can conscientiously and with due regard to duty and official oath decline the responsibility." For its part, the Supreme Court had long ago insisted "that the jurisdiction of federal courts is limited to actual cases and controversies; and that they have no power to give advisory opinions"; he then went on to enumerate a long list of cases, dismissed by the Court in recent years on this ground alone, which had sought to challenge the validity of important acts of Congress.[53]

Even when the Court did acknowledge jurisdiction of a case, according to Brandeis it also recognized "a series of rules" developed over many decades by which it was able to avoid "passing upon a large part of all the constitutional questions pressed upon it for a decision." The justices would not determine the validity of legislation "in a friendly, non-adversary proceeding"; nor would they "anticipate a question of constitutional law in advance of the necessity of deciding it." When such a decision did become necessary, the rule that was formulated would be no broader in scope than was "required by the precise facts" of the case at bar. If a case could be "decided on either of two grounds, one involving a constitutional question, the other a question of statutory construction or general law," the Court would opt for the latter. It would "not pass upon the validity of a statute upon complaint of one who fails to show that he is injured by its operation"; neither would it do so "at the instance of one who has availed himself of its benefits." Lastly, and perhaps most pertinently given the nature of the central issue at stake in *Ashwander*, when the validity of an act of Congress was seriously called into question, the Court was bound as "a cardinal principle" to "first ascertain" whether a construction of the statute was "fairly possible" by which the question of constitutionality might be avoided.

Having enumerated these "rules" and illustrated their application in numerous decisions, Brandeis's next task was to distinguish the particular circumstances of the present case from those prevailing in other stockholder suits where the Court had been ready to pass on important constitutional questions. "In most," he noted,

the statute challenged imposed a burden upon the corporation and penalties for failure to discharge it; whereas the Tennessee Valley Authority Act imposed no obligation upon the Alabama Power Company, and under the contract it received a valuable consideration. Among other things, the Authority agreed not to sell outside the area covered by the contract, and thus preserved the corporation against possible serious competition.

These points, together with other features of the present litigation, made it possible to differentiate *Ashwander* "from all the cases in which stockholders have been held entitled to have this Court pass upon the constitutionality of a statute which the directors had refused to challenge": a proposition that he proceeded to illustrate by analyzing the leading cases involved. None of these, he believed, was directly analogous; however,

> If, or in so far as, any of the cases discussed may be deemed authority for sustaining this bill [in equity], they should now be disapproved. This Court, while recognizing the soundness of the rule of stare decisis where appropriate, has not hesitated to overrule earlier decisions shown, upon fuller consideration, to be erroneous.[54]

From this bold assertion, and after a brief rehearsal of the reasons why he believed the plaintiffs were indeed estopped from bringing the suit, contra the opinion of the chief justice, Brandeis turned at length to his peroration. Here his primary theme was to be "the long established presumption in favor of the constitutionality of a statute—a venerable precept of American jurisprudence for which authorities as varied and respected as Chief Justice Marshall, Judge Cooley, and Professor Thayer were adduced in evidence. The burden of his argument was simple: "Even where by the substantive law stockholders have a standing to challenge the validity of legislation under which the management of a corporation is acting, courts should, in the exercise of their discretion, refuse an injunction unless the alleged invalidity is clear." In the present case it was not at all clear. Therefore, he concluded:

> The challenge of the power of the Tennessee Valley Authority rests wholly upon the claim that the act of Congress which authorized it is unconstitutional. As the opinions of this Court and of the Circuit Court of Appeals show, that claim was not a matter "beyond peradventure clear." The challenge of the validity of the act is made on an application for an injunction—a proceeding in which the court is asked to exercise its judicial discretion. In proceedings for a mandamus, where, also, the remedy is granted not as a matter of right but in the exercise of a sound judicial discretion, . . . courts decline to enter on the enquiry where there is a serious doubt as to the existence of the right or duty sought to be enforced. . . . A fortiori this rule should have been applied here where the power challenged is that of Congress under the Constitution.

It is easy to see in this opinion, as most commentators have, a statement capable of general application in which Brandeis managed to encapsulate for his brethren, and for a wider legal audience, the very essence of his judicial thought and outlook. "It will be a treasure-house of instruction for many a day," Justice Cardozo prophesied on the back of a draft copy circulated by its author. Alexander Bickel, linking it with concerns expressed in the justice's unpublished "memorandum" in *Atherton Mills v. Johnston*, written sixteen years before, saw it as "the crowning statement of one of the truly major themes in [his] judicial work: the conviction that the Court must take the utmost pains to avoid precipitate decision of constitutional issues, and that it must above all decide such cases only when it is absolutely unable otherwise to dispose of a case properly before it." To Felix Frankfurter, the Court's decision to accept jurisdiction in *Ashwander* appeared to reflect the political and economic importance of the case. "It would not be without historic warrant to conclude," he wrote in 1938, "that the scales were turned in favor of taking jurisdiction by the imponderable pressures of the public importance of the [statute] under review." Brandeis's dissent, on the other hand, in which Justices Roberts, Stone, and Cardozo concurred, struck the Harvard professor as "perhaps the most notable opinion expounding the rationale of jurisdiction in constitutional controversies," and, for him at least, clearly demonstrated "infringement of those rules of judicial self-limitation which alone gave coherence to the great body of precedents which he passed under review."[55]

Yet behind the specific procedural questions at issue between Hughes and Brandeis, Frankfurter was alone in discerning a broader theme: not merely the widening use of the stockholder suit as a conventional mechanism for "contesting the validity of regulatory and revenue statutes," but "the fecund possibilities of equity" procedures generally when used for that purpose.

> Just as equity, at common law, created its own jurisdictional problems with special reference to the avoidance of friction between two tribunals, so resort to equity for invalidating legislation generates its special problems, if needless friction between the judiciary and other branches of government is to be avoided. The evasion of the requirement for damage that cannot be compensated has a pungency of consequences in these public law controversies which strikingly underlines traditional equity practice. Public interest, however, exerts contradictory pressures. Considerations for abstention from decision, unless technical equity requirements are satisfied, are met with the temptation to make use of the flexible facilities of equity for prompt allaying of uncertainty. And so the cases reflect an oscillation between a very strict and a very easy-going attitude toward taking equity jurisdiction to decide constitutionality.

Moreover, to illustrate his point, Frankfurter was at pains to show that the Court's requirements in this regard had been growing steadily more lax, beginning with its decision to assume jurisdiction in *Pollock v. Farmers' Loan & Trust Co.* (1895) and reaching something of a watershed with its ruling in *Smith v. Kansas City Title & Trust Co.* (1921), which had sustained the Federal Farm Loan Act of 1916.[56]

The chief justice's holding in *Ashwander* relied heavily on precedents established by the *Pollock* and *Smith* decisions; and this may plausibly explain Brandeis's insistence that, were they to be considered authoritative in the present case, these and other similar judgments should be overruled. Despite appearances to the contrary, however, this was not a restatement of the Court's view of *stare decisis* but a redefinition of its author's own perception, and, more to the point, one that was decidedly ad hoc in its application. For Brandeis, like those of his colleagues who backed Hughes's opinion, was greatly impressed and arguably influenced by "the political and economic importance of the case" and by "the imponderable pressures of the public importance of the [statute] under review." Viewed from a broader perspective, therefore, his dissenting opinion needs to be read, not as disinterested representation of what current judicial practice actually was, but as an embattled assertion of what it ought to be. In other words, Riesman was not far wrong when he described his chief as "fighting a strategic action, a holding action, against the conservatives on the Court."[57]

In short, by 1936 if not before, Brandeis had come to recognize a flexible standard of judicial review where due process issues were concerned. When labor or welfare legislation of which he approved was threatened by the abstract liberties subsumed under *substantive* due process, he generally reacted by seeking to persuade the Court to set aside its rigid legal formulas and to consider instead the social context in which the facts of the case were embedded. When more concrete "civil" liberties were challenged, he remained concerned to ensure a full consideration of the relevant facts, yet regarded such inquiries as ultimately less important than the Court's responsibility to uphold rights he considered "inseparable from citizenship." But when the TVA, his favorite New Deal agency, was challenged because of the socioeconomic impact it was having in a broad region of the South affected by its operations, he quite simply reversed the order of his priorities and insisted on the inviolability of a legal formula without regard to the facts of the case at all.[58]

By a grand irony, the task of writing the "Brandeis opinion" in *Ashwander* was taken up by Justice McReynolds, his most unrelenting opponent among the so-called "four horsemen." The former attorney general found no difficulty in accepting that the petitioners had presented the Court with a justiciable controversy, and on grounds far more substantial than those pertaining to the *Smith* case. "We may not with propriety," he lectured his brethren, "avoid disagreeable duties by lightly forsaking long respected precedents and established practice." His concern was with another constitutional principle (ignored by Brandeis here though not elsewhere) that the federal government should not "in fact undertake something not intrusted to them . . . under pretence of exercising granted power"; to wit the commercial generation of electric power disguised as the improvement of inland navigation.[59]

The Circuit Court of Appeals had taken, he believed, "too narrow a view of the purpose and effect of the contract," which had in reality gone "far beyond the mere acquisition of transmission lines for proper use in disposing of power legitimately developed." Like all contracts, it needed to be "considered as a whole, *illumined by surrounding circumstances*." These he went on to elucidate in the remainder of the opinion, citing with damning effect the statements of policy contained in TVA's annual reports for 1934 and 1935. Here, and in the findings of fact made in the trial court, the government's purpose was explicitly revealed: "to provide a 'yardstick' of the fairness of rates charged by private owners, and to attain 'no less a goal than the electrification of America.' 'When we carry this program into every town and city and village, and every farm throughout the country, we will have written the greatest chapter in the economic, industrial and social development of America.'" McReynolds had no doubt about the standing in court of plaintiffs faced with such a prospect:

> No abstract question is before us; on the contrary, the matter is of enormous practical importance to [the] petitioners—their whole investment is at stake. Properly understood, the pronouncements, policies and program of the Authority illuminate the action taken. They help to reveal the serious interference with the petitioners' rights. Their property was in danger of complete destruction under a considered program commenced by an agency of the National Government with vast resources subject to its discretion and backed by other agencies likewise intrusted with discretionary use of huge sums. The threat of competition by such an opponent was appalling. The will to prevail was evident. No private concern could reasonably hope to withstand such force.

In other words, the power company's actions had been coerced not by "legal duress" but by an overwhelming display of political and economic muscle. The plaintiffs were entitled to an injunction because the accretion of power represented by TVA had been created without a constitutional mandate. Despite a persuasive rationale that in different circumstances would have been sufficient to carry the Court's conservatives with him, on this occasion McReynolds was alone in voting to uphold the decree of the District Court; and if Brandeis was made at all uncomfortable by the use of his own forensic methods against him, his unease is nowhere recorded.

Although it would be unwarranted to assume that Brandeis cherished no genuine scruples about jurisdictional issues, it would be naïve to assume that such concerns always outweighed more pragmatic considerations at stake in the exercise of his judicial function. Questions of jurisdiction were not merely "questions of power between States and Nations," as he had suggested to Frankfurter; they were also questions of power between the different branches of government and especially between the jarring ideologies represented by the all-too-human members of Brandeis's own court. Viewed alongside his own performance in the *Walters*, *Thompson*, and *Tompkins* cases, it simply makes no sense to portray him as regarding any particular set of legal or constitutional propositions as fundamental—as first principles to be defended for their own sake—when seeking to understand his underlying motivations as a judge. For behind and beneath them at every turn lay the even more elemental values of justice, liberty and democratic participation—values that, in his view at least, both underpinned and fashioned the institutions and objectives of a free society. "L.D.B. saw all the choices," wrote another former law clerk twenty years after the justice's death, "but, on the issues that mattered to him, and on which his reputation rests, he had such deep convictions that choice was easy. His great courage lay in his willingness, indeed zeal, to advocate many choices that were highly unpopular."[60]

However, the all but insuperable difficulty for those who would agree with the estimate of Brandeis implied by Frankfurter's "judicial biography" project—namely that he was at bottom and in matters of relevance to posterity an essentially juristic thinker—is that these choices were not determined by a uniquely "juristic" set of values, but by generalized articles of social, economic and political faith that derived as much from the gleanings of literature, history, and the social sciences as they did from the study of law. Chief Justice Stone was surely closer to the truth when he spoke of his old colleague's conviction that "the law itself was but the means to a social end." To explore the nature of that end, and to evaluate the success with which Brandeis managed to reconcile his ideal of judicial coherence with his perceived reality of bitter sociopolitical conflict will, therefore, be among the principal tasks of this book's final chapter.[61]

7

The Vision of Isaiah

By all means let the sages strengthen the Past at the expense of
the Future. The "Prophets" will follow, and will build a strong
Future on the Foundations of the Past. . . . Far more danger-
ous . . . is that other section, which seeks salvation in a Future
not connected with our Past. . . .
                                        —Ahad Ha-Am, *Selected Essays*

Did the social philosophy that informed Brandeis's jurisprudence during his years as a justice of the Supreme Court take for its model an image of how America had been in the past or a vision of what she might become in the future? Could the one be disconnected from the other? The answers to these questions are far from obvious. Although there can be no doubt that he was profoundly hostile to many key features of the industrial capitalism that had been evolving rapidly in the United States since the 1880s, and scarcely more that he considered the America of his youth to have been a more civilized society on many counts, we possess only the most meager evidence to indicate precisely which aspects of that society he thought might profitably be revived or reconstituted in the decades that lay ahead. Moreover, the difficulty of investigating the issues involved is compounded by the overlapping phases of his intellectual development considered at length in earlier chapters, which render the use of conventional shorthand labels such as "liberal," "radical," "conservative," or "reactionary" an exercise fraught with semantic hazards.

Brandeis's upbringing in Kentucky had launched him into adult life with a clearly defined set of moral values but a much less finely developed sense of how these might be made operational, either in his professional life or in his personal response to contemporary public issues. In so far as he had imbibed any coherent socioeconomic philosophy in his youth, it was a largely quiescent creed: one whose central tenets amounted to a complacent ideology of laissez-faire. Only on the single issue of abolition could his family be considered radicals. Building on this narrow conceptual foundation, his years of training as a lawyer and the first fifteen years or so of his career at the bar saw him adopt an attitude toward the prospects for social amelioration characterized by a naïve commitment to the traditional civic virtues of free trade, sound money, and honesty in public administration. He accepted without reservation the Jeffersonian maxim that the best government was that which governed least.

With time and application, his outstanding professional skills enabled him to become a very wealthy man who might without risk of opprobrium have gone on assimilating his own socioeconomic outlook and personal interests to those of his commercial clientele. That he did not can be explained variously by reference to the awakening of dormant liberal ideals; to a conscience disturbed by the mounting inequalities thrown up by runaway industrial development and urbanization; or even to a sympathetic identification with the experience of recent immigrants from Europe, especially his fellow Jews. Yet just as important as any of these factors may have been the realization that a growing number of his business clients were themselves predisposed toward reform. This may in turn help explain the fact that the progressive reevaluation of his views during the turbulent 1890s, and his widening involvement with reformist campaigns after 1900, proved no bar whatsoever to his amassing a considerable personal fortune, even if the public profile he engendered in the process did perhaps stimulate a measure of anti-Semitism. In 1894 his capital assets stood at around \$125,000; by the time of his appointment to the Supreme Court some twenty-two years later he was worth over \$2 million. What can be maintained with some certainty is that by the opening years of the new century, absolute financial security had combined with a self-conscious limitation of personal wants to free Brandeis from all forms of external obligation and to give him the independence he needed to pursue the campaigning activities that soon earned him the title of the "people's lawyer."[1]

More than anything else, it was the materialistic system of values and the patterns of conspicuous consumption associated with America's newly rich that first served to alienate him from the prevailing trends in twentieth-century life, though it must be added that he was appalled too by the slide into political and industrial plutocracy that their domination of corporate enterprise seemed to threaten. In this respect he was indeed backward looking; for even in his most radical scenarios for the taming of "bigness," he never failed to keep one eye fixed firmly on the precorporate business economy that had flourished briefly in the decades of his youth and early manhood. "Mr. Justice, I think you are a conservative," observed a prominent labor leader jovially after talking with Brandeis in his later years. "I have always so regarded myself," came back the amiable rejoinder. Likewise, in conversation with Harry Shulman in 1933, the justice did not demur at his law clerk's suggestion that the breaking up of large concentrations of corporate wealth meant "attempting to do the impossible, to turn the clock back." "Why shouldn't we turn the clock back," he retorted?

We just turned the clock back on a "noble experiment," which was unanimously adopted in the country and was being tried for some time [i.e., Prohibition]. At any rate whether the program can be executed or not is a separate question. To have that objection raised only confuses the proponent and directs his mind away from the real issue. First we must determine what is desirable to do and then we can find ways and means to do it.

In a literal sense, then, Brandeis's socioeconomic orientation was retrospective; it located the optimum level of organization in industry and commerce at a definable point in the relatively recent past, and regarded all developments in terms of size and concentration beyond that point as false steps that ought to be deliberately retraced.[2]

Nevertheless, he remained fully aware that to restore economic activity to something resembling the scale and configuration he considered socially desirable, and to ensure the future stability of such arrangements, profound changes would be needed, not only in the economic but also in the political and legal spheres, with institutional results that plainly had no historical counterpart. To this extent Brandeis's ideas were as radical as they were visionary in terms both of the ultimate ends sought and of the mechanisms envisaged for their achievement. "He warns against the concentration of power in few hands, whatever the source," noted another observer who met him during the 1930s, and then went on to examine the reasoning he felt lay behind the justice's admonitions.

> Inevitably, persons wielding such power will seek to perpetuate and increase it. They who hold our economic fate control our liberties. Colossal industrial enterprises are not only inefficient, but are changing a nation of independent business men, free workers, and sturdy farmers into a population dependent upon a few people for their daily bread. Government, as the representative of all, may redress the balance. But there are limits to government also. No individuals are wise enough to exercise arbitrary power over the rest of us. Even if such wisdom existed, the result would be bad. The capacity of citizens to direct their own lives should not be permitted to atrophy through disuse.

Such, in a nutshell, was the conceptual matrix underpinning not merely the socioeconomic prescriptions that Brandeis continued to offer politicians and administrators throughout his time as a justice of the Supreme Court, but also many of the opinions that more properly resulted from his tenure of high judicial office.[3]

Perhaps even more perceptive regarding his ideological orientation, and certainly better placed to see how he managed to reconcile the imperative elements of this social philosophy with his functions as a judge, was Dean Acheson, who served as his law clerk during the 1919 and 1920 sessions of the Court. Midway through his second year, the future secretary of state presented Felix Frankfurter with an estimate of his chief's social outlook. In it he insisted that there was a widespread misconception of Brandeis in those early postwar years: that he was a tribune of the people, a "plumed knight," calling on the masses to loose their chains; a true believer in the need for intelligent planning in the development of human institutions. A year's close acquaintance had been enough to convince him that such an assessment was completely erroneous.

> On the emotional side he has, of course, human sympathy. But it is a sympathy with people who are suffering, not with potential gods who are being held back in their development. He doesn't believe much in chains, and that sort of thing. And he isn't more than wistfully moved by the possibility of applying intelligence to life on a large scale because he knows there isn't that much intelligence to apply. . . . I don't think that the Justice puts the slightest faith in mass salvation through universal Plumb Plans. People haven't the intelligence for that sort of thing. They have only the intelligence to operate in small personal groups which deal with the things with which they are intimately acquainted. . . . His goal seems to be by the use of intellect to gain a purely negative freedom from interference for people who want to use their intellects.[4]

Acheson was aware too of the extent to which this underlying orientation helped direct Brandeis's judicial actions. The justice, he recalled later in his memoirs, "was not a simple man" and did not approach the business of opinion writing in a simple fashion. Keeping in mind that a majority opinion was of vital interest to members of the bar generally, as well as to counsel in the case and his colleagues on the bench, he aimed at more than the production of "a scholarly and sound rationalization of the Court's decision"; when writing a dissent he was always conscious that his potential audience had widened to include "the politically sophisticated public" as well. He tacitly recognized that the nation's highest tribunal was now not merely (perhaps not even primarily) a *judicial* forum but in constitutional cases at least had developed during the nineteenth century into an essential part of the *political* process. In Acheson's view, this was why he remained so steadfastly opposed to Taft's scheme for removing the scene of its activities from the Old Senate Chamber in the Capitol to a purpose-built site across the park:

> He found more than symbolic importance in having the Supreme Court midway between the Senate and the House, almost directly under the dome of the Capitol, accessible to the main flow of life through the old building. He thought it a great mistake to give the Court, the other branches of government, and the country the sense of its aloofness which came from setting it apart in a palace of its own.

Above all, whether writing for the Court or in dissent, Brandeis's essential purpose was to educate and persuade. According to Acheson, because he "understood the philosophical principle of antinomy: that inferences drawn from principles equally true may be in direct contradiction with one another," he was ready to agree with Justice Holmes's dictum that "general propositions do not decide concrete cases" and thus tried to make each case at bar seem as concrete as possible. In relation to his more educable brethren, his object in dealing with contentious subjects "was to narrow the issue and, with it, the area of judicial choice, of judicial discretion"; to this end he seemed willing to countenance a wide measure of *legislative* discretion. But when "judicial choices" did have to be made—say, which of two conflicting principles ought to prevail, or which view of the facts presented by counsel should be accepted—his former clerk doubted whether the purely "legal" issue facing the justices could always be guaranteed to "lie at the heart of the matter." Not unreasonably, he suspected the existence of "a deeper and more subtle judgment or intuition directing or, at least, affecting analysis"—what his friend Frankfurter, referring specifically to Brandeis, once termed "an understanding that transcends merely logical analysis."[5]

These conceptions of education and persuasion presuppose, however, that the person proposing to take on the job of educating and persuading has a truth to teach; in his years on the Court, it is evident that Brandeis believed himself possessed of such a truth. Acheson subsequently related how, on a visit to the old man's California Street apartment one evening in the twenties, he managed to maneuver a luckless friend into expounding his views on the relativeness of moral principles. "The eruption was even more spectacular than I had anticipated," he continued.

> The Justice wrapped the mantle of Isaiah around himself, dropped his voice a full octave, jutted his eyebrows forward in a menacing way, and began to prophesy. Morality was truth; and truth had been revealed to man in an unbroken, continuous flow by the great prophets and poets of all time. He quoted Goethe in German and from Euripides via Gilbert Murray. On it went—an impressive, almost frightening, glimpse of an elemental force.

Yet even as he recalled the details of this rhapsodic outburst across a gap of forty years, Acheson rejected any suggestion that such passionately held beliefs might have exerted a material influence on the choices that his erstwhile boss was called on to make during his time as a judge. For him, at least, more surprising by far than the discovery that Brandeis had "absolutist convictions on the nature of truth" was the extent to which "he kept his beliefs and emotions so sternly, even rigidly, disciplined and controlled in the performance of his judicial duties."[6]

Just how well placed, though, were Acheson and his fellow law clerks to determine the constituent elements of Brandeis's sociopolitical agenda during the 1920s and 1930s, or to assess the weight he was prepared to allow nonjudicial factors in the exercise of his judicial function? Can the written and oral accounts of these and others who met and talked with him during the last two decades of his life be used to illumine the key elements of his personal vision? Before answering these questions, we need to examine carefully the evidence provided by such intimate observers, and to reach an objective assessment of its accuracy, consistency, and perceptiveness. Above all, we need to establish precisely what viewpoint is actually represented by their accounts. Paul Freund, for example, is like Acheson an informed and articulate witness; but although several of his observations clearly convey the genuine responses of the recent Law School graduate, others may owe not a little to the greater detachment and experience of the Harvard scholar.

Freund's first meeting with Brandeis was in the fall of 1932 when, after a year's postgraduate study, he arrived in the capital, "called at his home and started work." The justice expected his clerks to work long hours, though just how and when they worked was left largely up to them. "It wasn't a nine-to-five or nine-to-six job—as long as you kept up with him—but it had become a tradition to work very early." Brandeis himself liked to work at the very beginning of the day. "I think he did his best work before dawn," Freund recalled.

> Just when he rose, of course, I don't know, but there was circumstantial evidence. When I would arrive around nine, there would generally be stacks of books in his adjoining office, showing that he had been there for some time. He had by then usually gone down one flight to his apartment, leaving a note—"Please see me when you come in"—which always made me feel uncomfortable. Here was this man, who was then seventy-six, waiting for me, and when I strolled in at my leisure, after he had put in maybe four hours of work. He did not work at night, and that was a matter of principle with him, because he thought that most of the blunders that were made were owing to fatigue, and he didn't really trust himself to work at night when he was tired. So the evenings were left for reading. . . . His wife did a lot of reading aloud. They would go through a book.[7]

On mundane matters of this nature, the details can be readily corroborated. Acheson's memory, though rather more extensive in its range than Freund's, is to much the same effect: that the justice took the hard work of his clerks for granted, and that he himself "worked long and hard" while making sure that he did so "with a fresh mind and at top efficiency." He adds the observation that Brandeis was generally as terse in the allocation of blame as he was in the distribution of praise and records how he encouraged his young assistants to participate in the opinion-writing process—thereby, incidentally, following the pattern that we saw established during his own clerkship with Horace Gray some forty years before. Once an assignment slip had been received from the chief justice, indicating the cases in which he was expected to write the opinion of the Court according to the votes previously taken in the Saturday conference, Brandeis would start writing some of them himself while letting his clerk experiment with some of the others. As Acheson explains in his memoirs:

> When he reached a point where he wanted his draft checked, he would give it to me and take mine from me in whatever state it was; sometimes using parts of it, sometimes not. My instructions regarding his work were to look with suspicion on every statement of fact until it was proved from the record of the case, and on

every statement of law until I had exhausted the authorities. If additional points were to be made, I was to develop them thoroughly. Sometimes my work took the form of a revision of his; sometimes of a memorandum of suggestions to him. He was remarkably tolerant of physical alteration and often dissection of his sheets.

That all of these processes were replicated in the work of other secretaries can be confirmed by reference to the ample evidence of drafts, notes, and memoranda surviving among Brandeis's Court papers.[8]

It is also supported by other pieces of evidence. Fourteen years after Acheson, in the spring of 1935, Nathan Nathanson was also collaborating with Brandeis in the drafting process, albeit in his own mind with rather indifferent results. "As we start on each opinion," he told Frankfurter, "I take a tremendous oath that I shall have the whole thing worked out, with the inevitable First, Second, and Third, before the Justice gets through stating the facts; as we finish, I clutch for solace some footnote gems, and a few scattered sentences." Later that same year, David Riesman could observe how working on opinions gave him an opportunity to see the way Brandeis worked and thought. "We have had several good scraps about policy," he reported, "but . . . I don't push him when I see his mind is made up—as it generally is. I still have the feeling as to policy at least that I'm no use to him." A good deal of Riesman's time was spent collecting facts, but this scarcely helped reduce his feelings of inadequacy. "Much of my work," he wrote, "is still waste motion, with some days little to show him for much grubbing or thinking; as time goes on, I will get a better idea of what he wants and how to go about finding it." Even Freund could write of having "the best judge in the land to correct my errors," though fortunately also "the gentlest and kindest of men."[9]

The fact is that, by involving them directly in the writing of his opinions, Brandeis was being of considerably more help to his young protégés from Harvard than they were to him. Except for a few outstanding clerks, their main usefulness was in the time-consuming exercise of gathering contextual information, seeking out legal precedents and checking citations. Twelve months was barely long enough to break in even the most promising assistant. As he informed Frankfurter toward the close of 1920: "Acheson is doing much better work this year, no doubt mainly because of his greater experience; partly, perhaps, because I talked the situation over with him frankly." He recognized that the young man's career development would require him to find a more exacting job at the end of this second year, but still regretted the impending loss. "If I consulted my own convenience," he confided, "I might be tempted to ask him to stay." Thereafter, no other secretary remained with Brandeis for longer than his allotted term.[10]

For most, nonetheless, their year with the justice proved a seminal influence on their lives, not merely because of the invaluable professional experience it afforded, but because of the contact with the man himself. Physically, they found him a compelling, some might say charismatic, figure. Like many others, Acheson noted the resemblance to Lincoln: "the same boldness and ruggedness of features, the same untamed hair, the eyes of infinite depth under bushy eyebrows, which in moments of emotion seemed to jut out. As he grew older, he carried a prophetic, if not intimidating aura." Indeed, the image of "Isaiah" may well have been deliberately cultivated, for Brandeis was apparently fond of quoting his fellow Kentuckian's maxim that "at forty every man is responsible for his [own] face." His voice too was impressive, especially when delivering his opinions in Court. "It is a marvellous performance," commented an otherwise skeptical Riesman, "dampened somewhat by my sorrow that there are few, perhaps none, in the audience of rubbernecks and waiting counsel who know how fabulously good it is, who have the opinion with them, to know how dramatic, how resonant, he has made a case dealing with accounting, or with berry boxes." And he went on to speculate how, in earlier days, Brandeis "must have been the perfect advocate, clear and full in exposition of facts, pungent and brief in elucidation of law." There seems to have been a widespread feeling, best articulated by Marion Frankfurter, that he was one of the very few men who gave "the appearance of greatness." Paul Freund pondered her remark often during his first few weeks in harness, as he later confided to her husband. "I wonder how many people," he added, "on coming away from meeting him, have had the feeling that they did 'see Shelley plain,' and that he did 'stop and speak' to them. For me, the experience comes not once but daily; and yet it always brings new exhilaration."[11]

This, however, was the problem: Young men like Acheson, Freund Riesman, and the rest arrived in Washington already in awe of the man for whom they were going to work, and he in turn insisted on maintaining the formality of his dealings with them throughout their year of service. He was the master, they the apprentices: The relationship between them was a tutorial one. It was not an ideal perspective from which to gain a rounded impression of the older man's views and objectives. "During the recess, I have a perfectly glorious time," wrote Nathanson, "because I see the Justice every day, and talk about the work, (and occasionally about other things, though not as much as I would like) and every task assumes the dignity with which he is so wondrously able to endow it." But when the Court was in session, they scarcely met at all; the clerk called it his "grass-widower period." "[I] go about the business of reading cases, with good intentions," he lamented, "but soon grow to feeling stale and dull, and let the weeks slip by in unproductive reverie, meditating on various unpleasant things." Needless to say, this was hardly a basis for penetrating intellectual analysis.[12]

Thus, while there is substantial agreement among the law clerks about the justice's working arrangements, and even about their own feelings in his presence, their interpretations of his thought and motivation, even in familiar social contexts, are far less deep and consistent. For example, one of the law clerk's duties was to organize the Sunday or Monday afternoon teas (even the day is disputed) that the Brandeises were in the habit of giving at their apartment each week while the Court sat. Freund regarded these sessions as the justice's "lifeline to the outside world." The guests tended to be a diverse bunch, he remembered: "The teas didn't follow protocol. It wasn't the case of embassy people one week and university people another week." There would generally be a mixture of ages as well as of vocations, and certain people would be invited a set number of times during the year: "the Danish minister, for instance, or a departmental librarian who had been helpful with research, or certain old friends and comrades in arms of earlier days—like Norman Hapgood, if he was in Washington." Then there were celebrities of the hour, people "who had recently done something which struck Brandeis as noble or heroic, taken a position, or made a speech, or introduced a bill," who were invited as a tacit sign of the justice's approval, as "kind of mark of recognition."[13]

Others besides the clerks have recorded their impressions of these gatherings. For Robert L. Stern, in the mid-1930s a young lawyer in the Justice Department, teas with the Brandeises stood out in memory as the most memorable social events he attended during his years spent working for the New Deal. He, like many of the secretaries, viewed the justice with awe: "I remember that my reaction on meeting [him] was that this was the closest I was ever going to get to meeting God in person." However, David A. Morse, who worked with Freund and Alger Hiss in the Solicitor General's office, was far less lyrical in his reaction to the tea parties. "They were really Spartan," he recalled, "as if you were in a prison: bare walls, a little bit of furniture, a threadbare rug, and a little bitty sandwich. The Justice would pick out somebody and have a conversation with him, and then you'd go home."[14]

These sessions served a dual purpose for Brandeis, enabling him to keep himself informed on current issues and to pass on his own general views about the state of the world. "He would draw people out, usually one on one, about what they were doing," Freund remembered, "and he would ask questions that would force the guest to think hard about what he was doing." The justice would then contribute his own observations, which were "characteristically of a very general philosophical sort," rather than of a prescriptive nature. During the 1920s his two favorite themes were apparently "the Greek Genius" and "the Curse of Bigness"; even with reference to the New Deal years, Freund remained adamant about the limited significance of the teas:

I think there's been a lot of misunderstanding about these conversations, as if Brandeis was plotting the tactics of various agencies by conversing with these people, but it was like a phonograph record being played over and over again. [He] cautioned them against their doing too much, against the limitations of the human mind, and against fatigue, and in time to go back to their home communities where they were needed. It was that kind of talk.

As an example of the sort of thing that went on he recited the experience of Joe Fanelli, a young protégé of Frankfurter's employed in the Social Security Administration. After enquiring about his job, the justice, true to character, advised him not to overstay his time in Washington but to return home.

> The next year, the same little ritual: "Go back to your home community." The third year, Fanelli was determined to break the monotony, and so when Brandeis said "Go back to your home community," Fanelli countered, "But Mr. Justice, my home community is New York city." Brandeis said, "That's your misfortune," and walked off.[15]

Several observers have noted that Alice Brandeis played an important role in carefully stage managing these encounters, especially in later years, partly to conserve her husband's dwindling resources of energy, and partly to ensure that he got to talk with as many people as he wished. He would be seated at one end of a sofa with his speaking companion of the moment placed next to him. "If she thought that one person was taking up too much of the Justice's time," recalled Freund, "she would come in and, quite without ceremony, wheel him away, or she'd bring up someone else to take his place, indicating it was time for a change." She also went out of her way to be kind to the clerks, taking a greater interest in their personal lives than her husband and inviting people to the apartment she thought they would like to meet. Moreover, in the early twenties, when her sisters were more frequent visitors and old friends from the campaigning days were rather more numerous in the assembled company, she had tended to provide them with a rival focus of attention, leaving a small semicircle of younger disciples and their wives to form up around her engaging spouse. "Though she gave signs of pleasure when this occurred," Acheson later recalled, "she kept it under strict control."

The justice, though, was always her main priority; she was seen to fuss over him "like a mother hen," and not only at the tea sessions. For example, whenever the weather turned inclement, she would take care to see that he was properly dressed—wearing rubber overshoes, scarf round his neck—to which regime, in Freund's recollection, he submitted himself "without a whimper." So it was in other matters too. For instance, Alice did not like him to have his hair cut; so while they were living at Stoneleigh Court, Brandeis got into the habit of visiting Charlie Laudano's barbershop in the basement twice a week, greeting its proprietor with the admonition: "Charlie, the invisible haircut!" In the domestic sphere at least, her word was a rule of law which all had to obey. At one Saturday afternoon conference of the Court that had dragged on rather longer than expected, Brandeis reportedly rose at 5:00 P.M. and addressed himself to the chief justice: "I am sorry, Mr. Chief Justice, but your jurisdiction has expired and that of Mrs. Brandeis has begun." Upon which he gathered up his papers and left.[16]

On the face of it, these accounts seem to provide us with a reasonable portrait of a much-respected elder statesmen, if not yet senile or decrepit, nonetheless slipping further into a cozy, quaint and sometimes cranky dotage as the twenties became the thirties. The anecdotes, so frequently retold, apparently testify to a marked hardening of the intellectual arteries and an increasing mental rigidity; at the same time, however, most seem to take for granted a continuing commitment to the established corpus of Progressive-liberal values familiar from earlier decades, and to something approaching the spiritual purity of the patriarch and prophet.

This is a picture susceptible to modest subversion, however. For one thing, Acheson's account of the Brandeis tea parties is alone in placing them squarely within their proper social context. The Washington in which this ritual became established was, after all, a place where stylish horse-drawn carriages still outnumbered cars: "a small, gangling southern city." In the early 1920s, the Brandeises would drive out every morning at ten o'clock sharp to take the air "in a smart runabout behind a handsome and spirited hackney." This steed was the romantically named Sir Gareth who, when eventually forced from the streets by the dangers of motorized traffic, would end his days on the Achesons' family farm in Maryland. It was this personal loss, as much as any profound social analysis, which hardened the justice's heart against the onrush of an "automobile culture" in the United States.

As for the teas themselves, as Dean Acheson explains, these were but the remnant of "a *fin de siècle* institution," which continued to be observed widely in the nation's capital during the 1920s.

This was the "at home" day of ranking ladies of our officialdom, when the rest of us paid respectful homage. Monday was always Supreme Court day. Cabinet wives, senatorial wives, high-ranking military wives at Fort Meyer and the Naval Observatory, each group had its day when cards were left . . . and ceremonial tea consumed. Most of these occasions were as tepid as the tea.

The justice and his wife were thus far from being in any sense innovative in their hosting of such gatherings. Again to quote Acheson's memories of 1920:

The Brandeises' "at home" was purposeful and austere. The hostess erect on a black horsehair sofa, presided at the tea table. Above her, an engraved tiger couchant, gazing off over pretty dreary country, evoked depressing memories of our dentist's waiting room. Two female acolytes, often my wife and another conscripted pupil of Mrs. Brandeis's weekly seminar on child education, assisted her. The current law clerk presented newcomers.

In short, a fairly typical "Edwardian" scene, presided over by a fairly typical "Edwardian" matron.[17]

Yet in some respects such appearances may be deceptive, because in
other ways the Brandeises were far from typical. For instance, Washington
at this date was not only a small town but also a racially segregated one. The
justice caused something of a stir, therefore, when on moving to a new
apartment in Florence Court West he insisted that Edward G. Poindexter,
the black Court messenger who also doubled as a family retainer, be
allowed to use the building's main elevator rather than the back stairs set
aside for "coloreds." Some, of course, might be tempted to dismiss this as a
feeble gesture toward equality, more or less on a par with his leading the
black maid Lizzie into the ocean at Mattapoisset in 1882; certainly, though-
out his long career, Brandeis never took a *public* stand on the issue of racial
discrimination. Moreover, when the National Association for the Advancement of Colored People (NAACP) approached him during the fall of 1914
concerning the operation of "Jim Crow" laws on interstate railroad cars, he
declined to investigate the situation in detail, pleading pressure of other
business.[18]

The limited advice that he was prepared to offer on that occasion does,
nevertheless, seem to suggest both an underlying sympathy with the plight
of America's blacks and a reason why he wished to avoid greater involvement. Having earlier proposed that petitions should be filed with the Interstate Commerce Commission, "seeking redress for failure to provide reasonable accommodations on such railroads as appeared to be particularly
serious offenders," he subsequently admitted to the NAACP's attorney that he
doubted whether the commission would be willing to "enter upon a general
investigation of conditions of service to colored people on interstate trains."
Though little discussed, race was already one of the most emotive issues in
American political life and calls to end discrimination fell on stubbornly deaf
ears, even in otherwise liberal circles. Brandeis's estimation of the Interstate
Commerce Commission's response may not have been especially heroic, but
it was realistic. What is more, at a personal level, he doubtless feared that
the open advocacy of so unpopular a cause would prove to be the graveyard
of his campaigning reputation. He therefore remained silent. The issue of
civil rights did not feature prominently in the Court's docket during his time
on the bench, and apart from casting votes against scandalous prejudice in
the Scottsboro cases he had few public occasions to distance himself from
outright bigotry. Only in private, where he possessed the power to make
small differences, were the ideals of his "uncle the abolitionist" called to
mind, impelling him to act as his conscience dictated.[19]

The justice and his wife were equally unusual in the way they brought up
their two daughters, Susan and Elizabeth. Prevented as much by poor health
as by the social conventions of her day from pursuing a career outside the
home, it was Alice who took the lead in raising the Brandeis girls to be
strong willed and independent. Both were "educated" as much by contact
with their parents and family friends as they were by formal schooling, and

each went on to achieve considerable academic and professional success. Susan took a law degree at the University of Chicago after graduating from Bryn Mawr College and entered legal practice in New York City, later becoming one of the first women to argue a case before the United States Supreme Court. Elizabeth went first to Radcliffe College and then, after five years spent working for the District of Columbia Minimum Wage Board, enrolled as a graduate student in economics at the University of Wisconsin, eventually obtaining her doctorate in 1928. She subsequently became one of the principal contributors to the monumental *History of Labor in the United States* (1918–35), edited by John Roger Commons, writing the section devoted to labor legislation for the years between 1896 and 1932. At a time, in short, when most women of their background and class were expected to content themselves with the acquisition of social and domestic accomplishments, both the Brandeis children were encouraged to identify fully with their parents' public interests and to pursue independent professional careers, even after marriage.[20]

At times, however, it had looked as if this progressive strategy might backfire, especially with their elder daughter. Entering law school during the Great War, Susan quickly adopted a decidedly Bohemian appearance and took up with a set of radical students opposed to America's involvement in the conflict. When she considered joining a peace group, and her boyfriend of the moment began talking about registration as a conscientious objector, the justice counseled them earnestly against taking any measure that might bring them into conflict with the law. But his disapproval was always tempered with affectionate concern. "Your happiness and worldly development . . . are my deep longing," he wrote in July 1917 once she had returned to Chicago after a particularly tense visit home. "Whatever I can do to advance them, you may rely upon. And yet I recognize how little there is that I can do." Explaining the situation to Alice, who had been staying with friends in Boston, he was even more resigned. "[S]he really does not belong to our world," he observed. "Perhaps it is really a kind of Providence leading her into another where she will fit better." Despite being painfully aware of what he considered to be her "many defects," Louis refused to interfere in her life. Likewise in 1925, when she announced her intention of marrying Jack Gilbert, a less than outstanding New York attorney, he regarded her choice as "unambitious" but still refrained from expressing open hostility. The advice contained in his frequent letters, however, was clearly intended to steer her toward an energetic career in public life. "You have been happily born into an age ripe for change," he told her on her birthday in 1919; "and your own horror of injustice properly beckons you to take an active part in effecting it." He did not consider her gender a bar to eventual success; only perhaps her impetuosity.

In laying your plans—bear in mind that time, the indispensable, is a potent factor—and that your own effectiveness is to be measured in terms of a life-time; —And that you should have before you half-a-century of persistent, well-directed effort with ever growing power and influence. Be not impatient of time spent educating yourself for the task, nor at the slowness of that education of others which must precede real progress. Patience is as necessary as persistence and the undeviating aim.

He was well aware that this all sounded "fearfully solemn" for a day that ought to be filled with "joy and sunshine"; but freely confessed that he could "never think of your future without this view of a noble, useful and significant life."

In any event, Susan managed to make a success of both her career and her marriage, delighting her father particularly by the enthusiasm that she and her husband later showed for the Zionist cause. These were not areas of the justice's life and complex psychological makeup into which his law clerks possessed much insight; however, they do nevertheless afford a helpful shift of perspective from which to consider his ideals and social outlook.[21]

Yet another means of getting behind the Brandeis mystique is provided by examining the recollections of those who found themselves less than enthraled by it. One such hold-out, as we have already seen, was David Riesman, who, admittedly with the benefit of hindsight, would recall a rather less cozy image of his former chief than that presented by his other secretaries. The justice did not discuss his socioeconomic ideas with Riesman at all, and whatever sense of his thinking the latter was able to form depended entirely on his being present when Brandeis was talking to others. What he thought he detected in his boss was an implacable hostility toward the rich and the stylish, and particularly toward big business. "There was a strong Populist strain in his thought, as expressed in his writings and in his early vision of himself as the 'people's advocate,'" he remembered, and that led him to regard ordinary folk in a romantic and idealized light. This was in sharp contrast to the greater realism of Felix Frankfurter, often regarded as the justice's alter ego, whose experience of the Palmer Raids after World War I and the Sacco-Vanzetti case in the 1920s had left him acutely aware of "how 'the people' could behave." Yet Riesman could find in Brandeis no trace of any sentimental affection for the down-trodden, and his interpretation of the anecdotal evidence is a good deal less charitable than that of his peers:

> There was also in Brandeis a punitive and even a bloodthirsty side. It outraged him that those on unemployment insurance in Detroit could smoke cigarettes and be able to drive cars. In fact, with his anti-urban bias, he would just as soon have seen Detroit disappear. Another aspect of what the British call bloody-mindedness came out dramatically one time when he was visited by Harold Laski. He told the latter, to the latter's shock, that he hoped that the Nazis and the British would all kill each other. The reason for his hatred for both was rooted in his Zionism. . . . Early on in my experience with Justice Brandeis, I had the nerve to tell him that I

thought Zionism was a form of Jewish fascism. He said I did not know anything about Jewish history, which was quite correct, and he refused to discuss the subject further.

Nevertheless, Riesman did manage to formulate his own impression of Brandeis's general philosophy. "I had in college come across the Southern Agrarians," he explained in 1981, "and shared their generally culturally conservative and politically decentralist outlook. In thinking of Justice Brandeis both at the time I was with him and later, I have always defined him as a Southern Agrarian." As illustrated by their essay collection *I'll Take My Stand* (1930), the Southern Agrarians were social conservatives, whose assertion of bucolic, "Jeffersonian" values seemed to find an echo in the justice's own enthusiasm for the rural conservation programs of the TVA. Indeed, Brandeis wanted Riesman to go to Tupelo, Mississippi, "and work on behalf of the Southern Agrarian reforms sponsored by the TVA"; however, the latter disappointed him by declaring his intention of returning to work with Professor Carl Friedrich of Harvard's Government Department, while practicing law for a year with a Boston firm. "His attitude," he recalled, "was that as somebody who had had many advantages, I should go to a place which needed those advantages, such as Tupelo. . . . All my interest in the art and music and general culture of Boston he considered decadent."

On a broader front, he believed that the justice was essentially hostile to the objectives of the Roosevelt administration. While conceding that Brandeis's predilection for participatory democracy and individual self-reliance could be "thought of as ultra-Left in some anarchist and individualist constellations," he was adamant that this was not the intellectual context of the 1930s:

> the arguments that swirled about the New Deal . . . were between federalizers and states' righters. The former were those who thought of themselves as on the Left. And in the Washington of the New Deal, it was protégés of Felix Frankfurter, as well as academics from Columbia and Yale, who were almost without exception— indeed, I cannot think of an exception—federalizers. A number were either openly or . . . covertly Stalinist, impatient with the liberal centralizers for not moving fast enough. . . . I knew no socialists who were not centralizers, even though they were Social Democrats. . . . Thus it is in the context of the centralizing impulses of the New Deal, combined with his scorn if not hatred for Felix Frankfurter's admired Franklin D. Roosevelt, that Brandeis appeared "reactionary."

For his own part, thought Riesman, the justice was looking to a very different kind of future from that held out by the New Dealers: one in which rural life and the small-town community might be revivified. "He would have liked to see a country of self-reliant yeomen and small artisans." It was to further these aspirations, he believed, that Brandeis supported schemes like TVA. He really cared about the fabric of rural society. Riesman recalled being introduced by him to the Rust brothers, inventors of the mechanical cotton-picker; he remembered also the justice's efforts at persuading them not to put it on the market "because he feared the uprooting of Southern sharecroppers and small farmers were it to come into wide use."[22]

It is not necessary to agree with every detail of Riesman's analysis to appreciate the importance of the interpretative issues that it raises. For the composite picture of Brandeis that he presents is far removed from that painted by those of the justice's law clerks who muster in the respect-bordering-on-worship school. The Brandeis we are offered here is a "conservative decentralist," whose deep concern to uphold states' rights and preserve the social values of small-scale, rural communities imbued him not only with a pronounced anti-urban prejudice, but also with a real and lasting antipathy toward the centralizing thrust of the New Deal. Furthermore, he continued to be, for good measure, a fervent Zionist; a man who hated the British as much as he did the Nazis; and whose domestic ideology had little to distinguish it from that of other Southern conservative intellectuals. None of these alleged facets of his makeup can be dismissed out of hand; all of them will have to be addressed more or less squarely in the pages that follow.

We need, then, to reconsider in some detail the substantive elements of Brandeis's social vision; to identify with greater precision than hitherto his requirements for civilized living; to discover what, in short, his hopes for the future of mankind really were. To begin with, his strictures about institutional scale and his forthright advocacy of small competitive units were not confined to, nor were they directed primarily toward, the rural and agrarian context in which Riesman places them. Neither, happily, do they have to be assessed in isolation; for as the justice himself indicated to economist Emanuel Goldenweiser in a 1934 interview, his views on the efficiency of small units, indeed his entire socioeconomic outlook, had to be understood in the wider context of his ideas about democracy and the prime objective of encouraging human potentiality to the fullest possible extent. His thinking in these areas was predicated on a belief in the desirability of decentralized, local development, and the participation of individual citizens in decisions that affected their own lives. Acheson was thus absolutely correct when he wrote of Brandeis in 1920:

> He believes that when all is said the effect of any man's life is imperceptible except where it is combined with the lives of a handful of chosen spirits in a community which is not too big to be moved. He denies any validity in large units and says that differentiated communities will be the measure above which our civilization cannot rise.

Just precisely what the justice had in mind when he spoke of a nation of "differentiated communities" has been explored obliquely in earlier chapters, and will be considered more directly in due course. For the moment let us confine our attention to his ideas concerning the nature of democracy itself.[23]

In its mature form, his conception of political liberty was indeed, as many observers have suggested, decidedly Jeffersonian in its configuration. He was profoundly suspicious of power concentrated in the hands of a narrow elite, and he distrusted all those ("the world's wise") who claimed the right to direct and control the lives of others, be it on the basis of wealth, breeding, or expertise. Yet as we have seen, this had not always been his attitude; for in the early years of his manhood, he had felt a strong inclination to side with those in positions of authority. "I trusted only expert opinion," he admitted to a journalist-interviewer in 1913, adding ruefully that "experience of life" had made him democratic. "I began to see that many things sanctioned by expert opinion were wrong." He then went on to cite unemployment, particularly as caused by the irregularity of work, as an example of the kind of thing he had in mind.

He was aware, nonetheless, that thinking along these lines was far from universal; that despite the ubiquity of democratic forms and libertarian rhetoric, real power in the United States, certainly economic power, was vested in relatively few hands. Thus it must be stressed that his celebration of democracy and the central position reserved for it within his system of social thought was not merely a pious evocation of the American way of life: something that every citizen could take for granted. On the contrary, it represented a tenuous ideal to which most Americans had little hope of attaining. Only a fundamental reordering of the dynamic relationships within American society could make this ideal a reality for the majority of ordinary working people. "What a democracy demands," he told Frankfurter in 1934, "is not necessarily 'distribution of wealth'—but 'distributing power': consumer power, economic power, political power and the power of human creative development."[24]

Yet it was not sufficient either to put one's trust in the "masses" over the "classes"; for if democracy implied rights, it also imposed responsibilities. As far as Brandeis was concerned, democracy was less an abstract concept in political theory than a concrete proposal for conducting the affairs of men in the real world, and as such made weighty demands on the intelligence and commitment of all who would make it work. "Democracy in any sphere is a serious undertaking," he counseled in 1922, and proceeded to detail its obligations:

It substitutes self-restraint for external restraint. It is more difficult to maintain than to achieve. It demands continuous sacrifice by the individual and more exigent obedience to the moral law than any other form of government. Success in any democratic undertaking must proceed from the individual. It is possible only where the process of perfecting the individual is pursued. His development is attained mainly in the processes of common living.

Most important of all, though, he realized that in a civilized society true democracy could not be equated with each and every whimsical expression of the general will as molded by rabble-rousing demagogues or mediated by prejudiced legislative majorities. He shared with Aristotle and the other political philosophers of Ancient Greece the realistic apprehension that when defined in this way, democracy could all too readily degenerate into abject tyranny. What, then, did he regard as the essential features of a democratic society; and, once one were established, how was its vitality to be preserved?[25]

Part of the answer to these questions—and in the American context it was a large part—lay in the willingness of all citizens to accept, and function within, the framework of republican contraints set out in the federal Constitution. The concept of "government under law," he believed, was not intended to prevent the nation's legislative and judicial institutions from operating flexibly; neither did it preclude the need for politicians and judges to approach every new social situation with all the resourcefulness and creative experimentation they could muster. Its proper function, in fact, was twofold: to establish fixed rules of procedure for handling socioeconomic conflicts, regardless of the specific guise in which each appeared; and to define more or less precisely a series of legal rights considered so fundamental to civil society that neither temporary expediency nor the mere weight of numbers would be thought sufficient reason to set them lightly aside.

In Brandeis's view, however, constitutional government was not just a piece of impersonal machinery for the automatic settling of disputes or the enforcement of consensual values; it was a delicate, organic structure, whose potential for development and growth depended less on the wisdom of those actively involved in administration than on the good sense and intelligence of an informed general public. It was this perception that, in 1920 at least, led him to hold Great Britain in especially high regard. "England is joyously interesting," he informed Dean Acheson while getting ready to return home from the Zionist conference in London. "The struggle onward is proceeding intelligently and in good temper. Public opinion is an omnipresent potent factor; and one feels himself in a land where there is real democracy, manfully applied." He was clearly no more in sympathy with the ideas about the direct implementation of popular sovereignty then in vogue among American liberals than he had been when decrying similar mechanisms in his lectures at the Massachusetts Institute of Technology twenty-eight years earlier. As he told his clerk, there were

> None of your "democratic facades" here—nor constitutional cure-alls of initiative, referendum and recall or primary elections—and like machinery, as a substitute for thought and attention to matters of public interest. I would swap the whole job-lot of them for a few letters to the Times, backed by the determined spirit of men who protest when their supposed rights are being infringed upon.

Not that England was a hot-bed of radicalism; in fact, there was "very little real redness." However, as he noted wryly, "most of the British world are dyed with a very faint pink which color blind Americans might take for scarlet."[26]

In light of such opinions it is hardly surprising that he placed a high priority on the need for a good standard of public education in its widest sense. As the young David Riesman observed, Brandeis had considerable faith in the potential of most ordinary people for self-improvement and personal development. "For him the separation of powers is not only the means for assuring freedom but a device for giving the maximum number of citizens an opportunity for creative responsibilities." He felt it was the duty of reformers to prepare the people for their role; thus his approach to education was essentially democratic as well. "Unlike most of my Harvard friends," continued Riesman, "his emphasis would not be on the good standing but on the average, an average which is capable of being raised. He is not interested in bettering the supposed best as much as in improving the supposed mediocre." Yet as the Great Depression demonstrated only too clearly, the issues facing governments in industrial society were both complicated in their ramifications and inherently difficult to understand, even for experts. Undaunted by the difficulty of explaining such complexities to the general public, perhaps because he feared the alternatives even more, the elderly justice stuck to his guns. "We might as well abdicate on democracy," he told Frankfurter candidly in 1932, "if we are unwilling to take up the task of educating the American people on fundamental problems."[27]

As Riesman also noted in the memorandum he wrote for Frankfurter in 1936, the justice possessed "an extraordinary faith in the possibilities of human development." He thought of men more or less equal in their potentialities; where they differed, he believed, was in their advantages. The need, therefore, from a reformist standpoint anyway, was to afford the maximum number of people not only the abstraction of freedom but something more concrete as well: "an opportunity for creative responsibilities." This meant achieving democracy in the workplace as well as in public life. Brandeis had long viewed the trend toward institutional giantism as the most baleful factor operating in modern American life, and this in turn had led him irresistibly toward the forthright advocacy of both worker and consumer cooperatives, and thence into the uncharted rigors of a thorough-going industrial democracy.[28]

Not that he envisaged workers controlling the means of production in traditional leftist terms: Neither state ownership nor syndicalism held any attractions for him whatever. Industrial councils and profit-sharing schemes were much more to his liking. Key to any new institutional arrangement, however, was the improvement of the workingman himself. During the years of Progressive optimism before the war, Brandeis had readily embraced the notion that a higher material standard of living for American workers would necessarily involve further mechanization, and, subject to democratic controls, the widespread application of scientific-management techniques as well. By these means, he believed, physical well-being could be secured and spiritual growth promoted—both within a societal framework dependent on the successful harmonization of industrial efficiency and workers' choices. In fact, the theoretical balance between economic advantage and social acceptability implicit in this model was rarely found operating in practice, and the idealized clarity of his abstractions frequently bore little or no resemblance to the harsh realities of modern industrial capitalism: a fact that he himself belatedly came to realize.

The steel and coal strikes of 1919 brought those realities into sharp focus and were to prove something of a watershed in the development of his thinking on these issues. At first he seemed confident that an outcome guaranteeing workers the right to organize and negotiate freely with their employers was a foregone conclusion. "The struggle for rights is over," Acheson recorded him as saying in October, as Judge Elbert H. Gary of U.S. Steel agreed to participate in an industrial conference. "They are now recognized as much as anything ever is in a world where you cannot expect unanimity. The thing to preach now is the correlative duty to one's mates and to the job." When the talks collapsed, however, his confidence began to waver; and when reports began coming in of a police crack-down against labor and socialist groups connected with the strike, he confessed himself "deeply humiliated and filled with a sense of sin that we with the greatest possibilities of any people should waste ourselves on these age-old methods of oppression."

His principal fear was that such crude attempts to smash union organization might serve to "drive labor into radical leadership." By the end of November, with the coal situation worsening daily, Acheson was prophesying revolution and even the justice was growing pessimistic about the outcome. "There will be a reaction of protest all right," he agreed. "The situation is forcing it. We are being governed by a set of insane men—inanity [sic] is not the word for this sort of thing. They have lost all power to see and weigh consequences." A day later, though, he had recovered something of his equilibrium. When his clerk asked whether he thought there was still a way out, he replied: "Yes, and the men will find it, if only their money holds out and the west freezes for a couple of weeks." As for the injunctions taken out against the strikers, he considered these of little account:

> They can't arrest everyone. I wish they would get out four thousand injunctions and see that they are all perfectly useless. We shall never get anything better until

our people are convinced of that. The conduct of the miners has been most wonderful—every possible provocation, all the forces of the Government, capital and the press against them, and yet they have kept their heads and maintained perfect order. It's wonderful!

To his boss's repeated insistence that all would be well, provided the money held out, Acheson answered that he was "an incurable optimist." "Oh, yes. Oh, yes," came back the rejoinder.[29]

This interesting exchange provides an ideal backdrop against which to interpret not only Brandeis's reasoning in the numerous unionization cases coming before the Supreme Court in the early twenties but also the more considered suggestions aimed at ending industrial conflict that he sent to Felix Frankfurter in the fall of 1922. The court cases will be considered shortly. His peace proposals were formulated in the midst of a new round of strikes in the mines and on the railways, prompted by management attempts to impose wage cuts. The justice's general position was made clear from the start. Once the present disputes were ended, he wrote,

a rational people should begin to think how a recurrence of like situations can be prevented. Clearly it is not by prohibiting strikes by compulsory arbitration or by crippling trade unions. It is not by physical force or by legal coercions. As long as these industries are privately owned or operated strikes in them must be permitted; and, even if publicly owned and operated, their employees must be free to join the unions. The promise of better conditions lies in industrial sanitation, not dosing.

In this regard, he had two specific recommendations to offer. First, it was essential that trade unionism "should be frankly accepted and all war upon it, direct and indirect, by employers must cease." Second, the use of private detectives and armed guards by employers should be prohibited, and their right to enjoin the actions of their work force discontinued, forthwith. "Civil redress by the employer should be had only through action for damages; and violations of criminal law should be vigorously prosecuted." These steps, he believed, would bring several immediate benefits to the industrial relations scene. Most of the causes of discontent would be swept away, especially "the general conviction that the powers of the government are perverted by and in aid of the employers"; at the same time, a necessary "belief in the impartiality of courts" would be restored. More important, once stripped of the "delusive protection" presently afforded by equitable relief and the tactics of physical confrontation, management would be forced to sit down with workers and to discuss the outstanding differences between them in a "constructive" fashion. "Nine-tenths of the injustices of which workers complain in the country," Brandeis argued, "could be removed by persistent application of the inventive mind to the situations involved in the relation of Employer & Employee. But for the delusive 'easier way,' necessity would again prove itself the mother of social-industrial invention."

If such a climate of cooperation could be generated, capital as well as labor could expect to gain from the new arrangements, because the losses to employers, and to the community at large, previously resulting from arbitrary behavior on the part of unions would be greatly reduced. But in any event, society was entitled to look to its own interests and to protect itself as best it could from all excesses, whichever side of industry was responsible for them. "Investors of ordinary prudence have learned to insure against accident, error and wrongdoing by not putting all their eggs in one basket," the justice explained. "But our unreasoned passion for bigness and for integration has led us to disregard in social-industrial life that wise warning." The answer, he believed, lay in a different set of priorities: "in diversity, in decentralization, financial and territorial, with protective federations, in maintaining independent supplies of substitutes." The potential for "arbitrariness on the part of coal barons or miners" should be balanced, as far as possible, by the development of alternative sources of energy such as hydroelectric power, oil, or natural gas. Similarly, those expecting to be held to ransom in the event of arbitrary action on the railroads should seek protection in the enhancement of "water transportation, the trolley, the auto and the air service."

In all of these proposals, Brandeis had a single objective in view: to restrict "the field of necessary conflicts of interest between employers and employees . . . to relatively small and hence manageable proportions." However, if, in exceptional cases, "adjustment as a result of negotiation" should prove unattainable, the proper solution, he insisted, lay not in a resort to physical or legal force but in "passive resistance."

> The remedy for the arbitrary demand of an excessive price for an article or service is doing without. Employers and consumers must have courage and must exhibit their powers of endurance when emergencies arise. Walls, mercenaries and laws have never succeeded in affording for long protection to a fear-ridden, comfort-loving people. Employer and consumer must show that they love justice and independence more than they do goods or ease. In the exercise of these qualities, the true preparedness indicated above, and vigorous enforcement of the criminal law if need be, lies the democratic way out.[30]

Freed from bitter disputes that warped their judgment and prevented their moral development, he believed, workingmen could at last focus their attention on increasing output and thus improving the quality of their lives. At first, as indicated earlier, he appeared to regard the embracing of higher levels of technology as an essential part of this developmental process; however, by the early 1920s, with the wide extension of production-line working and fully automatic processes, his support for technical advance was beginning to grow more qualified. To Harold Laski he spoke critically of "our unbounded faith in the efficiency of machinery and our worship of the false god of Bigness"; and through Frankfurter he sought to encourage the

New Republic to ascertain "whether [the] prevailing tendency toward labor saving is really cost saving." With increased plant charges for interest, repairs, depreciation, and obsolescence, with frequent failure to operate at full capacity, and the increased expense of organization and supervision, he suspected that unit costs might not be reduced to the degree that manufacturers generally hoped. Might not "the limit of machinery & organization efficiency in substitutions for human labor . . . have been exceeded"? His intuition told him to be pessimistic: "The tendency toward substitution of machine-tenders for skilled operatives etc. is certainly anti-social. I doubt whether (except in factories like Ford's) it is not, in large measure, also uneconomic." Henry Ford was in any case "a genius & a 'sport', the exception which tends to prove the rule." Brandeis was not alone, of course, in worrying about the possibilities of technological unemployment; however, if his microeconomic concerns now seem narrow and unnecessarily gloomy, his social apprehensions were both humane and prophetic.[31]

Although Brandeis was by no means an uncritical supporter of every action undertaken by trade-union activists during the 1920s, neither was he in any sense hostile to what he considered the legitimate demand of workers to play a part in the running of the companies that employed them. Indeed, with regard to what he considered the pressing need for a massive extension of industrial democracy in America, his views changed little between the testimony he gave to the Industrial Relations Commission in 1915 and the onset of the Great Depression some fifteen years later. Indeed, the publication of Berle and Means's *The Modern Corporation and Private Property* (1932) seemed to provide a quantified analysis of the economic concentration he had always feared. His dissenting opinion in *Liggett Company v. Lee*, delivered in the following year, would cite their finding that a quarter of the nation's wealth was controlled directly by 200 nonbanking corporations, and that these in turn, though nominally controlled by some 2,000 directors, were in practice dominated by a few hundred individuals. This, he insisted, was "the negation of industrial democracy." Moreover, other writers had shown that, coincident with the growth of these giant corporations, a pronounced concentration of personal wealth had also occurred. The resultant maldistribution of wealth and income had served to paralyze initiative and lessen human happiness; most serious of all, it had been one of the principal causes of the nation's devastating economic slump. There was a widespread belief, declared Brandeis,

> that by the control which the few have exerted through giant corporations, individual initiative and effort are being paralysed, creative power impaired and human happiness lessened; that the true prosperity of our past came not from big business, but through the courage, the energy and the resourcefulness of small men; that only by releasing from corporate control the faculties of the unknown many, only by reopening to them the opportunities for leadership, can confidence in our future be restored and the existing misery be overcome; and that only

through participation by the many in the responsibilities and determinations of business can Americans secure the moral and intellectual development which is essential to the maintenance of liberty.[32]

One little-noticed aspect of the *Liggett* dissent was its concluding emphasis of the attractions of cooperative enterprise as an alternative to corporate capitalism. The Florida anti-chain-store statute that gave rise to the case had itself taken notice of the recent growth of cooperative merchandizing, and in setting its license-fee rates had formally recognized the desirable features of this phenomenon. Moreover, Brandeis maintained that the state's legislators had been fully entitled to do so, because it was a legitimate exercise of their reserved powers to establish, preserve, or bring to an end whatever social or economic institutions they chose. They could, if they wished, control giant corporations as they now controlled public utilities, or they could engage in business on their own account. Indeed, this did not exhaust the possibilities open to them, for to "Americans seeking escape from corporate domination" there remained available "under the Constitution another form of social and economic control—one more in keeping with our traditions and aspirations." This was the "way of co-operation," which Brandeis saw as leading

> directly to the freedom and the equality of opportunity which the Fourteenth Amendment aims to secure. That way is clearly open. For the fundamental difference between capitalistic enterprise and the co-operative—between economic absolutism and industrial democracy—is one which has been commonly accepted by legislatures and the courts as justifying discrimination in both regulation and taxation.

In footnotes compiled by Paul Freund the justice provided his readers not only with an appropriate legal citation in support of this contention, but also with a long and comprehensive bibliography of recent writing on the subject of cooperation that included Laski's 1928 classic: *The Recovery of Citizenship*.[33]

In fact, Brandeis's interest in the cooperative movement had a long history. During the Progressive period he had kept a file on the subject, the earliest item in which was the program of a meeting held in Boston's Faneuil Hall at the beginning of 1904 "for the purpose of organizing a co-operative exchange"; whether he attended himself is uncertain. He did, though, assist employees of the New Haven Railroad to organize several cooperative stores, and by 1911 could describe himself as "a thorough believer in consumers' cooperation." Much of his motivation, echoed subsequently in the *Liggett* opinion, came from a deeply felt hostility toward the rapid development of retail chains. "I value the cooperative association," he wrote at the year's close, "not merely as reducing the cost of living, but as eliminating in part the evil of capitalistic exploitation"; and he went on to cite the recent merger of two drugstore chains as a prime example of what could be expected from the arrival of bigness in retail marketing. It is clear that he saw the cooperative movement as a means of reversing this disturbing trend. Eighteen months later, therefore, he was greatly encouraged by a magazine article that argued that in several European countries the center firms of several industries had been forced to offer more favorable terms to their customers solely on account of the competition engendered by cooperative producers and wholesalers.[34]

His most comprehensive statement on the future development of cooperative enterprise came in the first of a series of memoranda which he sent to Felix Frankfurter in September 1922 as a suggested policy platform for the *New Republic*. Entitled "What to do about Capitalism," it encapsulated in a few terse pages all the major strands of his mature thought about economic issues. It began with a striking testament of liberal faith:

> We recognize the evils and abuses of Capitalism. But we do not believe in Communism; we do not believe in State Socialism; and we do not believe in Guild Socialism. We do believe in consumer cooperation. But we also believe that private capital has now and at least for a long time to come must have an important part to play in the best development of America and its ideals. We believe that the part of private capital may be a beneficent one and should be confined in a sphere which is desirable or necessary.

This being said, it soon became clear that the role he envisaged for consumer cooperatives was a wide one, extending into "every field of commerce, industry, finance or service" where it was or might become feasible. "So far as it can, from time to time, supersede privately owned businesses," he wrote, "it should be encouraged to do so. It is essentially democratic." It put the consumer in control of the market, and by so doing helped develop in him a vital sense of responsibility. Properly conducted, he maintained, such enterprises would "eliminate wastes & particularly the excessive spread between cost of production and price to the consumer."

For similar reasons, producer cooperatives ought to be encouraged. "They limit the power of the capitalists and of the middle man," he asserted, "and lessen the abuses common in the use of private capital." They achieved this "by enabling small private capitalists, like the consumers, to help themselves." They too were democratic, distributing "the responsibility, as well as the right to profits, among those directly interested as producers," thereby promoting their personal development. "Ultimately," he believed, "the producers' cooperatives to a large extent merge into consumers' cooperatives, that is, the consumers through their cooperatives should become also producers." To facilitate this and other desirable outcomes, the third sphere of operations in which he saw an important role developing for cooperation was banking. By the widespread use of cooperative banks and credit unions, he insisted, "the menacing power" of America's financiers might be lessened. Once again the principal appeal of such institutions was seen as lying in their inherently democratic features: "The direct gains from the capital go to those whose capital is used. The owners of the capital have the ultimate responsibility for its proper use. And the responsibility develops those upon whom it rests." In short, for Brandeis, support for cooperation was a logical progression from positions he had first adumbrated in *Other People's Money* almost a decade before.[35]

That cooperation held out a valid social alternative to corporate capitalism, he seems to have had no doubts, and in *Frost v. Corporation Commission of Oklahoma* (1929) he addressed the issue squarely with reference to the two kinds of organization—stock and nonstock corporations—established under state laws to further the development of agricultural cooperation. As he saw it, farmers sought through both mechanisms "to secure a more efficient system of production and distribution and a more equitable allocation of benefits." But this "was not their only purpose," for by these methods they hoped "to socialize their interests" as well as to promote their own financial advantage; "to require an equitable assumption of responsibilities while assuring an equitable distribution of benefits." In short, the farmers' aim was "economic democracy on lines of liberty, equality and fraternity." Brandeis then proceeded to explain how, in order to "accomplish these objectives, both types of co-operative corporations [*sic*] provide for *excluding capitalist control*. As means to this end, both provide for restriction of voting privileges, for curtailment of return on capital and for distribution of gains or savings through patronage dividends or equivalent devices." The whole tone of this dissent indicates that he thought highly of such mechanisms as constituting a useful antidote to the worst excesses of competitive business activity.[36]

In view of what has just been said, it will come as little surprise that the justice received with enthusiasm *The Recovery of Citizenship*—a detailed study of the cooperative movement written by Harold Laski, which, as noted earlier, was to feature prominently in the footnotes of his *Liggett* dissent. "You have dealt with a much neglected field," he told its author toward the end of 1928, "and perhaps the most important of all, economically and politically." He was especially cheered by the book's reference to the most recent successes of cooperation, and concluded: "In most instruments of social-economic advance the credits have set against them debits—sometimes heavy ones. In the Cooperatives there are only credits;—and the problem is merely one of occupying the field, and of overcoming defects, of perfecting the instrument."[37]

Nevertheless, despite the socioeconomic potential he considered immanent in cooperative forms of organization, Brandeis was well aware throughout the 1920s that, for the time being at any rate, the most pernicious obstacle to the implementation of greater industrial democracy was not the remaining imperfections of cooperation but the barely legitimate status of

American labor unions in the eyes of the law. Beginning in the 1890s, and continuing for more than four decades thereafter, the federal courts led by the Supreme Court itself intervened repeatedly in the industrial relations field with a clear and consistent object in view: to define and restrict the occasions on which, the reasons for which, and the tactics by which combinations of workers might lawfully take action against their employers. To achieve this goal, the courts not only drew heavily on common-law rules designed in a simpler age to protect property against "maliciously inflicted harm," but likewise distorted the purposes of more recent antitrust legislation by defining hitherto accepted forms of labor organization and activity as conspiracies in restraint of trade. Furthermore, these judicial determinations were generally obtained neither in the course of criminal proceedings nor by civil suits for damages but by means of prophylactic injunctions issued according to the ancient principles of equity, any violation of which rendered union leaders liable to fine or imprisonment for contempt without recourse to a jury trial.[38]

As might be anticipated from what we already know about his views, Brandeis was at odds with his Supreme Court colleagues on a wide variety of labor-related issues. Though he spoke for his brethren in *Dorchy v. Kansas* (1926), by holding that "a strike may be illegal because of its purpose" and that "neither the common law nor the Fourteenth Amendment confers the absolute right to strike," he was generally more convinced than they by the need to treat labor's aspirations sympathetically and to define its proper sphere of action broadly. As regards the "restraint of trade" argument, he reminded the Court in *Bedford Cut Stone Company v. Journeymen Stone Cutters' Association* (1927) that only "*unreasonable* restraints upon interstate commerce" were outlawed under the Sherman Act, and that as in other contentious areas a proper definition of "reasonableness" could only be reached "by the application of common law principles as administered in the federal courts, unaffected by State legislation or decisions." Dissenting in the case at bar, he left his fellow justices in no doubt about his own perception of what was at stake. "If a small craft of workmen," he wrote, "may be enjoined from refraining to work upon materials prepared in shops in another State operated by employers of the same craft, combined in as association aggressively opposed to the union, then Congress created by the Sherman Law and the Clayton Act an instrument for imposing restraints upon labor which remind of involuntary servitude."[39]

Although Brandeis wrote many opinions on labor issues during his years on the bench, two in particular from the early twenties are worthy of closer consideration. In *Duplex Printing Press Company v. Deering* (1921) he dissented vehemently from a majority ruling that the Clayton Act's attempted guarantee of the right to strike or picket did not extend to "secondary" disputes, and that therefore an injunction when sought could lawfully issue. As we have already seen, and as Alexander Bickel has correctly observed,

"Brandeis believed that some control needed to be exercised over labor's methods of economic warfare. But the heart of the matter for him was that the problem was properly a legislative one": a point made crystal clear in the concluding paragraph of his dissenting opinion in the case. "Because I have come to the conclusion," he wrote,

> that both the common law of a State and a statute of the United States [i.e., the Clayton Act] declare the right of industrial combatants to push their struggle to the limits of the justification of self-interest, I do not wish to be understood as attaching any constitutional or moral sanction to that right. All rights are derived from the purposes of the society in which they exist; above all rights rises duty to the community. The conditions developed in industry may be such that those engaged in it cannot continue their struggle without danger to the community. But it is not for judges to determine whether such conditions exist, nor is it their function to set the limits of permissible contest and to declare the duties which the new situation demands. This is the function of the legislature which, while limiting individual and group rights of aggression and defense, may substitute processes of justice for the more primitive method of trial by combat.[40]

In 1913, though, even before the passage of the Clayton Act, the first Arizona legislature had chosen to act in this area by undertaking to prevent the courts of that state from enjoining the right of workers to strike or picket peacefully against their employers, setting aside in the process a common-law prohibition against picketing previously enforced within its boundaries. In the case of *Truax v. Corrigan*, twice argued before the Supreme Court and ultimately decided at the end of 1921, this statute was declared invalid as being a violation of both the due process and equal protection clauses of the Fourteenth Amendment. Angered especially by Chief Justice Taft's use of the equal protection clause, which he later characterized as "dreadful," and by the unequivocal use of the term "property" to describe business activity, Brandeis focused on three principal issues in his dissent: the conditions ordinarily operating to limit the rights of employers, the wide diversity of legal rules governing relations between employer and employee, and the freedom of state legislatures to extend or curtail the availability of equitable remedies as they saw fit.

Regarding the first, he readily accepted the existence of a legal right to carry on a business for profit, as well as the subsidiary rights of securing and retaining customers, setting the price of goods or services sold, and buying "merchandise and labor" likewise at an appropriate price. "This right to carry on a business—be it called liberty or property—has value," he maintained; "and he who interferes with the right without cause renders himself liable." Where cause existed, though, such rights could not only be interfered with but in certain circumstances might even be destroyed. Competitors might "make inroads upon his trade"; suppliers or workers might do the same upon his profits.

What methods and means are permissible in this struggle of contending forces is determined in part by decisions of the courts, in part by acts of the legislatures. The rules governing the contest necessarily change from time to time. For conditions change; and, furthermore, the rules evolved, *being merely experiments in government*, must be discarded when they prove to be failures.

When such changes affected relations between employers and their work force, some abridgement of the standards of liberty or property then prevailing was inevitable; but their enactment remained, notwithstanding, a legitimate use of the police powers reserved to the several states, and might only be ruled invalid on due process grounds if adjudged arbitrary or unreasonable in a court of law. Viewed in the light of "the contemporary conditions—social, industrial, and political—of the community to be affected," and the wide disparities of existing practice and interpretation between different states with reference to the legality of strikes, picketing, boycotts, and the like, the Arizona statute did not appear to him either arbitrary or unreasonable. Neither could changes relating exclusively to employers and employees such as those contained in it be held "violative of the equal protection clause, merely because the liberty or property of individuals in other relations to each other (for instance, as competitors in trade or as vendor and purchaser) would not, under similar circumstances, be subject to like abridgement. Few laws," declared Brandeis emphatically, were "of universal application." Indeed, it was a characteristic of the Anglo-American legal tradition that it "dealt not with man in general, but with him in relationships." Consequently, he was clear in his own mind that "a peculiar relationship of individuals" was a sufficient "legal basis for classification," and fully capable of satisfying the requirements imposed on states by the Fourteenth Amendment.[41]

Perhaps the most far-reaching result of the Court's reactionary stance in relation to labor disputes—a stance exemplified by Taft's holding in *Truax v. Corrigan*—was the final elimination of Brandeis's earlier enthusiasm for judicial law making via the creative application of equitable procedures. As we observed when considering the initial orientation he received from his teachers at Harvard, he had been especially impressed by Professor Charles Smith Bradley, formerly chief justice of the State of Rhode Island, who stressed the importance of equity pleading within the framework of America's common-law tradition. He had also imbibed from Bradley an early prejudice against the use of juries in civil suits, preferring to rely instead on he professional competence of judges. Over the years, however, he had grown increasingly suspicious of judge-made law, and at the same time had come to appreciate that, although the principles of equity might well facilitate the attainment of justice when used on behalf of the weak and oppressed, they might just as readily serve to frustrate it when applied on behalf of powerful vested interests.[42]

Discussing the vexed question of labor injunctions in his *Truax* dissent, Brandeis addressed the problem in large part by means of indirection, many of his most telling points being couched as the mere rehearsal of a long-running controversy. Once the use of such injunctions became "extensive and conspicuous" in the mid-1890s, he wrote:

> The equitable remedy, although applied in accordance with established practice, involved incidents which, it was asserted, endangered the personal liberty of wage-earners. The acts enjoined were frequently, perhaps usually, acts which were already crimes at common law or had been made so by statutes. . . . The effect of the proceeding upon the individual was substantially the same as if he had been successfully prosecuted for a crime; but he was denied, in the course of the equity proceedings, those rights which by the Constitution are commonly secured to persons charged with a crime.

Typically, an alleged and usually insignificant danger to property was exploited so as to expedite the often cumbersome processes of the criminal law, thereby denying to individuals the substantive and procedural protections guaranteed them by the Bill of Rights. Judges not only usurped the proper functions of the jury, but frequently of the police department and the legislature as well, incidentally abridging constitutional rights "to free speech, to a free press, and to peaceful assembly" as they did so.

> It was urged that the real motive in seeking the injunction was not ordinarily to prevent property from being injured nor to protect the owner in its use, but to endow property with active, militant power which would make it dominant over men. In other words, that, under the guise of protecting property rights, the employer was seeking sovereign power. And many disinterested men, solicitous only for the public welfare, believed that the law of property was not appropriate for dealing with the forces beneath social unrest; that in this vast struggle it was unwise to throw the power of the State on one side or the other according to principles deduced from that law; that the problem of the control and conduct of industry demanded a solution of its own; and that, pending the ascertainment of new principles to govern industry, it was wiser for the State not to interfere in industrial struggles by the issuance of an injunction.

In Arizona, boycotts were held to be legal at common law, and in Brandeis's opinion the state's legislators had been fully entitled to render peaceful picketing legal by statute; but even if his brethren now wished to rule otherwise and decide that employers had "a constitutional right to be free from interference by such a boycott, or that the picketing practiced was not in fact peaceful," he could still see no reason whatever why the state should "lack the power to refuse to protect that right by injunction." The "refusal of an equitable remedy for a tort" was clearly not ipso facto, nor in the circumstances of the case at bar, a denial of due process. Moreover, the "acknowledged legislative discretion exerted in classification, so frequently applied in defining rights," extended equally, he believed, to the question of appropriate remedies. It was "for the legislature to say—within the broad limits of the discretion it possesses—whether or not the remedy for a wrong shall be both criminal and civil, and whether or not it shall be both at law and in equity."[43]

Ten days after the *Truax* decision was handed down, Brandeis sent copies of the opinions in this and the *Duplex* case to Woodrow Wilson, knowing, he said, how deeply interested the former president had been "in the labor provisions embodied in the Clayton Act." A month later, in an unsigned editorial in the *New Republic*, Felix Frankfurter placed the chief justice's ruling at the end of a long line of Supreme Court decisions which, in his opinion (and most certainly in Brandeis's also), were in danger of totally emasculating the legislative power of state and nation alike. "The simple fact of the matter," the Harvard professor asserted, "is that in a decision like *Truax v. Corrigan*, the Court, under the guise of legal form, exercises political control. That the courts are especially fitted to be the ultimate arbiters of policy is an intelligent and a tenable doctrine," he went on disingenuously. "But let them and us face the fact that five Justices of the Supreme Court *are* conscious molders of policy instead of the impersonal vehicles of revealed truth."[44]

The developing contours of Brandeis's thought concerning the most appropriate mechanisms for achieving industrial peace in America were paralleled by a continuing movement of his attitude toward the state and local regulation of business activity. As we saw in the last chapter, his experience on the Court made him familiar with a wide variety of cases involving exercise of the states' reserved powers, and what he saw and heard drove him increasingly to favor an interventionist role for state government in the affairs of industry and commerce. As a consequence, his enthusiasm for federal activity in these areas, never particularly high, waned steadily. "Do not believe that you can find a universal remedy for evil conditions or immoral practices," he warned a correspondent in 1922. "And do not pin too much faith in legislation. Remedial institutions are apt to fall under the control of the enemy and to become instruments of oppression." The Clayton Act's fate at the hands of politicians, administrators, and judges alike was responsible in large measure for this renewed cynicism. Likewise, in 1933, with reference to Senator George Norris's proposals for the federal licencing of corporations, he was able to comment: "In that sort of a measure I see only danger. . . . It looks to me like infantile faith in regulation—to which the Berle-Means et al. association are addicted." By 1937, if not before, his disillusionment was complete: "I get little encouragement from the announcement that [Senator] Borah will work on Anti-trust with F. D. [Roosevelt]," he told Frankfurter. "47 years of the Sherman Law futility ought to be . . . convincing."[45]

The rationale behind his increasingly negative attitude toward federal action was stated plainly as early as 1922. Antitrust laws had failed, he believed: first, on account of their refusal to recognize size as a danger, and a consequent emphasis on combinations; and, second, because of the adoption of prohibition and criminal penalties. "Illegal combination," he observed ruefully, "was inherently difficult to prove. Furthermore, it was not deemed by the community a wrong. Size should not be prohibited, should not be treated as criminal, but should be discouraged by supertaxes & by being thus made less profitable." In 1938, this theme was developed further in an unusually candid telegram sent to veteran muckraker Frederic C. Howe. Asked to provide details of "taxation or other devices to limit corporation size and intercorporate abuses to encourage small enterprise," Brandeis responded by suggesting an "annual excise tax rapidly progressive in the rate as the total capitalization of the corporation rises," the total amount of such capital to be reckoned by adding to the par value of the company's own issues "the aggregate value of the stocks, bonds and other securities of all subsidiary or other corporations" in which it held more than 20 percent of all outstanding obligations.[46]

This support for *state* action is perhaps best demonstrated by reference to his opinion in *New State Ice Company v. Liebmann* (1932), where he dissented vehemently from the majority decision invalidating an Oklahoma statute that required all those wishing to engage in the manufacture and sale of ice to obtain a license from the state's Corporation Commission. The keynote of his argument was that the Fourteenth Amendment should not be used to prevent experimentation aimed at correcting the twin economic evils of "technological unemployment and excess productive capacity," which had "attended progress in the useful arts." With the American economy rushing headlong toward utter collapse, those who argued otherwise took on themselves "a grave responsibility."

> Denial of the right to experiment may be fraught with serious consequences to the Nation. It is one of the happy incidents of the federal system that a single courageous State may, if its citizens choose, serve as a laboratory; and try novel social and economic experiments without risk to the rest of the country. This Court has the power to prevent an experiment. We may strike down the statute which embodies it on the ground that, in our opinion, the measure is arbitrary, capricious or unreasonable. We have power to do this, because the due process clause has been held by the Court applicable to matters of substantive laws as well as to matters of procedure. But in the exercise of this high power, we must be ever on our guard, lest we erect our prejudices into legal principles. If we would guide by the light of reason, we must let our minds be bold.[47]

It should first be noticed that the socioeconomic ideas underpinning this dissent were thoroughly consistent with the general position Brandeis took in the postwar years: namely that, while an overall framework of limitations could and should be provided by the federal government, making indirect use of its commerce and taxing powers for regulatory ends, it was properly the right and responsibility of the states to experiment with ways of providing for the welfare of their citizens; and that this clearly comprehended the right to regulate both corporate competition and corporate monopoly. The particularities of a case were always of great importance to Brandeis, but as we have seen this rarely prevented him from seeking the widest possible powers of discretion for state legislatures. Though recognizing fully that a regulation valid for one kind of situation might not be appropriate in another, "since the reasonableness of every regulation is dependent upon the relevant facts," he had no reservations whatever about recognizing the *power* of the states to regulate wherever the public interest required them to do so. For as he explained in an earlier section of his ice-case dissent, there was

> no difference, in essence, between a business called private and one called a public utility. . . . In my opinion, the true principle is that the State's power extends to every regulation of any business reasonably required and appropriate for the public protection. I find in the due process clause [of the Fourteenth Amendment] no other limitation upon the character or scope of the regulation permissible.[48]

The thrust of this argument, with its focus (as in *Truax*) on the right of the states to experiment, may have struck later commentators as both parochial and irrelevant; but by those attempting to grapple effectively with the dire socioeconomic consequences of the depression, it was viewed as both timely and courageous. Social pundit Max Lerner, writing to Brandeis just a few days after its delivery, regarded it as "distinctly one of your greatest opinions—cogent, comprehensive, unflinching and withal possessed of a gathering passion." He was particularly pleased to find that the justice had been ready to set out so clearly his "views with regard to the theory of the public interest as the basis of state regulation." Other correspondents read the opinion as a manifesto. "I really feel," wrote Brookings economist Isador Lubin after reading it, "that your dissent is going to be something to which we of the younger generation are going to turn to [sic] with pride in future years when the law finally comes into accord with economic reality."[49]

Brandeis's view of "economic reality" was not generally a popular one, however, focusing attention as it did on the stifling effects of "bigness" on the lives of ordinary working people. Progress in the development of human potential could only proceed, as he told Laski in 1921, "from the aggregate of the performances of individual men," each of whom was "a wee thing, despite the aids and habiliments with which science, invention and organization have surrounded him." Man might have only limited intelligence, but if he could be made aware of his own limitations he nonetheless possessed "vision, wisdom and ingenuity enough" to adjust the size of his undertakings, and particularly his institutions, to human scale. Physical and spiritual development had already become inseparable objectives for Brandeis before the 1920s, the first being seen as an essential prerequisite for the second. "In order to live," he had written in 1914, "men must have the opportunity for developing their faculties; and they must live under conditions in which [these] may develop naturally and healthily." They needed leisure in which to reflect and grow. Shorter working hours, regular days of rest, the abolition of child labor, and the elimination of "sweated" conditions for adults were thus not merely an ethical consideration but a social and spiritual necessity.[50]

If working people were to "live under conditions conducive to health and moral development," then poverty had to be eradicated; and while the redistribution of existing wealth was desirable, if only to reduce discontent, the long-term improvement of social conditions could only come as the result of substantial increases in productivity. Here he was highly optimistic of success: "I believe that the possibilities of human advancement are unlimited," he had told an interviewer in 1913.

> I believe that the resources of productive enterprise are almost untouched, and that the world will see a vastly increased supply of comforts, a tremendous social surplus out of which the great masses will be apportioned a degree of well-being that is now hardly dreamed of. . . . But precisely because I believe in this future in which material comfort is to be comparatively easy of attainment, I also believe that the race must steadily insist upon preserving its moral vigor unweakened.

For Justice Brandeis, moral and spiritual development went hand in hand with the betterment of material well-being; the latter made the former possible. "The development of the individual is . . . both a necessary means and the end sought," he told the Federal Council of Churches in a rare public statement in 1922. "For our objective is the making of men and women who shall be free—self-respecting members of a democracy—and who shall be worthy of respect. Improvement in the material conditions of the workers and ease are the incidents of better conditions—valuable mainly as they may ever increase opportunities for development."[51]

The main question, though, was how this improvement in material well-being, this "tremendous social surplus," could best be generated. Traditional interpretations of Brandeis, extrapolating backward from the last years of his life, have tended to be misleading. Most early commentators saw his ideas in this area as plainly outmoded, harking back solely to the moribund values and tarnished verities of the preindustrial era. "His faith in smallness was too stark and vigorous," wrote Arthur Schlesinger. "When he decried the automotive industry on the ground that Americans ought to walk more, he was speaking for an America that was dead. His words were morally bracing but socially futile." Likewise Ray Moley, Brains Trust adviser to Franklin Roosevelt, sought to identify Brandeis with the notion "that if America could once more become a nation of small proprietors, or corner grocers and smithies under spreading chestnut trees, we should have solved the problems of American life."[52]

Even Laski was ready to label him "intellectually, as to ends, a romantic anachronism"; though admittedly he went on to soften the force of this criticism somewhat by adding that "his method of analysis does magnificently relate law to the life of which it is the expression." Brandeis, he observed in 1933, "is really a Jeffersonian Democrat, trying to use the power of the State to enforce an environment in which competition may be really free and equal": a goal the English Socialist deemed impossible of attainment. In fact, though this assessment accurately identifies the justice's "criterion for all action" as "an ethical individualism" firmly rooted in a wider social philosophy, it is only partially correct in seeking to locate the core of that philosophy in America's past; the truth was rather more complicated.[53]

Interpretations such as these contain just enough authenticity to retain a semblance of credibility but are nevertheless gross oversimplifications: polemic rather than history, a travesty of Brandeis's social and economic thinking. As the best of his biographers have shown, and as will shortly become evident, his ideal society was less the rustic austerity of Jefferson's Virginia or, for that matter, Thoreau's New England, than it was the experimental community of Lilienthal's Tennessee Valley or Ben-Gurion's Palestine. For although his attitude toward technology was always subtle and ambivalent, at no time is there evidence to support the view that he longed to see America restored to the museumlike condition of horse-and-buggy communications and handicraft industries. If any mode of transport should stand as a metaphor for his ideal level of technological sophistication, it is less the horse-drawn carriage than the railroad train. His adult mind was not formed after all in the placid, bucolic 1830s but in the speeding, shrieking 1870s. Though he might at times have wished it otherwise, he was not at bottom the scion of pastoral Kentucky but the adopted son of industrial Massachusetts.

Nevertheless, one idea that he firmly rejected was that bigness was in some way an inevitable feature of modern economic life. He liked to quote Machiavelli's dictum that "Fate is inevitable only when it is not resisted." In reality, far from resisting the onset of bigness, Americans had actually fostered the conditions in which it could develop. Bigness was "man-made" and "authorized" by the corporation statutes; and, as he would add wryly, "that which is man-made can be unmade." The dissenting opinion he wrote in *Liggett Company v. Lee* included a lengthy historical account of state incorporation laws. Corporations, he explained, had initially been subject to strict limitations as to the amount of authorized capital, the scope of their powers and the range of activities they were permitted to undertake. These limitations had been removed, not because the fears that had given rise to them had been allayed, nor because of any widespread belief that they were no longer desirable or necessary, but because a few irresponsible states like New Jersey and Delaware had chosen to make themselves attractive to corporate businesses by abandoning restrictions altogether. Others, powerless to prevent the outflow of capital and jobs, and thus of revenue, had been forced with much reluctance to follow suit. The fact remained, however, that corporations owed their existence to state laws, and this, in Brandeis's opinion, justified the states in imposing whatever levies and controls they considered appropriate in return for the privilege of doing business in corporate form.[54]

That it *was* a privilege, and not a right, he had no doubt. "The prevalence of the corporation in America," he suggested in an early draft of his dissent, had led men of that generation to act at times as if the right of incorporation "were inherent in the citizen, like liberty of contract"; they were in error. Paul Freund, his law clerk for that session, found the analogy unfortunate. "It may be unwise to exalt liberty of contract," he commented in a memorandum to the justice. "Besides, the proposition is true only to the extent that the natural rights theory of the 18th century is accepted as authoritative. . . . Is it really necessary to commit yourself to an espousal of any privilege inherent in the citizen?" The justice evidently agreed that it was not, and the words "like the liberty of contract" were omitted from the definitive version. It is interesting to speculate, however, whether this omission represented the conscious denial of all natural rights as a legitimate basis for judicial reasoning, or merely a characteristic unwillingness to offer hostages to fortune.[55]

As previously indicated, the *Liggett* case concerned a piece of anti-chain-store legislation passed by the State of Florida in 1931, containing the novel provision that a heavier license fee should be charged on stores with a single owner but not located within the same county. Five of the plaintiffs, Brandeis observed, were among the two hundred largest nonbanking corporations in America. Their assets totaled $820 million; between them they operated 19,718 stores—one alone operated sixteen thousand. Against these and the owners of other multiple chains, the individual retailers were engaged in a struggle for their independence, and perhaps their existence. How had the Florida legislature responded to this situation? Brandeis offered the following interpretation:

> The citizens of the state, considering themselves vitally interested in this seemingly unequal struggle, have undertaken to aid the individual retailers by subjecting the owners of multiple stores to the handicap of higher licence fees. They may have done so merely to preserve competition. But their purpose may have been a broader and deeper one. They may have believed that the chain store, by furthering the concentration of wealth and of power and by promoting absentee ownership, is thwarting American ideals; that it is making impossible equality of opportunity; that it is converting independent tradesmen into clerks; that it is sapping the resources, the vigor and the hope of the smaller cities and towns.[56]

When, as was customary, copies of the completed opinion were circulated among his fellow justices, Harlan Fiske Stone, explaining why he could offer the dissent only limited support, wrote back: "I think you are too much an advocate of this kind of legislation." It was a damning charge, and one to which the following postscript added by another former law clerk adds a certain credence. Shortly after the delivery of this opinion, Henry Friendly, his secretary during the 1927–28 session of the Court, passed through Washington on his way home following a stay in Tallahassee, Florida's state capital. In the course of a visit to his old chief, he ventured to suggest that the anti-chain-store law had only been passed because of pressure from powerful groups associated with the drugstore industry. Lewis Paper relates the story as follows:

> Friendly saw an amusing contrast between the logic of Brandeis's opinion and the realities of legislative behavior. "You know," he told his former boss. . . , "I was down watching the Florida Legislature, and I don't think they had any of those social benefits in mind that you discussed. I think they were just influenced by the drug lobby." Brandeis did not smile or respond in any way. He just moved on to a new subject.[57]

Factually wide of the mark or not, the principal features of this dissenting opinion remained characteristic of Brandeis's strictures on, and remedies for, the evils of bigness throughout the 1930s. He opposed federal incorporation but approved of legislation to prevent businesses from incorporating in one state and doing the greater part of their business in another; and he favored taxation over antitrust suits as the best means of breaking up industrial and marketing combines. On the issue of precisely which authorities should be empowered to regulate and control the corporations, he preferred state to federal action, but was ready to countenance both. In his view, the depression "had come about because of the failure of Government to impose controls to prevent a breakdown." Now it was up to government to redeem itself by devising and applying appropriate limitations. "I would leave a lot of power to the states," he told Harry Shulman at the end of 1933, "and have the federal government help and direct the States by appropriate taxation." The objective was simple enough: "to make men free." Yet a measure of caution was necessary. "The federal government must not become too big just as corporations should not be permitted to become too big. You must remember," he warned Shulman, "that it is the littleness of man that limits the size of things we can undertake. Too much bigness may break the federal government as it has broken business."[58]

To categorize such a position as unchanged from the "laissez-faire conservatism" of his youth would clearly be absurd; neither (*pace* Riesman's observation about the Southern Agrarians) was it simply a restatement of the traditional states rights philosophy of the Old South. Brandeis was by no means opposed to the idea, or indeed the practice, of an interventionist governmental authority during his later years, but he believed profoundly that such interventionism should occur only within the framework of a constitutional separation of powers—operating not only between federal and state authorities but between their different branches as well. Only by the strictest adherence to such separation could civil servants be assured of their independence, politicians be kept responsive to the will of the people, and the evils of bigness in government be avoided. A few weeks after the Supreme Court unanimously denied President Roosevelt's right to dismiss Republican Federal Trade Commissioner William E. Humphrey in May 1935, Brandeis expressed his satisfaction to an unidentified confidant. "If men on the Federal Trade Commission and similar government agencies are not allowed to exercise their independent judgment we should have in effect a dictatorship or a totalitarian state. What would happen to us if Huey Long were President and such a doctrine prevailed?"[59]

While his position on the appropriate spheres for the federal and state regulation of competition seems to have developed rapidly in the decade after 1912, and more especially once he joined the Court, his position on monopoly and the possibility, even desirability, of public ownership matured more slowly. In 1922, as in the article penned for *Harper's Weekly* almost ten years earlier, he continued to see some form of public ownership as inevitable: "The sphere of private capitalistic control is now and will necessarily be, from time to time further narrowed, through the assumption by the nation, state or municipality of functions which the public or community concludes cannot properly be performed by or be entrusted to private ownership or management."[60]

It seems evident, though, that he continued to regard regulation as the preferable option, and that by 1932 he believed he had discovered a mechanism capable of controlling "essential" or "natural" monopolies without having resort to outright public ownership—an alternative altogether less threatening to the private-property traditions of American capitalism. This was the legal device known as a "certificate of public convenience and necessity." Early in March that year, John Frances, the law librarian at the Library of Congress, sent him a memorandum detailing recent references to such certificates in the legal literature on public utility regulation, and the substance of this research was quickly incorporated into his *New State Ice* dissent. The certificate was a technical instrument "unknown to the common law," he told his brethren.

> It is a creature of the machine age, in which plants have displaced tools and businesses are substituted for trades. The purpose of requiring it is to promote the public interest by preventing waste. . . . [Its] introduction in the United States . . . marked the growing conviction that under certain circumstances free competition might be harmful to the community, and that, when it was so, absolute freedom to enter the business of one's choice should be denied.

It was no valid objection to the Oklahoma statute involved in the case that it fostered monopoly, for that is precisely what it was designed to do; however, the requirement of a licensing certificate made it possible, at least in theory, to keep that monopoly under effective control, by vesting in a state commission the power to terminate the license whenever the public interest might be served thereby. Henceforth, the elderly justice would consistently view such novel methods of administrative control as a sound, practical alternative to public ownership, even where natural monopolies were involved, and state regulation as accordingly more effective, if properly conducted, than its federal counterpart.[61]

None of those close to Brandeis politically in the thirties were willing to accept the logic of the argument presented in *Liebmann* at face value—that in this rightly celebrated specimen of the jurist's art he might actually have been signaling his willingness to make peace with regulated monopoly as the necessary price to be paid for controlling bigness. Paul Freund surely spoke for all Frankfurter's Harvard-trained disciples when he contrived to see in it a classic example of the justice's ability to "write massive opinions in support of the constitutionality of measures with which as a matter of legislative policy he had no sympathy." It was, he wrote, "a resounding argument for the constitutional right of a state to experiment with economic measures for which there was some rational support, even though they seemed misguided and destined to failure."[62]

Yet not everyone perceived its purpose in this light. Max Lerner expressed surprise, but not disbelief, at Brandeis's "clear utterances about competition in this opinion," observing that he now seemed "less concerned with the value of maintaining competition than with the effective administration of a service." Milton Handler of Columbia University was even more forthright. "I was very much interested in your defense of monopoly," he wrote in March 1932 after reading the opinion.

> I was somewhat troubled by the statement which you made when I spoke to you in September, in which you said that it was futile to attempt control of [i.e., prevent] monopoly. The important thing was to avoid it. I should be very reluctant to see competition disappear in industries such as ice and coal since I have little faith in the sort of people who man our commissions. What likelihood is there of a commission issuing a certificate to introduce competition against an inefficient company with a local monopoly, where there is close political connection between the commission and the existing units in the industry? But of course these are no reasons for denying the power of the state to utilize this method of control.

If he remained personally skeptical about its likely effectiveness, Handler clearly saw no reason to doubt the justice's own sincere commitment to the idea of administrative regulation.[63]

In fact, as we saw in an earlier chapter, Brandeis's early anxieties about monopoly began to abate as his worries about the effects of bigness began to develop. The implication here of a major ideological shift is more apparent than real, though; for it was actually his deep-seated concern for the preservation of democratic ideals that underpinned both the earlier and the later emphases. This would always be his primary criterion for measuring the efficiency of institutional structures. Looking back from the standpoint of 1931, he located the first public presentation of this view around 1911–12. "You may recall," he told a correspondent, "that in my testimony before the Clapp Committee and the Stanley Committee . . . I brought out particularly 'the limit of greatest efficiency' economically and socially." He had expressed a similar notion in *Other People's Money* (1913), and again much later in the dissent he wrote in *Quaker City Cab Company v. Pennsylvania* (1928). Indeed, he may have been moving toward the concept as early as 1907. Then, in the midst of his fight to prevent the New Haven-Boston & Maine merger, he had argued that: "There is for a community a general limit where efficiency can be reached by consolidation. To that point I am in favor of it. . . ." By 1912, however, his ideas were much more fully articulated:

> A large part of the American people . . . [have] learned that efficiency in business does not grow indefinitely with the size of the business. Very often a business grows in efficiency as it grows from a small business to a large business; but there is a unit of greatest efficiency in every business at any time, and a business may be too large to be efficient, as well as too small.[64]

Initially, of course, Brandeis's grasp of this idea was essentially intuitive, but over the years he became more and more concerned to amass empirical evidence that might support his contention. Thus in 1921, for instance, he wrote congratulating Harold Laski on his new book, *The Foundation of Sovereignty*, and urged him to "develop further the cult of the unit of greatest efficiency and spread further the truth that progress must proceed from the aggregate of the performances of individual men." By the time of his 1933 dissent in the Florida chain-store case, he was able to assemble, with the assistance of his law clerk, Paul Freund, a formidable array of footnote references to the theoretical arguments over the relationship of efficiency to size. Yet as Freund commented ruefully in the middle of his researches, it was "much harder to find respectable authority for these points than it is, e.g. for planned production." As late as 1939, he could be found encouraging Morris Ernst to "do a book on the economic factors of excessive size in business and government and cities," hoping that the New York City lawyer "would explore the optimum point of efficiency of a coal company, a city, a savings bank, a steel factory, et cetera." The fact remains nevertheless that the concept had already been fully developed in the justice's mind long before any empirical evidence was marshaled in support of it, thereby placing yet another question-mark against the authenticity of his celebrated inductive methodology.[65]

Still, knowing as much as he undoubtedly did about the facts and figures of American industry, Brandeis could never be wholly dogmatic about the relative merits and demerits of bigness—at any rate, not in the economic sphere. There was, as he told Frankfurter rather surprisingly in 1935, "much to be said for bigness." One of its principal recommendations he had conceded as early as 1914. The large industrial corporation enjoyed enormous advantages in the gathering of market information and in the carrying out of research and development. "Laboratories are maintained, and they can be maintained, only by great concerns." He went on, though, to link this discussion with his wider aspirations for enlarging the political and industrial democracy of the nation:

> It is the relatively small man who pre-eminently needs the aid and the solicitous care of industry and of government. We have . . . to bear all the time that democratic view in mind that education does not end with the common school, nor does it end with the university. We are beginning throughout the country to talk now of vocational training. But where shall vocational training end? Not merely with the training of the individual for the bit of work that he is to enter into. That training must continue throughout life, and that training must extend to every part of his business life.

From here he proceeded to draw an analogy between the experimental programs and educational services provided for farmers by the U.S. Department of Agriculture, and the kind of technical programs and services he believed ought to be performed on behalf of small businesses by other agencies of the federal government.

> What better could the Government of this country do than to extend to business that care and solicitude and aid which it shows in the case of the farmer? To make it affirmatively the business of the Government to extend to the manufacturer throughout this country the opportunity of knowing about his particular line of manufacture the best that can be known.[66]

Nevertheless, a degree of open-mindedness about the precise point of balance between the efficiencies and wastes of scale did not prevent him from formulating early and definite opinions about the general desirability of small units. "It seems to me," he argued in 1914, "that the limit of efficiency in business is reached at a fairly early stage, and that the disadvantages of size outweigh in many respects the advantage of size." Whereas larger units were a common incident of monopoly, there was absolutely no reason for believing that competition necessarily resulted in units too small for efficiency. But what precisely was the limit of greatest efficiency, and how was it to be determined? According to Brandeis, the limit would "differ in different businesses and under varying conditions in the same business"; in every organization there would be a point at which it became "too large for efficient and economic management," just as there would be a point where it was "too small to be an efficient instrument." This was hardly a formula capable of scientific application, however; nor was it particularly illuminating. Perhaps Brandeis had in mind the prosperous merchants and small businessmen of Massachusetts, who had joined him in his fight against the trusts; or perhaps he had some other model for his postulate of the efficient small unit—in all likelihood some system of producer cooperatives. Whatever the concrete basis of these abstractions, the fact remains that he proffered no mechanism for ascertaining when these elusive "points of greatest efficiency" had been reached or surpassed. He did not even provide a working definition of efficiency. So far as direct evidence is concerned, the printed record is absolutely silent.[67]

Fortunately, there survives a good deal of inferential evidence. For example, in the eighth chapter of *Other People's Money* (titled, incidentally, "A Curse of Bigness") the smaller units referred to in the context of railroad companies were themselves businesses of substantial size, such as the Chicago, Burlington, and Quincy, which in 1901 possessed 7,912 miles of track and $109 million (par value) of outstanding stock. Likewise in 1915, testifying before the U.S. Commission on Industrial Relations, Brandeis at one stage spoke of a "corporation whose capitalization is very small as compared to those to which you refer, Mr. Chairman, but which runs into the millions." Likewise, in 1934 he commended the history of savings-bank life insurance in Massachusetts as "bearing upon the efficiency of small units," perhaps thereby providing a further tangential insight into the kind and scale of operations he favored.[68]

But it was in a discussion with Federal Reserve economist Emanuel Goldenweiser in the winter of 1933–34 that the justice supplied the most complete picture of what he envisaged, and why. As Goldenweiser noted after their meeting:

> He approaches the whole problem from the point of view of democracy. He feels that we haven't had democracy and that we ought to give it a trial. His conception of democracy is that there should be no forces strong enough to make it impossible for people to resist pressures. [His experience with the New Haven Railroad] . . . has made him feel confident that we ought not to have any large aggregations of capital either in the form of super-fortunes or super-corporations. He would approach the problem by way of taxation. He would tax very heavily all large fortunes and all large corporations. He is aware of the fact that "large" would mean a different thing for different lines of industry. He mentioned, for example, that the Campbell Soup Company has $200,000,000 capital. He feels that no soup company needs that much money. On the other hand, a steel company might very well need some such amount.[69]

Even when taken together, these inferences hardly form a detailed and comprehensive picture, but they do serve to explode the impression that Brandeis's "small unit" was a synonym, or perhaps even a euphemism, for preindustrial cottage industry. Whatever he conceived in his mind's eye— and his definition of small seems to have been a remarkably elastic one—it was certainly not "basket-weaving technology," nor "horse-and-buggy transportation," nor "smithies under spreading chestnut trees."

The Great Depression of the 1930s appeared to provide Mr. Justice Brandeis with a final opportunity to guide Americans away from the seductive path of corporate growth and federal government hegemony. As observed before, after 1916 the only reliable means of access to the true configuration of his mind is to be had through his private correspondence, his legal opinions delivered from the bench, and the notes and reminiscences of those with whom he talked. None is a perfect source. Yet from a detailed examination of these varied materials it becomes clear that the views which he had formulated and expounded before his appointment, and had further developed during his early years on the Court, underwent relatively little change during the remaining years of his life. Particulars were revised, new applications were elaborated, emphases were shifted somewhat; but in all essentials, the philosophical assumptions underlying his prescriptive advice to the New Dealers were identifiably similar to those he had developed during two decades of reforming activity after 1895, championed in his writings and other public pronouncements of that period, and sharpened to a fine precision during his time as a judge.

In 1933, the Supreme Court Justice was still making the same associations between bigness, nonparticipation, and social violence that the "people's attorney" had been making twenty years earlier. As he told his younger daughter Elizabeth, the curbing of bigness "is indispensable to true Democracy & Liberty. It is the very foundation also of wisdom in things human— 'Nothing too much.'" He hoped that her Progressive friends in Wisconsin would see the truth of this. Otherwise, though there might be some amelioration of economic hardship, there could not be "a working 'New Deal.'" If the efforts promised by the incoming Roosevelt administration were to fail, the consequence might be the appearance of "Fascist manifestations" in America. Size was the issue because it restricted human development and thwarted individual aspirations. "If the Lord had intended things to be big," he declared with unconscious triteness, "he would have made man bigger— in brains and character."[70]

Indeed, so confident was Brandeis that the views expressed by him in earlier years remained relevant to Americans in the context of economic dislocation and collapse, that he was at considerable pains to promote their republication throughout the thirties. The Wall Street Crash and its aftermath might in any event have stimulated a renewal of public interest in his most celebrated book, *Other People's Money*, first published in 1913. As the justice told his nephew in 1932: "The present depression, the debunking of the great financial kings, and the losses of those who followed them have made men think, and i[nter] a[lia] realise that 'Other Peoples Money' should have been heeded." As it was, a new hard-cover edition costing two dollars appeared later in the year, featuring a specially commissioned introduction by Norman Hapgood, but when it failed to sell, a cheap reprint was brought out by the National Home Library Foundation in 1933—100,000

copies retailing at fifteen cents each. Brandeis and those close to him worked assiduously to promote the volume's circulation, with Hapgood making a
special radio broadcast about it to coincide with the launch, the justice himself agreeing to underwrite the foundation's expenses with a check for
$2,200 and his elder daughter Susan hassling distributors in New York to get
it onto the city's subway newsstands. Sherman Mittell, its publisher, even
approached the Civilian Conservation Corps and the TVA "to have the
Government purchase books for the forgotten folk now in its employ, who
receive the least pay and have a need for good books." As a result of
their combined efforts, the entire edition sold out within five months of
publication.[71]

The reception accorded to *Other People's Money* on its reappearance was
generally favorable. John Maynard Keynes, who like many other opinion
formers was sent a complimentary copy, remarked to Hapgood "how extraordinarily well it reads after twenty years"; and in a letter to the editor of
the *Economist*, Felix Frankfurter dutifully echoed his mentor's own view
about the work's continuing importance. "I venture to suggest that this little
book will shed more light on the fundamentals of American banking and
financial history during the last twenty years than all the writings of techni-
cians on the workings of the Federal Reserve System," he observed. "Time
has completely vindicated Mr. Brandeis's proposed remedies, although
more far-reaching remedies must now be applied than those which he outlined twenty years ago." David Coyle, a consulting engineer with the new
Public Works Administration, who evidently became acquainted with the
justice at about this time, was even more exuberant in his praise. "You sure
swing a mean wallop," he wrote at the end of 1933, after reading the copy
given him by Brandeis's friend Lincoln Filene. "Of course it appears now
that you were somewhat ahead of your time in 1913,—and one may whisper
that just possibly der Tag hasn't really arrived even now: but in public we all
now raise a mighty shout and see if we can bring on the climax." It was
above all heartening, Coyle assured the old campaigner, "to see your keen
sword still flashing in the front line of battle."[72]

Also in 1933, a new edition appeared of that other Brandeis compilation,
Business—A Profession, for which an introduction by James C. Bonbright
was added to the two earlier versions written by Ernest Poole and Frankfurter respectively. But undoubtedly the most significant publication exercise
undertaken at this time was the brand new volume of previously uncollected
items, begun by New York attorney Clarence M. Lewis and completed after
his untimely death by Osmond K. Fraenkel. Initially favoring the evocative
title *Prophetic Powers* for this book, the publishers, Viking Press, were
eventually persuaded to accept a more prosaic alternative selected by the
justice himself—and so it appeared in the closing weeks of 1934, renamed
The Curse of Bigness.[73]

Less reticent than Brandeis about sending a copy to the White House,

Frankfurter regarded its publication as "a truly important event & extraordinarily timely on several counts." Reviewing it for the *New York Herald Tribune*, though, Max Lerner was a good deal less rapturous and in some ways more perceptive:

> If it were not for the New Deal this volume would not have half the interest it does have. On one topic after another . . . there is a substantial continuity between what Brandeis once said and what President Roosevelt is saying and trying to do. But the continuity is more apparent than real. Brandeis's central idea of the "curse of bigness" is not a popular one in a government whose great administrative effort is now directed toward co-ordinating further the many agencies huddled together in Washington but wielding a far-flung power. If this be taken as the core of Mr. Justice Brandeis' thinking . . . the striking fact becomes not the identity of the Brandeisian thought and the New Deal, but their discord.[74]

Lerner's observation cuts right to the heart of the problem facing anyone seeking to interpret the significance of Brandeis's exhortations to the New Deal's politicians and administrators. For quite plainly the rejection of bigness and celebration of the small unit, which together characterized much of the policy advice he gave to President Roosevelt and his colleagues during the 1930s, set him at odds not only with what David Riesman rightly termed the "federalizing" thrust of the New Deal, but with almost every dynamic tendency of twentieth-century life. And to make matters worse, the interpretations afforded by many historians, not to mention the more detailed studies of legal scholars and biographers, have frequently treated his ideas about institutional size in total isolation from the wider context of his social philosophy, leaving their readers with the erroneous impression that, by the 1930s at any rate, Brandeis was a single-issue thinker: a would-be atomizer of large-scale industry, a laissez-faire reactionary, a libertarian conservative, an apostle of smallness in all things.[75]

In fact, though unequivocal evidence for his thinking on the subject is difficult to come by, it seems impossible to sustain Riesman's view that Brandeis was uniformly hostile to the strategic objectives of the New Deal and uncompromisingly scornful of Roosevelt as its principal architect. It would be more accurate to say that he disagreed with many of the tactics and methods employed during the so-called First New Deal, and thought more or less highly of the president as the latter furthered or frustrated the programs that the justice himself was advocating—occasionally face to face but most commonly through intermediaries like Frankfurter and his young disciples in government. Briefly stated, Brandeis wanted the federal government to establish a stable economic framework within which the several states could work to discover the best means of ensuring a permanent return to prosperity. As made plain in the Oklahoma ice case, not Washington but the various state capitals were his preferred laboratories for experiments in social and economic reform.

The federal authorities were to remain important, however, as manipulators of the two great instruments of policy that Brandeis considered necessary to bring this state of affairs into being: namely, a major program of public works to end unemployment and restore purchasing power to consumers, and a new regime of corporate taxation aimed at rendering large-scale enterprises uneconomic. The first of these should be developed with imagination and deployed in every state, encompassing such things as flood control, afforestation, soil improvement, and adult education, in addition to more traditional kinds of civil engineering projects; the second should rely on excise taxes and a progressive tax on corporate incomes, both discriminating in favor of smaller units to achieve its goal. To these two primary weapons might be added a lesser armory that included postal-savings banks to extricate government (as well as millions of ordinary Americans) from the withering grip of the "money trust"; graduated federal taxes on incomes and inheritances to wear down and eventually eliminate completely the "super-rich"; and a system of social security to ameliorate the worst financial penalties associated with unemployment and old age.[76]

Measured against this standard, the New Deal measures of 1933–35 were a generally discouraging package. While the TVA and the Civilian Conservation Corps were on the whole compatible with the Brandeisian ethos, the Agricultural Adjustment Administration (AAA) and the National Recovery Administration (NRA), with their emphasis on federal power and central planning, were plainly not. It seemed as if the old Progressive battles between the New Freedom and the New Nationalism were being reenacted. Anxious now, though, not to become involved in domestic political squabbles, at least not in public, the justice preferred whenever possible to approach such matters obliquely, highlighting the differences between himself and the planners by reference to the contrasting socioeconomic regimes of Russia and Denmark.

In March 1917, he had expressed "elation" on learning of the Russian Revolution and animatedly repeated Charles Crane's belief "that Russia will teach the world democracy." In November 1918, unlike many Americans, he was prepared to wait and see what the Soviet Union might achieve under the Bolsheviks; considered it possible that the Russian people might "be earnestly trying to discover a way towards stabilization and recovery"; and believed that an economic mission should be sent to the country to assist with recovery. In the following decade he seems to have opposed military intervention, deplored the refusal to establish trade links, and favored international recognition. But he did not share the wave of enthusiasm for Russia's command economy, which seized many American liberals during trips to Moscow in the late twenties and early thirties. For him, the Soviets' development of collective farming was proof enough of their misguided commitment to bigness.[77]

THE VISION OF ISAIAH

Denmark, on the other hand, seemed to commend itself as a veritable model of community-based living and participatory democracy. As early as 1921, while looking for an alternative to "the packing monopoly," which he saw operating in the United States, Brandeis had been impressed by the Danish practice of having "many packing plants distributed . . . over the farming region" and run by cooperatives. It was only a decade later, however, as the depression deepened, that his interest in the country began to develop seriously. Beginning in 1932, the Danish minister in Washington was a frequent guest at the Brandeises' California Street apartment, and began supplying the justice with a steady stream of "material from his files and . . . more comprehensive reports from Denmark" itself. By October he had assembled enough information to suggest to Josephine Goldmark that they renew the partnership which, twenty-five years earlier, had produced the seminal brief filed in *Muller v. Oregon*. This time the project was to be a wide-ranging study of Danish social democracy: an enterprise that, he hastened to assure her, "should be no less interesting and prove equally important." The result, published four years later as *Democracy in Denmark*, combined an analysis of Danish society and institutions written by Josephine with a study of the Danish "folk high school" translated from the German by her sister, Alice Goldmark Brandeis, the justice's wife. It "points the way," Louis declared in a letter he wrote to Morris Ernst, enclosing a copy. To others he would henceforth observe rhetorically: "Why should anyone want to go to Russia when they can go to Denmark?"[78]

Privately, however, he found economic developments at home not only more difficult to fathom but, on the whole, far less encouraging. "As you may have imagined, I see little to be joyous about in the New Deal measures most talked about," he told his economist daughter in the spring of 1934; "N.R.A. and A.A.A. seem to be going from bad to worse." Moreover, he expected the advances promised by the tax bill then being steered through the Congress by "Young Bob" LaFollette to be "woefully small." But he was not yet an outright opponent of the National Recovery Administration, and as late as October could still write Norman Hapgood: "N.R.A. seems to be tending toward removal of price-fixing and production curtailment;—and toward the lowering of prices, which is essential to lessening unemployment. It is a pity we have wasted so much time in trodding [sic] false paths; but good to be on the right one now."[79]

Six weeks later, though, in December 1934, the so-called "hot oil" code came before the Supreme Court causing Brandeis to rethink his position completely. Indeed, from then on, it appears that any lingering readiness on his part to give NRA the benefit of the doubt was finally dispelled. He was never more deeply disillusioned with the New Deal than in the early months of 1935. "Things are working badly for liberalism and F. D.," he told Frankfurter in February; and by March the range of his discontent had widened to the point where he could lament both the state of the country in general and the errors of the agriculture secretary in particular. "The folly of Mr. Wallace's [crop] restriction program," he wrote Elizabeth, "is being seen now in the cotton price drop & development of growing elsewhere; and the cancelling of spring wheat restrictions for this year is impressive." He was marginally more heartened by the progress of ideas for a new social security system, which, despite intense lobbying from those in favor of a national scheme, at last seemed likely to be state based and to incorporate several features of the plan already operating in Wisconsin, which, since his daughter and son-in-law had been directly involved in its original development, he strongly approved of.[80]

This and other measures of the Second New Deal that passed into law during the spring and early summer of 1935 were generally more congenial to Brandeis than most of what had gone before, and his estimate of the president rose in proportion. In a series of letters written to Hapgood during July and August of that year, Roosevelt was variously described as having "no doubt about Big Business now"; "showing much wisdom"; "making a gallant fight"; giving "evidence . . . of growing firmness"; and "showing fine fighting qualities." Nonetheless, by November 1935, the justice was getting worried by the worsening political outlook as critics to both right and left of the administration began lining up to challenge the soundness of its recent measures. "This is certainly a period which must give concern to F. D. [Roosevelt] and his following—Liberals as well as Democrats," he told Hapgood. "Happily for F. D., it is nearly twelve months before election day. And happily also, the enemy has neither a leader nor measures."[81]

As regards the war against bigness, from time to time Brandeis thought he detected signs of understanding on the part of the president and his advisers. The Securities and Exchange Commission (SEC) appealed to him not so much as a *regulatory* agency, but because he felt it would be able to gather factual evidence to demonstrate the evils of great size; he also welcomed Roosevelt's move against public-utility holding companies as a first stage toward dethroning the "money power." As he observed in June 1935: "If F. D. carries through the Holding Company bill we shall have achieved considerable toward curbing Bigness—in addition to recent advances." A month later, he could cheerfully pronounce that bigness was "waning in many fields": in agriculture experts had recently predicted a return to "very small farms intensively cultivated"; in cities, some were now arguing that the days of the sky-scraper were definitely numbered; and on the railroads he thought the future would see "the light cars and small train . . . dominate" in both passenger and local freight services. Generally, however, he remained both gloomy and apocalyptic, reverting constantly to admonitions and exhortations to action. A lawyer from the SEC, visiting him in March 1935, reported his opinion that many of the New Deal's reforms were "of the court plaster type, and that so long as we suffered giant combinations to exist, reformers would always be outsmarted"; little that occurred in the months and years that followed gave him much cause to change his mind.[82]

In fact, these concerns about institutional scale were not so much the wellspring from which his policy prescriptions ultimately derived, as they were the end product of a chain of reasoning that found its origin in much deeper, more elemental beliefs and principles. As has been shown in the earlier chapters of this book, the twin pillars on which the intellectual system of his mature years rested were a pervasive awareness of human limitations, and an irreducible faith in the efficacy of laws for ordering the relationships between men and controlling the forces and institutions threatening always to blight or dominate their lives. As his interest in Denmark perhaps suggests, Brandeis believed that the most appropriate social context in which to preserve and develop the potential inherent in each citizen was the community. "The great America for which we long is unattainable," he had written as long ago as 1920,

> unless individuality of communities becomes far more highly developed and becomes a common American phenomenon. For a century our growth has come through natural expansion and the increase of the functions of the Federal Government. The growth of the future—at least of the immediate future—must be in quality and spiritual value. And that can come only through the concentrated, intensified strivings of smaller groups. The field for special effort should now be the State, the city, the village—and each should be led to seek to excel in something peculiar to it. If ideals are developed locally the national ones will come pretty near taking care of themselves.[83]

It was this belief that informed his decision in 1924 to help develop the University of Louisville into an institution capable of contributing more effectively to the education and culture of the city and state of his birth—a generous, if somewhat belated act of filial piety, which nevertheless grew directly out of deeply held convictions. That was the reason why he encouraged the brightest young men of his acquaintance to return to their home communities and to work selflessly for their improvement. When Willard Hurst returned to Madison in the fall of 1937, Alice Brandeis wrote to reassure him that he was making the correct choice. "We expect much of you in the years to come," she told him warmly, "for your spirit and fine purpose we know are of the finest." A few months later, as his erstwhile clerk began to voice doubts, the justice himself wrote that he should stay in Wisconsin. "My guess is that the next three or more years there will convince you that the East has nothing better to offer as a permanent matter," he observed. "And, in any event, the stay there will develop you and make you a more useful citizen." Despite tempting offers from the law schools of both Chicago and Yale, Hurst decided to remain at Madison to the obvious delight of his former chief, who seems to have drawn a genuine and vicarious pleasure whenever one of his clerks was persuaded to take up residence in the provincial hinterland, which he himself had abandoned in his youth, and especially when the individual in question opted to pursue the career in teaching on which his own back had once been turned.[84]

This pleasure was not so much hypocritical as it was wistful; for in old age Brandeis evidently possessed a set of moral priorities markedly different from the ones that had determined the choices before him in the 1880s—the product of a long lifetime of sometimes bitter experience. So when one former disciple later criticized the severe rationality of the justice's ethics, and asserted that his morality was "economic, not poetic, in its foundations," he could hardly have been further from the truth. More accurately it should be observed that his social and economic nostrums were always firmly rooted in an almost aesthetic sense of moral order; that, to use Dean Acheson's paraphrase, he believed "morality was truth."[85]

Regardless of their own ideological positions, all witnesses agree that at least one element of Brandeis's thinking remained as clear in his mind through the depression as it had been in the Progressive Era: his belief in the constraining force of human limitations. He remained firmly convinced that men possessed only a modest capacity for making weighty judgments, and that those whose decisions materially affected the lives of others should exercise their faculties with the greatest care and only after due consideration of all the facts available to them. The most obvious focus for this concern was the complex world of business and finance, where matters of judgment and competence had been brought into sharp relief by the events of 1929. "There ought to be a challenge of men being director[s] in many corp[oration]s," the justice told Frankfurter two weeks after Roosevelt's inauguration in 1933. "I doubt whether any man can really perform the duties of director of more than one—efficiently." The answer, he believed, was to set statutory limits on the number of directorships that could be held, thereby promoting not only greater efficiency but also greater honesty, since potential conflicts of interest would be avoided.[86]

Yet given such clearly articulated views on the management of business, it would have been remarkable had he not also expressed doubts about what he considered the equally limited capacities of government officials. Referring to the unprecedented atmosphere of intellectual excitement prevailing in New Deal Washington, he thought he detected a measure of impatience amid all the "noble thinking and high endeavor," and with it a tendency to forget that "The world's wise are not wise / claiming more than mortals know." It was perhaps characteristic that he should be worried about Roosevelt himself. As he told Frankfurter in August 1934: "the human limitations of the man on-top must give all his well-wishers concern."[87]

But the clearest expression of his attitude toward the burdens inseparable from public life are to be found in the notes of a conversation that Emanuel Goldenweiser had with him in May 1935. As Goldenweiser recalled:

He spoke of the limitations of human wisdom and [said] that was a reason why administrative machinery should not make demands upon human nature that are greater than human nature can meet. I said to him that his court had a pretty good record, and that that was due in part to the strong feeling of responsibility. He said that in addition to that there was the fact that his court had a very limited number of cases and no administrative responsibilities, so that the members of the court had a chance to do some thinking. He said that he only had one young man secretary whom he kept one year and then replaced by another one fresh out of law school and that he did not even have a stenographer and did all his writing in long hand; that that gave him the necessary freedom from interruptions and administrative detail, so that he could give his entire time to study and meditation.[88]

Such an immediate sense of human frailty made Brandeis uneasy about all agglomerations of power, whether economic or political. He instinctively distrusted those, "the world's wise," who claimed to possess sufficient knowledge, ability, and foresight to order or plan the lives of others. Such pervasive skepticism did not necessarily engender pessimism, though; for his mind was able to reach beyond the awareness of human limitations to a hopeful perception of human potentialities as yet unrealized so far as the great mass of ordinary men and women were concerned. In the memorandum he wrote for Frankfurter in 1936, Riesman, offered one of the more perceptive commentaries on this strand of the justice's thought. While noting his former chief's mistrustful attitude toward power and human abilities, he was quick to explain that this did not generate in him any sense of fatalism. "Justice Brandeis . . . does not believe that human beings are the prey of unconquerable forces," he wrote;

he puts his trust in reason but a skepticism of power and human limitations lies at the bottom of his constitutional philosophy; for him the separation of powers in all its forms . . . [is] the accretion of wisdom, since humans are limited and may be perverse. Since no man is wise enough nor good enough to run the whole show, freedom can only be attained in the interstices between competitive units, clashing, none large enough to dominate or disturb the state by too violent combat. As you say, he prefers freedom to efficiency but he also believes that in the long run freedom is more efficient since it utilizes better the human material and is able to cope with novel situations.[89]

This, at bottom, was what Brandeis found so appealing about the pioneer colonies he had seen in Palestine in 1919 and why he continued to support them throughout the remainder of his life. His efforts on behalf of Zionism occupied a good deal of the free time left him by his labors on the Court, but after the rejection of his leadership at the Cleveland Convention in 1921 they were directed into new channels. During the twenties and thirties the emphasis would be on raising the investment funds needed to develop Palestine along the lines set out in the Pittsburgh Platform and the Zeeland Memorandum. Certain aspects of the settlement task, such as the eradication of malaria, the generation of hydroelectric power, and the extraction of minerals from the Dead Sea, struck him as particularly worthwhile and so attracted his personal support; however, it was in the acquisition of land that his prophet's vision was to prove most significant for the future.[90]

When, in 1933, David Ben-Gurion presented him with a memorandum outlining the importance of the southern Negev region, and stressing the need for a major port on the Red Sea linking the future Israel with Asia, the justice immediately saw the point and gave him the $100,000 he required to establish the Jewish settlement at Eilat; and later in the decade he would secretly supply Ben-Gurion with the money needed to arm the Haganah defense units against Arab attacks. Convinced as he was that German Jews had no choice but to leave their country, and having no comparable sense of Arab nationalism, Brandeis easily grew exasperated when Jewish emigration was frustrated by the seeming intransigence and prejudice of other countries. It was probably what he regarded as Britain's mishandling of the mounting tension between Jews and Arabs in Palestine, and London's effective repudiation of the promises contained in the Balfour Declaration, which sparked off the outburst that Harold Laski found so shocking; but such displays of naked emotion were not typical. In fact, when Palestinian developments were involved, his most common expression of feeling was one of pride in the advances made by the fledgling national homeland, and especially by its young pioneers. At the end of 1939, for instance, he could be found encouraging the organizers of a Jewish educational program to carry out "a detailed study of recent and current achievements" there. "I know of nothing in Jewish history finer," he told his correspondent, "than the lives of many groups of young men and women in the agricultural settlements. Their remarkable achievements are the fruit of complete devotion to the cause of their people."[91]

Yet, to Brandeis, they had done more than to comport themselves like good Jews; they had sought to grapple with the limitations of strength and wisdom common to all human beings. For beneath the emotional attachments of shared ethnicity and an ancient cultural tradition, what the American Isaiah had helped create in Palestine was the archetypical "small unit" of his imagination—a living laboratory in which to experiment with the institutional forms and social values that lay at the heart of his vision for the future of all civilized men.

More concrete than such speculations, however, and rather more comprehensive in their scope than any number of fragmentary references to Roosevelt and his administration, were the cases that came before the Supreme Court in the mid-1930s including several brought to test the constitutional validity of New Deal measures. Here, Brandeis had to find some means of reconciling his own social and political preferences with the standards of judicial behavior and patterns of constitutional interpretation for which he had been fighting since his appointment in 1916. It must be said that he did not always succeed.

As noted earlier, it was not until the "hot oil" code came before the Court in *Panama Refining Company v. Ryan* (1935) that he appreciated fully the NRA's methods of doing business. The case concerned the president's authority under the terms of the National Industrial Recovery Act to issue orders prohibiting the transportation in interstate commerce of oil produced in violation of state regulatory legislation. During the oral arguments on 10 December 1934, Brandeis discovered that it was all but impossible for those affected by such orders to discover what they contained, and that the only copy of the industry code seen by the petitioners had been in the "hip pocket of a government agent sent down to Texas from Washington." The following day Paul Freund wrote Frankfurter to explain the significance of what had occurred in court. The justice's questioning of Assistant Attorney General Stephens about "the availability of orders and regulations" had been rigorous and telling, he believed, and at very least had proved "the need for an official gazette." But the issue had gone beyond this.

L.D.B. was chiefly concerned, on the constitutional side, with delegation under 9(c), which permits the President to declare acts a crime without making findings. Several of the others—Van D[evanter] most vigorously—were evidently with him on this. The hearing was really concerned with the fundamentals of representative and responsible government, not with the ills of the oil industry. All in all, a salutary approach, I think, though the oil boys and the Dep[artmen]t of Justice are sorrowful.

They were soon to be sadder still. Early in the New Year the chief justice ruled that the delegation of legislative power authorized under section 9(c) was invalid because of its breadth; only Justice Cardozo dissented.[92]

Although he did not write the opinion himself, Brandeis did have "a great deal to do" with it, as he later told Frankfurter; for having declined Hughes's invitation to take the job on, he then played a major role in "shaping" it "& setting my brethren on either side to ask some of their questions." In the Gold Clause cases, however, he deliberately distanced himself from the Court's decision. "I was very glad that I was not asked to write [the] opinion as well I might have been," he confided to the Harvard professor shortly afterward. The issue at stake here was the government's 1933 decision to abandon the gold standard and nullify the clauses in all public and private contracts specifying payment in gold. In *Norman v. Baltimore & Ohio Railroad Company* (1935) the Court upheld the move with regard to private transactions, but in *Perry v. United States* (1935) held that Congress lacked the power to repudiate its own obligations. Though prepared to vote with the majority in both cases, Brandeis was deeply unhappy about doing so. "[I] knew what my legal conclusions were, at the outset, & [was] so completely out of sympathy on matters of policy with what [the] Gov[ernmen]t did that I thought it best to say nothing," he explained later. The economics of the situation had been "doubtful at best," while the "morals were plain & most important. I don't know," he concluded gloomily, "whether we shall recover."[93]

If the *Panama* and *Perry* decisions had been bad news for the administration, even worse was to follow. On 6 May 1935, in *Railroad Retirement. Board v. Alton Railroad Company*, the Railroad Retirement Act was struck down by a majority of 5 to 4, with Brandeis this time numbered in the minority along with Hughes, Stone, and Cardozo. Speaking for the Court, Justice Roberts held that not only was the due process clause of the Fifth Amendment contravened by the act; it also failed to measure up as "a regulation of interstate commerce within the meaning of the Constitution." It was this latter aspect of the decision, in effect denying Congress the power to enact *any* compulsory pension plan for railroad employees, which particularly troubled the chief justice. "The power committed to Congress to govern interstate commerce does not require that its government should be wise, much less that it should be perfect," he observed.

The power implies a broad discretion and thus permits a wide range even of mistakes. Expert discussion of pension plans reveals different views of the manner in which they should be set up and a close study of advisable methods is in progress. It is not our province to enter that field, and I am not persuaded that Congress in entering it for the purpose of regulating interstate carriers, has transcended the limits of the authority which the Constitution confers.

Although there is no evidence to suggest that Brandeis took any part in the drafting of this dissent, it certainly followed the principle of judicial self-restraint elaborated in many of his own opinions down the years and was fully in line with his earlier thinking on the constitutionality of compensation laws generally.[94]

The Court's biggest blow to the policy objectives of the First New Deal fell three weeks later on 27 May, "Black Monday," when within the space of a few hours the government lost the NRA, the Frazier-Lemke Mortgage Relief Act, and, as noticed earlier, the right to dismiss administrators appointed to work with independent agencies. Brandeis voted with the majority in all three cases, and actually delivered the opinion of the Court in *Louisville Land Bank v. Radford*, observing that, by the terms of the Fifth Amendment, "private property shall not be . . . taken even for a wholly public use without just compensation," regardless of how great the supposed need of the nation. No call for bold experimentation here! Roosevelt and his officials were at first dismayed, then baffled, then downright angry.[95]

Brandeis, on the other hand, could scarcely contain his jubilation. Immediately after the decisions were handed down, he summoned Ben Cohen and Tommy Corcoran—two of his and Frankfurter's principal lieutenants within the administration—to a meeting in the anteroom of the Clerk's Office. "The Justice was visibly excited and deeply agitated," remembered Cohen the following day, and went on to recall the conversation that ensued.

> "You have heard," he gasped, "our three decisions. They change everything. The Court was unanimous. . . . You must phone Felix and have him down in the morning to talk to the President. You must see that Felix understands the situation and explains it to the President. You must also explain it to the men Felix brought into the Government. They must understand that these three decisions change everything. The President has been living in a fool's paradise."

When Corcoran interrupted him to suggest that the narrow definition of interstate commerce contained in the *Schechter* ruling might imperil the holding-company legislation then pending in Congress, Brandeis did not demur, but only repeated his remark about Roosevelt living in a fool's paradise. "'The Court unanimously has held that these broad powers cannot be exercised over matters within the States,'" he went on more lucidly.

> "All the powers of the States cannot be centralized in the Federal government. The Federal commissions exercise quasi-legislative and quasi-judicial powers. We have overruled much of what was said in the Meyers [*sic*] Case, and restricted the decisions to purely executive officers—officers performing ministerial acts which the President himself might perform if he had the time."

He repeatedly stressed how the unanimity of the Court meant that everything the administration had been doing would have to change. It was as though these three decisions had somehow coalesced in his mind to represent the vindication of every constitutional principle he held dear.[96]

Neither the unanimity nor the euphoria were to last long; for what linked the decisions of "Black Monday" was less a common thread of constitutional interpretation than an ephemeral coalition of the Court's warring factions held together by a shared hostility to what they regarded as executive arrogance and congressional incompetence. In Brandeis's case, a mounting distaste for the administrative malpractices of the recovery agency—coupled, it should be noted, with both a natural contempt for the sloppy draftsmanship of much early New Deal legislation and a long-standing desire to stem further federal encroachment on a sphere of operations constitutionally reserved for state action—was sufficient cause to side with the conservative doctrines enunciated in *Schechter*, albeit at the cost of setting aside, for the present at least, his customary unwillingness to second-guess the wisdom of legislative decisions. The legal principles invoked in *Radford* and *Humphrey's Executor*, by contrast, were essentially those of procedural due process and the separation of powers—matters that seldom divided the Court. Future cases would see the old divisions reassert themselves, however; for where such contentious issues as substantive due process or the government's powers of taxation were involved, or where petitioners sought judicial review of statutes by means of spurious claims in equity, Brandeis and his "liberal" colleagues would once again discover that they and the conservatives had few fundamental ideas in common.

He had been prepared to accept the chief justice s convoluted reasoning on the commerce clause in *Schechter* because he agreed with the conclusion Hughes was seeking to reach. But what would he do with a principle of law he regarded as truly sacrosanct, or with a piece of government legislation that he wished to uphold? In *United States v. Butler* (1936) it was his concern to sustain the government's taxing power which led him to join in Stone's minority opinion rather than any newfound enthusiasm for the AAA. Indeed, the extent of his political aversion to the New Deal's plans for agriculture was hardly less pronounced than his dislike for the NRA. This is evident from a letter he wrote to Frankfurter in February 1935 following news of Jerome Frank's removal from the Agriculture Department's legal division. This would have saddened him more, he confessed, had he not been convinced that the AAA's crop curtailment policy would soon prove disastrous. Quite apart from the main damage being done to the functioning of agricultural markets, he noted several regrettable "by-products" as well: "The 2,500,000 dispossessed; the Arkansas anti-free speech proceedings; the suppression of Mary Meyer's [sic] reports; the lessening of the traffic of the southern railroads"—all were deplorable. Nevertheless, when an opportunity presented itself in *Butler* to strike down the root cause of these ills by denying the government's right to levy the processing tax needed to fund the AAA's operations, this time he declined to bend his constitutional scruples to accommodate his political judgment.[97]

But his vote in *Butler* merely salved his conscience; it did not preserve the Agricultual Adjustment Act, which was struck down by a majority of 6 to 3. If other items of New Deal legislation that he considered more worthwhile were to be sustained in subsequent cases—such as the Tennessee Valley Authority Act, the Wagner Labor Relations Act, or the recent Social Security measures—an alternative strategy would have to be found. As we saw in the previous chapter, one promising avenue was that explored in the *Ashwander* case, where Brandeis urged his brethren to refuse jurisdiction. In fact this was not an isolated incident. A few months later, with the Guffey Coal Act at stake, he drafted a short memorandum re *Carter v. Carter Coal* (1936) in which a similar line of argument was attempted. However, the flimsiness of its reasoning and the lack of supporting legal authorities for its central contentions drew a scathing critique from David Riesman, and the effort was quickly abandoned. When the Court's decision was finally announced in May 1936, Brandeis was content to join Justice Cardozo's dissent on the merits of the case.[98]

The detailed examination of later New Deal cases falls outside the scope of the present study, for the simple reason that Brandeis refrained from writing his own opinion in any of them; and in view of what we know about his attitude toward the AAA, it would seem dangerous to draw specific lessons from his concurrence in the opinions of his colleagues when collateral evidence is wholly absent. Nevertheless, two general conclusions do seem appropriate regarding his last years on the Court. In the first place, Brandeis's legal dilemma with regard to the centralizing thrust of the New Deal was never satisfactorily resolved. It was a combination of F.D.R.'s resounding election victory in the fall of 1936 and his ill-fated Court-packing plan the following spring that protected the legislation of the Second New Deal from the kind of judicial mauling meted out to the earlier measures—not the motive force of Isaiah's constitutional reasoning in *Ashwander*, nor any sudden visceral conversion to the cause of activist government on the part of his more reactionary brethren.

Second, as we saw in the last chapter, those closest to Brandeis became increasingly conscious of a new and unsettling determination to reach decisions that were ideologically congenial to him, regardless of any consequences this might entail for previously cherished canons of judicial consistency. In some instances, such as the Oregon berry-box case that so disturbed Riesman, the result could perhaps be explained by the justice's choice of one constitutional principle over another: let us say the plenitude of a state's police powers as against the free flow of commerce between neighboring states. In others, though, Brandeis's more transparent purpose was to have the Court's new majority endorse a position he had previously elaborated in one or more dissenting opinions. For example, his ruling in *Senn v. Tile Layers Protective Union* (1937), which he delivered amid industrial-relations tensions heightened by the recent wave of sit-down strikes in the auto industry, saw the postulates he had expounded in *Truax v. Corrigan* recognized at last as the law of the land, whereas Taft's arguments in the earlier case were consigned to oblivion. This was an objective Brandeis considered important enough to justify the settling of a constitutional issue that had not even been raised by counsel at the original trial. In some men, the gulf separating the jurisprudential ethics adduced in *Ashwander* from those calmly set aside in *Senn* only a year later might be praised as evidence of a timely pragmatism; in such a self-conscious pillar of virtue as Brandeis, however, it was rather to be lamented as the sure sign of a rapidly advancing old age, of an almost desperate awareness that time was fast running out.[99]

"The wishes of youth are garnered in age." Thus runs the old German saying prefixed as a motto to the second part of Goethe's *Poetry and Truth*. In this part of his autobiography, the grand exemplar of German letters is contemplating the fate of youthful ambition. With single-minded determination to achieve his heart's desire, he believes, a man might at last avail himself of worldly wealth or intellectual preeminence, if either were the object of his adolescent dreams. Indeed, if favored by his circumstances and spurred on by the tenor of the times, he might reasonably aspire to success in both these areas, and with perseverance and application could feel confident of his ultimate good fortune. Doubtless, he observes,

> so many accidental hindrances join with human limitations, that here we have unfinished beginnings, there an empty grasp, and wish after wish crumbles away. But if these wishes have sprung from a pure heart, and are in conformity with the necessities of the times, we may composedly look on unfinished plans and frustrated efforts in the calm assurance that not only will the incomplete come to completion, the dropped threads be resumed, but that also many kindred things, things we have never attempted, never even thought of, will be brought to pass. And if, during our own lifetime, we see that performed by others, to which we ourselves felt an earlier call, but which we had perforce relinquished, with so much besides: then the inspiring feeling must be ours, that only mankind in its entirety is the true man, and that the individual can only then be joyous and happy when he has the courage to merge himself in the great whole.[100]

"Whenever one returns to Goethe one finds new revelations," Brandeis confided to his sister-in-law in October 1932, after rereading the poet's autobiography during his summer vacation at Chatham. "Writing was but an incident of his living." Coming as it did, therefore, from one of his favorite books, the justice would certainly have been familiar with the passage just quoted. It was one whose wisdom he had good cause to ponder in the closing years of a life which, though rich in achievement by most standards, had experienced more than its fair share of frustrated dreams and ill-founded optimisms. After his retirement from the Court in 1939, much of his time was taken up with family and friends, well away from the hurly-burly of public life, albeit that from time to time he felt constrained by the plight of the Jews in Europe and Palestine to reenter the fray on their behalf. In some ways it was a happy time; but it also brought inevitable regrets about what had not been achieved, and about how limited his power had become to influence events. "All I can do now," he told his niece Fannie sadly in May 1940, "is to let people talk to me and imagine I help them. I don't—but . . . ," and his voice trailed away into silence.[101]

Coda: The Wisdom of The World

O, not with knowledge is Wisdom bought;
And the spirit that soareth too high for mortals
Shall see few days: whosoever hath caught
At the things too great for a man's attaining
Even blessings assured shall he lose in the gaining.
— Euripides, *The Bacchae*

Louis Dembitz Brandeis died of a heart attack on 5 October, 1941, only a few weeks short of his eighty-fifth birthday. Two days later, a small group of family, friends, and professional colleagues gathered in the California Street apartment to pay their last respects. Much to the annoyance of Rabbi Stephen Wise, no religious service was held; instead a string quartet played selections from Beethoven, after which two of those closest to him stepped forward to say a few words in his memory. Speaking on behalf of the justice's former law clerks, Dean Acheson recalled not only his passion for truth, but, more surprisingly in the opinion of some, his personal sensibility as well. "We are the fortunate ones," he averred, "but what he has meant to us is not very different from what he has meant to hundreds of young men and women who have grown up under his influence." By Acheson's account, the seemingly austere prophet had also been a wise and much-loved mentor to those among the secretaries who had been willing and able to reach beyond his outward display of reserve. Their relationship

> was far more than that between young men and one of the greatest and most revered figures of our time. What gave it life, what gave it endurance was the depth of affection which the warmth of his interest and solicitude for us inspired. Throughout these years we have brought him all our problems and all our troubles, and he had time for all of us. In talk with him the problems answered themselves. A question, a comment, and the difficulties began to disappear; the dross and shoddy began to appear for what it was, and we wondered why the matter had ever seemed difficult. . . . I have heard him speak of some achievement of one of us with all the pride and of some sorrow or disappointment of another with all the tenderness of a father speaking of his sons. He entered so deeply into our lives because he took us so deeply into his.

In stark contrast to this intimate portrait, the second eulogist, Felix Frankfurter, uttered a few sober sentences about how Hebraism and Hellenism, two of the "dominant sources of our culture," had been so felicitously fused in Brandeis's mind; stressed his life-long commitment to upholding the moral law; and concluded with a passage from Bunyan's *Pilgrim's Progress* describing the death of Mr. Valiant-for-Truth.[1]

Listening in person to these very different addresses, Dr. Jonas Frieden-wald, one of Brandeis's younger Zionist associates, was in no doubt which version of Isaiah he preferred. As he explained to Frankfurter the following day,

> I was deeply moved by your talk. It had all the more passion in that it was so im-personal and seemed to me most fitting for there certainly was never anyone with a greater impersonal passion than LDB or one whose lack of ease in Zion was more impersonal. It seemed to me there was no word of truth in the picture of fond and sentimental paternalism which Acheson painted. Rather, I would have guessed, the Justice always fortified but never ameliorated his judgments by his emotions. I suspect that few if any people were ever fond of him in a cosy comfortable sort of way and that he mattered personally only to those few who knew how to reach love through veneration and respect.[2]

Was Acheson mistaken, then? David Riesman would certainly argue that he was; Paul Freund and Willard Hurst would probably declare that he was not. In so far as they relied on their own personal experiences, all would be correct. The future secretary of state was one of those who stayed in close touch with Brandeis once his clerkship was ended. When Alice was ill in the midtwenties—a time of great emotional stress for the justice—he was there as a much-needed friend and companion with whom the older man could share political gossip and forget his loneliness. Others, like Freund and Hurst, might well have recognized the description of a kindly patriarch solic-itous for their welfare, but it is difficult to picture Isaiah greeting them or any of his other young protégés with a cheery: "Dean, what is the latest dirt?" By the time he retired from the Court, almost all those with whom he had been on similar terms of intimacy were gone—Sam Warren in 1910, his brother Alfred in 1928, Bess Evans and Norman Hapgood in 1937; and with the exception of Frankfurter and Julian Mack none of those who worked as his lieutenants in later years, be it in Zionism or in sundry other causes, be-came close friends. Thus there were few left able to identify with Acheson's personal remarks.[3]

But what of the other main image proffered in his address: that of Bran-deis as a champion of absolute truth? As we have seen, this perception too was the product of firsthand experiences; however this time his words drew an outline that others less intimate with the justice were capable of recogniz-ing for themselves. "We are the generation which has lived during and be-tween two wars," Acheson observed darkly. To them had belonged "the desert years of the human spirit . . . the barren years of disillusionment"—years when the very existence of truth had been called into question. They had lived through a time in which "men with a little new-found knowledge believed that they had pried into the mainsprings of the human mind and spirit, and could make mankind work for any end by playing upon its fears and appetites." Perhaps some of those listening were reminded at this point of the justice's oft-repeated warning that "the worldly wise are not wise, claiming more than mortals know"? Whether they were or not, the speaker continued to develop his theme. "These were the years during which we were with the Justice and saw in action his burning faith that the verities to which men had clung through the ages were verities; that evil never could be good; that falsehood was not truth, not even if all the ingenuity of science reiterated it in waves that encircled the earth." Had they not heard Brandeis come close to echoing St. Paul's injunction to think on those things which were true, honest, just, pure, and of good report? Such was the vision of a latter-day prophet who knew that

> truth was less than truth unless it were expounded so that people could understand and believe. During these years of retreat from reason, his faith in the human mind and in the will and capacity of people to understand and grasp the truth never wavered or tired. In a time of moral and intellectual anarchy and frustration he handed on the great tradition of faith in the mind and spirit of man which is the faith of the prophets and poets, of Socrates, of Lincoln.[4]

Twenty years later, one of the clerks for whom Acheson had spoken so eloquently, returned once more to the theme of truth. In the spring of 1960, Judge Henry J. Friendly of the United States Court of Appeals was in Louisville to address members of the Mississippi Valley Historical Association on the subject of Brandeis's "general legal philosophy." Nearing the end of a detailed evaluation, which in its published version Frankfurter would subsequently regard as "just right and admirably expressed," he turned at last to consider Brandeis's thinking in the light of a quotation from the Gospel according to St. John: "the truth shall make you free." This he believed had been the essence of the justice's teaching. "He was the authentic child of the *Aufklärung*," Friendly believed, who harbored "none of today's doubts as to whether the truth could be ascertained." While he clearly did not accept the evangelist's contention "that this truth could be found by abiding in the Word or in becoming the disciple of any leader," neither did he expect to elicit it by means of "intuition or from speculation in metaphysics." In Brandeis's view, it could be discovered "only from the relentless, disinterested and critical study of facts." Yet despite a deliberate focus on the principles underpinning its subject's jurisprudence, Friendly's address, like those of Acheson and Frankfurter before it, dealt not in facts but in abstractions. For a more concrete assessment of the significance Isaiah's vision held for his contemporaries, we must look elsewhere.[5]

The justice's death had occurred precisely nine weeks before the Japanese attack on Pearl Harbor. By the time the Bar of the Supreme Court arranged its memorial tribute to him in December 1942, the United States had been at war for more than a year. It was not an involvement he had anticipated or advocated. Believing that western countries had no justification for controling Asia and hoping to witness soon their "orderly retreat," he had predicted back in 1921 that, left to themselves, it would be India and China rather than Japan that would emerge as the dominant powers in the continent. Thereafter, the focus of his international concerns had narrowed progressively, to the point where even the most momentous events stirring in the wider world tended to be interpreted solely in terms of their likely impact on the Jewish settlements in Palestine. Since Japanese expansionism could in no way directly threaten the Middle East, it made little obvious impression on his conscious mind.[6]

Although he had been unable to foresee America's active participation in a global conflict, he did nevertheless have some inkling of the sweeping social, economic, and political changes that such a war might bring ln its wake; they were, after all, but a quickening of the institutional revolution against which he had been inveighing for almost half a lifetime. Economic mobilization on a scale sufficient to guarantee democracy's victory over the Axis powers was soon to bring about the long-feared triumph of Bigness in almost every aspect of American life, and by a cruel irony would ensure that Brandeis's liberal vision became an ideological irrelevance for the rising generation. In short, the world war and its consequences were to erect an insurmountable barrier between the moral and practical aspirations of his idealistic philosophy and the tangible realities of the postwar world.

On that December morning in 1942, at least one of the speakers called on to address the select circle of lawyers gathered together in the Supreme Court Building was aware of the enormous gulf already existing between the dominant values of America's material culture and the righteous ethics of Isaiah's austere spirituality. There, Learned B. Hand, himself a highly respected member of the judiciary, provided the most perceptive of all the many eulogies uttered and written to the late justice's memory in the months and years following his death. Deeply conscious of the hazards attending any effort to disentangle the interwoven strands of a man's life, and of affording to any one isolated element of his makeup a disproportionate value, Hand sought nevertheless to identify the vital spirit that had animated Brandeis's thinking. The connecting thread singled out for particular scrutiny was what he described as his subject's "hatred of the mechanization of life," as a result of which he had come to live "at odds with much of the movement of his time."[7]

As Hand fully appreciated, Brandeis was less fearful of the artifacts produced by technology than of the crushing effect on humanity itself, which their mindless use seemed to foreshadow:

In many modern contrivances which to most of us seem innocent acquisitions of mankind—the motor car for instance—he saw a significance hostile to life's deeper, truer values. If he compromised as to a very few, the exceptions only served to emphasize the consistency of his conviction that by far the greater part of what passes for improvement, and is greedily converted into necessity, is tawdry, vain and destructive of human values.

His principal concern was not really with the dubious worth of so much gadgetry and mechanical convenience, but rather with the institutional structures needed to produce it—the giant corporations and finance houses, the sprawling bureaucracies—and with the evermore directed, homogeneous, and impersonal patterns of existence that these structures threatened to impose on individual citizens, now thought of increasingly as "workers" or "consumers." This was what he meant by "the curse of bigness." Although, as we have seen, he had long harbored empirical reservations about the actual efficiency of large industrial conglomerates, and always doubted the capacity of human minds to comprehend and control "such manifold and intricate structures," his skepticism in these areas was merely incident to a more fundamental perception. In Hand's view, what really mattered to Brandeis was "the inevitable effect of size on the individual," regardless of whether the efficiency of the enterprise was impaired or not.

At the same time, he believed the protection of individuality to be just as vital in the political as it was in the economic sphere, and this went a long way toward explaining the precise definitions of legitimate political action occurring so prominently in his pronouncements from the bench. For whereas the exercise of political power might constitute the only defense a vulnerable citizen possessed against the powerful forces in society always threatening to overwhelm him, it could also become his oppressor. Without a proper separation of powers, and a rigorous observance of the checks and balances afforded by the Constitution, the concentration of political power might eventually prove even more menacing than its economic counterpart. Thus, Hand observed, Brandeis's

determination to preserve the autonomy of the states—though it went along with an unflinching assertion of federal power in matters which he reckoned truly national—amounted almost to an obsession. Haphazard as they might be in origin, and even devoid of much present significance, the states were the only breakwater against the ever pounding surf which threatened to submerge the individual and destroy the only kind of society in which personality could survive.

The proper measure was not what the states currently were but what they might become.

Yet if he looked to state governments to provide a framework within which his conception of the "good life" might take form, it was on the existence and vitality of even smaller social units that his ideas about the development of human potentialities ultimately depended. "He believed," Hand declared, "that there could be no true community save that built upon

the personal acquaintance of each with each; by that alone could character
and ability be rightly gauged. . . . Only so could the latent richness which
lurks in all of us come to flower." Size was again seen as the destructive element. Once the social context in which men lived out their lives became too
big to facilitate "mutual contact and appraisal," the "flavour and significance" of everyday existence began to diminish apace; relationships became "standardized" leading people to ignore in their fellow citizens "all
those authentic features which mark, and which indeed alone create, an
individual."

Isaiah's vision was, Hand realized, a dual one; for while he had never
ceased to invoke in the minds of his disciples a picture of what the ideal society could be like, neither had he ever balked at warning all who would listen
what it was in the process of becoming. Stripped to its essentials, the substance of his admonition remained stark:

> The herd is regaining its ancient and evil primacy; civilization is being reversed, for
> it has consisted of exactly the opposite process of individualization—witness the
> history of law and morals. These many inventions are a step backward; they lull
> men into the belief that because they are severally less subject to violence, they
> are more safe; because they are more steadily fed and clothed, they are more
> secure from want; because their bodies are cleaner their hearts are purer. It is an
> illusion; our security has actually diminished as our demands become more ex-
> acting; our comforts we purchase at the cost of a softer fibre, a feebler will and an
> infantile suggestibility.

Aware as he was of Brandeis's message to contemporary industrial society,
though, Hand was equally sure of society's response: The city states of
Ancient Greece lay in ruins, and Jefferson's ideal commonwealth of sturdy
yeomen had proven a mirage in his own lifetime; the realities of preindustrial life had in any case been far removed from the virtuous harmonies of
Arcadian mythology and were well lost. Mankind, and especially those yet
to enjoy their full share of the material benefits that science and technology
could provide, would not forego "the vast command over Nature" that the
previous century had brought to pass. "The conquest of disease, the elimination of drudgery, the freedom from famine, the enjoyment of comfort, yes
even that most doubtful gift, the not too distant possession of a leisure we
have not yet learned to use—on these, having once tasted them, mankind
[would] continue to insist." Moreover, because all of these great advances
seemed predicated on "the cooperation and organization of great numbers,"
the case for returning to a smaller scale of operations would only prove
attractive if it could be shown that doing so was fully compatible with preserving, indeed with extending still further, the material progress already
gained.

These were powerful arguments, and ones that the eulogist himself found
it hard to contradict. "Societies small enough for their members to have

personal acquaintance with each other" were, he accepted, a thing of the past; and the "black art" of publicity, mediated through magazines, radio, cinema, and the press, had clearly to be recognized as a permanent substitute for personal judgments based on firsthand knowledge. Yet at the same time, he remained acutely conscious that manipulation of these same mass media was also an elemental buttress of totalitarian power and had indeed provided one of the primary mechanisms by which fascism became established in Europe. It was "the power of reiterated suggestion and consecrated platitude" which, perhaps more than any other factor, had brought Western civilization to its present "imminent peril of destruction." The principle most at stake in the war, the principle Brandeis had most treasured, was in fact the survival of individuality itself. The outcome of this titanic conflict would, he believed, finally determine "whether the ultimate value shall be this wistful, cloudy, errant, You or I, or that Great Beast, Leviathan, that phantom conjured up as an *ignis fatuus* in our darkness and a scapegoat for our futility."

Americans had now chosen their sides in this struggle and, in considering the life and teaching of Louis D. Brandeis, could surely refresh their faith in the rectitude of the decision taken. The message they would find there, however, was not one guaranteed to afford them comfort. "A great people," observed Hand, "does not go to its leaders for incantations or liturgies by which to propitiate fate or to cajole victory; it goes to them to peer into the recesses of its own soul, to lay bare its deepest desires; it goes to them as it goes to its poets and seers." Here was the role that Ahad Ha-Am had ascribed to the prophets of Hebrew tradition: men who must speak truth because they could not do otherwise. The form in which Isaiah's "truth" was couched mattered less now than its essential substance, Hand believed.

> If I have read it aright, this was that substance: "You may build your Towers of Babel to the clouds; you may contrive ingeniously to circumvent Nature by devices beyond even the understanding of all but a handful; you may provide endless distractions to escape the tedium of your barren lives; you may rummage the whole planet for your ease and comfort. It will avail you nothing; the more you struggle, the more deeply you will be enmeshed. Not until you have the courage to meet yourself face to face; to take true account of what you find; to respect the sum of that account for itself and not for what it may bring you; deeply to believe that each of you is a holy vessel unique and irreplaceable; only then will you have taken the first steps along the path of Wisdom. Be content with nothing less; let not the heathen beguile you to their temples, or the Sirens with their songs. Lay up your treasure in the Heaven of your hearts, where moth and rust do not corrupt and thieves cannot break through and steal."

True, the words of this summation were all Judge Hand's, but Louis Dembitz Brandeis would not have dissented from a single syllable.

Notes

Abbreviations Used in the Notes

BL   Melvin I. Urofsky and David W. Levy, eds., *Letters of Louis D. Brandeis* 5 vols. Albany: State University of New York Press, 1971–78.
FFLC   Felix Frankfurter Papers, Library of Congress, Washington, D.C.
LBHLS   Louis Dembitz Brandeis Papers, Harvard Law School Library, Cambridge, Mass.
LBLU   Louis Dembitz Brandeis Papers, University of Louisville Library, Louisville, Ky.
LDB   Louis Dembitz Brandeis.
SGBU   Susan Brandeis Gilbert Papers, Goldfarb Library, Brandeis University, Waltham, Mass.

Prelude: The Good Grey Judge

1. Melvin I. Urofsky, *A Mind of One Piece: Brandeis and American Reform* (New York: Scribner, 1971), p. xii, ascribes the phrase used in his title to Paul A. Freund. Harold J. Laski, *The American Democracy: A Commentary and Interpretation* (New York: Viking Press, 1948), p. 112.

2. *Other People's Money—And How the Bankers Use It* (New York: Stokes, 1914); *Business—A Profession* (Boston: Small, Maynard, 1914); Alfred Lief, ed., *The Social and Economic Views of Mr. Justice Brandeis* (New York: Vanguard Press, 1930); Osmond K. Fraenkel, ed., *The Curse of Bigness* (New York: Viking Press, 1934); Alfred Lief, ed., *The Brandeis Guide to the Modern World* (Boston: Little, Brown, 1941); Solomon Goldman, ed., *Brandeis on Zionism*, (Washington, D.C.: Zionist Organization of America, 1942). For subsequent reissues and new editions of the earlier collections, see inf., pp. 317–18.

3. Melvin I. Urofsky and David W. Levy, eds., *Letters of Louis D. Brandeis*, 5 vols. (Albany N.Y.: State University of New York Press, 1971–78); Frankfurter to Abraham G. Duker, 10 May 1956, FFLC, Box 127. For the erroneous inferences drawn from this source of material by Thomas K. McCraw, see inf., p. 148.

4. The most important of the early biographies are: Jacob De Haas, *Louis. D. Brandeis: A Biographical Sketch* (New York: Bloch, 1929); Alfred Lief, *Brandeis: The Personal History of an American Ideal* (New York: Stackpole, 1936); Alpheus T. Mason, *Brandeis: A Free Man's Life* (New York: Viking Press, 1946). The two specialist judicial studies are: Samuel J. Konefsky, *The Legacy of Holmes and Brandeis* (New York: Macmillan, 1956); Alexander M. Bickel, *The Unpublished Opinions of Mr. Justice Brandeis: The Supreme Court at Work* (Cambridge, Mass.: Harvard University Press, 1957). The biographical essays contained in Urofsky, *Mind of One Piece*, including a particularly good one (chap. 2) on LDB as a jurist, represent the

first modern attempt at a scholarly reappraisal. The 1980s saw publication of two new full-length biographies: Lewis J. Paper, *Brandeis: An Intimate Biography of One of America's Truly Great Supreme Court Justices* (Secaucus, N.J.: Citadel Press, 1983); Philippa Strum, *Louis D. Brandeis: Justice for the People* (Cambridge, Mass.: Harvard University Press, 1984). To these should also be added Allon Gal, *Brandeis of Boston* (Cambridge, Mass.: Harvard University Press, 1980), which limits its prime focus to the years before LDB's appointment to the bench. All three are excellent. Other, more specialized studies will be identified as appropriate in later notes.

5. Author's interview with Paul A. Freund, Harvard Law School, 25 April 1983.

6. Paul A. Freund, "The Liberalism of Justice Brandeis," *American Jewish Archives* 10 (1958): 4–5.

7. Interview with Freund, 25 April 1983.

8. Freund, "Liberalism of Justice Brandeis," pp. 5–6.

9. With the exception of Mason and Gal (see sup., n. 4), LDB's biographers have paid only passing attention to the first part of his life and his early career in the law. It is instructive to recall, though, that when he first became involved in the public campaigns of the Progressive Era he was already in middle life, his eventual eighty-five-year span being more than halfway toward completion.

10. LDB's "worldly wise" maxim is, in fact, a misquotation of the following lines from Gilbert Murray's translation of Euripides' play *The Bacchae*:

> "Hidden from the eyes of day,
>   Watchers are there in the skies,
>   That can see man's life, and prize
> Deeds done by things of clay.
>   *But the world's Wise are not wise,*
>   *Claiming more than mortal may.*
> Life is such a little thing."

Euripides: Translated into English Rhyming Verse (New York: Longman, Green, 1902), p. 96. Emphasis is added. A subsequent edition of Murray's translation was among the books on Greek history and culture that LDB and his wife were said to "cherish as daily companions": LDB to Adele Brandeis, 29 September 1924, *BL*, 5:140–41. The more literal Loeb translation of these lines is quoted in the epigraph on p. 333.

11. Quoted in Freund's introduction to Bickel, *Unpublished Opinions*, p. xv. In fact, the exegesis of these words offered here is almost as enigmatic as the original: "And so, surely, [his memoirs] had been [written]; for in a life whose impulsion was the duty of public persuasion the record is as open, in the main, as a book. Such a life is measured out in words: not words that are recollections in tranquility, not inert counters with which to symbolize experience, but words that are the actual signs of living encounters, fragments of fleece, in Holmes' phrase, left on the hedges of life." About Felix Frankfurter and his long professional and personal association with LDB, see especially Nelson L. Dawson, *Louis D. Brandeis, Felix Frankfurter, and the New Deal* (Hamden, Conn.: Archon Books, 1980); H. N. Hirsch, *The Enigma of Felix Frankfurter* (New York: Basic Books, 1981); Bruce A. Murphy, *The Brandeis/Frankfurter Connection: The Secret Political Activities of Two Supreme Court Justices* (New York: Oxford University Press, 1982); Michael E. Parrish, *Felix Franfurter and His Times: The Reform Years* (New York: Free Press, 1982); Leonard Baker, *Brandeis and Frankfurter: a Dual Biography* (New York: Harper & Row, 1984); Robert A. Burt, *Two Jewish Justices: Outcasts in the Promised Land* (Berkeley: University of California Press, 1988).

12. Frankfurter to Riesman, 11 March 1936, FFLC, Box 96.

13. Mason to Frankfurter, 22 January 1960, FFLC, Box 83. For the origin and development of his relationship with the justice, see Mason to LDB, 3 March 1931, *BL*, 5:473, and editors' notes, pp. 473–74. Paper, *Brandeis*, pp. 393–94, offers a brief discussion of the circumstances that surrounded the writing of Mason's book; however, the thorny issue of whether LDB did or did not instruct Frankfurter to deny Mason access to his Court papers seems rather more open to question than Paper suggests.

14. Frankfurter to Bickel, 4 February 1958, FFLC, Box 127. In his preface to *Unpublished Opinions*, published the previous year, Bickel also mentions Mark DeWolfe Howe as having been "granted access" to LDB's Court papers along with himself and Freund, but this was probably in connection with Howe's work on Mr. Justice Holmes.

15. Frankfurter to Freund, 4 December 1951, FFLC, Box 56; Frankfurter to Simon Noveck, 1 December 1958, ibid., Box 128. References to the "judicial biography" are scattered throughout the Frankfurter Papers, but see especially Frankfurter to Mason, 11 January 1960 and Mason to Frankfurter, 22 January 1960, ibid., Box 83.

16. Frankfurter to Jaffe, 18 March 1947, FFLC, Box 70. For a fuller development of Jaffe's views on this subject, see his article: "Was Brandeis an Activist? The Search for Intermediate Premises," *Harvard Law Review* 80 (1966–67); 986–1003.

17. Wise to Frankfurter, 19 November 1941, FFLC, Box 128. As well as expressing his concern about Goldman, Wise was equally perturbed at the suggestion that LDB's son-in-law, Jack Gilbert, might undertake to write the "Zionist" biography: "To me it is tragic to think that the coarse hand of Gilbert is to touch the exquisite contour of L.D.B.'s memory." For the justice's own relationship with Gilbert, and the latter's involvement in Zionist affairs, see Paper, *Brandeis*, pp. 315–17. Even more illuminating is their correspondence in SGBU, Boxes 19–21. A brief summary of Wise's career and his association with LDB can be found in *BL*, editors' note, 3:296–97.

18. Frankfurter, "Mr. Justice Brandeis," *Harvard Law Review* 55 (1941–42); 181; the Wise extract is quoted in *BL*, 3:296–97.

Chapter 1. The Wishes of Youth

1. A fascinating description of the way in which visitors to the Ohio Valley perceived the region during the century or so before the Civil War can be found in John A. Jakle, *Images of the Ohio Valley: A Historical Geography of Travel, 1740–1860* (New York: Oxford University Press, 1977).

2. For the care needed in employing the term "Forty-Eighter," see Carl Wittke, *Refugees of Revolution: The German Forty-Eighters in America* (Philadelphia: University of Pennsylvania Press, 1952), pp. 3–5.

3. Josephine Goldmark, *Pilgrims of '48: One Man's Part in the Austrian Revolution of 1848 and a Family Migration to America* (New Haven: Yale University Press, 1930), pp. 175–76, 194–95; *Reminiscences of Frederika Brandeis: Written for her Son, Louis, in 1880 to 1886*, translated by Alice Goldmark Brandeis (privately printed, 1948), pp. 4, 12–13, 17, 44. For the importance of the silk trade at this period in Lombardy and Piedmont, see Bolton King, *A History of Italian Unity*, 2 vols. (1924; reprint, New York: Russell & Russell, 1967), 1:60, 104. Josephine and Alice Goldmark were the daughters of Joseph Goldmark, a prominent member of the Vienna Reichstag, who fled to America with a price on his head following the collapse of the 1848 revolution; their mother was Regina Wehle, one of the younger

children of Gottlieb and Eleanore. Alice Goldmark and LDB, who were married in March 1891, were therefore second cousins. In letters to his brother Alfred, LDB was still referring to his mother-in-law as "Aunt Regina" as late as 1912.

4. Goldmark, *Pilgrims of '48*, pp. 179, 182, 191. For the activities of the *Carbonari* in Italy between 1815 and 1832, see King, *Italian Unity*, 1:13–40, 110–25, 144; 2:384–85. The nature and extent of Moritz Wehle's involvement in these events remains unclear.

5. Goldmark, *Pilgrims of '48*, pp. 65–67; Stanley Z. Pech, *The Czech Revolution of 1848* (Chapel Hill: University of North Carolina Press, 1969), pp. 18–19, 45–46, 68, 139–40, 293–94. The riots in Prague were not unique, however. There were also anti-Jewish episodes recorded in Baden, Franconia, Hessen, and Posen in Germany, and at Pressburg in Hungary: see Wittke, *Refugees Revolution*, p. 86.

6. For a detailed account of the June Uprising in Prague, see Pech, *Czech Revolution*, chap. 6, especially pp. 149–50; cf. Goldmark, *Pilgrims of '48*, p. 68. Well aware of her father's role in 1848, Josephine Goldmark, like some Austrian officials at the time, fails to distinguish adequately between the circumstances of the Prague and Vienna revolts. As Pech observes (p. 158): "One unofficial public rumour even credited the Jews with causing the [Czech] uprising, a view doubtless influenced by the prominence of Jews in Viennese radical circles but hardly borne out by reality, for in Prague the Jews' only concern was to escape, with as few blows as possible, the rising tide of fury and scorn directed against them by a segment of the public." The importance of this factor in hastening the Wehles' departure is further underscored by the fact that other members of the family, though unwilling to abandon Europe altogether, felt constrained nevertheless to leave Prague at around the same time and to relocate themselves in Vienna: see *Reminiscences of Frederika Brandeis*, p. 7.

7. *BL*, 1:4, n. 6; Goldmark, *Pilgrims of '48*, pp. 196–200. Despite the open anti-Semitism demonstrated by some of the Prague insurgents, Adolph Brandeis was not the only young Jew wanting to play an active part in the revolution. James Taussig, the brother of one of Adolph's closest friends and his son Louis's future employer, was forced to flee to America after serving as a member of Student Revolutionary Corps throughout the siege of the city by the Austrian forces: see A. E. Zucker, ed., *The Forty-Eighters: Political Refugees of the German Revolution of 1848* (New York: Columbia University Press, 1950), p. 347.

8. Goldmark, *Pilgrims of '48*, pp. 200–14. The two members of the group who did not go on to Madison were Frederika's father, who remained in Cincinnati to establish a medical practice, and her brother, who did likewise with a view to studying law. By the middle of the nineteenth century, the Ohio Valley was no longer a "frontier" environment: "Towns and cities and a mature agrarian landscape had evolved, and the frontier had become the region's past, its history." (Jakle, *Images of the Ohio Valley*, p. 103.) Though the Wehles were in the end persuaded to abandon their dreams of a farming Utopia in the West, a sizable number of Forty-Eighters no better equipped for the rigors of frontier life did try their hands at agriculture. For a discussion of these so-called "Latin farmers," see Wittke, *Refugees of Revolution*, pp. 111–21.

9. Goldmark, *Pilgrims of '48*, pp. 214–20.
10. *Reminiscences of Frederika Brandeis*, pp. 9–13, 17.
11. Ibid., passim, but especially pp. 11–17, 24–25, 27, 34, 38–39, 42–43, 46–47. Whenever a place referred to is located in present-day Poland but is given its German name in Frederika's account, the modern Polish equivalent will be found in brackets. For purposes of identification, I have relied upon *Brockhaus Encyclopädie*, vol. 21 [Karten] (Wiesbaden: F. A. Brockhaus, 1975).
12. *Reminiscences of Frederika Brandeis*, pp. 3, 18.
13. Ibid., pp. 22–23, 31.

14. Ibid., pp. 16, 25–26. The evening music at the *Färberinsel* was apparently played by a band of the grenadiers. A North-German visitor to Prague in 1841, arriving too late for their concert, encountered them returning to barracks and described the occasion thus: "They marched along the broad road of the island, playing a lively air. . . . By their side went some five or six boys with torches, and in front of the band, along the broad level path of the promenade, some ten or twelve merry couples were dancing away lustily. The band was playing one of Strauss's waltzes. . . . 'This is a really remarkable scene,' said I to my companion. 'It is an every-day one here,' was his reply." J. G. Kohl, *Austria* (London: Chapman & Hall, 1843), pp. 56–57; see also pp. 59–61.

15. *Reminiscences of Frederika Brandeis*, pp. 34–36.

16. Ibid., pp. 25–27, 36–37, 42–43, 45–47.

17. Ibid., pp. 4–5. For the numerical estimate of Prague's Jewish population, and for some interesting glimpses into the city's Jewish quarter in 1841, see Kohl, *Austria*, pp. 46–56.

18. Theodore Wehle, "Notes on the Wehle Family and their Connection with the Frank Movement," quoted in Goldmark, *Pilgrims of '48*, pp. 191–94. For a concise but illuminating account of the Shabbatean movement, and of Frankism as the last stage in its development, see *Enyclopaedia Judaica*, 16 vols. (Jerusalem: Encyclopaedia Judaica, 1971–72), 7: cols. 55–72; 14: cols. 1219–54. It should be observed that not all those hostile to the Frankists shared Gottlieb Wehle's view of their high moral purpose, and scurrilous reports concerning deviant sexual practices were widespread.

19. *Reminiscences of Frederika Brandeis*, pp. 8–9. Note that in Alice Goldmark Brandeis's English translation, the term "Shabbatean" has been transposed rather misleadingly into the word "Sabbatarian."

20. *Reminiscences of Frederika Brandeis*, pp. 24, 32–33. During their travels in Poland, the differences between Frederika's parents and other Jews would have been even more marked. "The dress of the Polish Jews is purely oriental," noted a contemporary traveler. "It is totally different from that of their German brethren, and bears no resemblance to that of the Poles. But throughout Poland, from the Pontus to the Baltic, it never varies; a uniformity the more remarkable in a nation that has no political unity." For this and other observations on the distinctive characteristics of the Polish Jews, see Kohl, *Austria*, pp. 458–63; the quotation is on p. 462.

21. *Reminiscences of Frederika Brandeis*, pp. 26–27, 32–33, 47; Kohl, *Austria*, p. 53. For more on the career of Dr. Sachs, see *Encyclopaedia Judaica*, 14: col. 595.

22. Mason, *Brandeis*, p. 23. For a detailed discussion of the commercial environment into which the company of Brandeis & Crawford was launched, see Lewis E. Atherton, *The Frontier Merchant in Mid-America* (Columbia, Mo.: University of Missouri Press, 1971), especially chaps. 3–4.

23. Goldmark, *Pilgrims of '48*, p. 221.

24. Wittke, *Refugees of Revolution*, pp. 31, 34–35, 73–75, 95, 98. Kossuth also spoke in Madison, where Gottlieb Wehle introduced him to the assembly: see Goldmark, *Pilgrims of '48*, p. 226. For an excellent general discussion of the political turmoils of the decade, see Michael F. Holt, *The Political Crisis of the 1850s* (New York: Wiley, 1978). For a useful case study of religious divisions within the German fraternity elsewhere in Ohio, see Joseph M. White, "Religion and Community: Cincinnati Germans, 1814–1870" (unpublished Ph.D. diss., University of Notre Dame, 1980), especially pp. 333–59.

25. Wittke, *Refugees of Revolution*, pp. 151, 163–66, 187–88, Holt, *Political Crisis*, p. 160.

26. See Wittke, *Refugees of Revolution*, pp. 191–220, especially pp. 199–201; Holt, *Political Crisis*, 139–217, especially pp. 176–81.

27. Wittke, *Refugees of Revolution*, pp. 88–89, Goldmark, *Pilgrims of '48*, pp. 226–31.

28. For the European context of "bourgeois-liberal" sentiments among the Forty-Eighters, and especially their fears of the new proletariat, see Wittke, *Refugees of Revolution*, pp. 23–26; Pech, *Czech Revolution*, p. 20.

29. The one major exception is Alpheus T. Mason, but even he draws few conclusions from his depiction of LDB's European heritage; see *Brandeis*, pp. 11–32. For the assertion that "Mozart was my favorite in the days when as a boy I essayed the violin," see LDB to Susan Brandeis Gilbert, 2 February 1934, SGBU, Box 18, no. 1897.

30. *Reminiscences of Frederika Brandeis*, pp. 3, 32.

31. Mason, *Brandeis*, p. 24; Lief, *Brandeis*, pp. 15–16. Both rely heavily on Bert Ford, "Boyhood of Brandeis—An Early View of the Man," *Boston American*, 4 June 1916, part 4, pp. 1–2. References to Emma as the "class beauty" seem impossible to reconcile with evidence that LDB attended an all-male high school.

32. Wittke, *Refugees of Revolution*, pp 300–305; Mason, *Brandeis*, 25–26; Lief, *Brandeis*, p. 19.

33. The first references to specific books and authors read by LDB come in letters written during the 1870s and 1880s, but several are couched in terms that assume an earlier familiarity. See, for example, LDB to Otto A. Wehle, 12 November 1876, *BL*, 1:12; LDB to Amy Brandeis Wehle, 2 January 1881, *BL*, 1: 60–62; LDB to Alfred Brandeis, 31 October 1884, ibid., pp. 66–67. Cf. the reading habits of the younger Wehles in Madison and New York during the 1850s, including LDB's future mother-in-law Regina, in Goldmark, *Pilgrims of '48*, pp. 238–41.

34. LDB to Fannie Brandeis, 11 June 1926, *BL*, S:223; Lief, *Brandeis*, p. 15; *Reminiscences of Frederika Brandeis*, pp. 20–21; LDB to Alfred Brandeis, 7 October 1920, *BL*, 4:488; author's interview with Paul A. Freund, 25 April 1983.

35. LDB to Jacob Billikopf, 25 January 1915, *BL*, 3:412; Ford, "Boyhood of Brandeis," p. 2. The "Professor James" reference is to William James, the pioneering psychologist and Harvard professor generally considered to have been the leader, if not the founder, of the "pragmatic" school of philosophy in the United States.

36. Bureau of he Census, *Ninth Census of the United States: Statistics of Population* (Washington, D.C.: Government Printing Office, 1872), 1:150: Table 3: Population, 1870–1850, by Civil Divisions Less than Counties; ibid., pp. 380, 386–91: Table 8: Nativity, 1870, Fifty Principal Cities. These figures almost certainly underestimate the size of the total population, since it is generally conceded by scholars that the census returns from this period seriously undercount blacks and the poor.

37. Except where otherwise indicated, the details supplied in this and the following five paragraphs are taken from George C. Wright, *Life Behind a Veil: Blacks in Louisville, Kentucky, 1865–1930* (Baton Rouge: Louisiana State University Press, 1985), pp. 1–49. The quotation about the "head" and "heart" of Kentucky is from an article dated 25 December 1868, reprinted in Arthur Krock, ed., *The Editorials of Henry Watterson* (Louisville: Louisville Courier Journal, 1923), p. 21.

38. Frederick Law Olmsted, *The Cotton Kingdom: A Traveller's Observations on Cotton and Slavery in the American Slave States*, ed. Arthur M. Schlesinger (New York: Knopf, 1962), p. 541, n.

39. Quoted in Ernest Poole, "Brandeis: A Remarkable Record of Unselfish Work Done in the Public Interest," in Louis D. Brandeis, *Business—A Profession* (1914; reprint, New York: Kelley, 1971). Not all German Jews shared the Brandeises' feelings about slavery. As late as 1861, Isaac Mayer Wise, the leader of Reformed Judaism in the United States, was still characterizing abolitionists as "fanatics" and "demagogues": see Wittke, *Refugees of Revolution*, p. 193.

40. Harlan was appointed to the United States Supreme Court in 1877 and is best

remembered for his celebrated dissent in *Plessy v. Fergusson* (1896), where he came out strongly against the constitutionality of racial segregation. Bristow held several posts in state and federal government, including that of U.S. solicitor general, 1870–72, and secretary of the treasury, 1874–76. See LDB to Otto A. Wehle, 3 August 1879, *BL*, 1:48, n. 4.

41. For the career of Henry Watterson, see Isaac F. Marcosson, *Marse Henry* (New York: Dodd, Mead, 1951).

42. Mason, *Brandeis*, p. 24.

43. LDB to Otto A. Wehle, 3 August 1879, *BL*, 1:47.

44. Ford, "Boyhood of Brandeis," p. 2. In spite of the stylized representation of black speech patterns in this article, and its tendency to depict Lizzie (who is not even allowed the dignity of a surname) as a stereotypical "black mammy," the point of her story clearly rises above any such distortions of voice or convention.

45. Mason, *Brandeis*, pp. 24–25.

46. For an insightful treatment of America's "island communities" at midcentury, as well as of the crisis that engulfed them a few decades later, see Robert H. Wiebe, *The Search for Order, 1877–1920* (New York: Hill & Wang, 1967), especially pp. xiii–xiv, 2–5, 44–75. None of the backcountry farming communities likely to have been visited by Adolph Brandeis and his sons has been the subject of serious historical investigation, but a measure of comparative enlightenment may be gained from Don Harrison Doyle's excellent discussion of the institutional foundations of community in *The Social Order of a Frontier Community: Jacksonville, Illinois, 1825–70* (Urbana: University of Illinois Press, 1978). Doyle stresses the social control functions that voluntary institutions of all kinds exercised over their members in small towns, and the seeming paradox of common forms of social organization coexisting alongside the potentially divisive forces of religion, ethnicity, and class: see especially pp. 12–15, 155. From the vantage point of urban middle age, however, it was changes to the rural landscape rather than any diminution of community that struck LDB most forcibly when he revisited his home state. "Tobacco culture is driving out much of the beauty," he wrote from Versailles, Kentucky, at some point between 1900 and 1909. "The beautiful pastures with the scattered great trees are being converted into tobacco fields—which resemble great cabbage patches with less color—and as every bit of sun is desired for tobacco, the trees had to go.—Even along the road side." LDB to [Alice Goldmark Brandeis?], undated, SGBU, Box 23, no. 2426.

47. Mason, *Brandeis*, p. 28.

48. Wittke, *Refugees from Revolution*, chap. 22, especially pp. 351–59; LDB to Frederika Brandeis, 7 September 1870, *BL*, 1:3. The assertion that Adolph Brandeis wanted his son "to study medicine and remain in Europe," a society whose "ease and culture" he contrasted with "the rough-and-tumble character of America," is made in Lief, *Brandeis*, p. 20. No evidence is offered to justify this contention; but cf. Poole, "Brandeis," p. xi, where it is suggested that an academic career was being contemplated.

49. Mason, *Brandeis*, 29–32.

50. Quoted in Poole, "Brandeis," p. xi.

Chapter 2. The Spirit of the Law

1. James Willard Hurst, *The Growth of American Law: The Law Makers* (Boston: Little, Brown, 1950), p. 4.

2. Idem, *Law and the Conditions of Freedom in the Nineteenth-Century United States* (Madison: University of Wisconsin Press, 1956), pp. 10–15.

3. Ibid., pp. 7–10.

4. Mason, *Brandeis*, p. 33. The 12th ed. of Kent's *Commentaries*, edited by LDB's future friend and Supreme Court colleague, Oliver Wendell Holmes, Jr., had been published as recently as 1873. For the assessment of Kent, see Lawrence M. Friedman, *A History of American Law* (New York: Simon & Schuster, 1973), pp. 290–92.

5. See Mason, *Brandeis*, p. 34; *BL*, 1:8, n. 2. For detailed descriptions and evaluations of the new system of legal education introduced at Harvard by Langdell, see Arthur E. Sutherland, *The Law at Harvard: A History of Ideas and Men. 1817–1967* (Cambridge, Mass.: Harvard University Press, 1967), pp. 162–205; Robert B. Stevens, *Law School: Legal Education in America from the 1850s to the 1980s* (Chapel Hill: University of North Carolina Press, 1983), pp. 35–72; Franklin G. Fessenden, "The Rebirth of the Harvard Law School," *Harvard Law Review* 33 (1919–20): 493–517; Anthony Chase, "The Birth of the Modern Law School," *American Journal of Legal History* 23 (1979): 329–48. The "later acquaintance" was Edward F. McClennen; see his "Louis D. Brandeis as a Lawyer," *Massachusetts Law Quarterly* 33 (1948): 7. Sent to the journal by McClennen but not published until after his death, the essay was based substantially on a memorandum written in November 1941 at Mason's request. For a copy of the original document, "Brandeis—The Lawyer," and the correspondence between McClennen and Mason, see LBLU, WB (Unnumbered) [20–27]

6. Brandeis, "The Harvard Law School," *The Green Bag* 1 (1889): 18–21. Langdell's introduction of the case method into legal studies was in fact modeled on developments in clinical education that had occurred earlier in the field of medicine, and his "scientific" approach corresponded closely with, and indeed was largely dependent on, President Eliot's general reform plans for Harvard as a whole: see Chase, "Birth of the Modern Law School," pp. 331–46. It would be a mistake, though, to overstate the completeness of the Eliot-Langdell revolution during the years in which LDB was a student at Harvard. As he noted, "several of the professors declined for many years to adopt the system" advocated by their dean, and these included his own principal mentors, Thayer and Bradley: see Sutherland, *Law at Harvard*, pp. 179, 185.

7. Sutherland, *Law at Harvard*, p. 185; Chase, "Birth of the Modern Law School," passim, but especially pp. 332–43.

8. Fessenden, "Rebirth of Harvard Law School," pp. 498–503.

9. Sutherland, *Law at Harvard*, pp. 177–78. But cf. the observation that "Ames would set up his own reasoning against that of a legion of judges and scores of text-writers": LDB to Otto A. Wehle, 12 November 1876, *BL*, 1:11.

10. Sutherland, *Law at Harvard*, pp. 170–74, 180–83.

11. Ibid., pp. 182, 184–90; Gurney's letter to Eliot, which is undated but from internal evidence must have been written between 8 January and 14 May 1883, is printed verbatim on pp. 187–90. LDB to Otto A. Wehle, 12 November 1876, *BL*, 1:10–12; when LDB writes that he is "afraid those Supreme Court Judges will be refused admittance into paradise for the bad law they have been promulgating in this life. Many of them surely deserve the most dreadful punishment"—one wonders whether his tongue is stuck firmly in his cheek, or whether this represents just the kind of cocksure remark about which Gurney was so apprehensive.

12. Sutherland, *Law at Harvard*, pp. 190–91.

13. Ford, "Boyhood of Brandeis," p. 2; LDB to Wehle, 12 March 1876, *BL*, 1:6. For Langdell's efforts to improve the Law School's library, see Sutherland, *Law at Harvard*, pp. 191–93. LDB's enthusiasm for a formal legal education never wavered or waned. Forty years later, having just embarked on the judicial phase of his own career, he would write his eldest daughter, by then at the law school of the Univer-

sity of Chicago: "There is only one place to study law . . . and that is at the law school. To spend time next summer 'studying law' in [a law office]—or at home—would be time absolutely wasted.—I have given similar advice to law students galore—for a score of years or more." LDB to Susan Brandeis, 15 October 1916, SGBU, Box 11, no. 1057.

14. LDB to Wehle, 12 March 1876, *BL*, 1:6–8; Fessenden, "Rebirth of Harvard Law School," pp. 504–5. Although such clubs had been in existence at Harvard since the 1820s, the Pow-Wow was a new creation in 1870–71. The term "Kit's Freshmen" was coined at about the same date to identify members of the initially small coterie of pro-Langdell men; whether it was still current in 1875–76 is not clear: see Sutherland, *Law at Harvard*, pp. 179–80.

15. LDB to Wehle, 12 November 1876, *BL*, 1:10–11.

16. Mason, *Brandeis*, p. 47. On the question of LDB's grades, Sutherland observes (*Law at Harvard*, p. 198, n. 44): "Notation of excellence on a scale of 100 has varied over the years, so that a grade of 90-odd in 1878 is not convertible into the same figures in 1967; [nevertheless] the astonishingly high quality of Brandeis' work is still entirely evident."

17. Mason, *Brandeis*, pp. 28, 33, 45, 48; Strum, *Brandeis*, pp. 22, 24–25; Lief, *Brandeis*, p. 22.

18. See, for example, Mason, *Brandeis*, p. 46; and cf. the apparently derivative account in Paper, *Brandeis*, pp. 12, 15. Mason is in fact our only source for the claim that LDB was a sickly youth, about whose health his parents were always concerned; however, incomplete footnoting in this section of his text makes his authority for such an assertion less than clear. Although LDB may not have been as stoutly built as his elder brother, that is not the same thing as congenital weakness.

19. Mason, *Brandeis*, p. 46; LDB's letter to Wehle, dated 31 August 1876 and quoted here, was not printed in *BL*, vol. 1. In his 1879 report on the inadequacies of Dane Hall, Dean Langdell observed: "[T]he library and lecture-room are each lighted from four different directions; and it would probably be safe to say that a year has never passed in which the cross-lights of these two rooms have not ruined, or seriously injured, the eyes of one or more persons": see Sutherland, *Law at Harvard*, p. 194.

20. LDB to Douglas, 31 January 1878, *BL*, 1:21–22; LDB to Alfred Brandeis, 28 June 1878, ibid., pp. 23–24. For information about Douglas, Richards, Keener, and Warren, see the editors' notes in *BL*, 1:18, 19, 22.

21. LDB to Wehle, 12 November 1876, *BL*, 1:12; LDB to Douglas, 31 January 1878, ibid., p. 22. For Marcou, see editors' note, p. 15.

22. Mason, *Brandeis*, pp. 38–44; though consulted by both Mason and Gal, neither the *Index Rerum* nor the literary notebook could be located when I visited Louisville in 1984.

23. LDB to Amy Brandeis, 5 April and 2 December 1877, *BL*, 1:15–17, 19–20; ibid., p. 13, n. 11; LDB to Alfred Brandeis, 28 June and 5 July 1878, ibid., 23–25. The artists and "celebrities" are identified, ibid., p. 25 n. 7 and p. 21 n. 4, respectively.

24. Not many of the letters which LDB wrote from Cambridge as a student have survived, but most of those that do are printed in *BL*, 1:5–28. A few of the letters sent to him by his father and mother are quoted in Mason, *Brandeis*, pp. 43–45, and in Strum, *Brandeis*, p. 13. Regarding the mounting conflict between railroad workers and their employers, see Philip S. Foner, *The Great Labour Uprising of 1877* (New York: Monad Press, 1977); the situation in Louisville is discussed on pp. 124–28, 220–24, 258. For LDB's bland recollection of his own activities in the summer of 1877, see Mason, *Brandeis*, pp. 47–48. His reactions to the violent clashes between workers and Pinkertons at the Homestead steelworks in 1892 will be considered fully inf., pp. 109–12.

25. McClennen, "Brandeis as a Lawyer," pp. 4–7. McClennen worked closely with LDB between 1895 and 1916, first as an employee and later as a partner in the firm of Brandeis, Dunbar and Nutter.

26. For the best discussion of LDB's months in St. Louis, see Mason, *Brandeis*, pp. 48–54. McClennen, "Brandeis as a Lawyer," p. 8.

27. LDB to Warren, 30 May 1879, quoted in Mason, *Brandeis*, pp. 54–5; McClennan, "Brandeis as a Lawyer," p. 10.

28. Nagel to LDB, 5 July 1879, quoted in Mason, *Brandeis*, p. 57; LDB to Nagel, 12 July 1879, *BL*, 1:37–38. For a brief discussion of Gray's judicial attitudes and his contribution to the work of the United States Supreme Court, see Elbridge Davis and Harold A. Davis, "Mr. Justice Horace Gray: Some Aspects of his Judicial Career," *American Bar Association Journal* 41 (May 1955): 421–44, 468–71. Unlike LDB, however, Gray does not appear to have required his law clerks to undertake the initial research work for his opinions.

29. LDB to Walter B. Douglas, 6 July 1879, *BL*, 1:36; Unattributed letter, 17 March 1878, quoted in McClennen, "Brandeis as a Lawyer," p. 5; Nagel to LDB, 5 July 1879, quoted in Mason, *Brandeis*, p. 57; LDB to Nagel, 12 July 1879, *BL*, 1:39.

30. Mason, *Brandeis*, pp. 64–67.

31. LDB, "Harvard Law School," pp. 10–11; Mason, *Brandeis*, pp. 64–69; McClennen, "Brandeis as a Lawyer," pp. 8–9. For a fuller discussion of LDB's efforts on behalf of Harvard Law School, see James M. Landis, "Mr. Justice Brandeis and the Harvard Law School," *Harvard Law Review* 55 (1941–42), 184–90.

32. See Arnold M. Paul, *Conservative Crisis and the Rule of Law: Attitudes of Bar and Bench, 1887–1895* (Ithaca: Cornell University Press, 1960); William R. Brock, *Investigation and Responsibility: Public Responsibility in the United States, 1865–1900* (New York: Cambridge University Press, 1984). Brock provides much valuable information about the origins and activities of state administrative agencies in this period, but has little to say about the attitudes and motives of those who opposed their introduction.

33. "The Watuppa Pond Cases," *Harvard Law Review* 2 (1888): 195–98.

34. Ibid., p. 203; the Shaw citation is from *Cummings v. Barrett*, 10 Cush., pp. 186, 188 (1852).

35. Ibid., pp. 196, 199–200.

36. Ibid., pp. 200–11, passim; emphasis in the quotation from p. 211 is added.

37. "The Law of Ponds," *Harvard Law Review* 3 (1889): 1; the quotation is from a footnote on p. 10. The piece to which they were responding can be found at *Harvard Law Review* 2 (1889): 316.

38. McClennen, "Brandeis as a Lawyer," p. 10; *Louisville Joint Stock Land Bank v. Radford*, 295 U.S. 555, 602 (1935).

39. For some modern assessments of the privacy doctrine enunciated by Warren and Brandeis, see Don R. Pember, *Privacy and the Press: The Law, the Mass Media and the First Amendment* (Seattle: University of Washington Press, 1972); Diane L. Zimmerman, "Requiem for a Heavyweight: A Farewell to Warren and Brandeis Privacy Tort," *Cornell Law Review* 68 (1983): 291; Richard F. Hixson, *Privacy in a Public Society: Human Rights in Conflict* (New York: Oxford University Press, 1987). What these academic lawyers have to say has been largely neglected by LDB's biographers.

40. "The Right to Privacy," *Harvard Law Review* 4 (1890): 193, 196. The article was reprinted in *The Curse of Bigness*, pp. 289–315.

41. Ibid., pp. 193–95; emphasis added. For the original context of the phrase "the right to be let alone," see Thomas M. Cooley, *A Treatise on the Law of Torts or the Wrongs which Arise Independently of Contract*, 4th ed., ed. D. A. Haggard (Chicago: Callaghan, 1932), 1:34.

42. "Right to Privacy," pp. 197–98 and n. 1.

43. Ibid., pp, 198–207, passim. As well as evaluating property rights as a legal basis for preventing publication, Warren and Brandeis also gave due consideration to cases in which jurisdiction was asserted, wholly or in part, on the ground of an alleged breach of trust or contract. After some discussion, though, they were obliged to conclude that this afforded an inadequate basis for their wider purposes. "The right of property in its widest sense, including all possession, including all rights and privileges, and hence embracing the right to an inviolate personality, affords alone that broad basis upon which the protection which the individual demands can be rested." See ibid., pp. 207–11.

44. Ibid., p. 213.

45. Mason, *Brandeis*, p. 70; LDB to Warren, 8 April 1905, *BL*, 1:302–3; E. L. Godkin, "The Rights of the Citizen: To His Own Reputation," *Scribner's* 8 (July 1890): 58–67; "The Right to Privacy," p. 195, n. 7. The New York case referred to was *Marion Manola v. Stevens & Myers* (1890). A penetrating discussion of the article's origins, which goes a long way toward debunking the myths about Warren's alleged harassment by the press, can be found in Paper, *Brandeis*, pp. 33–36; this in turn relies heavily on James H. Barron, "Warren and Brandeis, *The Right to Privacy*, 4 *Harvard Law Review* 193; (1890): Demystifying a Landmark Citation," *Suffolk University Law Review* 13 (1979): 875–907. However, Paper's suggestion that Warren's supposed animus against the *Saturday Evening Gazette* may have been the result of that newspaper's attacks against his father-in-law, Grover Cleveland's secretary of state, Thomas Francis Bayard, serves merely to substitute one irrelevance for another. The legal and moral issues raised in "The Right to Privacy" are substantive ones, and require no ulterior motive to explain their investigation.

46. E. B. Adams, "The Right to Privacy and Its Relation to the Law of Libel," *American Law Review* 39 (1905): 37, quoted in *BL*, 1:303 n. 1; Wilbur Larremore, "The Law of Privacy" *Columbia Law Review* 12 (1912): 693, quoted in Mason, *Brandeis*, p. 650 n. 23; Pound [to Senator William Chilton, 8 February 1916], quoted in McClennen, "Brandeis as a Lawyer," p. 18; LDB to Alice Goldmark, 29 November 1890, *BL*, 1:94–95; LDB to S. D. Warren, 8 April 1905, ibid., pp. 302–3; LDB to Judge Andrew J. Cobb, 17 April 1905, ibid., pp. 303–4; LDB to James B. Ludlow, 20 April 1905, ibid., p. 306. The Georgia case was *Pavesich v. New England Life Insurance Co. et al.*, 50 *Southeastern Reporter* 68 (1905). For a discussion of LDB's dissent in *Olmstead v. United States* (1928), see inf., pp. 246–48. LDB to Clarence M. Lewis, 21 March 1934, *BL*, 5:533–34.

47. LDB to Alfred Brandeis, 30 January 1884, *BL*, 1:66 and n.; McClennen, "Brandeis as a Lawyer," p. 10.

48. LDB to Alfred Brandeis, 11 September 1880, *BL*, 1:57; LDB to Alice Goldmark, 11 October 1890, ibid., p. 92; Mason, *Brandeis*, pp. 88–89.

49. *Reminiscences of Frederika Brandeis*, pp. 16, 20–21, 29, 32, 40–41, 47.

50. Ford, "Boyhood of Brandeis," p. 2.

51. Mason, *Brandeis*, p. 78.

52. McClennen, "Brandeis as a Lawyer," p. 14; LDB to Alfred Brandeis, 21 March 1887, *BL*, 1:72–73. See also LDB's letters of 11 September 1880 and 20 March 1886, ibid., pp. 55, 67–68.

53. McClennen, "Brandeis as a Lawyer," pp. 14–16; LDB to Dunbar, 19 August 1896, *BL*, 1:124–26; for a brief discussion of the complaints being voiced by LDB's younger associates around 1896, to which this letter was a direct response, see especially p. 126 n. 1. Cf. McClennen, "Brandeis as a Lawyer," pp. 23–24. Though McClennen's observations refer properly only to the firm of Brandeis, Dunbar and Nutter after 1897, they seem generally applicable to the later years of Warren and Brandeis as well.

54. McClennen, "Brandeis as a Lawyer," pp. 6, 22–23. The legal environment in

which LDB's forensic skills were honed is illuminated by the analysis in Robert A. Silverman, *Law and Urban Growth: Civil Litigation in the Boston Trial Courts, 1880–1900* (Princeton: Princeton University Press, 1981).

55. LDB quoted in Poole, "Brandeis," p. xii; LDB to Langdell, 30 December 1889, *BL*, 1:84–88.

56. McClennen, "Brandeis as a Lawyer," pp. 3–4, 7, 27–28.

57. A fuller discussion of the problems involved in accurately dating the text of these lectures will be found on pp. 109–10.

58. "M.I.T. Course on Business Law, 1892–4," LBLU, A 4–3.

59. Ibid., pp. 1–3, 10–11.

60. Ibid., pp. 187–88.

61. Ibid., pp. 10–11, 200.

62. Ibid., pp. 206–8. Cf. the modern account of these developments in Friedman, *History of American Law*, pp. 21–23, 47–48, 130–31, 185, 341, 346–47.

63. J. R. Carter quoted without reference, ibid., p. 201. LDB's use of Carter's biological analogy is representative of what has been termed "the common intellectual commitment to scientism" shared by Eliot, Langdell and many of their younger contemporaries: see Sutherland, *Law at Harvard*, pp. 166, 176–78.

64. Ibid., pp. 204–5. In a note on p. 205, LDB observed: "In all human affairs precedent has weight. It is natural for the human mind in all cases of doubt to inquire what has been the past human experience. . . . Among the English respect for precedent [was] far more developed than elsewhere."

Chapter 3. Constitutional Limitations

1. Philip B. Kurland, ed., *Felix Frankfurter on the Supreme Court: Extrajudicial Essays on the Court and the Constitution* (Cambridge, Mass.: Harvard University Press, 1970), pp. 220, 456–59. The common law was a component part of state not federal law, and came to be a concern of the United States Supreme Court only by virtue of its appellate jurisdiction. Cf. the remarks of Mr. Justice McLean quoted in Thomas M. Cooley, *A Treatise on the Constitutional Limitations which Rest upon the Legislative Power of the States of the American Union* (1868; reprint, New York: Da Capo Press, 1972), p. 20 n.: "It is clear there can be no common law of the United States. The Federal government is composed of . . . sovereign and independent states, each of which may have its local usages, customs and common law. There is no principle which pervades the Union, and has the authority of law, that is not embodied in the Constitution or laws of the Union. The common law could be made a part of our Federal system only by legislative adoption."

2. Sutherland, *Law at Harvard*, pp. 185–86, the list of elective courses in the 1870s is from Hurst, *Growth of American Law*, p. 5. Gray's remark is quoted in *Frankfurter on the Supreme Court*, p. 22.

3. Hurst, *Law and the Conditions of Freedom*, pp. 43–44 and passim. For further details of Shaw's career and legal philosophy, see Leonard W. Levy, *The Law of the Commonwealth and Chief Justice Shaw* (Cambridge, Mass.: Harvard University Press, 1957); G. Edward White, *The American Judicial Tradition: Profiles of Leading American Judges* (New York: Oxford University Press, 1976), pp. 35–63.

4. Hurst, *Law and the Conditions of Freedom*, pp. 71–108; White, *American Judicial Tradition*, pp. 84–149; Brock, *Investigation and Responsibility*, pp. 58–87.

5. The cases cited are *Powell v. Pennsylvania*, 127 U.S. 678, 685 (1888); *Chicago, Milwaukee & St. Paul Railway Co. v. Minnesota*, 134 U.S. 418, 458 (1890); *Munn v. Illinois*, 94 U.S. 113 (1877). The "two subsequent cases" were *Budd v. New York*,

143 U.S. 517 (1892) and *Brass v. Oregon*, 153 U.S. 391 (1894). On the relationship between "substantive due process" and the "implied limitations" of natural law grafted onto the Constitution between the 1890s and the 1930s, see J. A. C. Grant, "The Natural Law Background of Due Process," *Columbia Law Review* 31 (1931): pp. 56–81.

6. See *U.S. v. E.C. Knight Co.*, 156 U.S. 1 (1895); *Pollock v. Farmers' Loan and Trust Co.*, 157 U.S. 429 (1895) and (rehearing) 158 U.S. 601 (1895); *In re Debs*, 158 U.S. 564 (1895); *Cincinnati, New Orleans & Texas Ry. Co. v. I.C.C.*, 162 U.S. 184 (1896); *I.C.C. v. Alabama Midland Ry. Co.*, 168 U.S. 144 (1897); *Smyth v. Ames*, 169 U.S. 466 (1897); *Holden v. Hardy*, 169 U.S. 366 (1898). For an interesting commentary on the implications and consequences of the decision handed down in *Smyth v. Ames*, see *Corwin on the Constitution. Vol. 3: On Liberty Against Government*, ed. Richard Loss (Ithaca, 1988), pp. 70–72. The best discussion of the remaining cases, viewed in their contemporary ideological context, is in Paul, *Conservative Crisis*, pp. 178–220.

7. For the "crisis of the 1890s," see Wiebe, *Search for Order*, pp. 44–163; Arthur Lipow, *Authoritarian Socialism in America: Edward Bellamy and the Nationalist Movement* (Berkeley: University of California Press, 1982). A lively account of the rise and fall of Populism is offered by Lawrence Goodwyn in his provocative revisionist study, *Democratic Promise: the Populist Moment in America* (New York: Oxford University Press, 1976); the major conflicts of the decade between labor and capital are treated with committed yet informative clarity in Sidney Lens, *The Labor Wars from the Molly Maguires to the Sitdowns* (Garden City, N.Y.: Doubleday, 1973), pp. 67–149. For the views of the "legal progressives," see Paul, *Conservative Crisis*, pp. 39–60, 182–84; and for the differing strands of conservative legal opinion, see ibid., pp. 19–38, 61–103.

8. For fuller discussion of the "Mugwumps," see Richard Hofstadter, *The Age of Reform from Bryan to FDR* (New York: Knopf, 1955), pp. 131–72; John G. Sproat, *"The Best Men": Liberal Reformers in the Gilded Age* (New York: Oxford University Press, 1968); Gerald W. McFarland, *Mugwumps, Morals and Politics, 1884–1920* (Amherst: University of Massachusetts Press, 1975); McFarland, ed., *The Mugwumps, 1884–1900: Moralists or Pragmatists?* (New York: Simon & Schuster, 1976).

9. LDB to Alice Goldmark, 26 February 1891, *BL*, 1:100.

10. Williams to LD8, 27 December 1890, quoted in Mason, *Brandeis*, p. 89; LDB to Alice Goldmark, [late February] 1891, *BL*, 1:100.

11. LDB to Alice Goldmark, 9 February 1891, *BL*, 1:99.

12. Argument before the Joint Committee on Liquor Law of the Massachusetts legislature, 27 February 1891, quoted in Mason, *Brandeis*, p. 90.

13. The assessment of Cooley in this and the following paragraph follows closely the brief but incisive account in White, *American Judicial Tradition*, pp. 115–22; the quotations will be found on pp. 119–21. Cf. also two perceptive essays by Alan Jones: "Thomas M. Cooley and the Michigan Supreme Court, 1865–1885," *American Journal of Legal History* 10 (1966): pp. 97–112; and "Thomas M. Cooley and 'Laissez Faire Constitutionalism': A Reconsideration," *Journal of American History* 53 (1967): pp. 759–71. For an interesting perspective on Cooley's efforts to impose the rule of law on recalcitrant railroad companies during his years with the Interstate Commerce Commission, see Brock, *Investigation and Responsibility*, pp. 236–42.

14. Cooley, *Constitutional Limitations*, pp. 49–55. White sees "certainty" and "flexibility" as alternative rather than complementary concepts in the history of judicial interpretation, and consequently underestimates the degree of flexibility implicit in Cooley's view of the common law: see *American Judicial Tradition*, pp. 113–15, 121.

15. Livy S. Richard, "Up from Aristocracy," *The Independent*, 27 July 1914, quoted in Mason, *Brandeis*, p. 87.

16. Memorandum by Alice H. Grady, 30 April 1907, explaining how the typescript of "M.I.T. Course on Business Law, 1892–4" came to be compiled, LBLU, A 4–3; cf. footnote on the contents page of the latter document, emphasis added. For the explicit references to Homestead, see inf., p. 111. There can be no doubt that LDB did give a series of lectures in the session 1892–93, because a letter survives from a student querying his grade on the course: see Theodore Varney to LDB, 23 June 1893, LBLU, NMF 1–2.

17. Paper is the only Brandeis biographer to have focused any real attention on the Massachusetts Institute of Technology lectures and what they reveal about their author's early attitudes to labor and capital. However, by locating the Homestead strike in 1893 rather than 1892, he misses the implications of his discovery for the cause and timing of LDB's change of outlook. See Paper, *Brandeis*, pp. 38–39.

18. "Course on Business Law," pp. 159–65.

19. Ibid., pp. 165–66. LDB was factually inaccurate in suggesting that the Carnegie Company employed the Pinkertons to regain possession of property that had been seized by striking workers. The latter's occupation of the steel mills was a temporary expedient and was the consequence, not the cause, of the detectives' arrival. Even after the bloody confrontation along the shores of the Monongahela, union officials were scrupulous about vacating the plant and restoring the watchmen charged with guarding the company's possessions. For a detailed account of the whole affair, see Arthur G. Burgoyne, *The Homestead Strike of 1892*, afterword by David P. Demarest, Jr. (1893; reprint, Pittsburgh: University of Pittsburgh Press, 1979), especially pp. 15–101; but cf. also Henry David, "Upheaval at Homestead," in Daniel Aaron, ed., *America in Crisis* (New York: Knopf, 1952), pp. 133–70; Leon Wolff, *Lockout; The Story of the Homestead Strike of 1892* (New York: Harper & Row, 1965).

20. "Course on Business Law," pp. 93–94. Interestingly, though, "The Right to Privacy" concluded with a tentative suggestion that the privacy of the individual should receive additional protection from the criminal law, and even took the unusual step of of supplying a draft bill for the purpose, prepared by William H. Dunbar, a junior member of the authors' firm: see p. 219, especially n. 3. By 1905, Warren at least was firmly convinced that the subject was one that required legislation. see Warren to LDB, 10 April 1905, *BL*, 1:303 n. 3.

21. LDB to Adolph Brandeis, 30 November 1889, *BL*, 1:83; "Course on Business Law," pp. 166–67, 172, 175 For the socioeconomic legislation enacted between 1889–91, see William B. Shaw, "Social and Economic Legislation of the States in 1890," *Quarterly Journal of Economics* 5 (1891): pp. 385–96; Shaw, "Social and Economic Legislation of the States in 1891," ibid., 6 (1892): pp. 227–42; Richard T. Ely and L. S. Merriam, "Report on Social Legislation in the United States for 1889–1890," *Economic Review* 1 (1891): pp. 245–56.

22. "Course on Business Law," pp. 175–81. Measures intended to regulate wages and working conditions were given rather more summary treatment, but are still dealt with in sufficient detail to show that LDB strongly disapproved of them: see ibid., pp. 181–86.

23. Ibid., pp. 15–16. For a modern analysis of the developments discussed in this and subsequent paragraphs, see Glenn Porter, *The Rise of Big Business, 1860–1910* (Arlington Heights, Ill.: AHM Press, 1973).

24. "Course on Business Law," pp. 20, 71–2.

25. Ibid., pp. 20–34. The attitude of the courts in respect of each type of trading agreement identified by LDB is amply supported by relevant citations.

26. Ibid., pp. 31–32.

27. Ibid ., pp . 271–74.

28. Ibid., pp. 38, 41–42.

29. Ibid., pp. 42–44. Waite's opinion in *Munn v. Illinois* (1877) is quoted and discussed in Paul, *Conservative Crisis*, pp. 8–10.

30. "Course on Business Law," p. 44. The Buffalo grain elevator case cited by LDB was *Budd v. N.Y.*, 143 U.S. 517 (1892): see Paul, *Conservative Crisis*, pp. 72–74.

31. For a useful discussion of Field's legal thinking, see White, *American Judicial Tradition*, pp. 84–108.

32. "Course on Business Law," pp. 50, 53–57.

33. Ibid., pp. 57–60. LDB went on to note ways in which the scope of state regulatory legislation could also be limited in certain circumstances by the commerce clause; he cited the case of an Iowa prohibition statute that was declared void because it had sought to prevent liquor produced elsewhere from entering the state: see ibid., pp. 60–65.

34. Ibid., p. 66. Cf. especially "The Watuppa Pond Cases," *Harvard Law Review* 2 (1888): pp. 195–211 passim.

35. "Course on Business Law," pp. 75–89, 114–15.

36. The observations of Mary Kenney O'Sullivan, Josephine Goldmark, and Alfred Lief are all quoted in Gal, *Brandeis of Boston*, pp. 56–59. It is not necessary to accept Gal's argument about LDB's social marginality in Boston to perceive the importance of the links that he identifies.

37. For example, Gal, *Brandeis of Boston*, p. 56; Mason, *Brandeis*, p. 141. Mason goes on to observe (ibid.): "Probably more instructive to Brandeis than books and speeches was actual labor warfare . . . and the acute labor troubles of his own industrial clients." LDB to Edwin D. Mead, 9 November 1895, *BL*, 1:121–23.

38. Strum, *Brandeis*, p. 95; see also *Notes on Business Law*, 2 vols. (privately printed, 1894–96), 2:1–59 and "Course on Business Law," pp. 158–86. Direct comparisons are difficult, because each of the later printed volumes is a casebook and commentary, whereas the earlier typescript appears to represent verbatim lectures. LDB to Nathan Abbott (paraphrase), 25 January 1894, *BL*, 1:117; cf. "Course on Business Law," p. 1.

39. LDB to Amy Brandeis Wehle, 1 February 1895, *BL*, 1:120; LDB to Evans, 6 August 1896, ibid., pp. 123–24. LDB's wife was away on vacation when Bryan delivered his "cross of gold" speech, and he was dismayed enough by its euphoric reception to send her a copy. "It must have been the voice and the manner—and above all the general temper of the audience than [*sic*] carried all away," he wrote. "There is a general sadness in the situation—and I have not thought out yet just how I feel about it—although I am clearer about what I shall do." LDB to Alice Goldmark Brandeis, 13 July 1896, SGBU, Box 1, no. 4. His conservative attitude toward the free coinage of silver had been reinforced, if not indeed formed, by reading *The Silver Situation in the U.S.* (New York: Putnam, 1893) by Harvard economist Frank W. Taussig, who was brother to Alfred Brandeis's wife Jennie. For his subsequent efforts in the anti-Bryan cause, see inf., p. 149.

40. LDB to Charles Nagel, 12 July 1879, *BL*, 1:40; LDB to Alfred Brandeis, 19 May 1881, *BL*, 5:656. For his attitude toward women generally, cf. the relevant comments in LDB to Alfred Brandeis, 28 June 1878 and 30 July 1881, *BL*, 1:24, 64; LDB to Amy Brandeis Wehle, 4 December 1879, 25 November 1880 and 2 January 1881, ibid., pp. 49, 59, 61–62; LDB to Elizabeth G. Evans, 5 August 1887, ibid., p. 73.

41. LDB to Alice Goldmark, 4 December 1890, *BL*, 1:95. Only limited extracts of the correspondence between Louis and Alice have been made available to historians

(ibid., pp. 92–101), members of the Brandeis family having chosen to exercise their "right to privacy" regarding materials perceived as too intimate and personal for general disclosure. Within these restrictions, the most perceptive and sensitive treatment of their courtship and early married life is to be found in Paper, *Brandeis*, pp. 43–48.

42. *Report of the Committee of the Whole Board of Aldermen on the Care and Management of Public Institutions*, vol. 3 (1894), quoted in Mason, *Brandeis*, pp. 90–91, cf. Paper, *Brandeis*, pp. 39–40. The wider ramifications of late nineteenth-century welfare policy are ably explored in Michael B. Katz, *In the Shadow of the Poorhouse: a Social History of Welfare in America* (New York: Basic Books, 1986). It should be noted that, whereas most reformers advocated work for paupers on account of its profitability and/or deterrent effect (ibid., pp. 31–32), LDB stressed its role in restoring their self-respect.

43. Both the report on the committee's proceedings and the letter of William L. Garrison, Jr., printed in the *Boston Herald*, 12 January 1897, are quoted in Mason, *Brandeis*, p. 92. If LDB regarded "moral growth" as a strictly individual potentiality during the early 1890s, after thirty years of successful campaigning experience he was ready to link it with more generalized postulates about the human condition. "No doubt my standards seem to some exacting," he told his daughter in 1925; "but my insistence results largely from my faith in man's possibilities and in his perfectibility." LDB to Susan Brandeis, 17 February 1925, SGBU, Box 12, no. 1196. Whether that "faith" survived the disappointments and frustrations of the 1930s is open to doubt.

44. McClennen, "Brandeis as a Lawyer," p. 17.

45. LDB to Alice Goldmark, 13 October 1890, *BL*, 1:92–93; *Frankfurter on the Supreme Court*, pp. 252–53.

46. *Felix Frankfurter Reminisces; An Intimate Portrait as Recorded in Talks with Dr. Harlan B. Phillips* (New York: Reynal, 1960), pp. 209–301.

47. James B. Thayer, "The Origin and Scope of the American Doctrine of Constitutional Law," *Harvard Law Review* 7 (1893): 133, 156.

48. Ibid., pp. 135–37.

49. Ibid., p. 138.

50. Ibid., pp. 139–42; *Marbury v. Madison*, 1 Cranch (5 U.S.) 137 (1803); Tilghman, Ch.J., in *Commonwealth [Penna.] v. Smith*, 4 Bin. 117 (1811); Charlton, J., in *Grimball v. Ross*, Charlton 175 (1808).

51. Thayer, "Origin and Scope," p. 148.

52. Ibid., pp. 151–52.

53. For the influence of Thayer on LDB, Holmes, et al., see *Frankfurter Reminisces*, p. 299. For a more wide-ranging consideration of the intellectual origins of the "Brandeis Brief," see inf., pp. 145–47.

54. See, for example, the exchange between LDB and Commissioner Weinstock (1915) in *Curse of Bigness*, p. 88; Gal, *Brandeis of Boston*, pp. vii–viii, 9–11, 23–25.

55. Frankfurter to W. L. R. Emmet, 5 February 1936, FFLC, Box 52; Gal, *Brandeis of Boston*, pp. 11–22.

Chapter 4. Toward a New Freedom

1. The literature on Progressivism is, of course, too vast to cite exhaustively, but the following items are of particular relevance to the issues raised in this chapter: Richard Hofstadter, *The Age of Reform* (New York: Knopf, 1955); Samuel P. Hays, *The Response to Industrialism, 1885–1914* (Chicago: University of Chicago Press, 1957); Robert Wiebe, *The Search for Order. 1877–1920* (New York: Hill & Wang,

1967); Otis L. Graham, Jr., *The Great Campaigns: Reform and War in America, 1900–1928* (Englewood Cliffs, N.J.: Prentice Hall, 1971); Arthur A. Ekirch, Jr., *Progressivism in America: A Study of the Era from Theodore Roosevelt to Woodrow Wilson* (New York: New Viewpoints, 1974); Martin J. Sklar, *The Corporate Reconstruction of American Capitalism, 1890–1914: the Market, the Law and Politics* (New York: Cambridge University Press, 1988).

2. The growing pressures on the urban environment and the response of reformers to them are ably considered in Blake McKelvey, *The Urbanization of America, 1860–1915* (New Brunswick: Rutgers University Press, 1963). On the "muckraking" phenomenon generally, see Cornelius C. Regier, *The Era of the Muckrakers* (Chapel Hill: University of North Carolina Press, 1932); Herbert Shapiro, ed., *The Muckrakers and American Society* (Boston: D. C. Heath, 1968). The best introduction to Sinclair's Progressive writings is Floyd Dell, *Upton Sinclair: A Study in Social Protest* (New York: AMS Press, 1970). The influence of Steffens is best understood by looking at *The Autobiography of Lincoln Steffens*, 2 vols. (New York: Harcourt, Brace, 1931), but Justin Kaplan, *Lincoln Steffens: A Biography* (New York: Simon & Schuster, 1974) is also valuable for its insights.

3. For the complex relationships between genteel reform and Progressivism, see Gerald W. McFarland, *Mugwumps, Morals and Politics, 1884–1920* (Amherst: University of Massachusetts Press, 1975).

4. For widely differing estimates of the role of businessmen in the Progressive movement, see Marguerite Green, *The National Civic Federation and the American Labor Movement, 1900–1925* (Washington, D.C.: Catholic University of America Press, 1956); Robert Wiebe, *Businessmen and Reform* (Cambridge, Mass. Harvard University Press, 1962); Gabriel Kolko, *The. Triumph of Conservatism: A Reinterpretation of American History, 1900–1916* (New York: Free Press of Glencoe, 1963); James Weinstein, *The Corporate Ideal in the Liberal State, 1900–1918* (Boston: Beacon Press, 1968).

5. On social workers and the development of Progressive Era welfare policies, see Allen F. Davis, *Spearheads for Reform: The Social Settlements and the Progressive Movement, 1890–1914* (New York: Oxford University Press, 1967); Michael B. Katz, *In the Shadow of the Poorhouse: A Social History of Welfare in America* (New York: Basic Books, 1986), especially pp. 113–205. For Christian ministers as reformers, see C. Howard Hopkins, *The Rise of the Social Gospel in American Protestantism, 1865–1915* (New Haven: Yale University Press, 1940); Henry May, *The Protestant Churches and Industrial America* (New York: Harper, 1949); Ronald C. White, Jr., and C. Howard Hopkins, *The Social Gospel: Religion and Reform in Changing America* (Philadelphia: Temple University Press, 1976). Full references to the relevant works of Hofstadter, Hays, Wiebe, Kolko and Weinstein will be found in n. 1 and 4 sup.

6. The regulatory posture of the New Nationalism is best approached through the writings of its chief proponents: see, for example, Herbert Croly, *The Promise of American Life* (New York: Macmillan, 1909); Charles R. Van Hise, *Concentration and Control: A Solution to the Trust Problem* (New York: Macmillan, 1912); *The Works of Theodore Roosevelt*, 20 vols., ed. Harman Hagedorn (New York: Scribner, 1926), vol. 17, *Social Justice and Popular Rule: Essays, Addresses, and Public Statements Relating to the Progressive Movement (1910–1916)*, especially pp. 245–356. The significance of Croly's book in Roosevelt's the developing conception of the New Nationalism is ably discussed in Eric Goldman, *Rendezvous with Destiny: A History of Modern American Reform* (New York: Knopf, 1952), pp. 188–207. The most sympathetic discussion of the New Freedom is still that provided in Arthur Link, *Wilson: The New Freedom* (Princeton: Princeton University Press, 1965).

7. Richard M. Abrams, *Conservatism in a Progressive Era: Massachusetts Politics, 1900–1912* (Cambridge, Mass.: Harvard University Press, 1964), pp. 55–56.

8. Ibid., passim, but especially pp. vii–xii, 1–24, 53–79. On the distinction between "center" and "peripheral" firms within the national economy, see Thomas K. McCraw, *Prophets of Regulation: Charles Francis Adams, Louis D. Brandeis, James N. Landis, Alfred E. Kahn* (Cambridge, Mass.: Harvard University Press, 1984), pp. 72–4. The "constitutional historian" was Edwin S. Corwin: see Loss, ed., *Corwin on the Constitution*, 3:59.

9. The references to LDB's supposed views on labor injunctions and women's suffrage are in Abrams, *Conservatism in a Progressive Era*, p. 58. The most detailed account of LaFollette's career, which includes several references to his relations with LDB, is Belle Case LaFollette and Fola LaFollette, *Robert M. LaFollette*, 2 vols. (New York: Macmillan, 1953). On Johnson, see Spencer Olin, *California's Prodigal Sons: Hiram Johnson and the Progressives, 1911–1917* (Berkeley: University of California Press, 1968). On the "cult of efficiency" generally, and on Frederick W. Taylor in particular, see Samuel Haber, *Efficiency and Uplift: Scientific Management in the Progressive Era, 1890–1920* (Chicago: University of Chicago Press, 1964). For LDB's enthusiastic advocacy of Taylor's scientific management techniques, see "Organized Labor and Efficiency," 22 April 1911, printed in *Business—A Profession*, pp. 37–50; LDB to H. C. DeRan, 12 February 1912, *BL*, 2:543. LDB first became acquainted with Taylor in 1910. It is even possible that LDB was responsible for coining the expression "scientific management": see LDB to Ray Stannard Baker, 3 December 1910, ibid., pp. 390–91; Dan Clawson, *Democracy and the Labor Process: The Transformation of U.S. Industry, 1986–1920* (New York: Monthly Review Press, 1980), p. 203. On T. R., Croly, and Lodge, see, respectively: John Blum, *The Republican Roosevelt* (Cambridge, Mass.: Harvard University Press, 1954); Charles W. Forcey, *The Crossroads of Liberalism: Croly, Weyl, Lippmann and the Progressive Era* (New York: Oxford University Press, 1961); John A. Garraty, *Henry Cabot Lodge: A Biography* (New York: Knopf, 1953).

10. Undated memorandum quoted in Mason, *Brandeis*, p. 69.

11. LDB to William H. Dunbar, 2 February 1893, *BL*, 1:106–109. For Dunbar's reply see Mason, *Brandeis*, pp. 80–82.

12. LDB to Jacob M. Rudy, 14 April 1913, *BL*, 3:62–63.

13. "Opportunity in the Law," 4 May 1905, printed in *Business—A Profession*, pp. 315–316.

14. LDB to Samuel Merwin, editor of *Success Magazine*, 21 September 1909, LBLU, WB 17740 [12–1]; LDB to Mark Sullivan, 4 June 1910, *BL*, 3:341; LDB to N. Hapgood, 30 July 1912, ibid., p. 656.

15. "The Nomination of Mr. Justice Brandeis" in Kurland, *Frankfurter on the Supreme Court*, p. 46.

16. McClennen, "Brandeis as a Lawyer," pp. 16–19. For a perceptive estimate of the *Muller* case, see John W. Johnson, *American Legal Culture, 1908–1940* (Westport, Conn.: Greenwood Press, 1981), pp. 28–36, 39–40.

17. Pound to Senator William E. Chilton, 8 February 1916, quoted in McClennen, "Brandeis as a Lawyer," p. 18.

18. McClennen, "Brandeis as a Lawyer," pp. 18–19. See also the opinions in *Holden v. Hardy*, 169 U.S. 366 (1898) and *Lochner v. New York*, 198 U.S. 45 (1905).

19. A. L. Todd, *Justice on Trial: The Case of Louis D. Brandeis* (New York: McGraw-Hill, 1964), pp. 56–59. For the full text of LDB's brief, including the evidence assembled by Josephine Goldmark, as well as the opinion of the Court and a short introduction by Leon Stein and Philip Taft, see Brandeis and Goldmark, *Women in Industry* (1908; reprint, New York: Arno Press, 1969), produced for the

National Consumers' League. To apply the term "sociological jurisprudence" to LDB's forensic methodology in *Muller v. Oregon* is perhaps to help perpetuate a misnomer. As Johnson rightly observes (*American Legal Culture*, p 35): "Although Brandeis's innovative appellate technique has been justly lauded for its legal utility, the brief in the *Muller* case did not offer very sophisticated social science analysis." Most of the data offered in support of its central hypotheses "was assembled in an unsystematic fashion. No attempt was made to control or isolate any of the multitude of independent variables affecting health, safety, morals, and the general welfare." The hypotheses themselves were completely untested. Yet as he concludes, "the Brandeis-Goldmark method of classification and assembly of data was no worse than much of that which passed for social science in the period. In fact, one commentator's characterization of Brandeis's *Muller* brief as "nascent social science" is an apt appraisal of the quality of the brief and the research out of which it sprang."

20. McCraw, *Prophets of Regulation*, p. 84.

21. Geoffrey Blodgett, *The Gentle Reformers: Massachusetts Democrats in the Cleveland Era* (Cambridge, Mass.: Harvard University Press, 1966), pp. 86, 224–26. Prominent among those who went over to Bryan in 1896 was fellow Mugwump, Congressman George F. Williams, who had sought to enlist LDB's active participation in the Democratic politics of the commonwealth in 1890: see ibid, pp. 212–41, 271–79. Concerning LDB's "retrospective sympathy" for the Populists, see LDB to Alice Goldmark Brandeis, 28 November 1899, SGBU, Box 1, no. 28.

22. Ibid , pp. 272–73.

23. Walter H. Reynolds to LDB, 21 February 1893, quoted in Mason, *Brandeis*, pp. 106–7; LDB to Amy Brandeis Wehle, 1 February 1895, *BL*, 1:120.

24. The account of the West End and Boston Elevated campaigns offered in this and the next two paragraphs is drawn principally from Abrams, *Conservatism in a Progressive Era*, pp. 61–73; the quotation is on p. 81. But cf. Mason, *Brandeis*, pp. 106–17.

25. LDB's 1911 remarks are quoted in Poole, "Brandeis," p. xviii.

26. For a brief outline of the LDB's fight against the Boston gas combine, see Abrams, *Conservatism in a Progressive Era*, pp. 138–40; a fuller version can be found in Mason, *Brandeis*, pp. 126–41.

27. LDB's "How Boston Solved the Gas Problem," November 1907, reprinted in *Business—A Profession*, pp. 93–108, remains the most informative account of the Boston sliding scale; the quotations are from pp. 101–2 and 93–94 respectively.

28. This and the next three paragraphs rely heavily on the discussion in Abrams, *Conservatism in a Progressive Era*, pp. 190–216.

29. *Second Hearing before [the] Joint Special Committee on Railroad and Street Railway Laws, 11 July 1905* (hereafter cited as *Street Railway Hearings*; copy preserved in LBLU, NMF 1B-1), pp. 17–19.

30. There are excellent accounts of LDB's battles against Mellen and the New Haven in Mason, *Brandeis*, pp. 177–214, and Paper, *Brandeis*, pp. 93–111. LDB's own writings on the New Haven episode include "The New Haven Transportation Monopoly," 11 February 1908, printed in *Business—A Profession*, pp. 255–78; "The New Haven—An Unregulated Monopoly," 13 December 1912, reprinted ibid., pp. 279–305; "The Failure of Banker Management," 16 August 1913, reprinted in *Other People's Money*, pp. 189–200.

31. Between 1908 and 1916, LDB repeated the approach first adopted in the *Muller* case by filing briefs defending maximum-hours and minimum-wage statutes in more than a dozen courts. The most important cases were *Ritchie v. Wayman*, 244 Ill. 509 (1910); *Ex parte Anna Hawley*, 85 Ohio 495 (1911); *People v. Eldering*, 245 Ill. 579 (1912); *Hawley v. Walker*, 232 U.S. 718 (1914); *Stettler v. O'Hara*, 69 Ore. 519 (1914); *People v. Schweinler Press*, 214 N.Y. 395 (1915); *Stettler v. O'Hara*, 243

U.S. 629. For discussion of the "Brandeis briefs" entered in these and similar cases, see Mason, *Brandeis*, pp. 245–53; Johnson, *American Legal Culture*, pp. 36–39. For a fuller discussion of the Garment Trades Protocol, see inf., pp. 181, 198.

32. These remarks supposedly uttered by Haywood are recorded in an undated memorandum in FFLC, Box 128. The context suggests they were noted down by Felix Frankfurter for possible use in the war of words that surrounded LDB's nomination hearings in 1916. Although their authenticity must be considered suspect, the sentiments expressed may be accepted with safety as the reflection of a widely held perception of LDB's attitudes toward labor at the time. Strum, who quotes the remarks verbatim (*Brandeis*, pp. 167–68), has no difficulty accepting their ascription to Haywood. The fullest discussion of LDB's extensive involvement with Savings Bank Insurance over many decades is Alpheus T. Mason, *The Brandeis Way: A Case Study in the Workings of Democracy* (Princeton: Princeton University Press, 1938); but cf. Paper, *Brandeis*, pp. 80–91; Strum, op. cit., pp. 74–93.

33. There is no historiographical consensus as to the degree of Ballinger's "guilt" or "innocence" in respect of the allegations made against him. Alpheus T. Mason, *Bureaucracy Convicts Itself: The Ballinger-Pinchot Controversy of 1910* (New York: Viking Press, 1941), evidently shares LDB's conviction that both Taft and his interior secretary acted reprehensibly; James L. Penick, Jr., *Progressive Politics and Conservation: The Ballinger-Pinchot Affair* (Chicago: University of Chicago Press, 1968) is somewhat more skeptical. Rather more concise discussions, with pertinent quotations from the hearings, can be found in Mason, *Brandeis*, pp. 254–89; and Paper, *Brandeis*, pp. 112–34. For a brief assessment of the debate and other relevant citations, see *BL*, 2:307–8 n. 1. The "most sensational controversy of the Progressive Era" quote is from McCraw, *Prophets of Regulation*, p. 88.

34. Grady to Alfred Brandeis, 13 May 1910, LBLU, NMF 33–2. Alfred, though, was less impressed by his brother's behavior: see Paper, *Brandeis*, p. 127.

35. That LDB did have serious ideas about the need for a federal policy to reconcile the conflicting needs of resource development and conservation is evident from subsequent comments he made on the situation in Alaska: see LDB to Robert M. LaFollette, 29 July 1911, *BL*, 2:467–72; LDB to Gifford Pinchot, 29 July 1911, ibid., pp. 473–74. The mining combination against which LDB might have chosen to move in 1910 was what he referred to in these letters as the "Morgan-Guggenheim Syndicate."

36. Gal, *Brandeis of Boston*, pp. 47–51, 177.

37. *Street Railway Hearings*, pp. 19–20.

38. LDB to Clapp, 24 February 1912, *BL*, 2:551–60. The fullest discussion of LDB's relations with the United Shoe Machinery Company is in Mason, *Brandeis*, 214–29; for a more succinct view, see Paper, *Brandeis*, pp. 221–24. McElwain's death in 1908 at the age of forty "greatly distressed" LDB, who not only appreciated his qualities as an enlightened businessman but also regarded him as a personal friend. A few days after his passing, Louis wrote to his brother Alfred (12 January 1908, LBLU, A 1–4): "He was in my opinion really the greatest man of my acquaintance—and the greatest loss to the Commonwealth—possessing the rare charm of great ability, courage, high character and personal charm." Most of his efforts had been devoted to building up the successful shoe-manufacturing company, which he had started from nothing in 1895; however, if he had lived, in LDB's estimation "he would soon have emerged from business into the field of his higher ideals and become a commanding figure in the Commonwealth." As it was, LDB believed him to have been "a sacrifice to overwork—to the perfecting of his business organization—for he had no love or even respect for money as such." In short, McElwain seems to have personified the perfect combination of professional competence and public idealism to which LDB himself aspired. Cf. his remarks about

McElwain and the Filene family, which constitute the greater part of the title essay (October 1912) in *Business—A Profession*, pp. 5–12.

39. *Purchase of Stock in the Boston and Maine Railroad. Hearing by the Legislative Committee on Railroads, Senator Faxon Presiding, Boston, 10[–11] June 1907* (hereafter cited as *B. & M. Hearings*; copy in LBLU, NMF 1B–1), p. 18. The rather garbled paraphrase of LDB's remarks that appeared in the *Boston American*, 10 June 1907, is quoted without comment in *BL*, 1:596 n. 7.

40. *B. & M. Hearings*, pp. 19–20.

41. Ibid., pp. 239–40, 243. Cf. LDB's *Argument . . . before the Commission on Commerce and Industry, In Opposition to the Merger. . . , 22 November 1907* (transcript in LBLU, NMF 1C–4).

42. Johnson to LDB, 12 August 1910, LBLU, NMF 33–2; LDB to Johnson, 16 August 1910, ibid. A fragment of LDB's reply as subsequently printed in the *Louisville Herald* is in *BL*, 2:369–70; the "committee of 100" apparently became formalized as the Citizens Public Utility Club and Alfred Brandeis became a member of its executive committee.

43. LDB to Louis B. Wehle, 1 October 1910, *BL*, 2:380–81. Because of increasingly heavy commitments elsewhere, LDB did not investigate the Louisville situation himself but passed Johnson's data over to Joseph B. Eastman, who since 1905 had served as executive secretary of the Public Franchise League. For his exhaustive analysis of the issues involved, and specific recommendations regarding appropriate future action, which were forwarded to Johnson by LDB without amendment, see Eastman to LDB, 5 October 1910, LBLU, NMF 33–2. A full and competent evaluation of Eastman's career is provided in Claude M. Fuess, *Joseph B. Eastman: Servant of the People* (New York: Colombia University Press, 1952); for a briefer assessment, see Abrams, *Conservatism in a Progressive Era*, pp. 59–60.

44. *The Curse of Bigness*, pp. 114–15. For an illustration of the practices LDB objected to, see ibid., pp. 105, 138–40.

45. *New State Ice Company v. Liebmann*, 285 U.S. 262 (1932). LDB's dissent is printed in *The Curse of Bigness*, pp. 143–60; see especially pp. 144, 149–52.

46. *The Curse of Bigness*, p. 105–6, 109.

47. Ibid., pp. 105, 115; and see also "Competition that Kills," 15 November 1913, printed in *Business—A Profession*, pp. 236–54. His oral argument in the *Stettler* case (1914) would suggest that he regarded minimum wage laws *inter alia* as a means of regulating cutthroat competition: see *The Curse of Bigness*, pp. 62, 68.

48. LDB to LaFollette, 17 May 1911, *BL*, 2:435; LDB to William B. Colver, 22 May 1911, ibid., pp. 435–36. The case in question was *Standard Oil Co. of New Jersey et al. v. U.S.*, 221 U.S. 1 (1911).

49. LDB to Edwin A. Grozier, 19 September 1911, *BL*, 2:495–96. Two weeks after the *Standard Oil* decision, the Court had again employed the "rule of reason" in an antitrust suit brought against the Tobacco Trust: see *U.S. v. American Tobacco Co.*, 221 U.S. 106 (1911). The Court actually found against both companies, but in terms that led to reorganization rather than fragmentation of their assets.

50. LDB to LaFollette, 26 May 1911, *BL*, 2:442–43. The editors somewhat overstate the degree of LDB's success in converting the senator to the views espoused in this letter.

51. For LDB's thoughts about criminal penalties, see ibid., p. 443.

52. Samuel to LDB, 3 January 1912, LBLU, NMF 43–4; LDB to Samuel, 15 January 1912, ibid. The LDB article referred to was "An Illegal Trust Legalized," *The World Today* 21 (December 1911), 1440–41. According to Melvin Urofsky, "Wilson, Brandeis and the Trust Issue, 1912–1914," *Mid-America* 49 (1967):7, LaFollette was already calling for a program of "strong government by the people to assault the citadels of corporate power through discriminate taxation, railroad reg-

ulation, and strong anti-trust laws. Brandeis agreed with the aims, but not with all the means." For LDB's subsequent adoption of the taxation weapon, see inf., pp. 306, 310–11, 316. Urofsky's article can be found reprinted with slight alterations in his *Mind of One Piece*, pp. 71–92.

53. LDB to Hapgood, 2 October 1912, *BL*, 2:694–96. Ross's letter is summarized in ibid, p. 512 n. 2–8.

54. LDB's copy of "Concentration in Industry," with the text heavily scored in pencil at points where he plainly disagreed with the argument, is in LBLU, NMF 43–4. Van Hise had hoped to see LDB in Boston on the day of his visit to Harvard, but found him out of town: see Alice H. Grady to Van Hise, 13 November 1911, ibid. The suggested reading on competition and monopoly is contained in Taussig to LDB, 18 November 1911, ibid. The books referred to in the text are Richard T. Ely, *Monopolies and Trusts* (New York: Macmillan, 1900); John Bates Clark, *The Control of Trusts: An Argument in Favor of Curbing the Power of Monopoly by a Natural Method* (New York: Macmillan, 1901).

55. LDB to Crane, 11 November 1911, *BL*, 2:510–12. In 1907 he had been ready to declare himself "a strong supporter" of the policies that Theodore Roosevelt was then pursuing, and to prophesy that he would be regarded by history "as one among the few great and beneficent American Presidents": see LDB to John W. Alling, 18 October 1907, LBLU, WB 15698 [10–3]. As late as 16 March 1912, he evidently still regarded Roosevelt in a positive light, telling George Rublee (*BL*, 2:568–69) that his influence was such "that in office or out he can contribute more than any other one man in the country to the proper solution" of the difficult social and industrial problems facing the nation. He still had hopes, however, that LaFollette would be able to wrest the Republican nomination from Taft, and opposed the former president's entry into the field and the establishment of the New Party. By the fall, however, with Roosevelt openly endorsing the program being proposed by Herbert Croly and Van Hise's Wisconsin group, LDB's sentiments had become decidedly hostile. "It is not only Col. Roosevelt's statements, but his acts, which speak his real opinion," he told Norman Hapgood (26 September 1912, LBLU, NMF 43–44). "His past attitude on the Steel Trust, the Harvester Trust, and the Sugar Trust, all confirm [it]." Cf. Van Hise to Hapgood, 23 and 28 September 1912, and Hapgood to Van Hise, 25 September 1912, ibid., in which Roosevelt's thinking on monopoly is considered in detail. However, even in the midst of these squabbles over policy, LDB did not lose sight of what was at stake for the reformers. "I am much grieved at the division among the progressives," he had told an associate of Gifford Pinchot's only a week before. "Instead of being distributed among three parties, or possibly four, they ought to be in one": see postscript of LDB to Philip P. Wells, 20 September 1912, NMF 51–57.

56. According to Urofsky, "Wilson, Brandeis and the Trust Issue," p. 20, Wilson himself had doubts about the feasibility of breaking up the trusts. For LDB's views on the effects of scale and "human limitations" on the viability of corporate enterprise, see F. Frankfurter to W. L. R. Emmet, 5 February 1936, FFLC, Box 52; *Other People's Money*, pp. 201–2, 204–7; *The Curse of Bigness*, pp. 71, 76. His belief that corporate executives should confine themselves to running only one business at a time remained unchanged into the 1930s: cf. LDB to Frankfurter, 17 March 1933, FFLC, Box 28.

57. *The Curse of Bigness*, pp. 116–17.

58. His views on "bigness" initially owed little to formal theory: see Gal, *Brandeis of Boston*, pp. 49–55, 96–106, 173–78. As discussed sup., LDB's growing interest in labor problems following the Homestead strike in 1892 was also of considerable importance in developing his attitude toward large corporate employers: cf. ibid., pp. 55–58.

59. *Other People's Money*, pp. 162–64; *The Curse of Bigness*, p. 77. In 1933, LDB

would draw enthusiastically on *The Modern Corporation and Private Property* (New York: Macmillan, 1932) to support his dissent in the Florida Chain-Store Case, describing its authors as "able, discerning scholars": see ibid., pp. 169–71.

60. LDB to Frank A. Fetter, 26 November 1940, *BL*, 5:648; LDB to R. S. Baker, 5 July 1931, ibid., p. 482. Cf. LDB to Frankfurter, 14 November 1937, FFLC, Box 28 . The summary of LDB's dissenting opinion in *Federal Trade Commission. v. Gratz*, 253 U.S. 421, 433 (1920) is in the "Digest of all opinions of Mr. Justice Brandeis," prepared by his law clerk, Harry Shulman, in August 1930 and subsequently added to by later clerks and by LDB himself: LBHLS, Paige Box 1 (3).

61. *The Curse of Bigness*, pp. 48–49, 86–88.

62. *Other People's Money*, pp. 149–52; *The Curse of Bigness*, pp. 118, 140–42. For the possible role of government in undertaking research and development, see below p. 315. LDB remained a supporter of technical education to the end of his life, particularly in Palestine: see LDB to Shlomo H. Bardin, 20 October 1939, *BL*, 5:626. *The Curse of Bigness*, p. 40.

63. *The Curse of Bigness*, pp. 49–51, 85–86.

64. Ibid., p. 41.

65. LDB to Alfred Brandeis, 30 January 1884, *BL*, 1:66; LDB to Amy F. Acton, 1 February 1905, ibid., p. 280; Maud Wood Park to LDB, 16 June 1991, LBLU, NMF 47–3. LDB's remarks of 14 June 1911 are quoted verbatim in a letter from Alice H. Grady to Martha Davies, 30 January 1912, ibid. Cf. LDB to the *Pittsburgh Sun* (telegram), 27 February 1912, for inclusion in its forthcoming edition on women's suffrage, ibid. There can be little doubt that LDB's attitudes toward women changed only slowly. "Man is best at work—unless it be at war—and women best at home (!!)" he told his wife, perhaps a little tongue in cheek, as he observed his fellow passengers on a ship bound for Rotterdam in 1899. (LDB to Alice Goldmark Brandeis, undated but endorsed "1899" in a separate hand, SGBU, Box 23, no. 2430.) Three years later, he was ready to "move for the wholesale admission of women to the bar—in order that they may satisfy the needs of women clients." (LDB to Alice Goldmark Brandeis, 30 December 1902, ibid., Box 1, no. 72.) By 1914, he was a good deal less patronizing but scarcely more optimistic about the careers that women could expect to enjoy in legal practice. "The profitable work in law is apt to be connected with important business transactions," he told his elder daughter, when she approached him on behalf of a female friend; "and there is little likelihood that in the near future men of business will take women for their lawyers—much as they may like them for assistants." Women doctors, he went on, had enjoyed a rather easier path in the medical profession, yet had still "advanced but slowly." (LDB to Susan Brandeis, 10 November 1914, ibid., Box 11, no. 1047.) Presumably, since inquiries were already being made about an appropriate law school for Susan, LDB intended using his own influence and connections to open doors that remained closed to other women.

66. Teresa A. Crowley to LDB, 23 and 28 February 1913, ibid.; LDB to Caroline I. Hibbard (telegram), 18 March 1913, *BL*, 3:48.

67. "Brandeis Points out Duty to Men," *Boston American* (Special Suffrage Campaign Issue) 17 April 1915. A clipping of this article is preserved in LBLU, NMF 47–3; cf. LDB to Mrs. F. W. Wile, 19 June 1915, *BL*, 3:535–36.

68. *The Curse of Business*, pp. 73, 80–81.

69. Ibid., pp. 35, 47.

70. LDB to Robert Bruere, 25 February 1922, *BL*, 5:46; *Brandeis of Boston*, p. 71. Indeed, as we saw in the previous chapter, LDB's original position regarding organized labor was rather more conservative than Gal suggests. His earliest positive, though still qualified, support for organized labor can be seen in "The Employer and Trade Unions," 21 April 1904, printed in *Business—A Profession*, pp. 13–27. For his later advocacy of the "preferential union shop" see Mason, *Brandeis*, pp.

294–304, 314–15. The detailed development of his thinking on organized labor can best be followed in Strum, *Brandeis*, pp. 94–113, 159–95.

71. *The Curse of Bigness*, pp. 72–74.

72. Acheson to F. Frankfurter, 16 November 1920, FFLC, Box 19; *The Curse of Bigness*, p. 107. See also LDB to William Howard Taft, 30 December 1911, *BL*, 2:531–36, for further speculation on the causes of labor violence and the steps needed to avoid it.

73. *The Curse of Bigness*, pp. 36, 74. For the unconvincing assertion that LDB adopted a consistent "antilabor" stance, see Kolko, *Triumph of Conservatism*, pp. 207–9.

74. *The Curse of Bigness*, pp. 79, 83–85. LDB's role in establishing and administering the New York Garment Trades Protocol is considered at length in Mason, op. cit., pp. 289–315.

75. *The Curse of Bigness*, p. 80.

76. Ibid., pp. 78–79.

77. Ibid., pp. 104, 130.

78. "Suggestions for Letter of Governor Wilson on Trusts" enclosed in LDB to Wilson, 30 September 1912, *BL*, 2:686–94. Cf. *Other People's Money*, p. 113: "The legal machinery must be greatly improved, and an administrative board of some kind, with fairly broad powers, must be created to supplement the powers of the courts in dealing with this subject."

79. Urofsky, "Wilson, Brandeis and the Trust Issue," pp. 11–14, 18–23; the quote from Hofstadter is on p. 12. For an analysis of LDB's thinking about economic regulation that differs considerably from both Urofsky's and my own, see McCraw, *Prophets of Regulation*, pp. 80–142.

80. "Suggestions . . . on Trusts" in LDB to Wilson, 30 September 1912, *BL*, 2:690–92. On the possibility of LDB's being offered the attorney-generalship in 1912–13 and his reactions to it, see Strum, *Brandeis*, pp. 204–7.

81. Urofsky, "Wilson, Brandeis and the Trust Issue," pp. 18–19.

82. Ibid., pp. 15–18; LDB to Lane, 12 December 1913, *BL*, 3:218–21; *Other People's Money*, p. 160. In his letter to Lane, LDB sets out his proposals for new legislation in considerable detail.

83. Urofsky, "Wilson, Brandeis and the Trust Issue," pp. 22–27. In light of LDB's comments to Wilson and Lane, it is difficult to sustain Urofsky's view that his unqualified endorsement of a strong Federal Trade Commission in June 1914 represented a surprising change of heart; he had in fact become reconciled to the need for an agency "to regulate competition" at least two years earlier. On the issue of trade agreements, LDB recommended the registration of all such arrangements with the proposed Federal Trade Commission, which could then rule on their permissibility; regarding railroads, he favored an amendment to the commodity clause of the Hepburn Act, passed in 1906 to deal specifically with matters of railroad regulation: see *The Curse of Bigness*, pp. 135–36, 138; *Other People's Money*, pp. 187–88. On the Hepburn Act itself, see Gabriel Kolko, *Railroads and Regulation, 1877–1916* (Princeton: Princeton University Press, 1965), pp. 127–54.

84. *The Curse of Bigness*, pp. 121–23, 135.

85. Ibid., p. 80.

86. Urofsky, "Wilson, Brandeis and the Trust Issue," p. 18.

Chapter 5. A Gift of Prophecy

1. For a full discussion of LDB's involvement with the setting of reasonable railroad charges between 1910 and 1914, see Mason, *Brandeis*, pp. 315–51; Paper, *Bran-*

deis, pp. 146–60. The broader context of railroad regulation during the Progressive Era is succinctly depicted in Ari and Olive Hoogenboom, *A History of the ICC from Panacea to Palliative* (New York: Norton, 1976), pp. 39–83.

2. Quoted in Ezekiel Rabinowitz, *Justice Louis D. Brandeis: The Zionist Chapter of His Life* (New York: Philosophical Library, 1968), pp. 48–49.

3. Quoted in ibid., pp. 49–50.

4. Mason, *Brandeis*, pp. 52–52. For other instances of government officials turning to LDB for advice at this time, see ibid., pp. 522–25. Mason offers no criticism of the constitutional propriety of this relationship with members of the executive branch; but cf. Bruce Allen Murphy, *The Brandeis Frankfurter Connection: The Secret Political Activities of Two Supreme Court Justices* (Garden City, N.Y.: Doubleday, 1983), especially pp. 16–72, where LDB's ethics are subjected to a rather more rigorous scrutiny.

5. The literature on LDB's Jewish identity and his involvement with Zionism is extensive. All of his biographers have much to say on the subject, but particularly incisive are the contributions in Baker, *Brandeis and Frankfurter: A Dual Biography* (New York: Harper & Row, 1984), pp. 70–80, 159–81; Paper, *Brandeis*, pp. 198–208, 259–74, 315–24, 386–89; and Strum, *Brandeis*, pp. 224–90. Jacob de Haas, *Louis D. Brandeis: A Biographical Sketch* (New York: Bloch, 1929), provides some interesting information, but its accuracy has sometimes been called into question; Rabinowitz, *Justice Brandeis*, contains some pertinent quotations but has little to offer by way of critical analysis. Gal, *Brandeis of Boston*, affords the fullest picture yet available of LDB's Jewish connections and affiliations in the years before his appointment as a Supreme Court judge, but the weight of interpretation placed on this evidence to the effect that LDB was marginalized in Boston because of his racial origins has not met with universal acceptance. A more recent treatment of the "social outcast" theme that draws somewhat different conclusions, can be found in Robert A. Burt, *Two Jewish Justices: Outcasts in the Promised Land* (Berkeley: University of California Press, 1988), passim, but especially chaps. 2 and 6. Among works with a broader focus, Yonathan Shapiro, *Leadership of the American Zionist Organization, 1987–1930* (Urbana: University of Illinois Press, 1971); and Melvin I. Urofsky, *American Zionism from Herzl to the Holocaust* (Garden City, N.Y.: Doubleday, 1975) are particularly relevant. Many of LDB's Zionist addresses and writings are printed in Solomon Goldman ed., *Brandeis on Zionism* (Washington, D.C.: Zionist Organization of America, 1942); and *BL*, vol. 3–5 are full of references to Zionist activity.

6. *Reminiscences of Frederika Brandeis*, pp. 32–34.

7. Baker, *Brandeis and Frankfurter*, pp. 21–22. Most other biographers have accepted uncritically Mason's assertion (*Brandeis*, p. 27) that LDB changed his middle name at some point in adolescence from David to Dembitz in honor of his uncle. Baker points out, however, that although no contemporary record of LDB's birth exists, his early school records already show his name as Louis *Dembitz* Brandeis. Nevertheless, Mason's version is given additional credence by his quotation (ibid., p. 66) of a letter from Dembitz to LDB, dated 16 April 1882, in which the writer explicitly refers to the name change, though not to himself as the cause of it. LDB's recollection of his uncle's religious observances is printed in Solomon Goldman, ed., *The Words of Justice Brandeis* (New York: H. Schuman, 1953), p. 160. In theological terms, however, Dembitz may not have been quite so orthodox as he has often been portrayed: see Gal, *Brandeis of Boston*, pp. 68–70. For LDB's conflation of the Jewish and Puritan traditions, see inf., p. 205.

8. Concerning the possibility of life after death, LDB reportedly got into a heated argument on the subject with his friend Glendower Evans, shortly before the latter's own untimely demise in 1886. According to the account given in Paper, *Bran-*

deis, p. 29: "Glen felt there might be something to it. Louis disagreed vehemently. Man's mind could not know what lies beyond the present life, Louis said. Religion was of no practical use." For his remarks about Uncle Lewis's intellectual range, see LDB to Stella and Emily Dembitz, 22 April 1926, *BL*, 5:219. Dembitz's scholarly credentials did, of course, include an impressive knowledge of the "history, ritual and theology" of Judaism: see Mason, *Brandeis*, p. 27. For LDB's continuing relationship with his uncle into adult life, see Gal, *Brandeis of Boston*, p. 2.

9. Gal, *Brandeis of Boston*, pp. 70–72.

10. Harold J. Laski, *The American Democracy: A Commentary and Interpretation* (New York: Viking Press, 1948), p. 320; the biblical quotation is from Prov. 29:18. Cf. Burt, *Two Jewish Justices*, pp. 124–25, where it is argued that it is the "vicarious . . . experience of alienation" rather than "productive interaction" which best characterizes LDB's relationship to the Jewish world. However, it is probable that Laski was thinking of LDB's "experience of the world" in a rather larger frame of reference than Burt's.

11. LDB to Adolph Brandeis, 29 November 1905, *BL*, 1:386, and editors' note, pp. 386–87.

12. The number of Jewish immigrants from Eastern Europe who chose to settle in Boston is difficult to estimate because the census lists them among those born in Russia and Poland, respectively, thereby confounding Jews with ethnic Russians, Poles, and Lithuanians. Considering this point, my colleague P. A. M. Taylor has suggested that the city's Eastern Jews (excluding Yiddish speakers recently arrived from Germany and the Austrian Empire) plausibly numbered around 1,500 in 1885; 5,000 in 1890; 13,000 in 1895; 18,000 in 1900; and 42,000 in 1910. If these figures are accurate, then in 1890 this group accounted for just 3.3 percent of Boston's foreign-born population. By contrast, the combined total for New York's Russian and Polish-born populations in the same year already stood at more than 55,000, or 8.7 percent of the foreign born; Chicago's stood at more than 31,000, or 7.1 percent: see *Compendium of the Eleventh Census: 1890*, 3 vols. (Washington, D.C.: Government Printing Office, 1892–97), 2:606. Turner's recollections are quoted in Sam B. Girgus, *The New Covenant: Jewish Writers and the American Idea* (Chapel Hill: University of North Carolina Press, 1984), p. 25.

13. Gal, *Brandeis of Boston*, pp. 43–46, 72–75; Strum, *Brandeis*, pp. 224–25.

14. All of the quotations in this paragraph can be found in Gal, *Brandeis of Boston*, pp. 125–26.

15. For LDB's early relationship with De Haas, see ibid., pp. 103, 127–30. Although they did not become close until the 1910s, it appears they were first introduced to one another more than a decade earlier: see LDB to Alice Goldmark Brandeis, 13 January 1900, SGBU, Box 1, no. 30. The *Jewish Advocate* published its interview with LDB in its issue of 9 December 1910, together with a slightly revised version of his 1905 address to the New Century Club; for quotations and discussion, see ibid., pp. 130–36.

16. LDB to Bernard G. Richards, 2 February 1911 and 26 April 1912, *BL*, 2:402, 611; Gal, *Brandeis of Boston*, pp. 132, 162–68. At the 14th Annual Convention of the Federation of American Zionists, held in Cleveland at the end of June 1912, it was announced that LDB had joined their ranks as a member. However, his 1911 and 1912 letters to Richards both refer merely to a $25 "contribution" rather than to the payment of membership dues, and it may be that the federation's leaders chose to interpret this as "joining" for their own publicity purposes. If so, LDB accepted the resultant minor coup as a *fait accompli*. The only evidence cited by Mason concerning the announcement is the *Jewish Advocate* for 7 March 1913: see *Brandeis*, pp. 443, 672. There is no evidence whatsoever to support Mason's further contention (ibid., p. 444) that "In 1912 and 1913 Brandeis appeared frequently on the speakers'

platform, practically making cross-country tours on behalf of Zionism." When he did address Jewish audiences during these years it was to promote the social and political causes in which he was interested: see, for example, Gal, *Brandeis of Boston*, p. 183.

17. LDB to Eugene N. Foss, 13 August 1912, *BL*, 2:659 and editors' note; LDB to Alfred Brandeis, 14 August 1912, ibid., p. 660; Gal, *Brandeis of Boston*, pp. 183–86. According to De Haas's own account (*Brandeis*, pp. 51–52; De Haas to LDB, 1 November 1926, LBLU, Z/P 33–1) his reference to Lewis Dembitz as "a noble Jew," and his subsequent story telling about Herzl and Zionism, occurred in December 1910 after the interview with LDB on savings-bank insurance, and was repeated at South Yarmouth in 1912 for the benefit of the Brandeis children. Among LDB's biographers, Paper and Baker are alone in accepting the likely accuracy of this explanation: see Paper, *Brandeis*, pp. 202, 420 n. 7; Baker, *Brandeis and Frankfurter*, p. 73. Were it correct, of course, it would reduce still further the importance of his meeting with De Haas as the key event leading to LDB's whole-hearted adoption of the Zionist cause, since during 1911 and 1912 his understanding of the issues involved remained minimal.

18. Strum, *Brandeis*, p. 229; "Memorandum of Interview in Mr. Balfour's apartment . . . [in Paris,] June 24, 1919," printed in Rabinowitz, *Justice Brandeis*, p. 113; Gal, *Brandeis of Boston*, pp. 186–87. Concerning the growth of anti-Semitism in the United States during the 1890s, see John Higham, *Send These to Me: Jews and Other Immigrants in Urban America* (New York: Atheneum, 1975), especially pp. 130–31.

19. LDB to Louis Lipsky, 18 and 23 July 1913, *BL*, 3:141, 147–48.

20. LDB to Sokolow, 1 August 1913, ibid., pp. 158–59.

21. A brief discussion of the Congress and the quotation from Ruppin's address can be found in Walter Laqueur, *A History of Zionism* (London: Weidenfeld & Nicolson, 1972), pp. 150–52.

22. Gal, *Brandeis of Boston*, pp. 178–81; LDB to Hapgood, *BL*, 3:117. LDB also wrote the obituary which, appeared in *The Maccabaean*, June 1919, under the title: "Aaron Aaronsohn, Product of Jewish Idealism." The likelihood of LDB having had the agronomist's stories in mind when he wrote to Sokolow about the development of the Jewish settlements in Palestine is surely enhanced by the fact that on the very same day he provided journalist Mary Boyle O'Reilly with a letter of introduction to Aaronsohn, whom he described as "an important source of information concerning conditions there": see LDB to Aaronsohn, 1 August 1913, *BL*, 3:157.

23. Quoted in Gal, *Brandeis of Boston*, p. 180; Strum, *Brandeis*, p. 273.

24. "The Jewish People Should Be Preserved," 30 August 1914, printed in *Brandeis on Zionism*, p. 44.

25. "The Fruits of Zionism," various addresses delivered during the fall and winter of 1914–15, ibid., pp. 49–50.

26. "The Jewish Problem, How to Solve It," June 1915, ibid., pp. 29–30.

27. "A Call to the Educated Jew," January 1915, ibid., pp. 63–64; cf. also "The Pilgrims Had Faith," 27–28 May 1923, ibid., p. 132. For LDB's deep admiration for characteristics displayed by native New Englanders and their Puritan ancestors, see especially Gal, *Brandeis of Boston*, pp. 80–83.

28. For a fuller discussion of Straus's historical researches and the views he derived from them, see Girgus, *New Covenant*, pp. 43–47, the quotations are on pp. 44 and 45–46, respectively. As Girgus points out (p. 4), Straus's thesis, that the institutions and values of America's political culture are themselves ultimately derived from Hebrew scriptures and Talmudic teachings, is supported by the more recent work of at least one scholarly interpreter of American Jewish culture: see Milton R. Konvitz, *Judaism and the American Idea* (Ithaca: Cornell University Press, 1978).

29. "The Victory of the Maccabees," December 1915, printed in *Brandeis on Zionism*, pp. 82–83.

30. Girgus, *New Covenant*, p. 47. Despite their differences of emphasis, Straus and LDB are both seen as part of Girgus's "New Covenant" tradition, whose members seek a solution to the problem of Jewish identity by embracing "the American idea." By this term Girgus would have us understand (p. 3): "the set of values, beliefs, and traditions of freedom, democracy, equality, and republicanism that are known as the American Way and that give America a unique identity in history."

31. Elias Bickerman, *The God of the Maccabees: Studies in the Meaning and Origin of the Maccabean Revolt*, English translation from the original German (Leiden: Brill, 1979), pp. 28–31, 90–91. For a wider-ranging discussion of the period of Hellenic rule, see John Bright, *A History of Israel*, 3d ed. (Philadelphia: Westminster Press, 1981), pp. 412–27.

32. Strum, *Brandeis*, pp. 237–42. Theodore Roosevelt was also given to praising *The Greek Commonwealth* as a great book, but when Zimmern accepted an invitation to discuss it over lunch, the former president subjected him to a resumé of what an *Encyclopedia Britannica* article had to say on the subject, complete with mistakes: see Eric Goldman, *Rendezvous With Destiny: A History of Modern American Reform* (New York: 1952), p. 189.

33. Bickerman, *God of the Maccabees*, pp. 90–91.

34. The "my people" reference occurs in LDB's 9 December 1910 interview with the *Jewish Advocate*, reprinted as "Sympathy for the Zionist Movement" in *Brandeis on Zionism*, p. 36. LDB's early appreciation of the importance of organization is discussed in Urofsky, *American Zionism*, pp. 144–45. LDB to *The Wahrheit*, 2 November 1915, *BL*, 3:626; even if this letter was drafted for LDB's signature by Louis Lipsky, as the editors suggest, it does nevertheless reflect accurately views that he was expressing elsewhere at the time.

35. LDB to Gustave Hartman, 16 June 1915, *BL*, 3:534–35. Although he declined to attend the founding conference of the American Jewish Emancipation Committee, two weeks later LDB did agree to become chairman of the Foreign Relations Committee of its international equivalent.

36. "The Common Cause," 24 January 1916, printed in *Brandeis on Zionism*, pp. 98–100.

37. Rabinowitz, *Justice Brandeis*, pp. 74–77. For LDB's involvement with the promotion, wording, and U.S. endorsement of the Balfour Declaration, see Strum, *Brandeis*, 272–73; Rabinowitz, (*Justice Brandeis*, pp. 54–73) reproduces many of the relevant documents. Weizmann's career as a Zionist leader is treated fully in Laqueur, *History of Zionism*, passim; for a brief but pertinent summary, see the editorial note in *BL*, 3:327–28.

38. LDB to Weizmann, 13 January 1918, *BL*, 4:335. The ascription of LDB's "Jeffersonian" vision of Palestine to Aaronsohn is rendered less speculative by an explicit reference elsewhere in this letter to recent talks between them; cf. discussion in Strum, *Brandeis*, 273–75.

39. The proceedings of the Pittsburgh Convention and their significance are ably digested in Urofsky, *American Zionism*, pp. 252–57; the quotation is from p. 256. For the Cleveland Convention of 1921 and the schism in American Jewry that resulted from it, see ; ibid., pp. 283–97. For a fuller discussion of the personalities and issues involved, see Ben Halpern, *A Clash of Heroes: Brandeis, Weizmann, and American Zionism* (New York: Oxford University Press, 1987), passim.

40. The fullest account of LDB's meetings with European Zionist leaders in 1919, and of his visit to Palestine, is in Strum, *Brandeis*, pp. 242–46; the quotations are on pp. 244 and 246, respectively.

41. "Memorandum of Interview with Balfour," 4 June 1919, printed in Rabinowitz, *Justice Brandeis*, pp. 113–14.

42. For the deterioration of relations between the Brandeis and Weizmann groups

during 1919–20, see Urofsky, *American Zionism*, pp. 267–79. "Memorandum of My Views As to Future Activities. 24 August 1920. On the Zeeland. [Concluded 23 September 1920]" is in FFLC, Box 162. For a printed version of the text, see De Haas, *Brandeis*, pp. 260–72.

43. "A Call to the Educated Jew," January 1915, ibid., pp. 63–65.

44. LDB's remarks about his mother's "sense of duty to the community" are quoted in Mason, *Brandeis*, p. 27.

45. "Flesh and Spirit," in Ahad Ha-Am, *Selected Essays*, translated from the Hebrew by Leon Simon (Philadelphia: Jewish Publication Society of America, 1912), quoted by LDB in "A Call to the Educated Jew," loc. cit., pp. 65–66. This was almost certainly the only volume of Ahad Ha-Am's essays that LDB had read before January 1915, but he evidently planned to continue his study of Ahad Ha-Am's writings while on vacation the following summer: see LDB to Israel Friedlaender, 25 June 1915, *BL*, 3:541.

46. See Leon Simon, *Ahad Ha-Am, Asher Ginzberg: A Biography* (Philadelphia: Jewish Publication Society of America, 1960); the quotations are from Louis Jacobs and Leon Simon in their respective introductions to L. Simon, ed., *Ten Essays on zionism and Judaism by Achad Ha-Am* (1922; reprint, New York: Arno Press, 1973), unpaginated and p. xxii. Zimmern too was aware of Ahad Ha-Am, at one point observing that on the question of assimilation he "preaches substantially the same doctrine as Herodotus." This is quoted by Strum (*Brandeis*, p. 241) who suggests that it may have been this reference that led LDB to read the Jewish philosopher's essays. However, she does not ascribe any particular significance to Ahad Ha-Am as an influence on LDB's thinking after 1914.

47. Ahad Ha-Am himself believed that true asceticism was essentially alien to the Jewish spirit; that it occurred only when individuals and societies came "to regard every material good thing of life as something evil and degraded, to be avoided by him who cares for his soul's health." He was careful to distinguish those consumed by such "hatred and contempt for the flesh" from those who practiced self-denial to avoid danger to their health or as a deliberate act of sacrifice. Far from showing disdain for the pleasures of the flesh, such actions betoken the high regard in which the body is held. See "Flesh and Spirit," *Selected Essays*, especially pp. 139–42, and Simon's introduction, ibid., p. 26. LDB's own inclination toward a frugal life-style certainly predates his reading of these essays, but it does appear to have become decidedly more pronounced in the last decades of his life.

48. See, for example, Laqueur, *History of Zionism*, pp. 458–61; Urofsky, *American Zionism*, pp. 246–98. Simon, ed., *Ten Essays on Zionism*, p. vii, indicates the limited range of this selection; but cf. the contents of the volume of Ahad Ha-Am's essays, translated into German from the original Hebrew by Israel Friedlaender and published under the title *Am Scheidewege* (Berlin: Jüdisher Verlag, 1913), which was sent to LDB by its author (see sup. 45) in 1915.

49. See Simon's introduction to Ahad Ha-Am, *Selected Essays*, pp. 13–14; "The Spiritual Revival," ibid, pp. 253–58.

50. Ibid., p. 262. Although these tendencies were already evident in LDB's writings before 1914, they became much more articulate thereafter.

51. For Ahad Ha-Am's cultural geneticism, see ibid., pp. 264–73 passim; the quotations are from p. 265 . But contrast the arguments in "The Wrong Way," *Ten Essays on Zionism*, pp. 20–21. LDB frequently referred to Jewish character traits and ideals in ways that implied their genetic transmission from a distant posterity.

52. "A New Savior," *Selected Essays*, p. 252.

53. "The Spiritual Revival," ibid., pp. 267–68, 288–90, 300.

54. See "Justice and Mercy," ibid., pp. 46–52; the quotations are from p. 48 and p. 52, respectively.

55. LDB to Frankfurter, 22 July 1927, *BL*, 5:297; "Flesh and Spirit," *Selected Essays*, pp. 143–48.

56. "Past and Present," *Selected Essays*, especially pp. 84–87; Simon's introduction, ibid., pp. 14–17.

57. "Priest and Prophet," ibid., pp. 130–31. For a more recent discussion of the differentiation between priests and prophets in the Jewish tradition, and moreover for one that specifically relates the distinctions being drawn to Frankfurter and LDB, see Burt, *Two Jewish Justices*, pp. 124–27.

58. Ibid., pp. 131–38; cf. "Moses," ibid, especially pp. 311–15.

59. For a modern interpretation of the prophetic role in early Jewish history, see Joseph Blenkinsopp, *A History of Prophecy in Israel: From the Settlement on the Land to the Hellenistic Period* (Philadelphia: Westminster Press, 1983).

60. Gal, *Brandeis of Boston*, pp. 134–35.

61. On the "Puritan jeremiad," and the Jewish-American writer as a "New Jeremiah," see Girgus, *New Covenant*, passim, but especially pp. 10–14; the quotation is on p. 12.

62. On the subject of LDB's "cultural pluralism," see ibid., pp. 57–58; Gal, *Brandeis of Boston*, pp. 147–57.

Chapter 6. Freedom and Justice for All

1. LDB to Alfred Brandeis, 22 October 1915, *BL*, 3:617–18. William Hitz to Felix Frankfurter, 17 December 1914, quoted in Mason, *Brandeis*, pp. 252–53. The case was *Stettler v. O'Hara*, 243 U.S. 629 (1914). Not all of LDB's auditors were equally impressed, however, an elderly member of the Clerk's Office staff remarking that "that fellow Brandeez has got the impudence of the Devil to bring his socialism into the Supreme Court": quoted in Mason, op. cit., p. 253.

2. Root to Frankfurter, 3 May 1916, FFLC, Box 128.

3. See for example: Benjamin N. Cardozo, *The Nature of the Judicial Process* (New Haven: Yale University Press, 1921). *The Growth of the Law* (New Haven: Yale University Press, 1924) and *The Paradoxes of Legal Science* (New York: Columbia University Press, 1928). For a discussion of LDB's legal articles, see sup. pp. 79–88. There is neither an index to nor a good compendium of his legal briefs. Given the volume of his polemical output before 1916, and the carefully crafted prose of his judicial opinions thereafter, it comes as something of a surprise to discover that LDB did not find the writing process easy. "The mere task of composition may continue difficult for you—as it has always been for me," he told his daughter, Susan in 1913. "The important thing is to have something to say and to learn how to say it." LDB to Susan Brandeis, 24 April 1913, SGBU, Box 11, no. 1041.

4. This and the following three paragraphs are drawn mainly from the summary of "The Living Law" provided in Mason, *Brandeis*, pp. 245–48. The full text can be found in *Illinois Law Review*, 10 (1916): 461–71. The 1905 address, "The Opportunity in the Law," was delivered to the Harvard Ethical Society and subsequently printed in *Business—a Profession*, pp. 313–27.

5. "Digest of Opinions," LBHLS, Paige Box 1. LDB clearly found Shulman's initial compilation useful, for until 1933 he and his clerks continued to insert additional entries. A complete listing of his opinions can be found in Linda A. Blandford and Patricia R. Evans, eds., *The Supreme Court of the United Statesm 1789–1980: An Index to Opinions Arranged by Justice*, 2 vols. (Millwood, N.Y.: Kraus International Publications, 1983).

6. Among the many estimates and analyses of LDB's judicial career, the fol-

lowing have proved especially useful: Felix Frankfurter, ed., *Mr. Justice Brandeis* (New Haven: Yale University Press, 1932); Paul A. Freund, "Mr. Justice Brandeis" in Allison Dunham and Philip B. Kurland, eds., *Mr. Justice* (Chicago: University of Chicago Press, 1956); Konefsky, *Legacy of Holmes and Brandeis*; Bickel, *Unpublished Opinions of Mr. Justice Brandeis*; David W. Levy, "The Lawyer as Judge: Brandeis's View of the Legal Profession," *Oklahoma Law Review* 22 (1969): 374–95; Janice Mark Jacobson, "Mr. Justice Brandeis on Regulation and Competition: An Analysis of His Economic Opinions" (Ph.D. diss., Columbia University, 1973); G. Edward White, *The American Judicial Tradition: Profiles of Leading American Judges* (New York: Oxford University Press, 1976), chap. 8; John W. Johnson, *American Legal Culture, 1908–40* (Westport, Conn.: Greenwood Press, 1981) especially chap. 3.

7. LDB to Otto A. Wehle, 12 March 1876, *BL*, 1:5–8.

8. Frankfurter, "The Supreme Court and the Public," reprinted in Kurland, *Frankfurter on the Supreme Court*, p. 220; "The Supreme Court," ibid., pp. 458–59.

9. The material contained in this and the following five paragraphs is based primarily on the address of Chief Justice Stone as printed in *Proceedings of the Bar of the Supreme Court of the United States and Meeting of the Court in Memory of Associate Justice Louis D. Brandeis. December 21, 1942* (Washington, D.C.: Government Printing Office, 1942), pp. 48–56; emphasis added.

10. Author's interview with David Riesman, Jr., Cambridge, Mass., 21 April 1983. Riesman's feelings of personal inadequacy were by no means unique among LDB's clerks. "When I am particularly troubled by my uselessness," wrote Nathan Nathanson, "I find Paul Freund a great comfort. He never fails to assure me that no matter what mistake I have made, someone else has made it before; and that he himself experienced similar difficulties." See Nathanson to Frankfurter, 4 March 1935, FFLC, Box 127. For a full discussion of the *Ashwander* case, see inf., pp. 266–73.

11. Riesman to the author, 13 April and 11 August 1981. The case in question was *Pacific States Box and Basket Company v. White*, 296 U.S. 176 (1935), and the materials that Riesman collected are preserved among LDB's Court papers at Harvard Law School, LBHLS, 99/3–10. The validity of his charges will be discussed more fully inf., pp. 262–66, 273–74, 331.

12. For a rather more objective appraisal of the confirmation hearings, see A. L. Todd, *Justice on Trial: The Case of Louis D. Brandeis* (New York: McGraw-Hill, 1968); for a more sanguine assessment of LDB's relations with the United Shoe Machinery Company, see Mason, *Brandeis*, chap. 14 passim. Additional light is cast on both subjects by John P. Frank, "The Legal Ethics of Louis D. Brandeis," *Stanford Law Review* 17 (1965): 683–709.

13. This and the next two paragraphs rely heavily on Riesman to Frankfurter, 22 May 1936, FFLC, Box 28, headed "Notes for an Essay on Justice Brandeis." In a letter to the author dated 11 August 1981, Riesman describes his letter to Frankfurter as containing "some disingenuousness," which he explains partly in terms of feeling guilty about offending Frankfurter and letting down Brandeis, and partly by associating his attitude toward the justice with the "over-admiration" he then felt for his own father. It is, however, plausible to assume that his reservations about Brandeis, voiced in 1936 as the opinions of his friends, have grown sharper and more "admissible" with greater maturity and self-assurance. However, yet another interpretation of his ex post facto criticism of LDB can be seen in a letter which Frankfurter addressed to Riesman more than twenty years after his clerkship, having just read a piece written by him in the *New Republic*: "I did not infer that you begrudged the 'indoctrination' that LDB gave you, but I wonder how much of it took, or perhaps I should say to what extent there has been a sociological counter-indoctrination making for an unfair imbalance, unfair at least to one with my outlook. Do you really think that Bran-

deis's series of rules for judicial restraint in his *Ashwander* opinion (297 U.S. 288, 346 et seq.) constitutes a code of 'peripheral' jurisprudence[?]" See Frankfurter to Riesman, 12 August 1957, FFLC Box 96.

14. It must, of course, be conceded that, where conflicting perspectives issue not from different observers but from the same observer at different times, the problem of reconciling them becomes one of a rather different order.

15. Variations and extensions of these principles are widespread in LDB's opinions, but Shulman's "Digest of Opinions" (LBHLS, Paige Box 1) facilitates identification of the most significant down to 1933. For the desirability of deciding cases on nonconstitutional grounds, see *Carey v. South Dakota*, 250 U.S. 118, 122 (1919); *Chastleton Corp. v. Sinclair*, 264 U.S. 543, 549 (1924); *Missouri Pacific R. Co. v. Boone*, 270 U.S. 466, 472 (1926); *Burns v. United States*, 274 U.S. 328, 337 (1927); *Hammond v. Schappi Bus Line*, 275 U.S. 164, 169 (1927); *Wuchter v. Pizzutti*, 276 U.S. 13, 26 (1928); *Herkness v. Irion*, 278 U.S. 92, 94 (1928); *Salomon v. State Tax Commission*, 278 U.S. 484, 492 (1929). Concerning the presumption of constitutionality, see *Hamilton v. Kentucky Distilleries & Warehouse Co.*, 251 U.S. 146, 161 (1919); *Eisner v. Macomber*, 252 U.S. 189, 238 (1920); *Untermyer v. Anderson*, 276 U.S. 440, 454 (1928); *O'Gorman & Young v. Hartford Fire Insurance Co.*, 282 U.S. 251 (1931); *Arizona v. California*, 283 U.S. 423 (1931). And about the importance of facts in determining the validity of statutes, see *Adams v. Tanner* 244 U.S. 590, 600 (1917); *Truax v. Corrigan*, 257 U.S. 312, 356 (1921); *Jay Burns Baking Co. v. Bryan*, 264 U.S. 504, 520, 533 (1924); *Dorchy v. Kansas*, 272 U.S. 306, 309 (1926); *Packer Corporation v. Utah*, 285 U.S. 105, 111 (1932).

16. *Washington v. Dawson & Co.*, 264 U.S. 219, 238 (1924); *Jaybird Mining Co. v. Weir*, 271 U.S. 609, 619 (1926); *Di Santo v. Pennsylvania*, 273 U.S. 34, 42 (1927). My exposition of LDB's argument in all of the cases referred to in this paragraph, and in the *Burnet* case in the next, draws heavily on the synopsis in Shulman's "Digest of Opinions," LBHLS, Paige Box 1, fols. 240v–41, where collectively they make up the section headed "Stare Decisis." For LDB's earlier discrimination between rules of property and rules of action, see sup. pp. 95–98.

17. *New State Ice Co. v. Liebmann*, 285 U.S. 262, 280 (1932); *Burnet v. Coronado Oil & Gas Co.*, 285 U.S. 393, 407, 412 (1932). Among several instances in the late 1920s and early 1930s of the Court overruling or disregarding previous decisions, particularly in tax cases, see *Quaker City Cab Co. v. Pennsylvania*, 277 U.S. 389, 403 (1928); *Macallen Co. v. Massachusetts*, 279 U.S. 620, 628 (1929); *Farmers Loan & Trust Co. v. Minnesota*, 280 U.S. 204, 212 (1930).

18. The full text of LDB's dissent, together with a full discussion of the circumstances in which it was written, can be found in Bickel, *Unpublished Opinions*, pp. 119–63. A unanimous Court eventually dismissed the case for want of jurisdiction: see *Stratton v. St. Louis Southwestern Railway Co.*, 282 U.S. 10 (1930). For the Taney opinion cited by LBD, see 7 How. 283 (1849).

19. Bickel, *Unpublished Opinions*, passim, but see especially pp. 21–33, 111–14, 210–13. The Frankfurter quote is on p. 29.

20. Melvin I. Urofsky, ed., "The Brandeis-Frankfurter Conversations," *Supreme Court Review* (1985): 309, 314–15, 317, 322, 327–30. Because of serious inaccuracies in the typescript transcription of Frankfurter's original manuscript notes (see "Conversations between LDB and F[elix] F[rankfurter]," [1921–26,] LBHLS, 114/14) Urofsky's version has generally been used for quotations. The reference to *Britt v. Zinc Co.* is obviously to *United Zinc & Chemical Co. v. Britt*, 258 U.S. 268 (1922). *Railway Commission v. Southern Pacific Railway*, 264 U.S. 331 (1924), is fully discussed, and LDB's suppressed opinion is printed in Bickel, *Unpublished Opinions*, pp. 205–10. See ibid., pp. 18, 199, for LDB's own reluctance to dissent repeatedly on issues about which he had already made clear his views in earlier opinions.

21. Jacobson, "Mr. Justice Brandeis on Regulation and Competition," affords a comprehensive study of LDB's judicial writings on socioeconomic matters.

22. *Myers v. United States*, 272 U.S. 52, 291 (1926); *Whitney v. California*, 274 U.S. 357, 374 (1927); *U.S. ex rel. Milwaukee Social Democratic Publishing Co. v. Burleson*, 255 U.S. 407, 431 (1920).

23. See *Burnap v. United States*, 252 U.S. 512, 515 (1920); *Burdeau v. McDowell*, 256 U.S. 465, 476 (1921). Cf. also the discussion of LDB's dissent in *Myers v. U.S.*, 272 U.S. 52, 240 (1926) in Paper, *Brandeis*, pp. 302–5.

24. In light of LDB's assertion about the responsibility of judges to keep abreast of technological innovation, it is worth noting that, in an early draft of his *Olmstead* opinion, the justice had mentioned television as one of the methods by which government might soon be able to intrude on an individual's privacy. His clerk, Henry J. Friendly, complained that the reference was not really appropriate. "Television doesn't work in a way so that you can take it and beam it across a street into an apartment or building and see what somebody is doing." Unabashed, Brandeis replied: "That's exactly how it works." Reference to television was deleted, though, from the version finally delivered in court. Quoted in Paper, *Brandeis*, p. 312.

25. *Olmstead v. United States*, 277 U.S. 438, 478–79, 485 (1928). Recalling the issues of the case in 1931, LDB commented: "One can never be sure of ends—political, social, economic. There must always be doubt and difference of opinion; one can be 51 per cent sure." Yet as to means there was not the same margin of doubt; fundamentals remained the same, and moral standards represented the accumulated wisdom of centuries. "Lying and sneaking are always bad," he declared, "no matter what the ends." Quoted in Mason, *Brandeis*, p. 569.

26. Undated "memorandum," [6 February 1928?] LBHLS, 48/3. Cf. the wording of the final version at 277 U.S. 438, 483–84. Successive stages in the drafting of this seminal opinion have been identified by Bickel, whose suggested dating of memoranda and explanatory notes about new phases of the argument added before each printing reveal clearly the sequential dynamics of it composition. For the influence of LDB's dissent on the Court's decision in *Katz v. United States*, 389 U.S. 347 (1967), see Paper, *Brandeis*, p. 314, who also provides (pp. 310–14) an excellent account of how LDB's thinking on the case developed. LDB to Frankfurter, 15 June 1928, *BL*, 5:345–46.

27. *Schenck v. United States*, 249 U.S. 47, 52 (1919); emphasis added.

28. *Schaefer v. United States*, 251 U.S. 466 (1920); *Pierce v. United States*, 252 U.S. 239 (1920). Quoted and discussed in Mason, *Brandeis*, pp. 561–63, Paper, *Brandeis*, pp. 282–83.

29. Urofsky, "Brandeis-Frankfurter Conversations," pp. 323–24. In the course of this discussion, LDB expressed himself as being strongly in favor of unlicensed forums like Speakers' Corner in London's Hyde Park, and told Frankfurter they should be "insisted upon" in places like Boston Common, if not in every municipal park in the country. For the upholding of Debs's conviction, see *Debs v. United States*, 249 U.S. 211 (1919).

30. This and the next four paragraphs are largely based on the opinions in *Gilbert v. Minnesota*, 254 U.S. 325 (1920); Paper, *Brandeis*, pp. 283–85. The other cases referred to are *Barron v. Baltimore*, 7 Pet. 243 (1833); *Slaughter House Cases*, 16 Wall. 36 (1873); *Twining v. New Jersey*, 211 U.S. 78 (1908) . For a masterly exposition of the process by which civil liberties eventually came to be protected from state action, though one that makes no specific reference to the *Gilbert* case, see Richard C. Cortner, *The Supreme Court and the Second Bill of Rights: The Fourteenth Amendment and the Nationalization of Civil Liberties* (Madison: University of Wisconsin Press, 1981), passim, but especially pp. 3–98.

31. *Gitlow v. New York*, 268 U.S. 652 (1925).

32. Landis to LDB, 16 August 1926, LBHLS, 44/7.

33. All quotations from the *Ruthenberg* opinion are taken from the latest draft, printed 4 November 1926, ibid., 44/10.

34. *Ruthenberg v . Michigan*, 273 U.S. 782 (1927); *Whitney v. California*, 274 U.S. 357, 372 (1927). For an early appreciation of the differences between the *Ruthenberg* and *Whitney* cases, see Landis to LDB, 21 August 1926, LBHLS, 44/7.

35. Urofsky, "Brandeis-Frankfurter Conversations," pp. 318–20, 325, 330. The night work case referred to was *Radice v. New York*, 264 U.S. 292 (1924). For a more detailed discussion of the profound constitutional disagreements exemplified in *Truax v. Corrigan*, 257 U.S. 312 (1921), see inf., pp. 302–5. On the Court's civil liberties record during the 1930s, see Michael E. Parrish, "The Hughes Court, the Great Depression and the Historians," *The Historian* 40 (1978): 306–7.

36. Urofsky, "Brandeis-Frankfurter Conversations," pp. 325–26. The Prohibition cases referred to are: *Ruppert v. Caffey*, 251 U.S. 264, 301 (1920); *Albrecht v. United States*, 273 U.S. 1, 11 (1927); *Barbour v. Georgia*, 249 U.S. 454, 459 (1919); *Lambert v. Yellowley*, 272 U.S. 581, 596 (1926).

37. LDB to Frankfurter, 7 October 1928, *BL*, 5:359; Mason, *Brandeis*, pp. 566–67.

38. LDB's memorandum for Wilson is quoted without reference in Mason, *Brandeis*, p. 567. Urofsky, "Brandeis-Frankfurter Conversations," pp. 307–8. LDB to Lief, 15 April 1934, quoted in Lief, ed., *The Brandeis Guide to the Modern World* (Boston: 1941), p. 70. Scholarly opinion differs considerably regarding the capacity of state and local governments in the 1920s and 1930s to assume the regulatory and welfare functions envisaged for them by liberal idealists such as LDB. James T. Patterson, *The New Deal and the States. Federalism in Transition* (Princeton: Princeton University Press, 1969), is scathing in his critique of their levels of competence, efficiency, and honesty; William R. Brock, *Welfare, Democracy and the New Deal* (New York: Cambridge University Press, 1988), though equally alive to their inadequacies, is rather more conscious of the potential for improvement.

39. LDB to Hapgood, 1 June 1922, quoted in Mason, *Brandeis*, p. 558. The child labor tax case was *Bailey v. Drexel Furniture Co.*, 259 U.S. 20 (1922) . For the possibility that there may originally have been a fragile majority on the Court in favor of upholding the Child Labor Tax Act in *Atherton Mills v. Johnson*, 259 U.S. 13 (1922), see Bickel, *Unpublished Opinions*, pp. 14–20; for LDB's suppressed opinion in the case, see ibid., pp. 5–14. His notion of a "dual sovereignty" shared between the state and federal levels of government has many features in common with the "concurrent sovereignty" theories developed in the antebellum period by Chief Justice Taney: for which see White, *American Judicial Tradition*, pp. 71–74, 95–98; Carl B. Swisher, "Mr. Chief Justice Taney" in Dunham and Kurland, *Mr. Justice*, pp. 205–7, 214–22, 228–29. There is much to ponder in Swisher's assertion (p. 203) that LDB "would have been proud in some, though not in all, respects to have been regarded as Taney's legal heir." On the subject of "dual federalism" generally and its demise in the era of the New Deal, see Loss, *Corwin on the Constitution*, 3:219–58.

40. Urofsky, "Brandeis-Frankfurter Conversations," p. 313. The issue of jurisdiction is well illustrated by the *Starbird* case, 243 U.S. 592 (1917), which is considered fully in Bickel, *Unpublished Opinions*, pp. 21–33; but cf. also the discussion of *Ashwander*, inf., pp. 266–73.

41. *Jay Burns Baking Co. v. Bryan*, 264 U.S. 504, 520, 533–34 (1924).

42. *Hutchison Ice Cream Co. v. Iowa*, 242 U.S. 153, 158 (1916); Urofsky, "Brandeis-Frankfurter Conversations," p. 313. Another factor doubtless exerting an important influence on the Court's "consistency" was the extensive changes of personnel that occurred between 1916 and 1924: Chief Justice White had been replaced by Taft, and Justices Day, Pitney, and Clarke had given way to Butler, Sanford, and Sutherland, respectively.

43. Nathanson to Frankfurter, 4 March 1935, FFLC, Box 127; Nathanson, "Mr.

Justice Brandeis: A Law Clerk's Recollections of the October Term, 1934," *American Jewish Archives*, 15 (1963): 14; *Nashville, Chattanooga & St. Louis Railway v. Walters*, 294 U.S. 405, 415 (1935). Cf. Paper, *Brandeis*, pp. 337–38. A "grade crossing" or "crossing at grade" is where railroad tracks and a road cross one another at ground level.

44. Frankfurter to Louis L. Jaffe, 2 October FFLC, Box 70. The case at issue here is *Southern Railway Co. v. Virginia ex rel. Shirley*, 290 U.S. 190 (1933).

45. Frankfurter to Jaffe, 2 October 1943; Jaffe to Frankfurter, 29 October 1943; Frankfurter to Jaffe, 1 November 1943: all in FFLC, Box 70. In *Morgan v. U.S.*, 298 U.S. 468 (1936), 304 U.S. 1 (1938) LDB twice joined in the Court's condemnation of the secretary of agriculture for failing to grant livestock brokers a full hearing of their case before fixing their commission fees. For a fuller account of Jaffe's views more or less contemporary with the *Southern Railway Company* case, see his "The Contributions of Mr. Justice Brandeis to Administrative Law," *Iowa Law Review* 18 (1932–33): 213–27.

46. Hurst to Frankfurter, 24 May 1938, FFLC, Box 127. For an illuminating discussion of LDB's behavior in *Erie Railroad Co. v. Tompkins*, 304 U.S. 64 (1938), see Paper, *Brandeis*, pp. 381–85; Johnson, *American Legal Culture*, pp. 63–64; cf. also Freund, "Mr. Justice Brandeis," pp. 111–12. More often referred to as *Erie* than as *Tompkins*, this decision overturned the ruling in *Swift v. Tyson*, 41 U.S. (16 Pet.) 1 (1842). For a comprehensive discussion of the issues raised by both cases, see Tony A. Freyer, *Harmony and Dissonance: The Swift and Erie Cases in American Federalism* (New York: New York University Press, 1981).

47. Hurst to Frankfurter, 24 May 1938, FFLC, Box 127. The arguments that disturbed Hurst in *Thompson v. Consolidated Gas Corp.*, 300 U.S. 55 (1937), will be found at pp. 74–81.

48. *Ashwander v. Tennessee Valley Authority*, 297 U.S. 288 (1936).

49. Hughes's opinion is at 297 U.S. 288, 315–40.

50. For a good summary of this and subsequent TVA litigation, see Thomas K. McCraw, *T.V.A. and the Power Fight, 1933–1939* (Philadelphia: J. B. Lippincott, 1971), chap. 6 passim. Despite the clouds still hanging over the agency's future, Director David E. Lilienthal was surprised and delighted by the outcome in *Ashwander*: "I had completely resigned myself to a bad decision," he wrote afterward, "only holding out hope that we would have some crumb of comfort in that unlike A.A.A. and N.R.A. we would not be swept completely out to sea, bag and baggage." Quoted ibid., pp. 114–15.

51. For an illuminating discussion of the intellectual rationale underlying the "Brandeis opinion," see Johnson, *American Legal Culture*, pp. 39–46; the quotations are from pp. 41 and 45, respectively. Cf. also Chester A. Newland, "Innovation in Judicial Technique: The Brandeis Opinion," *Southwestern Social Science Quarterly* 42 (1961): 22–31. The note on Clarke's "return" is in LBHLS, 1/1.

52. Unless otherwise indicated, the next four paragraphs are based on LDB's opinion printed at 297 U.S. 341–56.

53. The Cooley citation is to *Constitutional Limitations*, 8th ed., p. 332.

54. In support of the claim that he and his brethren had lately displayed a "keener appreciation of the wisdom of limiting our decisions rigidly to questions essential to the disposition of the case before the court," LDB cited the recent ruling in *U.S. v. Hastings*, 296 U.S. 188, decided earlier in that term; and in a terse footnote referred to the relevant literature on modified and overruled decisions.

55. Return of opinion dated 3 February 1936 from Cardozo, LBHLS, 96/7; Bickel, *Unpublished Opinions*, pp. 2–3. Frankfurter's article, "The Business of the Supreme Court at October Terms, 1935 and 1936," written jointly with Adrian S. Fisher, LDB's law clerk in 1938–39, was originally published in the *Harvard Law*

Review (1938) and is partially reprinted in Kurland, *Frankfurter on the Supreme Court*, pp. 338–57; the quotations here are from pp. 347 and 351, respectively.

56. Kurland, *Frankfurter on the Supreme Court*, pp. 342–50; the lengthy quotation concerning equity is on pp. 342–43. In light of Riesman's remark (letter to the author dated 13 April 1981) about LDB wanting to "pull down . . . the federal judges from their height," it is illuminating to compare his concerns here regarding equity with those he expressed elsewhere about "diversity of citizenship" cases. Concerning the latter, see LDB to Frankfurter, 2 April 1925, *BL*, 5:170.

57. Author's interview with Riesman, 21 April 1983.

58. Cf. Parrish, "The Hughes Court," pp. 305–6, where the idea of LDB supporting "a double standard of judicial review" is developed along similar, though not identical, lines. For a brief exposition of the opposing argument, that "Brandeis's masterful employment of procedural and jurisdictional rules was by no means simply a device for avoiding decisions by majority brethren who would have been opposed to his position on the merits," see Freund, "Mr. Justice Brandeis," p. 109. According to Hurst, quoted in Nelson L. Dawson, *Louis D. Brandeis, Felix Frankfurter and the New Deal* (Hamden, Conn.: Archon Books, 1980), pp. 81–82, LDB regarded the TVA as "a great achievement in human inventiveness and decentralization" and was "particularly interested in the 'grass roots' phase of the enterprise."

59. McReynolds's opinion, quoted in this and the following paragraph, is at 297 U.S. 356–72; emphasis added.

60. Henry Friendly to Frankfurter, 25 September 1961, FFLC, Box 56.

61. For Frankfurter's "judicial biography" project, and Stone's remark about law being "the means to a social end," see sup., pp. 25–27, 234.

Chapter 7. The Vision of Isaiah

1. Just how far LDB was the object of anti-Semitism during his years in Boston has been hotly debated by his biographers without any consensus emerging: see especially Urofsky, *Mind of One Piece*, pp. 9–12, 101–3; Gal, *Brandeis of Boston*, passim; Strum, *Brandeis*, pp. 225–34; Burt, *Two Jewish Justices*, pp. 35–36, 127, 138–39. The estimates of LDB's wealth can be found in Baker, *Brandeis and Frankfurter*, p. 27; Mason, *Brandeis*, p. 691.

2. Quoted in Freund, "Mr. Justice Brandeis" in Dunham and Kurland, *Mr. Justice*, p. 105; the "labor leader" was Sidney Hillman. Shulman's conversation with LDB occurred on 8 December 1933, and was recalled by him in a memorandum written on 1 February 1934, FFLC, Box 28. The mid-nineteenth-century economic environment that LDB seems to have favored, as well as its transformation into the corporate system he abhorred, is ably considered in Glenn Porter, *The Rise of Big Business, 1860–1910* (Arlington Heights, Ill.: AHM Press, 1973).

3. These observations are part of the undated draft of an article about LDB preserved in FFLC, Box 127. Contextual evidence suggests that it was written by Herbert B. Ehrmann, probably in the mid-1930s; see *BL*, 5:306 n. 1 and 2.

4. Acheson to Frankfurter, 16 November 1920, FFLC, Box 19, printed in Acheson, *Morning and Noon* (Boston: Houghton Mifflin, 1965), pp. 51–53.

5. Acheson, *Morning and Noon*, pp. 57, 83–85; Frankfurter to Shulman, 6 May 1935, FFLC, Box 102.

6. Acheson, *Morning and Noon*, pp. 95–96.

7. Author's interview with Paul Freund, 25 April 1983.

8. Acheson, *Morning and Noon*, pp. 78–81; cf. Acheson to Bickel, 7 December 1955, quoted in Bickel, *Unpublished Opinions*, p. 92.

9. Nathanson to Frankfurter, 4 March 1935, FFLC, Box 127; Riesman to Frankfurter, 21 November 1935, ibid.; Freund to Frankfurter, 15 November 1932, ibid., Box 56.

10. LDB to Frankfurter, 25 November 1920, *BL*, 4:510.

11. Acheson, *Morning and Noon*, pp. 46–47; Riesman to Frankfurter, 21 November 1935, FFLC, Box 127; Freund to Frankfurter, 15 November 1932, ibid., Box 56. In fact, LDB had long been at pains to compose his temperament as well as his image. The "general calm attitude towards every situation" that his daughter taxed him with in 1917 was, as he informed her, something that he had been cultivating for forty years. "I know it has, at times, been amazing to other ardent folk besides yourself. It does not imply criticism—but does involve a desire to know more." LDB to Susan Brandeis, 9 July 1917, SGBU, Box 11, no. 1069.

12. Nathanson to Frankfurter, 4 March 1935, FFLC, Box 127.

13. Interview with Freund, 25 April 1983.

14. Katie Louchheim, ed., *The Making of the New Deal: The Insiders Speak* (Cambridge, Mass.: Harvard University Press, 1983), pp. 83, 88.

15. Ibid., p. 103; Acheson, *Morning and Noon*, p. 50.

16. Interview with Freund, 25 April 1983; Riesman to Frankfurter, 21 November 1935, FFLC, Box 127; Acheson, *Morning and Noon*, pp. 41–42, 49–50. In fact, as we now know, Alice Brandeis enjoyed indifferent health throughout her married life, and in the mid-1920s suffered a devastating nervous breakdown from which she took years to recover fully: see Paper, *Brandeis*, pp. 291–93. For family correspondence relating to her most severe bouts of illness, see especially LDB to Alice Goldmark Brandeis, 28 December 1900 and 28 January 1901, SGBU, Box 1, nos. 37 and 47; LDB to Pauline Goldmark, 19 September 1906, ibid., Box 23, no. 2353; LDB to Susan and Elizabeth Brandeis, 7 August 1907, ibid., no. 2354; LDB to Susan Brandeis, 13 June 1922, 11 April 1923, and 14 October 1923, ibid., Box 11, nos. 1107, 1118, and 1122.

17. Acheson's picture of Washington, D.C., in the early 1920s can be found in *Morning and Noon*, chap. 3, especially pp. 41, 49.

18. Interview with Freund, 25 April 1983; LDB to May C. Nerney, 18 September 1914, *BL*, 3:297–98. For the Mattapoisset incident, see sup., pp. 89–90. Regarding Poindexter, only a few fragmentary references occur: see, especially, Acheson, *Morning and Noon*, p. 41; Paper, *Brandeis*, p. 247; editors' note in *BL*, 4:480, where he is described by LDB's younger daughter as "a very helpful member of the household"; Nathanson to Frankfurter, 4 March 1935, FFLC, Box 127, where the clerk refers to him as "my superior officer."

19. LDB to Chapin Brinsmade, 29 September 1914, *BL*, 3:305. The Scottsboro cases were *Powell v. Alabama*, 287 U.S. 45 (1932); *Norris v. Alabama*, 294 U.S. 587 (1935); *Patterson v. Alabama*, 294 U.S. 600 (1935). The first is treated briefly in Kurland, *Frankfurter on the Supreme Court*, pp. 280–85; its judicial context is explored more fully in Cortner, *Supreme Court and the Second Bill of Rights*, pp. 74, 124–26, 131–36, 201–3, 219. The best overall discussion of LDB's attitude to racial questions coming before the Court is in Strum, *Brandeis*, pp. 330–34, though the author does not perhaps appreciate the wider constitutional ramifications of the cases to which she refers.

20. Paper, *Brandeis*, pp. 45–48, editors' notes, *BL*, 1:111, 136. See Elizabeth Brandeis, "Labor Legislation" in John R. Commons et al., eds., *History of Labor in the United States*, 4 vols. (New York: 1918–35), 3:399–741.

21. This discussion relies heavily on the account in Paper, *Brandeis*, pp. 277–78, 315–16, from which the shorter quotes are also drawn. A vivid picture of LDB's sometimes stormy but always supportive relationship with his elder daughter emerges from the letters he wrote her during the 1910s and 1920s: see SGBU, Boxes

11–17, passim. His generally cordial correspondence with her husband will be found in ibid., Boxes 19–22. For the "birthday" advice, see LDB to Susan Brandeis, 24 February 1919, SGBU, Box 11, no. 1078.

22. The foregoing paragraphs are based on letters from Riesman to the author dated 13 April and 11 August 1981. See *I'll Take My Stand: The South and the Agrarian Tradition* by Twelve Southerners (New York: Harper, 1930).

23. Memorandum of a visit with LDB, 23 February 1934, Emanuel Goldenweiser Papers, LC, Box 7, Book AI; Acheson to Frankfurter, 11 December 1920, FFLC, Box 19. As the rest of the letter indicates, however, Acheson remained skeptical about LDB's ideas.

24. *The Curse of Bigness*, p. 40; LDB to Frankfurter, 10 January 1934, FFLC, Box 28. LDB's views on the evil of irregular employment were succinctly stated in a memorandum sent to A. Lincoln Filene, June 1911, *BL*, 2:444–50, copies of which circulated widely in later years; the topic is fully discussed in Mason, *Brandeis*, pp. 143–46, 308–9, 585–88, 621–22; Strum, *Brandeis*, pp. 96–99, 106–7, 169–70, 376–77, 381–83.

25. LDB to Robert Bruere, 25 February 1922, *BL*, 5:46.

26. "Mr. Justice Brandeis and the Constitution" in Kurland, *Frankfurter on the Supreme Court*, pp. 247–79; LDB to Acheson, 13 August 1920, *BL*, 4:476–77. For a brief assessment of the American liberal agenda in the years after the war, see Acheson, *Morning and Noon*, pp. 104–8, where LDB's letter is printed in full but is incorrectly dated.

27. Riesman to Frankfurter, 22 May 1936, FFLC, Box 28; LDB to Frankfurter, 9 December 1932, ibid.

28. Riesman to Frankfurter, 22 May 1936, ibid., Box 28.

29. Notes of ·conversations between LDB and Acheson, October-November 1919, printed in Àcheson, *Morning and Noon*, pp. 99–102. LDB's attitude toward the rights and wrongs of industrial disputes may not have been transformed overnight by events at Homestead in 1892; but by the time the street railway lines in Milwaukee were struck in 1896, his sympathies were clearly on the side of the workers— as they would be again in 1919. "All Milwaukee is talking of the Street Railway strike which has developed into a boycott," he wrote his wife from the city in May. When the employers had attempted to replace the striking workers, the community had responded by withdrawing its custom from the lines. Although he believed the company was "probably right in this particular issue," he also accepted that it had "a large area of sins," and that the public were "learning that these immortal creatures—who have the advantage of continuity—must be made to suffer for the sins of an earlier administration." He considered "the efficacy of the boycott" to be a "most cheering sight" and was impressed by the "perfect order" that prevailed. Then, in words foreshadowing those recorded by Acheson almost a quarter of a century later, he continued: "If the labor unions and their patrons have virtue enough to hold out a few weeks longer, the labor men will earn a great victory." The community was largely on their side, "and the capitalists of the town [felt] deeply humiliated by the condition of things." LDB to Alice Goldmark Brandeis, 18 May 1896 (2 letters), SGBU, Box 1, nos. 9 and 10.

30. LDB to Frankfurter, 4 September 1922, *BL*, 5:59–62. According to the editors, the contents of this letter were later to form the substance of an unsigned article in the *New Republic*, under the title "What to Do." Cf. also his proposed agenda for this revered organ of liberal opinion as outlined in LDB to Frankfurter, 6 September 1922, ibid., pp. 62–63.

31. LDB to Laski, 21 September 1921, *BL*, 5:17; memorandum on "The merits of labor saving devices," enclosed in LDB to Frankfurter, 30 September 1922, ibid., p. 71. For a full discussion of the actual industrial context against which LDB's re-

marks need to be interpreted, see Daniel Nelson, *Managers and Workers: Origins of the New Factory System in the United States, 1880–1920* (Madison: University of Wisconsin Press, 1975). The problem of technological unemployment only became a subject of serious academic discussion with the onset of the Great Depression: see, for example, Paul H. Douglas and Aaron Director, *The Problem of Unemployment* (New York: Macmillan, 1931), pp. 121–64; "Technological Change as a Factor in Unemployment," *American Economic Review* 22, Supplement (1932), 25–62. For LDB's remarks about Ford, see "The impoverishing spread," *BL*, 5:69. Despite Ford's virulent anti-Semitism (discussed in an editorial note, *BL*, 4:507–8), LDB had long been impressed by his business methods: see, for example, LDB to the Editor, *New York Times Annalist*, 5 January 1914, *BL*, 3:230; LDB to Alfred Brandeis, 26 September 1920, *BL*, 4:487–88.

32. For LDB's 1915 testimony on industrial democracy, see sup., pp. 178–82. Adolf A. Berle and Gardiner C. Means, *The Modern Corporation and Private Property* (New York: Macmillan, 1932). *Liggett Co. v. Lee*, 288 U.S. 517, 566, 568, 580 (1933).

33. 288 U.S. 517, 577–79. The citation was to LDB's own dissenting opinion in *Frost v. Corporation Commission*, 278 U.S. 515, 539 (1929), which will be considered further inf.; the bibliography regarding cooperation is in footnotes 67 and 69. See Harold J. Laski, *The Recovery of Citizenship* (London: E. Benn, 1928).

34. The file of materials on cooperation and profit sharing is in LBLU, NMF 20–3. LDB to C. H. Hubbert, 27 December 1911, *BL*, 2:529–30; LDB to Albert Sonnichsen, 16 July 1913, *BL*, 3:139.

35. Memorandum on "What to do about Capitalism," enclosed with LDB to Frankfurter, 30 September 1922, *BL*, 5:66–67.

36. *Frost v. Corporation Commission*, 278 U.S. 515, 536–37 (emphasis added); but cf. also the rather less guarded wording of these arguments on pp. 5–6 of the earlier draft dated "January—, 1929" in LBHLS 53/7. On the "return" dated 1 February 1929, ibid., 54/4, Justice Holmes wrote: "You have put too much work into this—more than was needed to lay out the opinion. But you certainly have killed it dead."

37. LDB to Laski, 29 November 1928, *BL*, 5:364.

38. Bickel, *Unpublished Opinions*, p. 77. For a sensitive, if sometimes rather one-sided, discussion of the industrial relations scene during the 1920s, see Irving Bernstein, *The Lean Years: A History of the American Worker, 1920–1933* (Boston: Houghton Mifflin, 1960), especially pp. 190–243, which deal with labor and the law.

39. *Dorchy v. Kansas*, 272 U.S. 306, 311 (1926), quoted in Bernstein, *Lean Years*, pp. 191–92. What Bernstein fails to make clear is the context of these phrases. Dorchy was prosecuted criminally for breaching a Kansas industrial relations statute that made it a felony for union executives to use the influence of their offices to persuade others to quit their employment in the mining industry. He had appealed his conviction on the ground that this provision denied him a liberty guaranteed under the Fourteenth Amendment. In fact, as the record showed, the strike that brought Dorchy before the trial court was not incident to any industrial dispute but was called to compel payment of a claim for $180 by a member of the local involved. This was the illegality against which LDB was ruling: "To collect a stale claim due to a fellow member of the union who was formerly employed in the business is not a permissible purpose." The words quoted as being from *Bedford Cut Stone Co. v. Stone Cutters' Association*, 274 U.S. 37, 58, 65 (1927), are actually those of Shulman's paraphrase in "Digest of Opinions," LBHLS, Paige Box 1, fol. 13 (emphasis added); though most if not all are LDB's own, they are here fitted together more pithily than in the original opinion.

40. *Duplex Printing Press Co. v. Deering*, 254 U.S. 443, 484 (1921), quoted in

Bickel, *Unpublished Opinions*, p. 96. The relevant section of the Clayton Act is printed and discussed in ibid., pp. 80–81. For connections between LDB's reasoning in this case and that of his suppressed dissent in *United Mine Workers v. Coronado Coal Co.*, 259 U.S. 344 (1922), see ibid., chap. 5, passim; Acheson, *Morning and Noon*, pp. 88–92.

41. Entry for 14 July 1923 in Urofsky, "Brandeis-Frankfurter Conversations," p. 318. *Truax v. Corrigan*, 257 U.S. 312 (1921); the passages from LDB's dissent quoted and paraphrased in the preceding three paragraphs are at pp. 354–56 (emphasis added). As well as providing a veritable barrage of case citations, from the U.S. courts, LDB also compared practice in England and the British Dominions.

42. See sup., pp. 68–69; LDB to Otto A. Wehle, 12 November 1876, *BL*, 1:10–11.

43. *Truax v. Corrigan*, 257 U.S. 312, 366–68, 372–73. Of course, LDB's assertions gloss over the fact that in *Barron v. Baltimore*, 7 Pet. 243 (1833), the protections of the Bill of Rights had been held not to protect citizens of the United States against actions taken by instrumentalities of the several states, and that the antilabor injunctions complained of were almost invariably granted by state courts applying equitable remedies made available under state laws.

44. LDB to Wilson, 28 December 1921, *BL*, 5:40. The *New Republic* editorial, conflated with two others, is printed with footnotes added in Kurland, *Frankfurter on the Supreme Court*, pp. 49–67; the quotation is on p. 65. For discussion of all the opinions in *Truax*, see Konefsky, *Legacy of Holmes and Brandeis*, pp. 124–29.

45. LDB to Robert W. Bruere, 25 February 1922, *BL*, 5:45; LDB to Frankfurter, 25 March 1933, FFLC, Box 28. Cf. LDB to Elizabeth Raushenbush, 19 November 1933, *BL*, 5:527, in which he reminded her of "the inevitable ineffectiveness of regulation." LDB to Frankfurter, 14 November 1937, FFLC, Box 28. There may be echoes here too of LDB's "pre-Homestead" hostility toward legislative reform, though now couched in terms of doubt about its effectiveness rather than of suspicion about the motives of the reformers.

46. "What to do about Capitalism," *BL*, 5:68. Copy of cablegram from Howe to LDB, 21 March 1938 and LDB to Howe, 22 March 1938, both in LBHLS, 114/12.

47. *New State Ice Co. v. Liebmann*, 285 U.S. 262 (1932); LDB's dissent begins at p. 280, and the passage quoted is at p. 311.

48. 285 U.S. 301–3.

49. Lerner to LDB, 26 March 1932, LBLU, SC 11–1; Lubin to LDB, 30 March 1932, LBHLS, 76/4.

50. LDB to Laski, 21 September 1921, *BL*, 5:17; *The Curse of Bigness*, p. 51. Cf. also LDB's remarks before the U.S. Commission on Industrial Relations in 1915, ibid., p. 81.

51. Ibid., pp. 45–46, 51; LDB to Bruere, 25 February 1922, *BL*, 5:46.

52. Arthur M. Schlesinger, Jr., *[The Age of Roosevelt:] The Politics of Upheaval* (Boston: Houghton Mifflin, 1960), pp. 387–88; Raymond Moley, *After Seven Years* (New York: Harper, 1939), p. 24.

53. Laski to O. W. Holmes, 12 August 1933, quoted in Burt, *Two Jewish Justices*, p. 134 n. 45.

54. LDB to Frank A. Fetter, 26 November 1940, *BL*, 5:648; cf. LDB to Frankfurter, 18 October 1935, FFLC, Box 28. *Liggett Co. v. Lee*, 288 U.S. 548–64. For a modern discussion of the "market" in state laws, see Lawrence M. Friedman, *American Law* (New York: Norton, 1984), pp. 131–33.

55. Draft opinion, 25 February 1933, LBHLS, 82/7; Freund to LDB, 26 February 1933, ibid., 81/5. Freund's reasoning about natural law theory turns on the meaning given the term citizen; if it is taken to mean a person living in civil society, then the rights referred to by LDB were not natural but civil or even constitutional rights.

56. *Liggett Co. v. Lee*, 288 U.S. 568–69.

57. Stone to LDB, 1 March 1933, LBHLS, 82/12; Paper, *Brandeis*, p. 335.

58. LDB to Frankfurter, 29 October 1934, FFLC, Box 28; John J. Burns to Frankfurter, 1 March 1935, ibid.; memorandum of conversation between LDB and Harry Shulman, 8 December 1933, ibid. For LDB's interpretation of the extent to which corporations were entitled to equal protection under the Fourteenth Amendment, see *Liggett Co. v. Lee*, 288 U.S. 575–77.

59. For a full and perceptive appraisal of the Southern Agrarians and their intellectual antecedents, see Richard Gray, *The Literature of Memory: Modern Writers of the American South* (London: Edward Arnold, 1977), pp. 1–105. The case referred to was *Humphrey's Executor v. U.S.*, 295 U.S. 602; Mr. Justice Sutherland rendered the opinion of the Court. LDB's remarks about Long and the possibilities for dictatorship are quoted by Mason (*Brandeis*, p. 619), who refers to "a confidential interview" on 23 June 1935 but fails to specify with whom.

60. "What to do about Capitalism," *BL*, 5:67.

61. Memorandum on "Certificates of Public Convenience and Necessity" enclosed with Frances to LDB, 1 March 1932, LBHLS, 75/3; *New State Ice Co. v. Liebmann*, 285 U.S. 281–2, 304. LDB had previously encountered Oklahoma's use of such certificates in *Frost v. Corporation Commission*, 278 U.S. 515, 536 (1929) but seems not to have appreciated their full potential. For a full discussion of LDB's attitude toward economic regulation during his years on the Court, see Jacobson, "Mr. Justice Brandeis on Regulation and Competition," passim; discussion of *Liebmann* is on pp. 102–12.

62. Freund, "Mr. Justice Brandeis" in Dunham and Kurland, *Mr. Justice*, p. 109.

63. Lerner to LDB, 26 March 1932, LBLU, SC 11–1; Handler to LDB, 25 March 1932, ibid., SC 12–1. The wider question of LDB's attitude toward administrative regulation generally is treated in Louis L. Jaffe, "The Contributions of Mr. Justice Brandeis to Administrative Law," *Iowa Law Review* 18 (1932–33): 213–27; G. Edward White, "Allocating Power between Agencies and Courts: The Legacy of Justice Brandeis," *Duke Law Journal* (April 1974): 195–244.

64. LDB to Ray Stannard Baker, 5 July 1931, *BL*, 5:482–83; testimony before a Massachusetts legislative committee, June 1907, quoted ibid., 1:596 n. 7, but also see sup., pp. 159–66, 171–73; *The Curse of Bigness*, p. 109; cf. also ibid., p. 105. For the fullest statement of these views, see LDB's dissenting opinion in *Quaker City Cab Co. v. Pennsylvania*, 277 U.S. 389, 410 (1928).

65. LDB to Laski, 21 September 1921, *BL*, 5:17; Freund to LDB, 24 February 1933, LBHLS, 81/5; Morris L. Ernst, *The Best Is Yet*, (New York: Penguin, 1947), pp. 24–25; the result of LDB's efforts in persuasion was Ernst, *Too Big* (Boston: Little, Brown, 1940).

66. LDB to Frankfurter, 12 March 1935, FFLC, Box 28; *The Curse of Bigness*, pp. 140–41. See Harold J. Laski, *The Foundations of Sovereignty and Other Essays* (New York: Harcourt, Brace, 1921).

67. *The Curse of Bigness*, pp. 116, 140–41; Gal, *Brandeis of Boston*, pp. 51–52.

68. *Other People's Money*, pp. 162–88, and especially pp. 174–75; *The Curse of Bigness*, p. 76; LDB to Frank A. Fetter, 24 May 1934, *BL*, 5:539. It is interesting to note that Professor Fetter was then working on a forthcoming book, *Democracy and Monopoly* (Princeton: Princeton University Extension Fund, 1939), whose subject matter was, of course, close to LDB's heart.

69. Memorandum of a visit with LDB, 23 February 1934, Goldenweiser Papers, Box 7, Book AI.

70. LDB to E. Brandeis Raushenbush, 19 November 1933, *BL*, 5:527. As well as representing a direct challenge to "Democracy & Liberty," bigness also contributed to the crushing drive toward uniformity that LDB regarded as one of the principal evils of twentieth-century life. Where he now saw this resulting in possible "Fascist

manifestations," three decades earlier his fear had been a "militarism" less specifically defined. "The true reason for the standing army—and the modern militarism," he told his wife, "is that the human male in masses looks well only in uniform. Hence, also the general tendency to uniformity in modern life. 'Tis but the concommitment [*sic*] of teeming millions." LDB to Alice Goldmark Brandeis, undated but endorsed "1899" in a separate hand, SGBU, Box 23, no. 2430.

71. LDB to Louis B. Wehle, 19 January 1932, *BL*, 5:494; LDB to Hapgood, 12 march 1932, ibid., pp. 499–500; Hapgood to Frankfurter, 19 March 1932, FFLC, Box 65. LDB to Frederick A. Stokes, 9 March and 25 July 1933; Sherman F. Mittell to Stokes (copy), 3 August 1933; Mittell to LDB, 23 August 1933—all in LBLU G 7–3. LDB to Mittell, 25 August 1933, *BL*, 5:519–20. Hapgood to LDB, 21 October 1933; Susan Brandeis Gilbert to Mittell, 17 January 1934; Mittell to Gilbert, 19 and 26 January 1934; Mittell to LDB, 23 January and 2 February 1934—all in ibid. Mittell to Gilbert, 1 March 1934; LDB to Mittell, 5 April 1934; Mittell to Gilbert, 18 April 1934—all in ibid. Further 100,000 copy editions were being discussed in 1934 and 1938, but nothing came of the idea: see Stokes to Hapgood, 5 June 1934, ibid; LDB to Stokes, 7 May 1938, *BL*, 5:599–600.

72. Keynes to Hapgood, 27 December 1933, LBLU, G 7–3; Frankfurter to the editor of the *Economist*, 21 March 1933, FFLC, Box 52; Coyle to LDB, 19 December [1933], LBLU, G 2–2. This last is just one item from an extensive file of correspondence, reviews, and other reactions to the book's reissue. "For Gosh sake, Dave, you haven't gone Brandeis, have you?" Jerome Frank is supposed to have remarked some time later, after reading one of Coyle's own articles about the evils of corporate capitalism. "Hell, I've always been Brandeis," was the engineer's reply. "The big battle is coming on, and them that is there will have the fun." Quoted in Ellis W. Hawley, *The New Deal and the Problem of Monopoly* (Princeton: Princeton University Press, 1966), pp. 290–91.

73. LDB to L. B. Wehle, 10 February and 9 July 1932, *BL*, 5:496, 504. For the origins of the Fraenkel collection and LDB's choice of a title, see LDB to C. M. Lewis, 21 March 1934, ibid., pp. 533–36; Bickel, *Unpublished Opinions*, p. 257 n. 9; Freund, "Mr. Justice Brandeis" in Dunham and Kurland, *Mr. Justice*, p. 120 n. 1.

74. Frankfurter to LDB, 17 November [1934], FFLC, Box 29; Lerner's review in *New York Herald Tribune*, 17 March 1935, Books Section.

75. Biographies and studies of LDB's legal thinking have been discussed elsewhere. Among New Deal historians, see, for example, Schlesinger, *Politics of Upheaval*, pp. 387–88, William E. Leuchtenburg, *Franklin D. Roosevelt and the New Deal* (New York: Harper & Row, 1963), p. 148; Frank Freidel, *Franklin D. Roosevelt: Launching the New Deal* (Boston: Little, Brown, 1973), pp. 345, 410. This list is not intended to be exhaustive.

76. The best brief summaries of LDB's reform agenda for the 1930s and his relationship to the New Deal are Paper, *Brandeis*, pp. 339–60; Strum, *Brandeis*, pp. 380–405. For two more detailed assessments, see Dawson, *Brandeis, Frankfurter and the New Deal*, passim; Murphy, *Brandeis/Frankfurter Connection*, pp. 98–185. For the justice's own explanation of what he wanted to see, especially in the area of public works policy, see "Memorandum of Talk with L. D. B., by Harry Shulman," 8 December 1933, FFLC, Box 28; LDB to Frankfurter, 3 August 1934, ibid.; cf. also Stephen W. Baskerville, "Frankfurter, Keynes and the Fight for Public Works, 1932–1935," *Maryland Historian* 9 (1978): 1–16.

77. "Memorandum of Views Expressed by Mr. Justice Brandeis on November 18, 1918," FFLC, Box 127; this is quoted verbatim in Mason, *Brandeis*, pp. 527–28, without a source being cited but with the additional information that LDB's conversation was with Herbert Hoover's secretary, Lewis Straus. LDB to Alice G. Brandeis, 13 June 1919, *BL*, 4:398–99; LDB to Alfred Brandeis, 23 March 1921, ibid., p. 546; LDB to Edwin A. Alderman, 11 May 1924, *BL*, 5:128; LDB to Frankfurter, 16

July 1926, ibid., p. 229; LDB to Hapgood (excerpt), 16 July 1935, ibid., p. 555. LDB may also have had the Russian Revolution of March 1917 in mind when he wrote his daughter a few weeks later: "I am sorry the war still looks depressing. To me the world seems more full of hope and promise than at any time since the joyous days of '48, when liberalism came with its manifold proposals." LDB to Susan Brandeis, 15 April 1917, SGBU, Box 11, no. 1061.

78. LDB to Alfred Brandeis, 5 November 1921, *BL*, 5:28; LDB to J. Goldmark, 8 January and 30 October 1932, ibid., pp. 492–93, 512–13. *Democracy in Denmark* (Washington, D.C.: National Home Library Foundation, 1936); LDB to Ernst, 24 December 1936, ibid., p. 585; LDB quoted in Schlesinger, *Politics of Upheaval*, p. 221. Some indication of the range of material gathered by LDB for the "Democracy in Denmark" project can be had from the correspondence preserved in LBLU, M 7–2.

79. LDB to E. B. Raushenbush, 22 April 1934, *BL*, 5:537; LDB to Hapgood, 27 October 1934, quoted in Mason, *Brandeis*, p. 618.

80. LDB to Frankfurter, 7 February 1935, FFLC, Box 28; LDB to E. B. Raushenbush, 26 March 1935, *BL*, 5:552–53.

81. Excerpts of letters from LDB to Norman Hapgood, 4 and 22 July, 2, 9, and 24 August, 28 November 1935, *BL*, 5:555–58.

82. LDB to Hapgood (excerpts), 15 June and 16 July 1935, ibid.; J. J. Burns to Frankfurter, 1 March 1935, FFLC, Box 28.

83. Letter from LDB in *The Survey*, 13 November 1920, quoted in Lief, *Brandeis Guide to the Modern World*, p. 4. Cf. similar remarks made eighteen months later with reference to the Court's recent child labor decisions: "I am convinced that the immediate loss will result in great gains later. If we may hope to carry out our idea to aid America—it will be by development through the State and local governments. Centralization will kill—but decentralization of social functions can help." In the previous century "nationalization" had been "the key work"; now the aim should be to "bring development in States and Cities." LDB to Susan Brandeis, SGBU, Box 11, no. 1105.

84. Bernard Flexner, *Mr. Justice Brandeis and the University of Louisville* (Louisville: University of Louisville Press, 1938); but cf. also Mason, *Brandeis*, pp. 588–93; Strum, *Brandeis*, pp. 398–401. Alice G. Brandeis to Hurst, 27 October [1937]; LDB to Hurst, 6 January and 22 May 1938, 13 May 1940—all in LBHLS, 114/20.

85. Charles E. Wyzanski, "Brandeis," *Atlantic Monthly*, 198 (November 1956), ?1. For a contemporary critique of Wyzanski's assessment, see Frankfurter to A. M. Bickel, 13 November 1956, FFLC, Box 23. For LDB's linkage of morality and truth, see Acheson, *Morning and Noon*, p. 96.

86. LDB to Frankfurter, 17 March 1933, FFLC, Box 28.

87. LDB to Alice P. Goldmark, 11 January 1934, *BL*, 5:531; the passage from Euripides quoted was coupled with another in German from Goethe's *Faust* to similar effect. Frankfurter to Frank W. Buxton (editor of the *Boston Herald*), 18 March 1934, FFLC, Box 28; LDB to Frankfurter, 28 August 1934, ibid.

88. Memorandum of a "Visit with Justice Brandeis," 19 May 1935, Goldenweiser Papers, Box 7, Book AI.

89. Riesman to Frankfurter, 22 May 1936, FFLC, Box 28.

90. This and the following paragraph afford only the briefest summary of LDB's later Zionist activities. For more detailed accounts, see Paper, *Brandeis*, pp. 316–24, 386–89, Strum, *Brandeis*, pp. 273–90; Urofsky, *American Zionism*, pp. 334–429.

91. Rabinowitz, *Justice Brandeis*, pp. 129–30; editors' note in *BL*, 5:532; LDB to Richard E. Gatstadt, 28 December 1939, LBHLS, 114/15. For a somewhat earlier example of manifest pride in the achievements of the Jewish settlements in Palestine, see LDB to Jacob DeHaas, 20 November 1930, SGBU, Box 23, no. 2381; another copy is printed in *BL*, 5:463–64.

92. Mason, *Brandeis*, p. 618; Freund to Frankfurter, 11 December 1934, FFLC, Box 56; *Panama Refining Co. v. Ryan*, 293 U.S. 388 (1935).

93. Entry for 25 February 1935, Urofsky, "Brandeis-Frankfurter Conversations," p. 337. There were, in fact, three gold-clause cases: *Norman v. Baltimore & Ohio R.R. Co.*, 294 U.S. 240 (1935); *Perry v. U.S.*, 294 U.S. 330 (1935); and, concerning the redemption of gold certificates, *Nortz v. U.S.*, 294 U.S. 317 (1935).

94. *Railroad Retirement Board v. Alton R.R. Co.*, 295 U.S. 330 (1935); Hughes's dissent begins at p. 374, and the passage quoted is at p. 392. For a detailed discussion of LDB's own thinking on different aspects the commerce clause, see Bickel, *Unpublished Opinions*, pp. 100–201. His attitude to workingmen's compensation laws is considered in Jacobson, "Brandeis on Regulation and Competition," pp. 181–87.

95. The three cases decided on "Black Monday" were *Schechter Poultry Corp. v. U.S.*, 295 U.S. 495 (1935); *Louisville Joint Stock Bank v. Radford*, 295 U.S. 555 (1935); *Humphrey's Executor v. U.S.*, 295 U.S. 602 (1935). All are discussed together in Jacobson, "Brandeis on Regulation and Competition," pp. 296–304. Cf. Richard Maidment, "The New Deal Court Revisited" in Stephen W. Baskerville and Ralph Willett, eds., *Nothing Else to Fear: New Perspectives on America in the Thirties* (Manchester: Manchester University Press, 1985), pp. 38–63, for an alternative perspective on these and the other New Deal cases dealt with by the Hughes Court.

96. Memorandum by Cohen of a "Conference with Justice Brandeis, at his request . . . 2 PM, May 27, 1935," FFLC, Box 28; the case referred to as largely overruled by the decision in *Humphrey's Executor* was *Myers v. U.S.*, 272 U.S. 52 (1926). Corcoran's characteristically less accurate but rather more colorful account of this interview is quoted in Schlesinger, *Politics of Upheaval*, p. 280.

97. *U.S. v. Butler et al.*, 297 U.S. 1 (1936); LDB to Frankfurter, 24 February 1935, FFLC, Box 28. On the suppression of Mary Conner Myers's findings about the way the AAA's cotton contract had been administered in Arkansas, see Paul E. Mertz, *New Deal Policy and Southern Rural Poverty* (Baton Rouge: Louisiana State University Press, 1978), pp. 33–34.

98. For a full discussion of LDB's *Ashwander* opinion, see sup., pp. 266–73. *Carter v. Carter Coal*, 298 U.S. 238 (1936); Cardozo's dissent begins at p. 324. LDB's undated "Memorandum" in this case, together with the two critical memoranda from Riesman dated 22–27 April and 27 April 1936, respectively, is preserved in LBHLS, 97/8. For a brief discussion of this case, and of its wider implications, see "The Orbit of Judicial Power" in Kurland, *Frankfurter on the Supreme Court*, pp. 351–53.

99. For the cases that concerned Riesman and others among LDB's later clerks, see sup., pp. 236, 262–66. *Senn v. Tile Layers Protective Union*, 301 U.S. 468 (1937); this case and the issues raised by it are considered in Paper, *Brandeis*, pp. 375–77.

100. Goethe, *Poetry and Truth*, 1:345–46.

101. LDB to Susan Goldmark, 7 October 1932, *BL*, 5:512. A concise picture of LDB's final years is provided in Paper, *Brandeis*, pp. 391–94, his remarks are from a memorandum by Fannie Brandeis, "Conversation with LDB," 19 May 1940, quoted in ibid., p. 394. Roosevelt's return to the White House for a third term obviously pleased him. "The English must be very much encouraged by FD's election," he wrote his son-in-law once the result was know; "also other Europeans democratically inclined." LDB to Jack Gilbert, 7 November 1940, SGBU, Box 21, no. 2282.

Coda: The Wisdom of the World

1. Mason, *Brandeis*, p. 637; the author's interview with Paul Freund, 25 April 1983. Acheson's address is reprinted as "Mr. Justice Brandeis" in *Harvard Law Review* 55 (1941): 191–92; Frankfurter's is summarized in Baker, *Brandeis and Frankfurter*, p. 373.

2. Friedenwald to Frankfurter, 8 October 1941, FFLC, Box 127.

3. For LDB's relationship with Acheson during the 1920s, see Paper, *Brandeis*, p. 292.

4. Acheson, "Mr. Justice Brandeis," p. 192.

5. Friendly, "Mr. Justice Brandeis: the Quest for Reason," *University of Pennsylvania Law Review*, 108 (1960): 985–99; the quotation is from pp. 998–99. Frankfurter to Friendly, 21 June 1960, FFLC, Box 56. For discussion of those aspects of the German *Aufklärung* which are most likely to have influenced LDB's thinking, see, for example, Eliza M. Butler, *The Tyranny of Greece over Germany* (Cambridge: Cambridge University Press, 1935); Humphrey Trevelyan, *Goethe and the Greeks* (Cambridge: Cambridge University Press, 1941); Victor Lange, *The Classical Age of German Literature, 1740–1815* (London: Edward Arnold, 1982).

6. LDB to Frankfurter, 13 November 1921, *BL*, 5:33. Though LDB was apparently in agreement with David Ben-Gurion's assessment (25 January 1934, ibid., pp. 531–33) that Germany and Japan were preparing to fight a world war as soon as the time was ripe, his primary concern was with the writer's ideas about the development of Palestine. The wider implication's of Ben-Gurion's analysis seem to have eluded him.

7. The material in this and the next six paragraphs is based primarily on the remarks of Judge Learned B. Hand, printed in *Proceedings of the Bar of the Supreme Court of the United States and Meeting of the Court in Memory of Associate Justice Louis D. Brandeis, December 21, 1942* (Washington, D.C.: Government Printing Office, 1942), pp. 19–25. For the contribution made by Chief Justice-Stone, see sup., pp. 233–35.

Bibliography

Archives

Franklin D. Roosevelt Library. Hyde Park, New York
Franklin D. Roosevelt Papers.

Goldfarb Library. Brandeis University. Waltham, Massachusetts
Susan Brandeis Gilbert Papers.

Harvard Law School Library. Cambridge, Massachusetts
Louis Dembitz Brandeis Papers.
Superior Court of the Pow Wow Papers.

Library of Congress. Washington, D.C.
Felix Frankfurter Papers.
Emanuel Goldenweiser Papers.

University of Louisville Library. Louisville, Kentucky
Louis Dembitz Brandeis Papers.

Interviews

Freund, Paul A. 25 April, 1983. Cambridge, Massachusetts.
Jaffe, Louis L. 21 April, 1983. Cambridge, Massachusetts.
Riesman, David, Jr. 21 April, 1983. Cambridge, Massachusetts.

Printed Primary Sources

Bickel, Alexander M., ed. *The Unpublished Opinions of Mr. Justice Brandeis: The Supreme Court at Work.* Cambridge, Mass.: Harvard University Press, 1957.

Brandeis, Frederika. *Reminiscences of Frederika Dembitz Brandeis: Written for her Son, Louis, in 1880 to 1886.* Translated by Alice Goldmark Brandeis. Privately printed, 1948.

Brandeis, Louis D. *Business—A Profession.* Boston: Small, Maynard, 1914.

———. *The Curse of Bigness.* Edited by Osmond K. Fraenkel. New York: Viking Press, 1934.

———. "The Harvard Law School." *The Green Bag,* 1 (1889): 10–25.

———. *Notes on Business Law.* 2 vols. Privately printed, 1894–96.

———. *Other People's Money—And How the Bankers Use It.* New York: Stokes, 1914.

————. "The Living Law." *Illinois Law Review* 10 (1916): 461–71.

————, and Goldmark, Josephine. *Women in Industry*. Reprint of 1908 ed. produced for the National Consumers' League. New York: Arno Press, 1969.

————, and Warren, Samuel D. "The Law of Ponds." *Harvard Law Review* 3 (1889–90): 1–22.

————, and Warren, Samuel D. "The Right to Privacy." *Harvard Law Review* 4 (1890–91): 193–220.

————, and Warren, Samuel D. "The Watuppa Pond Cases." *Harvard Law Review* 2 (1888–89): 195–211.

Goldman, Solomon, ed. *Brandeis on Zionism*. Washington, D.C.: Zionist Organization of America, 1942.

————, ed. *The Words of Justice Brandeis*. New York: H. Schuman, 1953.

Lief, Alfred, ed. *The Brandeis Guide to the Modern World*. Boston: Little, Brown, 1941.

————, ed. *The Social and Economic Views of Mr. Justice Brandeis*. New York: Vanguard Press, 1930.

Urofsky, Melvin I., ed. "The Brandeis-Frankfurter Conversations." *Supreme Court Review* (1985): 299–339.

————, and Levy, David W., eds. *Letters of Louis D. Brandeis*. 5 vols. Albany: State University of New York Press, 1971–78.

Secondary Sources

WORKS OF REFERENCE

Blandford, Linda B., and Evans, Patricia R., eds. *The Supreme Court of the United States. 1789–1980: An Index to Opinions Arranged by Justice*. 2 vols. Millwood, N.Y.: Kraus International Publications, 1983.

Brockhaus Encyclopädie, vol. 21 [*Karten*]. Wiesbaden: F. A. Brockhaus, 1975.

Bureau of the Census. *Ninth Census of the United States: Statistics of Population*. Washington, D.C.: Government Printing Office, 1872.

Bureau of the Census. *Compendium of the Eleventh Census: 1890*. 3 vols. Washington, D.C.: Government Printing Office, 1892–7.

Cases Argued and Decided in the Supreme Court of the United States [1–307 U.S.]. Lawyers' ed. 83 vols. Rochester, N.Y.: Lawyers Cooperative Publishing, 1917–39.

Encyclopaedia Judaica. 16 vols. Jerusalem: Encyclopaedia Judaica, 1971–72.

Mersky, Roy. *Louis Dembitz Brandeis, 1856–1941: A Bibliography*. New Haven, Conn.: Yale Law School, 1958.

Teitelbaum, Gene. *Justice Louis D. Brandeis: A Bibliography of Writings and Other Materials on the Justice*. Littleton, Colo.: Fred B. Rothman, 1988.

BOOKS

Abrams, Richard M. *Conservatism in a Progressive Era: Massachusetts Politics, 1900–1912*. Cambridge, Mass.: Harvard University Press, 1964.

Acheson, Dean. *Morning and Noon*. Boston: Houghton Mifflin, 1965.

Atherton, Lewis E. *The Frontier Merchant in Mid-America*. Columbia, Mo.: University of Missouri Press, 1971.

Baker, Leonard. *Brandeis and Frankfurter: A Dual Biography*. New York: Harper & Row, 1984.

Berle, Adolf A., Jr., and Means, Gardiner C. *The Modern Corporation and Private Property*. New York: Macmillan, 1932.

Bernstein, Irving. *The Lean Years: A History of the American Worker, 1920–1933*. Boston: Houghton Mifflin, 1960.

Bickerman, Elias. *The God of the Maccabees: Studies on the Meaning and Origin of the Maccabesn Revolt*. English translation from the original German. Leiden: Brill, 1979.

Blenkinsopp, Joseph. *A History of Prophecy in Israel: From the Settlement on the Land to the Hellenistic Period*. Philadelphia: Westminster Press, 1983.

Blodgett, Geoffrey. *The Gentle Reformers: Massachusetts Democrats in the Cleveland Era*. Cambridge, Mass.: Harvard University Press, 1966.

Blum, John M. *The Republican Roosevelt*. Cambridge, Mass.: Harvard University Press, 1954.

Bright, John. *A History of Israel*. 3rd ed. Philadelphia: Westminster Press, 1981.

Brock, William R. *Investigation and Responsibility: Public Responsibility in the United States, 1865–1900*. New York: Cambridge University Press, 1984.

———. *Welfare, Democracy and the New Deal*. New York: Cambridge University Press, 1988.

Burgoyne, Arthur G. *The Homestead Strike of 1892*. Reprint of 1893 ed. with an afterword by David P. Demarest, Jr. Pittsburgh: University of Pittsburg Press, 1979.

Burt, Robert A. *Two Jewish Justices: Outcasts in the Promised Land*. Berkeley: University of California Press, 1988.

Butler, Eliza M. *The Tyranny of Greece over Germany*. Cambridge: Cambridge University Press, 1935.

Cardozo, Benjamin. *The Growth of the Law*. New Haven: Yale University Press, 1924.

———. *The Nature of the Judicial Process*. New Haven: Yale University Press, 1921.

———. *The Paradoxes of Legal Science*. New York: Columbia University Press, 1928.

Clark, John Bates. *The Control of the Trusts: An Argument in Favor of Curbing the Power of Monopoly by a Natural Method*. New York: Macmillan, 1901.

Clawson, Dan. *Bureaucracy and the Labor Process: The Transformation of U.S. Industry, 1860–1920*. New York: Monthly Review Press, 1980.

Cooley, Thomas M. *A Treatise on the Constitutional Limitations which Rest upon the Legislative Power of the States of the American Union*. Reprint of 1868 ed. New York: Da Capo Press, 1972.

———. *A Treatise on the Law of Torts or the Wrongs which Arise Independently of Contract*. 4th ed. Edited by D. A. Haggard. Chicago: Callaghan, 1932.

Cortner, Richard C. *The Supreme Court and the Second Bill of Rights: The Fourteenth Amendment and the Nationalization of Civil Liberties*. Madison: University of Wisconsin Press, 1981.

Corwin, Edward S. *Corwin on the Constitution*. Vol. 3, *On Liberty Against Government*. Edited by Richard Loss. Ithaca: Cornell University Press, 1988.

Croly, Herbert D. *The Promise of American Life*. New York: Macmillan, 1909.

Davis, Allen F. *Spearheads for Reform: The Social Settlements and the Progressive Movement, 1890–1914*. New York: Oxford University Press, 1967.

Dawson, Nelson L., ed. *Brandeis and America*. Lexington: University Press of Kentucky, 1989.

———. *Louis D. Brandeis, Felix Frankfurter, and the New Deal*. Hamden, Conn.: Archon Press, 1980.

De Haas, Jacob. *Louis D. Brandeis: A Biographical Sketch*. New York: Bloch, 1929.

Dell, Floyd. *Upton Sinclair: A Study in Social Protest*. New York: AMS Press, 1970.

Douglas, Paul H., and Director, Aaron. *The Problem of Unemployment*. New York: Macmillan, 1931.

Doyle, Don Harrison. *The Social Order of a Frontier Community: Jacksonville, Illinois, 1825–70*. Urbana: University of Illinois Press, 1978.

Ekirch, Arthur A., Jr. *Progressivism in America: A Study of the Era from Theodore Roosevelt to Woodrow Wilson*. New York: New Viewpoints Press, 1974.

Ely, Richard T. *Monopolies and Trusts*. New York: Macmillan, 1900.

Ernst, Morris L. *The Best Is Yet*. New York: Penguin, 1947.

———. *Too Big*. Boston: Little, Brown, 1940.

Euripides: Translated into English Rhyming Verse. Translated by Gilbert Murray. New York: Longman, Green, 1902.

[The Plays of] Euripides. Translated by Arthur S. Way. 4 vols. Cambridge, Mass.: Harvard University Press, 1912.

Fetter, Frank A. *Democracy and Monopoly*. Princeton: Princeton University Extension Fund, 1939.

Flexner, Bernard. *Mr. Justice Brandeis and the University of Louisville*. Louisville: University of Louisville Press, 1938.

Foner, Philip S. *The Great Labor Uprising of 1877*. New York: Monad Press, 1977.

Forcey, Charles W. *The Crossroads of Liberalism: Croly, Weyl, Lippmann and the Progressive Era*. New York: Oxford University Press, 1961.

Frankfurter, Felix. *Felix Frankfurter Reminisces: An Intimate Portrait as Recorded in Talks with Dr. Harlan B. Phillips*. New York: Reynal, 1960.

———, ed. *Mr. Justice Brandeis*. New Haven: Yale University Press, 1932.

Freidel, Frank. *Franklin D. Roosevelt: Launching the New Deal*. Boston: Little, Brown, 1973.

Freyer, Tony A. *Harmony and Dissonance: The Swift and Erie Cases in American Federalism*. New York: New York University Press, 1981.

Friedman, Lawrence M. *American Law*. New York: Norton, 1984.

———. *A History of American Law*. New York: Simon & Schuster, 1973.

Gal, Allon. *Brandeis of Boston*. Cambridge, Mass.: Harvard University Press, 1980.

Garraty, John A. *Henry Cabot Lodge: A Biography*. New York: Knopf, 1953.

Girgus, Sam B. *The New Covenant: Jewish Writers and the American Idea*. Chapel Hill: University of North Carolina Press, 1984.

Goethe, Johann Wolfgang von. *Faust*. Translated by Philip Wayne. 2 vols. Harmondsworth: Penguin, 1959.

———. *Poetry and Truth from My Own Life*. Revised translation by Minna Steele Smith. 2 vols. London: G. Bell, 1913.

Goldman, Eric. *Rendezvous with Destiny: A History of Modern American Reform*. New York: Knopf, 1952.

Goldmark, Josephine. *Democracy in Denmark*. Washington, D.C.: National Home Library Foundation, 1936.

———. *Pilgrims of '48: One Man's Part in the Austrian Revolution of 1848 and a Family Migration to America*. New Haven: Yale University Press, 1930.

Goodwyn, Lawrence. *Democratic Promise: The Populist Moment in America*. New York: Oxford University Press, 1976.

Graham, Otis L., Jr. *The Great Campaigns: Reform and War in America, 1900–1928*. Englewood Cliffs, N.J.: Prentice Hall, 1971.

Gray, Richard. *The Literature of Memory: Modern Writers of the American South*. London: Edward Arnold, 1977.

Green, Marguerite. *The National Civic Federation and the American Labor Movement, 1900–1925*. Washington, D.C.: Catholic University of America Press, 1956.

Ha-Am, Ahad. *Am Scheidewege*. Translated into German from the Hebrew by Israel Friedlaender. Berlin: Jüdischer Verlag, 1913.

———. *Selected Essays by Ahad Ha-Am*. Translated from the Hebrew by Leon Simon. Philadelphia: Jewish Publication Society of America, 1912.

———. *Ten Essays on Zionism and Judaism by Achad Ha-Am*. Edited by Leon Simon. Reprint of 1922 ed. New York: Arno Press, 1973.

Haber, Samuel. *Efficiency and Uplift: Scientific Management in the Progressive Era, 1890–1920*. Chicago: University of Chicago Press, 1964.

Halpern, Ben. *A Clash of Heroes: Brandeis, Weizmann, and American Zionism*. New York: Oxford University Press, 1987.

Hapgood, Norman. *The Changing Years*. New York: Farrar & Rinehart, 1930.

Hawley, Ellis W. *The New Deal and the Problem of Monopoly*. Princeton: Princeton University Press, 1966.

Hays, Samuel P. *The Response to Industrialism, 1885–1914*. Chicago: University of Chicago Press, 1957.

Higham, John. *Send These to Me: Jews and Other Immigrants in Urban America*. New York: Atheneum, 1975.

Hirsch, H. N. *The Enigma of Felix Frankfurter*. New York: Basic Books, 1981.

Hixson, Richard F. *Privacy in a Public Society: Human Rights in Conflict*. New York: Oxford University Press, 1987.

Hofstadter, Richard. *The Age of Reform from Bryan to FDR*. New York: Knopf, 1955.

Holt, Michael F. *The Political Crisis of the 1850s*. New York: Wiley, 1978.

Hoogenboom, Ari, and Hoogenboom, Olive. *A History of the ICC from Panacea to Palliative*. New York: Norton, 1976.

Hopkins, C. Howard. *The Rise of the Social Gospel in American Protestantism, 1865–1915*. New Haven: Yale University Press, 1940.

Hurst, James Willard. *The Growth of American Law: The Law Makers*. Boston: Little, Brown, 1950.

———. *Law and the Conditions of Freedom in the Nineteenth-Century United States*. Madison: University of Wisconsin Press, 1956.

Jakle, John A. *Images of the Ohio Valley: A Historical Geography of Travel, 1740–1860*. New York: Oxford University Press, 1977.

Johnson, John W. *American Legal Culture, 1908–1940*. Westport, Conn.: Greenwood Press, 1981.

Kaplan, Justin. *Lincoln Steffens: A Biography*. New York: Simon & Schuster, 1974.

Katz, Michael B. *In the Shadow of the Poorhouse: A Social History of Welfare in America*. New York: Basic Books, 1986.

Kohl, J. G. *Austria*. London: Chapman & Hall, 1843.

Kolko, Gabriel. *Railroads and Regulation, 1877–1916*. Princeton: Princeton University Press, 1965.

———. *The Triumph of Conservatism: A Reinterpretation of American History, 1900–1916*. New York: Free Press of Glencoe, 1963.

Konefsky, Samuel J. *The Legacy of Holmes and Brandeis*. New York: Macmillan, 1956.

Konvitz, Milton R. *Judaism and the American Idea*. Ithaca: Cornell University Press, 1978.

Krock, Arthur, ed. *The Editorials of Henry Watterson*. Louisville: Louisville Courier Journal, 1923.

Kurland, Philip B., ed. *Felix Frankfurter on the Supreme Court: Extrajudicial Essays on the Court and the Constitution*. Cambridge, Mass.: Harvard University Press, 1970.

La Dame, Mary. *The Filene Store: A Study of Employees' Relation to Management in a Retail Store*. New York: Russell Sage Foundation, 1930.

LaFollette, Belle Case, and LaFollette, Fola. *Robert M. LaFollette, 1855–1925*. 2 vols. New York: Macmillan, 1953.

Lange, Victor. *The Classical Age of German Literature, 1740–1815*. London: Edward Arnold, 1982.

Laqueur, Walter. *A History of Zionism*. London: Weidenfeld & Nicolson, 1972.

Laski, Harold J. *The American Democracy: A Commentary and Interpretation*. New York: Viking Press, 1948.

———. *The Foundations of Sovereignty and Other Essays*. New York: Harcourt, Brace, 1921.

———. *The Recovery of Citizenship*. London: E. Benn, 1928.

Lens, Sidney. *The Labor Wars from the Molly Maguires to the Sitdowns*. Garden City, N.Y.: Doubleday, 1973.

Leuchtenburg, William E. *Franklin D. Roosevelt and the New Deal*. New York: Harper & Row, 1963.

Levy, Leonard W. *The Law of the Commonwealth and Chief Justice Shaw*. Cambridge, Mass.: Harvard University Press, 1957.

Lief, Alfred. *Brandeis: The Personal History of an American Ideal*. New York: Stackpole, 1936.

Link, Arthur. *Wilson: The New Freedom*. Princeton: Princeton University Press, 1965.

Lipow, Arthur. *Authoritarian Socialism in America: Edward Bellamy and the Nationalist Movement*. Berkeley: University of California Press, 1982.

Louchheim, Katie, ed. *The Making of the New Deal: The Insiders Speak*. Cambridge, Mass.: Harvard University Press, 1983.

McCraw, Thomas K. *Prophets of Regulation: Charles Francis Adams, Louis D. Brandeis, James M. Landis, Alfred E. Kahn*. Cambridge, Mass.: Harvard University Press, 1984.

———. *T.V.A. and the Power Fight, 1933–1939*. Philadelphia: J. B. Lippincott, 1971.

McFarland, Gerald W., ed. *The Mugwumps, 1884–1900: Moralists or Pragmatists?* New York: Simon & Schuster, 1976.

————. *Mugwumps, Morals and Politics, 1884–1920.* Amherst: University of Massachusetts Press, 1975.

McKelvey, Blake. *The Urbanization of America, 1860–1915.* New Brunswick, N.J.: Rutgers University Press, 1963.

Mann, Arthur. *Yankee Reformers in the Urban Age: Social Reform in Boston, 1880–1900.* Cambridge, Mass.: Harvard University Press, 1954.

Marcosson, Isaac F. *Marse Henry.* New York: Dodd, Mead, 1951.

Mason, Alpheus T. *Brandeis: A Free Man's Life.* New York: Viking Press, 1946.

————. *The Brandeis Way: A Case Study in the Workings of Democracy.* Princeton: Princeton University Press, 1938.

————. *Bureaucracy Convicts Itself: The Ballinger-Pinchot Controversy of 1910.* New York: Viking Press, 1941.

May, Henry. *The Protestant Churches and Industrial America.* New York: Harper, 1949.

Mertz, Paul E. *New Deal Policy and Southern Rural Poverty.* Baton Rouge: Louisiana State University Press, 1978.

Moley, Raymond. *After Seven Years.* New York: Harper, 1939.

Murphy, Bruce Allen. *The Brandeis-Frankfurter Connection: The Secret Political Activities of Two Supreme Court Justices.* New York: Oxford University Press, 1982.

Nelson, Daniel. *Managers and Workers: Origins of the New Factory System in the United States, 1880–1920.* Madison: University of Wisconsin Press, 1975.

Olin, Spencer. *California's Prodigal Sons: Hiram Johnson and the Progressives, 1911–1917.* Berkeley: University of California Press, 1968.

Olmsted, Frederick Law. *The Cotton Kingdom: A Traveller's Observations on Cotton and Slavery in the American Slave States.* Edited by Arthur M. Schlesinger. New York: Knopf, 1953.

Paper, Lewis J. *Brandeis: An Intimate Biography of One of America's Truly Great Supreme Court Justices.* Secaucus, N.J.: Citadel Press, 1983.

Parrish, Michael E. *Felix Franfurter and His Times: The Reform Years.* New York: Free Press, 1982.

Patterson, James T. *The New Deal and the States: Federalism in Transition.* Princeton: Princeton University Press, 1969.

Paul, Arnold M. *Conservative Crisis and the Rule of Law: Attitudes of Bar and Bench, 1887–1895.* Ithaca: Cornell University Press, 1960.

Pech, Stanley Z. *The Czech Revolution of 1848.* Chapel Hill: University of North Carolina Press, 1969.

Pember, Don R. *Privacy and the Press: The Law, the Mass Media and the First Amendment.* Seattle: University of Washington Press, 1972.

Penick, James L., Jr. *Progressive Politics and Conservation: The Ballinger-Pinchot Affair.* Chicago: University of Chicago Press, 1968.

Porter, Glenn. *The Rise of Big Business, 1860–1910.* Arlington Heights, Ill.: AHM Press, 1973.

Proceedings of the Bar of the Supreme Court of the United States and Meeting of the Court in Memory of Associate Justice Louis D. Brandeis, December 21, 1942. Washington, D.C.: Government Printing Office, 1942.

Rabinowitz, Ezekiel. *Justice Louis D. Brandeis: The Zionist Chapter of His Life.* New York: Philosophical Library, 1968.

Ransom, John Crowe et al. *I'll Take My Stand: The South and the Agrarian Tradition by Twelve Southerners*. New York: Harper, 1930.

Regier, Cornelius C. *The Era of the Muckrakers*. Chapel Hill: University of North Carolina Press, 1932.

Roosevelt, Theodore. *The Works of Theodore Roosevelt*. Edited by Herman Hagedorn. Vol. 17, *Social Justice and Popular Rule: Essays, Addresses, and Public Statements Relating to the Progressive Movement (1910–1916)*. New York: Scribner, 1926.

Schlesinger, Arthur M., Jr. *[The Age of Roosevelt:] The Politics of Upheaval*. Boston: Houghton Mifflin, 1960.

Shapiro, Herbert, ed. *The Muckrakers and American Society*. Boston: D. C. Heath, 1968.

Shapiro, Yonathan. *Leadership of the American Zionist Organization, 1897–1930*. Urbana: University of Illinois Press, 1971.

Silverman, Robert A. *Law and Urban Growth: Civil Litigation in the Boston Trial Courts, 1880–1900*. Princeton: Princeton University Press, 1981.

Simon, Leon. *Ahad Ha-Am, Asher Ginzberg: A Biography*. Philadelphia: Jewish Publication Society of America, 1960.

Sklar, Martin J. *The Corporate Reconstruction of American Capitalism, 1890–1914: The Market, the Law and Politics*. New York: Cambridge University Press, 1988.

Solomon, Barbara M. *Ancestors and Immigrants: A Changing New England Tradition*. Cambridge, Mass.: Harvard University Press, 1956.

Sproat, John G. *"The Best Men": Liberal Reformers in the Gilded Age*. New York: Oxford University Press, 1968.

Staples, Henry Lee, and Mason, Alpheus T. *The Fall of a Railroad Empire*. Syracuse, N.Y.: Syracuse University Press, 1947.

Steffens, Lincoln. *The Autobiography of Lincoln Steffens*. 2 vols. New York: Harcourt, Brace, 1931.

Stevens, Robert B. *Law School: Legal Education in America from the 1850s to the 1980s*. Chapel Hill: University of North Carolina Press, 1983.

Strum, Philippa. *Louis D. Brandeis: Justice for the People*. Cambridge, Mass.: Harvard University Press, 1984.

Sutherland, Arthur E. *The Law at Harvard: A History of Ideas and Men, 1817–1967*. Cambridge, Mass.: Belknap Press of Harvard University Press, 1967.

Taussig, Frank W. *The Silver Situation in the U.S.*. New York: Putnam, 1893.

Todd, A. L. *Justice on Trial: The Case of Louis D. Brandeis*. New York: McGraw-Hill, 1964.

Trevelyan, Humphrey. *Goethe and the Greeks*. Cambridge: Cambridge University Press, 1941.

Urofsky, Melvin I. *American Zionism from Herzl to the Holocaust*. Garden City, N.Y.: Doubleday, 1975.

———. *Louis D. Brandeis and the Progressive Tradition*. Boston: Little, Brown, 1981.

———. *A Mind of One Piece: Brandeis and American Reform*. New York: Scribner, 1971.

Van Hise, Charles R. *Concentration and Control: A Solution to the Trust Problem*. New York: Macmillan, 1912.

Weinstein, James. *The Corporate Ideal in the Liberal State. 1900–1918*. Boston: Beacon Press, 1968.

White, G. Edward. *The American Judicial Tradition: Profiles of Leading American Judges*. New York: Oxford University Press, 1976.

White, Ronald C., Jr., and Hopkins, C. Howard. *The Social Gospel: Religion and Reform in Changing America*. Philadelphia: Temple University Press, 1976.

Wiebe, Robert H. *Businessmen and Reform: A Study of the Progressive Movement*. Cambridge, Mass.: Harvard University Press, 1962.

———. *The Search for Order, 1877–1920*. New York: Hill & Wang, 1967.

Wilson, Woodrow. *The New Freedom: A Call for the Emancipation of the Generous Energies of a People*. New York: Doubleday, 1913.

Wittke, Carl. *Refugees of Revolution: The German Forty-Eighters in America*. Philadelphia: University of Pennsylvania Press, 1952.

Wolff, Leon. *Lockout: The Story of the Homestead Strike of 1892*. New York: Harper & Row, 1965.

Wright, George C. *Life Behind a Veil: Blacks in Louisville, Kentucky, 1865–1930*. Baton Rouge: Louisiana State University Press, 1985.

Zimmern, Alfred. *The Greek Commonwealth*. Oxford: Clarendon Press, 1912.

Zucker, A. E., ed. *The Forty-Eighters: Political Refugees of the German Revolution of 1848*. New York: Columbia University Press, 1950.

ARTICLES

Acheson, Dean. "Mr. Justice Brandeis." *Harvard Law Review* 55 (1941–42): 191–92.

Barron, James H. "Warren and Brandeis, *The Right to Privacy*, 4 Harvard Law Review 193 (1890): Demystifying a Landmark Citation." *Suffolk University Law Review* 13 (1979): 875–907.

Baskerville, Stephen W. "Frankfurter, Keynes and the Fight for Public Works, 1932–1935." *Maryland Historian* 9 (1978): 1–16.

Bernard, Burton C. "Brandeis in St. Louis." *St. Louis Bar Journal* 11 (1964): 54–60.

Brandeis, Elizabeth. "Labor Legislation." In *History of Labor In the United States*, edited by John R. Commons et al., 3: 399–741. 4 vols. New York: Macmillan, 1918–35.

Chase, Anthony. "The Birth of the Modern Law School." *American Journal of Legal History* 23 (1979): 329–48.

David, Henry. "Upheaval at Homestead." In *America in Crisis*, edited by Daniel Aaron, 133–70. New York: Knopf, 1952.

Davis, Elbridge, and Davis, Harold A. "Mr. Justice Horace Gray: Some Aspects of his Judicial Career." *American Bar Association Journal* 41 (May 1955): 421–44, 468–71.

Eliot, Charles W. "Langdell and the Law School." *Harvard Law Review* 33 (1919–20): 518–25.

Ely, Richard T., and Merriam, L. S. "Report on Social Legislation in the United States for 1889–1890." *Economic Review* 1 (1891): 245–56.

Evans, Elizabeth Glendower. "Mr. Justice Brandeis: The People' s Tribune." *Survey Graphic* 67 (1 November, 1931): 138–41.

————. "People I Have Known: Alice Goldmark Brandeis." *The Progressive* 1, no. 34 (1930): 3.

Fessenden, Franklin G. "The Rebirth of the Harvard Law School." *Harvard Law Review* 33 (1919–20): 493–517.

Ford, Bert. "Boyhood of Brandeis—An Early View of the Man." *Boston American* part 4 (4 June 1916): 1–2.

Frank, John P. "The Legal Ethics of Louis D. Brandeis." *Stanford Law Review* 17 (1965): 683–709.

Frankfurter, Felix. "Mr. Justice Brandeis." *Harvard Law Review* 55 (1941–42): 181.

————. "Mr. Justice Brandeis and the Constitution." *Harvard Law Review* 45 (1931–32): 33–111.

Freund, Paul A. "The Liberalism of Justice Brandeis." *American Jewish Archives* 10 (1958): 3–11.

————. "Mr. Justice Brandeis." In *Mr. Justice*, edited by Allison Dunham and Philip B. Kurland, Chicago: University of Chicago Press, 1956: 97–121.

Friendly, Henry. "Mr. Justice Brandeis: The Quest for Reason." *University of Pennsylvania Law Review* 108 (1960): 985–99.

Godkin, E.L. "The Rights of the Citizen: To His Own Reputation." *Scribner's* 8 (July 1890): 58–67.

Grant, J. A. C. "The Natural Law Background of Due Process." *Columbia Law Review* 31 (1931): 56–81.

Jaffe, Louis L. "The Contributions of Mr. Justice Brandeis to Administrative Law." *Iowa Law Review* 18 (1932–33): 213–27.

————. "Was Brandeis an Activist? The Search for Intermediate Premises." *Harvard Law Review* 80 (1966–67): 986–1003.

Jones, Alan. "Thomas M. Cooley and 'Laissez Faire Constitutionalism': A Reconsideration." *Journal of American History* 53 (1967): 759–71.

————. "Thomas M. Cooley and the Michigan Supreme Court, 1865–1885." *American Journal of Legal History* 10 (1966): 97–112.

Kaplan, Jacob J. "Mr. Justice Brandeis, Prophet." *The New Palestine* 32 (14 November, 1941): 27–28.

Kraines, Oscar. "Brandeis' Philosophy of Scientific Management." *Western Political Quarterly* 13 (1960): 191–201.

Landis, James M. "Mr. Justice Brandeis and the Harvard Law School." *Harvard Law Review* 55 (1941–42): 184–90.

Levy, David W. "The Lawyer as Judge: Brandeis's View of the Legal Profession." *Oklahoma Law Review* 22 (1969): 374–95.

————. and Murphy, Bruce Allen. "Preserving the Progressive Spirit in a Conservative Time." *Michigan Law Review* 78 (1980): 1248–98.

McClennen, Edward F. "Louis D. Brandeis as a Lawyer." *Massachusetts Law Quarterly* 33 (1948): 3–28.

Maidment, Richard. "The New Deal Court Revisited." In *Nothing Else to Fear: New Perspectives on America in the Thirties*, edited by Stephen W. Baskerville and Ralph Willett, Manchester: Manchester University Press, 1985. 38–63.

Nathanson, Nathan L. "Mr. Justice Brandeis: A Law Clerk's Recollections of the October Term, 1934." *American Jewish Archives* 15 (1963): 6–16.

Newland, Chester A. "Innovation In Judicial Technique: The Brandeis Opinion." *Southwestern Social Science Quarterly* 42 (1961): 22–31.

Parrish, Michael E. "The Hughes Court, the Great Depression and the Historians." *The Historian* 40 (1978): 286–308.

Poole, Ernest, "Brandeis: A Remarkable Record of Unselfish Work Done in the Public Interest." In *Business—A Profession*, edited by Louis D. Brandeis, Reprint of 1914 ed. New York: Kelley, 1971. ix–lvi.

Richard, Livy S. "Up from Aristocracy." *The Independent*, 27 July 1914.

Shapiro, Yonathan. "American Jews in Politics: The Case of Louis D. Brandeis." *American Jewish Historical Quarterly* 55 (1965– 66): 199–211.

Shaw, William B. "Social and Economic Legislation of the States ln 1890." *Quarterly Journal of Economics* 5 (1891): 385–96.

———. "Social and Economic Legislation of the States in 1891." *Quarterly Journal of Economics* 6 (1892): 227–42.

Shulman, Harry. "The Demise of *Swift v. Tyson*." *Yale Law Journal* 47 (1937–38): 1336–1353.

Swisher, Carl B. "Mr. Chief Justice Taney." In *Mr. Justice*, edited by Allison Dunham and Philip B. Kurland, 203–30. Chicago: University of Chicago Press, 1956.

Thayer, James B. "The Origin and Scope of the American Doctrine of Constitutional Law." *Harvard Law Review* 7 (1893–94): 129–56.

Urofsky, Melvin I. "Wilson, Brandeis and the Trust Issue, 1912–1914." *Mid-America* 49 (1967): 3–28.

White, G. Edward. "Allocating Power between Agencies and Courts: The Legacy of Justice Brandeis." *Duke Law Journal* (April 1974): 195–244.

Wyzanski, Charles E. "Brandeis." *Atlantic Monthly* 198 (November 1956): 66–72.

Zimmerman, Diane L. "Requiem for a Heavyweight: A Farewell to Warren and Brandeis Privacy Tort." *Cornell Law Review* 68 (1983): 291–367.

UNPUBLISHED WORKS

Jacobson, Janice Mark. "Mr. Justice Brandeis on Regulation and Competition: An Analysis of His Economic Opinions." Ph.D. diss., Columbia University, 1973.

White, Joseph M. "Religion and Community: Cincinnati Germans, 1814–1870." Ph.D. diss., University of Notre Dame, 1980.

Table of Cases Cited in the Text

Index